MOTOR MECHANICS

OTHER BOOKS AND INSTRUCTIONAL MATERIALS BY WILLIAM H. CROUSE AND *DONALD L. ANGLIN

The Auto Book*
Automotive Air Conditioning*
Automotive Automatic Transmissions*
Automotive Manual Transmissions and
    Power Trains*
Automotive Body Repair and Refinishing*
Automotive Brakes, Suspension, and Steering*
Automotive Dictionary*
Automotive Electronics and
    Electrical Equipment
Automotive Emission Control*
Automotive Engine Design
Automotive Engines*

Automotive Fuel, Lubricating, and
    Cooling Systems*
Automotive Mechanics
Automotive Engines Sound Filmstrip Program
Automotive Service Business
Automotive Technician's Handbook*
Automotive Tools, Fasteners,
    and Measurements*
Automotive Tuneup*
General Power Mechanics* (With Robert
    Worthington and Morton Margules)
Motor Vehicle Inspection*
Small Engine Mechanics*

AUTOMOTIVE ROOM CHART SERIES

Automotive Brake Charts
Automotive Electrical Equipment Charts
Automotive Emission Controls Charts
Automotive Engines Charts
Automotive Engine Cooling Systems, Heating,
    and Air Conditioning Charts

Automotive Fuel Systems Charts
Automotive Suspension, Steering, and
    Tires Charts
Automotive Transmissions and Power
    Trains Charts

AUTOMOTIVE TRANSPARENCIES BY WILLIAM H. CROUSE AND JAY D. HELSEL

Automotive Air Conditioning
Automotive Brakes
Automotive Electrical Systems
Automotive Emission Control
Automotive Engine Systems

Automotive Steering Systems
Automotive Suspension Systems
Automotive Transmissions and Power Trains
Engines and Fuel Systems

MOTORCYCLE MECHANICS

WILLIAM H. CROUSE
DONALD L. ANGLIN

GREGG DIVISION
McGRAW-HILL BOOK COMPANY

New York   Atlanta   Dallas   St. Louis   San Francisco
Auckland   Bogotá   Guatemala   Hamburg   Johannesburg   Lisbon
London   Madrid   Mexico   Montreal   New Delhi   Panama   Paris
San Juan   São Paulo   Singapore   Sydney   Tokyo   Toronto

Sponsoring Editor / Roberta Moore
Editing Supervisors / Paul Berk
                     Patricia Nolan
Design Supervisor / Caryl Valerie Spinka
Production Supervisor / Kathleen Morrissey

Technical Studio / Vantage Art, Inc.
Cover Designer / Caryl Valerie Spinka
                Judith Yourman

Library of Congress Cataloging in Publication Data

Crouse, William Harry, [Date]
  Motorcycle mechanics.

  Includes index.
    1. Motorcycles—Maintenance and repair. 2. Motor-
cycles.   I. Anglin, Donald L.   II. Title.
TL444.C76   629.28'775   81-217
ISBN 0-07-014781-7   AACR2

Motorcycle Mechanics

1 2 3 4 5 6 7 8 9 0   SMSM   8 9 8 7 6 5 4 3 2 1

ISBN 0-07-014781-7

CONTENTS

Part 5 MOTORCYCLE POWER TRAINS

Part 6 MOTORCYCLE CHASSIS

PREFACE

For a long time there has been a pressing need for a comprehensive, pedagogically sound, easily read, and interestingly written book on motorcycle mechanics. This need has been repeatedly stressed by those leaders in the teaching profession who are aware of the latest trends in technical education. Motorcycle dealers are turning to the technical-education schools more and more for good mechanics to service the motorcycles they sell. Motorcycle enthusiasts are seeking a comprehensive text that will fill their needs.

The authors of this textbook, *Motorcycle Mechanics,* have long been aware of these needs. But we decided not to rush into the market with a hastily conceived book. Instead, we first surveyed the field, to find out what the schools have been teaching about motorcycle service, and what motorcycle mechanics teachers felt was needed in the way of instructional material.

Then one author, a long-time performance-engine and motorcycle enthusiast, visited motorcycle service shops to catch up on the latest techniques and service tools. The other author researched the complete technical publication field, including manufacturers' service publications as well as the training material the various manufacturers and publishers have produced.

Together, the two authors prepared a comprehensive outline of what the book should be, and developed sample chapters for evaluation by experts in the teaching and servicing fields. Only after the completion of these reviews and tests of the material were the authors ready to spend the many months required to put together the textbook you now hold in your hands.

We believe that *Motorcycle Mechanics* covers, with a completeness never before achieved, the complex field of motorcycle design, construction, operation, maintenance, and repair. There are chapters on safety in and out of the shop, engine fundamentals, motorcycle classifications and types, motorcycle construction, two-cycle engines, four-cycle engines, engine measurements, gasoline and gasohol, motorcycle fuel systems, motorcycle carburetors, motorcycle fuel-system ser-

vice, exhaust emissions and air pollution, motorcycle engine oils, engine lubricating systems, lubricating system service, engine cooling systems, and much more.

Motorcycle electric and electronic equipment is covered in detail. There are comprehensive chapters on motorcycle maintenance, trouble diagnosis, and tune-up, two-cycle-engine top-end service, four-cycle-engine valve service, engine cylinder and crankshaft service.

Motorcycle Mechanics also has comprehensive chapters on motorcycle clutches and clutch service, motorcycle transmissions and transmission service, motorcycle final drives, motorcycle frames, suspension and steering, motorcycle brakes, and motorcycle wheels and tires.

The *Workbook for Motorcycle Mechanics* has been prepared to accompany the textbook. It includes the basic service jobs on motorcycles, outlining step-by-step how to do each job. To assist the motorcycle instructor, the *Instructor's Planning Guide for Motorcycle Mechanics* is available.

Motorcycle mechanics instructors are constantly aware of the need for congruency between the school curriculum and the future needs of students entering the motorcycle servicing field. These instructors know the minimum standards of competence demanded of entry-level employees by employers in this area. With this in mind, the instructor can and should tailor the learning experiences of students around tested and proven competency-based objectives. This will allow the students to develop the locally demanded career skills while mastering the necessary job competencies and performance indicators covered in *Motorcycle Mechanics.*

The aim of the authors and publisher of the *Motorcycle Mechanics* program is to supply authentic, comprehensive material that will enable the student, with the help of the teacher, to prepare for a rewarding and interesting servicing job in the motorcycle field.

William H. Crouse
Donald L. Anglin

ACKNOWLEDGMENTS

While preparing this book the authors were given invaluable aid and inspiration by many people in the motorcycle service field and in education. The authors gratefully acknowledge their indebtedness and offer their sincere thanks. All cooperated with the aim of providing accurate and complete information on how motorcycles are constructed, how they operate, and how to maintain and service them.

Special thanks must go to W. Kenneth Watts, Regional Training Administrator for American Honda Motor Company, for his review of the final manuscript and for his many valuable suggestions and contributions; and to Lory V. Curtis, Instructor at East High School, Salt Lake City, Utah, for his review of the final manuscript.

Also, special thanks must go to Jimmy Jarman, owner of Jarman's Sportcycles in Charlottesville, Virginia, for his technical assistance and for setting up and assisting in the photography required to illustrate the book.

Thanks are due to the following organizations for information and illustrations they supplied: AJS; American Garelli; ATW; Black and Decker Manufacturing Company; Castrol, Limited; Champion Spark Plug Company; Delco-Remy Division of General Motors Corporation; Federal Mogul Corporation; Firestone Rubber Company; General Motors Corporation; Harley-Davidson Motor Company; Heli-Coil Products Division of Mitre Corporation; Honda Motor Company, Ltd.; Husqvarna; Joseph Lucas, Ltd.; Kawasaki Heavy Industries, Ltd.; Kohler Company; Kwik-Way Manufacturing Company; Moto Laverda; Motorcycle Safety Foundation, Inc.; Neway Manufacturing, Inc.; Norton Triumph Corporation; Onan Corporation; Outboard Marine Corporation; Pacific Basin Trading Company; Penton; Phoenix International; Quaker State Oil Refining Corporation; Schwitzer Division of Wallace-Murray Corporation; Snap-on Tools Corporation; Sun Electric Corporation; Turbo Cycle Corporation; Suzuki Motor Company, Ltd.; Tecumseh Products Company; The Goodyear Tire and Rubber Company; TRW, Inc.; Union Carbide Corporation; Velosolex; Yamaha International Corporation; and Yuasa Battery Company, Ltd.

To all these organizations and the people who represent them, sincere thanks.

William H. Crouse
Donald L. Anglin

CHAPTER **1**

SAFETY IN AND OUT OF THE SHOP

After studying this chapter,
you should be able to:

1. Explain what safety on the job means.

2. Discuss shop layouts and describe the layout of the shop you work in.

3. Explain what to do in an emergency.

4. Discuss fire prevention and how to prevent fires.

5. List and discuss the 12 safety rules in the chapter.

6. Discuss the cautions you should use in operating power tools.

7. List the three laws of motorcycling safety and explain each.

1-1 SHOPWORK

Shopwork is varied and interesting. The shop is where you will learn how to service motorcycles, including adjusting brakes, checking charging systems, removing an engine and disassembling it, grinding valves on four-cycle engines, adjusting transmission linkages, and adjusting wheel spokes. These and many other basic motorcycle service jobs are discussed in this book.

Before you work in the shop, you must know about safety. Safety in the shop means protecting yourself and other workers from possible danger and injury. This chapter describes the rules you should follow in the shop to protect yourself from harm. When everybody obeys the rules, the shop is a much safer place than your home! Many more people are hurt in the home than in the shop.

In this chapter we also look at potential traffic hazards on the highway, on city streets, and off the highway. You must always think about safety and possible trouble when you test-ride a motorcycle. When riding a motorcycle, take every reasonable step to keep out of trouble. One of the most important steps is to always wear an approved safety helmet any time you are on a motorcycle.

1-2 SAFETY IS YOUR JOB

In the shop, you are "safe" when you protect your eyes, your fingers, your hands—all of yourself—from danger. Just as important, shop safety includes looking out for the safety of those around you. Important safety rules are listed and

discussed in the next few pages. Follow the rules—for your protection and for the protection of others. Do your part to keep any shop you are in a safe shop.

1-3 SHOP LAYOUTS

The term *shop layout* means the locations of workbenches, motorcycle stands, machine tools, and work stalls. Shop layouts vary. So the first thing you should do in a shop is to find out where everything is located. This includes the different machine tools, workbenches, exits, fire extinguishers, and work areas. In many shops, there are painted lines on the floor to mark off work areas. These lines guide customers and workers away from danger zones where machines are being operated. The lines also remind workers to keep their tools and equipment inside work-area lines.

Many shops have warning signs posted around machinery. These signs are there to remind you about safety and about how to use machines safely. Follow the posted instructions at all times. The most common cause of accidents in the shop is failure to follow instructions.

1-4 WHAT TO DO IN EMERGENCIES

If there is an accident and someone gets hurt in class, notify your instructor at once. Your instructor will know what to do and may apply first aid or may phone the school nurse, a doctor, or an ambulance. Be very careful in attempting first aid. You must know what you are doing. Trying first aid on an injured person can do more harm than good if it is done wrong. For example, a serious back injury could be made worse if the injured person is moved. However, quick mouth-to-mouth resuscitation may save the life of a person who has received an electric shock. Talk to your instructor if you have any questions about the shop safety plan.

Remember this about fires. The quicker you get at them, the easier it is to control them. But you have to use the right kind of fire extinguisher, and you have to use it correctly (Fig. 1-1). Again, ask your instructor if you have any questions.

1-5 FIRE PREVENTION

Gasoline is used so much in the shop that people forget it is very dangerous if not handled properly. A spark or a lighted match in a closed room filled with gasoline vapors can cause an explosion (Fig. 1-2). Always be careful with gasoline to prevent an accident. Here are some hints.

Suppose there are gasoline vapors because someone spilled gasoline or because a fuel line is leaking. Keep the shop doors open and/or keep the ventilating system running. Wipe up the spilled gasoline at once, and put the rags outside to dry. Never smoke or light cigarettes around gasoline. When you work on a leaky fuel line or carburetor, catch the leaking gasoline in a container or with rags, and put the soaked rags outside to dry. Fix

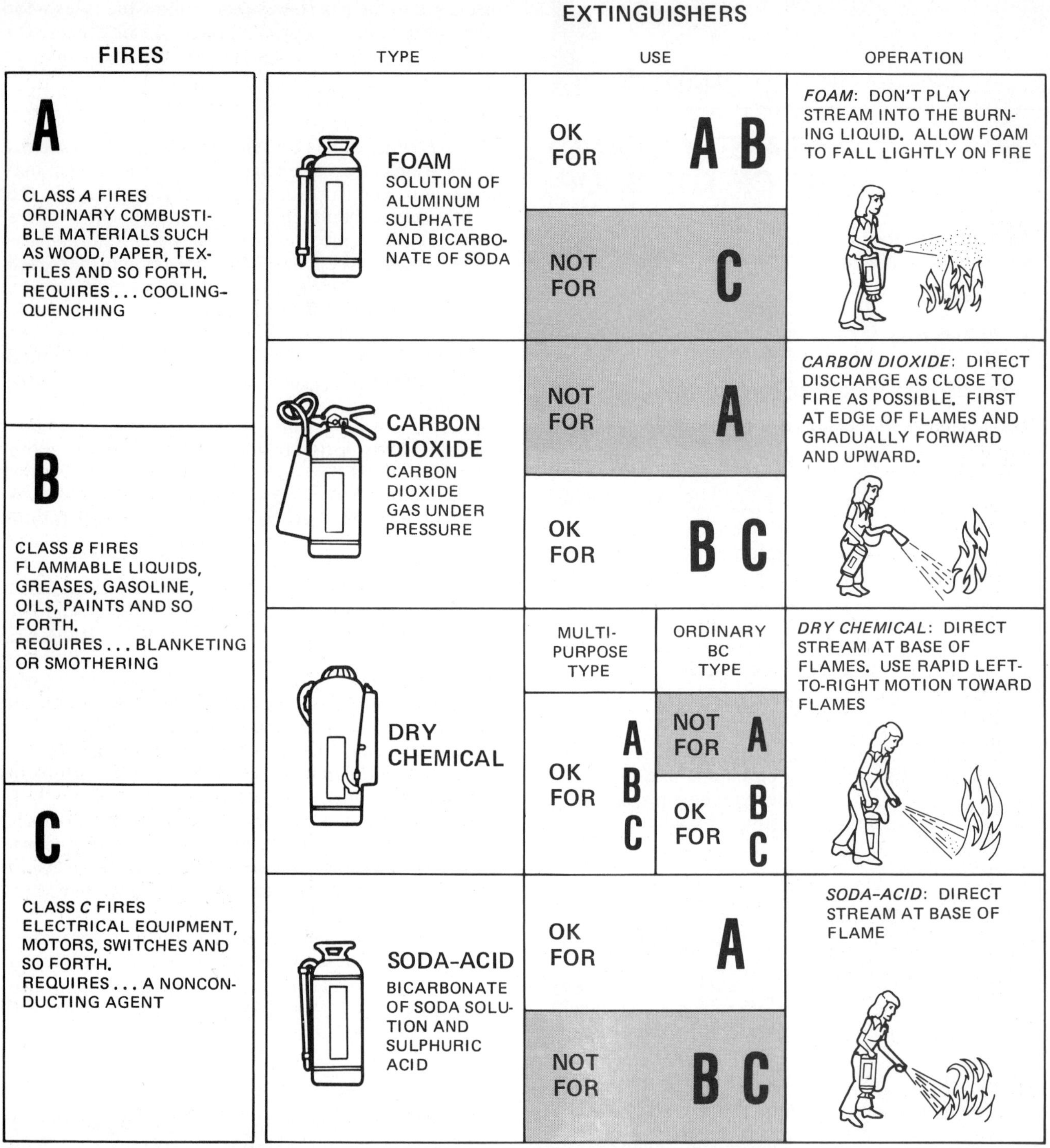

FIRES		TYPE	USE		OPERATION
A CLASS *A* FIRES ORDINARY COMBUSTIBLE MATERIALS SUCH AS WOOD, PAPER, TEXTILES AND SO FORTH. REQUIRES... COOLING-QUENCHING		**FOAM** SOLUTION OF ALUMINUM SULPHATE AND BICARBONATE OF SODA	OK FOR **A B** NOT FOR **C**		*FOAM:* DON'T PLAY STREAM INTO THE BURNING LIQUID. ALLOW FOAM TO FALL LIGHTLY ON FIRE
B CLASS *B* FIRES FLAMMABLE LIQUIDS, GREASES, GASOLINE, OILS, PAINTS AND SO FORTH. REQUIRES... BLANKETING OR SMOTHERING		**CARBON DIOXIDE** CARBON DIOXIDE GAS UNDER PRESSURE	NOT FOR **A** OK FOR **B C**		*CARBON DIOXIDE:* DIRECT DISCHARGE AS CLOSE TO FIRE AS POSSIBLE. FIRST AT EDGE OF FLAMES AND GRADUALLY FORWARD AND UPWARD.
C CLASS *C* FIRES ELECTRICAL EQUIPMENT, MOTORS, SWITCHES AND SO FORTH. REQUIRES... A NONCONDUCTING AGENT		**DRY CHEMICAL**	MULTI-PURPOSE TYPE OK FOR **A B C**	ORDINARY BC TYPE NOT FOR **A** OK FOR **B C**	*DRY CHEMICAL:* DIRECT STREAM AT BASE OF FLAMES. USE RAPID LEFT-TO-RIGHT MOTION TOWARD FLAMES
		SODA-ACID BICARBONATE OF SODA SOLUTION AND SULPHURIC ACID	OK FOR **A** NOT FOR **B C**		*SODA-ACID:* DIRECT STREAM AT BASE OF FLAME

Fig. 1-1 A chart showing some types of fire extinguishers, the correct way to use them, and the classification of fires.

the leak as quickly as possible. When you suspect the presence of spilled gasoline and fumes, don't make sparks around the motorcycle. For example, don't connect a test light to the battery.

Store gasoline in an approved safety container (Fig. 1-3). Never store gasoline in a glass jug. The jug could break, spilling the gasoline and causing an explosion or fire.

Oily rags can also be a source of fire. They can catch fire without a spark or flame. Oily rags and waste should be put into special closed metal containers, where they can do no harm.

1-6
SAFETY RULES Some people say, "Accidents will happen!" But safety experts do not agree. They say: "Accidents are caused—by careless actions, by inattention to the job, by using damaged or incorrect

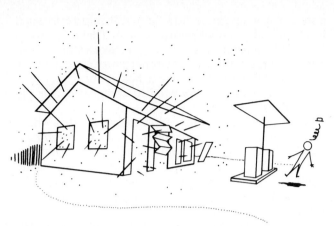

Fig. 1-2 An explosion can result from gasoline fumes.

GASOLINE
SAFETY
CONTAINER

Fig. 1-3 Store gasoline and all flammable liquids in approved safety containers.

tools. Sometimes accidents are caused by just plain stupidity!"

To help prevent accidents, follow these safety rules:

1. Work quietly and give the job your full attention.
2. Keep your tools and equipment under control.
3. Never indulge in horseplay or other foolish activities. You could cause someone to get seriously hurt.
4. Don't put sharp objects, such as screwdrivers, in your pocket. You could cut yourself or get stabbed.
5. Make sure your clothes are right for the job. Dangling sleeves or ties can get caught in machinery and cause serious injuries. Do not wear sandals or open-toed shoes. Wear full leather shoes, preferably with nonskid rubber heels and soles. Steel-toed safety shoes are best for shopwork.
6. Keep long hair out of machinery by wearing a cap.
7. If you spill oil, grease, or any other liquid on the floor, clean it up so that no one will slip and fall.
8. Never use compressed air to blow dirt from your clothes. Never point a compressed-air hose at another person. Flying particles could put out an eye.
9. Always wear goggles or a face shield when there are particles flying about. Always wear eye protection when using a grinding wheel.
10. Watch out for sparks flying from a grinding wheel or welding equipment. The sparks can set your clothes on fire.
11. To protect your eyes, wear goggles when using chemicals such as solvents. If you get a chemical in your eyes, wash them with water at once (Fig. 1-4). Then see the school nurse or a doctor as soon as possible.
12. Always use the right tool for the job. The wrong tool could damage the part being worked on and could cause you to get hurt.

CAUTION Never run an engine in a closed room that does not have a ventilating system. The exhaust gases contain carbon monoxide. Carbon monoxide is a colorless, odorless, tasteless, poisonous gas that can kill you! In a closed room the size of a one-car garage, enough carbon monoxide to kill you can collect in only three minutes.

1-7 TAKING CARE OF YOUR TOOLS Tools should be clean and in good condition. Greasy and oily tools are hard to hold and use. Always wipe tools clean before trying to use them. Do not use a hardened hammer or punch on a hardened surface. Hardened steel is brittle, almost like glass, and may shatter from heavy blows. Slivers may fly out and become embedded in your hand or in your eye. Use a soft hammer or punch on hardened parts.

1-8 USING POWER EQUIPMENT Many different types of power equipment are used in the motorcycle shop. The instructions for using any piece of equipment should be studied carefully before the equipment is operated. Hands and clothes should be kept away from moving machinery. Keep your hands out of the way when using any cutting device, such as a boring bar. Do not attempt to feel the finish while the machine is in operation. Keep your hands away from any rotating parts.

Fig. 1-4 If solvent or some other chemical splashes in your eyes, immediately wash your eyes with water.

Sometimes you will work on a part that uses compressed springs, such as a clutch or valves. Use care to prevent the springs from slipping and jumping loose. They may fly off at high speed and hurt someone.

Never attempt to adjust or oil moving machinery unless the instructions tell you that this should be done.

1-9 OPERATING THE MOTORCYCLE IN OR OUT OF THE SHOP
Motorcycles have to be moved around in the shop. They have to be tested, usually on the road or in a field. Different motorcycles have different operating characteristics, so make sure you know the motorcycle you are going to test before taking it out of the shop. When testing a bike outside the shop, know your territory. Know the area that you are riding in. Be alert to all traffic hazards. It is easy to become so involved in checking out the bike that you tend to ignore where you are going. Don't let that happen to you.

1-10 LAWS OF MOTORCYCLING SAFETY
There are three laws of motorcycling safety:

1. Know the motorcycle.
2. Know the territory—highway, street, or trail.
3. Know yourself.

Let's examine these three laws. First, you must know the motorcycle that you are riding. You would know the strong points and limitations of your own motorcycle. You would know how quickly it could reach 55 miles per hour (mph) [88 kilometers per hour (km/h)] in a passing situation and how quickly you could brake it to a stop. You would know how far to lean into a curve and how easily the rear wheel would skid. That's your own bike, and you know it. But when you take a strange bike out for a test, it may be another story. If the bike's engine is different, if the bike is heavier or lighter than your own, then you will need to compensate for the differences.

In a similar way, you need to know the area where you are going to test-ride a motorcycle. When you are checking out the shifts, you want to be on familiar territory. You don't want to be watching the traffic lights and dodging cars at the same time.

Most important of all, you must know yourself. Check up on yourself before you ride a motorcycle. If you are irritated about something, have overindulged or are very tired or ill, or are taking medication, you may be taking a big risk in riding a motorcycle. Riding when you are not fit can be very dangerous, especially if the bike you are test-riding is malfunctioning.

A motorcycle will do exactly what it is directed to do. If you are a little slow in sizing up a traffic situation, the bike will be a little slow in reacting. A spill or collision could result.

Never try to ride a motorcycle, for any reason, if your feet can't touch the ground when you are seated. Also, never get on a motorcycle and try to ride it if you really don't know how to ride and operate the controls. Many people have been seriously hurt because motorcycle riding looks so simple. But, in reality, a motorcycle is a very unforgiving machine. This book is not about motorcycle riding. It is about motorcycle mechanics. Many people work on motorcycles who ride seldom or not at all. If you honestly can't ride a motorcycle, for your own safety *stay off*.

CHAPTER 1 REVIEW QUESTIONS

1. What is the first precaution to observe when you are using a grinding wheel?
2. What is wrong with using gasoline to clean the floor or workbench when the shop doors are closed?
3. Why are oily rags dangerous?
4. What is wrong with operating an engine in a room when the doors are closed?
5. What is the purpose of the lines painted on the floor of the shop?
6. How many fire extinguishers are there in your shop, and where are they located?
7. What are the three laws of motorcycling safety?
8. Why should you never store gasoline in a glass jug?
9. Why must you never point the compressed-air hose at another person?

MOTORCYCLE CONSTRUCTION AND OPERATION

Before we get to the specific parts of a motorcycle, such as the engine fuel, lubricating, and cooling systems, clutches, transmissions, and final drives, we will look at the fundamentals of motorcycle construction and engine operation. Then we will study various types of engines, how they are constructed, and how their size and performance are measured.

There are six chapters in Part 1. They are:

Chapter 2   **Engine Fundamentals**

Chapter 3   **Motorcycle Classifications and Types**

Chapter 4   **Motorcycle Construction**

Chapter 5   **Two-Cycle Engines**

Chapter 6   **Four-Cycle Engines**

Chapter 7   **Engine Measurements**

CHAPTER 2

ENGINE FUNDAMENTALS

After studying this chapter,
you should be able to:

1. Explain what atmospheric pressure is and why it is essential to the operation of the engine.

2. Discuss and explain what a vacuum is.

3. Explain what the word *cycle* means.

4. Describe piston rings and their purpose.

5. Explain how the cranks on the engine crankshaft change reciprocating motion to rotary motion.

6. Discuss engine bearings and describe the different types.

2-1 INTERNAL COMBUSTION ENGINES

In this chapter we look at the fundamental physical principles that explain how engines work. There are two general kinds of power-producing engines—external combustion and internal combustion.

External means outside.
Internal means inside.
Combustion means burning.

An external combustion engine is an engine that burns fuel outside the engine. The steam engine is the major example. A boiler outside the engine is heated by the combustion of a fuel and produces steam. The steam goes into the engine and makes it run.

The internal combustion engine burns fuel inside the engine. All motorcycle and automotive engines are internal combustion engines. Therefore, the engines we describe in this book are all internal combustion engines. Figure 2-1 shows several motorcycle engines, cutaway so you can see their internal parts.

2-2 PRESSURE

Suppose we have a cylinder, which is a shape like a soda can (Fig. 2-2), filled with air and completely enclosed. When we heat it, the air expands inside the can, causing an increase in pressure.

Figure 2-3 shows how this applies to the engine. There, we have replaced the bottom of the can with a plug that is able to move up and down in the can. In the engine, the can is the engine cylinder and the movable plug is the piston. When the piston is pushed up to the top of the cylinder, the air above the piston is compressed. Now imagine that the air has gasoline vapor in it. Then we ignite, or set fire to, the air–gasoline-vapor

mixture. As the mixture burns, the temperature and pressure in the cylinder go up. The force against the top of the piston in a running engine can go as high as 4000 pounds (1814 kilograms [kg]) or more.

This force pushes the piston down, and that is how the engine produces power. We talk more about engine power and combustion later. But first, there still are some other fundamentals to cover.

2-3 ATMOSPHERIC PRESSURE

Engines won't run without the help of atmospheric pressure. The earth is covered with a blanket of air. This blanket is called the *atmosphere*. Normally we pay little attention to it. However, the atmosphere has weight, just as every other thing on earth has weight. The weight of anything on earth is the result of *gravity,* a force that tries to pull everything together. The gravity of the earth pulls down on every object, including the atmosphere.

When we measure the pull of the earth on the atmosphere, we find that the total pull, or the weight of the air, amounts to about 15 pounds per square inch (psi) [1.05 kilograms per square centimeter (kg/cm²)] at sea level. Fifteen pounds per square inch may sound like a lot of pressure, but it is very little compared with the pressure that develops in an engine cylinder. In the cylinder, during the power stroke of the piston, a pressure of more than 600 psi [42.18 kg/cm²] may develop. This means that the total downward push on the piston can reach 4000 pounds [1814 kg] or more.

NOTE In the metric system, pressure is also measured in a unit called the *kilopascal* (abbreviated kPa). A pressure of 1 psi is equal to 6.9 kPa.

2-4 VACUUM

A vacuum is an absence of air and any other matter. Astronauts on their way to the moon soon pass through the blanket of air that surrounds our earth. This blanket of air is our atmosphere. When the astronauts leave the atmosphere, they go into outer space, where there is no atmosphere. This is a vacuum.

The engine produces a partial vacuum in the cylinders as it runs. Atmospheric pressure then pushes the air-fuel mixture into the engine cylinders. This is one part of the operating cycle of the engine.

2-5 PISTON-ENGINE OPERATION

Now let's look into piston-engine operation. You have learned about combustion, heat, pressure, atmospheric pressure, and vacuum. Now, let's tie them all together and see what makes the engine work.

2-6 TWO-CYCLE AND FOUR-CYCLE ENGINES

Piston engines can be divided into two groups—two cycle and four cycle. In the two-cycle engine, it takes two piston movements, or strokes, to complete one cycle of engine operation. A stroke is a movement of the piston in the cylinder from top to bottom or from bottom to top (Fig. 2-4). The two limit-

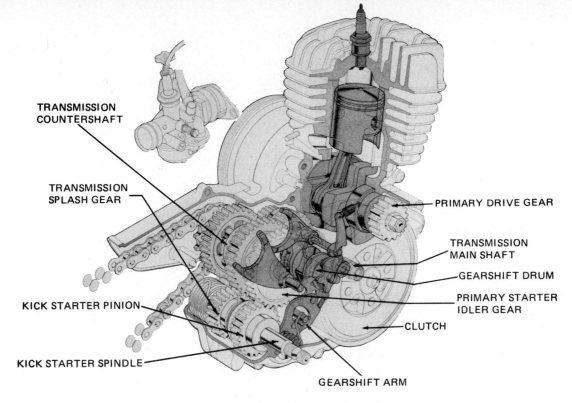

TRANSMISSION
COUNTERSHAFT

TRANSMISSION
SPLASH GEAR

KICK STARTER PINION

KICK STARTER SPINDLE

PRIMARY DRIVE GEAR

TRANSMISSION
MAIN SHAFT

GEARSHIFT DRUM

PRIMARY STARTER
IDLER GEAR

CLUTCH

GEARSHIFT ARM

(a) 50-cc ONE-CYLINDER TWO-CYCLE

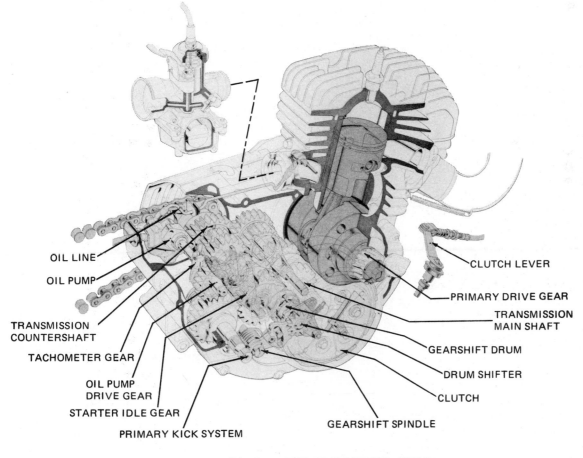

OIL LINE

OIL PUMP

TRANSMISSION
COUNTERSHAFT

TACHOMETER GEAR

OIL PUMP
DRIVE GEAR

STARTER IDLE GEAR

PRIMARY KICK SYSTEM

CLUTCH LEVER

PRIMARY DRIVE GEAR

TRANSMISSION
MAIN SHAFT

GEARSHIFT DRUM

DRUM SHIFTER

CLUTCH

GEARSHIFT SPINDLE

(b) 125-cc ONE-CYLINDER TWO-CYCLE

Fig. 2-1 The construction of several different motorcycle engines. (*Honda Motor Company, Ltd.*)

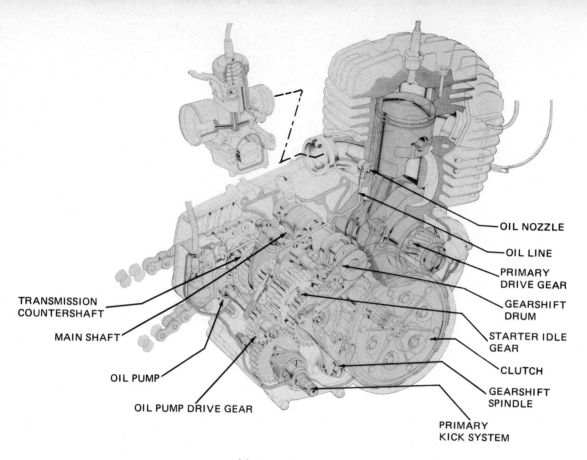

TRANSMISSION
COUNTERSHAFT

MAIN SHAFT

OIL PUMP

OIL PUMP DRIVE GEAR

OIL NOZZLE

OIL LINE

PRIMARY
DRIVE GEAR

GEARSHIFT
DRUM

STARTER IDLE
GEAR

CLUTCH

GEARSHIFT
SPINDLE

PRIMARY
KICK SYSTEM

(c) 250-cc ONE-CYLINDER TWO-CYCLE

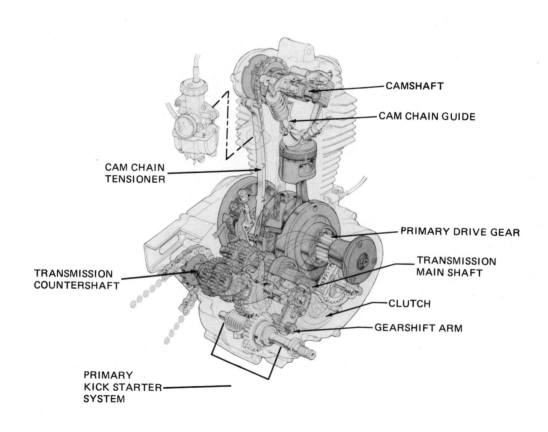

CAM CHAIN
TENSIONER

TRANSMISSION
COUNTERSHAFT

PRIMARY
KICK STARTER
SYSTEM

CAMSHAFT

CAM CHAIN GUIDE

PRIMARY DRIVE GEAR

TRANSMISSION
MAIN SHAFT

CLUTCH

GEARSHIFT ARM

(d) 125-cc ONE-CYLINDER FOUR-CYCLE

Fig. 2-1 (Continued)

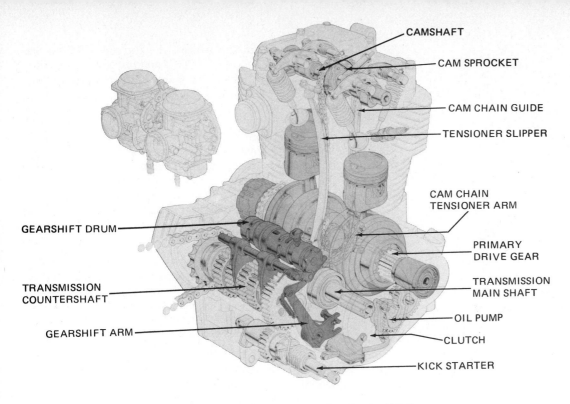

CAMSHAFT

CAM SPROCKET

CAM CHAIN GUIDE

TENSIONER SLIPPER

CAM CHAIN
TENSIONER ARM

PRIMARY
DRIVE GEAR

TRANSMISSION
MAIN SHAFT

OIL PUMP

CLUTCH

KICK STARTER

GEARSHIFT DRUM

TRANSMISSION
COUNTERSHAFT

GEARSHIFT ARM

(e) 360-cc TWO-CYLINDER FOUR-CYCLE

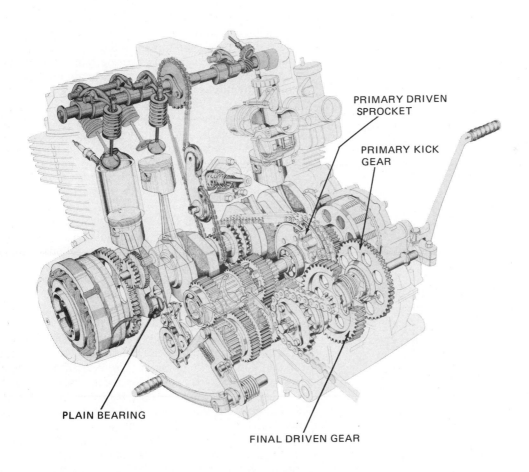

PRIMARY DRIVEN
SPROCKET

PRIMARY KICK
GEAR

PLAIN BEARING

FINAL DRIVEN GEAR

(f) 750-cc FOUR-CYLINDER FOUR-CYCLE

Fig. 2-1 (Continued)

Fig. 2-2 An engine cylinder is shaped like a soda can.

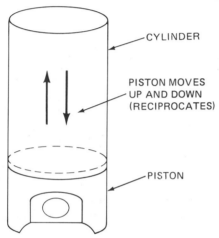

Fig. 2-3 In the engine, the piston moves up and down.

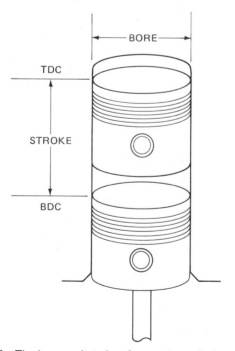

Fig. 2-4 The bore and stroke of an engine cylinder.

ing positions of the piston, the top and bottom, are called *top dead center* (TDC) and *bottom dead center* (BDC). These terms are used often in working with engines.

The piston in the two-cycle engine takes two strokes to complete one cycle. Every downward movement of this piston from TDC to BDC is a power stroke. Every upward movement of the piston from BDC to TDC is a compression stroke. When the piston moves up, it compresses a charge of the air-fuel mixture. Then, as the piston nears TDC, the charge is ignited by a spark from the ignition system. The ignited mixture burns, and the pressure pushes the piston down. In this way, every other stroke produces power (Fig. 2-5a).

NOTE The word *cycle* can mean several things. The way it is used in talking about engines, it means a series of events that repeat themselves. For example, the cycle of the seasons—spring, summer, fall, winter—is repeated every year. In a similar way, the two piston strokes in the two-cycle engine form a cycle that is repeated continuously as long as the engine runs.

The full name of the two-cycle engine is the *two-stroke-cycle engine*. Two piston strokes are required to complete one cycle. It is usually called a *two-cycle engine*, a *two-stroke engine*, or a *two-stroker*.

In the four-cycle engine (or the *four-stroke-cycle engine*) it takes four piston strokes to produce a single power stroke (Fig. 2-5b). Three of the piston strokes, or movements between TDC and BDC, are required to get the cylinder ready for the fourth stroke, which produces the power. In comparing the two-cycle with the four-cycle engine (☞6-13), we see that the four-cycle engine has several advantages in certain applications. This is why it is used in all modern automobiles, trucks, and buses.

The two-cycle engine is simpler in construction, easier to maintain, lighter in weight, and generally less expensive to manufacture. For these reasons, many air-cooled small engines, including many motorcycle engines, are two-cycle engines.

☞2-7
THE ENGINE CYLINDER Most motorcycle engines have from one to four cylinders. Benelli and Honda build motorcycles with a six-cylinder engine. Actually, there are no clear dividing lines between small engines, motorcycle engines, and the engines used in automobiles. Some so-called small engines and motorcycle engines actually are bigger than some engines that have been used in automobiles.

The cylinder is essentially a pocket closed at one end. It is like a can with one end cut out. The piston moves up and down in the cylinder (Fig. 2-3). The fit is loose enough to allow the piston to move up and down easily.

When the piston moves up, it traps a mixture of air and vaporized fuel ahead of it. When the piston gets near the top of the cylinder, an electric spark from the spark plug ignites the mixture. It burns, producing heat and high pressure. If it were not for other parts of the engine, the piston would be blown clear out of the cylinder. We will get to these other parts in later sections.

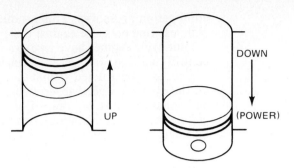

(a) TWO-STROKE CYCLE

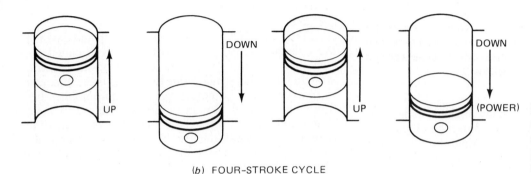

(b) FOUR-STROKE CYCLE

Fig. 2-5 (a) Two stroke. (b) Four stroke. In the two-cycle engine, every other piston stroke is a power stroke.

2-8
PISTON RINGS

The power that the engine produces depends on the pressure developed when the air-fuel mixture burns. If the piston is too loose to fit, much of this pressure would leak past the piston, as shown in Fig. 2-6. This leakage is called *blowby* because the high-pressure gases "blow by" the piston. Blowby reduces the pressure and the amount of power the engine can produce.

However, the piston cannot be made too tight a fit or it will stick in the cylinder. This could damage the engine.

The solution is to use piston rings. Figure 2-7 shows a set of piston rings. The piston rings form a good low-friction seal between the piston and the cylinder. The rings are installed in grooves cut in the piston.

To install the rings on the piston, the rings are expanded and slid down the piston until they drop into the piston grooves. You can see the piston rings in place on the engines shown in Fig. 2-1. When the piston-and-ring assembly is installed in the cylinder, the rings are com-

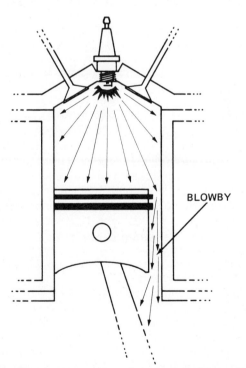

Fig. 2-6 If the piston is a loose fit in the cylinder, much of the pressure will be lost as the burning mixture leaks past or "blows by" the piston.

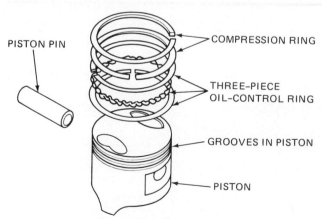

Fig. 2-7 A set of piston rings and a piston for a four-cycle motorcycle engine.

11

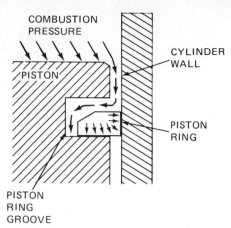

Fig. 2-8 Pressure in the combustion chamber above the piston, either from compression of the air-fuel mixture or from its combustion, presses the ring against the cylinder wall and the lower side of the piston-ring groove.

pressed into the grooves. In many engines, especially two-cycle engines, the rings must fit on the piston in a certain way. The split ends of a ring should almost touch. The gap formed by the split in the ring is called the piston-ring *end gap*.

The rings fit tightly against the cylinder wall and against the sides of the piston. They therefore form a good seal between the piston and the cylinder wall. But the piston and rings can slide up and down easily in the cylinder. The lubricating system, which is described later, coats the piston, piston rings, and cylinder wall with lubricating oil so the rings and piston can move up and down easily.

Figure 2-8 shows how the piston ring works to hold in the compression and combustion pressures. The arrows show the pressure from above the piston passing through the clearance between the piston and the cylinder wall. It presses down against the top and against the back of the piston ring, as shown by the arrows. This pushes the piston ring firmly against the cylinder wall and against the bottom of the piston-ring groove. As a result, there are good seals at both of these points. The higher the pressure in the combustion chamber, the better the seal.

Small two-cycle engines have one or two rings on the piston. Both are compression rings. Two rings are used to divide up the job of holding the compression and

combustion pressures. This produces better sealing with less ring pressure against the cylinder wall.

Four-cycle engines have an extra ring, called the oil-control ring (Fig. 2-9). As we explain later, four-cycle engines are constructed so that they get much more oil on the cylinder wall than do two-cycle engines. This additional oil must be scraped off to prevent it from getting into the combustion chamber, where it would burn and cause trouble. The oil-control ring does this job.

NOTE Some four-cycle-engine pistons have four rings because the engine design requires two oil-control rings for adequate oil control.

2-9
THE CRANK

The piston moves up and down in the cylinder. This up-and-down motion is called *reciprocating motion* (Fig. 2-3). The piston moves in a straight line. This straight-line motion must be changed to *rotary motion* in motorcycles and automobiles before it can be used. Rotary motion is required to make shafts and wheels turn. To change the reciprocating motion to rotary motion, a crank and connecting rod are used (Fig. 2-10). The connecting rod connects the piston to the crank.

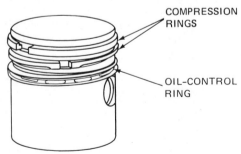

Fig. 2-9 The piston of the four-cycle engine has three rings. The upper two are compression rings, and the lower is an oil-control ring.

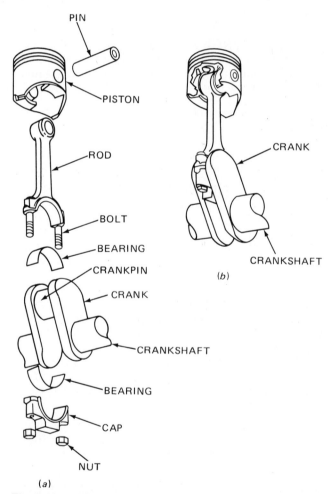

Fig. 2-10 (a) Piston, connecting rod, piston pin, and crank in disassembled view. (b) Piston and connecting-rod assembly, attached to the crankpin on the crankshaft.

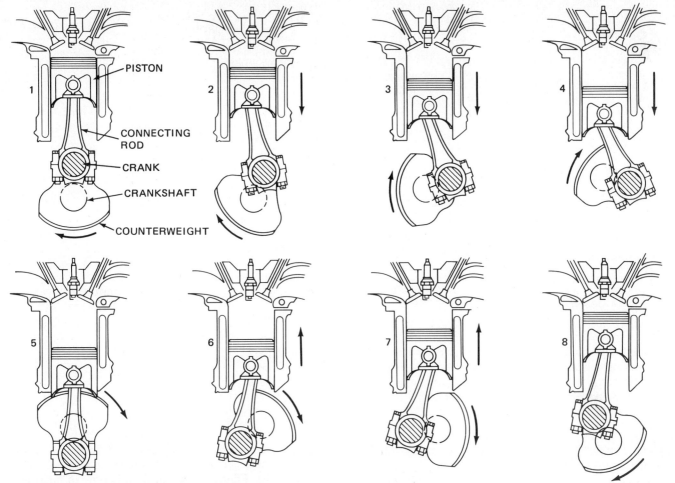

Fig. 2-11 The sequence of actions as the crankshaft completes one revolution and the piston moves from top to bottom to top again.

The crank is a simple device used in many machines. It is an offset part of a shaft. When the shaft rotates, the crank and crankpin swing in a circle. When the piston is pushed down in the cylinder by the pressure, the push on the piston, carried through the connecting rod to the crank, causes the crankshaft to turn. Figure 2-11 shows the motions that the piston, connecting rod, crank, and crankshaft go through. As the piston moves down and up, the top end of the connecting rod moves down and up with it. The bottom end of the connecting rod swings in a circle along with the crank.

The piston end of the connecting rod is attached to the piston by a piston pin, or wrist pin. The other end of the connecting rod is attached to the crankpin of the crank by a rod-bearing cap (Fig. 2-10). There are bearings at both ends of the connecting rod so that the rod can move with relative freedom. Bearings are discussed later.

NOTE The crank end of the connecting rod is called the rod *big end*. The piston end of the connecting rod is called the *small end*.

2-10
THE CRANKSHAFT
The crank is part of the crankshaft. As shown in Fig. 2-10, it is an offset section to which the connecting-rod big end is attached by a

bearing. The crankshaft is mounted in the engine on bearings which allow the crankshaft to rotate. As the crankshaft rotates, the crank swings in a circle (Fig. 2-11).

Crankshafts have counterweights, as shown in Fig. 2-11. These counterweights are used to correct the primary imbalance of the connecting rod, piston pin, Circlip, and piston. This reduces the tendency of the crankshaft to go out-of-round when it is rotating. The result is a smoother-running engine and less wear on the crankshaft bearings.

Crankshafts for motorcycle engines come in a variety of sizes and shapes. Some are automotive-type crankshafts of one-piece construction (Fig. 2-12a). Other crankshafts are of the built-up type (Fig. 2-12b). With the built-up type, a ball or roller bearing can be used, as explained in the following section.

2-11
ENGINE BEARINGS
The crankshaft is supported by bearings. The connecting-rod big end is attached to the crank of the crankshaft by a bearing. A piston pin at the rod small end attaches the rod to the piston (Fig. 2-10).

The piston pin rides in bearings. The crankshaft rides in bearings. Everywhere that there is rotary action in the engine, bearings are used to support the moving

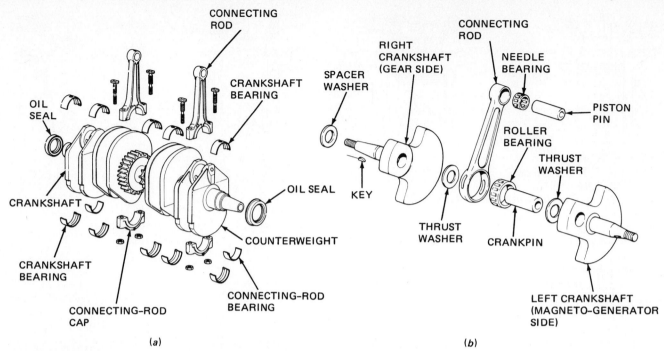

Fig. 2-12 Motorcycle crankshafts. (*a*) A one-piece crankshaft used in a four-cylinder motorcycle engine. (*b*) Disassembled view of a built-up crankshaft for a one-cylinder motorcycle engine. In this engine, the connecting rod has roller bearings at both ends. (*Harley-Davidson Motor Company*)

parts. The purpose of bearings is to reduce friction and allow the parts to move easily.

Bearings are lubricated with oil to make the relative motion easier. In a later chapter, we discuss friction and engine oil, and we look at the lubricating systems that deliver the oil to the moving parts.

Bearings used in engines are of two types, sliding or rolling, as shown in Fig. 2-13. The sliding type of bearing is called a *plain, bushing,* or *sleeve* bearing. It is in the shape of a sleeve that fits around the rotating journal, or shaft. Figure 2-12*a* shows this type of bearing. The sleeve-type connecting-rod big-end bearings—usually called *rod bearings*—are of the split-sleeve type. They must be split so they can be assembled in the engine.

The upper half of the bearing is installed in the rod;

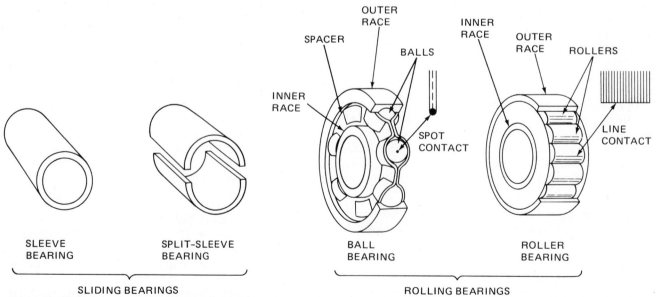

Fig. 2-13 Types of bearings used in engines.

the lower half is installed in the rod-bearing cap. When the rod cap is fastened to the rod, as shown in Fig. 2-10, a complete sleeve bearing is formed. Similarly, the upper halves of the main bearings are assembled in the engine. Then the main-bearing caps, with the lower halves, are attached to the engine to complete the sleeve bearings supporting the crankshaft (Fig. 2-12a).

The typical bearing half (Fig. 2-14) is made of a steel or bronze back to which a lining of relatively soft bearing material is applied. This relatively soft bearing material is made of several materials, such as copper, lead, tin, and other metals. Each of these metals has the ability to conform to slight irregularities of the shaft rotating against it. If wear does take place, it is the bearing that wears. Then, the bearing can be replaced instead of the much more expensive crankshaft or other engine part.

The rolling type of bearing uses balls or rollers between the stationary support and the rotating shaft, as shown in Fig. 2-12b. Since the balls or rollers provide rolling contact, the frictional resistance to movement is much less. In some roller bearings, the rollers are so small that they are hardly bigger than needles. These bearings are called *needle bearings*. Also, some roller bearings have the rollers set at an angle, so the races the rollers roll in are tapered. These bearings are called *tapered roller bearings*. A crankshaft supported by tapered roller bearings is shown in Fig. 2-15.

Some ball and roller bearings are sealed with their lubricant already in place. These bearings require no other lubrication. Other bearings require lubrication from the oil in the gasoline (two-cycle engines) or from the engine lubricating system (four-cycle engines).

As you study different motorcycle engines, you will find that all these types of bearings have been used in different engines. The type of bearing selected by the engineers depends on the design of the engine and the use to which the engine will be put. Sleeve bearings, being satisfactory and less expensive for most engine applications, are used in some four-cycle engines. In automobile engines, sleeve bearings are used almost

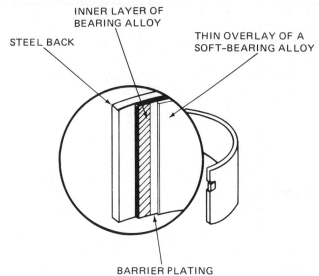

Fig. 2-14 The construction of an insert-type, or sleeve, bearing.

universally for the main, connecting-rod, and piston-pin bearings. But there are many motorcycle engines with ball and roller bearings to support the crankshaft and for the connecting-rod and piston-pin bearings.

**2-12
MAKING THE ENGINE RUN** The engine, in order to run, must be supplied with a mixture of air and gasoline vapor. This mixture must enter the cylinder and be compressed as the piston moves up. Then, a spark must occur in the cylinder so the mixture will be ignited.

The mixture burns rapidly, developing a high pressure which pushes the piston down. This push is carried through the connecting rod and causes the crankshaft to turn. Next, the burned gases must be removed from the cylinder and a fresh charge of the air-fuel mixture brought in. These actions continue as long as the engine runs. Later chapters discuss these actions in detail.

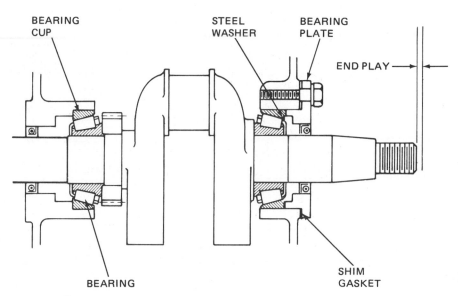

Fig. 2-15 A crankshaft mounted on tapered roller bearings.

CHAPTER 2
REVIEW QUESTIONS

1. What are the two general kinds of engines?
2. What is atmospheric pressure? What causes it?
3. What is a vacuum?
4. What are the two types of internal combustion engines that use pistons?
5. What does TDC mean?
6. What happens to the piston during a power stroke?
7. What is the purpose of the piston rings?
8. What two parts change the reciprocating motion of the piston to the rotary motion of the crankshaft?
9. What connects the piston to the crank? How is this part fastened to the piston? How is it fastened to the crank?
10. What supports the crankshaft?
11. What are two types of bearings?

CHAPTER **3**

MOTORCYCLE CLASSIFICATIONS AND TYPES

After studying this chapter,
you should be able to:

1. List and define the six major classes of motorcycles, from the moped to the dirt bike.

2. Explain what piston displacement means and how to figure it.

3. Define the nine basic classifications of motorcycle engines based on displacement.

4. Discuss engine classification by number and arrangement of cylinders.

5. Discuss motorcycle classification by use, defining mopeds, minibikes, street bikes, enduros, trials bikes, and trikes.

|←——— WHEELBASE ———→|

Fig. 3-1 The wheelbase of a motorcycle. (*Harley-Davidson Motor Company*)

3-1 THE VARIETY OF MOTORCYCLES
There are many different kinds of motorcycles and engines. There is more variety in engines, ignition systems, and other components in motorcycles than in automobiles. When you look at the different kinds of two-wheeled vehicles, at the bottom end of the scale you find inexpensive mopeds that can be lifted by one person. At the other end of the scale, there are large touring bikes that weigh over 700 pounds [318 kg] and cost as much as a small car.

3-2 WHAT IS A MOTORCYCLE?
There are several definitions, ranging from "a two-wheeler with an engine" to the more complete definition of the Uniform Motor Vehicle Code: "Any motor vehicle other than a tractor having a seat or saddle for the use of the rider and designed to travel on not more than three wheels in contact with the ground."

The Society of Automotive Engineers (SAE) has a slightly different definition. According to the SAE: "A motorcycle is any motor vehicle, other than a tractor, designed to operate on no more than three wheels in contact with the ground and weighing less than 1500 pounds [680 kg] curb weight."

Two basic measurements used to classify motorcycles are wheelbase (Fig. 3-1) and seat height (Fig. 3-2).

"Official," or engineering, definitions are important in racing, where you are competing against others. However, they may be less important when you are selecting a new bike or when you are servicing a bike.

When you select a motorcycle, you pick the model that fits your body size, your pocketbook, and your plans for using the bike. When you service bikes, you look at the service needs of each bike and don't worry too much about what class it falls into.

There are other motorcycle classifications. You can classify motorcycles by engine type and size, by performance, or by the type of use the machine was designed for. For example, a dirt bike is a different type of machine from a road bike, a moped, or a minibike. These are motorcycle classifications based on use. We will explain these terms later.

3-3 AN INTRODUCTION TO MOTORCYCLE TYPES
There are about 40 manufacturers, mostly in Japan and Europe, selling motorcycles in the United States. Each manufacturer offers from three to as many as 30 models. This means there are nearly 300 different models to classify. Generally, motorcycles can be put into one of six classifications. This is possible because most bikes are designed for one specific purpose only. For example, one type is for the road, another is for dirt, a third is for desert travel, and a fourth is for the trail. You should not take a road bike on the trail or into

SEAT HEIGHT

Fig. 3-2 The seat height of a motorcycle. (*Honda Motor Company, Ltd.*)

the desert. This is against the law and could damage the bike.

These six classes are listed and briefly discussed below. Later, we will describe each more fully and show you examples.

1. Moped. Theoretically, this is a motorized bicycle. The name comes from *mo*tor-*ped*al. It is a bicycle on which a small engine has been installed.

2. Minibike. This is a "child's" version of the real thing. Basically, a minibike is a motorcycle with smaller wheels, shorter wheelbase, and lower saddle height. It is not intended for use on the road or street. Usually it has no lights, turn signals, or horn.

3. Road, or street bike. This is the major classification of motorcycles. The road bike is for use on paved roads only. There are many different kinds of road bikes, but all are *street-legal*. This means they have headlights, taillights, horn, brakes front and rear, muffler, rearview mirror, and usually a battery-powered electric system. They are built in various models. The lightweight bike (under 200 pounds [91 kg]) is for short runs, such as commuting or going to the store or school. The mid-range bikes, with bigger engines and heavier construction, can go faster than 100 mph [161 km/h]. And at the top of this classification are the heavies, which may weigh more than 700 pounds [318 kg].

4. On-road, off-road bike. This is a compromise bike. It is not quite as good as a strictly road bike on the road and not quite as good as a strictly dirt bike on the dirt. But there is enough of both in the on-road, off-road bike so you can ride it on the highway and then cut across a field, away from highway traffic. This road-and-dirt type of bike is generally known as the *enduro*.

You can tell this class of bike by several characteristics. The front fender is several inches above the front tire to allow for the up-and-down movement of the wheel on rough terrain. The exhaust pipe or pipes are high or sweep upward to reduce the chance of grass fires being set by sparks from the exhaust gas. They do not have a large muffler or extra-large knobby tires.

5. Trail bike. Most trail bikes are motorcycles made strictly for trails. Some are designed for both trail and road, but they can take rough terrain and fields. Some models have extra-large tires. Some have three wheels; these are tricycles and commonly are called *trikes*.

6. Dirt bike. This is an off-road bike, designed for a particular purpose. Some dirt bikes are desert racers, some are for trials (not trails), some are motocrossers, and some are for scrambles. These are various types of competition events.

Not every bike falls neatly into one of the classifications. One of the major activities of many motorcycle riders (motorcyclists) is modification. The motorcycle owner may decide to modify the bike by installing a different engine, different tires, special brakes, or even a specially modified frame or steering system. The bike ends up with a different character and possibly falls into a different classification.

3-4 ENGINES AND PISTON DISPLACEMENT

A great many kinds of engines are used in motorcycles, from small single-cylinder engines to large six-cylinder engines that approach the size used in automobiles. These engines are not classified according to horsepower, but according to piston displacement. Now let's find out what this term means.

The engine produces power by means of pistons that move up and down in cylinders (Fig. 2-11). Piston displacement is the volume that the piston displaces as it moves from its bottom position to its top position, as shown in Fig. 3-3. The bottom position is called BDC (bottom dead center) and the top position is called TDC (top dead center).

Motorcycle piston displacements are all classified in the metric system in cubic centimeters (cc).

Piston displacement is a volume measurement. When we talk about volume, we mean what is inside an enclosed space. For example, we mean the volume of air in a room or the volume of water in a bottle. When comparing motorcycle engines, we talk of volume in terms of cubic centimeters (cc). One cubic centimeter is a cube measuring one centimeter (cm) on a side. There are 16.387 cc in 1 cubic inch. The engine in one model of motorcycle (Fig. 3-4) has a cylinder diameter (or *bore*) of 6.1 cm [61 millimeters (mm)], or 2.4 inches. The area of a circle of this diameter is 29.2 square centimeters (cm²), or 7.54 square inches.

To figure the volume, multiply the area by the *stroke* (the distance the piston moves from BDC to TDC). In the engine in Fig. 3-4, the stroke is 6.1 cm. This gives a volume of 178 cc for one cylinder. However, the engine has three cylinders. To find total engine displacement, multiply by 3 (3 × 178 = 534). Engine displacement is 534 cc. A 534-cc engine is a midsize motorcycle engine. It is rated by the manufacturer as producing 50 horsepower (hp) [37.3 kW] at 6500 revolutions per minute (rpm).

Think of piston displacement as the working space inside the engine. It is where all the action takes place as the piston moves up and down. The bigger the piston displacement, the greater the working space, and the

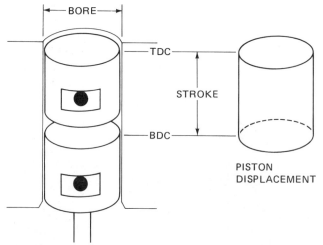

Fig. 3-3 The piston displacement is the volume the piston displaces, or takes the place of, as it moves from BDC to TDC.

more power the engine can produce. For example, one engine with a piston displacement of 97 cc is rated at 11 hp [8.2 kW] at 7000 rpm. Another engine, with 981-cc displacement, develops 80 hp [59.7 kW] at 7250 rpm. Later, in a chapter on engine measurements, we explain how piston displacement and engine horsepower are tied together. Also covered is the formula for calculating the piston displacement of any engine.

There are several ways to increase piston displacement and horsepower. The diameter of the engine cylinder, or bore, can be made larger. The distance the piston moves from bottom to top, or stroke, can be made larger. Also, the manufacturer can increase the number of cylinders in the engine.

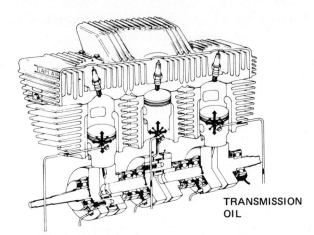

Fig. 3-4 A three-cylinder motorcycle engine. (*Suzuki Motor Company, Ltd.*)

3-5 ENGINE CLASSIFICATION BY PISTON DISPLACEMENT

The piston displacement of an engine, or simply *displacement*, is the piston displacement of one cylinder times the number of cylinders. Engines are made in such a variety of sizes that engine displacements are used to classify motorcycles. In the following list, note how one classification merges into another:

1. Under 100 cc. These are lightweight engines for lightweight motorcycles. Their primary use is for economy bikes and minibikes. Speed and acceleration are not very good, but the gasoline mileage is up to 140 miles per gallon (mpg). The main use for this engine is in bikes for pleasure-riding, around-town shopping, going to school, and off-road recreation.

2. 100 cc. The "hundred" may give up to 90 mpg. It is used in a wide variety of motorcycle models for street and off-road use.

3. 125 cc. This is the most commonly used engine size. It offers speed, acceleration, and fuel economy. It is not the most desirable engine for highway use because of its limited top speed and acceleration. This engine often is used in enduro and road-and-dirt motorcycles.

4. 175 cc. Engines in this general category vary from 171 to 199 cc. Road motorcycles with this engine may average about 55 mpg. However, most engines of this size are used in enduros and dirt bikes.

5. 250 cc. Engines of this size run from 200 to about 300 cc. Almost all motorcycle manufacturers have models in this category. This size engine is used in almost every type of motorcycle, including enduros and street, dirt, trail, and racing bikes.

6. 350 to 400 cc. Here is the beginning of the high-performance motorcycles. High speed, rapid acceleration, and relatively good gasoline mileage are delivered by these engines. This size engine is used in almost every type of motorcycle. It is very popular in the racing motocross bike. A motocross bike also is called an *Mx-er* Motocross racing is probably the most demanding, from rider and machine, of any sport.

7. 500 cc. This is an engine for the high-performance bike. When we get into this category, fuel economy is not very important. This size engine is fitted to many street models. It also is used in racing bikes.

8. 600 to 750 cc. These are street and touring motorcy-

cles that can weigh more than 500 pounds [227 kg]. The heavy weight is the reason they are not suitable for dirt, desert, motocross, or trail riding. You don't move a big, heavy motorcycle through a series of obstacles that demand instant response. Besides, picking up a 500-pound [227-kg] motorcycle, if it falls down, is very difficult.

9. Over 750 cc. These are the large touring motorcycles. Some models are classed as superbikes. They are used in motorcycles weighing as much as 700 pounds [318 kg]. Some of these are six-cylinder engines developing up to 90 hp [67 kg]. They compare in size and output to engines used in small cars. These engines can power a rider over the highway at 130 mph [210 km/h] and sometimes even faster. Fuel economy is considered poor. The price of a fully equipped large motorcycle can be higher than the price of a small car.

3-6 ENGINE CLASSIFICATION BY NUMBER AND ARRANGEMENT OF CYLINDERS

Many motorcycles use one-cylinder engines. These are often called *singles*. Other motorcycle engines have two or more cylinders, arranged in various ways (Fig. 3-5).

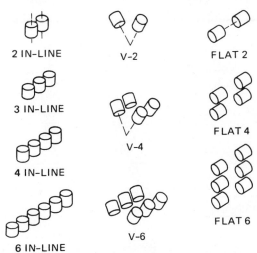

Fig. 3-5 Various cylinder arrangements used for motorcycle engines.

Two-cylinder engines are called *twins*. The two cylinders can be arranged in line (a *vertical twin*), in a V, or opposed.

Three-cylinder engines are often called *triples,* or *triplets*. The three cylinders are in a single line. Four-cylinder engines are called *fours,* and six-cylinder engines are called *sixes*. There are few sixes in motorcycles, but many motorcycles for street and touring have four-cylinder engines. The four cylinders may be arranged in a line, in two banks of two cylinders each set at an angle, or in two opposed banks of two cylinders each.

⌥ 3-7
ENGINE CLASSIFICATION BY STROKES
PER CYCLE   Another engine classification is by the operating cycle. There are two basic cycles—the two-stroke cycle and the four-stroke cycle. These were mentioned in ⌥ 2-6 and are discussed in detail in Chaps. 5 and 6.

⌥ 3-8
MOTORCYCLE CLASSIFICATION BY USE
Motorcycles also are classified according to their purpose, or the use to which they will be put. In ⌥ 3-3, we listed these categories—mopeds, minibikes, road bikes, dirt bikes, and so on. Now, let us look at each of these categories in detail.

⌥ 3-9
MOPEDS   *Moped* is pronounced as two syllables—*mo-ped*. Figure 3-6 shows mopeds. Basically, a moped is a bicycle on which a small engine has been installed.

The French firm Velosolex was probably the first company to produce a moped. They simply bolted a small engine on a bicycle frame in front of the handlebars (Fig. 3-6a). The engine drives a small rubber wheel. You start off with the engine disengaged, pedaling to get moving. Then you throw a lever and the engine moves down and forward so its rubber wheel comes in contact with the front tire. This starts the engine and it takes over. The engine is not very powerful, so you might have to help by pedaling up steep hills. According to the manufacturers, this moped can travel up to 150 miles on one gallon of gasoline.

Other mopeds drive the rear wheel with a chain or rubber V-belt (Fig. 3-6b). On these models, you start pedaling and then press a button for a few seconds. This starts the engine and it takes over.

Mopeds use the U-type, or step-through, frame you see on girls' bicycles. This provides the room needed for the engine. Suspension varies from springs in the seat to motorcycle-type suspension with the wheels separately sprung.

⌥ 3-10
NHTSA RULING ON MOPEDS   The National
Highway Traffic Safety Agency (NHTSA) has issued special rules that put mopeds in a slightly different category from the strictly motorcycle classification. The federal rules eliminated the necessity for the moped to have a foot-operated rear-wheel brake, turn signals, and lights that work when the bike is standing still. Instead, the federal rules permit:

1. Both brake levers to be installed on the handlebars
2. Use of a wheel-driven bicycle-type generator for lights
3. Elimination of turn signals and battery
4. Reduction of braking requirements for mopeds with top speeds of under 30 mph [48 km/h] to match bicycle braking requirements

(a)   (b)

Fig. 3-6   Mopeds. (*a*) A moped that has the engine mounted over the front wheel. (*b*) A moped with the engine on the frame. (*Velosolex; American Garelli*)

With these reduced requirements, the new category of mopeds was introduced. State and local regulations concerning mopeds vary greatly.

3-11 MINIBIKES

Minibikes (Fig. 3-7) are supplied in numerous sizes and models. Some can be fitted with bicycle-type trainer wheels. These are extra wheels attached to the sides of the minibike to keep it from falling over while the youngster learns to ride it.

Some minibikes are designed for off-road trail use only. Practically all have single-cylinder engines of under 100-cc displacement and under 10-hp [7.46-kW] output. Seat height is from 18 inches [457 mm] to 25 inches [635 mm]. This emphasizes the fact that some of these minibikes are for very *small* children.

Minibikes for trail use are not required to be equipped with lights and horn. Some minibikes can be used for both road and trail, and these are road-equipped. However, authorities advise against using minibikes on the highway. They are small and too easily overlooked, and they do not have the power to accelerate and keep up with fast-moving traffic.

3-12 ROAD, OR STREET MOTORCYCLES

This is the major category of motorcycles. There are a hundred or more street models to choose from, with a great variety of engine sizes. All have certain things in common. The front fender is close to the wheel. The tires have street tread and not the knobby or stud tread used on off-road motorcycles. We cover tires in later chapters. Street motorcycles are equipped with lights, horn, front and rear brakes, and license plates. The street bike is made in a variety of sizes—lightweight, or economy; middleweight, or midrange (including sports bikes); and heavyweight, or touring. In the heavyweight class there is also the superbike. Now, let's discuss each classification.

NOTE These classifications are not completely distinct. One class merges into another. Different manufacturers might classify the same motorcycle in different categories. Some motorcycles might fall into either one of two adjacent categories, according to how you might classify them. Also, an owner might modify a motorcycle in a way that would put it into a different category.

1. Lightweight, or economy. This is the least expensive street bike (Fig. 3-8). It is fully equipped with the legally required lights, brakes, and horn. It has an engine ranging in size from less than 100-cc to about 125-cc displacement. Almost all are single-cylinder. A few have two-cylinder engines. Because the engines are small, the bikes are not suitable for long highway trips. However, they are economical to operate and provide up to 125 mpg. You see these bikes around town—commuting, running errands, and going to and from school.

2. Middleweight, or midrange. In midrange street bikes, the engines range from 200 to 599 cc (Fig. 3-9). Many have one-cylinder engines, but there are twos, threes, and fours in this classification. Weights run from a little over 200 pounds [91 kg] to more than 400 pounds [181

Fig. 3-7 A 75-cc minibike. (*Kawasaki Heavy Industries, Ltd.*)

Fig. 3-8 A lightweight street bike. It has a 90-cc two-cycle single-cylinder engine. (*Kawasaki Heavy Industries, Ltd.*)

Fig. 3-9 A midrange street bike. The engine is a two-cylinder four-cycle engine with a displacement of 360 cc. (*ATW*)

kg]. The motorcycles in the lower engine-size and weight range are just about the smallest bikes you can safely use on the highway. They have adequate acceleration and speed needed to keep up with traffic.

3. Sports bikes. This is really a subcategory of the midrange motorcycle and includes the heavier and more powerful models. You get better performance with these motorcycles. Some models are among the most powerful bikes on the road today.

4. Heavyweights. Here are the largest, most powerful motorcycles, excluding the specials built for high performance and special competition events. A touring motorcycle is shown in Fig. 3-10. These motorcycles weigh from around 400 pounds to more than 700 pounds [181 to 318 kg]. They are built for highway and interstate travel. The suspension and seat will carry a rider and passenger all day without excessive fatigue. These motorcycles have electric starters. Engines range in

size from two to six cylinders. Displacements range from around 650 to 1200 cc. These bikes often are called *touring bikes* because that is what they are designed for—long hauls on the highway. There are several variations of heavyweights, as follows:

a. Superbikes. These are generally large motorcycles with performance that borders on the unbelievable! They may not be as comfortable as touring bikes, but they will outperform almost anything on the road.

b. Cafe racers. The story goes that motorcyclists in Paris, France, like to race from one cafe to another. For this friendly competition, modifications were made. The results were superbikes with a difference. The modifications included a sort of shielding, called fairing, which reduced wind resistance. The seats were moved back and the handlebars were redesigned so the rider could ride low in the saddle, shielded from the wind by the fairing. The result was a highly responsive and very fast motorcycle with a style of its own.

c. Chopper. This is another special category for customized motorcycles. What started out as the hobby of a few is now a separate category. The chopper owner usually is a person who wants something more than transportation. The result is a distinctive type of two-wheeler (Fig. 3-11). Note that the front wheel appears to be way out in front. The general impression is that of a low-slung, different sort of motorcycle. Engines in these bikes are usually multicylinder and of a fairly high displacement.

3-13 ENDUROS, OR DUAL-PURPOSE MOTORCYCLES
These are the motorcycles that can be used both on the highway and for dirt or trail riding (Fig. 3-12). Because enduros must be street-legal, they have lights, rearview mirror, horn, and brakes front and rear. You can tell an enduro from a strictly street bike at a glance. The enduro has a front fender

Fig. 3-10 A large touring bike with an engine displacement of 900 cc. (*Kawasaki Heavy Industries, Ltd.*)

Fig. 3-11 A chopper type of motorcycle. Note how the front wheel has been set forward.

several inches above the front wheel, as shown in Fig. 3-12. But strictly dirt and trail bikes have this high fender, too. However, the enduro also has the required street-legal equipment, and the dirt bike does not.

There have been, and probably will continue to be, arguments as to the merits of the enduro as compared with the strictly street or strictly dirt machine. The dirt machine should be as light as possible, consistent with the strength and power demands of the job it is called upon to handle. The good road machine is relatively heavy and also has enough power to provide a smooth and comfortable ride. The tires should be different for the two machines—knobby for dirt, relatively smooth for the road. The engine and transmission should be different for the two types of operation.

A street motorcycle should have an engine-transmission combination that provides high torque and power in the upper speed ranges. This gives the bike what it needs for high-speed maneuvering on the highway. The dirt bike moves at relatively low speeds. Its engine-transmission combination should deliver maximum torque and power at low bike speeds.

Therefore, the good enduro is a compromise motorcycle. Some models are more dirt than road. Others are more road than dirt. The cyclist who is shopping for an enduro has a lot to think about. There are two sub-classifications of enduros, as follows:

1. Road-trail enduro. These motorcycles tend to have higher ground clearance than other models because they are designed for rough travel on wilderness trails. Some have luggage racks because the road-trailer is often looking for a place to pitch a tent or at least sleep out for the night. These bikes can take to the highway, being street-legal, but their best performance is in the low-speed range. This means they have relatively poor performance on the highway, particularly at higher speeds. Also, because they are lightweight, they do not give a good ride at medium or high speed.

2. Road-wood enduro. These are similar to the road-trail enduro but are generally somewhat tougher. Usually, they have luggage racks. Some have special transmissions to provide maximum engine power at low bike speeds.

**3-14
SPECIAL-PURPOSE MOTORCYCLES** In this category are the bikes designed for off-road recreational or competition use exclusively. Each bike is designed for one special purpose and cannot compete in other categories. All have one thing in common. They must be trucked or carried on a trailer to the scene of the action, since they do not have to be street-legal. This means the bike has no lights, no horn, no mirror, no muffler. In this category are the motocrosser, the desert racer, the scrambler, and the trial (not trail) bike.

1. Motocrossers. Also known as *Mxs*, these are rugged machines (Fig. 3-13). Motocrossing is considered to be the most strenuous sport, with the possible exception of soccer. Therefore, the motorcycle has to be as tough as it can be made.

Fig. 3-12 A 175-cc enduro. (*Kawasaki Heavy Industries, Ltd.*)

The bikes are raced on a closed course that may be shorter or longer than a mile. The course is over rough terrain made even more difficult by the addition of obstacles. It can include steep hills, sand, water, mud, jumps over logs and other obstacles, sharp turns, deep ruts, and a long straight stretch which may be downhill. The engine and the motocross rider must be strong enough to take the punishment of the course. Motorcycle frames have broken during motocross competitions.

The rider also must be tough. A motocross course has many hazards and jumps (Fig. 3-13) which demand quick response from rider and machine. So the motor-

Fig. 3-13 An Mx is a motorcycle used for motocross racing.

Fig. 3-14 A tricycle, or all-terrain cycle. It has a single-cylinder four-cycle 90-cc engine. (*Honda Motor Company, Ltd.*)

cycle must have ease of handling and quick power response. All Mxs have a minimum of hardware, high front fenders, engine mounted high off the ground, a skid plate under the engine to protect it, and knobby tires. The Mx must be strong enough to take motocross-course punishment and light enough to get through the worst hazards. Also, it must be powerful enough to handle whatever comes up on the course at competition speeds.

2. Desert racers. These are found largely in the western states, because that is where the deserts are. Desert racers are very similar to motocrossers in general construction. However, they are built for long runs at top engine torque and power at intermediate to relatively high bike speeds. The engines are usually in the high displacement range.

3. Scramblers. These are bikes with high-performance engines that start quickly. They can take off fast and can keep going. The transmissions are geared to give high torque at low speeds.

4. Trial bikes. This type of motorcycle was first developed in Britain during the early 1900s. The purpose of the trial was to test the reliability of the motorcycle and, later, the skill of the rider. During the trial, unscheduled stops caused the rider to lose points. Today, a typical trial bike is a lightweight motorcycle with a 250-cc engine, reinforced frame, knobby tires, and exceptionally low gearing.

**3-15
TRICYCLES** The tricycle, or *trike,* is a motorcycle on which the rear wheel has been moved to one side to make room for a third wheel at the rear. A popular type of recreational trike is shown in Fig. 3-14. A motorcycle with a sidecar is another form of tricycle.

**CHAPTER 3
REVIEW QUESTIONS**

1. What is a moped?
2. What is a minibike?
3. What is a motorcycle?
4. What is seat height?
5. What measuring points on a motorcycle are used to determine wheelbase?
6. What equipment must be on a motorcycle to make it street-legal?
7. Why should a street bike not be ridden across fields?
8. What is an enduro model of motorcycle?
9. What is a dirt bike?

10. What are the smallest and largest piston displacements for motorcycle engines?
11. What is piston displacement?
12. What is the meaning of TDC?
13. What is the meaning of BDC?
14. What is the most common engine size for a motorcycle?
15. What types of motorcycles use knobby tires?
16. How does a motocross bike differ from others?
17. What is the difference between a trail bike and a trial bike?
18. What is a trike, or tricycle?

CHAPTER 4

MOTORCYCLE CONSTRUCTION

After studying this chapter,
you should be able to:

1. Describe various types of motorcycle frames.

2. Explain what the swinging rear fork is and how it works.

3. Define a shock absorber and explain how it works.

4. Discuss front suspension and steering.

5. Describe the different types of wheels and tires.

6. Discuss motorcycle brakes and explain how the different types work.

7. Describe the locations of the different controls on motorcycles and explain how they work.

8. Describe motorcycle power trains and define their purpose.

4-1
MOTORCYCLE CONSTRUCTION

A motorcycle consists of a frame, a steerable front wheel, an engine, a transmission, a final drive to carry engine power to the rear wheel, springs at the front and rear wheels, and brakes to slow or stop the motorcycle (Fig. 4-1). The basic shape and layout has changed little since about 1900.

A motorcycle has many other necessary and important components, such as the controls and the lights. Later chapters cover two-cycle engines, four-cycle engines, electric systems, wheels and tires, and other parts and systems in the motorcycle.

4-2
MOTORCYCLE FRAMES

The purpose of the motorcycle frame is to support the engine and rider. At the same time, the frame provides attachment points for the wheels. The front wheel must be mounted so that it can be pivoted from side to side for steering. The frame must be light but strong, rigid under stress, and formed so that the wheels, engine, and rider can be easily accommodated.

Several designs have been used for frames. The most common uses seamless steel tubing with welded joints and with lugs welded on to support the engine and transmission. Figure 4-2a is an example of this construction. This frame is called a *cradle frame* because the engine and transmission are cradled between the two lower frame loops. In some designs, no longer widely used, the engine and transmission form the lower part of the frame. The tubular parts end with lugs which are attached to the engine-transmission assembly to complete the frame.

In addition to the attachments for the engine, the frame includes the support for the front-wheel steering head. The rear end of the frame has a support for the pivoted fork that locates the rear wheel. We describe suspensions later. Figure 4-2b shows the tubular frame for one model of Kawasaki. In many frames, the tubular parts are welded together and the lugs are then brazed onto the frame at the proper locations.

Occasionally, rectangular or square tubing is used for motorcycle frames. The advantage of using a square or rectangular tube is that it has flat surfaces to which lugs can be more easily brazed or welded. In addition, it is easier to screw or bolt accessories to flat surfaces than

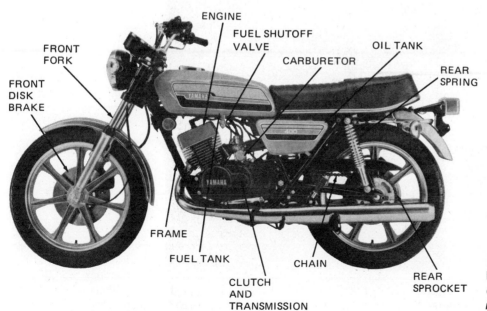

ENGINE

FUEL SHUTOFF VALVE

CARBURETOR

OIL TANK

FRONT FORK

REAR SPRING

FRONT DISK BRAKE

FRAME

FUEL TANK

CLUTCH AND TRANSMISSION

CHAIN

REAR SPROCKET

Fig. 4-1 The major components of the motorcycle. (*Yamaha International Corporation*)

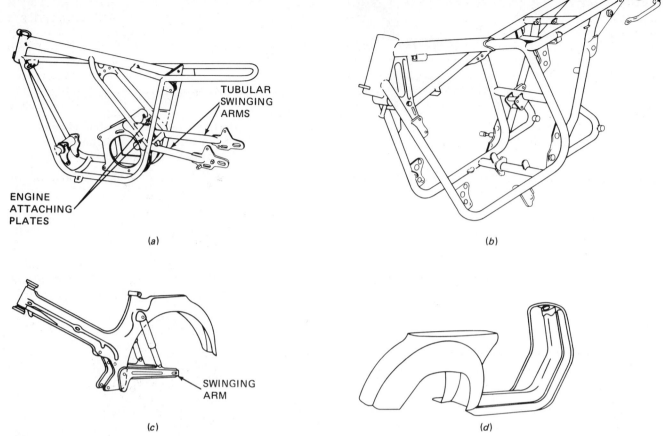

Fig. 4-2 Motorcycle frames. (*a*) Frame made of welded tubes. The tubular swinging arms are pivoted on the engine attaching plates. The plates are rubber-mounted to the frame. (*b*) Frame made of seamless steel tubing. (*c*) A spine frame. (*d*) A reverse-spine, or open, frame. (*Kawasaki Heavy Industries, Ltd.; Castrol, Limited*)

Fig. 4-3 The swing arm on a motorcycle that has monoshock rear suspension. (*Yamaha International Corporation*)

to round surfaces. A possible disadvantage is that square or rectangular tubing is not as strong as round tubing, on a comparative weight basis.

Another type of frame construction is called a *spine frame*. This name comes from the use of a single, strong, large-diameter tube, or box-section, that serves as the sole means of tieing together the front and rear wheels and the engine with the transmission. The spine frame shown in Fig. 4-2c is made of pressed heavy-gauge steel plate which has been welded together. The front end contains the support for the front-wheel steering head. The rear end, in the construction shown in Fig. 4-2c, includes the rear fender and the attachments for the pivoted fork that supports the rear wheel.

On some motorcycles, the spine doubles as an oil tank. Some spine frames use the engine and transmission assembly as an integral part of the frame itself.

The *reverse spine frame*, or *open frame*, shown in Fig. 4-2d, is used on motor scooters and lightweight bikes. The advantage of this design is that the rider sits "in" the bike, rather than straddling a frame member.

4-3
REAR SUSPENSIONS The swinging rear fork is used on almost every type of motorcycle. The swinging fork, or *swing arm*, has a single pivot point behind the engine on the frame (Fig. 4-3). This allows the rear wheel assembly to move up and down. It moves in an arc as it pivots around the attachment point on the frame. Travel of the rear wheel is controlled by one or two springs and shock absorbers. Construction of the rear swing arm and its effect on chain life are discussed in Chapter 30, "Motorcycle Frames, Suspension, and Steering."

A variety of rear springs have been used on motorcy-

cles. The most common arrangement includes a pair of coil springs, one on each side (Fig. 4-4). Each spring is combined with a shock absorber into a spring-damper assembly. The upper ends are attached to the frame on pivots. The lower ends are attached to the two legs of the swinging fork, just at or near the rear-wheel axle (Fig. 4-4). As the fork swings up and down, the springs compress and extend. Today, all motorcycles have some type of springing between the rear-wheel axle and the frame.

4-4
SHOCK ABSORBERS The purpose of the shock absorber, or damper, is to prevent excessive wheel movements and to damp out secondary movements of the wheel after any road irregularity has passed. The shock absorbers for the rear wheel are mounted inside the coil springs, as shown in Fig. 4-4. In the illustration, note the location of the adjusting cams. These can be adjusted to compress the spring varying amounts. This, in turn, will change the ride to soft, medium, or hard.

4-5
SEAT-POST SPRINGING In some motorcycles, the seat is sprung. It is supported on a post that moves up and down on springs. This improves riding comfort and gives a smoother ride. The springs absorb part of any up-and-down motion of the frame before the motion reaches the rider.

4-6
FRONT SUSPENSION AND STEERING A motorcycle must be steerable. This is accomplished by swinging the front wheel from side to side. At the same

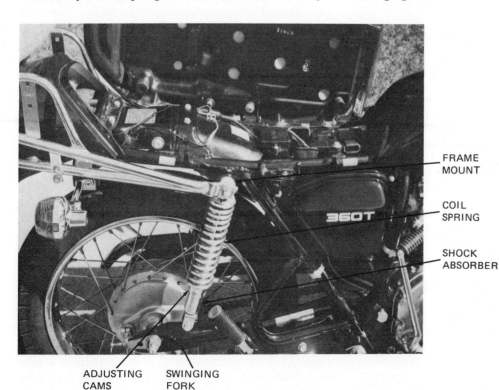

FRAME
MOUNT

COIL
SPRING

SHOCK
ABSORBER

ADJUSTING
CAMS

SWINGING
FORK

Fig. 4-4 The spring-damper mounts at the top to the frame and at the bottom to the swinging fork. (*Honda Motor Company, Ltd.*)

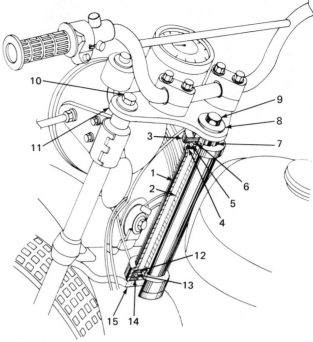

1. Head pipe	6. Inner race	11. Stem head
2. Steering stem shaft	7. Stem Locknut	12. Outer race
3. Stem cap	8. Washer	13. Ball bearing
4. Outer race	9. Stem head bolt	14. Inner Race
5. Ball bearing	10. Fork top bolt	15. Steering stem

Fig. 4-6 Details of the steering system. (*Kawasaki Heavy Industries, Ltd.*)

Fig. 4-5 A telescopic type of front fork that has the spring and shock absorber built into each leg. (*Honda Motor Company, Ltd.*)

time, the front wheel must be sprung. A spring must be interposed between the frame and the front wheel. Motorcycles have a front fork that supports the front wheel while permitting it to swing from side to side for steering.

There are various designs of front fork. Figure 4-5 shows the telescopic type. On each side of the wheel there is a smaller inside tube, or main tube. The lower end of the inside tube fits into the top of the larger tube (also called the *fork leg,* or *slider*). Inside the main tube are springs and a piston. The main tube is filled with oil. As the front wheel moves up and down, the springs expand and shorten to absorb the shock of the holes and bumps that the front wheel meets. At the same time, the oil in the tube is forced through small holes by the piston. This restricts the spring movement. The action is similar to the shock-absorber action in the rear suspension.

As every motorcycle (and bicycle) rider knows, there are two ways to steer. On the highway, body lean can be used for steering. But for low-speed maneuvering, directional changes must be made by turning the handlebars. When the handlebars are turned, the front fork turns with them. This changes the position of the front wheel, and the motorcycle steers in a new direction. Figure 4-6 shows a typical construction of the steering head and frame assembly.

4-7
WHEELS Most motorcycle wheels are of the spoke type, as shown in Fig. 4-7a. This type of wheel is made by lacing the spokes through holes in the hub and then fastening them through holes in the rim. The result is a strong, light, and flexible wheel that is held together by tension on the spokes. However, spoke wheels require periodic adjustment to be sure all spokes are equally tight. Another disadvantage of spoke wheels is that the holes in the rim prevent the use of tubeless tires. The air would leak out through the spoke holes.

Cast wheels are available on some motorcycles. These look like the mag wheels that are popular on cars and vans. Like the mag wheels for cars and vans, motorcycle mags for street use are usually made from cast aluminum. Real magnesium wheels are very expensive and are usually found only on racing bikes.

An advantage of mag wheels is that the rim is in one piece, without any holes. Therefore, tubeless tires can be used on mag wheels. A disadvantage of some cast mag wheels is that they are heavier than the spoke wheels they replace. Figure 4-7b shows a mag-style wheel used by Honda on some bikes. This wheel is assembled from aluminum parts and is lighter than cast aluminum wheels.

4-8
TIRES AND TUBES The tires used on most motorcycles are of the inner-tube type. An inner doughnut-shaped tube is put between the wheel rim and the tire itself to hold the air. The inner tube has an air valve, as shown in Fig. 4-7. When the tire and tube have been

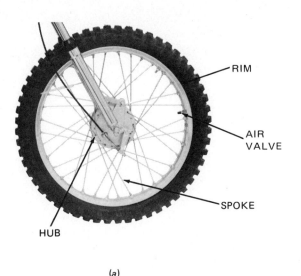

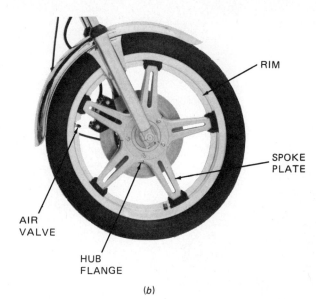

(a)

(b)

Fig. 4-7 Motorcycle wheels. (a) Most motorcycle wheels are of the spoke type. (b) A mag-type wheel that mounts a tubeless tire. (*Pacific Basin Trading Company; Honda Motor Company, Ltd.*)

installed on the rim, compressed air is forced into the tube through the air valve. On the motorcycle, the tire provides some shock-absorbing action, delivers engine power to the ground, and provides braking action to slow or stop the motorcycle when the brake for that wheel is applied.

A typical motorcycle tire is shown in cutaway view in Fig. 4-8. A motorcycle tire is different from a car tire in that the motorcycle tire has tread farther up the sidewalls. This design is needed to keep the tire in contact with the ground when the motorcycle is leaning into high-speed turns.

Tires come with a variety of treads, as shown in Fig. 4-9. A universal tread is shown to the left. The other treads are special-purpose designs. Knobby tread gives positive bite on soft or rocky hills. Motocross tread is for dirt, track, hill climbing, and cross-country driving. Street tread is for street and highway travel. Rib tread is especially designed for taking corners fast and has good road-holding ability. Stud tread is for scrambles, hill climbing, and heavy off-road use.

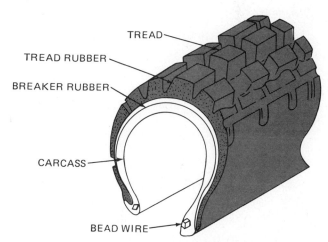

Fig. 4-8 A cutaway view of a motorcycle tire, showing its construction. (*Kawasaki Heavy Industries, Ltd.*)

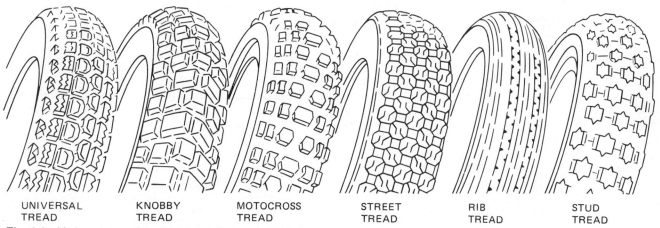

| UNIVERSAL TREAD | KNOBBY TREAD | MOTOCROSS TREAD | STREET TREAD | RIB TREAD | STUD TREAD |

Fig. 4-9 Various types of tire treads used on motorcycle tires.

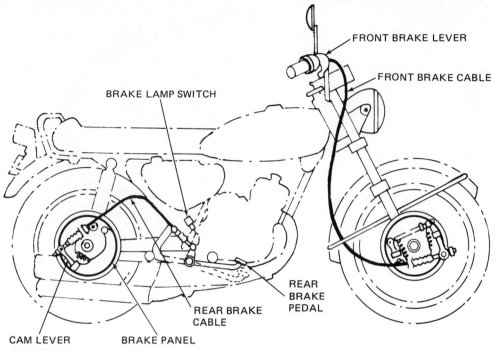

FRONT BRAKE LEVER

FRONT BRAKE CABLE

BRAKE LAMP SWITCH

REAR BRAKE PEDAL

REAR BRAKE CABLE

CAM LEVER

BRAKE PANEL

Fig. 4-10 The brake system on a motorcycle. The front-wheel brake is applied by a lever on the right handlebar. The rear-wheel brake is applied by a foot-operated brake pedal on the right side of the motorcycle. (*Kawasaki Heavy Industries, Ltd.*)

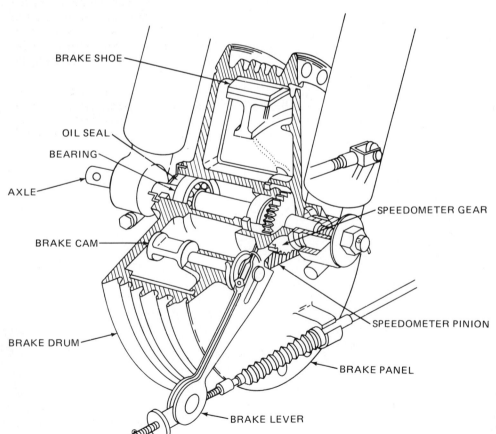

BRAKE SHOE

OIL SEAL

BEARING

AXLE

BRAKE CAM

BRAKE DRUM

SPEEDOMETER GEAR

SPEEDOMETER PINION

BRAKE PANEL

BRAKE LEVER

Fig. 4-11 A cutaway view of a front-wheel hub, showing the construction of a drum brake. (*Kawasaki Heavy Industries, Ltd.*)

4-9
BRAKES

Automotive-type brakes are used in motorcycles, which may have drum brakes, disk brakes, or one of each type. Front and rear brakes usually are controlled separately, as shown in Fig. 4-10. The front brake is applied by a lever on the right handlebar. The rear brake is applied by a foot pedal on the right side of the motorcycle (Fig. 4-10).

The brakes on many motorcycles are mechanically operated by cables that connect the handlebar lever to the front wheel, and the foot pedal to the rear wheel. Other motorcycles have brakes that are operated by an automotive-type hydraulic brake system.

The typical drum type of motorcycle brake is shown in Fig. 4-11. It has a pair of curved shoes, lined with a tough, heat-resistant material such as asbestos. When the brakes are applied, these shoe linings are forced outward and into contact with the smooth inner surface of the brake drum.

Disk brakes are installed on many motorcycles, especially larger and heavier motorcycles. Early installations were mostly on the front wheel, as shown in Fig. 4-12. Now disk brakes are used on both front and rear wheels. The disk brake on a motorcycle usually is hydraulically operated.

Figure 4-13 shows the hydraulic system for a front-wheel disk brake. The hydraulic system provides stronger braking and requires less hand or foot force to apply the brake. The complete hydraulic brake system includes a master cylinder on the right handlebar, a master cylinder for the right foot pedal, brake lines connecting the master cylinders to the calipers, and the caliper and disk at each wheel.

On the motorcycle, the caliper is stationary, and the disk rotates with the wheel hub. When the disk brake is applied, a piston in the master cylinder sends brake fluid through brake lines to the wheel caliper. The brake fluid in the wheel caliper causes a brake pad located on each side of the rotating disk to move against it. The effect is to clamp the disk between the two pads, slowing or stopping the disk. This gripping of the disk pro-

Fig. 4-12 A front-wheel disk brake on a motorcycle. (*Yamaha International Corporation*)

duces the braking action that slows or stops the motorcycle.

In later chapters, you will learn more about how brakes work and how to service them.

4-10
MOTORCYCLE CONTROLS

Until a few years ago, different motorcycle manufacturers placed the operating controls at different locations on the motorcycle. This caused some rider confusion. As a result, the Department of Transportation issued regulations that standardized the locations of motorcycle controls.

Today, the controls are located as shown in Fig. 4-14. The throttle is operated by rotating the right grip on the handlebar. The front brake lever also is on the right handlebar. A throttle cable runs from the handlebar grip

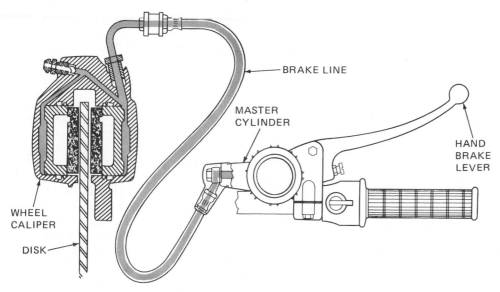

Fig. 4-13 A schematic diagram of a disk-brake system for the front wheel of a motorcycle. (*Castrol Limited*)

31

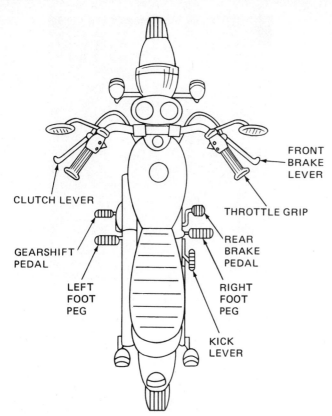

Fig. 4-14 The location of the operating controls on a motorcycle. (*Motorcycle Safety Foundation, Inc.*)

to the carburetor. On motorcycles with a mechanically operated front brake, another cable runs from the front brake lever to the brake at the front wheel.

The left grip on the handlebar does not move. Mounted in front of it is the clutch lever. Again, a cable

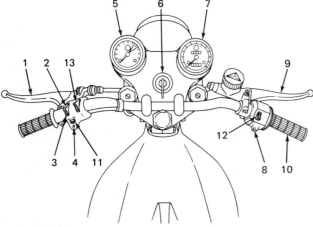

1. Clutch lever
2. Beam indicator
3. Low/high beam switch
4. Horn button
5. Tachometer
6. Key and ignition switch
7. Speedometer
8. Starter button
9. Front brake lever
10. Throttle twist grip
11. Turn signal switch
12. Engine stop switch
13. Headlight switch

Fig. 4-15 The handlebar controls on one model of motorcycle. (*Moto Laverda*)

connects the clutch lever on the handlebar with the clutch on the engine.

To shift gears, there is a foot-operated gear shift pedal on the left side of the motorcycle. On the right side of the motorcycle, there is the foot-operated rear-brake pedal. The gear shift pedal may have a short linkage connected to it. The brake pedal has a cable or linkage to transmit pedal movement to the rear brake.

CAUTION Never mount and attempt to ride an older motorcycle until you have checked out the locations of the controls and how they operate. Many older motorcycles that were manufactured before the locations were standardized are still in use.

Many other controls are mounted on the handlebars, as shown in Fig. 4-15. An engine stop button mounts on the right handlebar. On the left handlebar, the turn-signal switch, horn button, headlight switch, and headlight-beam selector switch are mounted.

While stands are not controls used when riding the motorcycle, almost every motorcycle has one or two stands attached to it. A stand is a device to support the motorcycle in an upright position while the rider gets off. Almost all motorcycles have a kick stand, or side stand, which can be kicked down quickly for parking. The motorcycle shown in Fig. 3-11 is resting against the kick stand. Many motorcycles also have a center stand. Figure 3-6b shows a moped with the center stand down. The center stand also raises the rear wheel off the ground so the motorcycle can be serviced easily.

**4-11
CONTROL CABLES** Figure 4-16 shows the front-brake cable, which is one of several control cables on a motorcycle. Control cables carry the movements of the rider's hands (and sometimes the feet) to the carburetor, clutch, and brakes. Cables are used for this job because they can transmit movements while bent in any direction. At the same time, the control cables allow for movement between the handlebars and the frame, and between the frame and the suspension.

A control cable contains an inner wire which is made up of many strands of fine wire wound together. The inner wire is covered with a flexible tube that is often made of heavier steel wire wrapped in a hollow spiral to form an outer tube, or casing. Then the casing is covered with plastic. Control cables of this type are called *Bowden cables.*

The inner wire of a control cable may have a nipple on each end. It fits into a matching hole or socket in the front brake lever or clutch lever on the handlebars. Some cable end-nipples are soldered onto the wire, some are crimped, and some are held in place with a locking screw.

The outer casing of the control cable is held stationary by cable stops. At the top, the cable fits into the stationary mount of the control lever on the handlebar. At the lower end, the outer casing is secured to a stationary bracket near the arm or other part that is to be moved when the cable is pulled. When the control lever is moved, the outer casing remains still. The control-lever movement is transmitted by the pulling action of the inner wire.

To provide proper adjustment and free play of the control cable, each control cable has an adjusting nut or a threaded adjuster and locknut at one end. Some control cables have adjustments at both ends. The adjuster and cable stops usually are slotted so that the complete cable can be replaced quickly and easily.

The Bowden cable type of control cable can be used to transmit pulling action only. The inner wire is returned to its original position by a spring. This is because a stranded wire cannot transmit a pushing motion. The wire would flex and the nipple ends would push out of their sockets.

☑ 4-12
ENGINES There are several ways to classify engines, based on design or construction features. Motorcycle engines frequently are classed by the number of cylinders, by the arrangement of the cylinders (in line, V, opposed) (Fig. 3-5), by two-cycle or four-cycle, by air-cooled or liquid-cooled, and by displacement.

☑ 4-13
IGNITION, FUEL, LUBRICATING, AND COOLING SYSTEMS For the engine to run, the cylinders must receive the air-fuel mixture and sparks. The air-fuel mixture comes from the fuel system. The sparks come from the ignition system. In addition to all this, the moving engine parts must be lubricated, and there must be some means of cooling the engine. Therefore, the engine needs four support systems to make it run. These are

1. The ignition system
2. The fuel system
3. The lubricating system
4. The cooling system

We cover these systems in detail in later chapters.

☑ 4-14
POWER TRAIN The power train of a motorcycle is shown in Fig. 4-1. It consists of three essential units: a clutch, a transmission, and a final drive such as a chain and sprockets to carry the engine power to the rear wheel. Some motorcycles have automatic transmissions just like automobiles. Other motorcycles use a drive shaft instead of a chain and sprockets for the final drive.

The purpose of the transmission is to allow for different speed ratios between the engine and the wheel. The transmission allows the engine to run fast while the

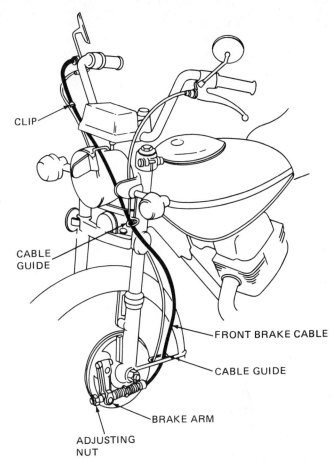

Fig. 4-16 The front-brake cable, one of several control cables on a motorcycle. (*Honda Motor Company, Ltd.*)

wheels turn slowly. This sends more power to the wheel so the motorcycle can accelerate, or pick up speed. Once the motorcycle is moving, the transmission gears can be changed, or shifted. This changes the difference between the engine and wheel speeds. The transmission can be upshifted several times. This means that the ratio between the engine speed and the wheel speed can be changed to provide for higher motorcycle speeds.

The purpose of the clutch is to momentarily interrupt the flow of power from the engine to the transmission whenever the gears are shifted. It is difficult to shift gears that have power flowing through them. Therefore, the power flow must be momentarily interrupted whenever a shift is made. The clutch does this job. Later chapters cover transmissions and clutches in detail.

CHAPTER 4
REVIEW QUESTIONS

1. What is the purpose of the motorcycle frame?
2. Name three types of frames.
3. What types of rear springs are used on most motorcycles today?
4. What is the purpose of the shock absorber?
5. What effect does a spring in the seat post have on rider comfort?
6. Describe the construction of a telescopic front fork.

7. What is a swinging fork?
8. Why are spoke wheels used on most motorcycles?
9. What is the difference between a spoke wheel and a cast wheel?
10. What type of wheels can be used with tubeless tires?
11. Why does a motorcycle tire have tread fairly high up on the sidewall?
12. What type of tire tread is best for soft dirt?
13. How is the front brake applied?

14. How is the rear brake applied?
15. What type of brakes are used on motorcycles?
16. What is the difference between a disk brake and a drum brake?
17. How does the rider on a motorcycle operate the throttle?
18. What are three ways to classify engines?
19. What types of control cables are used on motorcycles?
20. What three units make up the power train?

CHAPTER 5

TWO-CYCLE ENGINES

After studying this chapter,
you should be able to:

1. Describe the operation of a two-cycle engine.

2. Explain what a piston stroke is.

3. Discuss the actions of the ports in a two-cycle engine.

4. Describe the operation of the reed valve.

5. Explain why each cylinder in a multiple-cylinder engine must have its own sealed crankcase.

6. Describe the rotary valve and explain how it works in a two-cycle engine.

7. Discuss the advantages of the rotary valve.

8. Describe the construction of the two types of crankshaft—single-piece and built-up.

9. Explain why a flywheel is needed and how it works.

5-1 AN INTRODUCTION TO TWO-CYCLE ENGINES

Figure 5-1 shows a typical two-cycle motorcycle engine that has the clutch and transmission built into the crankcase. This is sometimes called *unit construction* because the engine, clutch, and transmission are combined into a single unit sharing a common crankcase. Other motorcycles have the clutch and transmission detached from the engine. On these motorcycles, the clutch and transmission mount in back of the engine and are driven by a primary chain from it. Figure 5-2 shows how the primary chain transfers power from the engine crankshaft to the transmission.

All motorcycle engines are internal combustion engines that burn gasoline or a similar fuel inside the cylinder. The pressure that results from this burning makes the piston move. The reciprocating (up-and-down) movement of the piston is changed to rotary motion by the connecting rod and crank on the crankshaft (Chap. 2). The rotary motion can then turn gears and sprockets so the rear wheel rotates and the motorcycle moves.

The two-cycle engine is simple in construction. It has only three major moving parts, the piston assembly, the connecting rod, and the crankshaft (Fig. 5-3).

5-2 SINGLE-CYLINDER TWO-CYCLE MOTORCYCLE ENGINES

Many motorcycles use a one-cylinder two-cycle engine. Figure 5-1 shows a motorcycle engine removed from the motorcycle. The complete engine assembly includes the engine itself and a two-part, or split, crankcase that houses the clutch and transmission assembly.

Figure 5-3 shows the cylinder and cylinder head removed from a similar engine. Notice that in the motorcycle engine shown in Figs. 5-1 and 5-3, the cylinder and cylinder head are separate parts. In many small two-cycle engines of the type used in power mowers, the cylinder and cylinder head are one piece.

Figure 3-1 shows a motorcycle with a one-cylinder two-cycle engine. Figure 4-1 shows a two-cylinder two-cycle engine in a street bike. Figure 3-4 shows, in cutaway view, a three-cylinder two-cycle engine. Engines with multiple cylinders (multicylinder engines) usually provide more power and flexibility than a large single-cylinder engine of the same size. Multiple-cylinder engines usually are used in street bikes.

Different sizes of single-cylinder two-cycle engines, complete with clutch and transmission, are shown in Fig. 2-1*a, b,* and *c.* The transmission and clutch are shown so that the transmission gears and clutch plates can be seen. These engines are similar to those shown in Figs. 5-1 to 5-4.

The parts of a one-cylinder two-cycle motorcycle engine are shown disassembled in Fig. 5-4. You can see from this illustration how the two halves of the crankcase are brought together to form the sealed crankcase needed to provide crankcase pressure. The crankcase pressure is needed to push the air-fuel mixture from the crankcase up into the cylinder. We discuss crankcase pressure later. The two castings that form the crankcase also support the clutch assembly and form the case for the transmission.

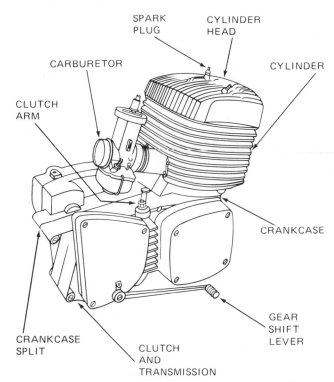

Fig. 5-1 A typical single-cylinder two-cycle engine. (*Husqvarna*)

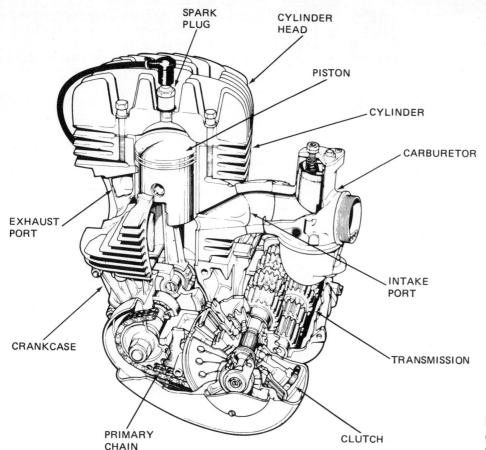

Fig. 5-2   A cutaway view of a single-cylinder two-cycle engine and transmission. (*AJS*)

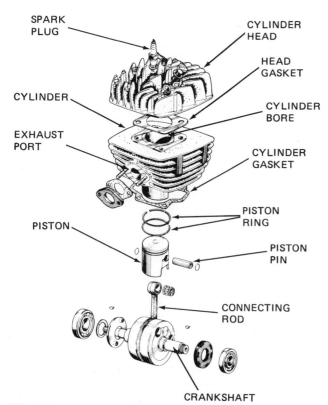

Fig. 5-3   The major parts of the top end of a single-cylinder two-cycle engine. (*Suzuki Motor Company, Ltd.*)

The major difference between the one-cylinder engine and the multiple-cylinder engine is that the multicylinder engine has more parts. Also, in the two-cycle multicylinder engine, each cylinder must have its own sealed or airtight crankcase.

5-3
THE PISTON STROKE   Figure 2-4 shows a piston stroke. It is the movement of the piston from TDC (top dead center) to BDC (bottom dead center) or from BDC to TDC. In describing the piston strokes of a two-cycle engine, every upstroke (from BDC to TDC) is considered a compression stroke, and every downward stroke (from TDC to BDC) is a power stroke.

During each upward stroke of the piston in a two-cycle engine, three separate events must take place. First, the burned gases remaining from the previous power stroke must be cleared from the cylinder. Second, a fresh charge of the air-fuel mixture must be brought into the cylinder. Third, this charge of the air-fuel mixture must be compressed in readiness for ignition. To accomplish all this, the engine has openings, or *ports,* in the side of the cylinder wall. The piston, as it moves up and down, opens or seals off these ports. The air-fuel mixture enters the cylinder through one of the ports. The burned gases leave through another port.

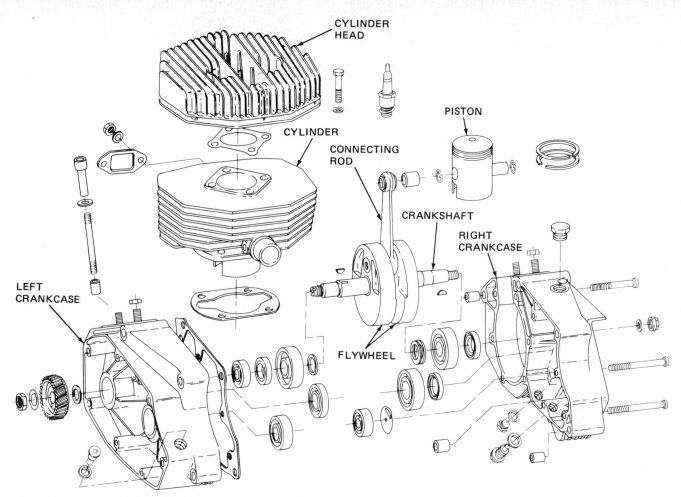

Fig. 5-4 A disassembled view of a one-cylinder two-cycle engine. The two halves of the crankcase enclose and support the crankshaft and the clutch and transmission. (*Penton*)

5-4
CYLINDER PORTS The three ports in the cylinder of a two-cycle engine can be seen when you look down into the cylinder from the top (Fig. 5-5). Figure 5-6 shows two views of a cylinder sliced in half so you can see the three ports. They are the *intake port,* the *exhaust port,* and the *transfer port.* The transfer port is a long passage in back of the cylinder wall which leads from the crankcase to the opening in the cylinder wall. The crankcase is the lower part of the engine where the crankshaft rotates.

5-5
PORT ACTIONS The piston, as it moves up and down in the cylinder, acts as a valve, blocking off and then opening the ports. Figure 5-7 shows the action. To the left (*a*) the piston has moved up to TDC and the compressed air-fuel mixture has been ignited. The power stroke starts and the piston is pushed down.

Notice in *a* that the air-fuel mixture is flowing into the crankcase. The reason it flows as shown is that a vacuum (see 2-4) is produced in the crankcase when the piston moves up. Atmospheric pressure causes air to

flow through the carburetor, pick up a charge of fuel, and then flow into the crankcase. The piston has moved above the intake port, so the port is open and allows the air-fuel mixture to enter the crankcase.

At *b* in Fig. 5-7, the piston has been pushed down almost to BDC. This has opened the exhaust port so that burned air-fuel mixture can begin to flow out, or *exhaust,* from the cylinder. When the piston has moved down to BDC, as shown at *c,* it has cleared the now-

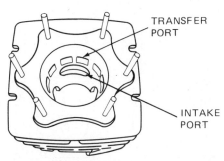

Fig. 5-5 The ports in the cylinder wall of a two-cycle engine. (*Suzuki Motor Company, Ltd.*)

37

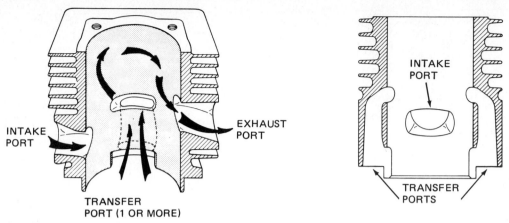

Fig. 5-6 Cutaway views of a cylinder of a two-cycle engine showing the locations of the three ports.

open transfer port. The air-fuel mixture in the crankcase flows up into the cylinder, as shown by the arrows. The reason it flows up is that the piston, in moving down, has put the air-fuel mixture in the crankcase under pressure.

Notice that in *b* the piston has closed off the intake port so that the crankcase is sealed. Therefore, as the piston moves down, it compresses the air-fuel mixture trapped below it in the crankcase.

Part *d* shows compression. The piston, in moving up, closes off the transfer and exhaust ports. The air-fuel mixture above the piston is therefore compressed by the upward-moving piston. As the piston nears TDC, as shown at *a,* ignition again takes place, and the whole cycle from *a* through *d* is repeated over and over for as long as the engine runs.

A port can be either one large opening or a series of smaller openings (Fig. 5-5). If the port is too large, the piston rings could catch on the side of the opening and break. To prevent this, a series of smaller openings is used in some engines.

Figure 5-8 shows the four steps, or *actions,* in a two-cycle engine in more detail. These illustrations show

sectional views of an actual engine. Refer to Fig. 5-6 and note that the transfer port (or ports) can be located 90° from the intake and exhaust ports. This is one arrangement. When a series of holes is used for the transfer port they may overlap the other ports, as shown in Fig. 5-5.

5-6
TWO-CYCLE ENGINES WITH REED
VALVES   Many two-cycle motorcycle engines have a reed valve (Fig. 5-9) installed in the intake-port passage between the carburetor and the crankcase (Fig. 5-10). The reed valve has a series of thin, flexible blades. The blades are shown bent back from their seated position in Fig. 5-9. When the piston is moving up, the vacuum in the crankcase causes atmospheric pressure to push the air-fuel mixture into the crankcase.

In a running engine, the reed valve acts like an automatically controlled flap. Changes in crankcase pressure cause the flap to open and close the intake port. This prevents blowback and preignition from reaching the carburetor. During crankcase compression, the

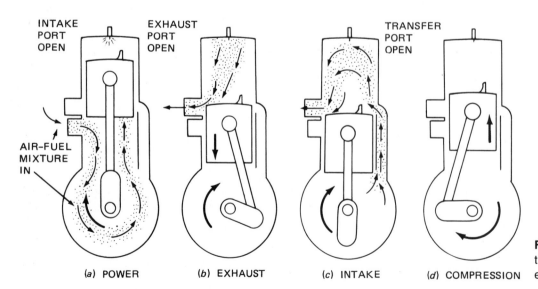

Fig. 5-7 The events in a two-cycle three-port engine.

(a) POWER   (b) EXHAUST   (c) INTAKE   (d) COMPRESSION

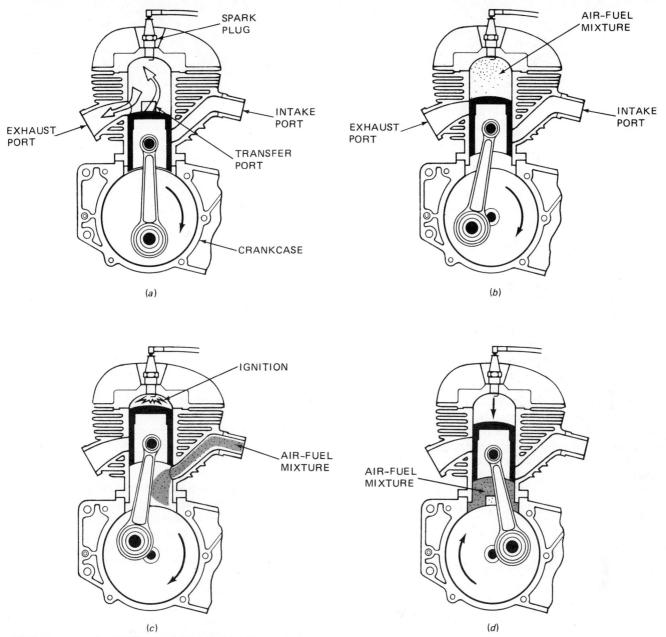

Fig. 5-8 The actions in a two-cycle engine. (*a*) Intake and exhaust: The piston is at BDC and the air-fuel mixture is entering the cylinder through the transfer port while the burned gases are leaving the cylinder through the exhaust port. (*b*) Compression: As the piston moves up the cylinder, it closes all the ports. Compression of the air-fuel mixture trapped in the combustion chamber begins. (*c*) Ignition: When the mixture is compressed, a spark ignites it and combustion occurs. At the same time, the upward movement of the piston has opened the intake port, and the air-fuel mixture enters the crankcase. (*d*) Power: The piston is pushed down, forcing the crankshaft to turn. At the same time, the downward-moving piston is compressing the air-fuel mixture trapped beneath it in the crankcase.

reed valve closes to prevent blowback, or air-fuel mixture from being pushed back out of the intake port at low speed. This improves the low-speed power of the two-cycle engine by making sure that a full charge of the air-fuel mixture gets into the cylinder.

The total movement of each petal or leaf of the reed valve is controlled by the *valve stopper* (Fig. 5-9). Un-

der the leaves there are holes, or ports, that connect the carburetor with the crankcase. Figure 5-10 shows the installation of the reed valve in a motorcycle engine. The reed valve mounts on the side of the cylinder between the carburetor and the intake port. When the reed valve is open, the air-fuel mixture flows through the intake port into the crankcase.

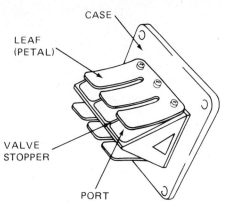

Fig. 5-9 A reed-valve assembly for a two-cycle engine.
(*Yamaha International Corporation*)

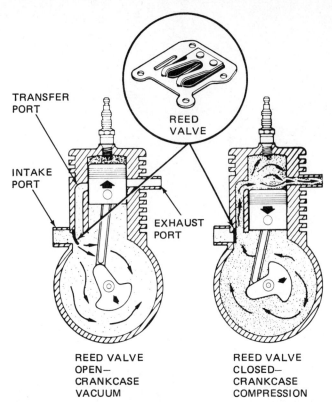

Fig. 5-11 The actions in a two-cycle engine with a reed valve.

When the piston moves up, a partial vacuum is created in the sealed crankcase (Fig. 5-11, left). Atmospheric pressure forces the reed valve off its seat and pushes the air-fuel mixture from the carburetor through the open reed valve into the crankcase.

After the piston passes TDC and starts down again, pressure begins to build up in the crankcase. This pressure closes the reed valve. Further downward movement of the piston compresses the air-fuel mixture that is trapped in the crankcase. The pressure which is built up on the air-fuel mixture then causes it to quickly flow through the transfer port into the engine cylinder. This occurs as soon as the piston moves down enough to clear the transfer port (Fig. 5-11, right).

5-7 CRANKCASES FOR MULTIPLE-CYLINDER ENGINES

In multiple-cylinder engines, each cylinder must have its own individual sealed crankcase to provide crankcase compression for that cylinder. In a three-cylinder two-cycle engine, for example, the crankcase is divided into three separate sealed compartments.

Figure 3-4 shows a three-cylinder two-cycle engine, cut away so you can see the internal parts. Note that the main bearings supporting the crankshaft are sealed ball bearings. The main bearings between the cylinders are double-row sealed ball bearings. The bearings divide the crankcase into three separate sealed compartments.

5-8 ROTARY-VALVE TWO-CYCLE ENGINES

In the engines discussed so far, the piston serves as the timing valve to open and close the ports. Longer port opening can be achieved with a rotary valve. This improves engine breathing and performance.

An engine with a rotary valve is shown in Fig. 5-12 with the side cover removed so the rotary valve can be seen. Notice that the intake port is located in the crankcase wall instead of in the cylinder. Rotation of the rotary valve opens and closes the intake port. The rotary valve is installed on the crankshaft and rotates with it.

Figure 5-12 shows the rotary valve as having just moved out from blocking the intake port. The piston is

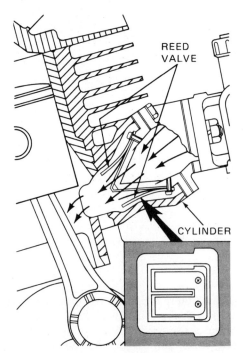

Fig. 5-10 A sectional view of a two-cycle engine which has a reed valve in the side of the crankcase wall, between the carburetor and the cylinder.

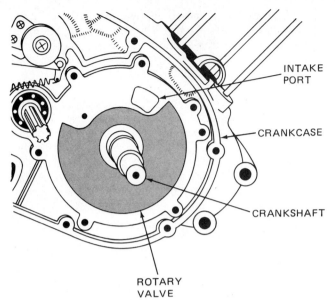

ROTARY VALVE

Fig. 5-12 The carburetor and side cover removed from a two-cycle engine to show the rotary disk valve, or rotary valve.

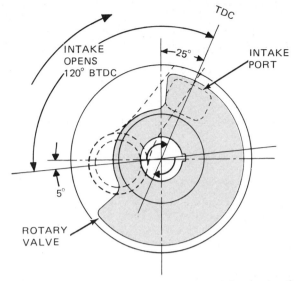

Fig. 5-13 The position of the rotary valve as it begins to open the intake port into the crankcase. (*Kawasaki Heavy Industries, Ltd.*)

moving up, producing a vacuum in the crankcase so that the air-fuel mixture can flow into the crankcase.

Figures 5-13 and 5-14 show the two limiting positions of the rotary valve. In Fig. 5-13, the rotary valve is just at the point of moving away from the intake port. In Fig. 5-14, the rotary valve has just moved to the position where the intake port is completely blocked off. Notice that in the example shown the intake port is open 175° [120° before TDC (BTDC) plus 55° after TDC (ATDC)]. This is the number of degrees the crankshaft and the rotary valve turn from the time the intake port starts to open until it is completely closed.

The transfer and exhaust ports for the rotary-valve engine are the same as for the engines described previously.

**5-9
THE ADVANTAGE OF THE ROTARY VALVE**   The advantage of the rotary-valve engine is that the rotary valve allows the intake port to be open for a longer time. In Figs. 5-13 and 5-14, the duration of intake-valve opening is 175°. This can be changed by installing a different rotary valve.

In the engines described in ☑ 5-5 and 5-6, the intake port is open a shorter time. Figure 5-15 shows the intake and exhaust timing for a piston-port engine. The intake port, in the example shown, is opened 71° BTDC and is closed 71° ATDC. This is called *symmetrical port timing*. The piston, in moving up, opens the intake port the same number of degrees before TDC as it closes the intake port after TDC. In the example shown, the total opening is 142° of crankshaft rotation.

When you contrast this 142° with the 175° for the rotary-valve engine (Figs. 5-13 and 5-14) you can see that, in the rotary-valve engine, the air-fuel mixture has a longer time to enter the crankcase. This means that more mixture gets in, and more mixture enters the cylinder, where it is compressed and burned. This pro-

duces a more powerful push on the piston, and therefore more power is produced.

In addition, the rotary valve opens and closes the intake port more quickly, as shown in Fig. 5-16. The curve for the rotary valve is shown as a solid line. It has a sharp rise and a sharp fall. This means the port can start to admit the air-fuel mixture more quickly and can cut it off more abruptly at the end of the intake period.

Also, the location of the rotary valve can be changed. It does not have to provide symmetrical port timing. This is shown by the position of the rotary-valve curve in Fig. 5-16. The leftward shift of the curve means that the intake port opens earlier to allow the air-fuel mixture more time to enter the crankcase as the piston moves up.

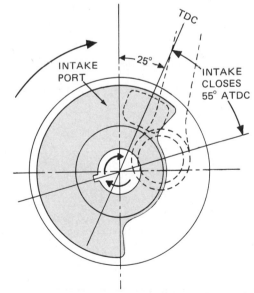

Fig. 5-14 The position of the rotary valve as it closes the intake port. (*Kawasaki Heavy Industries, Ltd.*)

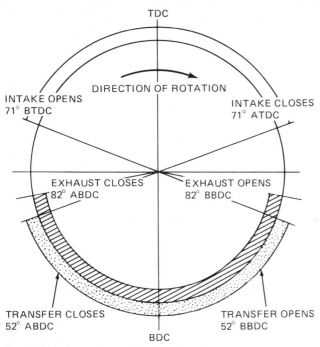

Fig. 5-15 A port-timing diagram for a piston-port type of two-cycle engine. (*Kawasaki Heavy Industries, Ltd.*)

5-10
CRANKSHAFT   In some motorcycle engines, the crankshaft is a single piece, as shown in Fig. 2-12a. In other engines, the crankshaft is built up from several pieces. Figure 5-17 is an example of a built-up crankshaft for a one-cylinder two-cycle engine. Figure 5-18 shows a similar crankshaft assembly in exploded view.

To build up, or assemble, the crankshaft, the crankpin is pressed into the holes in the two crankshaft halves, called *flywheels*. This arrangement permits the use of a roller bearing at each end of the connecting rod. A small roller bearing is used at the piston pin that has almost needle-size rollers. This bearing is called a *needle bearing*.

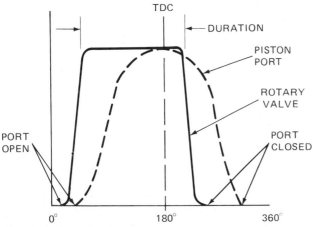

Fig. 5-16 A graph comparing the intake port opening in a rotary-valve engine (solid line) with that in a piston-port engine (dashed line). (*Kawasaki Heavy Industries, Ltd.*)

Multiple-cylinder two-cycle engines also may have built-up crankshafts. Figure 3-4, for example, shows a crankshaft in a three-cylinder two-cycle motorcycle engine.

5-11
FLYWHEEL   The power impulses resulting from the power strokes occur during less than one half of a revolution of the crankshaft in two-cycle engines. As the piston passes TDC, the high pressure from the combustion of the air-fuel mixture pushes down on the piston. This push does not last long. As soon as the piston passes the exhaust port, the pressure is relieved and the power stroke ends. This occurs 98° ATDC in the engine shown in Fig. 5-15.

During the rest of the cycle, as the piston passes BDC and starts back up, there is no power being produced. Only the momentum of the moving parts carries the piston up to TDC so another power stroke can take place. Therefore, a one-cylinder engine has a tendency to speed up during the power stroke and slow down the rest of the time. To smooth out this speed-up and slow-down action, the engine has a flywheel.

The flywheel in a typical single-cylinder two-cycle engine is shown in Figs. 5-17 and 5-18. In this type of engine, the flywheel is made of two thick, round, and heavy metal plates connected by the crankpin and enclosed by the crankcase. When the engine is running, the flywheel makes use of the property of *inertia* that all material things have.

An object that is moving tries to keep moving. That is inertia. An object that is stationary tries to remain still. That also is inertia. So the flywheel, once it is in motion, tries to keep moving. Then when the crankshaft tries to slow down during the nonpower part of the cycle, the flywheel helps to keep it moving. Also, when the power stroke occurs and the crankshaft tries to speed up, the flywheel helps to keep it from suddenly speeding up. The flywheel gives up energy to keep the crankshaft moving during the nonpower time, and then takes in and stores energy when the crankshaft tries to speed up.

Multiple-cylinder engines also use flywheels. The power strokes in these engines are arranged to follow one another in sequence, or overlap, to make a smoother-running engine. But they also need flywheels to further smooth out the engine. In some engines, such as automobile engines, a single-piece flywheel is attached to one end of the crankshaft outside of the crankcase.

5-12
OPERATING CHARACTERISTICS OF TWO-CYCLE ENGINES   Usually a two-cycle engine develops less power than a four-cycle engine of the same size. One reason for this is that there is a shorter *effective power stroke* in the two-cycle engine. In an engine, the distance the piston travels is defined as the *piston stroke*, or *total piston stroke*.

However, the effective stroke is not the same as the total stroke. The effective stroke is the distance that the piston travels while work is done on it by the expanding gases. This distance is shorter in a two-cycle engine. The exhaust port must be opened earlier than in a four-cycle engine to begin the *scavenging* process. Scavenging is the clearing of the burned exhaust gases from the cylinder and the filling of it with fresh air-fuel mixture. This shorter scavenging time is one of the reasons that a two-cycle engine develops less power than a comparable four-cycle engine.

Another operating characteristic of the two-cycle engine is the higher thermal load, or heat load, placed on it. This means that a two-cycle engine runs hotter than a comparable four-cycle engine. The two-cycle engine fires every time the piston reaches TDC. There are no "no-load" strokes, as there are in the four-cycle engine, to provide engine cooling. In a two-cycle engine, therefore, parts run hotter and may wear more quickly because of their higher operating temperature.

Chapter 16 covers engine cooling systems in detail, and ✍6-13 provides a further comparison of two-cycle and four-cycle engines.

✍5-13
TYPES OF CYLINDER SCAVENGING

There is another reason why a two-cycle engine produces less power than a comparable four-cycle engine. In the two-cycle engine, a smaller air-fuel charge is burned in the cylinder. At full throttle, the amount of air-fuel mixture may be only about half of the amount in a four-cycle engine.

Cylinder scavenging greatly affects the operation of a two-cycle engine. For example, in some two-cycle engines at full throttle, as much as 25 percent of the air-fuel mixture that enters the cylinder escapes through the exhaust ports before they are closed.

The two basic methods of cylinder scavenging used in two-cycle engines are *cross scavenging* and *loop*

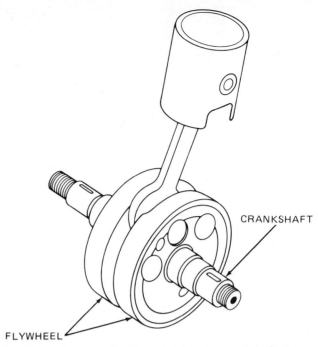

Fig. 5-17 An assembled two-cycle-engine crankshaft, showing the flywheels. (*Suzuki Motor Company, Ltd.*)

scavenging (Fig. 5-19). Most motorcycle engines are loop-scavenged, because the top of the piston runs cooler. Cross scavenging requires a deflector on the top of the piston. This system has been widely used in outboard engines and in some motorcycle engines.

In cross scavenging, the transfer and exhaust ports are opposite each other (Fig. 5-19, left). The deflector on the top of the piston faces the transfer port. As the

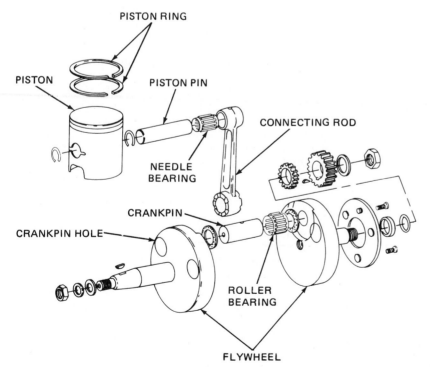

Fig. 5-18 A disassembled view of the crankshaft, connecting rod, and piston of a one-cylinder two-cycle engine. Roller bearings are used at both ends of the connecting rod. (*Kawasaki Heavy Industries, Ltd.*)

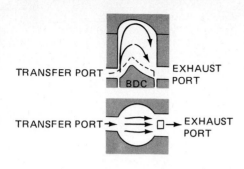

CROSS SCAVENGING
(DEFLECTOR PISTON)

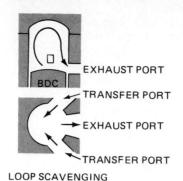

LOOP SCAVENGING
(FLAT PISTON)

Fig. 5-19 Types of cylinder scavenging used in two-cycle engines. (*Robert Bosch Corporation*)

fresh mixture enters the cylinder through the transfer port, the deflector routes the mixture up and across the top of the combustion chamber. This path is shown by the arrows in Fig. 5-19, left.

However, only the first part of the entering charge follows the cylinder wall. Then, while the piston is at BDC, the entering air-fuel mixture takes the shortest path. It flows almost straight across the top of the piston and out the exhaust port. This pattern may even allow part of the burned exhaust gases to remain in the cylinder.

Loop scavenging is shown in Fig. 5-19, right. The fresh air-fuel mixture flows into the cylinder from transfer ports on either side of the exhaust port. The entering air-fuel mixture is directed upward in the direction of the opposite cylinder wall by the shape and location of the transfer ports.

As the fresh air-fuel mixture enters the cylinder, the remaining exhaust gases are forced out. Because the incoming air-fuel mixture cannot take a shortcut, as with the cross-scavenging system, less of the fresh air-fuel mixture is lost. However, a small amount does escape from the cylinder. In addition, a core of burned exhaust gas may remain in the center of the cylinder.

CHAPTER 5
REVIEW QUESTIONS

1. Where are the clutch and transmission located in most two-cycle motorcycle engines?
2. What is an internal combustion engine?
3. How can a two-cycle engine operate without valves?
4. What is a port?
5. How often do power strokes occur in a two-cycle engine?
6. Why must a two-cycle engine have an airtight crankcase?
7. What is a piston stroke?
8. Describe what happens in a two-cycle engine during the upstroke of the piston.
9. Describe what happens in the two-cycle engine during the downstroke of the piston.
10. Name the ports in a two-cycle engine, and explain the purpose of each port.

11. What times the opening and closing of each port in a piston-port engine?
12. Why are some ports made of several smaller holes instead of a single large hole?
13. Why does the exhaust port usually open before the transfer port?
14. When does the power stroke end in a two-cycle engine?
15. Why must a two-cycle engine have pressure in the crankcase?
16. What is the purpose of the reed valve?
17. Describe the operation of the rotary valve.
18. What causes the rotary valve to operate?
19. How does the rotary valve allow the intake-port timing to be changed?
20. Why do engines need a flywheel?

CHAPTER **6**

FOUR-CYCLE ENGINES

After studying this chapter,
you should be able to:

1. Describe the construction of a four-cycle engine and explain how it differs from the construction of a two-cycle engine.

2. Discuss the four-stroke cycle and explain the actions during each piston stroke.

3. Describe the difference between a push-rod engine and an overhead-camshaft engine.

4. Explain how the valves are operated in the two types of engines.

5. Discuss the advantages of the overhead-camshaft engine.

6. Define valve float and explain how it can happen.

7. Describe valve timing and a typical valve-timing graph.

8. Explain what counterbalancers are and why they are needed.

9. Discuss piston rings and explain why the four-cycle engine needs an oil ring.

10. Compare two-cycle and four-cycle engines and explain why automotive engines are of the four-cycle type.

6-1 FOUR-CYCLE-ENGINE CONSTRUCTION

All automotive engines operate on the four-cycle principle. Many motorcycle engines also are four-cycle engines. The basic difference between two-cycle and four-cycle engines is in the way the air-fuel mixture gets into the engine cylinders and in the way burned gases are removed from the cylinders.

The previous chapter explained how the two-cycle engine does all this. There are intake, transfer, and exhaust ports in the cylinder. The piston, as it moves down and up, opens and closes ports. This allows the burned gases to escape and a fresh charge of the air-fuel mixture to enter.

The four-cycle engine also has intake and exhaust ports. However, they are opened and closed in a different manner, as explained in later sections.

In the four-cycle motorcycle engine, the cylinder head and the cylinder block are separate parts, as shown in Fig. 6-1. Figure 2-1*d, e,* and *f* shows cutaway views of four-cycle engines. Figure 6-2 shows the cylin-

der head of an in-line two-cylinder engine in exploded view. In Fig. 6-2, the two cylinders are parallel to each other and in a single line, or row. Motorcycle engines also are made with three, four, and six cylinders. Figure 3-5 shows different cylinder arrangements. In the engines shown in Figs. 6-1 and 6-2, the valves are installed overhead, or in the cylinder head. We describe valves and valve locations later.

There are many similarities between two-cycle and four-cycle engines. The pistons, cylinder, connecting rod, and crankshaft are very much alike (Fig. 6-3). However, there are several important differences, both in construction and in operation. Notice the much more complex cylinder head in the four-cycle engine (Fig. 6-2). Then compare Fig. 5-4, which shows a disassembled two-cycle engine, with Fig. 6-2. There are many more parts in a four-cycle engine than in a two-cycle engine.

6-2 THE FOUR-STROKE CYCLE

In the four-stroke-cycle engine, one out of every four piston strokes is a power stroke. The four-stroke-cycle engine is usually called a *four-cycle engine,* or a *four-stroker.* This engine requires at least two valves that open and close to permit intake and exhaust. Figure 6-4 shows the four strokes. We explain how the valves are opened and closed later.

In Fig. 6-4*a,* the piston is moving down on the intake stroke. The intake valve is open and the carburetor is delivering an air-fuel mixture to the cylinder. After the intake stroke ends, the intake valve closes. Now, the piston moves up on the compression stroke (Fig. 6-4*b*). The air-fuel mixture is trapped and therefore compressed in the top of the cylinder (the *combustion chamber*).

As the piston nears TDC on the compression stroke, the ignition system delivers a spark to the spark plug. This ignites the compressed air-fuel mixture, and the resulting high pressure forces the piston to move down on the power stroke, as shown in Fig. 6-4*c.* The downward push on the piston may total as much as 4000

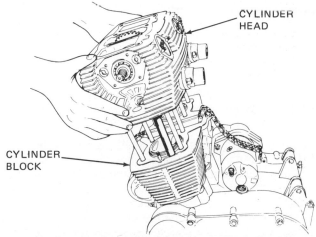

Fig. 6-1 In a four-cycle motorcycle engine, the cylinder block and the cylinder head are separate parts. (*Moto Laverda*)

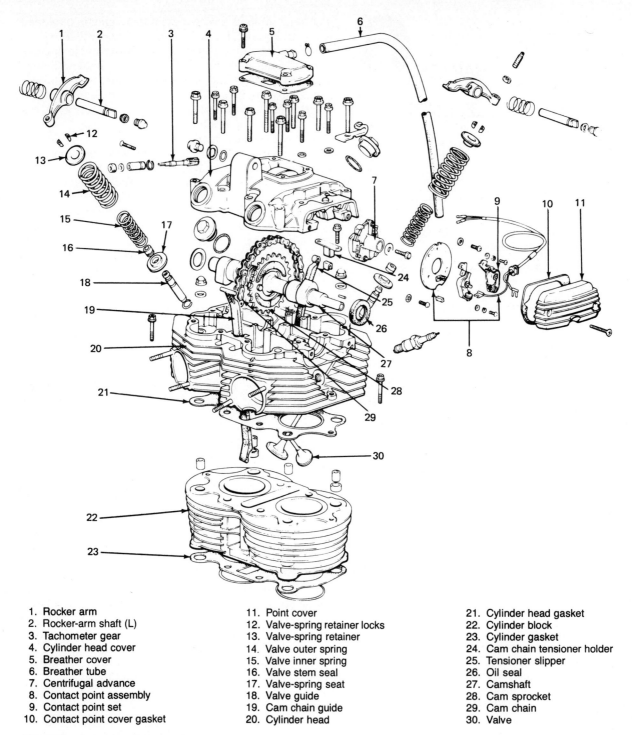

1. Rocker arm
2. Rocker-arm shaft (L)
3. Tachometer gear
4. Cylinder head cover
5. Breather cover
6. Breather tube
7. Centrifugal advance
8. Contact point assembly
9. Contact point set
10. Contact point cover gasket

11. Point cover
12. Valve-spring retainer locks
13. Valve-spring retainer
14. Valve outer spring
15. Valve inner spring
16. Valve stem seal
17. Valve-spring seat
18. Valve guide
19. Cam chain guide
20. Cylinder head

21. Cylinder head gasket
22. Cylinder block
23. Cylinder gasket
24. Cam chain tensioner holder
25. Tensioner slipper
26. Oil seal
27. Camshaft
28. Cam sprocket
29. Cam chain
30. Valve

Fig. 6-2 A disassembled view of a two-cylinder four-cycle motorcycle engine. (*Honda Motor Company, Ltd.*)

pounds [1814 kg] in a modern small engine. The powerful push is carried through the connecting rod to a crank on the engine crankshaft, as shown in Fig. 6-4c. The ignition system, which produces the spark at the spark plug, is explained in a later chapter.

The fourth stroke in the four-stroke cycle is the exhaust stroke. As the piston nears BDC on the power stroke, the exhaust valve opens. Now, as the piston passes BDC and moves up on the exhaust stroke, the

burned gases in the cylinder are forced out, as shown in Fig. 6-4d.

As the piston nears TDC on the exhaust stroke, the intake valve opens. Then, after TDC, the exhaust valve closes, and the whole cycle of events is repeated once again. The cycle is repeated continuously as long as the engine runs.

The valves are opened and closed at the proper times by the *valve train*. The valve train includes a camshaft

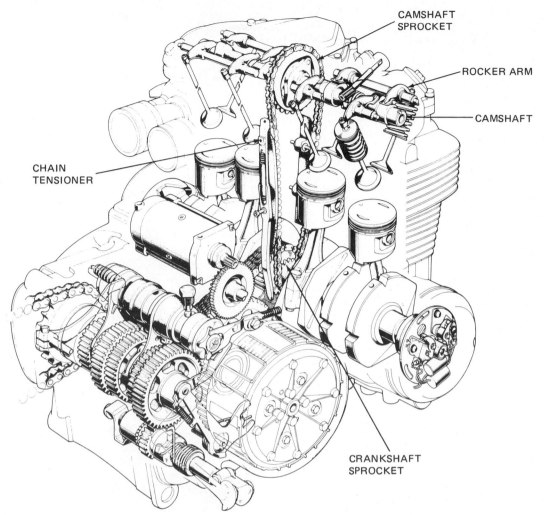

Fig. 6-3 A cutaway view of an in-line four-cylinder four-cycle motorcycle engine. (*Honda Motor Company, Ltd.*)

which is driven from the engine crankshaft. In some engines, the camshaft is located in the cylinder block, near the crankshaft. However, in most four-cycle motorcycle engines, the camshaft is located in the cylinder head, as shown in Figs. 6-2 and 6-3. Cams and valve trains are discussed later.

6-3 VALVES In most engines, there are two openings, or ports, in the top of the combustion chamber. One of these openings is the intake port. The air-fuel mixture flows in through this port when the intake valve is open (Fig. 6-4*a*). The other opening is the exhaust port. The burned gases flow out, or exit, through this port when the exhaust valve is open (Fig. 6-4*d*).

An engine valve is a long metal stem which is flared out at one end (Fig. 6-5). When a valve moves up into a valve port, the valve face seats on, or makes contact with, the valve seat in the cylinder head. The fit is so tight that no air or other gas can pass between the valve face and the seat when the valve is closed, or seated.

The intake valve is usually larger than the exhaust valve. The reason is that the only push behind the entering air-fuel mixture when the intake valve is open is atmospheric pressure. However, when the exhaust valve opens the burned gases are under high pressure from the combustion process. The intake valve is larger so that there will be more space for the air-fuel mixture to flow through when entering the cylinder.

6-4 OPERATING THE VALVES The valves must be moved at the right times to open and close the valve ports in the cylinder head. Figures 6-6 and 6-7 show typical valve operating arrangements used in four-cycle motorcycle engines. The valves move up and down in valve guides that are part of the cylinder head.

Each valve has a *valve spring* (Fig. 6-7) that puts tension on the valve and tries to keep the valve closed, or seated, on the valve seat. When the valve is closed, the port in the cylinder head also is closed. The valve spring is held between the cylinder head and a *valve-spring retainer* (Fig. 6-7). The spring retainer is attached to the valve stem by a *valve-spring retainer lock,*

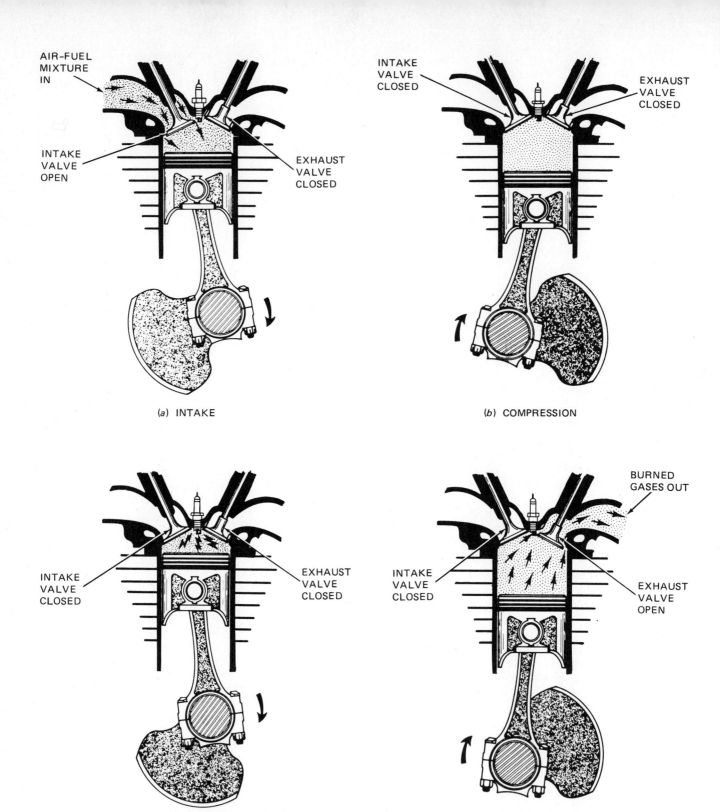

(a) INTAKE

(b) COMPRESSION

(c) POWER

(d) EXHAUST

Fig. 6-4 The strokes in a four-cycle engine. (*a*) The intake stroke: The intake valve, at left, has opened. The piston is moving downward, allowing fresh air-fuel mixture into the cylinder. (*b*) The compression stroke: The intake valve has closed. The piston is moving upward, compressing the mixture. (*c*) The power stroke: The ignition system produces a spark that ignites the mixture. As the mixture burns, high pressure is created, pushing the piston down. (*d*) The exhaust stroke: The exhaust valve, at right, has opened. The piston is moving upward, pushing the burned gases out of the cylinder.

which fits into grooves in the valve stem. You can see the retainer-lock grooves in the valves shown in Fig. 6-5.

NOTE Some engines use a torsion-bar valve spring instead of the coil-spring type shown in Fig. 6-7. Others close the valves with a cam and rocker-arm arrangement which acts against a plate around the valve stem. This positive-closing type of valve-operating mechanism is called *desmodromic*.

Above the valve stem is a *rocker arm*. The rocker arm rocks up and down on the rocker-arm shaft in the cylinder head. One end of the rocker arm rests on a cam which has a high spot, or lobe, on it, as shown in Fig. 6-6. The cam is part of the camshaft, which is driven by gears, a chain or a toothed belt from the crankshaft. Figure 6-3 shows a camshaft-drive arrangement for a four-cycle engine.

As the camshaft rotates, the cam lobe moves around under the rocker arm, causing it to be pushed upward and pivot around the rocker-arm shaft. This causes the other end of the rocker arm to push down on the end of the valve stem. This downward push overcomes the valve-spring tension so that the valve is pushed down off its valve seat. The valve is then open, and gas can pass through the opening between the valve seat and the valve.

If the open valve is the intake valve, the air-fuel mixture from the carburetor passes through the intake port into the cylinder. If the exhaust valve is open, then hot exhaust gases pass through the exhaust port on their way out of the cylinder.

As the piston continues its movement, the crankshaft and camshaft continue to rotate. The lobe on the cam moves out from under the rocker arm. Now, the valve spring forces the valve to close so that the port, or passage, is sealed.

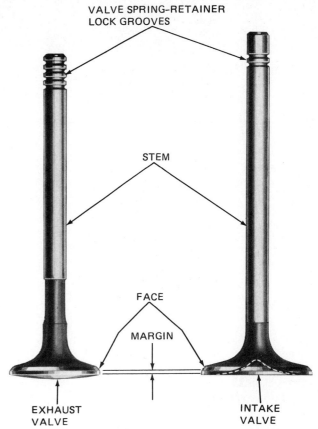

Fig. 6-5 Typical engine valves for a four-cycle engine.

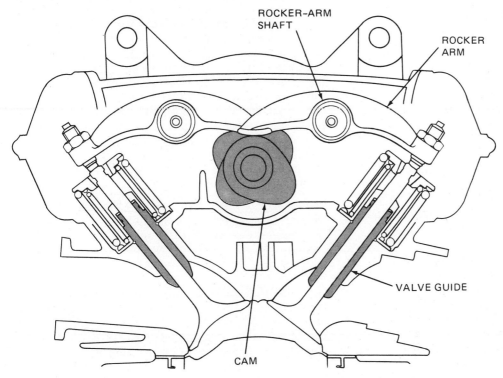

Fig. 6-6 A valve-operating mechanism for a four-cycle motorcycle engine.

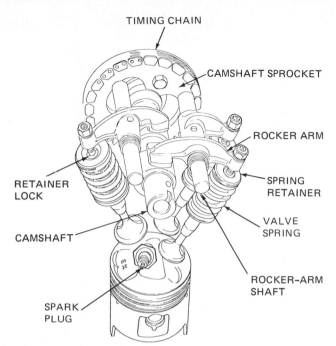

Fig. 6-7 A valve train for a four-cycle engine which has two intake valves and one exhaust valve for each cylinder. The additional intake valve improves engine breathing. More of the air-fuel mixture can enter, so stronger power strokes and higher power output result.

The gear or sprocket on the camshaft is twice as large in diameter as the gear or sprocket on the crankshaft. The camshaft must rotate at half the speed of the crankshaft. The crankshaft must turn two revolutions while the camshaft is turning only one revolution. One

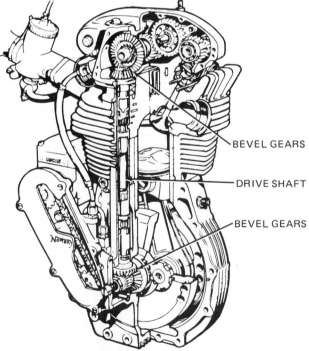

Fig. 6-8 An engine with a camshaft in the head driven by bevel gears and a driveshaft. (*Norton Triumph Corporation*)

camshaft rotation produces one opening and closing of each valve. Therefore, the intake and exhaust valves open once while the crankshaft is turning two times.

While the crankshaft is turning twice, each piston is making four strokes. During one of these four strokes, the intake valve is open. During another of these strokes, the exhaust valve is open. During the other two strokes, both valves are closed. To sum up, while the crankshaft is making two revolutions and the piston is taking four strokes, the camshaft is making one revolution and opening each valve once.

6-5 LOCATION OF THE CAMSHAFT

Most motorcycle engines have the camshaft mounted in the cylinder head, as already described (6-4) and illustrated (Figs. 6-2, 6-3, 6-6, and 6-7). In most engines, the camshaft is driven by sprockets and chain or by a neoprene toothed belt. A few engines with the camshaft in the head use bevel gears and a drive shaft to drive the camshaft (Fig. 6-8).

When a chain or a toothed belt is used, some form of chain or belt *tensioner* is required. You can see this tensioner in Fig. 6-3 and other illustrations of overhead-camshaft engines in the book. The purpose of the tensioner is to take up any looseness in the chain or belt. This prevents erratic valve action and minimizes chain noise.

Some motorcycle engines have the camshaft in the cylinder block or in the crankcase, near the crankshaft. Figures 6-9 and 6-10 show this arrangement. The cylinder in the engine shown in Fig. 6-9 is nearly horizontal. It has a push rod for each valve rocker arm. The camshaft end of the push rod is enclosed in a valve lifter, which takes the wear of the rotating cam. The camshaft is driven by gears from the crankshaft. The camshaft gear is twice as large as the crankshaft gear.

A two-cylinder, V-type engine is shown in Fig. 6-10. The camshaft is driven by gears from the crankshaft. There is a push rod for each valve. In this engine, the valve lifter has a roller which rides on the camshaft. This greatly reduces friction on and wear of the cam and the lifter foot. The push rods are enclosed in hollow tubes, or covers. These tubes form the return circuit for the lubricating oil. The oil is sent to the cylinder head by the oil pump through an oil line (41 in Fig. 6-10). The oil lubricates the upper end of the push rod, the rocker arms, and the valve stems. The oil then flows back down to the oil sump at the bottom of the engine through the push-rod tubes.

NOTE Engines using push rods are often called *push-rod engines*. Engines with camshafts in the cylinder head are called *overhead-camshaft (OHC) engines* or *overhead-cam engines*.

6-6 ROCKER ARMS

Most rocker arms are of the type that mount on a rocker-arm shaft in the cylinder head (Figs. 6-2, 6-3, 6-6, and 6-7). Some engines have rocker arms that are mounted on ball pivots (Fig. 6-11). These rocker arms work the same way as shaft-mounted rocker arms.

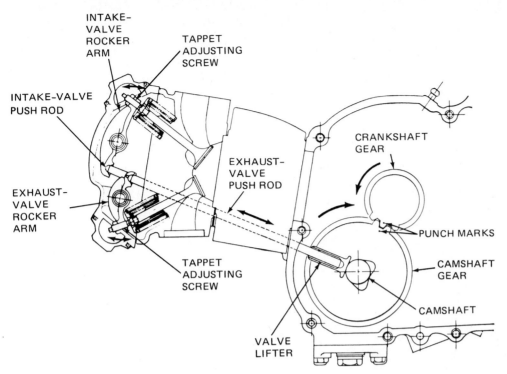

INTAKE-VALVE ROCKER ARM

TAPPET ADJUSTING SCREW

INTAKE-VALVE PUSH ROD

EXHAUST-VALVE PUSH ROD

CRANKSHAFT GEAR

EXHAUST-VALVE ROCKER ARM

PUNCH MARKS

CAMSHAFT GEAR

TAPPET ADJUSTING SCREW

CAMSHAFT

VALVE LIFTER

Fig. 6-9 A sectional view of an overhead-valve engine with a gear-driven camshaft. The camshaft is in the crankcase. The cam action is carried to the rocker arms by push rods. (*Honda Motor Company, Ltd.*)

6-7 LOCATION OF VALVES

Most valves are located in the cylinder head, as already explained and illustrated (Figs. 6-2 and 6-3). These engines are called *overhead-valve engines* or *I-head engines*. This is because the shape of the cylinder and combustion chamber with valves is roughly the shape of the letter I.

Some motorcycle engines have been made with the valves side by side with the cylinder (Fig. 6-12). These engines have the valve trains in the cylinder and crankcase. Such engines are called *side-valve engines, flat-head engines,* or *L-head engines.* The cylinder and combustion chamber form an inverted L.

6-8 ADVANTAGES OF THE OVERHEAD-CAMSHAFT ENGINE

Most modern motorcycle engines, and many of the latest automotive engines, have the camshaft in the cylinder head. Overhead-camshaft engines are more flexible, respond more quickly to power demands, and can often reach higher speeds than push-rod engines. This is because overhead-camshaft valve trains have fewer parts. They do not require valve lifters or push rods. This means there is less inertia in the valve train and fewer parts to bend or deflect.

Inertia is a property of all physical objects (6 5-11). It is the tendency to resist any change in direction or speed of motion. In a push-rod engine, for example, the valve lifter, push rod, and rocker arm are stationary until the cam lobe comes up under the valve lifter. When this happens, the valve lifter, push rod, and rocker arm are all set into motion. Their inertia resists this motion, and a slight bending of the parts can occur.

Therefore, it takes longer for the motion to reach the valve stem.

At higher engine speeds, this effect is greater, and the opening of the valve is delayed longer. Eliminating the push rod and rocker arm reduces this delay. The valve opens sooner and better performance results at high engine speeds.

Another factor is *valve float.* Valve float can occur at high speeds in push-rod engines because of the inertia of the moving push rod and rocker arm. Once they are set into motion, their inertia tends to keep them moving. At high speed this movement can keep pushing down on the valve stem even after the cam lobe has passed out from under the valve lifter. The result is that a clearance appears between the push rod, rocker arm, and valve stem. Then, as the valve spring takes control again, the parts all come together with a strong pounding effect.

Valve float means that the valve "floats" free from the rest of the valve train. Valve float can damage valve-train parts. Also, control of the valve itself is momentarily lost. To prevent this action, valve springs must be made strong enough to keep the valve from floating. The stronger springs can increase the wear of the cam and the valve-lifter foot. However, the design of push-rod engines and their valve trains generally takes into account all these factors. In this way, satisfactory engine performance and minimum wear of parts are achieved.

Because overhead-camshaft engines do not have push rods or, in many engines, valve lifters, there is less inertia in the valve train. Also, there is less deflection or bending of the valve-train parts. The result is that valve action is more uniform and quicker. The engine responds more quickly to power demands and can reach higher speeds.

51

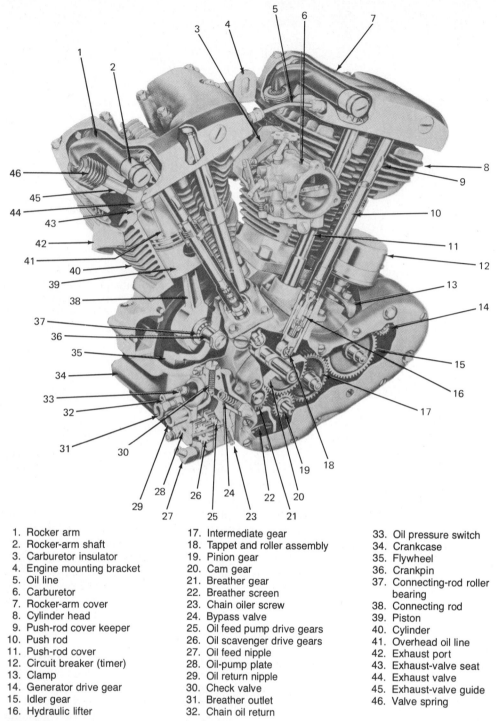

1. Rocker arm
2. Rocker-arm shaft
3. Carburetor insulator
4. Engine mounting bracket
5. Oil line
6. Carburetor
7. Rocker-arm cover
8. Cylinder head
9. Push-rod cover keeper
10. Push rod
11. Push-rod cover
12. Circuit breaker (timer)
13. Clamp
14. Generator drive gear
15. Idler gear
16. Hydraulic lifter

17. Intermediate gear
18. Tappet and roller assembly
19. Pinion gear
20. Cam gear
21. Breather gear
22. Breather screen
23. Chain oiler screw
24. Bypass valve
25. Oil feed pump drive gears
26. Oil scavenger drive gears
27. Oil feed nipple
28. Oil-pump plate
29. Oil return nipple
30. Check valve
31. Breather outlet
32. Chain oil return

33. Oil pressure switch
34. Crankcase
35. Flywheel
36. Crankpin
37. Connecting-rod roller bearing
38. Connecting rod
39. Piston
40. Cylinder
41. Overhead oil line
42. Exhaust port
43. Exhaust-valve seat
44. Exhaust valve
45. Exhaust-valve guide
46. Valve spring

Fig. 6-10 A cutaway view of a V-type two-cylinder four-cycle engine which has the camshaft in the crankcase. It uses push rods. (*Harley-Davidson Motor Company, Inc.*)

Some engines have a single overhead camshaft (SOHC). Others have two (double overhead camshaft, DOHC).

6-9 IMPROVING ENGINE BREATHING

Improving the breathing of the engine means allowing the engine both to take in the air-fuel mixture more easily and to exhaust burned gases more easily. One way of improving engine breathing is to use more valves. Figure 6-7, for example, shows the valve trains of a one-cylinder four-cycle engine that has two intake valves. Figure 6-13 is a cutaway view of a one-cylinder four-cycle overhead camshaft engine using four valves—two intake valves and two exhaust valves.

The additional valves allow more of the air-fuel mixture to enter, so that the power strokes are more powerful. The engine produces more power. We have more to say about engine breathing later in ✍ 7-14, "Volumetric Efficiency."

✍ 6-10 VALVE TIMING
While the engine is running, the valves open and close. They do not open and close at TDC and BDC, but some time before or after BDC and TDC.

For example, the intake valve starts to open several degrees of crankshaft rotation before TDC on the exhaust stroke. This is before the exhaust stroke is finished. This gives the valve enough time to reach the fully open position before the intake stroke begins. Then, when the intake stroke starts, the intake valve is already wide open and the air-fuel mixture can start to enter the cylinder immediately.

The intake valve remains open for several degrees of crankshaft rotation after the piston has passed BDC at the end of the intake stroke. This allows additional time for the air-fuel mixture to continue to flow into the cylinder. The fact that the piston has already passed BDC and is moving up on the compression stroke while the intake valve is still open does not affect the movement of the air-fuel mixture into the cylinder. Actually, the air-fuel mixture is still flowing in as the intake valve starts to close.

The reason for this is that the air-fuel mixture has inertia. The mixture attempts to keep on flowing after it once starts through the carburetor and into the engine cylinder. The momentum of the mixture then keeps it flowing into the cylinder even though the piston has started up on the compression stroke. This packs more of the air-fuel mixture into the cylinder and results in a stronger power stroke.

For a somewhat similar reason, the exhaust valve opens before the piston reaches BDC on the power stroke. As the piston nears BDC, most of the push on the piston has ended. Nothing is lost by opening the exhaust valve toward the end of the power stroke. This gives the exhaust gases additional time to start leaving the cylinder. Exhaust is well started by the time the piston passes BDC and starts up on the exhaust stroke.

The exhaust valve then stays open for several degrees of crankshaft rotation after the piston has passed TDC and the intake stroke has started. This makes good use of the inertia of the exhaust gases. They are moving rapidly toward the exhaust port. Leaving the exhaust valve open for a few degrees after the intake stroke starts gives the exhaust gases additional time to leave the cylinder. This allows more of the air-fuel mixture to enter on the intake stroke so that a stronger power stroke results.

The actual timing of the valves varies with different four-cycle engines. The timing of a typical high-performance motorcycle engine is shown in Fig. 6-14. Note that the intake valve opens 36° of crankshaft rotation BTDC (before TDC) on the exhaust stroke and stays open until 68° of crankshaft rotation after BDC on the compression stroke. The exhaust valve opens 68° before BDC on the power stroke and stays open 36° ATDC

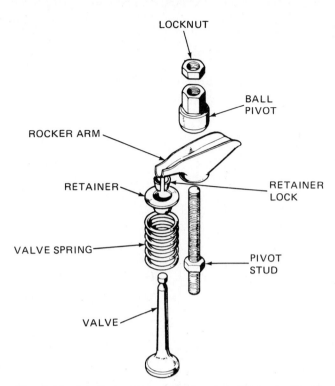

Fig. 6-11 A ball-pivot type of rocker arm for an overhead-valve engine. (*Honda Motor Company, Ltd.*)

on the intake stroke. This gives the two valves an overlap of 72° at the end of the exhaust stroke and beginning of the intake stroke. The duration, or length of time each valve is open, is 284°.

✍ 6-11 COUNTERBALANCERS
Single-cylinder and two-cylinder vertical-twin motorcycle engines have a fairly high level of vibration when they are running. This can easily tire the rider and places additional loads on the motorcycle frame, fasteners, and other parts.

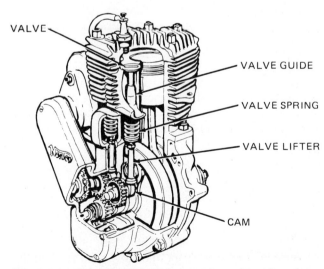

Fig. 6-12 A cutaway view of an engine with side valves. (*Norton Triumph Corporation*)

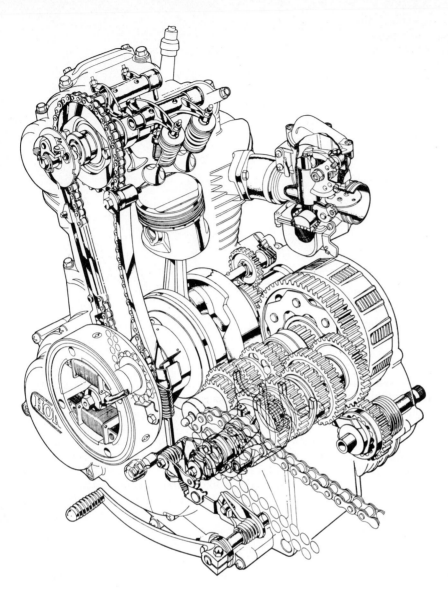

Fig. 6-13 A cutaway view of a one-cylinder overhead-camshaft engine using four valves—two intake valves and two exhaust valves. (*Honda Motor Company, Ltd.*)

To help reduce the vibration of these engines, some manufacturers put a counterbalancer into the crankcase. An engine of this type is shown in Fig. 6-15. Basically, the counterbalancer is made up of one or more weights on shafts that are driven by the crankshaft. The weights are designed and placed on the counterbalancer shafts so that as they rotate they tend to counteract, and thereby balance out, the vibrations that occur naturally in the engine as each cylinder fires. The result is a smoother-running engine.

6-12
PISTONS AND PISTON RINGS In many of the engines illustrated in this chapter the piston heads have a complex shape. Notches have been cut out of the piston heads to provide room for the valve heads. The notches prevent the piston from striking the valves as the piston approaches TDC. Therefore, the piston can be designed to move closer to the cylinder head on the compression stroke. This is an important factor in the design of high-compression engines.

A high-compression engine can produce more power than a low-compression engine of the same size. We will have more to say about high compression in Chapter 7.

Two-cycle engines use one or two piston rings, while the four-cycle engine uses three or four rings. The upper rings—the compression rings—in both types of engines work to hold the pressure in the combustion chamber. In the two-cycle engine, oil is mixed with the gasoline or with the air-fuel mixture to lubricate the piston rings and piston.

In many four-cycle engines a different method of lubricating the cylinder wall, piston, and rings is used. A supply of oil is kept in the bottom of the crankcase, or sump. This oil is splashed or pumped around so that droplets hit the cylinder wall and keep it oiled. At the same time, some of the oil is pumped to the cylinder head to lubricate the valve train. The oil also covers the bearings in the engine so they are adequately lubricated. Lubricating systems are covered in detail in a later chapter.

A lot of oil is splashed on the cylinder wall, and the

two compression rings alone would pass too much of it. This oil would then get into the combustion chamber where it would be burned. The burned oil would leave a carbon residue that would soon clog the valve ports and foul the spark plugs, preventing them from firing properly. Then the engine would begin to lose power and would soon stop working altogether.

To prevent problems caused by oil reaching the combustion chamber, the piston on a four-cycle engine is equipped with a third ring, called the *oil-control ring*, as shown in Fig. 2-7. Its purpose is to scrape excess oil off the cylinder walls on every downstroke of the piston. This oil drops back down into the crankcase instead of working its way up into the combustion chamber.

⚒ 6-13
COMPARING TWO-CYCLE AND FOUR-CYCLE ENGINES
The four-cycle engine is very similar in many ways to the two-cycle engine. In both engines, a piston moves up and down in the cylinder. The piston is attached to a crank on the crankshaft by a connecting rod. When ignition of the compressed air-fuel mixture takes place, the high pressure forces the piston down. This force, carried through the crankshaft, causes the crankshaft to rotate.

To this point, the actions are similar in both engines. However, in the two-cycle engine, the air-fuel mixture is admitted to the cylinder, and the burned gases leave the cylinder through openings, or ports, in the cylinder wall (Chap. 5). Also, in the two-cycle engine, the air-fuel mixture is compressed in the cylinder every time the piston moves up. Every time the piston reaches TDC, there is combustion and resulting high pressure to push the piston down. Only one crankshaft revolution and two piston strokes are required to complete the cycle of engine operation in the two-cycle engine.

The four-cycle engine does not have valve ports in the cylinder wall. Instead, this engine has movable metal valves. These valves are opened by cams on a camshaft. The intake valve opens to allow the air-fuel mixture to enter the cylinder. The exhaust valve opens to allow the burned gases to escape from the cylinder.

It takes two revolutions of the crankshaft to complete the four strokes in a four-cycle engine (Fig. 6-4). In the two-cycle engine, a power stroke occurs every two piston strokes—every crankshaft revolution (Fig. 5-8). Every downward movement of the piston is a power stroke. In effect, the intake and compression strokes are combined. Also, the power and exhaust strokes are combined.

You might think that because the two-cycle engine has twice as many power strokes as the four-cycle engine, it produces twice as much horsepower as a four-cycle engine of the same size and running at the same speed. However, this is not true. In the two-cycle engine, when the transfer and exhaust ports have been opened by the piston, there is always some mixing of the fresh charge and the burned gases. Not all the burned gases get out, and this prevents a larger fresh charge from entering. Therefore, the power stroke that follows is not as powerful as it would be if all the burned

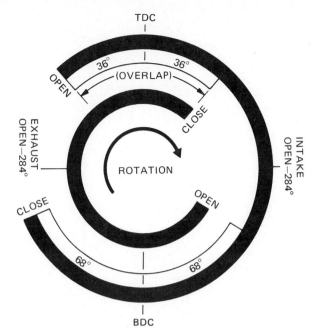

Fig. 6-14 The intake- and exhaust-valve timing in a high-performance motorcycle engine. The complete cycle of events is shown as two circles, which represent two complete crankshaft rotations. The timing for the valves differs among different engines. (*Yamaha International Corporation*)

gases were exhausted and a full charge of the air-fuel mixture entered.

In the four-cycle engine, nearly all the burned gases escape from the combustion chamber during the longer time that the exhaust valve is open. Almost a full charge of the air-fuel mixture can enter the cylinder because a complete piston stroke is devoted to the intake of the air-fuel mixture. Contrast that with the fact that in the

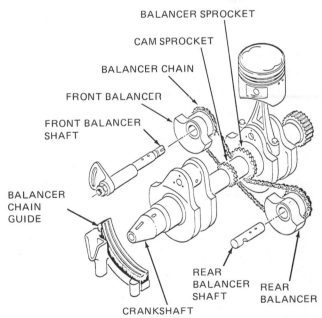

Fig. 6-15 An engine with counterbalancers in the crankcase. (*Honda Motor Company, Ltd.*)

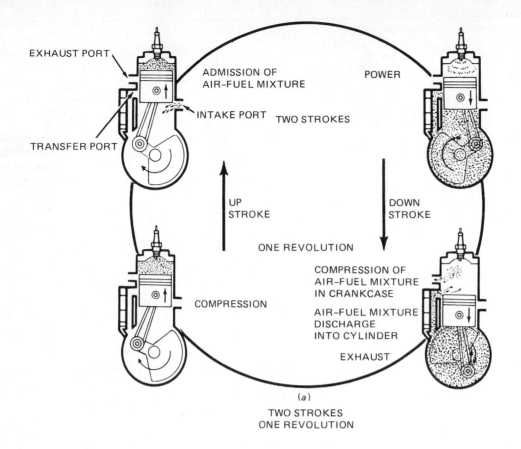

EXHAUST PORT

ADMISSION OF AIR-FUEL MIXTURE

POWER

INTAKE PORT TWO STROKES

TRANSFER PORT

UP STROKE

DOWN STROKE

ONE REVOLUTION

COMPRESSION OF AIR-FUEL MIXTURE IN CRANKCASE

COMPRESSION

AIR-FUEL MIXTURE DISCHARGE INTO CYLINDER

EXHAUST

(a)

TWO STROKES ONE REVOLUTION

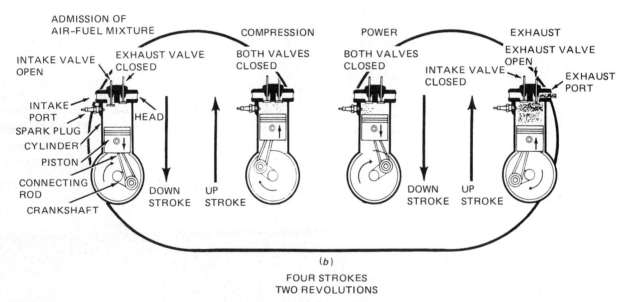

ADMISSION OF AIR-FUEL MIXTURE

COMPRESSION

POWER

EXHAUST

INTAKE VALVE OPEN

EXHAUST VALVE CLOSED

BOTH VALVES CLOSED

BOTH VALVES CLOSED

EXHAUST VALVE OPEN

INTAKE VALVE CLOSED

EXHAUST PORT

INTAKE PORT

SPARK PLUG

CYLINDER

PISTON

CONNECTING ROD

CRANKSHAFT

HEAD

DOWN STROKE

UP STROKE

DOWN STROKE

UP STROKE

(b)

FOUR STROKES TWO REVOLUTIONS

Fig. 6-16 Comparing the operation of the two-cycle engine and the four-cycle engine.

two-cycle engine only part of a stroke is available. Therefore, the power stroke in the four-cycle engine produces more power (Fig. 6-16).

Two-cycle engines are widely used as power plants for motorcycles, lawn mowers, motorboats, snow removers, model airplanes, motor scooters, power saws, and other equipment. Two-cycle engines usually are air cooled. Because they have no valve train or liquid cooling system, they are relatively simple in construction, relatively simple to service, and light in weight. These are desirable characteristics for engines used on small, lightweight equipment and vehicles such as motorcycles that must be handled and moved around.

CHAPTER 6
REVIEW QUESTIONS

1. What is the biggest difference between the construction of a two-cycle engine and the construction of a four-cycle engine?
2. In a four-cycle engine, what closes the valves?
3. When is the intake valve open?
4. When is the exhaust valve open?
5. Why does a four-cycle engine require more rings on the piston than a two-cycle engine?
6. What are the four strokes of the four-stroke cycle?
7. What causes the valves to open?
8. Explain the different methods used to drive the camshaft.
9. What is an I-head engine?
10. When is a rocker arm used?
11. What is a *ball-pivot* type of rocker arm?
12. Explain what makes an engine a *push-rod* engine.
13. How does inertia limit the flexibility of a push-rod engine?
14. What is valve float?
15. Why do some engines have more than two valves per cylinder?
16. Why are some piston heads notched?
17. What happens when excess oil gets into the combustion chamber?
18. What is valve timing?
19. Why don't the valves open and close to coincide with the piston strokes?
20. How does valve overlap help improve engine performance?

CHAPTER **7**

ENGINE MEASUREMENTS

After studying this chapter,
you should be able to:

1. Explain what work is.

2. Define energy.

3. Discuss power and define horsepower.

4. Define torque.

5. Explain what inertia is.

6. Describe friction.

7. Define bore, stroke, piston displacement, and compression ratio.

8. Explain what volumetric efficiency is and how it can be improved.

9. Compare bhp, ihp, and fhp and explain how they are related.

10. Explain how the brake horsepower and the torque of an engine are related.

11. Discuss the mechanical and thermal efficiency of an engine.

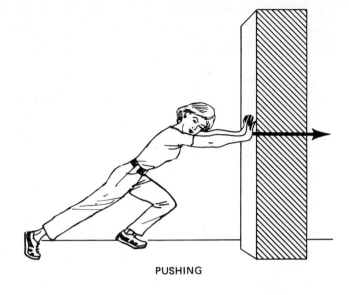

PUSHING

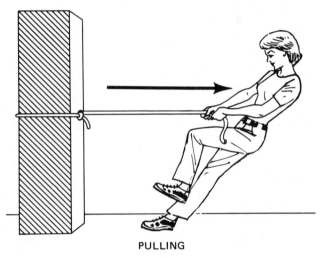

PULLING

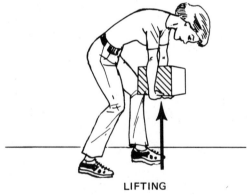

LIFTING

Fig. 7-1 When a push, pull, or lift moves an object, work is done on that object.

7-1
FUNDAMENTAL MEASUREMENTS Before we discuss physical and performance measurement of engines, let's look at some fundamentals, such as work, energy, power, torque, and horsepower. This will give you the background information to understand engine measurements.

7-2
WORK Work is the moving of an object against an opposing force. The object is moved by a push, a pull, or a lift, as shown in Fig. 7-1. For example, when a weight is lifted, it is moved upward against the pull of gravity. Work is done on the weight. When a coil spring is compressed, work is done on the spring.

Work is measured in terms of distance and force. If a 5-pound weight is lifted off the ground 1 foot, the work done on the weight is 5 foot-pounds (ft-lb), or 1 foot times 5 pounds. If the 5-pound weight is lifted 2 feet, the work done is 10 ft-lb. Work is equal to distance times force.

In the metric system, work has been measured in three different units. These units are the meter-kilogram (m-kg), the newton-meter (N-m), and the joule (J).

Using meter-kilograms, our example would be: Lifting a 5-kilogram (kg) [11-lb] weight 1 meter (m) [3.28 ft] requires 5 mkg [36.08 ft-lb] of work. If the 5-kg weight is lifted 2 m, the work done is 10 m-kg [72.16 ft-lb]. However, the joule is the proper metric measure for work.

7-3 ENERGY

Energy is the ability or capacity to do work. When work is done on an object, energy is stored in that object. Lift a 20-pound [9.072-kg] weight 4 feet [1.219 m] and you have stored energy in the weight. The weight can do 80 ft-lb [11.056 m-kg] of work. If a spring is compressed, energy is stored in it. When the spring is released, it can do work on another body. For example, when the rocker arm stops pushing on the valve stem, the valve spring pulls the valve up so the valve closes.

7-4 POWER

Work can be done slowly, or it can be done rapidly. The rate at which work is done is measured in terms of power. A machine that can do a large amount of work in a short time is called a high-powered machine. Power is the rate, or speed, at which work is done.

7-5 TORQUE

Torque is twisting or turning effort. You apply torque to the screw top of a bottle to loosen the top. You apply torque to the handlebars when you steer around a turn. The engine supplies torque to the motorcycle rear wheel to make it rotate.

However, torque must not be confused with power. Torque is turning effort which *may or may not result in motion*. Power is the rate at which work is being done. This means that something must be moving when power is being used.

Torque is measured in pound-feet (or lb-ft, not to be confused with ft-lb of work). For example, suppose you push on a crank with a 20-pound push, and the crank is 1½ feet long. You would be applying 30 lb-ft of torque to the crank, as shown in Fig. 7-2. You would be applying this torque regardless of whether or not the crank was turning. The torque is there as long as you continue to apply the 20-pound push to the crank handle.

NOTE In the metric system, torque is measured in kilogram-meters (kg-m) or newton-meters (N-m), and not pound-feet. Gradually, the newton-meter is replacing the kilogram-meter. It will eventually be the standard way to measure torque in the metric system.

7-6 HORSEPOWER

One horsepower (hp) is the power of one horse, or a measure of the rate at which a horse can work. For example, a 10-hp engine can do the work of 10 horses.

One horsepower is equal to 33,000 ft-lb of work per minute. Look at Fig. 7-3. In the illustration, the horse walks 165 feet in 1 minute, lifting the 200-pound weight. The amount of work done is 33,000 ft-lb (165 feet × 200 pounds). The time is 1 minute. If the horse did this work in 2 minutes, then it would be only "half" working. It would be putting out only 0.5 hp. One formula for horsepower is

$$\text{hp} = \frac{\text{ft-lb per minute}}{33,000} = \frac{L \times W}{33,000 \times t}$$

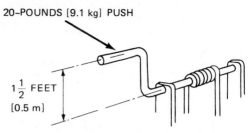

Fig. 7-2 Torque is measured in pound-feet (lb-ft). It is calculated by multiplying the push by the crank offset, or the distance of the push from the rotating shaft.

where

hp = horsepower
L = length, in feet, through which W is exerted
W = force, in pounds, exerted through distance L
t = time, in minutes, required to move W through L

In the metric system, power output from an engine often is measured in kilowatts (kW). This is the amount of electricity the engine could produce if it were used to drive an electric generator. To convert from one measurement system to the other, 1.34 hp is equal to 1 kW. One hp is equal to 0.746 kW. Therefore, a 100-hp motorcycle engine is equal to a 74.6-kW engine. A second formula for horsepower, which is more convenient to use with engines, is

$$\text{hp} = \frac{\text{torque} \times \text{rpm}}{5252}$$

This formula is more commonly used because engine-testing dynamometers (described later) measure engine performance in rpm (revolutions per minute), torque, and horsepower.

7-7 INERTIA

Inertia is a property of all material objects. It causes them to resist any change of speed or direction of travel. A motionless object tends to remain motionless. A moving object tends to keep moving at the same speed and in the same direction.

Consider the motorcycle. When it is standing still, its inertia must be overcome by applying power to make it move. To increase its speed, more power must be ap-

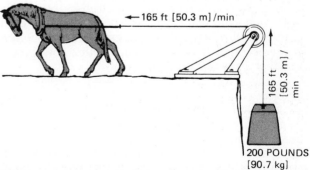

Fig. 7-3 One horse can do 33,000 foot-pounds of work per minute.

59

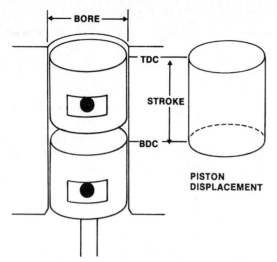

Fig. 7-4 Piston displacement is the volume the piston displaces, or takes the place of, as it moves from BDC to TDC.

plied. To decrease its speed, the brakes must be applied. The brakes must overcome the motorcycle's inertia to slow it down. Also, when the motorcycle goes around a curve, its inertia tends to keep it moving in a straight line. The tires on the road must overcome this tendency, or else the inertia of the motorcycle will send it into a skid.

7-8
FRICTION
Friction is resistance to motion between two objects in contact with each other. If you placed a book on a table and then pushed on the book, you would find that it took a certain amount of push, or force, to make the book move. If you placed a second book on top of the first book, you would have to push harder to slide the two books across the table.

If you put oil on the table, the books would slide on the oil. You could move the books much more easily, because the oil reduces the friction between the books and the table.

Friction, or resistance to motion, increases with the load. The higher the load, the greater the friction. There are three kinds of friction: dry, greasy, and viscous. These are discussed in detail in a later chapter.

In the engine, all moving parts are covered with oil, or lubricated, so that they will easily slip over one another. Even so, some power is used up in overcoming the friction to make them move. The power that is used in an engine to overcome friction is called *friction horsepower* and abbreviated fhp. Friction horsepower is further discussed in this chapter.

7-9
ENGINE MEASUREMENTS
Now we look at the physical measurements of an engine. These include the size of the cylinder, the distance the piston moves in the cylinder, the volume the piston displaces as it moves from BDC to TDC, and the compression ratio. Later, we will look into the performance measurements of an engine.

7-10
BORE AND STROKE
The size of an engine cylinder is given by its bore and stroke (Fig. 7-4). The bore is the diameter of the cylinder. The stroke is the distance the piston travels from BDC (bottom dead center) to TDC (top dead center). When giving the bore and stroke of an engine, the bore is always given first. For example, in a 3- by 2½-inch cylinder, the diameter, or bore, is 3 inches and the stroke is 2½ inches. These measurements are used to figure the piston displacement (7-11).

The bore and stroke of a motorcycle engine usually are given in the metric system in millimeters (mm). A cylinder that is "56 by 60" is a cylinder that has a 56-mm bore and a 60-mm stroke.

Years ago, most engines were built with a long stroke and a smaller bore, such as a 2- by 3-inch engine. In recent years, engines have been designed with a shorter stroke and a larger bore. For example, one popular small engine has a 2½-inch bore and a 2¼-inch stroke. Such engines are called *oversquare*. A *square* engine has a bore and a stroke of equal lengths. An example of this is the 49-cc Honda engine which has a bore and a stroke of 40 mm by 40 mm.

There are several reasons for the manufacturer to build an oversquare engine. With the shorter piston stroke, there is less friction loss and shorter piston-ring travel, which means less wear. Also, the shorter stroke reduces the loads on the engine bearings. However, shortening the length of the stroke also changes the torque-producing characteristics of the engine. Sometimes a long-stroke, or *undersquare*, design must be used to attain the desired performance from an engine. An undersquare engine with a long stroke burns cleaner and has less exhaust emissions than an oversquare engine.

7-11
PISTON DISPLACEMENT
Piston displacement is the volume that the piston displaces, or "sweeps out," as it moves from BDC to TDC (Fig. 7-4). For example, the piston displacement of a 3- by 2-inch cylinder is the volume of a cylinder 3 inches in diameter and 2 inches long. The piston displacement of the cylinder is equal to

$$1/4\pi \times D^2 \times L = 0.7854 \times 3^2 \times 2$$
$$= 0.7854 \times 9 \times 2$$
$$= 14.14 \text{ cubic inches}$$

where

$\pi = 3.1416$, a constant used to find the area of a circle
D = diameter, or bore, of cylinder
L = length of stroke

If the engine has four cylinders, the total displacement is 14.14 times 4, or 56.56 cubic inches.

In the metric system, piston displacement is given in cubic centimeters (cc). Therefore, a displacement of 56.56 cubic inches would be a displacement of 927 cc in metric measurements. Since 1000 cc equals 1 liter (L), 927 cc is 0.927 liter.

7-12 COMPRESSION RATIO

COMPRESSION RATIO The compression ratio of an engine is a measure of how much the air-fuel mixture is compressed in an engine cylinder (Fig. 7-5). It is calculated by dividing the air volume in one cylinder with the piston at BDC by the air volume with the piston at TDC.

NOTE The air volume with the piston at TDC is called the *clearance volume.* It is the clearance that remains above the piston at TDC.

For example, one cylinder of an engine has a volume of 42.35 cubic inches [694 cc] at BDC, as shown in A of Fig. 7-5.

It has a clearance volume of 4.45 cubic inches [73 cc], as shown in B of Fig. 7-5. Therefore, the compression ratio is 42.35 divided by 4.45 [694 ÷ 73], or 9.5 to 1, which is written as 9.5:1. During the compression stroke, the air-fuel mixture is compressed from a volume of 42.34 cubic inches [694 cc] to 4.45 cubic inches [73 cc], or to 1/9.5 of its original volume.

In recent years, the compression ratios of motorcycle engines have increased. This increase offers several advantages. The power and economy of an engine increase as the compression ratio goes up (within limits). This does not require an increase in engine size or weight.

An engine with a higher compression ratio "squeezes" the air-fuel mixture harder (compresses it more). This causes the air-fuel mixture to produce more power on the power stroke. Here is the reason: A higher compression ratio means a higher pressure at the end of the compression stroke. This means higher combustion pressure during the power stroke. The piston is pushed down harder. The burning gases also expand to a greater volume. It all adds up to this: There is more push on the piston for a longer time during the power stroke.

However, increasing the compression ratio does cause some problems. As the compression ratio goes up, detonation, or spark knock, becomes more of a problem. Detonation is discussed in a later chapter. In addition, higher compression ratios produce more pollutants in the exhaust gases and also cause the engine to be harder to crank.

7-13 ENGINE-PERFORMANCE MEASUREMENTS

ENGINE-PERFORMANCE MEASUREMENTS Let us now look at the measurements that can be taken on an operating engine. These include volumetric efficiency, horsepower, friction horsepower, and torque.

7-14 VOLUMETRIC EFFICIENCY

VOLUMETRIC EFFICIENCY The amount of air-fuel mixture taken into the cylinder on the intake stroke is a measure of the engine's volumetric efficiency. If the air-fuel mixture were drawn into the cylinder slowly, a full charge could get in. But the mixture must pass rapidly through narrow openings and bends in the carburetor and intake ports. In addition, the mixture is heated from engine heat. Therefore, the mix-

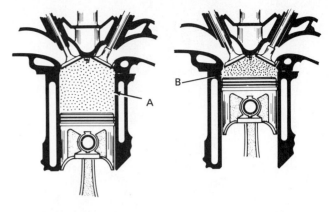

PISTON AT BDC   PISTON AT TDC

Fig. 7-5 Compression ratio is the volume in a cylinder with the piston at BDC divided by the volume with the piston at TDC, or A divided by B.

ture expands. The rapid movement and heating reduce the amount of the mixture that can get into the cylinder. A full charge of the air-fuel mixture does not enter, because the time is too short and the air is heated.

Volmetric efficiency is the ratio of the amount of the air-fuel mixture that actually enters the cylinder to the amount that could possibly enter. For example, a certain cylinder (Fig. 7-5a) has an air volume of 47 cubic inches [770 cc]. If the cylinder were allowed to completely fill up, it would take 0.034 ounce [0.964 g] of air. However, suppose that the engine is running at a high speed, so that only 0.027 ounce [0.765 g] of air can enter during each intake stroke. This means that the volumetric efficiency is only about 80 percent (0.027 is 80 percent of 0.034). Actually, 80 percent is a good volumetric efficiency for an engine running at medium-high speed. The volumetric efficiency of some engines may drop to as low as 50 percent at high speeds. This is another way of saying that the cylinders are only half-filled at high speeds.

This is one reason why engine speed and power output cannot increase without limit. At higher speed, the engine has a harder time breathing, or drawing in air. It is starved for air and cannot produce any further increase in power output.

To improve volumetric efficiency, intake valves can be made larger, or two intake valves can be used in each cylinder. Also, valve lift can be increased. This means that the lobe on the cam can be made larger so the valve opens wider. However, when this is done, there is danger of the piston head striking the valve head. Unless the engine design takes this into account, serious engine damage can result. Many piston heads are notched so that the piston head will not strike the open valves. In operation, there is a very small clearance between the valves and the pistons.

Volumetric efficiency also can be increased by making the intake ports and passages wider and as straight and short as possible. Also, the smoothness of the inside surfaces of the intake ports is important. Rough surfaces slow down the flow of the air-fuel mixture. Many motorcycle mechanics smooth the ports of the

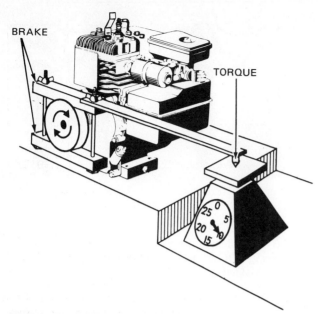

BRAKE

TORQUE

25
20 5
15 10

Fig. 7-6 An engine dynamometer is used to measure engine torque and brake horsepower.

engine, especially if it is to be raced. Another way to improve volumetric efficiency is to use more carburetors or to use carburetors with larger air passages, which improve engine breathing at high speed. All these changes help produce more power at high speeds because they improve volumetric efficiency.

7-15 BRAKE HORSEPOWER   The horsepower output of engines is measured in terms of brake horsepower (bhp). The name comes from the braking device that formerly was used to hold engine speed down while torque or horsepower was measured (Fig. 7-6). When an engine is rated at 30 hp [22.38 kW], for example, it is really brake horsepower that is meant. This is the amount of power the engine is able to deliver at certain speeds with a wide-open throttle.

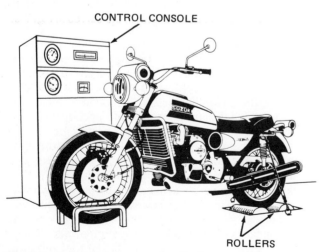

CONTROL CONSOLE

SUZUKI

ROLLERS

Fig. 7-7   A motorcycle on a chassis dynamometer.

The usual way to rate an engine is with a *dynamometer,* or *dyno* (Fig. 7-6). This device has a mechanism (an electric generator, water brake, or friction brake) which can put different loads on the engine. The engine dynamometer can measure the torque or shaft horsepower that the engine can develop under various operating conditions.

Some dynamometers are used to test engines by themselves. This type of dynamometer is known as an *engine dynamometer* and is shown in Fig. 7-6. The dynamometer usually found in the shop checks the engine with the engine in the motorcycle. This type of dynamometer is called a *chassis dynamometer* and is shown in Fig. 7-7. The rear wheel of the motorcycle is placed between the rollers. The engine drives the wheel, and the wheel drives the rollers. The rollers can be loaded or braked varying amounts so that the torque and horsepower available at the rear wheel (rear-wheel horsepower) can be measured.

From this information, the brake horsepower of the engine can be calculated. Meters on the dynamometer usually read engine rpm, torque, and horsepower. The torque and horsepower meters are connected to the forward roller of the chassis dynamometer.

The use of the chassis dynamometer is becoming more common in motorcycle service. The dynamometer can give a quick report on engine conditions by measuring engine power output at various speeds and loads. Also, adjustments can be made to the engine while it is running at any speed or load, and the results can be seen immediately.

Some motorcycle dynamometers are made so that high-performance engines can be tested while still in the motorcycle. On this type of dynamometer, the rear wheel is removed from the motorcycle. Then a drive chain is fitted around a driven sprocket on the dynamometer. This overcomes the wheel-spin problem which can occur when dyno checks are made on high-performance motorcycles. The high power at the rear wheel can cause the tire to spin on the rollers so that accurate measurements cannot be made.

When a shop is equipped with a dynamometer, road testing of motorcycles is not always necessary. The dyno quickly gives the mechanic troubleshooting and diagnosis information. In addition, the dyno improves shop safety and reduces the liability risk. Road testing is done in the shop instead of on the streets. Many shops that have a dynamometer use it to attract new customers by advertising "dyno tuning."

7-16 INDICATED HORSEPOWER   Indicated horsepower (ihp) is the power that the engine develops inside the combustion chambers during the combustion process. A special device is required to measure ihp. It measures the pressures in the engine cylinders. The four small drawings in Fig. 7-8 show the pressures in the cylinder during these four strokes. These pressures are used to figure ihp. Indicated horsepower is always higher than bhp. This is because some of the power developed in the cylinders is used up in overcoming the friction in the engine.

7-17 FRICTION HORSEPOWER

Friction horsepower (fhp) is the power required to overcome the friction of the moving parts in the engine. One of the major causes of friction loss (or fhp) is piston-ring friction. Under some conditions, the friction of the rings moving on the cylinder walls accounts for 75 percent of all friction in the engine. This points up one advantage of the short-stroke, oversquare engine. With a short stroke, the piston rings do not have as far to travel, and ring friction is lower. Figure 7-9 shows a curve of friction horsepower for one engine operating under certain specified conditions.

Friction horsepower goes up as engine speed goes up. The graph in Fig. 7-9 shows this. At low speeds, it takes only a few horsepower to overcome the friction in the engine. But as speed increases, the friction loss goes up until, at 8000 rpm, friction is using up 40 hp. As you can see in Fig. 7-9, that is a significant part of the power produced in the engine.

7-18 RELATING BHP, IHP, AND FHP

Brake horsepower is the power available to do work. Indicated horsepower is the power developed in the engine cylinders. Friction horsepower is the power lost due to friction in the engine. The relationship among the three is

$$bhp = ihp - fhp$$

The horsepower available from the engine (bhp) is equal to the horsepower developed (ihp) minus the horsepower lost as a result of friction (fhp).

7-19 ENGINE TORQUE

Torque is turning effort. When the piston is moving down on the power stroke, it applies torque to the engine crankshaft through the connecting rod. The harder the push on the piston, the greater the torque applied. This means that the higher the combustion pressures, the greater the amount of torque.

The dynamometer is normally used to check engine torque. Engine dynamometers frequently have direct-reading torque meters. Chassis dynamometers usually have direct-reading horsepower meters. To find the horsepower of an engine when the meter on the dynamometer reads torque, use the formula discussed in 7-6.

7-20 BRAKE HORSEPOWER AND TORQUE

The torque that an engine can develop changes with engine speed, as shown in Fig. 7-9. At intermediate speeds, volumetric efficiency is high. There is sufficient time for the cylinders to fill almost completely. This means that with the maximum amount of the air-fuel mixture, higher combustion pressures will develop. With higher combustion pressures, the engine torque is higher.

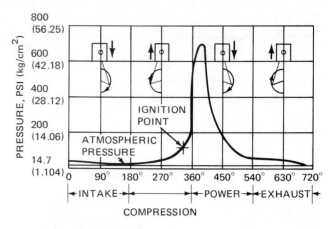

DEGREES OF CRANKSHAFT ROTATION AND PISTON STROKES

Fig. 7-8 Pressures in a four-cycle-engine cylinder during the four piston strokes. The four strokes require two crankshaft revolutions (360° each), a total of 720° of rotation. This curve is for a particular engine operating at one definite speed and throttle opening. Changing the speed and throttle opening would change the curve (particularly the power curve).

At higher speed, volumetric efficiency drops off. There is not enough time for the cylinders to become filled with air-fuel mixture. Since there is less of the air-fuel mixture to burn, the combustion pressures do not go as high. There is less push on the pistons, and engine torque is lower. Notice in Fig. 7-9 how the torque drops off as engine speed increases.

The bhp curve of an engine is different from the torque curve. Figure 7-9 also shows the bhp curve for the same engine for which the torque curve is shown. The torque curve starts at low speed and increases until a high engine speed is reached. But at a still higher speed, bhp drops off.

The drop-off of bhp is due to reduced torque at higher speed and to increased fhp at the higher speed. Figure 7-9 compares the curves of torque, bhp, and fhp for a four-cycle engine.

NOTE The curves in Fig. 7-9 are for one particular engine only. Different engines have different torque, bhp, and fhp curves. Peaks may be at higher or lower speeds, and the relationships may not be as shown in the curves in Fig. 7-9.

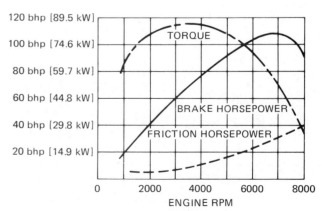

Fig. 7-9 Torque-bhp-fhp curves of an engine.

7-21 ENGINE EFFICIENCY

ENGINE EFFICIENCY The term *efficiency* relates the effort exerted and the results obtained. For engines, efficiency is the relation between the power delivered and the power that could be obtained if the engine operated without any power loss. Engine efficiency can be computed in two ways, as mechanical efficiency and as thermal efficiency.

Mechanical efficiency is the relationship between bhp and ihp:

$$\text{Mechanical efficiency} = \frac{\text{bhp}}{\text{ihp}}$$

EXAMPLE At a certain speed, the bhp of an engine is 116 and its ihp is 135. Mechanical efficiency is bhp/ihp = 116/135 = 0.86, or 86 percent. In this engine, 86 percent of the power developed in the cylinders is available to do work. The remaining 14 percent, or 19 hp [14.17 kW], is consumed as fhp.

Thermal efficiency (*thermal* means *of or related to heat*) is the relation between the power output and the energy in the fuel burned to produce this output.

Some of the heat produced by combustion is carried away by the engine cooling system. There is more about this in a later chapter. Some heat is lost in the exhaust gases, which are hot when they leave the cylinder. These are heat (thermal) losses that reduce the thermal efficiency of the engine. They do not add to the power output of the engine. The remainder of the heat is used by the engine to develop power. Because so much heat is lost during engine operation, thermal efficiency may be as low as 20 percent. In a gasoline engine, thermal efficiency seldom is higher than 25 percent.

CHAPTER 7 REVIEW QUESTIONS

1. Define work.
2. Define power.
3. Define energy.
4. Define horsepower. In what terms is horsepower measured in the United States Customary System? In the metric system?
5. An engine develops 25 lb-ft of torque at 4000 rpm. What is the horsepower?
6. What are the three kinds of friction?
7. What are the bore and the stroke of an engine? How are bore and stroke given in the metric system?
8. What is piston displacement? In what terms is piston displacement given in the metric system? How many cubic inches of displacement does a 1-liter engine have?
9. What does the term *kilowatt* mean?
10. What is volumetric efficiency?
11. Explain what can be done to the valves and intake ports to improve volumetric efficiency.
12. Will a two-cycle or a four-cycle engine give better volumetric efficiency? Why?
13. What is brake horsepower? How is it measured in the shop?
14. What is the compression ratio? How can it be increased in an engine?
15. What is ihp?
16. What is fhp? What is the major cause of fhp in an engine?
17. What is the relationship among bhp, ihp, and fhp?
18. What is mechanical efficiency?
19. What is thermal efficiency?
20. What is inertia?

PART **2**

MOTORCYCLE ENGINE SYSTEMS

To operate and to produce usable power, an engine requires more than just the ignition of a charge of air and fuel inside the cylinder. The engine must have fuel, lubricating, and cooling systems to run. While the engine runs, it burns gasoline and creates a certain amount of air pollution. In Part 2, we discuss the engine support systems that every engine must have, how the gasoline is burned, and the air pollution that results.

There are nine chapters in Part 2. They are:

CHAPTER 8

GASOLINE AND GASOHOL

After studying this chapter,
you should be able to:

1. Describe the makeup and properties of gasoline.

2. Explain what happens when gasoline burns and what happens when it is not completely burned.

3. Define *gasohol*.

4. Discuss volatility and explain why it is important in gasoline.

5. Discuss spark knock, or detonation, and what can be done to reduce or prevent it.

6. Define *octane*.

7. Explain the relationship between the compression ratio and detonation.

8. Define *preignition* and discuss its cause.

9. Explain pump octane ratings.

8-1
PROPERTIES OF GASOLINE   Gasoline appears to be a simple compound when you first look at it. It is a clear or colored liquid that evaporates quickly from a flat pan and burns violently in the open air. However, gasoline is not a simple compound. It is a complex mixture of several compounds. It is a blend of a number of basic fuels, each of which contributes its own characteristics to the mixture.

Gasoline is a *hydrocarbon* (HC). This means that gasoline is mostly made up of hydrogen and carbon. These two elements readily unite with oxygen, a common element that makes up about 20 percent of the air. When they unite, the process is called *combustion,* or *burning.* When hydrogen (H) unites with oxygen (O), water is formed. (The chemical formula for water is H_2O.) When carbon (C) unites with oxygen (O), carbon monoxide (CO) and carbon dioxide (CO_2) are formed.

If the gasoline in an engine burned completely, only water and carbon dioxide would remain. The trouble is that perfect combustion never happens. Not all the gasoline burns completely. As a result, hydrocarbons and carbon monoxide come out of the tail pipe and pollute the air.

NOTE   Gasoline is often referred to as *gas*. The sort of gas you burn in a gas stove or use to heat a house is a vapor that is delivered through gas lines or pipes. Therefore, there is "gas" that is a gas, and there is "gas" that is slang for the liquid fuel gasoline.

8-2
GASOHOL   To help conserve gasoline, alcohol can be mixed with gasoline. The blend is called gasohol (from *gaso*line and alco*hol*) and is usually a mixture of 90 percent gasoline and 10 percent alcohol. This extends the supply of gasoline by about 7 percent (*not* 10 percent, since more of the mixture must now be burned to develop the same power). Gasohol, which is available in various parts of the country, can be used in most engines without any changes in the engine or carburetor.

Gasohol will not harm the engine. However, gasohol may cause damage to the fuel-pump diaphragm, carburetor seals, and fuel-system O-rings in some engines. With continuous use of gasohol, fuel filters may require more frequent service.

8-3
SOURCE OF GASOLINE   Gasoline is made from crude oil, from which engine lubricating oil is also made. The crude oil goes through a process called *refining.* From the refining process come gasoline, lubricating oil, grease, fuel oil, and many other products.

During the refining process, several compounds, called additives, are added to gasoline to give it the characteristics of good gasoline. Good gasoline should have

1. Proper volatility, which determines how quickly gasoline vaporizes
2. Antiknock compounds, which provide resistance to spark knock, or detonation
3. Oxidation inhibitors, which prevent the formation of gum in the fuel system
4. Antirust agents, which prevent rusting of metal parts in the fuel system
5. Anti-icers, which fight carburetor icing and fuel-line freezing
6. Detergents, which help keep the carburetor clean
7. Dye, for identification

Let's talk about volatility and antiknock first.

8-4
VOLATILITY   After gasoline is mixed with air in the carburetor, the gasoline must vaporize quickly, before it enters the engine cylinders. If the gasoline is slow to vaporize, tiny drops of liquid gasoline will enter the cylinders. Because these drops do not burn, some of the fuel is wasted. It goes out the tail pipe and helps create smog. Also, the gasoline drops tend to wash the lubricating oil off the cylinder walls. This increases the wear on the cylinder walls, piston rings, and pistons.

The ease with which gasoline (or any liquid) vaporizes is called its *volatility*. A high-volatility gasoline vaporizes very quickly. A low-volatility gasoline vaporizes slowly. A good gasoline should have just the right volatility for the temperature of the outside air in which it will be used.

8-5
ANTIKNOCK   Spark knock is also called *detonation*. If you have ever been in a car or on a motorcycle

NORMAL COMBUSTION

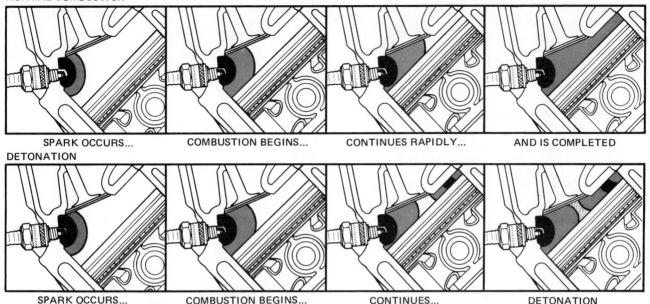

SPARK OCCURS...   COMBUSTION BEGINS...   CONTINUES RAPIDLY...   AND IS COMPLETED

DETONATION

SPARK OCCURS...   COMBUSTION BEGINS...   CONTINUES...   DETONATION

Fig. 8-1 Normal combustion without detonation is shown in the top row. The air-fuel mixture burns smoothly from beginning to end, providing an even, powerful push against the top of the piston. Detonation is shown in the bottom row. The last part of the air-fuel mixture explodes, or burns instantaneously, producing detonation, or spark knock. (*Champion Spark Plug Company*)

that had detonation, you have heard the sound. The engine pings. It sounds like someone is tapping the cylinder walls with a hammer. Look at Fig. 8-1. The horizontal row at the top of the figure shows what happens during normal combustion. The fuel charge—the mixture of air and fuel—starts burning as soon as the spark occurs at the spark plug. The flame sweeps smoothly and evenly across the combustion chamber, much like a balloon being blown up.

Now look at the horizontal row at the bottom of Fig. 8-1. The spark starts combustion in the same way. However, before the flame can reach the far side of the combustion chamber, the last part of the charge explodes. The result is a very quick increase in pressure. This is known as detonation, and it gives off a pinging sound.

Detonation can ruin an engine, because the heavy shocks on the piston put a great strain on the engine parts. Continued detonation can cause pistons and other parts to break (Fig. 8-2). So detonation must be avoided.

Gasoline refiners have various ways to make gasoline that does not detonate easily. A gasoline that detonates easily is called a *low-octane gasoline*. A gasoline that resists detonation is a *high-octane gasoline*.

8-6 INCREASING THE OCTANE

One way to increase the octane is to change the refining process. Another way is to add a small amount of tetraethyl lead, also known as *ethyl* or TEL. This additive tends to prevent the last part of the fuel charge from detonating. However, there are two problems with using tetraethyl lead.

One problem is that when gasoline containing TEL is burned, some of the lead gets into the air. Lead is a poison, and breathing air containing lead can cause lead poisoning. Lead poisoning can cause illness and death. Today there are laws limiting the use of lead in gasoline. The other problem is that the lead keeps exhaust-emission controls on cars from working as they should. These are two reasons why gasoline without lead is now required (by law) for most new cars and recommended for most new motorcycles.

8-7 COMPRESSION RATIOS AND DETONATION

Over the years the compression ratios of engines have gone up. The reason is that higher compression ratios give engines more power. The com-

Fig. 8-2 A piston damaged by detonation. Note the scoring on the skirt of the piston. (*ATW*)

67

Fig. 8-3 A piston damaged by preignition. The excessive temperature has melted a hole through the piston head. (*TRW, Inc.*)

pression ratio is the amount that the air-fuel mixture is compressed on the compression stroke (Fig 7-5). The more the air-fuel mixture is compressed, the higher the compression ratio.

But a high compression ratio can cause a problem. It increases the temperature of the air-fuel mixture. The higher heat of compression may cause the remaining air-fuel mixture to explode before normal combustion is completed. This must not happen. The compression ratio must be kept low enough to make sure that the fuel charge will not ignite from the heat of compression.

8-8
DETONATION AND PREIGNITION   Let's define these two terms. They describe the two most common forms of abnormal combustion.

Detonation—A secondary explosion that occurs in the combustion chamber after the spark at the spark plug. Detonation sets up a shock wave in the cylinder. This shock wave may be so severe that it will shatter or chip metal away from the top ring land of the piston. The ring lands are the metal bands that remain after the grooves are machined for the piston rings to fit into. Figure 8-2 shows a piston damaged by detonation. The detonation has knocked a hole through the center of the piston head.

Detonation produces a noise that is usually regular in character. It is most noticeable when the engine is accelerated or is under a load, as when climbing a hill. Under these conditions, the throttle usually is fully open, or nearly so. The engine is taking in a full air-fuel charge on every intake stroke. Volumetric efficiency is high. However, the high compression pressures that result can cause combustion problems.

Preignition—Ignition of the air-fuel mixture in the combustion chamber by some source of heat prior to the spark at the spark-plug gap. The sound of preignition is similar to a dull thud. Preignition causes excess heat in the combustion chamber. When the piston gets

too hot from preignition, a hole can melt through the top center of the piston. Figure 8-3 shows a hole in a piston caused by preignition.

There are other types of abnormal combustion, such as surface ignition and rumble. Surface ignition can originate from hot spots in the combustion chamber, such as on a hot exhaust valve or spark plug, or from combustion-chamber deposits. Sometimes the deposits may break loose and particles may float free and become hot enough to produce ignition. Surface ignition can occur before or after the spark occurs at the spark plug.

Surface ignition can cause engine rumble and rough operation, or mild to severe detonation. The hot spots can act as substitutes for the spark plugs, so that the engine will continue to run even after the ignition switch is turned off. This condition, called *dieseling*, can cause serious engine damage.

Preignition, surface ignition, and rumble are usually service problems. They result from inadequate servicing of the engine, such as the installation of the wrong spark plugs, which run too hot, and the use of incorrect fuels and lubricating oils for the engine and the type of operation. With incorrect fuel or oil, engine deposits may occur which will lead to surface ignition and rumble. Engine deposits can also increase the compression ratio, so that the engine becomes more likely to detonate.

8-9
OCTANE RATING OF GASOLINE   The octane rating of a gasoline is a measure of its resistance to detonation in the engine. An octane rating *does not* measure the energy in a gasoline, the quality of a gasoline, or whether a gasoline contains lead.

There are three ways of designating the octane rating of gasoline. The *research octane number* (RON) is determined by testing gasoline in laboratory engines running at low speed with wide-open throttle. This tends to give a high octane rating to a gasoline, such as 100 for premium and 94 for regular. The *motor octane number* (MON) is determined by testing gasoline in engines running at full throttle with high engine speed. This gives the gasoline a lower octane rating, such as 92 for premium and 86 for regular. In general, the RON for any gasoline is about eight numbers higher than the MON for the same gasoline.

Another octane rating is called the *antiknock index*, or *road octane number*. It relates reasonably well to the actual performance of gasolines in cars. This is the newest rating system and is the number that you are most likely to see on the pumps at service stations. Road octane number for a gasoline is found by adding together its RON and MON and dividing by 2. The formula is

$$\text{Road octane number} = \frac{\text{RON} + \text{MON}}{2}$$
$$\text{(antiknock index)}$$

The typical road octane number for gasoline is about 96 for leaded premium, 90 for leaded regular, and 87 for unleaded regular.

The owner's manuals for most motorcycles recommend unleaded or low-lead gasoline with a research octane number of 85 to 95. This means that for most motorcycles unleaded regular gasoline is the proper fuel to use. However, Harley-Davidson, for example, continues to recommend the use of leaded premium in its V-twin engines. When that is unavailable, use unleaded premium gasoline.

CHAPTER 8
REVIEW QUESTIONS

1. With perfect combustion, what two compounds would be formed when gasoline burns?
2. What is volatility? Why is it important in gasoline?
3. What does the term *antiknock index* mean?
4. What is heat of compression?
5. Explain how detonation is produced by a high heat of compression.
6. What effect does increasing the compression ratio have on detonation? Why?
7. Describe one method of measuring the antiknock index of a gasoline.
8. What does *octane rating* mean?
9. What is the difference between detonation and preignition?
10. Why has lead been removed from gasoline?
11. Name six gasoline additives.

MOTORCYCLE FUEL SYSTEMS AND TURBOCHARGERS

After studying this chapter,
you should be able to:

1. Discuss the purpose of the fuel system.

2. List and describe the components of a motorcycle fuel system.

3. Describe the operation of a gravity-feed fuel system.

4. Discuss the purpose of the float system and how it works.

5. Discuss the fuel tank and cap.

6. Explain why you should never fill the fuel tank while the motorcycle is inside your home, garage, or shop.

7. Discuss the fuel shutoff valve and its purpose.

8. Describe a pressure-feed fuel system and how it works.

9. Discuss exhaust systems and the special features they should have.

10. Describe the muffler, expansion chamber, and spark arrester, and explain what their purposes are.

11. Discuss motorcycle noise, how it is measured, and the legal limits on noise.

12. Discuss the turbocharger and how it works.

9-1 PURPOSE OF THE FUEL SYSTEM

The fuel system delivers a combustible mixture of air and vaporized fuel to the engine cylinders. It must change the proportions of air and fuel for different operating conditions. When the engine is cold, for example, the mixture must be rich (have a high proportion of fuel). This is because the fuel does not vaporize readily at low temperatures. The extra fuel is added so that enough fuel vaporizes to form a combustible mixture.

9-2 FUEL-SYSTEM COMPONENTS
The motorcycle fuel system consists of the following components:

1. The fuel tank, which stores the liquid gasoline
2. The fuel shutoff valve, which prevents or allows fuel to flow from the tank

3. The fuel filter, which filters out dirt particles from the gasoline
4. The fuel line, which carries gasoline from the shutoff valve to the carburetor float bowl
5. The carburetor, which mixes the gasoline with air
6. The intake port or intake manifold, which delivers the air-fuel mixture from the carburetor to the engine
7. The fuel pump (on some engines), which pumps the gasoline from the fuel tank to the carburetor

Two general types of fuel systems are used on motorcycle engines. These are the gravity-feed fuel system (Fig. 9-1) and the pressure-feed fuel system (Fig. 9-2). The most common type is the gravity-feed system. The pressure-feed system requires the use of a fuel pump. We discuss the fuel pump later.

9-3 GRAVITY-FEED FUEL SYSTEM
In a gravity-feed fuel system, gasoline flows down by gravity from the fuel tank to the fuel shutoff valve (Fig. 9-3). When the lever on the valve is in the open position, as shown in Fig. 9-3, gasoline can continue its flow down through the valve and into the fuel filter. In Fig. 9-3, the filter is combined with the fuel shutoff valve. Other motorcycles have a separate fuel filter.

From the filter, the gasoline flows through a fuel line to the carburetor float bowl. The purpose of the float system is to prevent the delivery of too much gasoline to the carburetor. Without the float system, all the fuel in the fuel tank would run down into the carburetor. The float system is made up of a small bowl, a float of metal or cork, and a needle valve that is operated by the float. Figure 9-4 is a simplified drawing of a float system. When gasoline from the fuel tank enters the float bowl, the float is raised. As the float moves upward, it lifts the needle valve into the inlet hole (called the *needle-valve seat*).

When the gasoline is at the proper height in the bowl, the needle valve is pressing tightly against its seat, so that no more gasoline can enter. When the carburetor withdraws gasoline to operate the engine, the gasoline level in the float bowl falls. The float and needle drop down, and more gasoline can enter. In operation, the needle valve holds a position that allows gasoline to enter at the same rate that the carburetor withdraws it. This keeps the level of gasoline in the float bowl at one height.

NOTE Some motorcycle carburetors do not have a float system. See Chap. 10, "Motorcycle Carburetors and Fuel Injection."

When the engine is running, air passes through the air cleaner on the way to the carburetor. In the carburetor, the air picks up a charge of gasoline. Then the air-fuel mixture flows through the intake port and enters the cylinder. Now let's look at the parts of a typical motorcycle gravity-feed fuel system.

9-4 FUEL TANK
The fuel tank (Fig. 9-5) normally is located in front of the rider and mounted on the frame of the motorcycle. The tank is made of sheet metal or

Fig. 9-1 A gravity-feed fuel system for a motorcycle. (*Honda Motor Company, Ltd.*)

plastic. Rubber grommets and damper pads (shown in Fig. 9-5) are used to help insulate the tank from the vibrations of the frame.

A typical motorcycle fuel tank holds 5 gallons [18.9 L] or less of fuel. During normal operation of most motorcycles, a small amount of fuel is retained in a reserve section of the tank. This reserve fuel is for use if the main fuel supply is used up. Sometimes a rider will allow the motorcycle to run out of gas, because most motorcycles do not have a fuel gauge. To check the fuel level in the tank, the rider must stop the motorcycle, remove the tank cap, and look into the tank to see the fuel level in it.

Figure 9-6 shows how one fuel tank provides a main

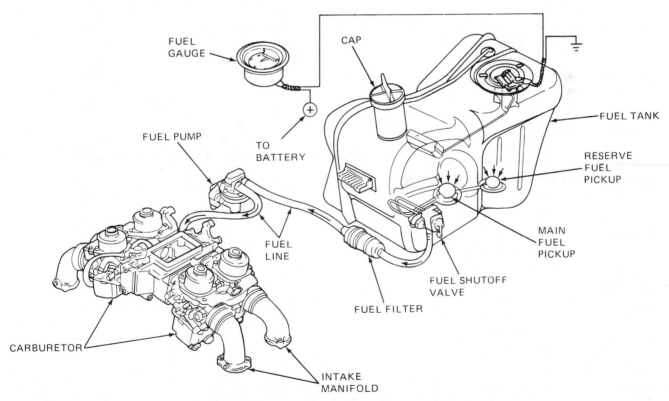

Fig. 9.2 A pressure-feed fuel system using a fuel pump. (*Honda Motor Company, Ltd.*)

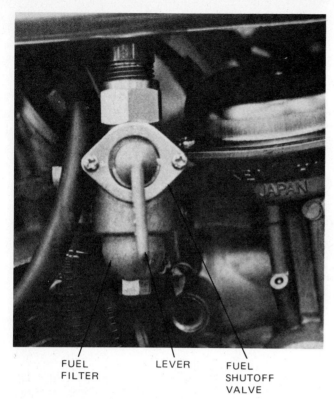

FUEL FILTER   LEVER   FUEL SHUTOFF VALVE

Fig. 9-3 The fuel shutoff valve and fuel filter. (*ATW*)

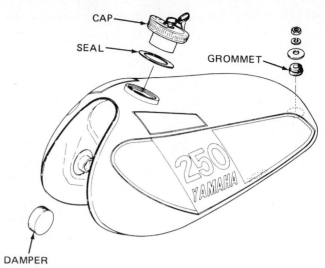

CAP
SEAL
GROMMET
DAMPER

Fig. 9-5 Fuel tank and cap for a motorcycle. (*Yamaha International Corporation*)

fuel supply and a reserve fuel supply. Notice that two fuel pickups are used. To operate the engine on the reserve fuel, the lever on the fuel shutoff valve is turned to the reserve position.

The filler opening of the tank is closed by a cap (Fig. 9-5). The cap, which is removed to add fuel, has a small hole in it for air to enter the tank as fuel is used up. A fuel strainer, or filter, at the tank outlet or in the fuel line filters out dirt and moisture that might have entered the tank. This prevents any contaminants from entering the carburetor, where they could clog the fuel passages and stop the engine.

On some motorcycles, a lock is built into or attached to the filler cap. Off-road motorcycles used in racing may have a tube attached to the air vent in the cap. The tube is routed down the frame of the motorcycle. This prevents any sloshing gasoline from spraying out of the hole in the cap and getting on the motorcycle or on the rider.

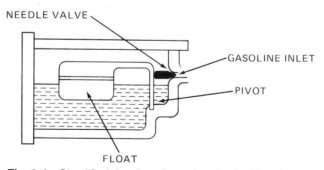

NEEDLE VALVE
GASOLINE INLET
PIVOT
FLOAT

Fig. 9-4 Simplified drawing of a carburetor float bowl.

Vaporized gasoline (HC) can escape from the fuel tank through the vent hole in the cap. It then contributes to the formation of smog. To prevent this, evaporative emission control systems, similar to those used on automobiles, have been proposed for motorcycles. Air pollution and emission control systems are discussed in Chap. 12.

CAUTION **Never fill the fuel tank or add gasoline to it while the motorcycle is inside your home, garage, or shop. Fumes from the gasoline could be ignited by any flame, as from a cigarette or a hot-water heater, and cause an explosion or a fire. Fill the tank at a service station or outside in the open. Use a funnel, if necessary, to prevent spilling the gasoline. Never fill the fuel tank completely to the top. Always leave at least ½ inch [13 mm] of space to allow for expansion of the fuel.**

9-5 FUEL SHUTOFF VALVE

A fuel shutoff valve (also called a *fuel valve,* a *fuel supply valve,* or a *fuel petcock*) is used in motorcycle fuel systems (Figs. 9-1 to 9-3). The purpose of the valve is to prevent engine flooding when the motorcycle is parked. Flooding can occur when liquid gasoline leaks out of the carburetor and runs into the engine. Since the tank of gasoline sits above the carburetor, a leaking needle valve in the carburetor will allow this to happen. But if the fuel shutoff valve is turned off, flooding cannot occur.

Here is what could happen if the engine is flooded. In a four-cycle engine, the gasoline may run down the intake port past the intake valve and get into the combustion chamber. The liquid gasoline could wet, or foul, the spark plug. This will prevent starting, or make starting very difficult.

Large amounts of gasoline in the combustion chamber will run down the cylinder wall and wash away the lubrication between it and the piston and rings. Then the gasoline will dilute the oil in the crankcase. When the engine is cranked, excessive piston ring and cylinder wall wear will occur. Also, the diluted oil may fail to provide other moving engine parts with adequate lubrication during starting. In a two-cycle engine, the gasoline may run from the carburetor directly into the crankcase.

Accumulations of liquid gasoline in the crankcase of any engine could cause a crankcase explosion. This would damage the engine and blow out gaskets and seals. When gasoline is found in the crankcase, it should be drained. Then refill the crankcase (of a four-cycle engine) with the proper grade and type of oil.

Figure 9-6 shows the fuel shutoff valve for the type of fuel tank shown in Fig. 9-5. Notice in Fig. 9-6 that there are two fuel pickup tubes located in the top of the valve. The longer pickup is for the main fuel supply. After it can no longer pick up gasoline, turning the lever on the fuel shutoff valve opens the reserve fuel pickup. Then it can deliver the remaining gasoline in the tank to the carburetor.

9-6 FUEL FILTER

A fuel filter, or *fuel strainer,* usually is installed in the fuel system of an engine. The filter mounts at the outlet of the fuel tank or in the fuel line between the fuel tank and the carburetor. In Fig. 9-3, the fuel system shown has a fuel filter under the fuel tank, in the bottom of the fuel shutoff valve. In Fig. 9-2, a fuel filter is shown installed ahead of the fuel pump in the fuel line from the fuel tank.

Regardless of the location of the fuel filter, its job is to filter out any dirt or water in the gasoline. This prevents these contaminants from getting into the carburetor. Dirt in the carburetor can clog the fuel nozzle and other very small passages. This can cause fuel starvation in the engine. The result is poor engine performance, stalling, or failure to start.

In-line fuel filters (Fig. 9-2) cannot be cleaned. They are replaced at regular service intervals. Other fuel strainers and filters usually can be disassembled and cleaned, as shown in Fig. 9-6. The procedure for servicing fuel filters is explained in Chap. 11.

9-7 FUEL LINE

On a typical motorcycle, a short piece of hose carries the gasoline from the fuel tank to the carburetor, as shown in Fig. 9-1. This short piece of hose is the fuel line. On a motorcycle that uses an in-line fuel filter and has a fuel pump, three separate sections of hose are used (Fig. 9-2). Clamps fasten the fuel line to the fuel shutoff valve and to the carburetor.

Because the fuel line carries gasoline, rubber hose must never be used. The gasoline will cause it to swell and crack. Only plastic or other special fuel-system hose should be installed.

The fuel line seldom requires service. However, it must be of the correct size to fit the connections on the fuel shutoff valve and on the carburetor. Also, the hose must be of the correct length. If the hose is too long, it may touch the engine or exhaust system. This could wear or burn a hole through the hose, allowing gasoline to leak out. Should this happen, there is always the possibility of fire.

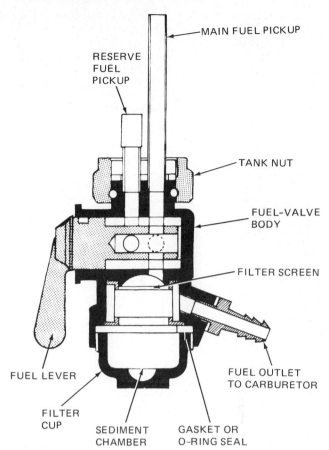

Fig. 9-6 Sectional view of a fuel shutoff valve, or petcock. (*Kawasaki Heavy Industries, Ltd.*)

9-8 CARBURETOR

In the gravity-feed fuel system, shown in Figs. 9-1 and 9-3, the fuel tank is located above the carburetor. The fuel feeds down to the carburetor float bowl by gravity. The carburetor works in just about the same way as the carburetors used in automobiles, and has many of the same systems. The construction and operation of carburetors are discussed in detail in Chap. 10.

9-9 INTAKE MANIFOLD

The intake manifold in multicylinder engines is a series of pipes, or passages, through which the air-fuel mixture can flow from the carburetor to the cylinders (Fig. 9-2). The fuel is mixed with air in the carburetor to form the combustible air-fuel mixture. This mixture then flows through the intake manifold to the intake valve that is open. Figure 9-2 shows an intake manifold for a four-cylinder engine.

The intake manifold is designed to avoid sharp corners and to make the passages to the intake valves as short and straight as possible. Also, the walls of the passages are smooth. Sharp corners and rough surfaces tend to obstruct the flow of the air-fuel mixture. The size and shape of the passages are designed to supply all cylinders with equal amounts of the air-fuel mixture. The operation of the auxiliary intake chamber for high-performance two-cycle engines is covered in 9-18.

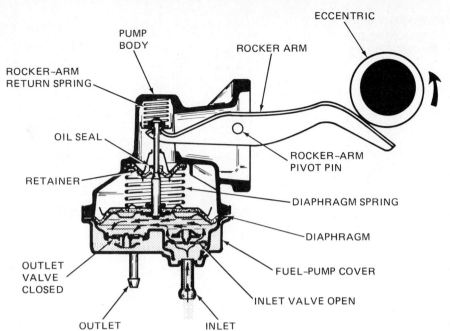

Fig. 9-7 When the eccentric rotates so as to push the rocker arm down, the arm pulls the diaphragm up. The inlet valve opens to admit fuel into the space under the diaphragm.

9-10
PRESSURE-FEED FUEL SYSTEM On engines where the fuel tank must be mounted on a level with or below the carburetor, a gravity-feed fuel system will not work. However, a fuel pump will deliver fuel to the float bowl of the carburetor regardless of their relative positions. Fuel pumps are used on all automobiles. The purpose of the fuel pump is to draw fuel from the fuel tank and deliver it to the carburetor float bowl.

The system using a fuel pump is called a *pressure-feed system*. A system of this type is shown in Fig. 9-2. A cam, or *eccentric,* on the camshaft forces a pump lever, or rocker arm, to move up and down. This action produces the pumping action in the pump. In larger engines, such as those used in automobiles, the rocker arm also is actuated by an eccentric on the engine camshaft. Some fuel pumps use a push rod from the eccentric on the camshaft to the pump lever.

9-11
FUEL-PUMP OPERATION Figure 9-7 shows schematically how the fuel pump works. When the pump rocker arm is pushed down by the high part of the eccentric, it lifts the diaphragm against the pressure of the diaphragm spring. This produces a vacuum in the pump chamber which lifts both the inlet and the outlet

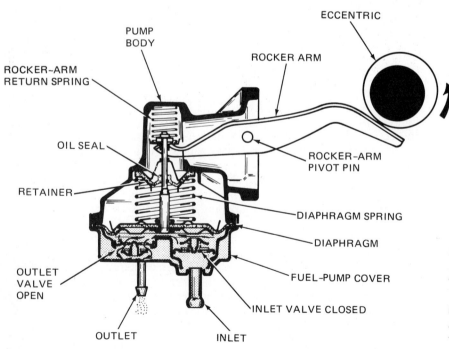

Fig. 9-8 When the eccentric rotates so as to allow the rocker arm to move up, the diaphragm is released so it can move down, producing pressure under it. This pressure closes the inlet valve and opens the outlet valve so fuel flows to the carburetor.

valves. The upward movement of the outlet valve closes it. The upward movement of the inlet valve opens it. Now, the vacuum will cause fuel from the fuel tank to flow into the pump chamber.

When the high part of the eccentric moves away from the rocker arm, the diaphragm spring pushes down on the diaphragm. This creates pressure in the pump chamber (Fig. 9-8). The pressure pushes down on both valves, causing the inlet valve to close and the outlet valve to open. The pressure then pushes fuel from the pump chamber through the fuel line into the carburetor float bowl.

Fuel-pump action is continuous as long as the engine runs. When the float bowl in the carburetor becomes sufficiently filled, the float rises and lifts the needle valve up into the seat. This shuts off any further delivery of fuel. We have already described how this works and showed a simplified float system in Fig. 9-4. When the float system refuses to take any further fuel, the diaphragm remains in its upper position, shown in Fig. 9-7. The diaphragm is held up even though the pump lever releases it and the spring pressure is trying to push it down.

In actual operation, the float needle-valve takes a position that allows just enough fuel to enter the float bowl to replace the fuel leaving. The pump operates to deliver just this amount of fuel and no more.

9-12 EXHAUST SYSTEM

After the air-fuel mixture has been burned in the engine cylinder, the burned exhaust gases are forced out of the cylinder through the exhaust port. From there they pass through the exhaust pipe (also called the *header pipe*) to the muffler and into the air.

Figure 9-9 shows a typical exhaust system for one cylinder of a two-cylinder four-cycle street-legal motorcycle engine. This is a separate, or independent, exhaust system. It serves only one cylinder of a multicylinder engine.

Note the *heat diffuser* (in Fig. 9-9) at the connection of the exhaust pipe to the cylinder head. The purpose of the diffuser, with its large fins, is to help cool the hot exhaust gases. Without the diffuser, on some engines the exhaust gas is so hot when it reaches the exhaust pipe that the pipe will turn blue. Some pipes can burn through at the first bend in the pipe. The use of the heat

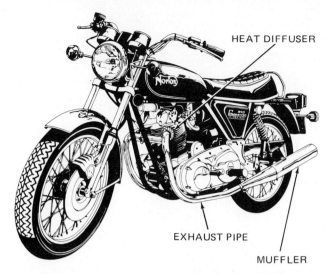

Fig. 9-9 An independent exhaust system for one cylinder of a two-cylinder four-cycle engine. (*Norton Triumph Corporation*)

diffuser helps prevent this, thereby prolonging the life of the exhaust pipe.

To help reduce the noise from some multicylinder engines the exhaust pipes from each cylinder are routed into a collector (Fig. 9-10). Then the exhaust gases pass through the collector and into a single large muffler. The system for four-cylinder engines is known as a *four-into-one* type of exhaust system. There also are *three-into-one* systems for three-cylinder engines and *two-into-one* systems for two- and four-cylinder engines. But the purpose of all of these exhaust systems is the same: to allow the engine to produce its best power while reducing exhaust noise to a minimum.

Exhaust systems usually are made of chrome-plated steel. However, some are finished with heat-resistant black paint.

The exhaust systems described above are the type used on four-cycle motorcycles that are ridden on the street. Figure 9-11 shows a typical exhaust system for a one-cylinder two-cycle engine used on an off-road motorcycle. Instead of the type of muffler shown in Figs. 9-9 and 9-10, a combination expansion chamber and muffler is used. Expansion chambers and mufflers are described in following sections.

An inner pipe can be removed from the end of the

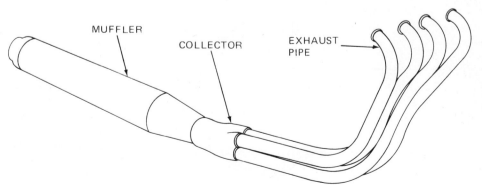

Fig. 9-10 A collector type of exhaust system in which separate exhaust pipes for each cylinder of a four-cylinder engine are routed into the collector. From the collector, the exhaust gas flows into a single large muffler.

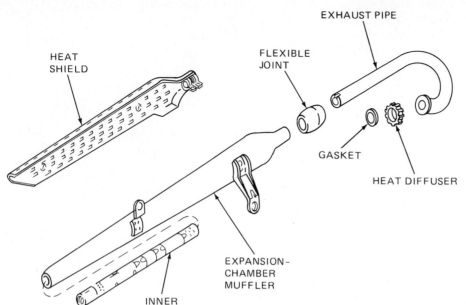

HEAT SHIELD

FLEXIBLE JOINT

EXHAUST PIPE

GASKET

HEAT DIFFUSER

EXPANSION–CHAMBER MUFFLER

INNER PIPE

Fig. 9-11 Exhaust system for a one-cylinder two-cycle engine using a combination expansion chamber and muffler. (*Pacific Basin Trading Company*)

expansion chamber for cleaning. A heat shield, made of stamped steel with holes in it for ventilation, is mounted to the muffler. The heat shield prevents the rider from being burned by touching the hot muffler while riding. In Fig. 9-11, a flexible joint is used to connect the exhaust pipe to the muffler. Flexible tubing or a flexible joint at this point will absorb vibration and help prevent cracking and breaking of the system. This can be a problem on two-cycle engines in heavy off-road use.

A great variety of exhaust systems is used on two-cycle engines. Figure 9-12 shows the heat shield and expansion chamber locations on an off-road motorcycle. The long, thin pipe at the end of the expansion chamber is a type of muffler called a *stinger*. Motorcycles for off-road use are equipped with a *spark arrester* to prevent hot carbon particles in the exhaust gas from igniting dry grass and brush.

9-13
MUFFLER The muffler (Fig. 9-13) contains a series of holes, baffles, and resonance chambers. They absorb and damp out the high-pressure surges that enter the exhaust pipe when the exhaust valve or exhaust port opens. This cools and quiets the exhaust gases, thereby reducing exhaust noise.

Some exhaust systems do not use a separate muffler. Instead, the exhaust pipe contains a series of scientifically shaped restrictions. The restrictions damp out the exhaust noise without interfering with the flow of exhaust gases.

To further reduce exhaust noise, some exhaust pipes are made of a special laminated, or layered, pipe. The laminate consists of two layers of pipe, one inside the other, or of a plastic film sandwiched between the two metal pipes. Laminated pipe has very good sound-

EXPANSION–CHAMBER HEAT SHIELD

STINGER

Fig. 9-12 Location of the heat shield and stinger on a two-cycle motorcycle. (*Kawasaki Heavy Industries, Ltd.*)

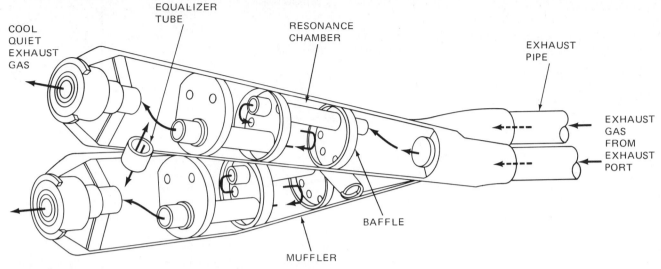

Fig. 9-13 Cutaway view of motorcycle mufflers for a multicylinder engine. The arrows show the flow of the exhaust gas through the mufflers. (*Honda Motor Company, Ltd.*)

deadening properties. It will quiet certain engine noises that otherwise would pass through the muffler.

Figure 9-13 shows the mufflers used on one side of a four-cycle four-cylinder motorcycle. Notice the use of a short equalizer tube between the mufflers. This allows the exhaust gas to leave from both mufflers, by passing into the muffler with the lowest pressure. The results are reduced back pressure in the exhaust system and higher engine power.

9-14 EXPANSION CHAMBER

The exhaust system on a two-cycle motorcycle engine must do more than just reduce noise. It must help scavenge the burned exhaust gases from the cylinder and help draw a fresh air-fuel charge into the cylinder. The fresh air-fuel mixture must momentarily be held in the cylinder while the exhaust port is open. This prevents the unburned air-fuel mixture from flowing out of the cylinder with the exhaust gases (Fig. 9-14). When this happens, engine power is reduced and air pollution increases.

Sound waves can be used to hold the air-fuel mixture in the cylinder while the piston has the exhaust port uncovered. Sound waves are simply traveling waves of air pressure. They travel through the air in much the same way that small waves or ripples travel across a pool of water when you toss a stone in it. The ripples travel from the center outward until they reach the side. Then they bounce off the side and are reflected back toward the center.

In a similar manner, sound waves from the cylinder travel outward at a very high rate of speed from the exhaust port as soon as it is opened. The sound waves travel through the exhaust pipe until they strike a baffle, which reflects them back toward their source (the exhaust port). This action is shown in Fig. 9-15.

The reflected sound waves reach the exhaust port just as some of the fresh air-fuel charge is ready to enter the exhaust pipe. The sound wave acts as an invisible

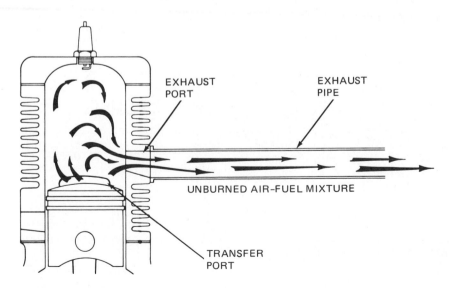

Fig. 9-14 Overscavenging of the cylinder in a two-cycle engine allows unburned air-fuel mixture to flow out the exhaust pipe. (*Kohler Company*)

77

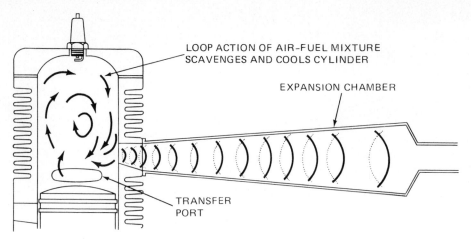

LOOP ACTION OF AIR-FUEL MIXTURE
SCAVENGES AND COOLS CYLINDER

EXPANSION CHAMBER

TRANSFER
PORT

Fig. 9-15 Actions of an expansion chamber, showing how the energy of the pressure wave is reflected back to the exhaust port to prevent over-scavenging. (*Kohler Company*)

barrier, as shown in Fig. 9-15. It blocks the port and holds the air-fuel mixture in the cylinder. This prevents overscavenging, in which part of the air-fuel mixture is carried out of the cylinder and into the exhaust system by the exiting burned exhaust gases. Overscavenging is a factor behind the failure of many two-cycle engines to meet the exhaust-emission standards for street-legal motorcycles. To do so, they require redesign and other modifications.

The muffler for some two-cycle engines is combined with the expansion chamber, as shown in Fig. 9-11. The purpose of the megaphone-like device is to amplify the sound. This increases the speed of the sound waves. It thereby improves scavenging by creating a low-pressure area behind each passing sound wave. The effect is to speed up the scavenging of the exhaust gases from the cylinder with fresh air-fuel mixture from the transfer port.

After the sound waves are amplified by the megaphone, they must pass through a series of baffles which provide maximum silencing and minimum back pressure. If the back pressure is too high, the fresh air-fuel mixture will flow too slowly through the transfer port to fill the cylinder completely. Also, the exhaust gases will not be completely scavenged from the cylinder. This

will result in less air-fuel mixture in the cylinder for the next combustion event, and the engine will deliver a weak power stroke.

Expansion chambers are used on many two-cycle motorcycle engines. The use of the expansion chamber improves cylinder scavenging and filling, thereby improving engine performance.

**9-15
SPARK ARRESTER** Figure 9-16 shows a two-cycle engine muffler with a spark arrester. In the muffler, fiberglass packing around the inside of the steel shell deadens the sound. After passing through the muffler, the exhaust gas enters the spark arrester. Exhaust gas from every motorcycle engine carries with it some red-hot carbon particles. On off-road motorcycles, to eliminate the danger of fires caused by these hot particles, a spark arrester must be used.

As the exhaust gas enters the spark arrester, angled blades cause the exhaust gas to swirl. When the gas swirls, the heavier carbon particles are thrown to the outside of the spark arrester, as shown in Fig. 9-16. There the carbon particles are trapped. Then the exhaust gas, free of hot carbon particles, flows through the center of the spark arrester into the outside air.

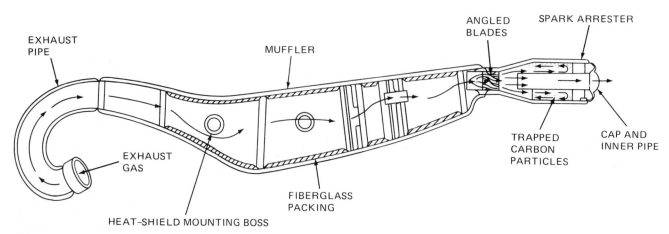

EXHAUST PIPE

MUFFLER

ANGLED BLADES

SPARK ARRESTER

EXHAUST GAS

TRAPPED CARBON PARTICLES

CAP AND INNER PIPE

HEAT-SHIELD MOUNTING BOSS

FIBERGLASS PACKING

Fig. 9-16 Muffler and spark arrester for a two-cycle engine. (*Honda Motor Company, Ltd.*)

As the engine runs, the spark arrester gradually fills up with carbon particles. On most spark arresters, the end cap and outlet pipe are removable so that the accumulated carbon can be cleaned out.

9-16 NOISE

Several states and the Environmental Protection Agency (EPA) have set or proposed noise standards for motorcycles. Although two-cycle engines generally are louder than four-cycle engines, no distinction is made in the standards for street motorcycles (Fig. 9-17). Large off-road motorcycles are allowed to be noisier than motorcycles with an engine displacement of 170 cc or less.

Most of the state noise laws are basically the same. They require that a motorcycle exhaust system must not be modified to increase the noise level above that of the original-equipment muffler and exhaust system. Many of the complaints about motorcycle noise are caused by large-displacement engines that are running without a muffler or with a loud muffler. Figure 3-11 shows a motorcycle with a modified exhaust system that is very loud.

Mopeds are virtually unaffected by the noise standards. However, some large motorcycle engines may require redesign to make them quieter. For example, a liquid-cooled motorcycle engine is quieter and has fewer exhaust emissions than an air-cooled engine. But more than the engine makes noise on a motorcycle. Shaft drive, used on some medium and large motorcycles, is quieter than chain drive.

Noise is measured on a decibel meter. A *decibel* (dB) is the unit used to measure the pressure of sound intensity, or the relative loudness of sound. Discomfort from a loud sound occurs at about 120 dB. An unmuffled snowmobile may cause the decibel meter to read 100 dB at 50 feet [15 m] away. With a muffler, the noise level can be lowered to about 83 dB.

A motorcycle that is manufactured as a competition model and labeled as such by its manufacturer is not required to meet the proposed EPA noise standards. These motorcycles are to be used only in closed-course competition events. All other off-road motorcycles must be muffled to meet the proposed standards.

Removing the muffler from an engine does not necessarily produce more power. For example, many two-cycle engines with a properly designed and positioned muffler and exhaust system may produce more power than engines with a straight pipe. Some of the reasons for this are discussed in the section on expansion chambers (9-14).

9-17 TURBOCHARGER

The turbocharger, or *blower,* is a rotary air pump used on some high-performance four-cycle motorcycle engines. It forces more of the air-fuel mixture into the engine cylinders. It includes a rotary compressor located between the carburetor and the intake manifold (Fig. 9-18). Inside the compressor is an impeller that looks like the impeller in the water pump of a liquid-cooled engine (Fig. 9-18). When the impeller spins, its blades act like a fan and

Motorcycle type	Production year	Noise limit, dB
Street motorcycles	1983	83
	1986	80
Off-road motorcycles, 170 cc or less	1983	83
	1986	80
Off-road motorcycles, over 170 cc	1983	86
	1986	82
Mopeds	1983	70

Fig. 9-17 Environmental Protection Agency (EPA) noise standards for motorcycles and mopeds.

send additional air-fuel mixture to the intake manifold and the engine cylinders. With more of the air-fuel mixture entering the cylinders, the engine develops more power.

Figure 9-19 shows how the impeller is driven. The impeller is mounted on the same shaft as a turbine wheel, which is in the line between the exhaust manifold and the exhaust pipe. Exhaust gases flowing from the engine cylinders through the exhaust manifold spin the turbine wheel. This spins the impeller so that more of the air-fuel mixture is forced into the engine cylinders.

On some engines, the impeller is in front of the carburetor and sends only air into the carburetor. When the air is under pressure, it picks up a greater quantity of fuel as it goes through the carburetor. The result is the same as when the impeller is located between the carburetor and the intake manifold. The cylinders get additional air-fuel mixture and develop more power.

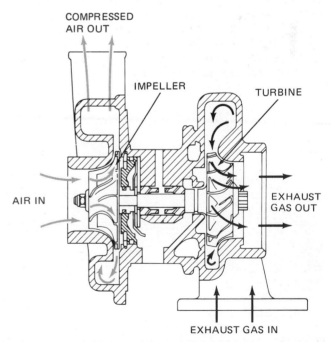

Fig. 9-18 Operation of a turbocharger. (*Schwitzer Division of Wallace-Murray Corporation*)

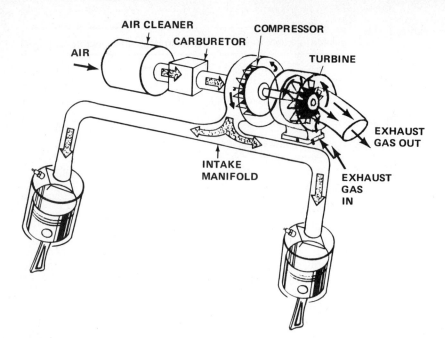

Fig. 9-19 Simplified drawing of a turbocharger which is driven by the exhaust gas from the engine.

NOTE A turbocharged engine is sometimes referred to as a *blown* engine. The turbocharger is "blowing" more air or air-fuel mixture into the cylinders. However, this term can be confusing because an engine sometimes *blows*, which means that the engine has stopped because of internal damage.

The advantage of using a turbocharger is that a smaller engine with low fuel consumption can produce high power when needed. The Kawasaki turbocharged engine (Fig. 9-20) is typical of motorcycle installations. Under normal riding conditions, the turbocharger does not develop pressure. But as the throttle is opened wide at about 4500 rpm, the engine manifold vacuum drops to zero. Now the turbocharger engages.

Fig. 9-20 A turbocharged Kawasaki, the world's fastest and quickest production motorcycle. (*Turbo Cycle Corporation*)

Using the exhaust gases coming from the cylinders to spin the turbine, the compressor impeller pressurizes the air-fuel mixture flowing into the intake manifold. With a pressure instead of a vacuum in the intake manifold, the cylinders take in an overcharge, or *supercharge,* of the air-fuel mixture. The engine produces much more power than it would without the turbocharger.

A turbocharged engine operates as a normal engine most of the time. The turbocharger does not add power at usual speeds. During normal riding, it is estimated to operate only about 5 percent of the time. To engage the turbocharger, the throttle must be wide open and engine speed about 4500 rpm.

9-18 AUXILIARY INTAKE CHAMBER

To improve low- and mid-range power in some high-performance two-cycle engines, an auxiliary intake chamber is used (Fig. 9-21). The chamber is connected to the intake manifold, between the carburetor and the reed valve, by a hose. As the chamber fills with the air-fuel mixture and then empties, the pulsing of air through the carburetor is reduced. As a result, engine power is increased.

During the intake stroke, crankcase vacuum pulls the air-fuel mixture through the intake manifold and past the end of the hose attached to the chamber. This creates a vacuum in the hose and chamber. When the reed valve closes, intake-manifold vacuum drops quickly. However, the chamber vacuum now acts to draw the air-fuel mixture from the carburetor into the chamber (Fig. 9-21, left).

When the intake stroke begins again, crankcase vacuum draws the air-fuel mixture from the chamber into the intake manifold (Fig. 9-21, right). There the additional mixture supplements the normal flow from the carburetor. This continual filling and emptying of the auxiliary chamber reduces the pulsing of air through the carburetor.

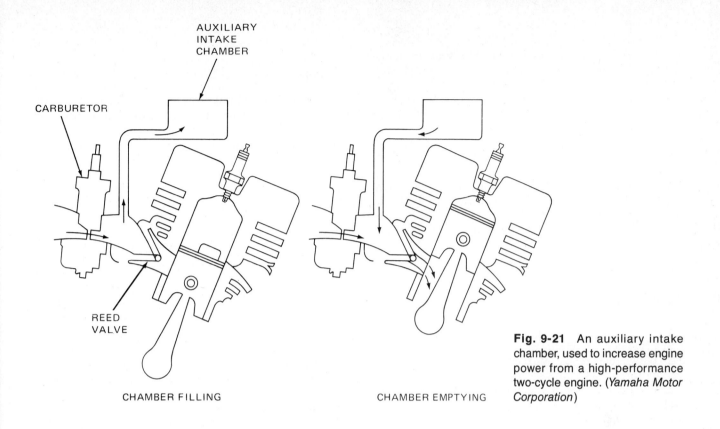

AUXILIARY
INTAKE
CHAMBER

CARBURETOR

REED
VALVE

CHAMBER FILLING

CHAMBER EMPTYING

Fig. 9-21 An auxiliary intake chamber, used to increase engine power from a high-performance two-cycle engine. (*Yamaha Motor Corporation*)

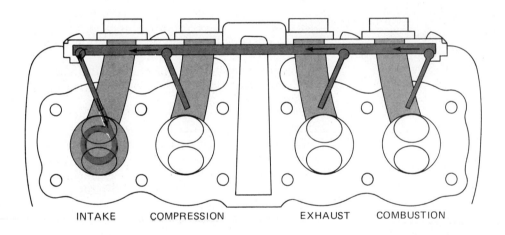

INTAKE   COMPRESSION   EXHAUST   COMBUSTION

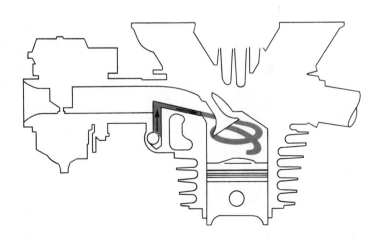

Fig. 9-22 An induction system on a four-cylinder four-cycle engine that uses smaller subintake ports to swirl the air-fuel mixture. (*Yamaha Motor Corporation*)

9-19
SWIRL-TYPE COMBUSTION CHAMBER

Some multicylinder four-cycle engines have an induction system with two intake ports for each cylinder. Figure 9-22 shows the system in operation on a four-cylinder four-cycle engine. The purpose of the system is to swirl the air-fuel mixture within the combustion chamber until burning is completed.

In the engine, a second set of smaller intake ports, called *subintake ports*, also deliver the air-fuel mixture to each cylinder. The subintake ports are about one-fourth the size of the main ports. The smaller ports open into the main ports just above the intake valve seat. They are aimed so that the flow of the air-fuel mixture from the smaller ports is directed around the walls of the cylinder. The result is that the air-fuel mixture swirls around as the mixture is compressed in the combustion chamber.

Figure 9-22 shows how the subintake ports for all four cylinders are interconnected. With only one cylinder in the engine on the intake stroke at any time, the air-fuel mixture is drawn from the other three carburetors and subintake ports. When the intake valve opens, the mixture flows about four times faster through the smaller ports than through the main ports. The result is faster, more complete burning of the air-fuel mixture in each cylinder. With this system, the distribution of the air-fuel mixture among the cylinders is much more even. Although the system has no moving parts, a 10-percent improvement in fuel economy has been reported.

CHAPTER 9
REVIEW QUESTIONS

1. What is the purpose of the fuel system?
2. List the components of the fuel system.
3. What two types of fuel systems are used on motorcycles?
4. Why does a motorcycle have a fuel shutoff valve?
5. Describe the operation of the needle valve and seat in the float bowl.
6. How much gasoline does a motorcycle fuel tank hold?
7. How is the level of gasoline in the fuel tank checked on most motorcycles?
8. Why is there a vent hole in the fuel-tank cap?
9. Describe how gasoline can get into the lubricating oil if the fuel shutoff valve is left on while the motorcycle is parked.
10. Which contaminants are trapped by a fuel filter or strainer?
11. How does water get into the fuel tank?
12. What is the difference between an intake port and an intake manifold?
13. What is the difference between a gravity-feed fuel system and a pressure-feed fuel system?
14. What operates the fuel pump?
15. What is the purpose of the heat diffuser used on some exhaust pipes?
16. On a four-cylinder engine, is there any advantage to using a four-into-one exhaust system?
17. Why are some mufflers and expansion chambers covered with a heat shield?
18. What is the difference between a muffler and an expansion chamber?
19. What is the difference between a stinger and a spark arrester?
20. How does a muffler quiet the noise of the exhaust gas?
21. What is the purpose of an expansion chamber?
22. Are expansion chambers used on two-cycle or four-cycle engines?
23. Which type of engine may use reflected sound waves to help prevent overscavenging?
24. Why must a spark arrester be used on off-road motorcycles?
25. How is noise measured?
26. Describe the operation of a turbocharger.

CHAPTER 10

MOTORCYCLE CARBURETORS AND FUEL INJECTION

After studying this chapter,
you should be able to:

1. Explain why the motorcycle engine needs different mixture richness for different operating conditions.

2. Describe how a fixed-venturi carburetor operates.

3. Explain how a variable-venturi carburetor works.

4. Discuss venturi action.

5. Explain the difference between the slide-valve variable-venturi carburetor and the constant-vacuum variable-venturi carburetor.

6. Explain how the float system works.

7. Describe the slide-valve variable-venturi carburetor and explain how the starting, slow, and main systems work.

8. Describe the fixed-venturi carburetor and explain how the choke, idle, accelerator, cruising, and full-power systems work.

9. Explain the construction and purpose of air cleaners.

10. Describe the difference between the carburetor and the fuel-injection types of fuel-delivery systems.

11. Describe the construction and operation of electronic fuel injection.

10-1
AIR-FUEL REQUIREMENTS
The internal combustion engine burns a mixture of air and fuel vapor in its cylinders to produce power. The fuel system delivers this air-fuel mixture to the engine cylinders.

The air-fuel mixture must have the proper proportions of air and gasoline for good engine operation. If the mixture does not have enough gasoline vapor (mixture too lean) or if the mixture has too much gasoline vapor (mixture too rich), the engine will not run properly. Also, to start a cold engine, the mixture must be enriched. It must have a higher proportion than normal of gasoline vapor in it. It is the job of the carburetor (Fig. 10-1) to supply the correct air-fuel mixture.

Motorcycle-engine fuel systems usually have a separate carburetor for each cylinder. For example, a three-cylinder engine has three carburetors. An exception to this is the Harley-Davidson V-twin (or V-2) engine, which uses a single carburetor. The placement of the two cylinders makes this possible. Adjustment and service of carburetors is covered in Chap. 11.

10-2
CARBURETOR TYPES
There are two basic types of carburetors: fixed-venturi and variable-venturi. The venturi is the restricted place in the air passage through which the air must flow. This restriction produces a partial vacuum, which causes a fuel nozzle to discharge gasoline. The gasoline mixes with the air to produce the combustible mixture that the engine needs to run.

Most carburetors installed on motorcycle engines are of the variable-venturi type. We will discuss these first. The fixed-venturi carburetor is used on most automobile engines. It also is used on Harley-Davidson V-twin engines.

10-3
CARBURETION
Carburetion is the mixing of gasoline with air to obtain a combustible mixture. The carburetor performs this job. It supplies a combustible mixture of varying richness, to suit engine operating conditions.

The mixture must be rich (have more fuel) for starting, acceleration, and high-speed operation. A less rich (leaner) mixture is desirable at intermediate speeds with a warm engine. The carburetor has several systems through which the air-fuel mixture flows during different operating conditions. These systems produce the varying mixture richness required for varying operating conditions. All this is explained in the sections that follow.

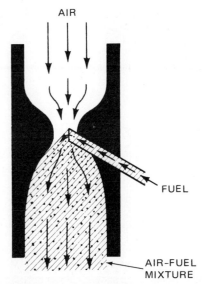

Fig. 10-1 The carburetor mixes air and gasoline to supply the engine with a combustible air-fuel mixture.

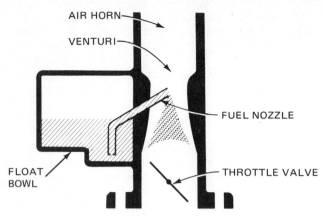

Fig. 10-2 A simple carburetor consists of an air horn, a fuel nozzle, and a throttle valve.

10-4 VAPORIZATION

When a liquid changes to a vapor, it is said to *evaporate,* or *vaporize.* Water placed in an open pan will evaporate. It changes from a liquid to a vapor. Wet clothes hung on a line become dry because the water evaporates out of the clothes. When the clothes are spread out, they dry more rapidly than when they are bunched together. This illustrates an important fact about evaporation. The greater the surface exposed, the more rapidly evaporation takes place. A pint of water in a tall glass takes a long time to evaporate. A pint of water in a shallow pan evaporates much more quickly.

10-5 ATOMIZATION

To vaporize the liquid gasoline more quickly, it is sprayed into the air passing through the carburetor (Fig. 10-1). Spraying the liquid turns it into many fine droplets. This effect is called *atomization,* because the liquid is broken up into small droplets. (But it is not actually broken into atoms, as the name implies.)

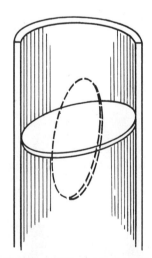

Fig. 10-3 The throttle valve in the carburetor. When the throttle valve is closed, as shown, little air can pass through. The air flow is throttled. But when the throttle valve is opened, as shown by the dashed lines, there is little throttling effect.

Each droplet is exposed to air on all sides. With so much surface exposed, it vaporizes very quickly. During normal engine operation, the gasoline vaporizes almost as soon as it is sprayed into the air passing through the carburetor.

10-6 CARBURETOR OPERATION

The carburetor is a mixing valve. It mixes gasoline with air to form an air-fuel mixture. The mixture then goes through the intake manifold or intake port to the engine cylinder. There, the air-fuel mixture is compressed and burned to make the engine run.

To illustrate carburetor action, we use the basic elements of the fixed-venturi carburetor. The fixed-venturi carburetor has an air horn, a fuel nozzle, and a throttle valve (Fig. 10-2). The air horn is a round tube, or barrel. The venturi is a narrow section in the air horn. The fuel nozzle is a small tube through which fuel can flow from the float bowl (the reservoir under the carburetor).

The throttle valve is a round disk mounted on a shaft. When the shaft is turned, the throttle valve is tilted. When it is tilted into the position shown by the dotted lines in Fig. 10-3, the throttle valve is open, and air can flow through the air horn freely.

When the throttle valve is tilted into the position shown by the solid lines in Fig. 10-3, the throttle valve is closed. Little or no air can get through the air horn. The throttle valve determines how much air gets through the carburetor. It is the amount of air passing through the carburetor that determines how much fuel flows to the cylinder.

The carburetor in Fig. 10-2 is a vertical carburetor. The air horn is in the vertical position. This is the type of carburetor used in almost all automobile carburetor fuel systems. However, the air horn can be turned to a horizontal position, as shown in Fig. 10-4, and the carburetor will work just as well. Most motorcycle carburetors use a horizontal air horn.

10-7 VENTURI EFFECT

The venturi causes fuel to flow out of the fuel nozzle when air flows through the air horn. The reason is that the air has to flow faster through the venturi than through the rest of the air horn. This faster flow of air produces a partial vacuum in the venturi. The partial vacuum then causes fuel to flow from the fuel nozzle (Fig. 10-5). The more air that flows through the venturi, the greater the vacuum. The greater the vacuum, the more fuel is discharged by the fuel nozzle.

Air is not a continuous fluid, or substance. It consists of separate particles, or molecules. When we keep this in mind, the venturi effect becomes more easily understood.

As air enters the air horn, all the air particles are moving toward the venturi at about the same speed. However, if all particles are to move through the constriction, or venturi, they will have to speed up and hurry through.

Suppose we watch two of the particles on their way through the venturi. One particle is slightly behind the

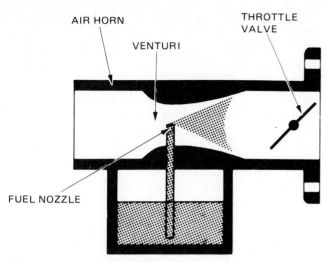

Fig. 10-4 If the air horn is turned to a horizontal position, the carburetor will work just as well.

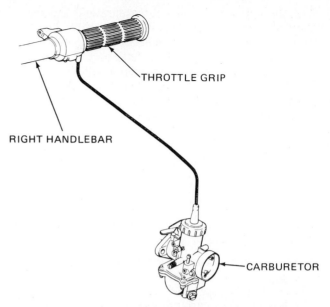

Fig. 10-6 The throttle valve in the carburetor is controlled by a cable which moves as the throttle grip is turned. (*Suzuki Motor Company, Ltd.*)

other. The leading particle, entering the venturi first, speeds up, tending to leave the second particle behind. The second particle, entering the venturi, also increases in speed. But the first particle has, in effect, a head start. The second particle cannot catch up. They are farther apart in passing through the venturi than they were in entering the air horn.

Now visualize a great number of particles going through the same action. You can see that in the venturi the particles are farther apart than they were when they first entered the air horn. This is another way of saying that a partial vacuum exists in the venturi. A partial vacuum is a thinning out of the air. This means that there is a more-than-normal distance between the air particles, or molecules.

There is a relationship among the amount the throttle is open, the amount of air going through the venturi, and the amount of fuel being discharged. This relationship keeps the ratio of air to fuel fairly constant. However, other systems and devices are needed to change the air-fuel ratio for different operating conditions.

10-8
FIXED AND VARIABLE VENTURIS
The carburetor we have been describing has a fixed venturi (Figs. 10-2 to 10-5). The size and shape of the venturi cannot be changed. However, the carburetors used on many motorcycle engines have a variable venturi. This type of carburetor is shown in Fig. 10-6. On these the size of the venturi can be changed. Figure 10-7 illustrates the principle.

The *piston*, or *slide valve*, is a round cylinder that can be moved up or down in a round bore to change the size of the venturi. In effect, the piston serves both as a device to change the size of the venturi and as a throttle valve. When the piston moves down, the venturi is made smaller. Also, the air flow is restricted, or throttled down. When the piston moves up, more air can

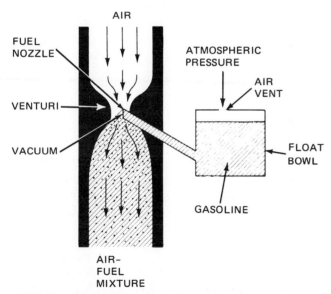

Fig. 10-5 The venturi, or narrowed section, causes a vacuum to develop in the air stream in the venturi. Then atmospheric pressure pushes fuel up and out of the fuel nozzle.

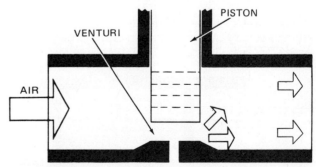

Fig. 10-7 Principle of the variable-venturi carburetor: The piston, or slide, can be moved up or down to change the size of the venturi.

flow through. In motorcycle carburetors, the movement of the piston is controlled by a cable from the throttle grip on the right handlebar (Fig. 10-6).

When the rider rotates the throttle grip, the grip pulls on the cable. The cable consists of a stiff wire inside a flexible metal cover. The wire can slide back and forth in the cover. This cable is sometimes called a *Bowden cable*. When the cable is pulled by the rotating grip, it pulls on the piston (slide valve) inside the carburetor. The farther the rider twists the grip, the farther the piston moves up. The upward movement of the piston increases the size of the venturi so that more of the air-fuel mixture can flow to the engine. More engine power results.

10-9 FUEL-NOZZLE ACTION

In the carburetor, a partial vacuum occurs in the venturi when air flows through. The fuel nozzle is located in the venturi. The other end of the fuel nozzle is in the fuel reservoir (the float bowl in most carburetors). Figure 10-5 shows the relationship between the venturi, the fuel nozzle, and the float bowl on a carburetor with a vertical air horn. Figure 10-8 shows the relationship on a carburetor with a horizontal air horn and a slide valve, or throttle piston. Regardless of the positions of the air horn and float bowl, the venturi action is the same.

With vacuum at the upper end of the fuel nozzle and with atmospheric pressure at the lower end, fuel is pushed up and out of the nozzle. The fuel leaves the nozzle in the form of a fine spray which rapidly turns into vapor as the droplets of fuel evaporate. The more air passing through, the faster it moves and the greater the vacuum at the venturi. This means that more fuel is discharged. Therefore, the proportions of air and fuel stay approximately the same from partly open to fully open throttle.

Carburetors for some motorcycle engines also include additional systems for feeding more fuel into the air when the throttle is suddenly opened for quick accel-

eration and for wide-open throttle operation. Also, carburetors have systems for supplying extra fuel for starting the engine.

10-10 AIR-FUEL RATIOS

When the engine is started, the air-fuel mixture must be rich. The mixture must have more fuel in it. A mixture of about 9 pounds [4.1 kg] of air to 1 pound [0.45 kg] of fuel, or a ratio of 9:1, is required for starting a cold engine. The reason is that only part of the gasoline vaporizes when the engine is cold. Therefore the engine has to be given more than enough fuel to make sure that enough will vaporize to ensure starting.

When the engine is idling, a less rich mixture is needed—about 12:1. During intermediate-speed, part-throttle operation, a relatively lean mixture of about 15:1 is needed. During high-speed, wide-open-throttle operation, a richer mixture of about 13:1 is needed.

These ratios are examples only. Different engines require different ratios for various operating conditions.

10-11 CARBURETOR SYSTEMS

The fixed-venturi carburetor may have up to six systems and other devices that provide the correct air-fuel mixture for different operating conditions:

1. The float system
2. The idle system
3. The main metering system
4. The power system
5. The accelerator-pump system
6. The choke system

The variable-venturi carburetors do not have all of these systems. Instead, they vary the air-fuel ratio to suit operating conditions by other means. We describe the systems in typical carburetors and discuss their operation in following sections.

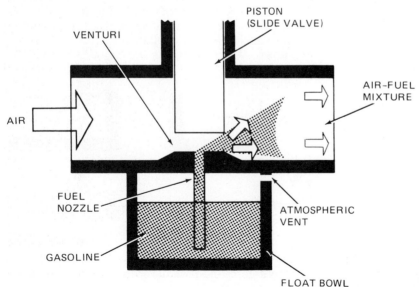

Fig. 10-8 In a carburetor with a horizontal air horn, the fuel reservoir or float bowl is placed beneath the air horn.

10-12
TYPES OF MOTORCYCLE CARBURETORS
Three different types of carburetors are used on motorcycle engines:

1. Slide-valve variable-venturi carburetors
2. Constant-vacuum variable-venturi carburetors
3. Fixed-venturi carburetors

The *slide-valve carburetor* is the most widely used on motorcycle engines. Because the slide valve is operated directly by the throttle cable (Fig. 10-6), this carburetor sometimes is called a *mechanical carburetor*. The slide-valve carburetor is used on almost every size of engine and on both two-stroke and four-stroke models.

In general, the *constant-vacuum carburetor* (also called the *constant-velocity carburetor*) is used on medium-to-large, two- to four-cylinder motorcycle engines. This type of carburetor has both a disk-type throttle valve, or *butterfly valve* (Fig. 10-2 to 10-4), and a slide valve, or piston (Fig. 10-7).

The *fixed-venturi carburetor* (Figs. 10-2 to 10-4) is used on the Harley-Davidson V-twin engines. This carburetor is very similar in operation to the typical carburetor on automobile engines.

10-13
SLIDE-VALVE VARIABLE-VENTURI CARBURETORS
The slide-valve carburetor is the simplest type of motorcycle carburetor. Figure 10-9 shows in simplified view a slide-valve variable-venturi carburetor. Figure 10-10 shows a typical slide-valve carburetor on a single-cylinder two-cycle engine. The throttle cable is attached to the top of the movable piston, or slide valve. When the throttle grip is rotated, the slide valve moves up or down in its bore (☞ 10-7). This varies the size of the venturi.

The position of the slide valve controls the amount of air passing through the carburetor. Also, it controls the amount of fuel being discharged. A tapered needle valve (often called a *jet needle* because it fits into the needle jet) is attached to the lower end of the slide (Fig. 10-9). The needle moves up and down with the slide valve. This changes the size of the fuel passage through the main jet. As a result, the amount of fuel that flows from the main jet into the air passing through the venturi varies.

When the slide valve is up, more air flows through. At the same time, more fuel flows because the tapered needle valve is also up. This maintains a relatively constant air-fuel ratio throughout the speed range.

Notice the spring in Fig. 10-9. As the slide valve is pulled up by twisting the throttle grip, the spring is compressed. When the throttle grip is released, the spring expands. This pushes the slide valve down to the engine idle position. The spring also pulls the throttle grip back to the closed throttle position.

10-14
VARYING THE VENTURI
The venturi is the space between the floor of the air horn and the bottom of the slide valve (Fig. 10-11). When the slide valve

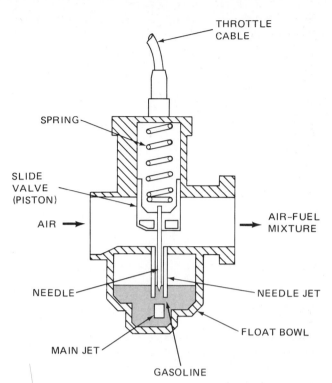

Fig. 10-9 Simplified view of a slide-valve carburetor.

moves down, it reduces the size of the venturi. When the slide valve moves up, it increases the size of the venturi.

Figure 10-12 shows the size of the venturi with various positions of the slide valve. The view is what you would see if you looked directly into the air horn.

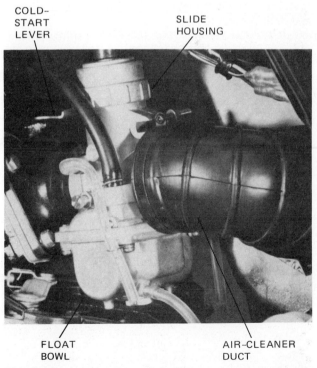

Fig. 10-10 A slide-valve carburetor on a single-cylinder two-cycle engine (*ATW*)

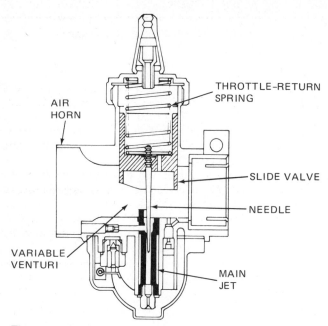

Fig. 10-11 The size of the venturi is the space between the bottom of the slide valve and the floor of the air horn. (*Kawasaki Heavy Industries, Ltd.*)

the slide valve down and returns the throttle grip to the idle position. This is why on most motorcycles the engine returns to idle when the throttle grip is released.

10-15
OPERATION OF A SLIDE-VALVE VARIABLE-VENTURI CARBURETOR
Now let's look at the operating systems in slide-valve carburetors. These systems include the float system, the starter system, the slow system, and the main system. An exploded view of one model of slide-valve carburetor is shown in Fig. 10-13.

Float System The slide-valve carburetor has a float system. The purpose of the float system is to maintain a constant level of gasoline in the float bowl. Figure 9-4 is a simplified view of a float bowl. The parts in the float system are shown at the bottom of Fig. 10-13. Figure 10-14 shows the float system in cutaway view.

As the fuel level rises in the float bowl, the float also rises. This pushes the needle valve up into the valve seat and shuts off the flow of fuel. When the fuel level falls, the float also falls. This allows the needle valve to open so more fuel can enter the float bowl. In operation, the needle valve and the float take positions that allow fuel to enter at the same rate that it is leaving. This maintains a constant level of fuel in the float bowl.

The reason it is important to maintain a constant level of fuel in the float bowl is this: If the fuel level is too high, too much fuel would flow out of the fuel jet, or nozzle. The air-fuel mixture would be too rich. Fuel would be wasted, and the engine would run poorly or stall. The exhaust gas would have a high percentage of hydrocarbons (HC) and carbon monoxide (CO), both of which are atmospheric pollutants.

If the fuel level is too low, not enough fuel will flow from the fuel jet, or nozzle. The mixture will be too lean, and the engine will run poorly or stall.

Notice how moving the slide valve up increases the size of the venturi, going from left to right in Fig. 10-12.

The position of the slide valve is controlled by the movement of the throttle grip on the right handlebar (Fig. 10-6). To raise the slide, the throttle grip must be twisted. This increases the size of the venturi. Now more air can flow through it, and more fuel can discharge from the main jet (Figs. 10-11 and 10-12).

To lower the slide valve the throttle grip is turned or released. A compressed spring in the carburetor above the slide valve expands (Fig. 10-11). The spring pushes

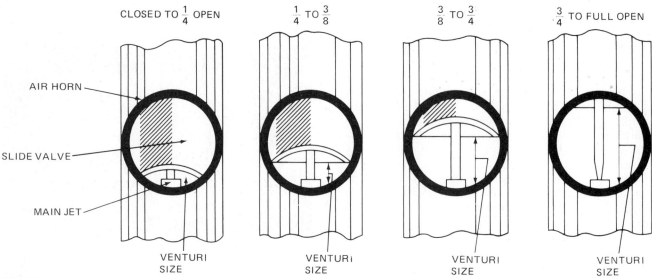

Fig. 10-12 Various positions of the slide valve in a variable-venturi carburetor. (*Kawasaki Heavy Industries, Ltd.*)

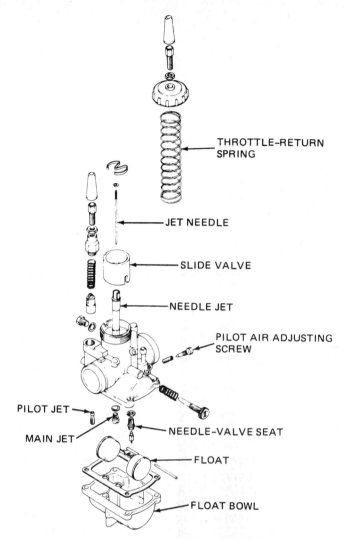

THROTTLE-RETURN SPRING

JET NEEDLE

SLIDE VALVE

NEEDLE JET

PILOT AIR ADJUSTING SCREW

PILOT JET

MAIN JET

NEEDLE-VALVE SEAT

FLOAT

FLOAT BOWL

Fig. 10-13 Exploded view of a typical slide-valve carburetor. (*Suzuki Motor Company, Ltd.*)

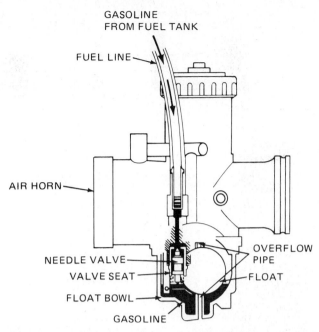

GASOLINE FROM FUEL TANK

FUEL LINE

AIR HORN

NEEDLE VALVE

VALVE SEAT

FLOAT BOWL

GASOLINE

OVERFLOW PIPE

FLOAT

Fig. 10-14 The float system of a slide-valve carburetor. (*Suzuki Motor Company, Ltd.*)

NOTE Not all carburetors have a float system. For example, the carburetor shown in Fig. 10-25 does not use floats. Instead, it has a fuel reservoir which is called a *fuel chamber.*

Notice the overflow pipe in Fig. 10-14. Its purpose during normal operation is to act as an air vent. Atmospheric pressure is admitted to the float bowl through this pipe. This causes the fuel to flow from an area of high pressure (atmospheric pressure) to an area of low pressure (the vacuum in the venturi). Also, if the fuel level in the float bowl temporarily gets too high, the excess fuel will drain away through the overflow pipe.

Starting System The cold starting system in the carburetor is also called the *starter system.* Regardless of its name, its purpose is to provide a rich mixture for starting a cold engine. There are two general types of cold starting systems, the *choke valve* and the *mixture enricher.* The difference is in their basic operation. The choke valve produces a richer mixture by partially choking off, or blocking, the air flow into the carbure-

tor. Then, when the engine is cranked, more fuel is discharged into less than the normal amount of air. The resulting richer mixture provides easier starting of a cold engine.

Instead of choking off the air flow through the carburetor, the other type of cold starting system opens an additional fuel passage. This system is often called the *mixture enrichment* type of cold starting system.

Figure 10-15 shows a variable-venturi carburetor that has a choke valve. When the choke valve is closed, little air can enter the air horn. This produces a partial vacuum when the engine is cranked. The vacuum causes the carburetor jet to supply fuel to the air that does get through. This produces the rich mixture needed for starting.

The choke valve may be a butterfly valve or a disk-type valve that pivots on a shaft (Fig. 10-15). Or a slide-type valve may be used that is pushed into the air passage to restrict the air. Either type may have a *relief valve* in it. The relief valve opens as the vacuum behind it increases during engine cranking. By opening, the relief valve prevents an excessively high vacuum that might cause excessive fuel discharge and a flooded engine.

Figure 10-16 shows the mixture-enricher type of cold starting system in a variable-venturi carburetor. This system is often used on two-cycle engines.

When the starter lever is operated, the starter plunger is pulled up. This opens the starter system so that air can flow through the starter air passage (Fig. 10-16). At the same time, the vacuum in the air horn causes fuel to be pulled up through the starter jet. The fuel mixes with air entering the air bleed at the top of the float bowl. The mixture then moves up to the starter air passage. This produces the rich mixture needed to start a cold engine.

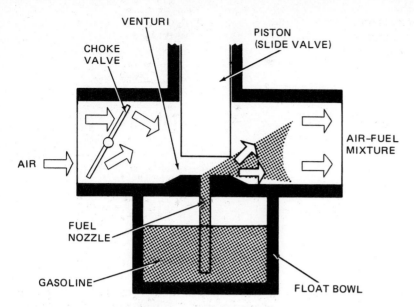

Fig. 10-15　Choke valve in a variable-venturi carburetor.

NOTE When cranking an engine with the mixture-enrichener type of cold starting system, do not rotate the throttle grip on the handlebar. This will raise the slide in the carburetor, open the venturi, cause a loss of vacuum at the fuel discharge port, and reduce the air flow through the starter air passage. The additional air will also lean the rich air-fuel mixture from the starting system so much that the engine may be difficult to start.

Other variable-venturi carburetors use a primer, or *tickler system,* to provide a rich mixture for starting. The tickler system has a plunger that is pushed down to provide extra fuel for starting.

Slow System The slow system controls the air-fuel mixture from idle to low speed. It is also called the *idle system,* the *low-speed system,* or the *pilot system.*

When the slide valve is nearly closed all fuel feeds from the *idle port* (Fig. 10-17). The venturi is very small,

producing a high vacuum at the idle port. The high vacuum also draws air through the air inlet into the idle system. This air mixes with the fuel flowing up from the idle jet so that a very rich mixture exits from the idle port. The mixture is leaned out by the additional air flowing through the venturi. This produces the proper air-fuel mixture needed for idling. The air flow into the idle system, and therefore the mixture richness, can be adjusted by turning the idle air screw, shown in Fig. 10-17.

As the slide valve is raised, additional air can flow through the venturi. Increasing the size of the venturi reduces the vacuum at the venturi. Now the idle port delivers less fuel.

However, the additional air flowing through the venturi passes over the *low-speed port* and causes it to begin delivering fuel. This is the condition shown in Fig. 10-17. Both the idle and the low-speed ports are delivering fuel.

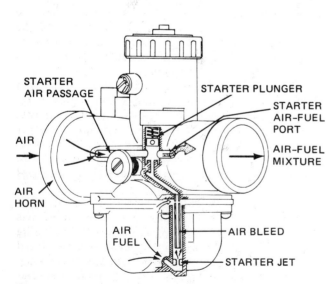

Fig. 10-16　Choke system, or starting system, for cranking a cold engine. (*Suzuki Motor Company, Ltd.*)

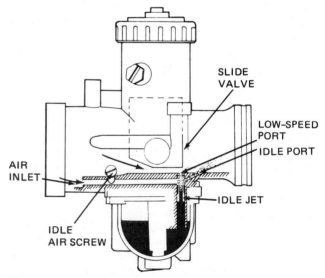

Fig. 10-17　Slow system which controls the air-fuel mixture from idle to low speed. (*Suzuki Motor Company, Ltd.*)

As the venturi opens further (slide valve moves up), the additional air flowing through creates enough of a vacuum that the main jet starts to discharge fuel. The tapered needle moves up with the slide valve, so the amount of fuel discharged is proportional to the amount of air flowing through the venturi. Therefore, the correct air-fuel ratio is maintained.

The idle, low-speed, and main jet actions overlap. At idle, only the idle port delivers fuel. Then at slightly above idle, the low-speed port starts to deliver fuel. Further opening of the slide valve causes the main jet to discharge fuel. But at the same time the idle and low-speed ports reduce or stop their fuel delivery.

The small air inlet in the floor of the carburetor continues to carry air to the needle jet (Figs. 10-17 and 10-18). The air bleeds into the fuel before it discharges from the needle jet. This premixes the fuel with some air so the mixture emerges from the needle jet as a fine mist, as shown in Fig. 10-18. In the air horn, the fuel further mixes with the large volume of air flowing through the venturi. This produces the proper air-fuel mixture for medium engine speed. With fuel beginning to flow from the needle jet, the main system is phasing into operation as engine speed increases.

To adjust the idle or slow-speed air-fuel ratio, most carburetors have a screw-type needle valve. The screw is located either before or after the idle or slow-speed air bleed. When the screw is located in the air passage before the air bleed, the screw is often called an *air adjustment screw*. When the screw is located in the passage carrying the air-fuel mixture after it leaves the air bleed, the screw is known as a *fuel adjustment screw* or a *mixture screw*.

The air screw is turned in, or clockwise, to richen the air-fuel mixture. To richen the mixture with a fuel adjustment screw, the screw is turned out, or counterclockwise. The procedures for setting and adjusting the screws are covered in Chap. 11.

Air Bleeds In the carburetor there are small passages or perforated tubes that permit air to enter or *bleed* into the fuel passages. This premixes the fuel with air. As a result, atomization of the fuel is improved, and the air-fuel ratio can be more accurately controlled. This occurs because throttle opening and engine speed determine the speed and volume of air entering the carburetor. They in turn govern the amount of air that bleeds into the fuel passage through the air bleed.

The air bleed also combats the tendency for excessive fuel to feed through the main jet when air speed through the carburetor is high. Under these conditions, considerable air bleeds into the main jet. When air speed through the carburetor is low, less air bleeds into the main jet. This compensates for the reduced vacuum in the venturi, which tends to pull less fuel from the fuel-discharge port.

Air-bleed passages are also used in idle systems to permit some air to bypass the closed throttle valve and mix with the fuel feeding through the idle system. These passages are also sometimes called *antisiphon systems* because they act as air vents to prevent the siphoning of fuel from the float bowl at low engine speeds.

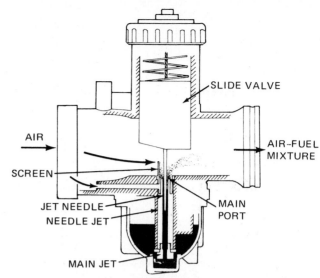

Fig. 10-18 Main-system operation provides fuel in the medium- to high-speed range. (*Suzuki Motor Company, Ltd.*)

In motorcycle carburetors, air bleeds are used in the idle and low-speed system and in the main system. Many motorcycle carburetors have an air adjustment screw which controls the amount of air flowing through the air bleed. Turning the screw in or out changes the idle air-fuel ratio, as discussed earlier.

Another purpose of air bleeds is to compensate for changes in altitude. At higher elevations, atmospheric pressure is less. Therefore, less air (by weight) enters the carburetor and the resulting air-fuel mixture is richer. One way to readjust the air-fuel mixture is to install smaller fuel jets in the carburetor. However, air bleeds can be designed into the carburetor to automatically correct the air-fuel ratio as altitude changes. Some carburetors have an *altitude compensator* knob that can be pulled out at high elevations. This opens an additional air passage into the carburetor, thereby preventing an excessively rich mixture.

Main System The main system is also called the *main-metering system*, the *cruising system*, and the *high-speed system*. In the carburetor, the main system provides the air-fuel mixture needed by the engine in the medium- to high-speed range.

When the slide valve is raised further, to the position shown in Fig. 10-18, the vacuum at the venturi is reduced so much that the idle port no longer discharges fuel. However, the jet needle has been raised further out of the needle jet so that its fuel passage is larger. Additional fuel now discharges from the main jet to take care of the additional air passing through the enlarged venturi.

When the throttle has been fully opened for full-speed or maximum-power operation, the venturi has increased to its largest size. A full flow of air is passing through. At the same time, the jet needle has been lifted almost clear of the needle jet. Fuel can flow freely from the float bowl to the main jet. This provides the relatively rich mixture required by the engine when developing maximum power.

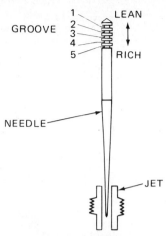

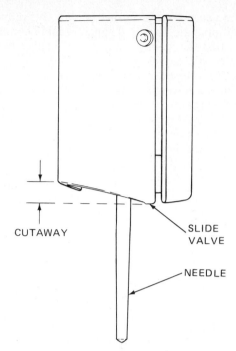

Fig. 10-19 Grooves on the slide-valve end of the jet needle provide adjustment for the richness of the air-fuel mixture.

Notice the small screen shown in Fig. 10-18. In this carburetor, the screen is attached to the top of the needle jet. When air is flowing through the venturi, the screen blocks a small amount of the air. This causes a slight turbulence which helps provide better atomization of the fuel.

Fig. 10-20 Slide valve, showing the area that has been cut away. (*Kawasaki Heavy Industries, Ltd.*)

10-16
NEEDLE AND SLIDE SHAPES The shape of the needle and how it is mounted in the slide valve determine the amount of fuel that will flow from the

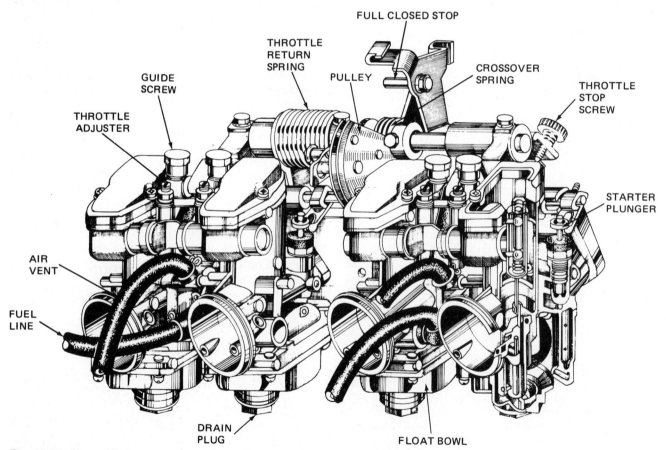

Fig. 10-21 Four carburetors used on a four-cylinder four-cycle engine. (*Kawasaki Heavy Industries, Ltd.*)

main port during various operating conditions. Manufacturers supply needles with different tapers to meet varying requirements. In addition, many needles have a series of grooves cut in their upper end, as shown in Fig. 10-19. The attachment point of the needle to the slide valve can be varied. The first step in Fig. 10-19 would have the needle at its lowest point. This would result in the leanest mixture. If the attachment point were at the fifth step in Fig. 10-19, it would place the needle at its highest point. This would result in the richest mixture.

The amount the throttle valve is cut away on its front edge can change the air flow and the vacuum at the venturi and the two ports—main and idle. Figure 10-20 shows the portion that is cut away on a typical slide valve. Proper design of the cutaway prevents flat spots on acceleration between idle and low-speed system operation and between low-speed and main system operation.

The size of the main jet at the bottom of the needle can also be changed to change the richness of the mixture. Most main and low-speed jets are threaded and can be replaced with a screwdriver. Usually a series of jets are available with larger and smaller diameters than standard. By changing the jet size, the amount of fuel that can pass through is increased or decreased. A jet with a larger diameter will have a higher number stamped on it. This will enrich the air-fuel mixture. To lean the mixture, install a jet with a smaller diameter. It will have a lower number.

10-17 MULTIPLE-CARBURETOR INSTALLATIONS

Most multiple-cylinder motorcycle engines have multiple carburetors—one carburetor for each cylinder. Figure 10-10 shows the carburetor on a single-cylinder two-cycle engine. Figure 10-21 shows the four carburetors used on a four-cylinder four-cycle double-overhead-camshaft engine. With multiple carburetors, special linkage is used so that all throttle valves or slide valves will be opened or closed together. Also, a special linkage is required to the choke or starter system of each carburetor.

Figure 10-22 shows the cables to the three carburetors used on a three-cylinder two-cycle engine. The cables are attached to the tops of the slide valves. When the throttle grip is turned to open the throttles, all three cables pull the three slide valves up at the same time.

Note the cable running to the oil pump in Fig. 10-22. The oil pump delivers varying amounts of oil to the three cylinders, according to the throttle opening. This oil is sprayed into the ingoing air-fuel mixture. Engine lubricating systems are covered in Chap. 14.

The purpose of having a carburetor for each cylinder is to assure the best possible air-fuel ratio for each cylinder. When a single carburetor is used on a four-cylinder engine, for example, a manifold is required. The manifold is a series of pipes running to the four cylinders. Because they must be different lengths, the four cylinders do not get exactly the same amount of the air-fuel mixture, and the richness of the mixture varies between cylinders. With a carburetor for each cylinder, all cylinders will receive the same amount of the air-fuel mixture, and the mixtures will be uniform in richness.

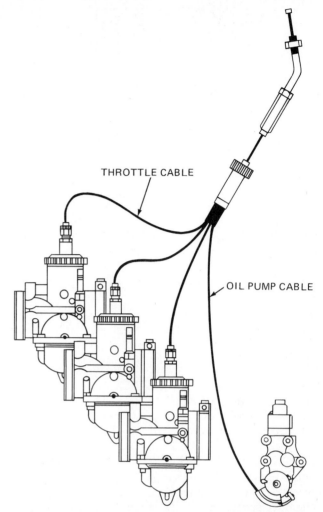

Fig. 10-22 Cables linking the throttle grip to the slide valves in the three carburetors. (*Kawasaki Heavy Industries, Ltd.*)

Another reason for using a separate carburetor for each cylinder is to save space. An intake manifold usually is large and bulky. Take a look at the intake manifold on a four-cylinder automobile engine. Most motorcycles do not have the space available for an intake manifold and a carburetor large enough to service all cylinders of a multicylinder engine.

10-18 CONSTANT-VACUUM CARBURETORS

The constant-vacuum variable-venturi carburetor is also known as a *constant-velocity carburetor* and as a *dash-pot carburetor*. It is used on a variety of medium-sized and large engines. In this carburetor, both a slide valve and a disk type of throttle valve (Figs. 10-2 to 10-4) are used. Unlike what happens in the slide-valve carburetor, the slide valve is not operated by the throttle cable. Instead, the throttle cable is connected to the disk-type throttle valve. The slide valve is controlled by an attached vacuum diaphragm or a vacuum piston (Fig. 10-23). The vacuum device moves the slide valve in response to changes in air pressure, or vacuum.

Now let us see how this carburetor (Fig. 10-23) works. The piston is an assembly of two basic parts: the

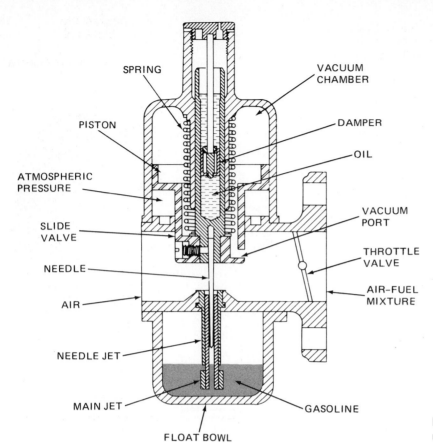

SPRING

VACUUM CHAMBER

PISTON

DAMPER

OIL

ATMOSPHERIC PRESSURE

VACUUM PORT

SLIDE VALVE

THROTTLE VALVE

NEEDLE

AIR-FUEL MIXTURE

AIR

NEEDLE JET

MAIN JET

GASOLINE

FLOAT BOWL

Fig. 10-23 Sectional view of a constant-vacuum variable-venturi carburetor.

outer two-diameter piston and the inner oil-damper reservoir. The piston moves up and down in the piston chamber according to how much vacuum there is between the piston and throttle valve. When the piston moves down, it reduces the size of the venturi. Reducing the size of the venturi reduces the amount of air that can flow through. At the same time, the tapered needle attached to the slide valve also moves down into the jet. This reduces the amount of fuel that can flow.

When the engine is idling and the throttle valve is closed, the piston is at its lowest point, pushed down by the piston spring. When the throttle is opened, intake manifold vacuum is introduced into the air horn. This vacuum draws air from the space above the piston, acting through the vacuum port in the lower part of the piston (Fig. 10-23). The piston is raised by the vacuum, partly compressing the piston spring.

As the piston is raised, more air can pass through the venturi. At the same time, the needle is lifted from the jet, allowing more fuel to flow. The additional air-fuel mixture satisfies the part-throttle condition. As the throttle is opened further, the piston and needle are lifted further. Therefore, the amount of air-fuel mixture delivered is proportional to the throttle opening. The piston spring and vacuum, working together, determine the size of the venturi.

To prevent the piston from being too sensitive and moving up and down too much from slight changes in vacuum, an oil damper is built into the inner diameter of the piston (Fig. 10-23). As the piston moves up and

down, a small amount of light oil must flow past the damper. This action does not noticeably change the operation of the piston. A device which prevents the throttle from opening or closing too quickly is called a *dash pot*. The oil damper is a form of dash pot, and this is why the carburetor is sometimes called a *dash-pot carburetor*.

10-19
FIXED-VENTURI CARBURETORS Fixed-venturi carburetors have been used mostly on the big Harley-Davidson V-twin engines. Figure 10-24 shows that this type of carburetor has the basic features of an automobile-engine carburetor.

Figure 10-25 shows a typical Harley-Davidson fixed-venturi carburetor in sectional view.

A special feature is a spring-balanced lever that is controlled by a diaphragm instead of a float bowl. As gasoline enters the fuel chamber, the gasoline tends to push the diaphragm down. This action allows the spring-loaded lever to pivot and force the inlet needle valve up into the valve seat, shutting off the flow of fuel into the chamber.

In operation, the inlet needle is positioned to allow just enough fuel to enter to balance the fuel leaving the chamber. This system operates at any tilt angle and resists vibration, either of which can cause a float-type control to become unbalanced. The carburetor has the following systems for operating under varying conditions:

1. A choke system
2. An idle system
3. An accelerator system
4. A cruising system
5. A high-speed system

Now let's discuss how each of these carburetor fuel systems operates.

Choke System   For starting a cold engine the choke lever is set so the choke valve is in the closed position. Now, when the engine is cranked for starting, the vacuum produced by the engine causes fuel to feed into the small amount of air that gets past the choke valve. The fuel feeds from the idle port, from the off-idle (or secondary idle) port, from the idle air bleed, and from the main nozzle (Fig. 10-25).

This provides the engine with a very rich mixture for starting. As fuel is withdrawn from the fuel chamber, atmospheric pressure, acting under this diaphragm, pushes the diaphragm up. This causes the control lever to pivot so the inlet needle moves down to allow more fuel to enter. The fuel flows down from the fuel tank, which is above the carburetor, by gravity.

When the engine starts, the additional air demands of the engine cause the spring-loaded top half of the choke valve to pivot inward. This allows more air to flow in. Then, as the engine starts to run, the choke should be moved to about half open. Later, when the engine warms up, the choke should be opened fully.

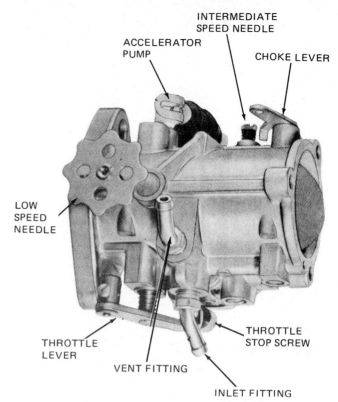

Fig. 10-24   A fixed-venturi carburetor. (*Harley-Davidson Motor Company, Inc.*)

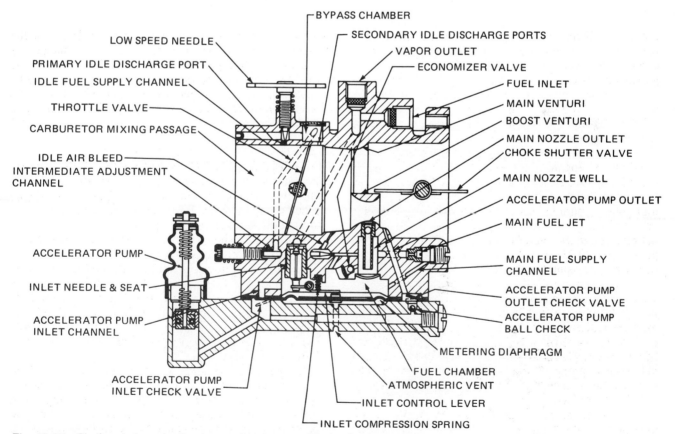

Fig. 10-25   Sectional view of a fixed-venturi carburetor. (*Harley-Davidson Motor Company, Inc.*)

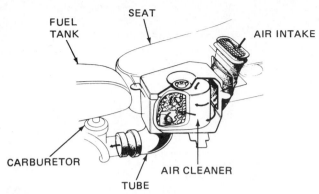

Fig. 10-26 On most motorcycles, the air cleaner is located under the seat. (*Honda Motor Company, Ltd.*)

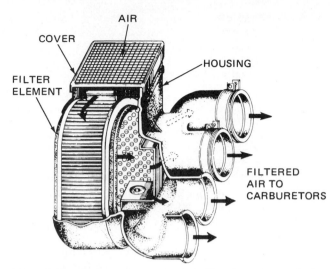

Fig. 10-28 A dry-paper type of air filter for a four-cylinder engine. (*Kawasaki Heavy Industries, Ltd.*)

Idle System   The throttle valve is slightly open when the engine is idling. Not enough air is flowing through the air horn and venturi to cause the main nozzle to discharge fuel. Instead, the primary idle-discharge port provides sufficient fuel during this condition. The vacuum created by the engine causes the idle port to discharge fuel. This mixes with the air passing the edges of the throttle to provide the air-fuel mixture the engine requires.

When the throttle is slightly open, the edge of the throttle valve moves past the secondary, or off-idle, port (Fig. 10-25). Now engine vacuum can work on this port, also, so it discharges fuel.

Accelerator System   The accelerator pump provides additional fuel when the throttle is opened. This additional fuel is needed because when the throttle is opened, there is a sudden inrush of additional air. The main-metering system and the main nozzle cannot in-

stantly respond with additional fuel. Therefore, without the accelerator system, the air-fuel mixture would suddenly lean out. This could cause the engine to misfire and stumble. However, the accelerator system supplies the additional fuel needed to maintain sufficient mixture richness and prevent stumble.

Figure 10-25 shows the accelerator system. The accelerator pump is operated by the lever shown in Fig. 10-24. When the throttle is opened, the accelerator-pump plunger is forced downward. This pushes fuel through the accelerator system so it discharges into the boost venturi. During this time, the other nozzle and ports may also be discharging fuel. Note the pump outlet check valve to the lower right in Fig. 10-25. The valve includes a check ball, which rests on a seat when the accelerator system is not in operation. This prevents atmospheric pressure from working backward toward the pump and upsetting carburetor operation.

Note also the pump inlet check valve toward the lower left in Fig. 10-25. Its purpose is to prevent accelerator-pump pressure from forcing fuel back up into the fuel chamber rather than out the pump outlet port. When pump pressure develops, this check valve closes to shut off the line to the fuel chamber.

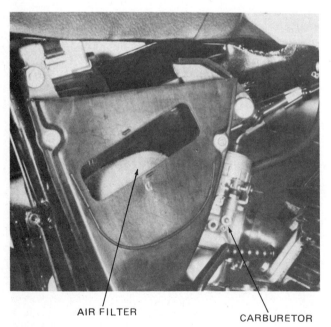

Fig. 10-27 Location of the air cleaner in a motocross bike. (*ATW*)

Cruising, or Intermediate-Speed, System   This system is in operation when the throttle valve has opened enough to produce a vacuum at the boost venturi. In this case, the main nozzle begins to discharge fuel. At the same time, if the throttle is open, the vacuum at the idle and off-idle ports may become too low to cause these ports to discharge fuel. They may discharge some fuel, but generally the fuel for intermediate speed and cruising comes from the main nozzle.

High-Speed, Full-Power Operation   When the throttle is fully open, its edge moves close to the boost venturi. This directs the engine vacuum more completely to the boost venturi. The additional vacuum

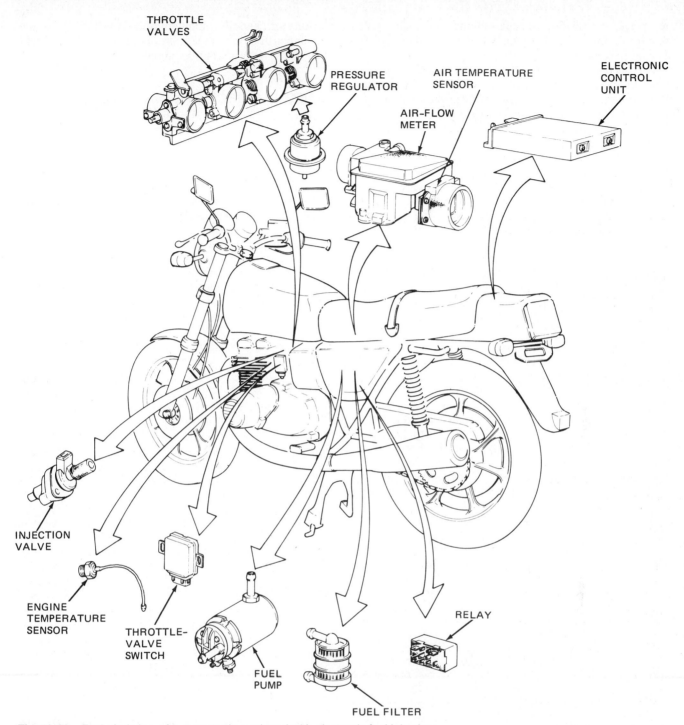

THROTTLE
VALVES

PRESSURE
REGULATOR

AIR TEMPERATURE
SENSOR

AIR-FLOW
METER

ELECTRONIC
CONTROL
UNIT

INJECTION
VALVE

ENGINE
TEMPERATURE
SENSOR

THROTTLE-
VALVE
SWITCH

FUEL
PUMP

FUEL FILTER

RELAY

Fig. 10-29 Exploded view of a motorcycle equipped with electronic fuel injection.
(*Kawasaki Motors Corporation*)

applied to the main nozzle causes it to supply more fuel. Therefore, the air-fuel mixture is enriched to allow the engine to produce more power for high-speed operation.

Chapter 11 describes the adjustments that can be made on this carburetor. There are three basic adjustments (Fig. 10-24): low-speed needle, intermediate-speed needle, and throttle-stop screw for engine idle speed.

**10-20
AIR CLEANERS** A large volume of air passes through an engine when it is running. The air usually contains dust and grit particles which float around in it. This dirt, if it gets into the engine, can seriously damage and rapidly wear moving engine parts. Dust on bearings can gouge them and scratch the shaft journals rotating in the bearings. This leads to early bearing and shaft failure. Dust on the piston and piston rings can scratch

the rings, the piston, and the cylinder wall. This will result in rapid wear of the rings and wall and in loss of engine performance.

Dirt in the air entering the carburetor can clog the very small fuel and air-bleed passages. In addition, the dirt can cause wear and sticking of the slide valve and the piston in the carburetor. To keep the dust and dirt from entering the engine, an air cleaner or air filter is installed on the carburetor.

All air entering the engine through the carburetor must first pass through the air cleaner. The upper part of the air cleaner contains a ring of filter material composed of fine-mesh metal threads or ribbons, special paper, cellulose fiber, or polyurethane. The air must pass through this ring, which traps most of the dust particles.

The air cleaner also muffles the noise of the intake of air through the carburetor and ports. This noise would be more noticeable if it were not for the air cleaner. In addition, the air cleaner acts as a flame arrester, if the engine backfires through the carburetor. Backfiring may occur if the air-fuel mixture is ignited in a cylinder before the intake valve or port closes. When this happens, there is a momentary flashback of flame through the carburetor. The air cleaner keeps the flame from leaving the carburetor and igniting gasoline fumes outside the engine.

On many motorcycles, the air cleaner is located under the seat. Figure 10-26 shows a typical arrangement. Figure 10-27 shows the location of the air cleaner on a one-cylinder two-cycle motocross bike. In the picture, the number plate has been removed so the filter element can be seen. This is a polyurethane filter element which is installed around a wire-mesh guide.

Motorcycles often use an air cleaner which is not directly mounted to the carburetor but is connected by a hose or tube. Figure 10-28 shows this type of air cleaner for a four-cylinder engine. On multicylinder engines which have more than one carburetor, the air cleaner is connected by separate hoses or tubes to each

carburetor. The filter element shown in Fig. 10-28 is a dry-paper filter element. It is similar to the type widely used today on automobile engines.

10-21
FUEL INJECTION

The engine must have a continuous supply of combustible air-fuel mixture to run. In most motorcycle engines, the carburetor supplies this mixture. However, gasoline fuel injection has been used for several years on various models of automobile engines. Now fuel injection is beginning to appear on motorcycle engines.

The basic difference between the carburetor and fuel injection is in where and how the fuel enters the airstream. In the carburetor, the air flow through it causes the fuel to discharge and mix with the air. Then the intake passages carry the air-fuel mixture into the engine. With fuel injection, only air enters the intake passages after passing through a throttle valve. Fuel sprays, under pressure, from a nozzle or injection valve into the air just before it reaches the intake valve (on four-cycle engines). When the intake valve opens, the air-fuel mixture flows on into the cylinder. Combustion follows in the normal manner.

Fuel injection has been used on some experimental and racing motorcycle engines for many years. However, the first production motorcycle engine with fuel injection was a four-cylinder four-cycle engine introduced by Kawasaki in 1980. This system is an *electronic fuel injection* (EFI) system. It uses an electronic control unit to vary the length of time that the injection valves remain open. Figure 10-29 shows the system, as used by Kawasaki, in exploded view.

A fuel-injection system replaces the carburetors on an engine. With EFI, the air-fuel ratio is controlled electronically. Air flow through the throttle valves is measured continuously and directly to determine the air-fuel ratio needed by the engine.

Sensors in the system continually monitor engine speed, engine temperature, intake air flow, and intake air temperature. This information is sent to the electronic control unit, which processes these signals and determines the fuel requirements of the engine.

Then the electronic control unit generates an electric signal which is sent to the fuel-injection valves. This electric signal opens the electromagnetic injection valves. Now exactly the amount of fuel needed by the amount of air entering the engine sprays out. How long the injection valve is held open determines how much fuel is injected. The injection-valve nozzle is designed to deliver a finely atomized fuel charge, for even and complete combustion.

Three basic parts make up the electronic fuel-injection system. These are the air-intake system, the fuel-delivery system, and the electronic control system.

10-22
AIR-INTAKE SYSTEM

Figure 10-30 shows the air-intake system. The incoming air passes through the air cleaner to the air-flow meter. In the air-flow meter, the air-flow rate and the air temperature are measured. Then the air enters the *surge tank,* which distributes the

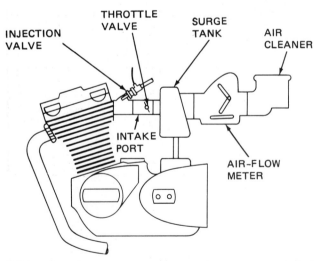

Fig. 10-30 Air-intake system on an engine with electronic fuel injection. (*Kawasaki Motors Corporation*)

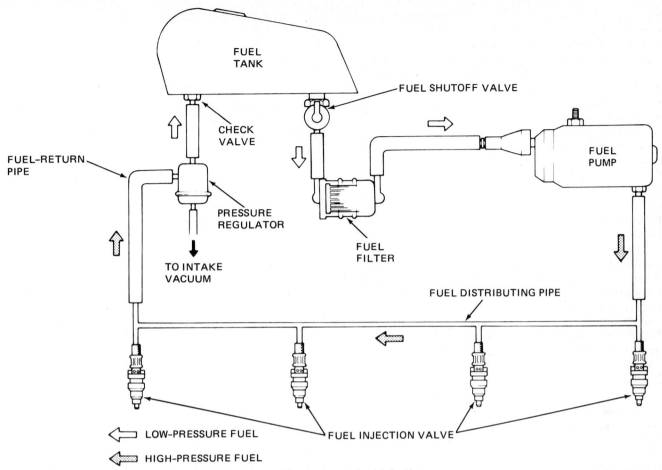

Fig. 10-31 Fuel-delivery system on an engine with electronic fuel injection. (*Kawasaki Motors Corporation*)

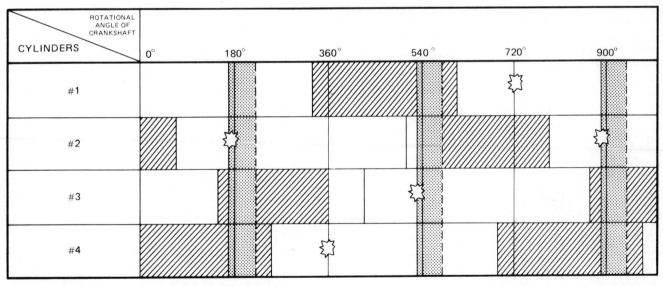

IGNITION

DURATION OF INTAKE VALVE OPENING

DURATION OF FUEL INJECTION

Fig. 10-32 Injection-timing chart for a four-cylinder four-cycle motorcycle engine. (*Kawasaki Motors Corporation*)

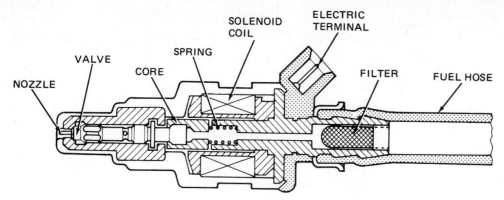

Fig. 10-33 Sectional view of a solenoid-operated injection valve. (*Kawasaki Motors Corporation*)

air to the cylinder intake ports. A throttle valve in each intake port controls the air flow to each cylinder.

The surge tank has two functions. First, it reduces the effects of air-flow pulsations on the air-flow meter. Second, it acts like a manifold to distribute the incoming air to each cylinder.

10-23
FUEL-DELIVERY SYSTEM
The fuel-delivery system is shown in Fig. 10-31. When the fuel shutoff valve is opened, fuel flows from the tank through the

valve to the fuel filter. An electric fuel pump pulls the fuel from the filter, pressurizes the fuel, and delivers it under higher pressure to the fuel-distributing pipe. The fuel-distributing pipe is connected to each of the four fuel-injection valves.

When the signal from the electronic control unit opens the injection valves, fuel sprays out. Fuel injection continues as long as the signal from the electronic control unit holds the injection valve open. The injectors are wired electrically in parallel to the electronic control unit. Therefore, all injectors open and close at

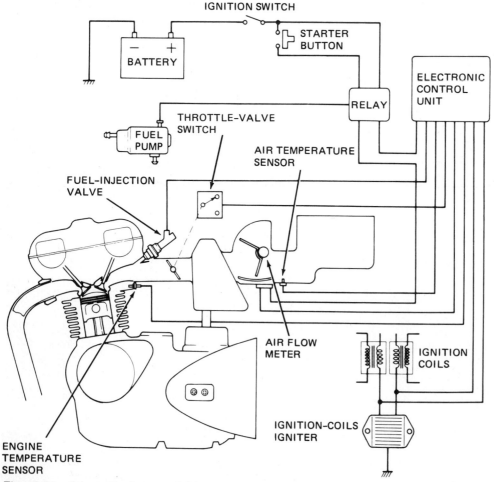

Fig. 10-34 Schematic diagram of the electronic control system on a motorcycle with electronic fuel injection. (*Kawasaki Motors Corporation*)

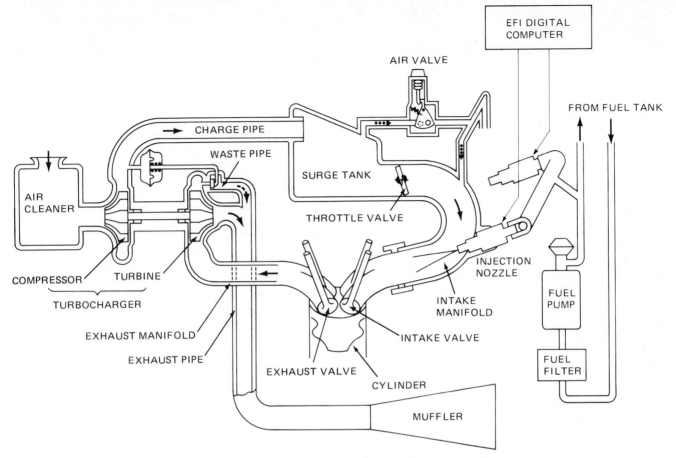

Fig. 10-35 Schematic diagram of a combined electronic fuel-injection and turbocharger system developed by Honda for a prototype motorcycle. (*Honda Motor Company, Ltd.*)

the same time. This occurs once during every crankshaft rotation, or twice between consecutive intake valve openings. Figure 10-32 shows an injection-timing diagram. The duration of the intake-valve opening is always the same. However, the duration of fuel injection changes. Fuel injection always begins at the same time, but the time of the closing of the injection valve changes. This lengthening and shortening of the fuel-injection duration acts to keep the air-fuel ratio at the ratio desired by the electronic control unit. Also, longer fuel injection provides the additional fuel needed for higher speeds and greater loads.

Excess fuel is returned to the fuel tank through the pressure regulator. The pressure regulator controls the pressure of the fuel in the fuel-distributing pipe.

The solenoid-operated fuel-injection valve, or fuel injector, is shown in sectional view in Fig. 10-33. Normally the valve is held closed by the valve spring, which pushes the core and valve against its seat in the nozzle. But when the electronic control unit sends a current pulse to the solenoid, the current flows through the solenoid coil. This creates a magnetic field which pulls the core in towards the solenoid. As the core moves, the valve is lifted off its seat. This allows the fuel to spray out of the nozzle into the intake air.

Fuel injection continues as long as current flows

through the solenoid coil to hold the valve open. As soon as current flow stops, the spring closes the valve and fuel injection ends. In the running engine, this sequence is repeated by each fuel injector once during every crankshaft revolution.

10-24 ELECTRONIC CONTROL SYSTEM

Figure 10-34 shows the electronic control system. The following signals are electrically sent to the electronic control unit from the various sensors:

1. Engine speed, which is picked up at the ground sides of the primary windings of the ignition coils.
2. Air-flow rate, which is measured by the air-flow meter.
3. Start signal, which is picked up at the positive side of the starter relay.
4. Throttle-valve position, which is picked up by a switch on the throttle-valve shaft to signal when the throttle valves are in the idle and full-load positions.
5. Engine temperature, which is picked up by the engine-temperature sensor in the cylinder head.
6. Air temperature, which is measured by the air-temperature sensor built into the air-flow meter.

In operation, the electronic control unit receives these signals as input data and processes them in accordance with a predetermined program. The electronic control unit then computes the duration of fuel injection required to meet the needs of the engine. A signal pulse of the proper width is sent to the injectors. Each fuel-injection valve opens for the duration that the pulse is received. This allows the correct amount of fuel to be injected into each intake port.

This type of electronic fuel-injection system is called an *air-flow-sensitive system*. The air flow into the engine is measured before it reaches the cylinders. This allows the electronic control unit to compute the proper amount of fuel before it is needed.

10-25
BENEFITS OF ELECTRONIC FUEL
INJECTION Electronic fuel injection provides better driveability, better fuel economy, low exhaust emissions, and low maintenance. However, it usually is a more complicated and expensive fuel-delivery system to manufacture.

The system automatically compensates for changes in the engine that could affect the air-fuel ratio. For example, carbon deposits in the combustion chamber cause less space to be available for filling with fresh air-fuel mixture. Therefore, less air passes through the throttle valves. This is immediately sensed by the air-flow meter, which signals the electronic control unit. The electronic control unit, in turn, generates a shorter signal pulse for the fuel-injection valves. This reduces the amount of fuel delivered, thereby maintaining the desired air-fuel ratio.

Figure 10-35 shows in schematic view the combined electronic fuel injection and turbocharger system on a prototype motorcycle developed by Honda. By using the turbocharger (☞9-17), high performance can be obtained from the 500-cc engine. With a 5 psi [0.35 kg/cm²] boost from the turbocharger, the engine produces 76 bhp. This gives the motorcycle a top speed of 125 mph [201 km/h]. To eliminate the throttle lag that is characteristic of many turbocharged engines, the electronic fuel-injection system is used.

CHAPTER 10
REVIEW QUESTIONS

1. What are the two basic types of carburetors?
2. What is a carburetor?
3. How is the throttle controlled on a motorcycle?
4. Describe the venturi effect.
5. What is the difference between a fixed venturi and a variable venturi?
6. What causes fuel to flow from a fuel nozzle?
7. When does the engine require the richest air-fuel mixture?
8. Why is a float system necessary on most carburetors?
9. Is there a difference between a slide valve and a throttle valve?
10. Which motorcycle uses a fixed-venturi carburetor?
11. In a slide-valve carburetor, what causes the throttle to return to the idle position when the rider releases the throttle grip?
12. How is the slide valve connected to the throttle grip?
13. Explain the operation of the needle valve and seat in the float system.
14. Why is an overflow pipe used on motorcycle carburetors?

15. What is another name for the choke system in a carburetor?
16. Describe the operation of the main system in the slide-valve carburetor.
17. How can the air-fuel ratio be changed in a carburetor that uses a tapered jet needle?
18. On multicylinder motorcycle engines, why are separate carburetors used for each cylinder instead of one large carburetor?
19. What is the difference between a slide-valve carburetor and a constant-vacuum carburetor?
20. In a constant-vacuum carburetor, what operates the slide valve?
21. Why do constant-vacuum carburetors have an oil damper?
22. How does the fixed-venturi carburetor used by Harley-Davidson operate without a float bowl?
23. What controls the amount of fuel discharged from the jets of a fixed-venturi carburetor?
24. Why do motorcycle engines require an air cleaner?
25. Where is the air cleaner located on most motorcycles?

11

MOTORCYCLE FUEL-SYSTEM SERVICE

After studying this chapter,
you should be able to:

1. Discuss the precautions to observe in fuel-system work.

2. Explain how to service air cleaners.

3. Describe fuel-line and fuel-shutoff-valve service.

4. Discuss fuel-tank and cap service.

5. Explain how to service fuel pumps.

6. Describe how to purge the spark arrester.

7. Discuss decarboning the muffler and exhaust pipe.

8. Discuss various carburetor troubles and their possible causes. Eleven troubles are listed in the chapter.

9. Describe carburetor adjustments, including float adjustments.

10. Explain how to rebuild a carburetor.

11. Diagnose troubles in an electronic fuel-injection system.

11-1 FUEL-SYSTEM TROUBLE DIAGNOSIS

Fuel-system troubles usually show up in engine operation. They cause poor acceleration, hard starting, missing, loss of power, stalling, and other problems. These conditions are discussed in Chap. 23, "Motorcycle Maintenance, Trouble Diagnosis, and Tuneup."

In the fuel system, water and sediment may collect in the bottom of the fuel tank, in the fuel filter, and in the carburetor float bowl. Cleaning of these parts and other fuel-system services are covered in the following sections.

11-2 PRECAUTIONS TO OBSERVE IN FUEL-SYSTEM SERVICE

Refer to Chap. 1 for safety precautions to observe in shop work. The following precautions are especially important in fuel-system work:

1. Even a trace of dirt in a carburetor or fuel pump can cause fuel-system and engine trouble. Be very careful about dirt when repairing these units. Your hands, the workbench, and the tools should be clean.

2. Gasoline vapor is very explosive. Wipe up spilled gasoline at once, and then put the cloths outside to dry. Never smoke or bring an open flame near gasoline!

3. When using the solvent tank, be careful not to splash solvent in your eyes. If solvent or some other chemical gets in your eyes, wash them out with water (Fig. 1-4). Do not add gasoline to the solvent tank. This increases the danger of fire. Dump any gasoline from the carburetor or fuel pump in a container before cleaning them in the solvent.

4. When air drying parts with the air hose, handle the hose with care, as noted in Chap. 1. Also follow the other safety precautions listed in that chapter.

11-3 AIR-CLEANER SERVICE

When the air cleaner is dirty, too little of the air-fuel mixture may get into the engine. Air-cleaner service recommendations vary with different motorcycles and how they are used. Check the manufacturer's service manual and maintenance schedule for service procedures and intervals. Here are sample recommendations and service procedures for two types of air cleaner:

1. **Paper air-filter element** (Fig. 11-1). A typical recommendation is that the paper filter element should be inspected and cleaned every 3600 miles [6000 km] and replaced every 7200 miles [12,000 km]. If the motorcycle is operated in dusty areas or in heavy-duty service (for example, police use), the filter element should be inspected and cleaned more often. To remove the element on many motorcycles, raise the seat and take out the tool tray. Then lift the element out of the air-cleaner case.

Examine the filter element carefully. If the element is partly saturated with oil, discard it. To clean the element, use a compressed-air hose as shown in Fig. 11-1, blowing from the inside out. Hold the nozzle at least 2 inches [51 mm] away from the inside.

NOTE Never use compressed air on the outside of the element. This embeds dust particles in the paper and damages the element.

2. **Oiled-foam air-filter element.** In the oiled-foam air cleaner, shown in Fig. 11-2, the filter element consists

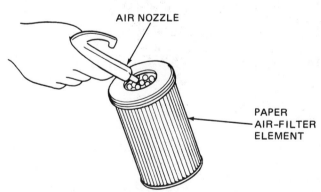

Fig. 11-1 Cleaning a paper air-filter element. (*Suzuki Motor Company, Ltd.*)

Fig. 11-2 Washing a polyurethane air-cleaner element.

of a polyurethane-foam pad soaked in oil. The air must pass through the foam. Dirt particles are trapped by the oily surface as they pass. One manufacturer recommends cleaning this type of air filter every 3600 miles [6000 km], under normal conditions.

To service this type of air cleaner, remove the filter element from the engine. Then wash the filter element in solvent. Squeeze the foam repeatedly with your hands to get out all the old oil and dirt.

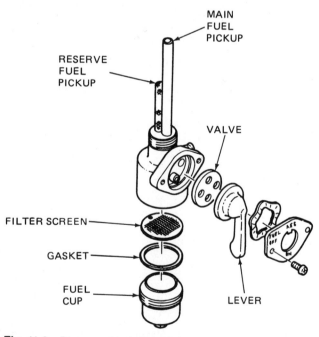

Fig. 11-3 Disassembled view of the fuel valve, showing the location of the filter screen. (*Yamaha International Corporation*)

NOTE Do not wash the element in solvent containing acetone or similar compounds or a hot degreaser. Do not violently wring, shake, or swing the element. Any of these may damage it.

Squeeze the element until no more solvent drips out of it. Coat the element with clean SAE 30 oil, or gear oil, as specified by the manufacturer. Finally, squeeze the foam between your hands and let the excess oil drip off. Failure to do this may cause the excess oil to choke the engine, and it may fail to start.

Air filters which are not installed directly on the carburetor are connected to it by a tube or hose. This hose must be connected airtight to both the air cleaner and the carburetor. The hose must have no cracks, punctures, or loose connections that could leak unfiltered air into the carburetor.

11-4
FUEL LINE AND FUEL SHUTOFF VALVE SERVICE   The fuel line from the tank to the carburetor should be inspected for leaks, kinks, and loosening of the retaining clips. Replace any defective fuel line.

Check the operation of the fuel valve (Fig. 9-3) by turning the lever to the OFF position. Disconnect the fuel line at the carburetor and hold a container under the line. No fuel should leak from the line. If fuel does drip out, the valve seal is defective and should be replaced.

Turn the fuel lever to the ON position (Fig. 9-3) and then to the RES position. Gasoline should flow freely from the line in both positions. Insufficient flow in either position indicates that a defective seal, dirt in the filter screen, or water in the filter cup is restricting the flow. Check the fuel strainer first, and then, if necessary, check the seal in the fuel valve.

A fuel valve in sectional view is shown in Fig. 9-6. Another type of fuel valve has a diaphragm operated automatically by engine vacuum. This fuel valve also is checked and serviced as discussed in this section.

CAUTION Whenever gasoline is spilled on an engine, the gasoline must be completely wiped off before starting the engine. Gasoline on an engine may catch fire when the engine is cranked. When cleaning the fuel strainer or when checking the fuel valve for fuel flow, gasoline should not be permitted to spill on the floor. Spilled gasoline is a fire hazard.

On many motorcycles, the fuel strainer is located in the lower part of the fuel valve, as shown in Fig. 11-3. To service the filter, turn the fuel lever to OFF and unscrew the strainer cup. Then take out the filter screen. Clean the screen and cup. If the screen remains partially clogged after cleaning, replace it. When a new screen is required, always use a new O-ring seal.

If water is found in the filter cup, there may be more water in the fuel tank. To drain any water from the tank, place the fuel line in a container. Turn the fuel lever to reserve, and allow the tank to drain until only clean gasoline runs out.

After cleaning or replacing the screen and seal, screw the fuel cup into the fuel valve. Then turn the fuel lever to ON and check for leaks.

11-5
FUEL-TANK AND CAP SERVICE
Fuel tanks require very little service. However, some moisture and dust enter the fuel tank during normal use. These contaminants can get into the fuel system and clog the filter screen. In addition, the moisture can cause the inside of a metal fuel tank to rust. To prevent these problems, some manufacturers recommend periodically rinsing out the tank with a mixture of oil and gasoline.

All fuel tanks have an air vent to admit air as the fuel level drops. Generally, the vent is in the fuel-tank cap. Sometimes, the vent will get plugged. This prevents air from entering, which means fuel cannot flow out. The result is that the engine starves for fuel and stops running.

Check the vent hole in the fuel-tank cap to make sure that it is not clogged or restricting the free flow of air. Figure 11-4 shows three types of fuel-tank caps. On the cap shown in Fig. 11-4a, the air vent can be checked by blowing through it. With some of the plastic off-road caps, shown in Fig. 11-4c, you should be able to see through the hole when you remove the cap. Also, on this type of cap, the plastic vent hose must be checked for cracks and obstructions. If the vent hose is cracked or clogged, replace it. The flip-up cap, shown in Fig. 11-4b, usually must be removed from the fuel tank to check the air vent.

When there is any trace of gasoline around the fuel tank, check the tank for leaks. In some tanks, leaks tend to occur at the tank seams. If the tank is damaged in any way, it should be repaired or replaced with a new tank. Plastic tanks often can be fixed by patching with fiberglass. The manufacturers recommend replacing a damaged metal tank.

11-6
FUEL-PUMP SERVICE
On engines equipped with a fuel pump, the fuel-pump pressure and capacity can be checked with a fuel-pump tester (Fig. 11-5), which is a combination vacuum and pressure gauge. Low pump pressure causes fuel starvation and poor engine performance. High pressure will cause an over-rich mixture, excessive fuel consumption, and such troubles as fouled spark plugs, rings, and valves (from excessive carbon deposits).

Fuel-pump testers are connected into the fuel line from the pump. They measure either the pressure that the pump can develop (Fig. 11-5), or the volume of fuel the pump can deliver during a timed interval. The vacuum that the fuel pump can develop should also be checked. This is done by connecting the tester to the vacuum side of the pump. Specifications are given in manufacturers' service manuals.

Most fuel pumps are serviced by complete replacement. They are relatively cheap. It may cost more in labor to repair an old pump than to buy a new one.

You can make a quick check of the fuel pump to see if it works by killing the ignition and disconnecting the fuel line to the carburetor. Then crank the engine while holding a small container under the fuel line to catch any gasoline that appears. If gasoline flows out strongly

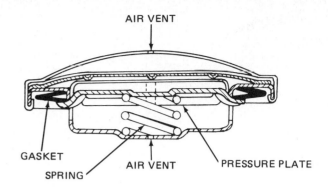

(a) SCREW-TYPE CAP

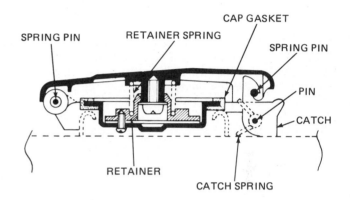

(b) FLIP-UP TYPE CAP

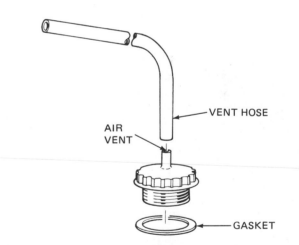

(c) PLASTIC OFF-ROAD TYPE CAP

Fig. 11-4 Three types of fuel-tank caps. (*Kawasaki Heavy Industries, Ltd.; Yamaha International Corporation*)

and in regular squirts, the fuel pump is working okay. If gasoline flow is weak or erratic, there is something wrong with the fuel pump.

On fuel pumps that are assembled with screws, remove the screws and examine the check valves. A small

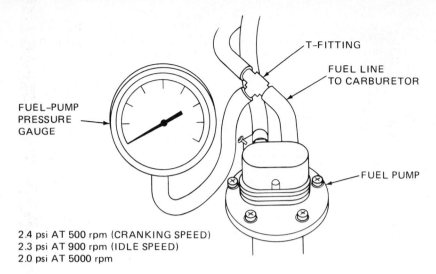

FUEL-PUMP PRESSURE GAUGE

T-FITTING

FUEL LINE TO CARBURETOR

FUEL PUMP

2.4 psi AT 500 rpm (CRANKING SPEED)
2.3 psi AT 900 rpm (IDLE SPEED)
2.0 psi AT 5000 rpm

Fig. 11-5   Checking the fuel-pump pressure.

particle of dirt may be lodged in one of the valves, holding it open. However, if you can see that the diaphragm is torn or has a hole in it, replace the fuel pump.

To remove the old pump, disconnect the fuel lines and take out the screws holding the fuel pump on the engine. Lift the fuel pump off, observing the position of the rocker arm (above or below the eccentric). Install the new pump, making sure the rocker arm goes on the correct side of the eccentric. Then attach the fuel lines and tighten the attaching screws.

11-7 FUEL-GAUGE SERVICE
Fuel gauges require very little in the way of service. Defects in the dash unit, the instrument cluster, or the tank unit usually require replacement of the unit. Details of operation and service of the fuel gauge are covered in Chap. 22.

11-8 PURGING THE SPARK ARRESTER (OFF-ROAD MOTORCYCLES)
Off-road motorcycles designed to travel through forests and on trails are equipped with a spark arrester. It keeps hot sparks from flying out of the muffler. This reduces the chance that

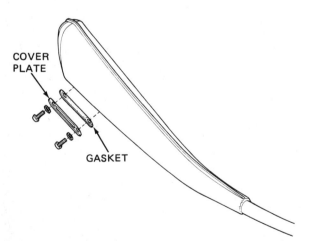

COVER PLATE

GASKET

Fig. 11-6   To purge the carbon deposits from the spark arrester, remove the cover plate. (*Honda Motor Company, Ltd.*)

hot carbon in the engine exhaust gas will cause a brush fire.

The spark arrester must have the carbon deposits cleaned, or purged, from it. Some spark arresters have a removable end cap that is removed to clean out the carbon (Fig. 9-16). Other spark arresters have a small slot or hole covered by a removable plate (Fig. 11-6).

To purge the spark arrester, remove the coverplate from the lower back end of the muffler, as shown in Fig. 11-6. This opens the port from the spark arrester. Follow the procedure recommended by the manufacturer. One way is to start the engine and accelerate it rapidly about 20 times. Most of the carbon deposits will be blown out of the spark arrester through the open port with the exhaust gas. Then reinstall the coverplate.

CAUTION Do not attempt to remove the coverplate screws if the engine and exhaust system are hot. You can easily be burned. Never do this job close to combustible materials or gasoline. The hot sparks from the spark arrester could start a fire.

11-9 DECARBONING THE MUFFLER AND EXHAUST PIPE (TWO-CYCLE ENGINE)
The muffler and exhaust pipe also accumulate carbon and should have the carbon removed periodically. A typical recommendation is to do this job every 4000 miles [6000 km] on a street motorcycle. The service interval and procedure vary according to the exhaust-system design and how the motorcycle is used.

On one type, you must remove the inner pipe of the muffler (Fig. 9-16). Carbon can be cleaned from the inner pipe by tapping it lightly or by using a wire brush. If the carbon is too thick to come off easily, it can be burned off by carefully using a torch. Then wash the pipe in solvent.

The exhaust pipe (Fig. 9-16) can be cleaned with a long screwdriver or by pulling an old chain through it. A used speedometer cable in a drill motor also works well. Follow the procedures recommended in the manufacturers' service manuals for cleaning the various types of exhaust systems.

NOTE Do not operate the engine without the muffler. Removing the muffler cuts down on engine performance and may cause engine damage. Also, the excessive noise of the un-muffled engine is illegal.

11-10 CARBURETOR TROUBLE DIAGNOSIS

Various engine troubles and possible fuel-system causes of these troubles are discussed in Chap. 23. Engine troubles can come from many things besides problems in the fuel system. Many times the carburetor is blamed for troubles that are in the electric system. Check the ignition system first. In Chap. 23, on engine trouble diagnosis, we list and describe engine troubles and their possible causes. Now, let us focus on the carburetor and see what troubles can be related to conditions inside the carburetor itself.

1. Excessive fuel consumption can result from:
   a. A dirty air filter
   b. A high float level or a leaky float
   c. A sticking or dirty float needle valve
   d. A worn jet or needle
   e. Idle too rich or too fast
   f. A stuck accelerator-pump check valve
   g. A leaky carburetor
2. Lack of engine power, acceleration, or high-speed performance can result from:
   a. The needle not clearing the jet
   b. Dirt or gum clogging the fuel nozzle or jet
   c. A low float level
   d. A dirty air filter
   e. The choke stuck or not operating
   f. Air leaks into the manifold or port
   g. The throttle valve or slide valve not fully opening
   h. A rich mixture, due to causes listed under item 1, above
3. Poor idle can result from low compression, a leaky vacuum hose, a missing carburetor vacuum plug or cap, or retarded timing. It can also result from an incorrectly adjusted idle mixture or idle speed, a clogged idle system, or any of the causes listed under item 2, above.
4. Failure of the engine to start unless primed could be due to no gasoline in the fuel tank or carburetor, the wrong tank cap, or a clogged tank or cap vent. The last causes a vacuum to develop in the tank, which prevents delivery of fuel to the carburetor. Holes in the fuel-pump vacuum line may allow air leakage which prevents fuel delivery. In addition, carburetor jets or lines clogged, a defective choke, a clogged fuel filter, or air leaks into the manifold or port could prevent normal starting.
5. Hard starting with the engine warm could be due to a defective choke or a closed choke valve.
6. Slow engine warm-up could be due to a defectively operating choke.
7. A smoky, black exhaust is due to a very rich mixture. Carburetor conditions that could cause this are listed in item 1, above.
8. If the engine stalls as it warms up, this could be due to a defective choke or a closed choke valve.
9. If the engine stalls after a period of high-speed driving, this could be due to an improperly adjusted carburetor or linkage.
10. If the engine backfires, this could be due to an excessively rich or excessively lean mixture. If the backfire is in the exhaust system, it is usually caused by an excessively rich mixture in the exhaust gas. Lean mixtures usually cause a popback in the carburetor.
11. If the engine runs but misses, there may be a leaky carburetor, intake port, or intake-manifold gasket. Or it could be that the proper amount of the air-fuel mixture is not reaching the engine or that the air-fuel ratio is not right. This might be due to a clogged or worn carburetor jet or needle or to an incorrect fuel level in the float bowl.

Some of the conditions listed above can be corrected by carburetor adjustment. Others require removal of the carburetor from the engine so that it can be disassembled, repaired, and reassembled. Following sections discuss carburetor adjustments and servicing procedures.

11-11 CARBURETOR ADJUSTMENTS

The carburetor has the job of mixing air and gasoline vapor in the proper ratio to provide good engine operation. If the carburetor is properly adjusted to give this correct air-fuel ratio, it is not likely to go too far out of adjustment in normal operation. However, screws can loosen and throw the adjustment off. In addition, fuel lines and jets in the carburetor can clog. This can mean that a partial disassembly of the carburetor for cleaning is needed, which then requires a carburetor adjustment. Carburetor servicing is divided into two parts: (1) adjustments and (2) removal and rebuilding (see 11-13).

At one time, there were several adjustments that could be made on certain carburetors. However, in recent years emission-control laws have been passed which limit carburetor adjustments on street-legal motorcycles. The only procedure now recommended for late-model motorcycles during tuneup is adjustment of the idle speed.

The idle mixture is preset at the factory. The adjustment specifications are listed on an emission-control information decal which is located on the seat base or near the engine. The owner's manual and the service manual list the steps that must be followed. However, if some carburetor trouble has occurred which requires disassembling the carburetor, the idle mixture may be readjusted.

Correction of rough running on a motorcycle engine with multiple carburetors may require synchronization, or balancing, of the carburetors. This means adjusting the carburetors so that they are all delivering the same amount of the air-fuel mixture to each cylinder. The procedure may be performed on late-model motorcycles, if required.

To check the choke, operate the choke through the full operating range. It should move smoothly. Adjust the linkage, if necessary. Start the engine and allow it to

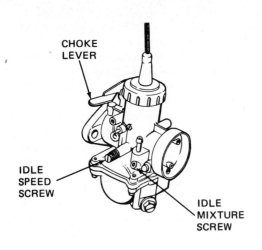

(a) SLIDE-VALVE CARBURETOR

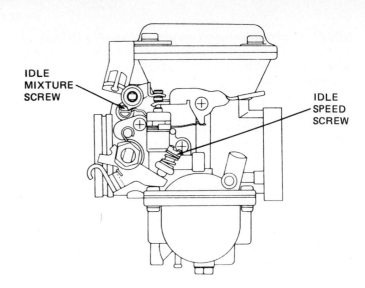

(b) CONSTANT-VACUUM CARBURETOR

Fig. 11-7 Locations of the idle-mixture screws and the idle-speed screws. (*Suzuki Motor Company, Ltd.; Yamaha International Corporation*)

warm up. With the engine idling, close the choke fully. If the engine does not stall, the choke probably is not closing completely.

If it is necessary to adjust the choke valve, check the clearance between the choke valve and the air horn with the choke valve fully closed. For example, on one model of motorcycle the clearance should be about 0.020 inch [0.5 mm].

The engine idle speed is checked and set with the engine warm and idling. The choke must be fully open. Find the specified idle speed for the engine by referring to the decal on the motorcycle, the owner's manual, or the manufacturer's service manual. Then check the tachometer to see if the idling speed is correct. The tachometer needle should be steady. Many motorcycle engines idle at about 1000 rpm. If the speed is not correct, adjust the *idle-speed screw* (also called the *throttle-stop screw*). On multiple-carburetor installations, turn all idle-speed screws equally. Typical locations of idle-speed screws are shown in Fig. 11-7.

Connect a vacuum gauge to each carburetor intake port and measure the vacuum at idle (Fig. 11-8). Each gauge should read within the range of 7.9 to 8.7 inches Hg [20 to 22 cm Hg]. No gauge needle should swing excessively. Adjustment is made by turning the *idle-mixture screw* (also called the *pilot air screw*) and the idle-speed screw. These are shown in Fig. 11-7.

Operate the throttle grip slowly and then rapidly to

Fig. 11-8 A vacuum-gauge set is used to adjust the carburetors. The fuel tank and the frame are not shown. (*Honda Motor Company, Ltd.*)

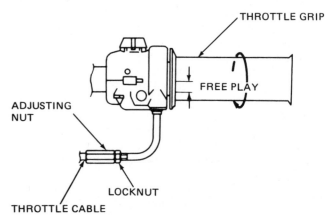

Fig. 11-9 Checking and adjusting the free play in the throttle cable. (*Yamaha International Corporation*)

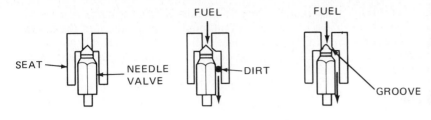

Fig. 11-10 Conditions of the needle and seat. Left, proper seating. Center, dirt holds the needle valve open. Right, a groove worn in the needle valve prevents it from closing completely. (*Suzuki Motor Company, Ltd.*)

see if the engine response is smooth. Perform the same check with the handlebar turned fully to the right and then to the left. If turning the handlebar causes a change in engine speed, the throttle cable is misrouted or improperly adjusted. Make the necessary corrections.

The throttle grip should have a certain amount of free play (Fig. 11-9). A typical specification is from ⅛ to ¼ inch [2 to 6 mm] of free play. If the free play is not within specifications, adjust the throttle cable. An adjusting nut and locknut are located at the end of the cable close to the throttle grip.

11-12 FLOAT ADJUSTMENT

Engine flooding indicates that something is probably wrong with the float system in the carburetor. That is why too much gasoline is getting into the engine. Sometimes you can see gasoline dripping from around the float-bowl gasket. A spark plug wet with gasoline may indicate that too much gasoline is running into the cylinder. On some carburetors, the float level can be set with a special gauge. Removing the float bowl is not required.

Usually, adjustment of the float level will correct a flooding problem. However, there are three other conditions to look for in the float system after removing the carburetor and the float bowl: (1) The needle valve may get dirt in it and be held open (Fig. 11-10, center). (2) The needle valve may get a groove worn in it so that the valve cannot close completely (Fig. 11-10, right). (3) The float itself may spring a leak (metal type) or get saturated (cork and plastic types) and sink to the bottom of the float bowl. This fully opens the needle valve.

Check the float to make sure it is in good condition. If it is of the hollow metal type, shake it to find if there is gasoline inside. If there is, the float is leaking and should be replaced. Also, make sure the needle valve can work freely in the valve seat. If the needle valve hangs, perhaps because of a dirt particle (Fig. 11-10,

center), the valve will not close completely. Fuel will continue to flow into the float bowl. This can cause an overrich mixture, which in turn could carbon the piston, piston rings, spark plugs, valves and ports, and exhaust system.

If none of the above conditions is causing the flooding, then the float should be adjusted so that the proper level of gasoline will be maintained in the float bowl. This adjustment is called *setting the float level*. Normally, this adjustment will not change. However, if the carburetor requires repair, then this adjustment should be checked.

The procedure of checking the float level on one model of slide-valve carburetor is shown in Fig. 11-11. The float should be parallel to the body mounting surface with the body gasket in place and the needle valve and float installed. If necessary, bend the tang on the float to bring the float to parallel.

Measure the distance from the top of each float to the gasket surface on the air horn (A in Fig. 11-11). Some manufacturers require that the float-bowl gasket be in place when this measurement is taken. Bend the float tang as necessary until the correct measurement is obtained. The specification for the correct float level is given in the manufacturer's service manual. Note that the float shown in Fig. 11-11 has two chambers. In carburetors that have a float with a single chamber, the adjustment of the float level is the same.

11-13 CARBURETOR REBUILDING

Carburetors are often blamed for engine problems that they don't cause. Be sure that an internal carburetor problem is indicated before completely disassembling the carburetor. When overhauling a carburetor, disassemble it only as much as is necessary for proper cleaning.

Disassembly and assembly procedures on carburetors vary according to the type of carburetor. In gen-

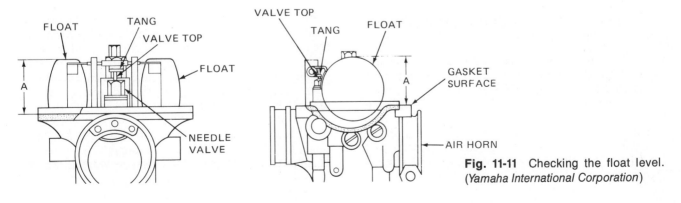

Fig. 11-11 Checking the float level. (*Yamaha International Corporation*)

eral, all slide-valve carburetors are disassembled similarly. Most constant-vacuum carburetors also are disassembled similarly. The manufacturer's procedure for disassembly and rebuilding should be carefully followed. On motorcycle carburetors, few special tools are required.

Complete carburetor overhaul or repair kits are available for many carburetors. These kits contain all the parts required (gaskets, washers, etc.) to overhaul the carburetor. The kit, properly installed, should restore the carburetor to its original performance. However, cleaning a carburetor can be done using only a gasket set. It is much cheaper than the kit and may be all that is needed. Other carburetor parts, such as a scored slide valve, will have to be obtained separately, perhaps through special-ordering by the parts department in a motorcycle dealership.

CAUTION When removing and handling a carburetor, be extremely careful to avoid spilling gasoline. The carburetor float bowl will have gasoline in it, so keep the carburetor upright. Gasoline is extremely flammable. Any gasoline that is spilled should be wiped up immediately. Put the gasoline-soaked towels outside the building in a safe area to dry.

Disassembly and assembly procedures on carburetors vary according to their design. What follows are general service procedures used on most carburetors:

1. Disassemble the carburetor. Note carefully the position of each part as it is removed. Place the parts in small pans. A completely disassembled slide-valve carburetor is shown in Fig. 10-13. Exploded views of other carburetors are shown in the manufacturer's service manuals.
2. Thoroughly clean the carburetor castings and metal parts in clean solvent. Be sure that both the inside and the outside of the castings are clean.

CAUTION Do not splash solvent or other carburetor cleaner in your eyes. It can seriously harm them. Wear goggles to protect your eyes.
Never soak any fiber, rubber, or plastic parts in carburetor cleaner. Wipe these parts with a clean, dry shop towel.

3. Blow off all parts with air until they are dry. Blow out all passages in the castings with compressed air. Make sure all jets and passages are clean. Do not use drills or wires for cleaning out fuel passages or air bleeds. This may enlarge the openings. Instead, clean out the openings with a chemical cleaner.

CAUTION Use the air hose with care. Wear goggles while blowing out the carburetor.

4. Check all parts for damage and wear. If damage or wear is noted, the part or assembly must be replaced. Check the float needle and seat for wear. Check the float hinge pin for wear and the floats for dents or distortion. Shake metal floats to see if they have water or fuel in them. Slide valves that are scored or burned should be replaced. Check the throttle-shaft and choke-shaft bores for wear and out-of-roundness.

5. Inspect the idle-mixture screw for burrs or grooves. These conditions require replacement of the screw.
6. Check the inside of the float bowl for dirt and water. Corrosion or deep pits require replacement of the float bowl.
7. Carefully inspect the main jet, jet needle, throttle valve, and air horn. If any parts are loose or damaged, replace them. Inspect all gasket mating surfaces for nicks or burrs. Repair any damage to the gasket mating surfaces. Inspect the remaining carburetor parts for damage or excess looseness. Replace any parts that are worn, damaged, or excessively loose.
8. Be sure your hands, the workbench, and your tools are clean. Then assemble the carburetor in proper order. Install all the gaskets and parts contained in the overhaul kit.
9. Use a new gasket to assure a good seal between the carburetor and the intake port. Put the carburetor into position and attach it with the nuts or bolts. Connect the fuel line and any other lines to the carburetor. Install the air cleaner. Make the idle-speed, idle-mixture, and other adjustments as described in ☑ 11-11.

☑11-14
☑FUEL-INJECTION SYSTEM TROUBLE DIAGNOSIS
Always make a complete and thorough visual inspection before attempting to check out or service the fuel-injection system using tools or test instruments. The two major problems to look for when inspecting the fuel-injection system are fuel leaks and air leaks. Either of these can cause driveability problems, as well as engine damage and excessive emissions. A fuel leak is a fire hazard.

1. Fuel leaks. Check carefully that there are no fuel leaks from any fuel line, from any connection, or from around the electric fuel pump (see Fig. 10-31). Layers of dirt may make fuel leaks and their sources difficult to find. New hose and fittings should be installed to replace any that leak. Clean all fuel-line connections thoroughly before they are opened.
2. Air leaks. No air leaks must occur in the air-intake system. Air leaks cause an excessively lean air-fuel mixture to be delivered to the cylinders. This is because air drawn in through the leak is not metered by the air-flow sensor. Replace any defective hoses, gaskets, or other parts.

Figure 11-12 is a trouble diagnosis chart for the Kawasaki electronic fuel-injection system. The chart lists the more frequent complaints and their possible causes. Many of the checks or corrections to be made are self-explanatory and can be performed quickly and easily. Others required the use of testers, and reference to the manufacturer's service manual.

One of the biggest problems in working with electronic fuel injection is to locate and identify each component of the system on the motorcycle. The trouble diagnosis chart (Fig. 11-12) tells you what to check. Information on how to check each component is in the

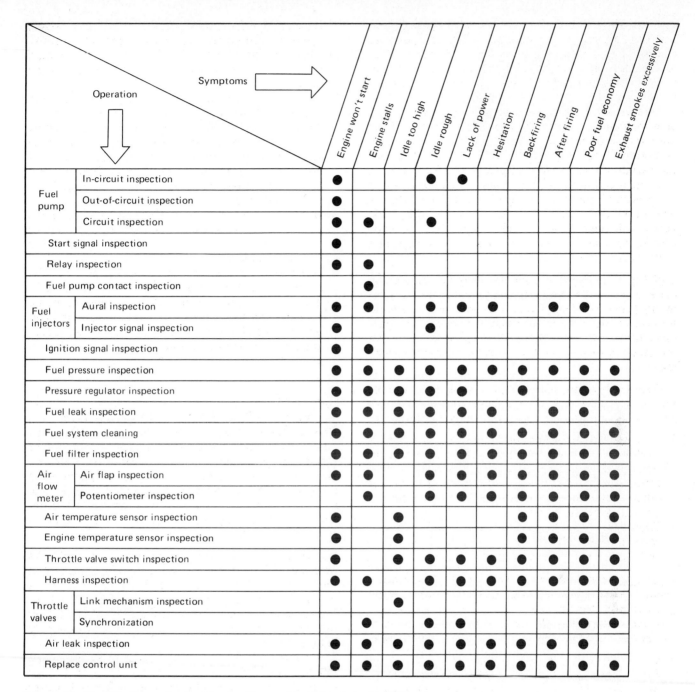

Operation		Engine won't start	Engine stalls	Idle too high	Idle rough	Lack of power	Hesitation	Backfiring	After firing	Poor fuel economy	Exhaust smokes excessively
Fuel pump	In-circuit inspection	●			●	●					
	Out-of-circuit inspection	●									
	Circuit inspection	●	●		●						
Start signal inspection		●									
Relay inspection		●	●								
Fuel pump contact inspection			●								
Fuel injectors	Aural inspection	●	●		●	●	●		●	●	
	Injector signal inspection	●			●						
Ignition signal inspection		●	●								
Fuel pressure inspection		●	●	●	●	●	●	●	●	●	●
Pressure regulator inspection		●	●	●	●	●		●		●	●
Fuel leak inspection		●	●	●	●	●	●			●	●
Fuel system cleaning		●	●	●	●	●	●	●	●	●	●
Fuel filter inspection		●	●	●	●	●	●	●	●	●	●
Air flow meter	Air flap inspection	●	●		●	●	●	●	●	●	●
	Potentiometer inspection		●		●	●	●	●	●	●	●
Air temperature sensor inspection		●		●				●	●	●	●
Engine temperature sensor inspection		●		●				●	●	●	●
Throttle valve switch inspection		●		●	●	●	●	●	●	●	●
Harness inspection		●	●		●	●	●	●	●	●	●
Throttle valves	Link mechanism inspection			●							
	Synchronization		●		●	●				●	●
Air leak inspection		●	●	●	●	●	●	●	●	●	
Replace control unit		●	●	●	●	●	●	●	●	●	●

Fig. 11-12 Trouble diagnosis chart for the Kawasaki electronic fuel-injection system. (*Kawasaki Motors Corporation*)

manufacturer's service manual. Figure 10-29 shows where each component is located on the motorcycle.

After performing any service on or repairing an electronic fuel-injection system, the ignition timing, idle speed, and idle mixture should be checked. They should be readjusted, if necessary, before returning the motorcycle to the customer.

The solenoid-operated injection valve in electronic fuel-injection systems can be checked with an ignition oscilloscope. Special fuel-injection scopes and special probes for other ignition scopes are available for this purpose. However, a quick check of the fuel-injector operation can usually be made with almost any type of shop scope.

To hook up the scope, first connect the proper primary lead to ground. Then connect the fuel-injection probe, or other primary lead, to the electric terminal on the injector. Figure 11-13 shows a typical pattern during operation of the injection valve. Any variation from this basic pattern indicates trouble.

The operation of the fuel injector can also be checked with a shop stethoscope or with a long screwdriver.

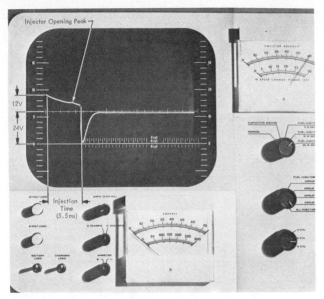

Fig. 11-13 Typical scope pattern showing the operation of the fuel injector. (*Autoscan, Inc.*)

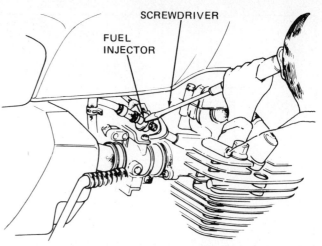

Fig. 11-14 Using a screwdriver to listen for the clicking sound from the injector. (*Kawasaki Motors Corporation*)

Place the tip of the screwdriver against an injector, as shown in Fig. 11-14. Put your ear against the top of the handle and listen. You should hear the injector making a clicking sound at regular intervals. The faster the engine is running, the shorter the time between clicks. This indicates that the injector is good. Now perform the same test on the other injectors. If the engine won't start, the injectors can be checked while cranking the engine with the starting motor.

Remove the electric connectors from the injectors, and connect a test light from the connector terminal to ground. Now crank the engine and watch the light. If the light flickers at regular intervals, the wiring is good. If the light flickers, but the injector does not make a clicking sound, install a new fuel injector. If the light does not flicker while cranking the engine, the wiring and connectors must be checked. If no problem is found, the injection signal must be checked.

CHAPTER 11
REVIEW QUESTIONS

1. How can dirt and water in the gasoline cause an engine to stop?
2. Where is the air cleaner located on most motorcycles?
3. How is the polyurethane air-filter element cleaned?
4. When no fuel flows from the fuel line to the carburetor, what is the first check that you make?
5. How do you check the air vent in the fuel-tank cap?
6. Describe how to check a fuel pump.
7. What is meant by *purging the spark arrester?*
8. Explain how to decarbon the muffler and exhaust pipe on a two-cycle engine.
9. List the conditions that can cause excessive fuel consumption.
10. What is the only adjustment that can be made today on carburetors on late-model motorcycles?
11. Explain how to check the choke.
12. What is wrong when the engine speed increases as the handlebars are turned to the right or left?
13. List three problems to look for in the float system.
14. Explain how to check and set the float level.
15. What is the difference between a carburetor repair kit and a carburetor gasket set?
16. How do you clean the plastic and rubber parts of a carburetor?

CHAPTER 12

EXHAUST EMISSIONS AND AIR POLLUTION

After studying this chapter,
you should be able to:

1. Explain what smog is and where the name comes from.

2. Discuss air pollution and the harm it can cause.

3. Describe the pollutants that come from motorcycles and list those that are legally limited.

4. Explain what the crankcase emission system is and how it works.

5. Discuss exhaust emission control systems and explain how they work.

6. Describe evaporative control systems and explain how they work.

12-1 SMOG

Exhaust emissions is another name for the air pollutants in the engine exhaust gas. Exhaust emissions from internal combustion engines can cause smog.

The word *smog* comes from *smoke* and *fog*. Smog is a sort of fog with other substances mixed into it. Smog has been around for a long time. Billions of years ago, when our earth was young, there were many volcanoes. They sent millions of tons of ash and smoke into the air. Winds whipped up clouds of dust. Animal and vegetable matter decayed and sent polluting gases into the air.

When humans came along, they began to produce their own kind of air pollution. At one time, people in cities (London, for example) burned soft coal to heat their homes. The smoke from their fires combined with moisture in the air to produce dense layers of smog. The smog would blanket the cities for days, particularly in winter. The heat generated in large cities tends to produce air circulation within a dome-like shape (Fig. 12-1). This traps the smog and holds it over the city.

Smog and the substances in it can be harmful—even deadly. Smog blurs vision. It irritates the eyes, the throat, and the lungs. Eyes water, throats get sore, and people cough. Smog can make people ill, and it can make sick people sicker.

Air pollution has been linked to such human ills as eczema, asthma, emphysema, cardiovascular difficulties, and lung and stomach cancer. It also has a harmful effect on the environment. Food crops and animals suffer. Paint may peel from houses. Scientists tell us that we must do everything possible to reduce people-made atmospheric pollutants and smog. This includes reducing atmospheric pollution caused by motorcycles.

12-2 AIR POLLUTANTS

Smog, along with smoke, is the most visible evidence of atmospheric pollution. But some atmospheric pollution is not visible and may not become visible until it is mixed with moisture. Lead compounds from leaded gasoline, hydrocarbons (unburned gasoline), carbon monoxide, and other gases may pollute the air without being seen.

All air is polluted to some extent. It carries some polluting substances. Many of the pollutants come from natural causes, such as smoke and ash from volcanoes, dust stirred up by the wind, compounds given off by growing vegetation, gases given off by rotting animal and vegetable matter, and salt particles from the oceans.

People add to these pollutants by burning coal, oil, gas, gasoline, and many other things. It is these added substances that we are concerned with in this chapter—especially those that come from the motorcycle.

Before we discuss the motorcycle, however, let us review the combustion process. Most fuels, such as coal, oil, gasoline, and wood, contain hydrogen and carbon in various chemical combinations. During combustion, oxygen from the air unites with the hydrogen and carbon to form water (H_2O), carbon monoxide (CO), and carbon dioxide (CO_2).

In addition, many fuels contain sulfur, which produces sulfur oxides (SO_x) when it burns. Also, in the heat of combustion, some of the nitrogen in the air combines with oxygen to form nitrogen oxides (NO_x). Some of the fuel may not burn completely. Then, smoke and ash are formed. Smoke is particles of unburned fuel and soot (called *particulates*) mixed with air.

All together, it is estimated that 200 million tons of pollutants enter the air every year in the United States alone. This is about 2000 pounds [907 kg] for every man, woman, and child in the country!

The clean-air laws are aimed at the pollution that is created by people.

12-3 POLLUTION FROM THE MOTORCYCLE

If not controlled, the motorcycle can give off pollutants from four places (Fig. 12-2). Pollutants can escape from

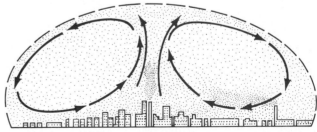

Fig. 12-1 The heat generated within a large city tends to produce a circulatory air pattern which traps smog within a "dome."

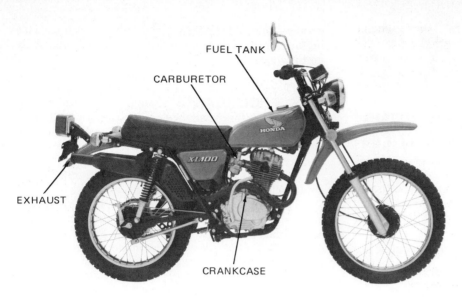

FUEL TANK

CARBURETOR

EXHAUST

CRANKCASE

Fig. 12-2 Sources of air pollution from a motorcycle. (*Honda Motor Company, Ltd.*)

the fuel tank, the carburetor, the crankcase, and the exhaust system. The fuel tank and the carburetor emit gasoline vapor. The crankcase of a four-cycle engine gives off partly burned air-fuel mixture that has blown by the piston rings. The pollutants coming from the exhaust system are partly burned gasoline (HC), carbon monoxide (CO), nitrogen oxides (NO_x), and—if there is sulfur in the gasoline—sulfur oxides (SO_x).

HC and CO appear in the exhaust gases because of incomplete combustion of the fuel (HC) in the engine cylinders. The high combustion temperature produces the nitrogen oxides (NO_x).

Automobiles must meet the emission standards for all three of the pollutants (HC, CO, and NO_x). However, the total emissions of NO_x from all motorcycles is so small that the Environmental Protection Agency (EPA) does not plan to set a standard for it. The requirement is that all street-legal motorcycles with an engine displacement larger than 49 cc manufactured on or after January 1, 1978, must meet federal standards for hydrocarbon (HC) and carbon monoxide (CO) emissions. Off-road and racing motorcycles are unaffected by these emission standards.

The emission regulations divide all street-legal motorcycles into three categories based on engine size. There is a different set of standards for each engine

displacement of 1978 and 1979 models. The categories are

50 to 169 cc
170 to 749 cc
750 cc and larger

Figure 12-3 is a chart showing the 1978-79 and 1980 emission limits for each size of motorcycle, based on the engine displacement. To meet these emission limits, most 1978 and later-model motorcycles with four-cycle engines are equipped with a crankcase emission-control system and an exhaust emission-control system. Many two-cycle engines have so much unburned gasoline (HC) in the exhaust gas that they cannot meet the standards. This is why the motorcycle manufacturers have been phasing out two-cycle engines in street-legal motorcycles.

**12-4
CRANKCASE EMISSION-CONTROL SYSTEMS** The crankcase is the lower part of the engine, the part that contains the crankshaft. The bottom of the crankcase (in many four-cycle engines) holds the engine oil. In operation, the lubricating system (Chap. 14) sends oil from the crankcase or oil tank to all moving parts in the engine.

	Engine displacement	Emissions, grams per mile [g/km]	
		Hydrocarbons (HC)	Carbon monoxide (CO)
1978–1979	50–169 cc	8.0 [5.0]	27.4 [17.0]
	170–749 cc	8.0*–22.5 [5.0–14.0]	27.4 [17.0]
	750 cc and larger	22.5 [14.0]	27.4 [17.0]
1980	All motorcycles 50 cc and larger	8.0 [5.0]	19.3 [12.0]

*This number depends on engine displacement.

Fig. 12-3 The emission limits for motorcycles. (*Suzuki Motor Company, Ltd.*)

The crankcase must be ventilated. During engine operation, some of the air-fuel mixture and burned gases leak down into the crankcase past the piston rings. This is called *blowby* because the gases "blow by" the rings. In addition, water and liquid fuel appear in the crankcase during cold-engine operation. All of these must be cleared from the crankcase before they cause trouble. In earlier engines, the crankcase was ventilated by an opening or a vent tube. Since 1978 closed-crankcase systems have been used on all street-legal four-cycle motorcycle engines. Instead of being discharged into the air, crankcase vapors are carried by a tube to the air cleaner and carburetor. Any blowby, water vapor, or unburned fuel is sent back through the engine to be burned.

NOTE A separate crankcase emission-control system is not required on a two-cycle engine. Two-cycle engines already have a sealed crankcase. Any blowby gas mixes with the fresh air-fuel mixture and is carried with it into the cylinder.

Unless the water, gasoline, and blowby are removed from the crankcase (in four-cycle engines), sludge and acids will form. Sludge can clog oil lines and prevent oil from getting to the engine parts. This could mean a ruined engine. Also, if no vent is provided, blowby will cause a pressure buildup in the crankcase. If the pressure is not relieved, it will cause oil leaks as it forces the oil out past the gaskets and seals.

A typical closed type of crankcase emission-control system for a motorcycle engine is shown in Fig. 12-4. Here's how the system works. The blowby gas escapes past the piston and rings into the crankcase. As the crankcase fills up, the blowby travels through the openings in the cylinder and collects in the valve cover. A

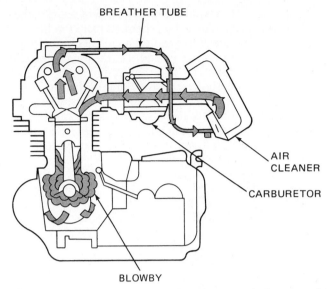

Fig. 12-4 A typical closed type of crankcase emission-control system. (*Kawasaki Heavy Industries, Ltd.*)

breather tube from the valve cover carries the blowby gas to the air cleaner. There the blowby gas is picked up and carried into the engine by the fresh air entering the air cleaner.

Sometimes oil vapor and mist can be carried along with the blowby gas. The oil will collect on the air filter and clog it, resulting in an excessively rich air-fuel mixture entering the cylinder. To prevent this problem, the system shown in Fig. 12-4 separates the oil from the blowby gas by the way the blowby gas is routed from the crankcase to the air cleaner.

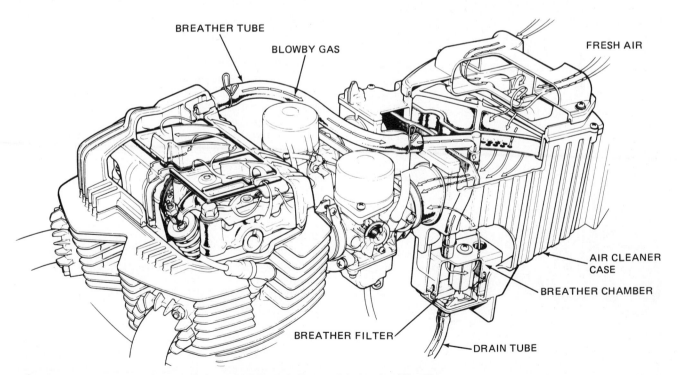

Fig. 12-5 A crankcase control system using a breather filter and drain tube. (*Honda Motor Company, Ltd.*)

Figure 12-5 shows another system in which a breather chamber is used. The oil is separated from the blowby gas by the breather filter and then collects in the drain tube. Then when service is required, the plug in the end of the tube is removed and the accumulated oil (and sometimes water) is drained out. Some drain tubes have a transparent section, so that you can tell by a quick visual inspection if draining is necessary. In general, positive-crankcase-ventilating (PCV) valves, used on automobile engines, are not installed on motorcycle engines.

12-5 EXHAUST EMISSION-CONTROL SYSTEMS
In an engine there are three methods of cleaning the exhaust gas (Fig. 12-2):

1. Controlling the air-fuel mixture
2. Controlling combustion
3. Treating the exhaust gas

Methods 2 and 3 are widely used on automobile engines. As yet, only method 1, controlling the air-fuel mixture, has been required on motorcycle engines.

Basically, controlling the air-fuel mixture means modifying the carburetor to deliver a leaner air-fuel mixture. The major change has been in the elimination of carburetor-mixture adjustments. Now the carburetor is preset at the factory by specialized test equipment. Only the idle-speed screw may be adjusted on 1978 and later model motorcycles. Carburetors are discussed in detail in Chap. 10.

On two-cycle engines, exhaust emissions may be increased by the use of the wrong type of oil. Also, the engine may be damaged when the wrong type of oil or the wrong oil-fuel ratio is used. This could happen because the carburetor jetting is leaner, which tends to raise the heat of combustion. The heat could cause the wrong oil to fail to provide adequate lubrication, and the engine could be damaged.

Some two-cycle engines have trouble meeting exhaust-emission standards. Motorcycle manufacturers have taken many steps to keep their new two-cycle engines within the exhaust-emission limits. For example, on one model of 250-cc motorcycle, Suzuki made the following changes:

1. Installed a close-tolerance carburetor with leaner jetting
2. Changed the port timing
3. Modified the shape of the piston
4. Increased the oil-pump volume
5. Lowered the compression ratio
6. Modified the design of the cylinder head
7. Installed a longer-reach spark plug
8. Made a smaller front fender to increase cooling
9. Modified the secondary muffler
10. Changed the first-gear ratio

In addition, the setup and tuneup specifications and procedures were changed. Without all these changes, the motorcycle would not meet exhaust-emissions standards and could not be sold in the United States.

12-6 EVAPORATIVE CONTROL SYSTEMS
Both the fuel tank and the carburetor can lose gasoline vapor if the vehicle has no control system (Fig. 12-2). The fuel tank "breathes" as temperature changes. As the tank heats up, the air inside it expands. Some air is forced out through the tank vent tube or through the vent in the tank cap. This air is loaded with gasoline vapor. Then, when the tank cools, the air inside it contracts, and air enters the tank from outside.

This breathing of the tank causes a loss of gasoline vapor. The higher the tank temperature goes (for example, when the motorcycle is parked in the sun), the more gasoline vapor is lost.

The carburetor can also lose gasoline by evaporation. The carburetor float bowl is full whenever the engine is running. When the engine stops, engine heat evaporates some or all of the gasoline stored in the float bowl. Without an evaporative control system, this gasoline vapor would escape into the atmosphere.

An evaporative control system captures these gasoline vapors and prevents them from escaping into the air. It thereby helps to reduce atmospheric pollution. All modern cars are equipped with evaporative control systems.

Motorcycles are not now required to have an evaporative control system. However, the use of such systems on motorcycles has been proposed. Basically, the evaporative control system collects the gasoline vapors and stores them while the engine is off. When the engine is started the vapors are routed into the cylinder and burned. Some motorcycles are equipped with a special sealed fuel cap that prevents vapor loss through it.

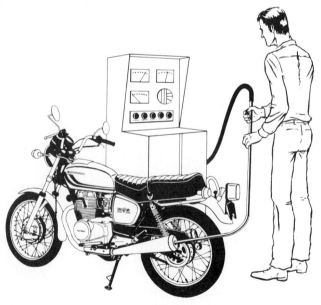

Fig. 12-6 Using an infrared exhaust-gas analyzer to check the pollutants in the exhaust gas from a motorcycle engine. (*ATW*)

12-7 EXHAUST-GAS ANALYZER

At one time, the major use of the early type of exhaust-gas analyzer was to adjust the carburetor on cars. It is still used for that purpose. However, today a newer type of infrared exhaust-gas analyzer has the added job of checking the operation and effectiveness of the emission controls on the car. Their main purpose is to cut down on carbon monoxide (CO), hydrocarbons (HC), and oxides of nitrogen (NO_x) in the exhaust gas. The infrared type of exhaust-gas analyzer can also be used in the same way to check the exhaust-gas emissions from the motorcycle.

Figure 12-6 shows an infrared type of exhaust-gas analyzer. It is used by sticking a pickup tube or probe into the exhaust pipe of the motorcycle (Fig. 12-6). The probe draws out some of the exhaust gas and carries it through the analyzer. Two dials on the face of the analyzer (Fig. 12-7) tell you how much HC and CO are in the exhaust gas. The HC meter shows parts per million (ppm). The CO meter reports a percentage. Federal, state, and local laws set the maximum legal limits on the amount of HC and CO permitted in the exhaust gas of a vehicle.

A different kind of tester is required for NO_x, but it works in the same general way. It draws exhaust gas from the exhaust pipe and runs the gas through the analzyer. The result is reported in terms of the amount of NO_x in the exhaust gas. Generally, NO_x testers are available only in testing laboratories. They are not used today in either automotive or motorcycle service shops.

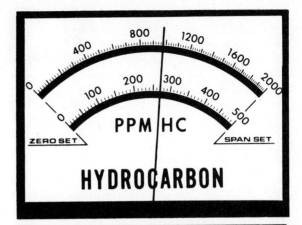
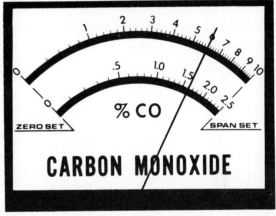

Fig. 12-7 Typical HC and CO meter faces on an infrared exhaust-gas analyzer. (*Sun Electric Corporation*)

CHAPTER 12
REVIEW QUESTIONS

1. What is smog?
2. What causes air pollution?
3. What pollutants can the motorcycle produce?
4. What is the crankcase emission-control system and how does it work?
5. How can emissions in the exhaust gas be controlled?
6. What is the evaporative control system and how does it work?

CHAPTER 13

MOTORCYCLE ENGINE OILS

After studying this chapter,
you should be able to:

1. Explain the purpose of engine oil in four-cycle and two-cycle engines.

2. Describe the oil for four-cycle engines.

3. Discuss oil viscosity and the viscosity ratings.

4. Explain oil-service ratings.

5. Discuss the oil additives used in four-cycle-engine oil.

6. Discuss the two different types of oil used in two-cycle engines and explain why they are different.

13-1
PURPOSE OF ENGINE OIL Engine oil flows in slippery layers onto engine parts, preventing metal-to-metal contact. Metal-to-metal contact would cause heat and very rapid wear; engine parts could be ruined in a few minutes. The oil greatly reduces friction and wear between moving parts. Friction is discussed in 7-8 and 7-17. In addition, engine oil

1. Removes heat from the engine (four-cycle engines). In four-cycle engines, the oil circulates between the hot engine parts and the cool oil pan or reservoir. Therefore, it continuously removes heat from the engine.

2. Absorbs shock between bearings and other engine parts. Layers of oil between metal parts, such as rotating journals and bearings, resist squeezing out when loads are applied. The layers act as cushions to absorb shock loads (for example, when combustion starts and pressures suddenly go up).

3. Forms a seal between the piston rings and the cylinder wall. The oil fills up little irregularities in the cylinder wall. It also clings to the cylinder wall and piston rings to form a good seal.

4. Acts as a cleaning agent (in four-cycle engines). The oil circulates between the engine's moving parts and the oil pan or reservoir. It picks up particles of carbon and other dirt and carries it to the oil pan or reservoir. Therefore, the oil acts as a cleaning agent.

13-2
ENGINE OIL There are four basic types of oil: animal, vegetable, mineral, and synthetic. The difference is in the source of the raw material from which the oil is refined. In the motorcycle engine, mineral oil and synthetic oil are the most frequently used. In addition, engine oil for four-cycle engines is different from

the oil for two-cycle engines. We cover these two types of oil in later sections. Most of the engine oil used today is made from natural crude oil (called petroleum). Petroleum comes from oil wells drilled deep into the earth. Petroleum must be refined to make gasoline, kerosene, lubricating oil, and many other products.

In recent years, synthetic oils have been introduced. These are claimed to have superior lubricating properties. Actually, there are three basic types of synthetic oils. The type most widely used at present is produced from organic acids and alcohols (from plants of various types). A second type is made from coal and crude oil. A third type is made from crude oil.

Four-cycle engines usually use lubricating oil refined from crude oil. Some two-cycle engines using oil-injection systems use synthetic oils. One claim made for synthetic oil is that it does not leave carbon deposits in the combustion chamber or on the spark plug. However, a synthetic oil may not mix with a petroleum-base oil. This can cause trouble. To use such an oil in an engine previously run on petroleum-base oil, you must drain all the old oil and flush out the engine with a suitable flushing oil.

13-3
OIL FOR FOUR-CYCLE ENGINES Oil for four-cycle engines has certain special characteristics and additives that are not important for two-cycle–engine oil. These include viscosity, service ratings, and the special chemicals (additives) put into the oil.

13-4
OIL VISCOSITY Viscosity refers to the ability of a liquid to flow. An oil with high viscosity is very thick and flows slowly. An oil with low viscosity flows easily. Oil gets thicker when cold. This is why it is harder to start an engine in cold weather. The cold increases the viscosity of the oil.

Oil viscosity is rated in two ways by the Society of Automotive Engineers (SAE). It is rated for (1) winter driving and for (2) summer driving. Winter-grade oils come in three grades: SAE 5W, SAE 10W, and SAE 20W. The "W" stands for "winter grade." The viscosity grade for "W" oils is determined by testing at $-0.4°F [-18°C]$. For other than winter use, the grades are SAE 20, SAE 30, SAE 40, and SAE 50. These oils are tested at $212°F [100°C]$. The higher the number, the higher the viscosity (the thicker the oil). All these grades are called single-viscosity oils.

Many oils have multiple-viscosity ratings. For example, SAE 10W-40 has the same viscosity as SAE 10W when it is cold and the same viscosity as SAE 40 when it is hot.

The engine manufacturer specifies the viscosity of oil for the engine. For example, for a certain four-cycle engine Honda recommends the use of SAE 10W-40 oil. But if that oil is not available, then the recommendations shown in Fig. 13-1 can be followed. The table shows how outside temperature affects the viscosity of oil that an engine needs. If you study the table, you will see that the higher the outside temperature, the higher the viscosity rating specified.

The 10W oil is good for starting and riding in very low outside temperatures. If higher temperatures are expected, a 20 or 20W oil should be used because it will hold its viscosity in the higher temperatures. A 20 or 20W oil will not thin out too much as it heats up. For riding in outside temperatures above 50°F [15°C], SAE 30 oil should be used.

13-5
SERVICE RATINGS
The service rating indicates the type of service for which the oil is best suited. For four-cycle gasoline engines, the service ratings are SA, SB, SC, SD, SE, and SF. Here is a brief description of each of these ratings:

SA Acceptable for engines operated under the mildest conditions

SB Acceptable for minimum-duty engines operated under mild conditions

SC Meets requirements of gasoline engines in 1964–1967 model passenger cars and trucks

SD Meets requirements of gasoline engines in 1968–1970 model passenger cars and some trucks

SE Meets requirements of gasoline engines in 1972 and later cars and certain 1971 model passenger cars and trucks

SF Meets requirements of gasoline engines in 1980 and later passenger cars and some trucks.

You will notice that this is an "open-end" series. If the engine manufacturers and oil producers see the need for other types of oil, they can bring out SG and SH service-rated oils.

Four-cycle-engine manufacturers recommend the use of a high-detergent oil. A high-detergent oil is designated by HD on the can or bottle. Here HD means *high detergency,* as well as *heavy duty.* See 13-6 for an explanation of *detergent.*

NOTE Do not confuse the viscosity and the service ratings of oil. A high-viscosity oil is not necessarily a heavy-duty oil. Viscosity ratings refer to the thickness of the oil. Thickness is not a measure of heavy-duty quality. Each engine oil has two ratings, viscosity and service. Therefore, SAE 10 oil can be an SC, SD, or SE oil. Likewise, an oil of any other viscosity rating can have any of the service ratings.

Figure 13-2 shows the recommendations of Harley-Davidson for the oil to use in their (four-cycle) motorcycle engines. Notice that the chart shows the grades of oil as 75, 58, and 105. These are not the SAE grades. They are testing-laboratory grades stated in Saybolt Universal Seconds (SUS). The number given by

Above 59°F [15°C]	SAE 30
32° to 59°F [0° to 15°C]	SAE 20 or 20W
Below 32°F [0°C]	SAE 10W

Fig. 13-1 A chart showing how the viscosity selection of an engine oil is based on the outside temperature in which the motorcycle will be ridden. (*Honda Motor Company, Ltd.*)

Harley-Davidson is the time in seconds that it takes 60 milliliters of the oil at a temperature of 210°F [99°C] to flow through a small calibrated hole in a special tester.

In Fig. 13-2, we have inserted in parentheses the equivalent SAE grade for each oil. If the use of a multi-viscosity oil is preferred in a Harley-Davidson, an SAE 20W-50 four-cycle motorcycle oil can be used.

13-6
OIL ADDITIVES
Certain chemical compounds, called *additives,* are added to the oil. The purpose of these additives is to give the oil special properties it does not have in its original refined state. Additives put into oil for four-cycle engines include the following:

1. Viscosity improver. This compound lessens the tendency for the oil to thin out as it gets cold. This is the compound that gives oil a multiple-viscosity rating, such as SAE 10W-40.

2. Pour-point depressants. These compounds help the oil flow at low temperatures. They depress the tendency of the oil to thicken.

3. Inhibitors. These are compounds that fight corrosion, rust, and oil oxidation.

4. Antifoaming compound. This compound fights foaming of the oil in the crankcase. Foam would put air in the lubricating system and this would block oil circulation; then, serious trouble caused by wear could occur.

5. Detergent dispersants. These compounds prevent dirt or other harmful substances from depositing on engine parts. The detergent acts like soap and, in effect, washes foreign substances from the engine parts. The dispersant prevents the particles from clotting and forming large particles which could clog the system and prevent normal oil circulation. The oil filter in the lubricating system removes these particles as the oil circulates through it.

6. Extreme-pressure compounds. Today's engines are built with heavy valve springs that put high pressure on the valve-train parts. Combustion pressures are also high. The extreme-pressure compounds added to oil help to resist the very high pressure between the engine

Harley-Davidson oil	Use grade	Air temperature (cold engine starting conditions)
Medium heavy	75 (SAE 40)	Above 40°F [4.4°C]
Special light	58 (SAE 20W-20)	Below 40°F [4.4°C]
Regular heavy	105 (SAE 50)	Severe operating conditions at high temperatures

Fig. 13-2 A chart showing the oil to use in a Harley-Davidson motorcycle engine. (*Harley-Davidson Motor Company*)

Fig. 13-3 A plastic 1-quart bottle of two-cycle motorcycle engine oil. A fuel-oil ratio mixing chart is printed on the back of the bottle. The sides of the bottle are marked in pints, fluid ounces, and cubic centimeters to aid in proper mixing. (*Quaker State Oil Refining Corporation*)

parts. The extreme-pressure additives fight *squeezing out* by furnishing lubrication even during extreme pressures.

13-7 TWO-CYCLE MOTORCYCLE ENGINE OIL

Two-cycle engines use a *total-loss* lubricating system. In this system, the oil is not recovered, as it is in four-cycle engines, but is burned in the combustion chamber. For this reason, the lubricating oil used in two-cycle engines does not need all of the additives listed in ⌦ 13-6. Two-cycle oil must be clean burning and leave a minimum of ash and carbon deposits. Special oils and some synthetic oils (see ⌦ 13-2) have been developed for two-cycle motorcycle engines.

There are two different types of two-cycle–engine lubricating systems (⌦ 14-2). In one, the oil is mixed with the gasoline (premixed). In the other, the oil is injected into the air-fuel mixture as it flows into the engine. These two types of two-cycle lubricating systems require two different types of oil. Both oils are basically similar because both oils have the same job to do. However, the oil for use in injector systems is different from the oil used as a premix. Here is the reason for the difference.

When the oil is mixed with the gasoline in the fuel tank, the oil is diluted with the gasoline. It is not affected by the outside temperature. But in the injector system, the oil is stored in a separate tank. In cold weather, the oil can get so cold that it gets thick and will not flow properly. Therefore, in making the injector oil, solvent is added. The oil flows easier and the injector system functions better in cold weather. This oil is called a *prediluted oil*.

Not all motorcycle manufacturers allow the use of prediluted oils in their two-cycle engines with oil injection. For example, in some dirt bikes Suzuki recommends the use of their own brand of two-cycle injector oil. If it is not available, then a nondiluted two-cycle oil of good quality should be used. Yamaha recommends their brand of oil. If that brand of oil is not available, then any brand of two-cycle oil with the designation BIA TC-W on the container may be used. BIA TC-W means that the oil is certified by the Boating Industry Association (BIA) for use in two-cycle water-cooled (TC-W) outboard engines. There are several different two-cycle motorcycle engines in which this oil may be used.

As you can tell from reviewing the oil recommendations above, not all two-cycle motorcycle engines can use the same oil. Therefore, for trouble-free service and long engine life, follow the oil recommendations for the engine listed in the motorcycle owner's manual for the motorcycle.

Figure 13-3 shows a 1-quart plastic bottle of two-cycle-engine oil. It is very handy and widely used. There is a mixing table for various fuel-oil ratios printed on the back of the bottle. Also, the sides of the bottle are marked in pints, fluid ounces, and cubic centimeters to aid in proper mixing.

CHAPTER 13 REVIEW QUESTIONS

1. What is friction?
2. Why can't lubricating oil be kept in the crankcase of a two-cycle engine?
3. Name the two methods of engine lubrication used in two-cycle engines.
4. What prevents metal-to-metal contact of moving parts in the engine?
5. What is the difference between a regular petroleum-based oil and a synthetic oil?
6. What are the compounds called that are added to lubricating oil?
7. Which oil has the higher viscosity, SAE 10W or SAE 20W?
8. How does Harley-Davidson rate the oil recommended for use in their engines?
9. What are five major oil additives?
10. Name five jobs that the oil does in the engine.
11. Where does the oil get rid of the heat it picks up from the parts of a four-cycle engine?

CHAPTER # 14

ENGINE LUBRICATING SYSTEMS

After studying this chapter,
you should be able to:

1. Describe the purpose of the lubricating system.

2. Discuss the premix and the oil-injection systems for two-cycle engines and explain how each works.

3. Explain the construction and operation of a pressure-oiling system for a two-cycle engine.

4. Describe the construction and operation of a two-cycle-engine oil pump.

5. Explain how the oil-recycling system works.

6. Describe four-cycle-engine lubricating systems, and explain the difference between dry-sump and wet-sump systems.

7. Discuss the oil pumps used in four-cycle engines and explain how they work.

8. Explain the purpose of oil filters and how they work.

14-1 PURPOSE OF THE LUBRICATING SYSTEM

The purpose of the engine lubricating system is to get oil to all moving engine parts so it can do its four jobs (13-1). The oil gets to the moving engine parts in different ways, according to whether the engine is a two-cycle or a four-cycle unit. Chapters 5 and 6 describe the two types of engine.

In the two-cycle engine, the oil is either premixed with the gasoline or injected into the ingoing air-fuel mixture (13-7). In the four-cycle engine, the oil is circulated between the engine moving parts and an oil pan or reservoir. We describe both systems in this chapter.

14-2 TWO-CYCLE-ENGINE LUBRICATING SYSTEMS

Many two-cycle engines are lubricated by mixing oil with the fuel. The oil enters the crankcase as a mist, and this lubricates the bearings, piston, piston pin, rings, and cylinder wall. This system works satisfactorily for some engines.

The amount of oil used in the fuel can be adjusted to provide best results. However, this fuel-oil mixing is not quite satisfactory for all two-cycle engines used in motorcycles. The reason is this: The engine needs more oil at high speed than at low speed. If the mixture is right

for high speed, it will be too rich in oil at low speed. This can lead to waste of oil and rapid accumulation of carbon in the engine. Carbon accumulation can seriously reduce engine performance. Often, the carbon will increasingly block the exhaust port in the cylinder wall so it becomes harder and harder for the exhaust gases to get out of the cylinder. The result is a falling off of engine power. In other sections, we will explain how such carbon accumulations can be removed.

It may be even more damaging to the engine if the mixture is right for low speed. In this case, the engine can be short of oil at high speed. The result can be insufficient lubrication at high speed, and this can cause engine failure. The bearings, piston, rings, and cylinder wall may not get enough oil. Moving parts will wear rapidly. Even worse, parts can overheat so much from the excessive friction that they may seize.

For example, if the piston seizes in the cylinder, the connecting rod can break and punch through the cylinder. In spite of this, many two-cycle racing bikes use premix, proportioning the mix for high-engine speed. One advantage is that the system has no moving parts, or anything else to get out of adjustment during a race.

Today, many two-cycle motorcycle engines use an oil-injection pressure lubricating system. In many of these systems, the oil is fed through nozzles into the air-fuel mixture coming from the carburetor. Also, oil may be delivered in a continuous flow directly to the engine bearings. The amount of oil fed through these two paths depends on engine speed and throttle opening. Before discussing oil pumps and oil-injection systems, let's take a closer look at the simple and reliable premix system and how it works.

14-3 PREMIX LUBRICATING SYSTEM

Some two-cycle motorcycle engines are lubricated by the premix system. In this system, a certain amount of oil is premixed with the gasoline before it is added to the fuel tank. Then the oil enters the crankcase as an oil mist carried along with the air-fuel mixture from the carburetor.

After compression in the crankcase, the air-fuel mixture travels to the combustion chamber, where it is burned. But part of the oil mist stays in the crankcase, where the oil droplets lubricate the bearings, piston, rings, and cylinder walls. Some of the oil does get into the combustion chamber, where the oil is burned along with the air-fuel mixture. This is why some two-cycle engines have a smoky exhaust. Figure 2-1a shows an engine that is lubricated with a fuel-oil premix.

The grade and amount of oil to be mixed with the gasoline is very critical. The manufacturer's recommendations should be carefully followed. Adding too much oil will cause the exhaust ports to become clogged very quickly. Also, carbon deposits will form on the piston and rings. This causes poor engine performance. Adding too little oil will deprive the engine of adequate lubrication, so it will wear out much sooner and may seize during hard running.

The typical mixture ratio for a motorcycle engine using premix is 20:1. Usually the manufacturer will specify the type and octane rating of the gasoline that should be used and the type and viscosity of the oil. Mix the gasoline and the oil by pouring the oil into an empty gasoline can. Add the amount of gasoline necessary to make a premix of the correct properties. Shake the can several times.

This procedure will result in the gasoline and oil being thoroughly mixed. Oil that is not fully mixed with the gasoline can block the carburetor jet, and the engine will not run.

One disadvantage to premix is that the lubricating qualities of the fuel-oil mixture do not last long. If the premix is being used in a racing bike, then a fresh mixture should be made up for each day of racing. Do not leave the premix in the motorcycle fuel tank for a long time. If the motorcycle is to be stored, or not used or ridden, completely drain the premix from the fuel system.

Motorcycle manufacturers also caution against mixing a mineral-base or petroleum oil with a vegetable oil. The two oils will not always mix. This could cause a premix that is too thick. Then the engine will lose power and possibly be damaged from lack of lubrication.

A two-cycle engine that is lubricated by premix usually will have needle bearings for the piston pin and the crankpin, and ball or roller bearings for the crankshaft. Figure 14-1 shows the parts that require lubrication in an engine lubricated with premix.

In an engine that is lubricated with premix, the big end of the connecting rod usually has slots around the center of the bearing area. Also, there are notches spaced around the sides of the rod. This allows the oil droplets contained in the air-fuel mixture to pass through the bearing. The drops of oil coat the bearing and provide it with the needed lubrication.

☑14-4 OIL-INJECTION SYSTEM

Figure 2-1c shows a single-cylinder two-cycle engine that has an oil pump to spray oil into the air-fuel mixture. This engine is very similar to engines that use premix. Both types of engines have an oil mist in the air-fuel mixture as it enters the crankcase. However, when an oil pump is used, the oil is not mixed with the gasoline before it is added to the fuel tank. Only gasoline is carried in the fuel tank. A separate, smaller oil tank, as shown in Fig. 4-1, carries a quantity of oil.

A pressure-oiling system is shown in Fig. 14-2. When the engine is running, oil from the tank fills the oil pump. The pump forces the oil under pressure through the oil line to an oil injector, or nozzle, in the intake port. As the air-fuel mixture from the carburetor passes the nozzle, the proper amount of oil is sprayed into the mixture.

The amount of oil spray is regulated by the oil-pump control lever, which is controlled by engine speed and throttle opening. This means that the fuel-oil ratio for the engine is varied as the operating conditions of the engine require. This results in less carbon deposits and less exhaust smoking than when premix is used.

Circulation of the air-fuel mixture containing the oil mist remains the same as with the premix. However, some of the air-fuel mixture must pass through the

bearings and get on the cylinder walls. Then the oil mist can provide the needed lubrication. An advantage to pressure oiling is that only gasoline passes through the jet in the carburetor. This improves control of the air-fuel mixture and prevents oil from blocking the jet. When premix is used, the lubricating oil passes through the carburetor with the gasoline.

If the oil pump fails in an engine with this type of lubricating system, the motorcycle can still be ridden, if necessary. A fuel-oil premix with a ratio of 20:1, as discussed in ☑14-3, can be used in the fuel tank. The premix will not damage the engine. However, premix must not be used in an engine that has pressure-lubricated bearings and crankshaft, as discussed in ☑14-5 and 14-6. The operation and control of the oil pump is discussed later.

☑14-5 PRESSURE-OILING SYSTEM

Figure 14-3 shows the lubricating system for a one-cylinder two-cycle engine. It is very similar to the system for the oil-injection system described in ☑14-4, except that there are two oil lines carrying oil from the oil pump.

One oil line carries oil to the intake port, where the oil is mixed with the air-fuel mixture from the carburetor. This oil then goes into the crankcase to provide lubrication for the piston, piston pin, piston rings, and cylinder walls. The second oil line carries oil from the oil pump to the crankshaft bearing and crankpin bearing. The amount of oil sent to these parts varies with engine speed and throttle opening, as we explain later.

The oil pump delivers oil to the intake port of the cylinder through a ball check valve. The oil pump also delivers oil, through another check valve, to one of the crankshaft bearings. This oil flows from the crankshaft bearing through oil holes drilled in the crankshaft to the crankpin bearing. From there, the oil sprays out to provide lubrication for the cylinder walls, piston, piston rings, and piston pin. In the engine shown in Fig. 14-3, one of the two crankshaft bearings is lubricated by oil from the transmission.

Figure 14-4 shows the path the oil follows from the oil pump to the crankshaft bearing and to the crankpin. After leaving the oil pump, the oil passes a check valve. This valve includes a spring-loaded ball. When oil-pump pressure increases, it pushes the ball up off the seat. This allows the oil to pass through the valve. The purpose of the check valve is to prevent oil from draining back down out of the bearings when the engine is stopped. Because of the check valve, oil is retained in the bearings to provide immediate lubrication when the engine is started.

After the oil passes through the check valve (Fig. 14-4), the oil flows through a hollow bolt into the crankshaft bearing, which is a ball bearing. Oil flows through the ball bearing to a hole drilled in the crankpin. A second hole drilled from the journal into the crankpin hole allows oil to flow out into the roller bearing that supports the connecting-rod big end.

Figure 14-5 shows the gear train that drives the oil pump. Note that there is considerable gear reduction between the crankshaft and the oil pump. Figure 14-6

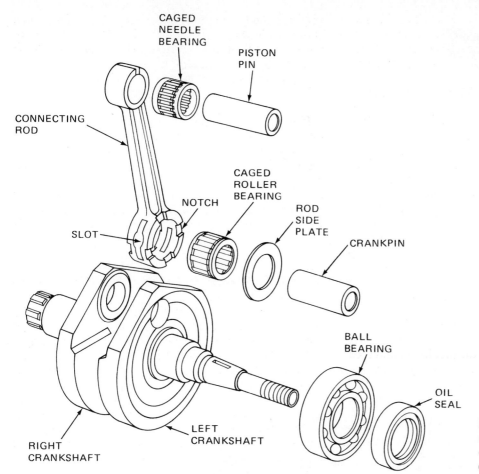

Fig. 14-1 Crankshaft, connecting rod, and bearings for an engine lubricated with premix. (*Honda Motor Company, Ltd.*)

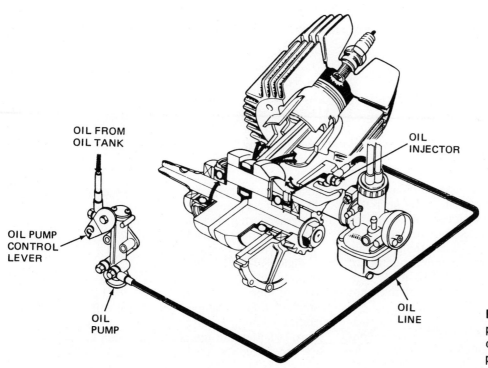

Fig. 14-2 A two-cycle-engine pressure-oiling system, using an oil pump and a nozzle in the intake port.

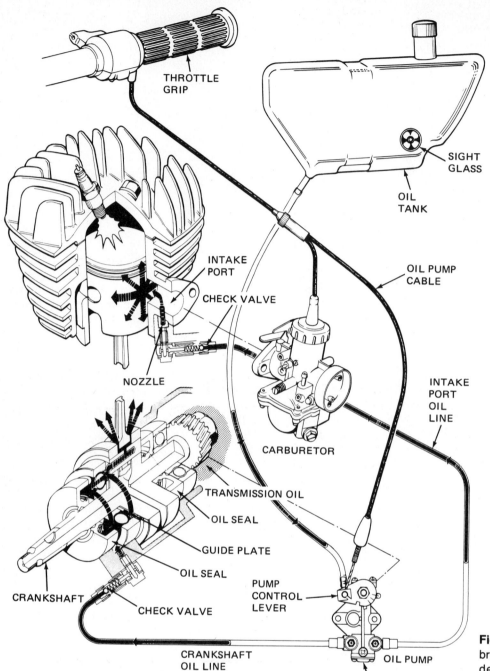

THROTTLE GRIP

SIGHT GLASS

OIL TANK

INTAKE PORT

CHECK VALVE

OIL PUMP CABLE

NOZZLE

INTAKE PORT OIL LINE

CARBURETOR

TRANSMISSION OIL

OIL SEAL

GUIDE PLATE

OIL SEAL

CRANKSHAFT

CHECK VALVE

PUMP CONTROL LEVER

CRANKSHAFT OIL LINE

OIL PUMP

AIR BLEED SCREW

Fig. 14-3 Complete pressure-lubrication system for a one-cylinder two-cycle engine. (*Suzuki Motor Company, Ltd.*)

shows the gear train in place in the engine. You can see that the kick-starter drive gear is the same gear that drives the oil-pump shaft. The kick lever is connected to the kick-starter shaft with a ratchet. After the engine is started and the kick lever is released, the gear train shown in Figs. 14-5 and 14-6 can run independently of the kick lever, driving the oil pump. This drive continues as long as the engine runs, even if the clutch is not engaged.

This same type of lubricating system is used for two-cylinder two-cycle motorcycle engines. The two-cylinder system is similar to the lubricating system for the one-cylinder engine. However, additional oil lines are

installed to carry oil directly to the second cylinder and to the center main bearings and second connecting-rod big-end bearing. The main bearing next to the transmission is lubricated by transmission oil, just as in the single-cylinder engine.

Figure 14-7 shows the lubricating system for a three-cylinder two-cycle motorcycle engine. It is the same type of lubricating system as for the two-cylinder and single-cylinder engines. The basic difference is that additional oil lines have been added to take care of the third cylinder and the additional main bearings. As in the other engines, the main bearing next to the transmission is lubricated by transmission oil.

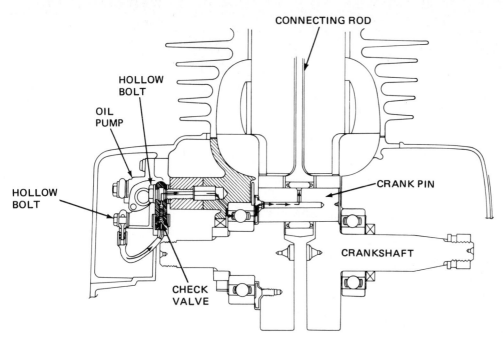

CONNECTING ROD
HOLLOW BOLT
OIL PUMP
HOLLOW BOLT
CRANK PIN
CRANKSHAFT
CHECK VALVE

Fig. 14-4 The oil-delivery system for the crankshaft and bearings of a one-cylinder two-cycle engine. (*Kawasaki Heavy Industries, Ltd.*)

14-6 TWO-CYCLE-ENGINE OIL PUMP

The typical oil pump for the engines described in ▧ 14-5 is shown in Fig. 14-8. Figure 14-5 shows the gear train that drives the oil pump. The pump is a reciprocating, or plunger-type, pump. The pump plunger is moved up and down by a worm gear that rotates on the end of the kick-starter shaft. This rotation is provided through the gear train described in ▧ 14-5 and shown in Figs. 14-5 and 14-6.

In operation, the pump plunger (Fig. 14-8) is held against the control cam by a spring, acting through the differential plunger. As the pump plunger moves up and down in the pump body, the differential plunger also moves up and down. It is pushed down by the pump plunger and up by the spring which was compressed on the downstroke. The downstroke of the differential plunger pressurizes the oil trapped between it, the differential cylinder, and the bottom of the pump. This pumping action sends oil through oil lines to the engine, as previously described.

The control lever on the pump is connected by a cable to the throttle grip, as shown in Fig. 14-3. As the throttle grip is twisted, the control lever is rotated. This causes the control cam to change its position inside the pump. By moving the offset of the control cam, the stroke of the pump plunger is increased. This increases the amount of oil that the pump discharges. As a result, the engine gets the right amount of oil for all operating speeds.

Figure 14-9 shows the fuel-oil ratio for a 250-cc single-cylinder two-cycle engine. The pump is set to deliver an oil-fuel mixture that varies from 50:1 at idle to 36.5:1 at 7000 rpm. Although less oil is delivered by each plunger stroke at high speed, there are more strokes per second; so the engine gets the additional oil it needs at high speed.

The oil pump in a two-cycle engine is not mounted in the crankcase, but on one side of the engine. This position allows easy access for checking and setting of the plunger stroke, which is adjustable.

Figure 14-10 shows the amount of oil discharged from the pump for one engine as the throttle is moved from idle to full open. Notice that a small amount of oil is sent to the crankshaft at all speeds, even when the engine is running and the throttle is closed. This prevents engine damage and possible seizure from oil starvation while the throttle is closed and the motorcycle is coasting downhill.

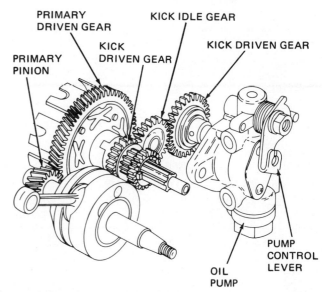

PRIMARY DRIVEN GEAR
KICK IDLE GEAR
PRIMARY PINION
KICK DRIVEN GEAR
KICK DRIVEN GEAR
OIL PUMP
PUMP CONTROL LEVER

Fig. 14-5 The gear train required to drive the oil pump. (*Suzuki Motor Company, Ltd.*)

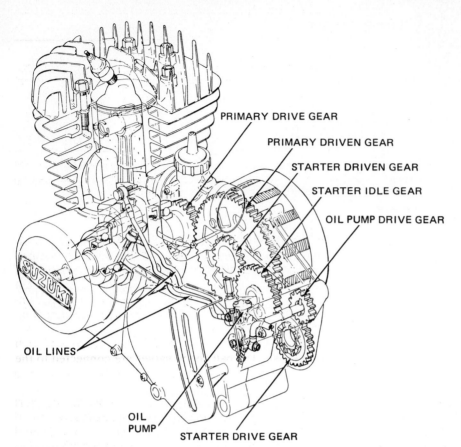

PRIMARY DRIVE GEAR
PRIMARY DRIVEN GEAR
STARTER DRIVEN GEAR
STARTER IDLE GEAR
OIL PUMP DRIVE GEAR

OIL LINES

OIL PUMP

STARTER DRIVE GEAR

Fig. 14-6 A one-cylinder two-cycle engine partly cut away to show the complete drive train for the oil pump. (*Suzuki Motor Company, Ltd.*)

In Fig. 14-10, notice that the amount of oil sent to the intake port increases more than 10 times as the throttle grip is twisted from idle to full throttle. The oil-pump performance chart shown in Fig. 14-10 is for a 75-cc single-cylinder engine. The increase in oil delivery is not so much due to a change in the length of plunger stroke as to the greatly increased number of strokes per second at high speed. Larger displacements and multiple-cylinder engines require higher oil-pump capacities.

Neither the oil pump nor the check valves (🖻 14-7) are to be disassembled for service. About the only

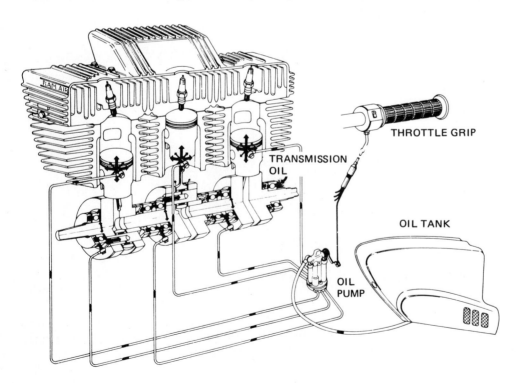

THROTTLE GRIP

TRANSMISSION OIL

OIL TANK

OIL PUMP

Fig. 14-7 The lubricating system for a three-cylinder two-cycle engine. (*Suzuki Motor Company, Ltd.*)

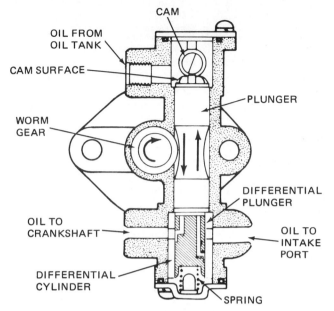

Fig. 14-8 Construction of a plunger-type oil pump. (*Suzuki Motor Company, Ltd.*)

Throttle valve position	Engine rpm					
	1100	3000	4000	5000	6000	7000
Closed idle	50:1	—	—	—	—	—
Half	—	48:1	40:1	34:1	35:1	39.5:1
Three quarters	—	40:1	40.5:1	44:1	37.5:1	35:1
Full	—	41:1	41.5:1	42:1	38:1	36.5:1

Fig. 14-9 A chart showing how the oil-injection pump varies the fuel-oil ratio as engine speed and the throttle opening change. (*Honda Motor Company, Ltd.*)

14-7 OIL-RECYCLING SYSTEM

In some multi-cylinder two-cycle engines, after the oil has lubricated the moving engine parts, the oil drops to the bottom of the crankcase. This is shown in Fig. 14-11. To prevent excessive accumulations of oil, the three-cylinder engine shown in Fig. 14-7 has an oil-recycling system (Fig. 14-11).

A ball check valve is located at the bottom of each crankcase. The ball check valves are connected to the transfer ports of other cylinders by oil lines, as shown in Fig. 14-11.

When a partial vacuum develops in the transfer port of the connected cylinder, any oil that has accumulated in the crankcase is pulled out by the vacuum. The oil passes into the combustion chamber of the other cylinder and is burned on the next power stroke. This system prevents the accumulation of oil in the crankcase.

repair permitted on the pump is replacement of the O-rings and pump-shaft (worm-gear) oil seal. If there is internal trouble, the complete pump should be replaced. If the check valves need cleaning, solvent should be squirted through them with a squirt can. Never use compressed air on a check valve, for this may distort the valve spring and ruin the valve.

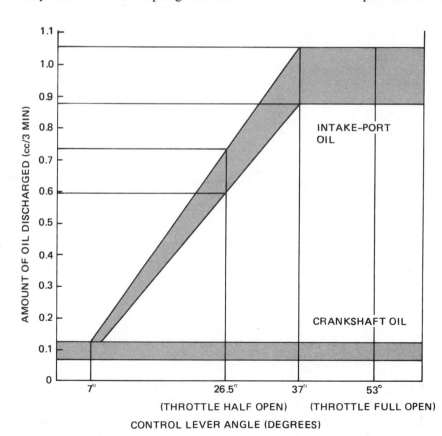

Fig. 14-10 Oil-pump performance chart for a one-cylinder two-cycle engine. (*Suzuki Motor Company, Ltd.*)

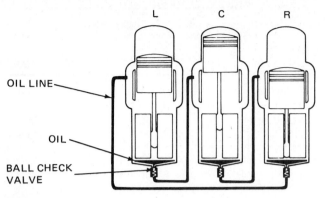

OIL LINE

OIL

BALL CHECK
VALVE

L   C   R

Fig. 14-11 Oil-recycling system for a multicylinder two-cycle engine. (*Suzuki Motor Company, Ltd.*)

14-8 FOUR-CYCLE-ENGINE LUBRICATING SYSTEMS

The two-cycle engine uses a *total-loss* lubricating system. This means that the oil is not recovered and reused. When oil goes into a two-cycle engine, the oil is burned along with the fuel. However, the four-cycle engine has a reservoir of lubricating oil which circulates constantly through the engine. The oil pump continuously sends oil from the crankcase through oil lines to all moving engine parts. The oil then drops back down into the crankcase where it is stored until it is picked up by the pump and recirculated again.

There are two types of lubricating systems for four-cycle engines, the *dry sump* and the *wet sump*. Both types require about 1 to 4 quarts of oil to lubricate the engine. We will now look at both of these systems.

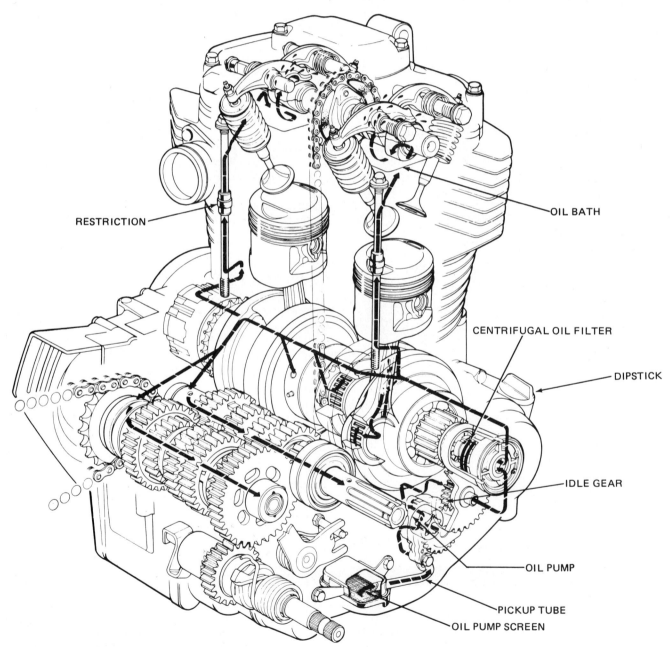

RESTRICTION

OIL BATH

CENTRIFUGAL OIL FILTER

DIPSTICK

IDLE GEAR

OIL PUMP

PICKUP TUBE

OIL PUMP SCREEN

Fig. 14-12 Lubricating system for a two-cylinder four-cycle motorcycle engine. (*Honda Motor Company, Ltd.*)

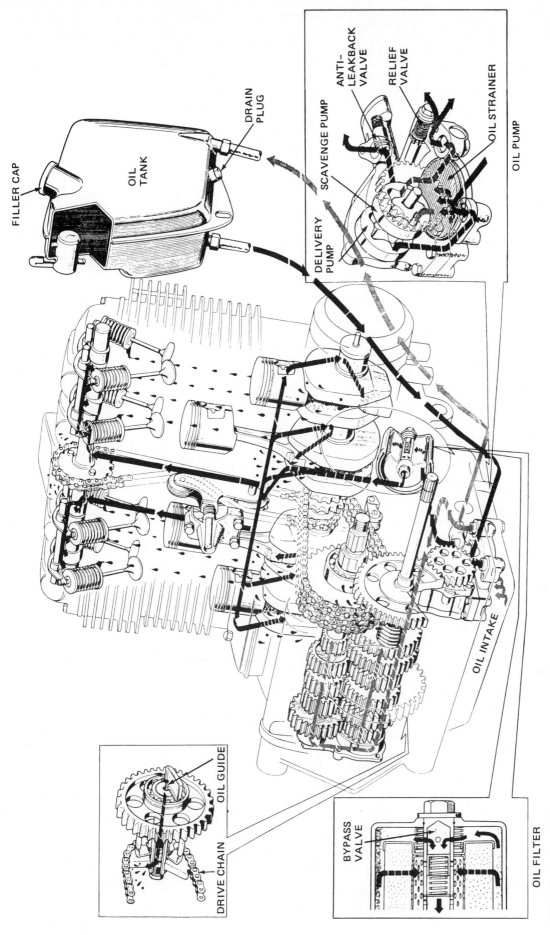

FILLER CAP

DRAIN PLUG

OIL TANK

ANTI- LEAKBACK VALVE

RELIEF VALVE

SCAVENGE PUMP

OIL STRAINER

DELIVERY PUMP

OIL PUMP

OIL GUIDE

DRIVE CHAIN

OIL INTAKE

BYPASS VALVE

OIL FILTER

Fig. 14-13 A dry-sump lubricating system for a four-cylinder four-cycle engine. *(Honda Motor Company, Ltd.)*

14-9
WET-SUMP LUBRICATING SYSTEM

Automobile engines and many four-cycle motorcycle engines use the wet-sump system. The sump is the area at the bottom of the crankcase. It is called a *wet sump* because the engine oil is stored in the crankcase under the crankshaft.

Figure 14-12 shows a two-cylinder four-cycle engine with a wet-sump lubricating system. An oil pump sends oil from the crankcase up through galleries and passages to the moving engine parts. After lubricating, cleaning, and cooling these parts, the oil drops back down into the crankcase. The oil pump keeps the oil circulating continuously while the engine is running. Variations of this system are described later in this chapter.

14-10
DRY-SUMP LUBRICATING SYSTEM
While most four-cycle dirt bikes today are wet sump, some engines are dry sump. This system has been used especially on four-cycle engines that are moving over rough terrain and operating at various angles from the vertical. Under these conditions, excessive oil can splash up over the lower part of the engine. Also, when the engine is tilted at an angle, the oil runs over to one side of the sump. Under these circumstances, the oil-pump intake will often be above the oil in the sump. Then the oil pump will not be picking up any oil or sending oil to the upper part of the engine. As a result, the engine will soon fail.

To prevent this, a dry-sump lubricating system has been used. In addition, some tall motorcycle engines have a dry-sump system simply to provide adequate ground clearance.

Some four-cycle motorcycle engines in street bikes and in dirt bikes are equipped with dry-sump lubricating systems. Figure 14-13 shows a four-cylinder four-cycle motorcycle engine that has a dry sump.

The dry-sump system uses a double pump that works like two separate oil pumps. One is a scavenge pump and the other is the pressure, or delivery, pump. As oil drops down from the engine into the crankcase, one pump picks up the oil and sends it through an oil line to the oil tank. From there, the second pump pressurizes the oil and delivers it to the moving engine parts.

With this system, the oil tank always is kept full. No oil remains in the crankcase. Therefore, the pressure pump always is full of oil. All moving parts are properly lubricated at all times, except when the check valve fails and allows the engine to wet sump. A disadvantage to having a remotely mounted oil tank is that it raises the center of gravity of the motorcycle. This may affect handling. Specific dry-sump lubricating systems are discussed later. Now let's discuss the parts of a typical lubricating system for a four-cycle motorcycle engine.

14-11
OIL PUMPS
The main purpose of the engine lubricating system is to supply oil to all the moving parts in the engine. The oil pump does this job. It sits in or near the crankcase and pumps oil from the crankcase to the engine parts. Figures 14-12 through 14-14 show the location of the oil pump and the gears that drive it. Figure 14-12 shows the complete wet-sump lubricating system for a two-cylinder engine. Figure 14-13 shows the complete dry-sump lubricating system for a four-cylinder engine.

Now let's follow the flow of lubricating oil through the engine, as shown in Fig. 14-14. The engine is a four-cylinder wet-sump engine with overhead camshaft.

The oil pump picks up oil from the bottom of the crankcase and sends the oil through the oil filter, as shown in Fig. 14-14. We discuss the oil filter later. The oil then passes through oil passages to the crankshaft bearings and crankpin bearings. Some of the oil, instead of going to the crankshaft, flows on to the cylinder head and lubricates the camshaft bearings, rocker arms, and valves. These passages are shown by black lines in Fig. 14-14. Then the oil drains back down to the crankcase.

Three types of oil pumps are used in motorcycle engines. These are the plunger type (discussed in 14-6), the gear type, and the rotor type. The two types commonly used in four-cycle engines are the gear type and the rotor type. Let's discuss the gear type first.

The gear-type oil pump includes a pair of spiral gears. As the shaft turns, the attached drive gear turns the driven gear. The spaces between the gear teeth are filled with oil from the oil inlet of the pump. As the gear teeth mesh, the oil is forced out through the oil outlet.

The other type of oil pump used in engines is the *trochoidal,* or rotor type. It has a pair of rotors, as shown in Figs. 14-12 and 14-13. The inner rotor has four lobes. The outer rotor has four recesses into which the four lobes fit. The outer rotor is offset so that on one side there is space between the lobes of the inner rotor and the recesses of the outer rotor. The inner rotor rotates, driven by the gear on the kick-starter shaft. The inner rotor forces the outer rotor to rotate along with it. The spaces between the lobes and the recesses fill with oil from the oil inlet. Then, as the lobes move into the recesses, the oil is forced out through the pump outlet.

14-12
RELIEF VALVES
The faster the engine runs, the faster the gears or rotors turn in the oil pump. This means that without relief, the oil pressure would go very high. To prevent too much pressure, oil pumps contain a relief valve. This valve contains a ball or plunger (Fig. 14-13) which is held in place by a spring. When the pressure starts to go too high, the relief valve pushes the ball or plunger back against the spring tension. This opens up a relief hole, which allows part of the oil to flow back down into the crankcase. The pressure is relieved and engine problems are avoided.

Figure 14-13 also shows the anti-leakback valve in the oil pump. The purpose of the anti-leakback valve is to prevent oil from flowing back down from the oil tank into the engine when the engine is stopped. When the engine is running, oil pressure from the oil pump keeps the valve open so oil from the sump can be pumped up into the oil tank.

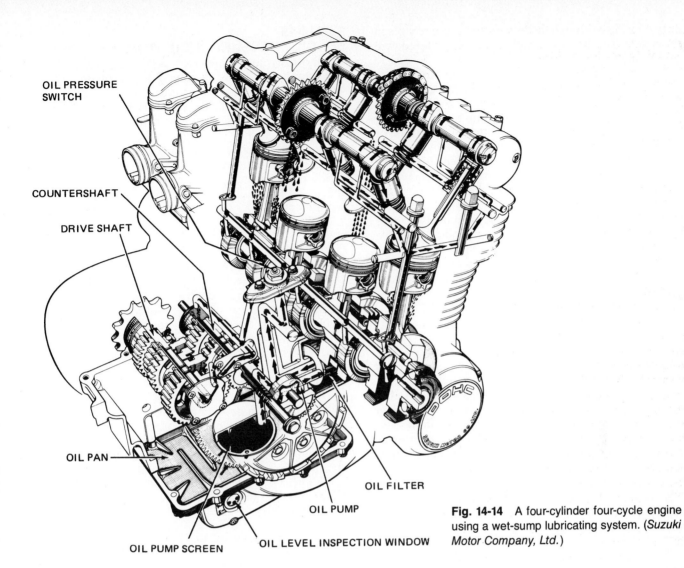

OIL PRESSURE SWITCH

COUNTERSHAFT

DRIVE SHAFT

OIL PAN

OIL PUMP SCREEN

OIL FILTER

OIL PUMP

OIL LEVEL INSPECTION WINDOW

Fig. 14-14 A four-cylinder four-cycle engine using a wet-sump lubricating system. (*Suzuki Motor Company, Ltd.*)

14-13
OIL FILTERS

In most motorcycle engines, the oil from the oil pump must first pass through an oil filter before it goes up to the engine. The oil filter is the engine's main protection against dirt. The filter removes particles of carbon, dirt, and metal so they do not get into the engine and damage bearings and other parts.

The automotive type of oil filter is widely used on motorcycle engines. This type of filter contains a filtering element made of pleated paper or fibrous material. The oil passes through the filter, and the paper or fibers trap the dirt particles.

Figure 14-13 shows a cutaway view of a full-flow oil filter. The filter material is in a replaceable element that can be thrown away when it becomes loaded with dirt. In the engine, the filter has a bypass valve, which consists of a spring-loaded ball or plunger.

If the oil cannot pass through the filter, the pressure buildup in the filter causes the bypass valve to open. This allows oil from the pump to bypass the filter and go directly to the engine. Engine damage from lack of lubrication is avoided. However, before this happens, the oil and filter should be replaced. If they are not, then

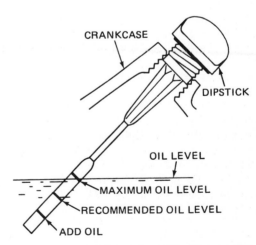

CRANKCASE

DIPSTICK

OIL LEVEL

MAXIMUM OIL LEVEL

RECOMMENDED OIL LEVEL

ADD OIL

Fig. 14-15 Using a dipstick to check the oil level in the crankcase of a four-cycle engine. (*Yamaha International Corporation*)

dirty oil will go through the bypass and cause trouble in the engine. The dirty oil, which is not being filtered, will cause rapid wear of the moving parts.

The engine shown in Fig. 14-12 uses a centrifugal, or rotary, oil filter. This filter works on the centrifugal principle. As oil from the oil pump enters the filter rotor through the guide, the oil is picked up by the spinning vanes inside the rotor. Foreign matter, such as dust or metallic particles, is separated from the oil by centrifugal force and sticks to the outer wall of the rotor. The cleaned oil then is fed to the engine parts through the outlet port in the center section of the filter cap.

The oil-filter element should be replaced before it stops working properly. Motorcycle manufacturers recommend that oil filters be replaced periodically. Some manufacturers require replacing the oil filter during the first oil change at 500 miles [800 km] and during every second oil change after that, at 2000-mile [3000-km] intervals.

14-14
OIL COOLERS
In some engines, the oil does not lose enough heat to the crankcase. Because these engines require additional oil cooling, a separate radiator, or heat exchanger, is used. This device is called an *oil cooler*. It is similar to the radiator in an automobile-engine cooling system. The oil cooler has a series of passages through which the hot oil can flow. It has another series of passages through which cool air can flow. The cool air flowing through the oil cooler carries away the excess heat from the oil and thereby lowers its temperature.

14-15
OIL-PRESSURE INDICATOR
Many four-cycle motorcycle engines now are equipped with an indicator light to show the rider if there is oil pressure in the engine. If the oil pressure is too low, the light will be on to warn the rider that the engine is not being properly lubricated. Continued operation at low oil pressure will damage the engine. The indicator light warns the rider to stop the engine before damage occurs.

Instead of an indicator light, some motorcycles have an oil-pressure gauge. Indicator lights and gauges are discussed in the chapter covering motorcycle electric equipment.

14-16
OIL-LEVEL INDICATOR
A dipstick (Fig. 14-15) is used to check the level of oil in the crankcase of a wet-sump four-cycle engine. To use the dipstick, the engine should be warm and the motorcycle upright and level. Unscrew the dipstick and wipe it clean. Then place the dipstick in the hole, but do not screw in the cap. Now remove the dipstick and read the oil level in the crankcase. The oil level should be between the upper and lower marks on the dipstick. If the oil level is below the lower mark, oil must be added.

The oil level in dry-sump engines and two-cycle engines with oil tanks can be checked in one or two different ways. Removing the oil-filler cap from the tank and seeing how much oil is in the tank is one way. Another way is to check the oil-level sight glass that is in the lower part of some oil tanks (Fig. 14-3). When the oil level is below the mark on the sight glass, more oil should be added.

CHAPTER 14
REVIEW QUESTIONS

1. Why can't oil be allowed to collect in the crankcase of a two-cycle engine?
2. What is premix?
3. Name three types of two-cycle-engine lubricating systems.
4. What is the typical fuel-oil ratio for a motorcycle engine?
5. Why doesn't premix last indefinitely?
6. Why are ball and roller bearings used so frequently in two-cycle engines?
7. Why are some two-cycle engines pressure-oiled?
8. What advantage is there to oil-injection over premix?
9. What type of oil pump frequently is used with the pressure-oiling system?
10. What controls the output of the pump in a pressure-oiling system?
11. Which gets more oil from the pump, the intake port or the crankshaft?
12. How is the oil pump serviced?
13. How does the oil-recycling system work in a multi-cylinder two-cycle engine?
14. Name the two general types of lubricating systems in four-cycle engines.
15. What is the difference between a wet sump and a dry sump?
16. Why does the dry-sump system require the use of a double pump?
17. In the flow path for the oil, where is the oil filter located?
18. What three types of oil pump are used in four-cycle engines?
19. Explain how a relief valve works.
20. What is an anti-leakback valve?
21. Describe the difference between a full-flow oil filter and a rotary oil filter.
22. When is an oil cooler needed?
23. How can you tell if a motorcycle engine has oil pressure when the motorcycle is not equipped with an oil-pressure indicator?
24. Explain how to read the engine-oil dipstick in a motorcycle engine.

CHAPTER 15

LUBRICATING-SYSTEM SERVICE

After studying this chapter,
you should be able to:

1. Discuss the two four-cycle-engine lubricating-system complaints.

2. Explain what could cause low oil pressure in a four-cycle-engine lubricating system.

3. List and describe five basic four-cycle-engine lubricating-system services.

4. Explain how to change engine oil in a four-cycle engine.

5. Explain how to clean the oil-pump screen in a four-cycle engine.

6. Discuss the servicing of two-cycle-engine lubricating systems.

15-1 LUBRICATING-SYSTEM TROUBLE DIAGNOSIS (FOUR-CYCLE ENGINE)

Two complaints related to the four-cycle-engine lubricating system are

1. That the engine is using too much oil.
2. That the indicator light is acting up (or the oil-pressure gauge shows low pressure).

There are many possible causes of excessive oil consumption. Two main factors that affect oil consumption are (1) engine speed and (2) the amount that engine parts have worn. If oil consumption is high, both of these factors must be considered. For example, if the oil is leaking from the engine because of a faulty gasket, then oil usage will be high. Also, worn bearings can cause high oil usage. If seals are worn, then excessive amounts of oil will leak past them out of the engine.

The second complaint is erratic indicator-light or oil-pressure-gauge action. If the light comes on part of the time, or if the pressure gauge sometimes shows low pressure, there are three possible causes. Either there is not enough oil in the engine, the oil pump is defective, or the oil pickup is not consistently picking up oil. This could result from the oil pickup falling off or becoming clogged.

If the light stays on all the time, or if the pressure gauge consistently reads low, then the first check is to see if the engine oil is low. If it is at normal height, check the oil-pressure sending unit. Remove it and install a pressure gauge to check for pressure with the engine running. If the pressure is okay, then the trouble is a

defective sending unit. If the pressure is low, there probably is trouble in the engine itself. An experienced mechanic often can tell by listening if the oil pressure is low. The noise of the bearings running without oil is a warning sound that the oil pressure is low. An engine operating for only a few seconds without oil pressure is a damaged engine.

Causes of low oil pressure include

1. A weak relief-valve spring
2. A worn oil pump
3. A broken or cracked oil line
4. Obstructions in the oil lines
5. Insufficient or excessively thin oil
6. Bearings that are so badly worn that they can pass more oil than the oil pump is capable of delivering
7. A defective oil-pressure indicator that may be reading low

Excessive oil pressure may result from

1. A stuck relief valve
2. An excessively strong valve spring
3. A clogged oil line
4. Excessively heavy oil
5. A defective oil-pressure indicator that may read high

15-2 LUBRICATING-SYSTEM SERVICE (FOUR-CYCLE ENGINE)

There are certain lubricating-system jobs that are done more or less automatically when an engine is rebuilt. For example, the crankcase is cleaned during an engine-overhaul job such as replacing bearings. When the crankshaft is removed, check and clean out the oil passages in the crankshaft. Also, the oil passages in the crankcase should be cleaned out. All these services are described in later chapters on engine service. Sections that follow describe such lubricating-system service jobs as

1. Checking the oil level
2. Changing the oil
3. Changing the oil filter
4. Servicing the oil-pressure relief valve and the crankcase ventilating system
5. Servicing the oil pump and the oil-pressure indicator

15-3 CHECKING THE OIL LEVEL (FOUR-CYCLE ENGINE)

Most engines use a bayonet type of oil-level gauge called the *dipstick* (Fig. 14-15). It is withdrawn from the crankcase or oil tank to determine the oil level (14-16).

The appearance of the oil should be noted to see whether it is dirty, thin, or thick. A few drops of oil can be placed between the thumb and fingers and rubbed to detect particles of dirt or metal. If the oil level is low, oil should be added. If the oil seems dirty, thin, or thick, it should be drained, and clean oil should be added.

NOTE If the engine has just been shut off, wait a few minutes for the oil to drain back down into the crankcase before checking the oil.

15-4
CHANGING THE ENGINE OIL (FOUR-CYCLE ENGINE)

Always follow the motorcycle manufacturer's recommendations for the time or mileage intervals between oil changes. Usually the oil filter should be changed the first time the oil is changed for a new engine, and every other oil change thereafter.

Oil should be changed more frequently during cold weather, particularly if most trips are short. With short-trip operation, the engine operates cold a greater part of the time. This increases the formation of water and sludge in the crankcase. More frequent oil changes remove this sludge before excessive amounts can collect.

When the motorcycle is operated in very dusty areas, the oil should be changed more frequently. Manufacturers recommend that a motorcycle that has been driven through a dust storm should have the oil changed immediately. It does not matter how recently the last oil change was made. At the same time, the air filter should be cleaned and the oil filter (if used) changed. When the engine oil is changed, the other maintenance points on the engine and chassis should be lubricated.

Changing the oil in many motorcycle engines is more important than it is in automobile engines. In the automobile engine, the engine oil has only the important job of lubricating the engine. However, many four-cycle motorcycle engines use the engine oil to lubricate and cool the clutch and the gears and bearings in the transmission. A different transmission oil is not used, as in the automobile.

In a wet-sump engine, the oil is carried in the crankcase. This type of engine is shown in Fig. 14-12. To drain the oil, remove the drain plug from the bottom of the crankcase.

In a dry-sump engine, the lubricating oil is contained in a separate oil tank, as shown in Fig. 14-13. To drain the oil, the drain plug in the bottom of the oil tank is removed. In addition, in a dry-sump engine, the crankcase drain plug must be removed to drain out any oil that may have settled there.

When changing the oil, the engine should be warm. If it is cold, operate it for 10 minutes to bring it up to the required temperature. There are two reasons for changing the oil while it is hot. First, hot oil will run out of the crankcase freely and quickly. Second, more of the contaminants in the oil will drain with it before they have time to settle out.

Next, note the position of the drain plug in the crankcase. When the drain plug is located in the center of the crankcase, many manufacturers recommend placing the motorcycle on its center stand to drain the oil. Other motorcycles have the drain plug on the left side of the crankcase. On these, the oil is drained with the motorcycle resting on its side stand.

Remove the oil-filler cap. Then place the drain pan under the drain plug and remove it.

CAUTION **Do not allow the draining oil to strike your hand. The oil may be hot enough to burn you.**

To change the oil in a four-cycle engine with a separate oil tank, place drain pans under the oil tank and the crankcase. Then remove the drain plugs and allow the oil to drain into the pans.

With the ignition off and the transmission in neutral, operate the kick starter several times. This will allow any oil trapped in pockets or passages in the engine to drain out.

While the oil is draining, clean and inspect each drain plug. If the sealing washer is cracked, distorted, or deeply grooved, replace it. A defective sealing washer may leak oil after it is reinstalled.

When the oil has finished running from the drain hole, wipe the hole clean with a rag or shop towel. Check the drain-plug mating surface on the crankcase to make sure there is a good sealing surface for the drain-plug washer. Burrs or grooves may cause oil leaks. Also, check for cracks around the hole. These may be caused by overtightening of the drain plug.

After all the oil has drained out and the above checks have been made, install and tighten the drain plug. A drain plug that is installed too loosely may vibrate out after the engine is running. An overtightened drain plug may split the sealing washer or crack the crankcase. Either type of improper drain-plug installation may result in oil leaking from around the drain-plug hole.

Pour the proper quantity and grade of oil in the engine, as specified by the motorcycle manufacturers. Start the engine. After the oil light goes off, run the engine at a fast idle for 1 to 2 minutes. Check for oil leaks from around the drain plug.

Stop the engine and check the engine oil level with the dipstick, as shown in Fig. 14-15. Add more oil if necessary to bring the oil level up to the FULL mark.

For a street motorcycle, many manufacturers recommend the first oil change at about 500 miles [800 km]. Thereafter, the oil should be changed at 1500-mile [2500-km] intervals, as specified in the manufacturer's maintenance schedule. The maintenance schedule is printed in both the owner's manual and the service manual for the motorcycle.

15-5
CHANGING THE OIL FILTER (FOUR-CYCLE ENGINE)

Oil filters are serviced by replacing the oil-filter element or the complete filter, according to the type. Oil screens are serviced by flushing out collected sludge and dirt.

As the oil filter becomes clogged, it passes less and less oil. The condition of a spin-on type of oil filter can be determined by feeling it after the engine has been operated for a short time. If the filter is hot to the touch, oil is flowing through the filter. If it is cold, the filter is probably clogged and is not passing oil. Replace the filter at the specified intervals. The usual recommendation is to replace the filter every other time the engine oil is changed. More frequent replacement should be made if the motorcycle is operated in unusually dusty conditions.

On some engines, the filter element and the container are replaced as a unit. This is the automotive type of spin-on filter. To use it on a motorcycle engine, an adapter is installed. Then, to replace the filter, the old filter can be unscrewed and a new filter screwed into

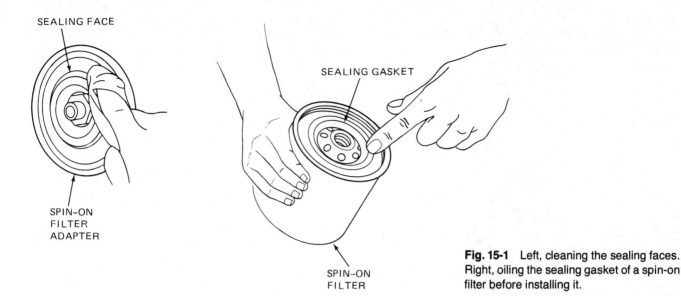

SEALING FACE

SPIN-ON FILTER ADAPTER

SEALING GASKET

SPIN-ON FILTER

Fig. 15-1 Left, cleaning the sealing faces. Right, oiling the sealing gasket of a spin-on filter before installing it.

place by hand. A drain pan should be placed under the old filter as it is removed to catch any oil that runs out.

With the old filter off, the recess and sealing face of the filter adapter should be wiped with a clean cloth (Fig. 15-1, left). Then the sealing gasket of the new filter should be coated with clean oil (Fig. 15-1, right). Finally, the new filter should be hand-tightened until the gasket comes up against the sealing face of the adapter. Then hand-tighten the filter another half turn. After installation, the engine should be run at fast idle to check for oil leaks. Check the oil level in the engine, and add oil if necessary.

NOTE The engine oil should be changed before the new filter is installed. A new filter should always start out with new oil.

Most oil filters on motorcycle engines have replaceable filter elements (Fig. 15-2). This type of filter is located in one of two places. It is either in the crankcase or attached to the crankcase. Figure 14-14 shows the filter installed inside the crankcase. To change the filter element, a bolt is removed from the center of the cover. Then the spring and filter element are removed from the crankcase.

In the other widely used filter installation, the filter element is located inside a finned cover that fastens to the crankcase. Usually, the cover is attached to the front of the engine. The fins on the cover dissipate heat to help control the temperature of the oil. Figure 15-2 shows this filter in exploded view.

To change the filter element, take off the filter cover by removing the bolt from its center. Then pull the cover off of the engine and take out the element. The old O-ring seals and filter element are discarded. Wipe the inside of the cover with a clean cloth. Be sure no traces of lint or dirt remain.

Install the new filter element in the cover with new O-rings. They are in the package with the new filter element. Then install the oil-filter cover on the engine.

Start the engine and check for oil leaks around the cover. Be sure the oil warning light goes out in a few seconds. If it does not, stop the engine immediately and find out why. If the engine has an oil-pressure gauge, note whether the oil pressure has changed. With a clean, new filter element, which will pass more oil, the pressure may be lower.

Stop the engine and check the oil level. Add oil if necessary. Installing a new filter element will require additional oil to bring the engine oil level to the proper height. Some manufacturers give two different oil-fill specifications. One is for the amount of oil to be added when only the oil is changed. The other is used when the filter element is changed along with the oil. This re-

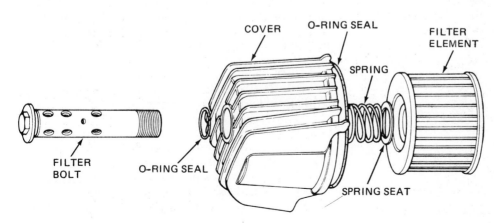

COVER   O-RING SEAL   FILTER ELEMENT

SPRING

FILTER BOLT   O-RING SEAL   SPRING SEAT

Fig. 15-2 Replaceable type of oil-filter element. (*Honda Motor Company, Ltd.*)

quires a larger quantity of oil, including the oil required to fill up the oil filter while maintaining the engine oil level at the FULL mark. For example, one model of motorcycle specifies the oil fill as 3 quarts [2.8 L] when only the oil is changed. But when the filter element also is changed, 3.4 quarts [3.2 L] are required.

The oil-filter element should be changed according to the maintenance schedule for the motorcycle. Usually the recommended interval is every other oil change. However, some owners change the oil-filter element every time the oil is changed.

15-6
CLEANING THE OIL-PUMP SCREEN (FOUR-CYCLE ENGINE)
In the four-cycle engine, an oil pump is used to send oil to the various moving parts of the engine. To clean the oil, an oil filter is used. As the oil leaves the pump, dirt and other contaminants are removed by the filter element (Chap. 14). This prevents excessive wear and damage that dirty oil can cause to moving engine parts.

However, the oil filter cleans the oil only after it passes through the oil pump. The oil filter does not protect the pump itself from dirt and other contaminants which get into the oil in the crankcase. The oil-pump screen (Fig. 15-3) or strainer does this job. It protects the pump, which also has close clearances and rapidly moving parts, from being damaged by dirty oil passing through it.

Basically, the oil-pump screen is a wire-mesh strainer fitted around the pickup tube of the oil pump, as shown in Fig. 14-14. As the oil in the crankcase is drawn into the pump, the oil must first pass through the screen. Dirt, metal particles, and sludge are trapped on the screen. This allows only clean oil to enter the oil pump.

In most engines the oil-pump screen is located inside the crankcase under the oil pump. To clean the screen, drain the oil from the crankcase of a wet-sump engine. Then remove any levers, cables, or exhaust pipes that are in the way. Take off the crankcase oil pan or the crankcase cover, as required. Remove the oil-pump

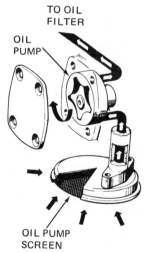

TO OIL FILTER

OIL PUMP

OIL PUMP SCREEN

Fig. 15-3 The oil-pump screen strains the oil before it goes to the oil pump.

screen from the oil pump or pickup tube. Clean the screen and oil pan or cover with solvent. Carefully scrape away any traces of gasket material on the oil pan or cover. Wipe out any dirt and sludge with a clean cloth.

Fit the screen to the pickup tube or to the pump and install it. On some engines, one or more new O-rings must be used to seal various openings. Be sure the O-rings are properly positioned when installed.

Install the oil pan or crankcase cover, using a new gasket if required. Then install any other parts removed earlier. Check the condition of the crankcase drain plug. If its condition is good, install it. Then fill the crankcase with the specified quantity and grade of oil. Start the engine and check for oil leaks. Stop the engine and check the oil level.

Cleaning the oil-pump screen is recommended every 12 months or 6000 miles [10,000 km] by some manufacturers. When the motorcycle is run in very dusty areas, the screen should be cleaned more often.

15-7
OIL PUMPS (FOUR-CYCLE ENGINE)
Oil pumps require little service in normal operation. If a pump is badly worn, it will not maintain oil pressure and should be removed for repair or replacement. In such a case, refer to the manufacturer's shop manual for details of servicing.

Relief valves are not usually adjustable, although springs of different tension may be installed to change the regulating pressure. However, this is not usually recommended. A spring of the proper tension was originally installed on the engine. Any change of pressure is usually brought about by some defect that requires correction. For example, badly worn bearings may pass so much oil that the oil pump cannot maintain normal pressure in the lines. Installing a stronger spring in the relief valve would not increase oil pressure. The relief valve does not operate under these circumstances.

15-8
CHECKING THE ENGINE OIL PRESSURE (FOUR-CYCLE ENGINE)
The oil pressure can be checked by removing an oil-gallery plug from the crankcase. Then use the necessary fittings and adapters to connect the pressure gauge. Start the engine and run it at about 3000 rpm. When the oil temperature is about 140°F [60°C], a typical specification is for the oil pressure to be 50 to 64 psi [3.5 to 4.5 kg/cm²]. If the oil pressure is not within specifications, check the oil pump as outlined in the manufacturer's service manual.

15-9
OIL-PRESSURE INDICATORS (FOUR-CYCLE ENGINE)
Oil-pressure indicators are discussed in Chap. 14. These units seldom require service. Defects in either the instrument-cluster unit or the engine unit usually require replacement of the defective unit. If the indicator is not functioning normally, a new engine unit may be temporarily substituted for the old one. This will determine whether the fault is in the engine unit or the instrument-cluster unit.

15-10 SERVICING THE CRANKCASE BREATHER (FOUR-CYCLE ENGINE)

Some water and oil may accumulate in the drain tube of the crankcase-breather system. Periodically the drain tube should be emptied. This is done by removing the drain plug and allowing any liquid to run out (Fig. 15-4). Then check that the breather tube is not clogged or collapsed.

On the type of system that has a crankcase-breather separator, the separator is removed from the engine. Take out the flow restrictor and drain the separator. Then reinstall the restrictor and put the separator back on the engine.

A routine service interval for draining the crankcase breather is every 3600 miles [6000 km]. Riding in the rain and at full throttle can cause water to accumulate in the crankcase-breather system. Under these conditions, the system should be drained more frequently, and whenever moisture can be seen in the clear plastic drain tube.

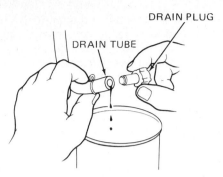

Fig. 15-4 Draining the crankcase-breather system.

15-11 TWO-CYCLE-ENGINE LUBRICATING SYSTEMS

Three different types of lubricating systems are used on two-cycle engines. These are the premix, oil-injection, and pressure-oiling systems. On engines that require gasoline and oil to be premixed, no additional lubricating-system service is required. The oil and gasoline are mixed according to the manufacturer's instructions. Details of preparing premix are given in Chap. 14.

Engines using oil-injection and pressure-oiling systems have an oil pump. Its operation is described in Chap. 14. On many motorcycles, the oil pump is located behind the right or left side cover of the engine.

Failure of the oil pump on a two-cycle engine seldom occurs. However, the pump may get out of adjustment. Then it will deliver either too much or too little oil to the engine. When too little oil is delivered, engine failure may occur before you know there is a lubrication problem. Excessive oil delivery often causes smoke in the engine exhaust at steady speed.

When little or no oil is reaching the engine, first check the oil tank. A glance at the sight glass (Fig. 14-3) in the tank will tell you if the tank is empty and if more oil should be added. If so, add the oil recommended in the manufacturer's service manual. Problems that can result from the use of the wrong oil are discussed in ⌧ 13-7.

Where there is oil in the tank, and no oil delivery to the engine, examine the oil line for kinks and cracks. A quick check of the oil line can be made by removing it from the pump. With the line disconnected, oil should flow freely from the line. If no oil flows, check the pump.

The output from the pump is controlled by a cable from the throttle grip (Fig. 14-3). Wear and stretching of the cable allows the pump to get out of adjustment. If the cable is too tight, too much oil is discharged. Carbon deposits may accumulate in the cylinder and ports and on the spark plug. An oil-pump cable that is too tight also could prevent the throttle valve in the carburetor from opening fully. When the cable is too loose, not enough oil will reach the engine. As a result, piston and cylinder scoring and other types of engine failure may occur.

To adjust the oil-pump cable on one motorcycle, adjust the throttle cable to have 0.020 to 0.040 inch [0.5 to 1.0 mm] of free play. This adjustment is made by turning the throttle-cable adjuster located at the upper end of the cable, close to the throttle-grip housing.

Next, remove the right side cover from the engine. Hold the throttle wide open. Set the oil pump by turning the pump-cable adjuster until the adjusting marks align, as shown in Fig. 15-5. The procedure for adjusting the oil pump varies on different motorcycles. Follow the steps in the manufacturer's service manual for the motorcycle you are servicing.

Sometimes air can get trapped in the oil pump or oil lines. This can occur after an oil pump or oil line is replaced, when the tank is drained or runs empty, and if a line cracks and the pump begins to draw in air. Getting the air out requires bleeding the oil pump.

Most oil pumps have a special air-bleed screw (Fig. 14-3). When it is removed, oil should run out of the hole. If no oil appears, manually operate the oil pump with

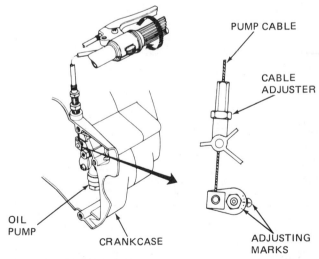

Fig. 15-5 Adjusting the oil pump in a two-cycle engine. (*Suzuki Motor Company, Ltd.*)

the pump control lever at full output until oil flows from the hole. As soon as a steady flow of oil, without any bubbles, runs from the hole, install the air-bleed screw.

Air trapped in the oil-pump discharge line sometimes can cause a problem. To eliminate air in this line, disconnect the line from the pump. Then use a plastic squeeze bottle or oil can to completely fill the line with oil.

CHAPTER 15
REVIEW QUESTIONS

1. What are the two main complaints about the engine lubricating system?
2. List the possible causes of low oil pressure.
3. Explain how to check the oil level in an engine.
4. When should the oil be changed in a four-cycle engine?
5. How is the oil changed in a dry-sump engine?
6. Why does an oil change include an inspection of the drain plug and washer?
7. What can cause an oil leak at the drain plug?
8. Describe the procedure for replacing an oil-filter element.
9. What is the difference between the oil-pump screen and the oil filter?
10. How often should the oil-pump screen be cleaned?
11. Explain how to check the oil pressure on a motorcycle that does not have an oil-pressure gauge.
12. What service does the crankcase breather require?
13. What can cause the oil pump on a two-cycle engine to get out of adjustment?
14. Describe how to bleed the air from an oil pump.

16

ENGINE COOLING SYSTEMS

After studying this chapter,
you should be able to:

1. Discuss air cooling of engines and explain how it works.

2. Describe liquid cooling of engines and explain how it works.

3. Explain the purpose of the various components of the pressurized liquid-cooling system, including the water pump, cooling fan, radiator, thermostat, and radiator pressure cap.

4. Discuss antifreeze solutions and the job they do.

5. Explain how to service an air-cooled-engine cooling system.

6. Discuss liquid-cooling-system troubles and their causes.

7. Describe nine liquid-cooling-system tests.

8. Explain how to clean the cooling system.

9. Describe how to locate and repair radiator leaks.

Fig. 16-1 An air-cooled motorcycle engine. (*ATW*)

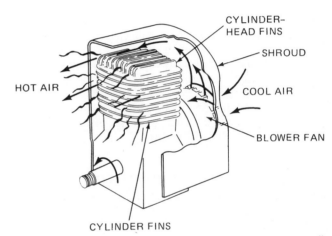

Fig. 16-2 Forced-draft type of air-cooling system on a small engine.

16-1 AIR-COOLED ENGINES

Most motorcycle engines are air cooled. Movement of the air around the engine carries off excess heat. A few motorcycle engines, and all automotive engines, are liquid cooled. In these, a coolant—water mixed with an antifreeze such as ethylene glycol—circulates inside the engine to carry away excess heat. We deal with air-cooled engines first in this chapter.

The air-cooled engine has fins on the cylinder head and cylinders (Fig. 16-1) which dissipate the heat. There are two types of air-cooling systems. The simplest is the open or open-draft system used on most motorcycle engines. This system is shown in Fig. 16-1. The second type of air-cooling is the forced-draft system, used on most other small engines (Fig. 16-2). This uses a blower or fan and a shroud to direct the forced air to flow around the fins and improve cooling. This system is not used on motorcycles, except for the engines on some minibikes.

The purpose of the cooling system is to remove excess heat from the engine so it does not overheat and damage itself. In the engine, the combustion temperatures may reach 3600°F [1982°C] (Fig. 16-3). Some of this heat gets to the cylinder wall. The upper part of the cylinder wall may reach 1200°F [649°C]. Much of this heat leaves the cylinder through the cooling fins of an

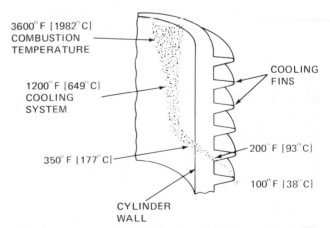

Fig. 16-3 Path of heat travel from combustion gases to the cooling fins. This is an example of heat transfer by conduction.

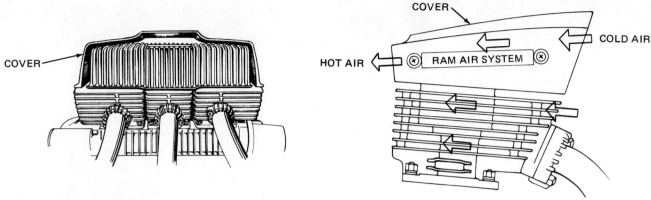

Fig. 16-4 An air-cooled engine that has a cover, or shroud, to direct air around the center cylinder. (*Suzuki Motor Company, Ltd.*)

air-cooled engine. But heat does travel down the length of the cylinder wall, as shown in Fig. 16-3. Most of the heat has traveled away by the time it reaches the bottom fin.

The cylinder heads and cylinders for motorcycle engines are usually made from aluminum. Aluminum is much lighter than a metal such as cast iron. Also, it is a much better conductor of heat than cast iron. However, aluminum is relatively soft. For this reason, the piston and rings cannot run directly on an aluminum cylinder wall. The aluminum would quickly wear away. Therefore, either the cylinder bore is chrome plated or a cast-iron sleeve is installed inside the bore. Either the chrome or the cast iron can take the piston and ring movement without undue wear.

16-2 AIR-COOLED-ENGINE CONSTRUCTION
In an air-cooled engine, each cylinder is semi-independent, surrounded by its own cooling fins (Fig. 16-4). To assist in cooling, some multiple-cylinder motorcycle engines have shrouds, or covers, to direct air around the cylinder fins (Fig. 16-4).

Fins are arranged in various ways to make best use of the air passing by. As you look at the various pictures of motorcycle engines in this book, note the different shapes and positions of fins. As a rule, two-cycle engines have larger fin areas than four-cycle engines. The reason is that the two-cycle engine has twice as many power strokes (to create heat) as the four-cycle engine when both are running at the same speed.

16-3 LIQUID-COOLED ENGINES
Liquid-cooled motorcycle engines are used on two-cycle racing bikes and on medium-to-large street-legal touring bikes. A liquid-cooled engine of this type is shown in Fig. 16-5. The arrows in Fig. 16-5 show how the coolant circulates between the engine and the cooling-system radiator.

Figure 16-6 shows the operation of the system. In the engine, the coolant circulates through water jackets. The water jackets are openings between the cylinder walls and cylinder heads and the outer shells of the cylinders and heads. As the coolant passes through the water jackets, it picks up heat and gets hot. Taking heat from the cylinder walls and head in this way keeps the walls and head relatively cool.

In some liquid-cooling systems, the radiator is mounted in front of the steering stem. To improve the air flow through the radiator, a cowl, or shroud, is placed in front of it. Coolant flows from the engine water jackets to the radiator and back to the water pump through rubber hose, the frame downtube, and the steering stem. Because the hollow tubing of the frame and steering stem is used to carry coolant, the only hoses required are two sections that carry liquid between the engine and the frame.

The liquid is water mixed with an antifreeze compound which is usually the chemical ethylene glycol. This mixture is called the *coolant*. The antifreeze lowers the freeze point of the liquid mixture, raises the boiling point, and helps prevent corrosion of the metal water-jacket surfaces. A widely used mixture for coolant is 50 percent water and 50 percent ethylene glycol.

As the coolant circulates, it picks up heat from the engine and carries this heat to the radiator. The radiator then cools the coolant. The radiator transfers the heat from its fins to the air passing between them. The coolant, water jackets, radiator size, and other details of the cooling system are designed so as to maintain the cylinder walls, head, pistons, and other working parts at efficient, but not excessive, temperature. Two types of liquid-cooling systems are used. These are (1) the natural-circulation, or thermosiphon, system and (2) the forced-circulation system.

Thermosiphon cooling is not widely used. In this system, the coolant circulates because hot coolant is thinner and lighter than cool coolant. So the hot coolant rises and the cool coolant sinks. This produces the circulation.

16-4 FORCED CIRCULATION
In the forced-circulation system, a water pump is used to assure continuous circulation of the coolant. Figure 16-6 shows the cooling system for a three-cylinder two-cycle engine. The water pump, driven by the engine, keeps

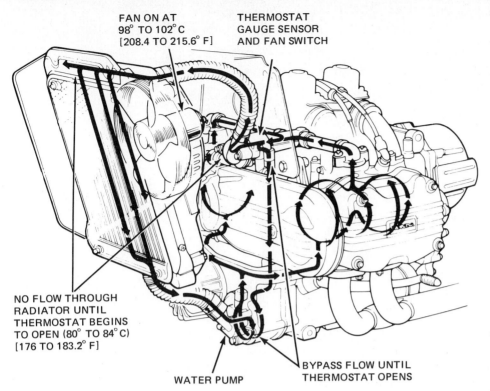

FAN ON AT
98° TO 102° C
[208.4 TO 215.6° F]

THERMOSTAT
GAUGE SENSOR
AND FAN SWITCH

NO FLOW THROUGH
RADIATOR UNTIL
THERMOSTAT BEGINS
TO OPEN (80° TO 84°C)
[176 TO 183.2° F]

WATER PUMP

BYPASS FLOW UNTIL
THERMOSTAT OPENS

Fig. 16-5 A liquid-cooled four-cylinder motorcycle engine. The arrows show the flow of coolant through the cooling system. (*Honda Motor Company, Ltd.*)

the coolant circulating while the engine is running. Note where the water pump is located in this engine. The coolant flows from the bottom of the radiator to the water pump. There the coolant is pressurized and forced up through the water jackets in the cylinders and cylinder head. The water pump, cooling fan, and radiator are discussed in the following sections.

16-5
WATER PUMP
Water pumps are of the impeller type. They are mounted in the cooling system between the engine and the radiator (Fig. 16-6). The pump consists of a housing, with a coolant inlet and outlet, and an impeller. The impeller is a flat plate mounted on the pump shaft with a series of flat or curved blades. When the impeller rotates, the coolant between the blades is thrown outward by centrifugal force and is forced through the pump outlet and into the cylinder block. The pump inlet is connected by a hose to the bottom of the radiator. Coolant from the radiator is drawn into the pump to replace the coolant forced through the outlet.

The impeller shaft is supported on one or more bearings. A seal prevents coolant from leaking out around the bearing. The water pump shown in Fig. 16-6 is driven by the starter-clutch gear from the engine crankshaft.

16-6
COOLING FAN
When the motorcycle is not moving, and under certain other conditions, the engine may begin to overheat. To prevent this, the liquid-cooling system includes a fan that is driven by an electric motor or by the engine crankshaft. The purpose of the fan is to provide a flow of air through the radiator to

improve engine cooling. The fan shown in Fig. 16-6 has four blades which, in rotating, pull air through the radiator. The fan motor turns on automatically when the coolant temperature gets too high.

Some engines are equipped with a fan shroud that improves fan performance. The shroud increases the efficiency of the fan. With the shroud, most or all of the air pulled back by the fan must first pass through the radiator.

16-7
RADIATOR
The radiator holds a large volume of coolant in close contact with a large volume of air so that heat will transfer from the coolant to the air. The radiator core is divided into two separate and intricate compartments. Coolant passes through one, and air passes through the other. The actions in one type of radiator are shown in Fig. 16-7.

There are several types of radiator construction. The *tube-and-fin radiator* shown in Fig. 16-7 consists of a series of tubes extending from the top to the bottom of the radiator, or from the upper to the lower tank. This is called a *down-flow radiator*. Fins are placed around the tubes to improve heat transfer. Air passes around the outside of the tubes and between the fins, picking up heat from the coolant in passing.

There is a coolant chamber, or tank, at the top or side of the radiator, into which hot coolant is delivered from the engine. Figure 16-6 shows a radiator with a top tank. A radiator cap on the tank can be removed and coolant added to replace any lost by evaporation or leakage.

The tank above or on the side of the radiator serves two purposes. It provides a reserve supply of coolant, and it provides a place where the coolant can be sepa-

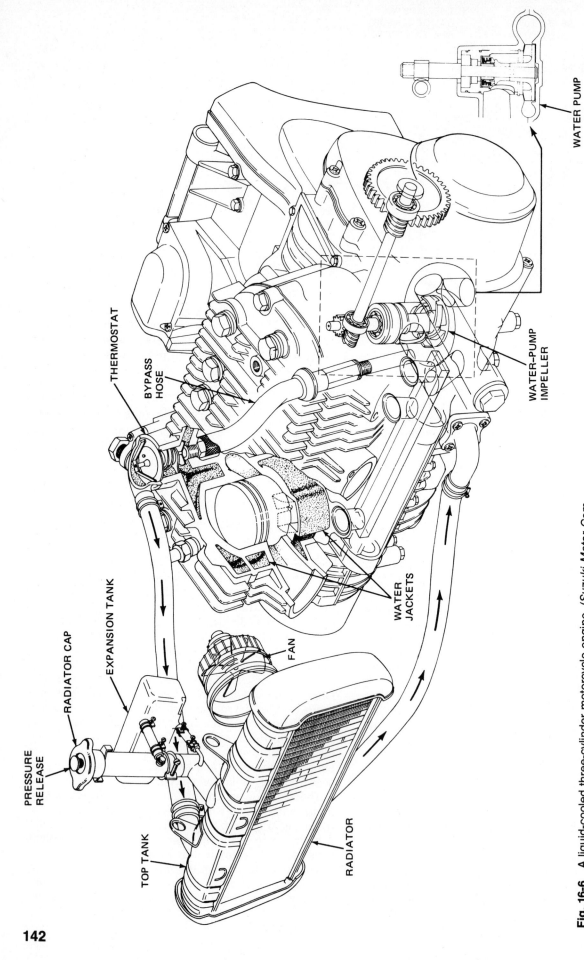

Fig. 16-6 A liquid-cooled three-cylinder motorcycle engine. (*Suzuki Motor Company, Ltd.*)

WATER PUMP

WATER-PUMP IMPELLER

WATER JACKETS

THERMOSTAT

BYPASS HOSE

RADIATOR CAP

PRESSURE RELEASE

EXPANSION TANK

TOP TANK

FAN

RADIATOR

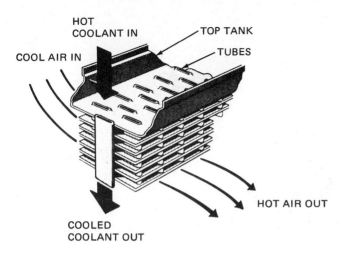

Fig. 16-7 Circulation of air and coolant through a tube-and-fin radiator. (*Union Carbide Corporation*)

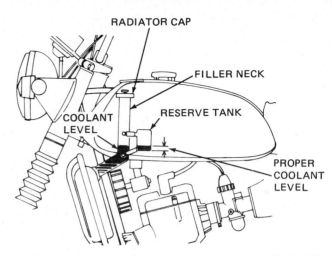

Fig. 16-8 Proper coolant level in the filler neck of a liquid-cooled engine. (*Suzuki Motor Company, Ltd.*)

rated from any air that might be circulating in the system.

Some liquid-cooling systems have a separate expansion tank, or reserve tank, as shown in Figs. 16-6 and 16-8. The expansion tank is partly filled with coolant and is connected to the radiator filler neck. The coolant in the engine expands as the engine heats up. This sends some of the coolant into the expansion tank instead of leaking it out on the ground.

16-8 THERMOSTAT

A thermostat is located in the passage between the cylinder head and the upper radiator tank. Figure 16-6 shows the thermostat location in the engine. The thermostat contains a temperature-sensitive wax pellet connected to a valve.

When the engine is hot, the wax pellet expands, opening the valve to allow coolant to pass freely into the radiator. But when the engine is cold, the wax pellet contracts, closing the valve. This closes the coolant return line to the radiator. Now, the coolant in the engine water jackets cannot leave. Therefore, the coolant and the engine both heat up very rapidly. This is desirable because the engine should heat up as rapidly as possible after starting. When an engine is operated cold, the lubricating oil flows so slowly that moving parts may not be fully lubricated. This promotes excessive wear. Also, water vapor in the air condenses and drips down into the crankcase. All this is minimized by the action of the thermostat.

As the engine warms up, the wax pellet expands and opens the valve to permit coolant to circulate between the engine and the radiator. With the thermostat open, normal coolant circulation and cooling of the engine take place.

16-9 PRESSURIZED COOLING SYSTEM

Liquid-cooled motorcycle engines have a pressurized-cooling system. Here's how it works. A special radiator cap, called a *pressure cap* (Fig. 16-9), is used on the

radiator. The cap has a pressure valve. When the cap is locked onto the radiator filler neck, the pressure valve seals the cooling system from the outside air.

As the engine warms up, the temperature of the coolant increases. The increased temperature causes the coolant and air trapped in the radiator to expand. But because of the pressure cap on the radiator, they

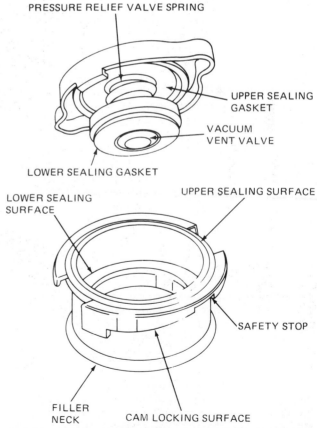

Fig. 16-9 A radiator pressure cap and filler neck, showing the locking arrangement.

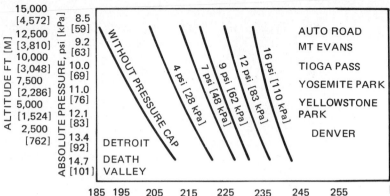

Fig. 16-10 Relationship between pressure and the boiling point of water, showing how pressure caps of various capacities can increase the boiling point.

can't get out. As a result, the pressure rises in the cooling system. This prevents boiling at normal temperatures. It also allows the cooling system to operate at a higher temperature so it is more efficient.

Water boils at about 212°F [100°C] at sea level. If the pressure on water is increased, it will not boil until a higher temperature is reached. Without pressurizing, the cooling system must be designed to prevent water from reaching 212°F [100°C]. But if the system is pressurized, water temperature can safely go up to almost 250°F [121°C] without boiling. This higher temperature allows the cooling system to operate more efficiently. Each added 1 psi [0.07 kg/cm²] increases the boiling point of water about 3¼°F [1.8°C].

Figure 16-10 shows the relationship between pressure and the boiling point of water. The cooling system shown in Fig. 16-6 uses a pressure cap on the radiator that allows the pressure to build up to a maximum of about 12 psi [0.84 kg/cm²].

16-10
RADIATOR PRESSURE CAP To pressurize a liquid-cooling system, a pressure cap is used on the radiator. A pressure cap is shown in Fig. 16-9. The pressure cap contains two spring-loaded valves. One, called the *pressure valve*, opens if the pressure gets too high. This prevents excessive pressure from damaging the radiator. The other valve is the *vacuum valve*. It operates when the engine cools. When this happens, a partial vacuum could form in the cooling system. The vacuum valve prevents this by opening to admit air from the outside. If a high vacuum formed, it might cause the radiator to partly collapse, pushed in by atmospheric pressure.

The radiator cap shown in Fig. 16-6 has a third valve—a *pressure-release valve*. Normally, it is not necessary to remove the radiator cap while the engine is warm. A sudden release of pressure could cause the coolant to start boiling. Boiling coolant and steam would spray out of the filler neck. They could burn your hands.

Some radiator caps, such as the one shown in Fig. 16-6, have a pressure-release valve. If you must remove the radiator cap from a warm engine, press the pressure-release button first. This releases the pressure and directs any steam and boiling coolant away from you. However, the safest procedure is to allow the engine to cool before removing the radiator cap.

16-11
ANTIFREEZE SOLUTIONS Liquid-cooling systems do not use plain water. They use coolant, which usually is a mixture of half antifreeze and half water. This mixture ratio has a boiling point of about 222°F [105°C] at atmospheric pressure. In a pressurized cooling system, the coolant enters the radiator at a higher temperature. Therefore, the temperature difference between the coolant and the surrounding air is greater. This causes a greater heat transfer.

Water freezes at 32°F [0°C]. If water freezes in the engine cooling system, it stops coolant circulation. Some parts of the engine will overheat, and this could seriously damage the engine. What is worse, when water freezes, it expands. Water freezing in the cylinder block could expand enough to crack the block. Water freezing in the radiator could split the radiator seams. Both conditions are serious. A cracked cylinder block cannot be repaired satisfactorily. A split radiator is also hard to repair.

To prevent freezing, antifreeze is added to the water. A mixture that is about one-half water and one-half antifreeze will not freeze even if the temperature drops to −34°F [−37°C]. It seldom gets that cold anywhere in the United States. Higher concentrations of antifreeze in water will prevent freezing of the coolant at temperatures as low as −84°F [−64°C]. The most commonly used antifreeze is ethylene glycol.

16-12
TEMPERATURE INDICATORS There are two kinds of temperature indicators: lights and a gauge. The light system includes a light that comes on when the engine temperature gets too high. This is a warning to the rider that something is wrong, so the engine can be stopped before serious damage occurs.

The other system has a gauge in the instrument cluster. A needle or pointer moves across the gauge to show the actual temperature of the coolant in the engine. The operation and service of temperature indicators is covered in Chap. 22.

144

16-13
SERVICING AIR-COOLED-ENGINE
COOLING SYSTEMS   Fins on the head and cylinder provide large surface areas from which heat can be dissipated. The heat flows from the inside of the cylinder, through the cylinder metal, to the fins, which transfer it to the outside air, as shown in Fig. 16-3.

If the fins become dirty and covered with oil or mud, the heat cannot get through. The accumulations act as a blanket to hold heat in the engine. As a result, the engine becomes overheated. The oil film on the engine parts becomes less effective, or actually fails. The result is that engine parts wear rapidly and engine life is shortened. Therefore, it is essential for long engine life to clean the engine when needed.

Another purpose of periodically cleaning the engine is to check for loose nuts or bolts and loose, broken, cracked, or otherwise damaged parts. One way to clean the engine is to use a stiff brush and water. This will get into all the crevices where dirt can accumulate and will clean away most of the mud and oil that can cause trouble. For a complete cleaning job, use a degreasing compound.

CAUTION **Do not clean a hot engine. Wait until it is cool. Water thrown on the hot engine can cause the head or cylinder to crack. Some cleaning solutions are flammable and could burst into flames if sprayed on a hot engine. Also, make sure that there is adequate ventilation. Some fumes from cleaning solutions are unhealthy to breathe.**

Three substances for cleaning the cylinder and head can be used—a degreaser, a solvent, or live steam. As a first step, use a wooden stick to scrape away all the accumulated trash, dirt, and grease. Do not use a metal tool because this will scratch the cylinder and head and encourage accumulations of dirt.

Then use the material you have available to finish the cleaning job. Degreasing compound comes in pressure-spray cans or in larger containers. To use live steam, you need a steam cleaner. This will be available in many shops.

While cleaning the cylinder and head, check for oil leaks, which usually show up as a heavy accumulation of dirt. Check also for cracks or other damage. Then apply the solvent on the areas to be cleaned. The degreaser in the pressure can is very easy to use. Other types of solvent can be applied with a bristle brush. After about five minutes, flush off the solution with a stream of water from a hose. If you have used solvent, use a solution of soapy water brushed on and then flushed off.

16-14
LIQUID-COOLING-SYSTEM TROUBLE
DIAGNOSIS   Two common complaints related to the liquid-cooling system are engine overheating and cooling-system leaks. If the engine is slow to warm up, this could also be a fault of the cooling system. Possible causes of these complaints are discussed in following sections. Detailed testing of the system is covered later in the chapter.

16-15
OVERHEATING   The rider may notice that the red light stays on or the temperature gauge registers in the overheating zone. Also, the rider may complain that the engine boiled over. Possible causes of engine overheating include:

1. A low coolant level resulting from leakage of coolant from the system, as described in 16-16.
2. Accumulations of corrosion, rust, and scale in the system, which prevent normal circulation of coolant. This can occur if plain water without antifreeze is used in an aluminum radiator and engine.
3. Collapsed hoses which prevent normal coolant circulation.
4. A defective thermostat which does not open normally and blocks circulation of coolant. If the engine overheats without the radiator becoming normally warm and if the fan is not running, then the thermostat is probably at fault. Also, the fan may be operating improperly.
5. A defective water pump which does not circulate enough coolant through the engine. One of the more common causes of a defective water pump is bearing failure.
6. Afterboil. The coolant may start to boil after the engine has been turned off. This could happen, for example, after a long, hard ride. The engine has so much heat in it that, after the engine is turned off, the coolant starts to boil.
7. Boiling caused by a frozen radiator. This hinders or stops the circulation of coolant. Then the coolant in the engine becomes so hot that it boils. Freezing of the coolant in the radiator, cylinder block, or head may crack the block or head and can open up seams in the radiator. A frozen engine may be damaged seriously.

NOTE   There are other causes of engine overheating which have nothing to do with conditions in the cooling system. High-altitude operation, insufficient oil, overloading of the engine, hot-climate operation, improperly timed ignition, long periods of slow-speed or idling operation—any of these can cause overheating of the engine. See Chap. 23 on engine-trouble diagnosis for additional information.

16-16
LOSS OF COOLANT   Leaks are usually obvious, for two reasons. First, the radiator requires frequent refilling with coolant. Second, the point of the leak usually shows up as telltale scale or water marks below the leak. If it is a cylinder-head-gasket leak, the gasket may require replacement. Attaching bolts or nuts should be tightened to the correct torque.

If the leak is in the radiator, the radiator should be removed and either repaired (see 16-27) or replaced.

If the leak is at a hose connection, the hose connection should be tightened. If a hose is leaking, it should be replaced.

Pressure-testing the cooling system to locate leaks is described in 16-25.

16-17
SLOW WARMUP

The probable cause of slow engine warmup is a thermostat that is stuck open. This open position allows the coolant to circulate between the engine and radiator even though the engine is cold. Therefore, the engine has to run longer to reach operating temperature. As a result, engine wear will be greater because the engine operates cold for a longer time.

16-18
LIQUID-COOLING-SYSTEM TESTS

Liquid-cooling-system tests include

1. Checking the coolant level
2. Checking the coolant antifreeze strength
3. Testing the thermostat
4. Checking the hose and hose connections
5. Testing the water pump

6. Checking for exhaust-gas leakage into the cooling system
7. Pressure-testing the cooling system and cap
8. Checking the fan
9. Checking the cooling system for accumulations of rust and scale

These are covered in detail in the following sections.

16-19
CHECKING THE COOLANT LEVEL

Use care when removing a radiator cap, especially when the engine is hot. Cover the cap with a cloth to protect your hand and turn the cap only to the first stop. Any pressure in the system will be released through the overflow tube. Then turn the cap further to remove it.

Some manufacturers warn against taking the cap off when the engine is hot and there is pressure in the cooling system. They state that if the cap is turned slightly and you hear a hissing sound, you should retighten the cap at once. The cap should be left tight until the engine has cooled and the pressure has dropped. They also say that it should not be necessary to check the coolant level in the system unless the engine has been overheating.

With the pressure relieved from the cooling system, remove the radiator cap. Then look down the filler neck. In the cooling system shown in Fig. 16-8, there is a white level plate located in the filler neck. The coolant should be about even with the level plate. If a small amount of liquid is needed, you can add distilled water. When a large amount of coolant is needed, the proper mixture of water and distilled water and antifreeze should be added.

16-20
TESTING ANTIFREEZE STRENGTH

The strength of the antifreeze solution must be great enough to protect against freezing at the lowest expected temperatures. The strength of the antifreeze can be checked with any of three testers. One is the *hydrometer* (Fig. 16-11). The higher the float rises in the coolant, the higher the percentage of antifreeze in the coolant. To use the hydrometer, put the rubber tube into the coolant and then squeeze and release the rubber bulb. Note how high the float rises in the coolant. Check the lower scale, which shows the temperature of the coolant and how low the temperature must drop before the coolant will freeze.

A second tester has several balls in a glass tube. Coolant is drawn into the tube by squeezing and releasing a rubber bulb. The stronger the solution, the more balls will float.

A third tester, called a *refractometer,* uses the principle of light refraction (bending of light rays) as light passes through a drop of the coolant.

CAUTION Coolant is poisonous. It can cause serious illness and even death if it is swallowed. Never put coolant or the hydrometer tube in your mouth.

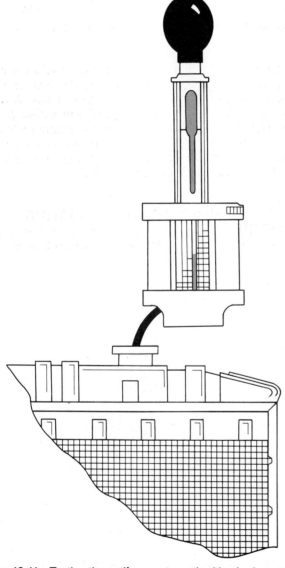

Fig. 16-11 Testing the antifreeze strength with a hydrometer.

16-21
TESTING THE THERMOSTAT To test the thermostat, remove it from the cooling system. Examine the thermostat for damage. If the complaint was slow warmup, the thermostat may be leaking. Hold the thermostat up to the light to see if the valve is closing completely. If there is a gap between the valve and the valve seat in the thermostat, replace the thermostat.

If your examination shows that the thermostat does not appear to be damaged, suspend the thermostat in a pan of water with a thermometer, as shown in Fig. 16-12. Heat the water on a stove burner or a hot plate. Watch the thermometer as the temperature rises. At about the temperature stamped on the thermostat or given in the manufacturer's service manual—usually 180°F [82°C]—the valve in the thermostat should begin to open. Continue heating the water to a temperature of 25°F [14°C] above the specification. At this temperature the thermostat should be fully open. Then, when cooled, the thermostat should close completely. If the thermostat does not open and close properly, it is defective and must be replaced.

16-22
CHECKING THE HOSE AND HOSE CONNECTIONS The appearance of the radiator hose and hose connections often indicates their condition. To check a radiator hose, squeeze the hose. It should feel firm. When you release the hose, it should quickly spring back into its original shape. If the hose is rotten and soft and collapses easily when squeezed, it should be replaced. Radiator hose must be in good condition, and connections should be properly tightened to avoid leaks.

16-23
TESTING THE WATER PUMP The operation of the water pump can be checked with the engine running. To make this test, substitute a clear plastic hose for the upper radiator hose. Then, when the engine is running, you can see how much coolant is circulating.

16-24
CHECKING FOR EXHAUST-GAS LEAKAGE INTO THE COOLANT A defective cylinder-head gasket may allow exhaust gas to leak into the cooling system. This is very damaging. Strong acids can form as the gas unites with the water in the coolant. These acids corrode the radiator and other cooling-system parts. A test for exhaust-gas leakage can be made with a tester installed in the radiator filler neck, as shown in Fig. 16-13.

The test is made with the engine running and then squeezing and releasing the bulb. This draws an air sample from the cooling system up through the test fluid. The test fluid is ordinarily blue. But if combustion gas is leaking into the cooling system, the test fluid will change to yellow. If a leak is indicated, the exact location can be found by removing one spark-plug wire at a time and retesting. When a leaking cylinder is firing, the liquid will change to yellow. When only nonleaking cylinders are firing, the liquid will remain blue in color.

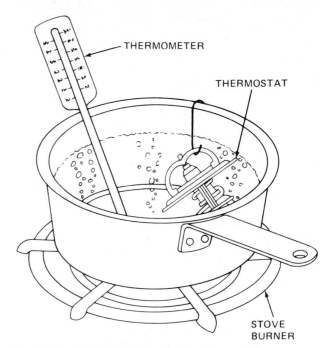

Fig. 16-12 Testing a cooling-system thermostat.

Undetected combustion leaks in the valve areas can cause cracked valve seats and cylinder heads. The coolant is forced away from the cracked area during heavy acceleration by the leakage of combustion gases through the leak. This causes excessive heat buildup. Then, when acceleration stops, the diverted coolant rushes back to the overheated area. The sudden cooling of the area can crack the head and valve seat.

16-25
PRESSURE-TESTING THE COOLING SYSTEM Some leaks in the cooling system are easy to find. They cause liquid to spray out of a hole or to drip

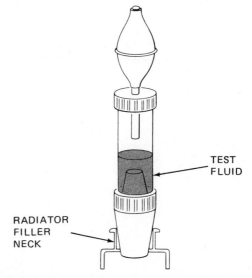

Fig. 16-13 Using a tester to check for exhaust-gas leakage into the cooling system.

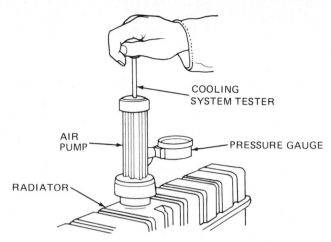

Fig. 16-14 Using the pressure tester to check the cooling system for leaks.

on the ground. To find other leaks, it is necessary to pressurize the cooling system.

To pressure-test the cooling system, apply pressure to it with a cooling-system tester (Fig. 16-14). The tester quickly shows a leaky cooling system. To use the tester, remove the radiator cap, fill the radiator to the proper level (but do not overfill it), wipe the filler-neck sealing surface, and attach the tester. Then operate the pump to build up the pressure to the capacity of the radiator cap. If the pressure holds steady, the cooling system is not leaking. But if the pressure drops, there are leaks. Look for liquid spraying or dripping from external leaks at hose connections, from hose, from water-pump and cylinder-head gaskets, or from the radiator.

If no external leaks are visible, remove the tester and start the engine. Run the engine until the normal operating temperature is reached. Reattach the tester, apply the specified pressure, and increase the speed to about half throttle. If the pressure-gauge needle fluctuates, it indicates an exhaust-gas leak, probably through a cylinder-head gasket. On a V-type or opposed engine, you can determine which bank, or side, is at fault by grounding the spark-plug leads on one bank.

When the needle does not fluctuate, sharply accelerate the engine several times and check for coolant being

blown out through the muffler. This would indicate a cracked block or head or a defective head gasket.

The pressure tester shown in Fig. 16-14 can be used with an adaptor to check the radiator pressure cap. Figure 16-15 shows how the adapter and the cap are attached to the tester. Then the rated pressure is applied to the cap. If the cap will not hold its rated pressure, it should be discarded.

16-26 CLEANING THE COOLING SYSTEM

Periodically check the radiator for mud, paper, and insects that may accumulate and block the air flow through the radiator. One way to remove most of the debris that catches on the radiator is to spray water through the radiator from the back side. Bent or damaged radiator fins should be straightened. When 20 percent of the radiator is obstructed, it cannot provide adequate cooling and the engine will overheat.

The cooling system should be cleaned periodically to remove collected rust and scale and to restore the system to proper operating condition. Most manufacturers recommend that the system be drained and flushed every 2 years. Coolant with new antifreeze should be put in at that time. Follow the procedure in the manufacturer's service manual.

16-27 LOCATING AND REPAIRING RADIATOR LEAKS

Leaks in a radiator leave telltale scale marks or coolant stains on the outside of the core below the leaks. An accurate way to locate radiator leaks is to remove the radiator from the motorcycle and drain out all the coolant. Then close the openings at top and bottom and immerse the radiator in water. Air bubbles will escape from the core through any leaks.

Small leaks can sometimes be repaired without removing the radiator from the motorcycle. Certain liquid compounds, when poured into the radiator, seep through the leaks. They harden on contact with the air, sealing off the openings. A more effective way of repairing leaks is to solder them. If there are leaks at various places in the core, it may not be worthwhile to attempt repair. The core is probably corroded to a point where other leaks will soon develop. Motorcycle radiators usually are made of aluminum to reduce weight. They corrode easily when tap water is used in the cooling system.

NOTE Radiator repair is usually done in a shop that specializes in radiator service.

16-28 WATER-PUMP SERVICE

Water pumps require little service in normal operation. They have sealed ball bearings that require no lubrication. If the pump develops noise or leaks or becomes otherwise defective, it must be removed for repair or replacement. Refer to the manufacturer's shop manual for details of the servicing procedure to be followed.

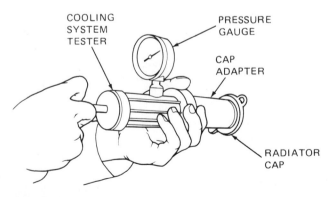

Fig. 16-15 Testing a radiator pressure cap.

CHAPTER 16
REVIEW QUESTIONS

1. What is the purpose of the cooling system?
2. Name the two types of cooling systems used on motorcycle engines.
3. What are the two types of air-cooling systems?
4. Define *heat*.
5. How do fins help remove heat from an air-cooled engine?
6. What method of heat transfer is used in engine cooling systems?
7. In a liquid-cooling system, what is the job of the water pump?
8. Explain why various arrangements of fins are used on air-cooled engines.
9. Which types of motorcycles have liquid-cooled engines?
10. How does the boiling point of coolant change when the cooling system is pressurized?
11. When does the cooling fan operate?
12. Should the thermostat be open or closed when the engine is cold?
13. Why is antifreeze used in the liquid-cooling system?
14. Name the two types of temperature indicators.
15. Explain how to clean the fins on an air-cooled engine.
16. What are the two major complaints about liquid-cooling systems?
17. How can the thermostat cause slow warmup?
18. Explain how to check the coolant level in an engine.
19. Why should the antifreeze strength be tested periodically?
20. Explain how to test a thermostat.
21. How do you check a radiator hose?
22. What can happen if exhaust gas seeps into the cooling system?
23. Explain how to pressure-test the cooling system.

PART

MOTORCYCLE
ELECTRIC EQUIPMENT

In Part 3 we cover the electric system used in motorcycles. First, we discuss electricity and electronics. We look at some of the actions of electricity and then describe diodes, transistors, and other solid-state devices. Next, we cover batteries, starters, charging systems, and ignition systems. For each of these, we describe their construction, their operation, troubleshooting, and servicing. Part 3 ends with a look at other electric units on the motorcycle, including headlights, horns, and indicating devices.

There are six chapters in Part 3. They are:

Chapter 17   Electricity and Electronics

Chapter 18   Batteries and Battery Service

Chapter 19   Starters and Starter Service

Chapter 20   Charging Systems

Chapter 21   Ignition Systems

Chapter 22   Electric Instruments and Wiring

CHAPTER 17

ELECTRICITY AND ELECTRONICS

After studying this chapter,
you should be able to:

1. Discuss the jobs that electricity does on the motorcycle.

2. Explain what electric current is, what causes it to flow, and how it is measured.

3. Describe the ammeter and how it works.

4. Discuss voltage and what it means in terms of current flow.

5. Explain the purpose of insulation.

6. Discuss Ohm's law.

7. Explain the difference between alternating current and direct current.

8. Discuss electronics and the two basic electronic devices.

9. Explain what *ground* means and why the motorcycle frame is used as the return electric circuit.

10. Describe the purpose of fuses and circuit breakers.

17-1 ELECTRICITY AND MOTORCYCLES

Figure 17-1 shows the complete electric system on a motorcycle. Electricity does several special jobs for motorcycles. One job is to operate the ignition system, which supplies electric sparks to the spark plugs in the engine cylinders. These sparks set fire to, or ignite, the air-fuel mixture. The mixture burns to produce heat and move the piston. This produces the power from the engine.

Many motorcycles have electric starters. These are small electric motors that spin the engine crankshaft to start the engine. A battery is required if an electric starting motor is used. The battery is an energy storage device. It stores chemical energy which, under certain conditions, can provide a flow of electric current. When a battery is used, a battery charging system is required to keep the battery charged. The charging system includes a generator, or alternator, which produces electricity when the engine is running. This electricity flows into the battery to restore the chemicals depleted during starting.

Also, motorcycles may be equipped with lights and a horn. Both of these require electricity. In this and following chapters we learn about electricity and look at the battery, starting, charging, and ignition systems.

Some variations of these systems are much like the systems used on automobiles. For example, motorcycle batteries and automobile batteries work in exactly the same way. The major difference is that the batteries used in most motorcycles are much smaller.

17-2 ELECTRICITY

Electricity is made up of many billions of tiny particles called *electrons*. Electrons are so small that it would take billions and billions of them, all piled together, to make a spot big enough to be seen through a microscope. Electrons are all around us. For example, in 1 ounce [28 g] of iron, there are about 22 million billion billion electrons. Electrons are normally locked up in the elements that form everything in the world.

17-3 ELECTRIC CURRENT

If electrons are forced to move together in the same direction in a wire, there is a flow, or *current*, of electrons. We call this flow an *electric current*. The job of the battery and alternator is to start the electrons moving in the same direction. When many electrons are moving, there is a high current. When relatively few are moving, the current is low.

17-4 MEASURING ELECTRIC CURRENT

The movement of electrons, or electric current, is measured in *amperes*, or *amps*. One ampere is a small flow of current. A battery might deliver 100 to 200 amperes as it operates the starting motor. A motorcycle headlight can draw 5 amperes or more. One ampere is a flow of about 6.28 billion billion electrons per second.

To determine the amount of current flowing in a wire, we use an ammeter. The ammeter uses one special effect of electron flow. This is that a flow of electrons produces magnetism.

17-5 MAGNETISM

There are two forms of magnetism: natural and electric. Natural magnets are made of iron or other metals. Electrically produced magnets are called *electromagnets*. Natural magnets and electromagnets act in the same way. They attract iron objects. Here are two important facts about magnets:

1. Magnets can produce electricity.
2. Electricity can produce magnets.

17-6 AMMETER

The ammeter is used to measure current. The simplest kind is shown in Fig. 17-2. This is the kind of ammeter used in the instrument cluster of some motorcycles. Its purpose is to tell the rider whether the alternator is charging the battery.

NOTE Some motorcycles have a voltmeter instead of an ammeter. The voltmeter indicates the *state of charge* of the battery. The ammeter indicates how much current is flowing into or out of the battery.

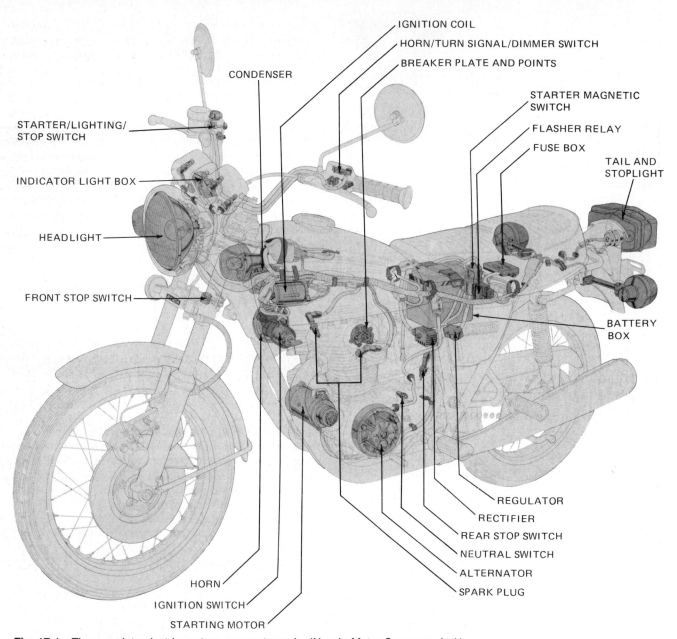

CONDENSER

STARTER/LIGHTING/
STOP SWITCH

INDICATOR LIGHT BOX

HEADLIGHT

FRONT STOP SWITCH

IGNITION COIL

HORN/TURN SIGNAL/DIMMER SWITCH

BREAKER PLATE AND POINTS

STARTER MAGNETIC
SWITCH

FLASHER RELAY

FUSE BOX

TAIL AND
STOPLIGHT

BATTERY
BOX

REGULATOR

RECTIFIER

REAR STOP SWITCH

NEUTRAL SWITCH

ALTERNATOR

SPARK PLUG

HORN

IGNITION SWITCH

STARTING MOTOR

Fig. 17-1 The complete electric system on a motorcycle. (*Honda Motor Company, Ltd.*)

The conductor in the ammeter (Fig. 17-2) is connected into the electric circuit between the alternator and the battery. When the battery is being charged, the current flows one way through the conductor. When current is being taken out of the battery, the current flows in the other direction through the conductor.

When current flows through any conductor, a magnetic field is produced around the conductor. An oval-shaped piece of iron, called an *armature,* is mounted above the conductor. A pointer is attached to the armature. A permanent magnet is positioned as shown so its ends are close to the armature. The permanent magnet attracts the armature and tends to hold it horizontal so the pointer points to zero.

If the motorcycle headlight is turned on when the engine is not running, current will flow from the battery, through the ammeter conductor, to the headlight. This causes a magnetic field around the conductor. This magnetic field attracts the armature and causes it to swing to the left, toward discharge, to show that the battery is being discharged.

If the engine is started so the alternator begins to work, the alternator sends current back through the conductor to the battery, charging it. Now the current is flowing through the conductor in the opposite direction. As a result, the magnetic field around the conductor also is reversed. The reversed magnetic field causes the armature and pointer to swing to the right, showing that the battery is being charged.

17-7
MAKING ELECTRONS MOVE To produce an electric current—which means to make electrons move—we have to concentrate a great many electrons

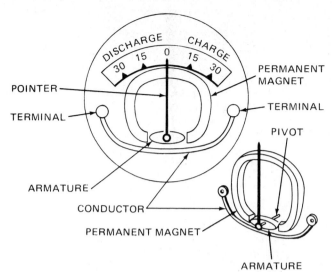

Fig. 17-2 Simplified drawing of an ammeter and its interior construction.

in one spot and remove electrons from another spot. Electrons try to balance out. They always try to move from areas where there are many electrons to areas where there are few electrons.

The battery or alternator has metal terminals. They concentrate electrons at one terminal and take them away from the other terminal. As a result, if the two terminals are connected by an electric circuit, electrons (current) will flow from the terminal with many electrons to the terminal with few electrons.

NOTE The terminal with many electrons is called the negative, or minus (−), terminal. The terminal that lacks electrons is called the positive, or plus (+), terminal. This is just the opposite of what you might think. The reason is that the electrons have negative, or minus, charges.

17-8 VOLTAGE
The difference in the concentrations of electrons at the two terminals is measured as *voltage*. When there is a great excess of electrons at one terminal and a great shortage at the other terminal, we say the voltage is high. What this means is that the pressure on the electrons to move from the "too many" terminal to the "too few" terminal is high.

High pressure is high voltage. Low pressure is low voltage. Motorcycle batteries are 12-volt units—low voltage. The spark at the spark-plug gap can reach 30,000 volts or more. That is high voltage—but not nearly as high as the voltage on the power lines that carry electricity from power plants to homes and factories. The voltage on cross-country power lines is several hundred thousand volts.

17-9 INSULATION
If electrons are lost from the wire in which they flow, electric power is lost. That is the reason that wires are covered with insulation. Insulation is material that will not allow electrons to flow through it. However, if the insulation goes bad, electric

current will flow where it is not supposed to. For example, if the insulation on the wire to a household appliance or a lamp is damaged, a fire could result. A person who touches the wire could get an electric shock.

The wires between the battery, alternator, and other electric devices on the motorcycle are all covered with insulation (Fig. 17-1). If the insulation fails, current can take a shortcut instead of flowing where it is supposed to. Such a shortcut is called a *short circuit*. It can cause trouble, as we learn later.

17-10 RESISTANCE
An insulator has a high resistance to the movement of electrons through it. A conductor, such as copper wire, has a very low resistance. Electrons can flow through it easily.

Resistance is measured in *ohms*. A long wire has more ohms of resistance than a short wire because the electrons have to travel farther. A thin wire has more ohms of resistance than a thick or heavy wire because the electrons have a harder time going through a thin wire. The electron path is smaller.

17-11 OHM'S LAW
The relationship between amperes (flow of current), voltage (electric pressure), and ohms (electric resistance) is this: Voltage is equal to amperage (I) times ohms (R).

$$V = I \times R$$

As voltage goes up, it can force more current (amperes) through a resistance (ohms). And as resistance goes up, a given voltage can force less current through. This last is important in motorcycle electricity. For example, if a battery connection goes bad, the resistance at that connection goes up. This means less current can flow (battery voltage stays the same). Perhaps not enough current could get through to crank the engine for starting. Or the bad connection (high resistance) might not let enough current get to the battery to recharge it. The battery would run down.

17-12 ALTERNATING CURRENT AND DIRECT CURRENT
Most of the electricity generated and used is alternating current (ac). The current first flows in one direction and then in the opposite direction. The electricity you use in your home changes direction, or alternates, 60 times a second. It is called 60-cycle ac (60 hertz).

Most electric devices on a motorcycle cannot use alternating current. For example, the battery is a direct-current (dc) unit. Other electric devices on the motorcycle also require direct current.

17-13 ELECTRONICS
The science of electronics has created a world of new electric devices. These include pocket radios, wristwatch calculators, pocket comput-

ers, small television sets, electronic controls in automobile and space vehicles, and many more.

An electronic device is any device operated by a flow of electrons. Electronic devices are used on motorcycles in battery-charging systems and ignition systems. We discuss these in later chapters.

◑ 17-14
BASIC ELECTRONIC DEVICES
Two basic electronic devices are the *diode* and the *transistor*. A diode allows current to flow in one direction but not in the other. Suppose a diode is connected into a circuit between an alternator (which produces alternating current) and a battery. The diode will allow current from the alternator to flow in one direction only (direct current)—the charging direction (Fig. 17-3). Changing alternating current to direct current is called *rectification*.

A transistor is a diode with some added semiconductor material. This turns the diode into a transistor, which can amplify electric current. Figure 17-4 shows how. When the electric switch is closed, a small amount of current can flow from the battery to the base of the transistor (0.35 amperes). In effect, this closes a switch inside the transistor. The transistor then permits 4.15 amperes to flow through the transistor—from the emitter to the collector.

If the switch is opened (Fig. 17-5), no current flows to the base. In effect, this opens the switch inside the transistor so no current can flow.

◑ 17-15
WIRING CIRCUITS
Wiring circuits in modern motorcycles can be rather complicated (Fig. 17-6). To simplify the wiring assembly, separate wires are grouped together as shown in Fig. 17-1. They are wrapped in insulation, with the various terminals coming out at the right places to connect to the various electric devices. These assemblies are called *wiring harnesses*. Terminal connectors of three types are shown in Fig. 17-7. Figure 17-8 shows some of the basic symbols used in wiring circuits to indicate different devices.

Note that in Fig. 17-8, upper right, there are two symbols for ground. These mean that the device or wire is connected to the motorcycle frame, or chassis. The frame then forms the return circuit for the electric current. Using the frame as the return circuit greatly reduces the amount of wiring the electric system requires. While we in the United States call the connection to the frame *ground*, many foreign countries call it *earth*. Both mean the same thing.

◑ 17-16
FUSES AND CIRCUIT BREAKERS
Fuses and circuit breakers are connected into electric circuits to protect them from damage in case a short circuit or ground develops. A short circuit or ground could allow a very high current to flow. For example, if you short circuited the battery by connecting across the battery

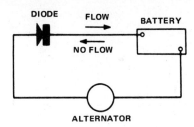

Fig. 17-3 Alternating current from an alternator can be rectified, or changed to direct current, by a diode so that the current can charge a battery.

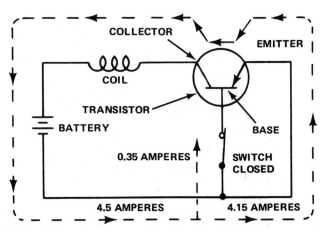

Fig. 17-4 When the switch is closed, current flows.

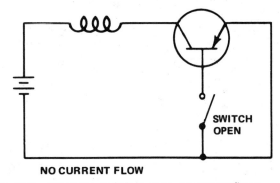

Fig. 17-5 When the switch is open, no current flows.

terminals, you would have a very high current flow of hundreds of amperes.

One type of fuse, a cartridge fuse, is shown in Fig. 17-9. It has a strip of soft metal connected between the two end caps and enclosed in a glass tube. If a short or ground develops, the high current overheats the metal strip and it melts, or "blows." This opens the circuit. If this should happen, you should first check the system to find and eliminate the cause. Then you should install a new fuse.

Circuit breakers do the same job as fuses. But they do not "blow." Instead, they open contact points when high current starts to flow. This opens the circuit. When the condition that causes the high current to flow is eliminated, the contact points close to complete the circuit again.

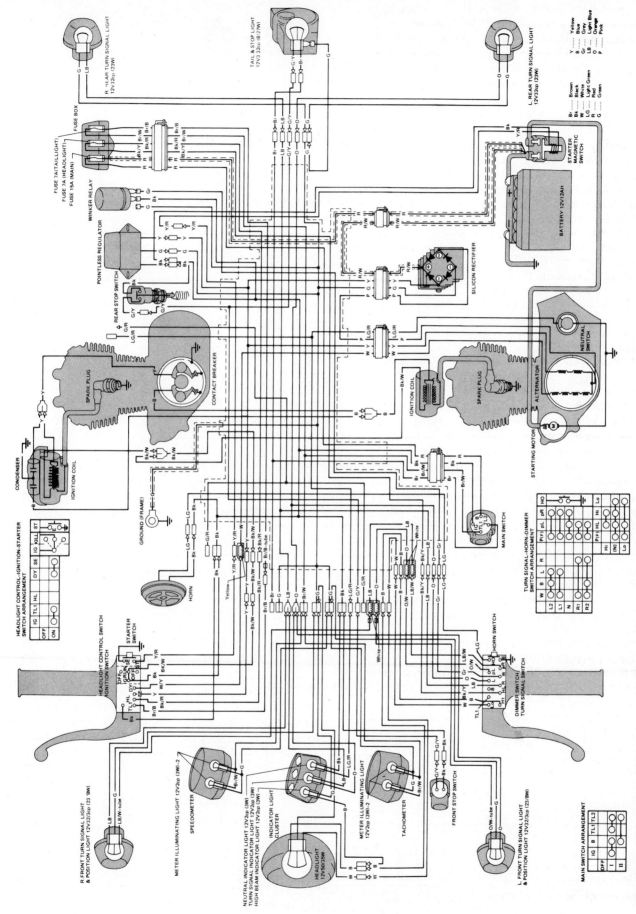

Fig. 17-6 Wiring diagram for the motorcycle shown in phantom view in Fig. 21-1. *(Honda Motor Company, Ltd.)*

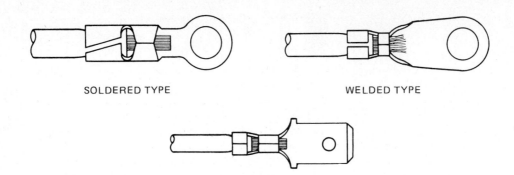

SOLDERED TYPE   WELDED TYPE

CRIMPED TYPE

Fig. 17-7 Types of wire terminals.

	ELECTRICAL SYMBOLS			
SYMBOL	REPRESENTS	SYMBOL	REPRESENTS	
(A)	AMMETER	⊣⊱	GROUND—CHASSIS FRAME	(Preferred)
⊣⊦	BATTERY—ONE CELL	⊣⊪	GROUND—CHASSIS FRAME	(Acceptable)
⊣⊩⊢	BATTERY—MULTICELL	(lamp)	LAMP or BULB	(Preferred)
12 V ±⊣⊩⊢	(Where required, battery voltage or polarity or both may be indicated as shown in example. The long line is always positive polarity.)	(lamp)	LAMP or BULB	(Acceptable)
		(MOT)	MOTOR—ELECTRICAL	
⊣⊢	CABLE—CONNECTED	—	NEGATIVE	
⊣ or ⊰	CABLE—NOT CONNECTED	+	POSITIVE	
⊣)⊢	CAPACITOR	⟋W⟍	RESISTOR	
⟍	CONNECTOR—FEMALE CONTACT	⟋	SWITCH—SINGLE THROW	
→	CONNECTOR—MALE CONTACT	⟋	SWITCH—DOUBLE THROW	
≪	CONNECTORS—SEPARABLE—ENGAGED	•—	TERMINATION	
⌒	FUSE	(V)	VOLTMETER	
(GEN)	GENERATOR	⚊⚊ or ⌒⌒	WINDING—INDUCTOR	

Fig. 17-8 Commonly used electrical symbols. (*General Motors Corporation*)

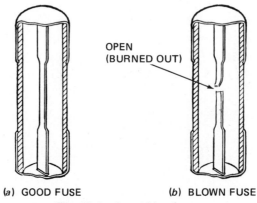

OPEN (BURNED OUT)

(*a*) GOOD FUSE   (*b*) BLOWN FUSE

Fig. 17-9 A cartridge fuse.

156

CHAPTER 17
REVIEW QUESTIONS

1. What do you call a flow of electrons all moving in the same direction in a wire?
2. Name two sources of electric current in a motorcycle.
3. The ampere is a measurement of what?
4. Can magnets produce electricity?
5. Can electricity produce magnets?
6. What device is used to measure current?
7. What makes electrons move in a wire?
8. What is voltage?
9. What is the purpose of insulation?
10. What is a short circuit?
11. What is resistance? How is it measured?
12. What is Ohm's law?
13. What is direct current (dc)?
14. What is alternating current (ac)?
15. What is a diode?

CHAPTER **18**

BATTERIES AND BATTERY SERVICE

After studying this chapter,
you should be able to:

1. Explain the purpose of the battery.

2. Discuss the relationship between battery size and battery capacity.

3. Describe the construction of a 12-volt battery.

4. Explain the purpose and composition of electrolyte.

5. Discuss battery ampere-hour rating and what it means.

6. Discuss the various conditions that can cause battery voltage to go up or down.

7. Describe six steps in battery maintenance.

8. Discuss the cautions to follow when working around batteries.

9. Explain why and how much battery specific gravity varies with temperature.

10. Discuss eight battery troubles and their causes.

11. Explain how to charge a motorcycle battery.

12. Explain how to activate a dry-charged battery.

18-1
PURPOSE OF THE BATTERY Lead-acid storage batteries are used in automobiles, in many motorcycles, and with many small engines. The battery is an electrochemical device. It produces electricity by converting chemical energy into electric energy.

The purpose of the battery is to operate the starting motor and the ignition system when the engine is being started. The battery also supplies current for lights, horns, and other electric accessories when the alternator is not generating enough current to handle the electric load. The amount of current the battery can supply is limited by its capacity. Capacity, in turn, depends on the amount of chemicals the battery contains. A large battery contains more chemicals and can produce more current for a longer time.

When the battery is supplying electric current, chemical actions in the battery push electrons out through one terminal and take them back in through the other terminal. After these chemical actions have gone on for a while, the battery becomes *discharged,* or *run down.* Now, current (electrons) from an alternator or generator must be pushed back through the battery in the reverse direction. This reverses the chemical actions in the battery so that the battery becomes *recharged.* It is then ready to supply electric current again.

18-2
SIZE OF BATTERIES On a motorcycle the battery usually is located under the seat. The seat is hinged so it can be raised to provide access to the battery. The size of the battery determines its capacity (how much current it can supply and for how long). Look at Fig. 18-1, which shows the size of typical automotive and motorcycle batteries. Both have six cells and are 12-volt batteries.

The automobile needs a large battery. This is because its large engine requires a strong starting motor which needs more current for starting. The automobile usually has many electric devices that require more current than the alternator can supply at idle or slow speeds.

The motorcycle has an engine that does not require as large a starting motor. Therefore, less current is needed for starting. Also, the motorcycle does not have as many electric devices as the automobile. The battery and starting motor are designed to be of a size that will work satisfactorily with the engine and vehicle in which

Fig. 18-1 Comparison of an automotive battery (left) and a motorcycle battery (right).

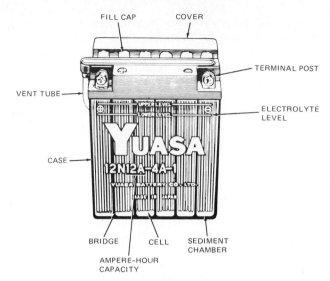

Fig. 18-2 Typical motorcycle battery. Its internal construction is the same as that of the larger batteries used in automobiles and trucks. (*Honda Motor Company, Ltd.*)

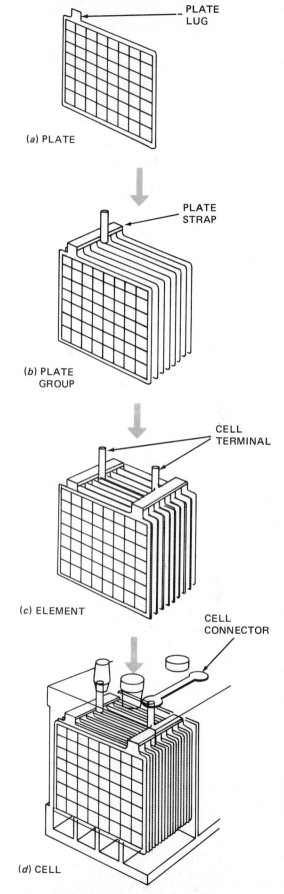

Fig. 18-3 Major parts that make up a battery cell.

they are installed. Figure 17-1 is a phantom view of a motorcycle, showing the locations of the battery (under the seat) and the electric equipment on the motorcycle. Regardless of size, all lead-acid batteries operate in the same manner.

18-3
BATTERY CELLS
Motorcycles use either a 6-volt battery or a 12-volt battery. Some motorcycles form a 12-volt battery by using two 6-volt batteries connected together. The 6-volt battery is made up of three cells of 2 volts each. A 12-volt battery is made up of six 2-volt cells.

Figure 18-2 shows a 12-volt motorcycle battery with the parts named. An easy way to tell a 6-volt battery from a 12-volt battery is to count the fill caps on the top of the battery. A 6-volt battery has three caps. Twelve-volt batteries have six fill caps, as shown in Fig. 18-2.

In a battery, the internal construction and operation of all cells are identical. The cells are enclosed in compartments in the battery case. The case is made of hard rubber or a plastic which is acid- and shock-resistant.

As shown in Fig. 18-3, each cell consists of an element submerged in a mixture of sulfuric acid and water (electrolyte) in an acidproof container having a hard-rubber cover. The cover is sealed in place with an acidproof compound.

The element is made up of two groups of plates, positive and negative, nested together. Each plate is insulated from adjacent plates by a separator, as shown in Fig. 18-4.

Many batteries sold by dealers as replacement batteries are *dry charged*. Acid is not added until the battery is sold. Such batteries are made as already described but have no electrolyte in them. Since they have no electrolyte and are sealed to prevent the entrance of moisture, they are chemically inert. They can be stored for months without deterioration.

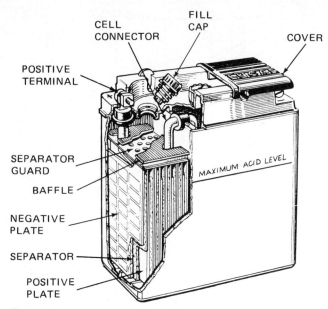

Fig. 18-4 Cutaway view of a 12-volt motorcycle battery. (*Joseph Lucas, Ltd.*)

18-4 BATTERY ELECTROLYTE

Battery electrolyte is made up of about 60 percent water and 40 percent sulfuric acid (in a fully charged battery). Here is what happens when electric current is taken out of a battery. The sulfuric acid gradually goes into the battery plates, which means the electrolyte gets weaker. As this happens, the battery runs down, or goes "dead." It then has to be recharged. The recharging job requires a battery charger.

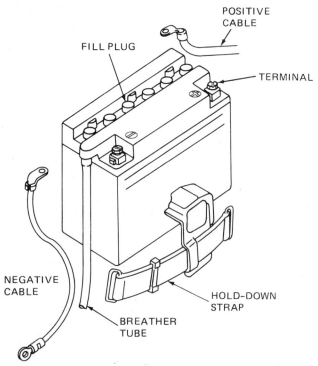

Fig. 18-5 A motorcycle battery that has screw-type terminals. (*Honda Motor Company, Ltd.*)

The charger pushes a current of electricity through the battery, restoring the battery to a charged condition (◢ 18-22). The current is pushed into the battery in a direction opposite to the direction from which it was taken out.

18-5 CELL CONNECTORS

The individual cells in a battery are connected in series so that their voltages add. The cell connectors are heavy lead bars attached to the cell terminals. In motorcycle batteries, the cell connectors are located above or in the cell covers. When they are in the cell covers, they are protected with an insulator or a heavy coat of sealing compound. This construction helps prevent current leakage across the tops of the cell covers.

The two terminals are on top (Figs. 18-1 and 18-2). Most motorcycle batteries use screws, as shown in Fig. 18-5, to fasten the cables to the terminals on the battery. Connecting cables to the terminals backward could cause damage to the electric system. Figure 18-5 also shows a battery-mounting arrangement. With this battery, it is difficult to connect the cables backward. When the battery is put into the motorcycle, the battery must be installed so that the terminals are closest to the cables. The two cable connectors will then be in position to be attached to the proper terminals. The cables may not reach the terminals if the battery is installed backward.

However, always mark or tag the cables as you remove them if there is any possibility of confusion. When removing a battery, disconnect the ground cable first. When installing a battery, connect the ground cable last.

18-6 FILL PLUGS

Fill plugs either push into plain holes or screw into threaded holes in the cell covers. A screw-type fill plug is shown in Fig. 18-4. The plugs can be removed so that water can be added to the cells when necessary. Water is lost during normal battery action. Some water evaporates and some is converted into gases (hydrogen and oxygen) as the battery charges. The battery has a vent hose (Fig. 18-5), or breather tube, to permit these gases to escape.

CAUTION Always check that the vent hose is open. If the vent hose is bent, twisted, or clogged, pressure will build up in the battery and may crack the case or blow out the fill plugs.

If too much water is added to the battery cells, electrolyte will be forced out the vent tube when the battery is charged (because of gassing). Electrolyte is corrosive and will damage engine and motorcycle parts. Also, this electrolyte loss reduces the operating ability of the battery.

To prevent the loss of electrolyte due to overfilling, various nonoverfill devices are now in use. These devices are normally incorporated in the cell covers. They usually provide some means of visually observing the electrolyte level so you will not overfill the battery.

Some batteries have cases made of transparent plastic (Fig. 18-1). It is easy to see the electrolyte level in these batteries. This battery has two marks on its side to show the upper and lower levels, or limits, of electrolyte. When the battery electrolyte drops down close to the lower-level mark, water should be added. But the electrolyte level must not be raised above the upper-level mark.

18-7 BATTERY VOLTAGE

Each battery cell has a voltage of about 2 volts. When three battery cells are connected in series, as shown in Fig. 18-6, their voltage adds up to 6 volts. Connecting six cells in series makes a 12-volt battery.

The actual voltage of a battery cell is about 2.1 volts. A six-cell battery will test, when fully charged, about 12.6 volts. However, it is called a 12-volt battery.

18-8 RECHARGING THE BATTERY

In the motorcycle, an alternator supplies charging current (Fig. 17-1). If the battery is run down so the engine cannot be started, or if the battery is removed from the motorcycle for service, a battery charger is used (Fig. 18-7). Battery charging is described in ☑18-22.

18-9 BATTERY RATINGS

The amount of current that a battery can deliver depends on the total area and volume of active plate material. It also depends on the amount and strength of the electrolyte. The strength is the percentage of sulfuric acid in the electrolyte. Factors that influence battery capacity include the number of plates per cell, the size of the plates, cell size, and the quantity of electrolyte.

Batteries may be rated in several ways. However, the capacity of most motorcycle batteries is given in *ampere-hours*. This is the number of amperes of current that a battery with an electrolyte temperature of 80°F [26.7°C] can deliver for 10 hours without cell voltage dropping below 1.75 volts. For example, the battery shown in Fig. 18-2 has a 12 ampere-hour capacity. This means that it can deliver a current of 12 amperes for 1 hour (12 × 1 = 12). It could also deliver a current of 3 amperes for 4 hours (3 × 4 = 12) or any other combination of current and time that equals its ampere-hour rating of 12.

Battery capacity may be judged by comparing the ampere-hour rating of two or more batteries. The larger battery will have the larger ampere-hour capacity. Some motorcycle batteries are so large that they are rated in ampere-hours by their 20-hour rating. The 20-hour rating system is used for automobile batteries.

18-10 VARIATIONS IN TERMINAL VOLTAGE

Because the battery produces voltage by chemical means, the voltage varies according to a number of conditions. These conditions and their effects on battery voltage may be summed up as follows:

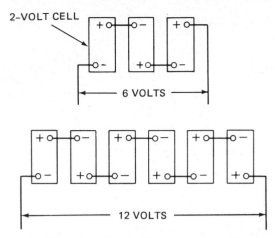

Fig. 18-6 When three 2-volt cells are connected in series, the battery of three cells produces 6 volts. Likewise, six cells connected in series produce 12 volts.

1. When the battery is being charged the terminal voltage increases with
   a. An increase in the charging rate: To increase the charging rate (amperes input), the terminal voltage must go up.
   b. An increasing state of charge: As the state of charge goes up, voltage must go up to maintain the charging rate. For example, a voltage of approximately 2.6 volts per cell is required to force a current through a fully charged battery. This is the reason that voltage regulators operate at about 15 volts (2.5 volts per cell)—slightly below the voltage required to continue to charge a fully charged battery. This setting protects the battery from overcharge. Regulators are covered in Chap. 20.
   c. A decreasing temperature: Lower battery temperatures require a higher voltage to maintain a charging rate.

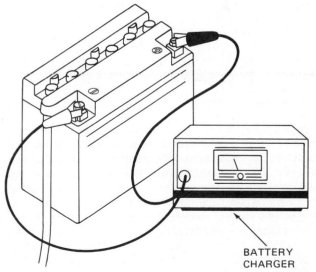

Fig. 18-7 A battery charger is used to recharge a battery when the engine cannot be started. (*Honda Motor Company, Ltd.*)

2. When the battery is being *discharged* the terminal voltage decreases with

   a. An increasing discharge rate: As larger amounts of current are taken from the battery, the chemical activities cannot penetrate the plates so effectively. Battery efficiency and voltage are reduced.

   b. A decreasing state of charge: With less active materials and sulfuric acid available, less chemical activity can take place, and the voltage drops.

   c. A decreasing temperature: With lower temperatures, the chemical activities cannot go on so effectively, and the voltage drops.

18-11 INTRODUCTION TO BATTERY SERVICE

Batteries wear out. They are subjected to variations in temperature, to motion, and to repeated discharge-recharge cycles. The chemicals in the plates tend to take on a permanent "set," or else the plate material flakes off and falls to the bottom of the battery in the sediment chambers. You can see the sediment chambers at the bottom of the battery in Fig. 18-2.

The length of a battery's life depends on its original design and manufacture. It also depends on the care and maintenance the battery gets during its lifetime. Now, we discuss the things that should be done to ensure long and trouble-free battery life.

18-12 BATTERY MAINTENANCE

Most people tend to forget about their motorcycle battery. They forget it until one cold morning when they try to start: the battery won't do its job, and the engine won't start. Battery failure is one of the more common motorcycle troubles.

If people would check their batteries once in a while, much battery trouble could be avoided. Here are the things that should be done:

1. Visually inspect the battery.
2. Check the electrolyte level in all the cells periodically.
3. Add water if the level is low.
4. Clean off corrosion around the battery terminals and top.
5. Check the condition of the battery with a testing instrument.
6. Recharge the battery if the charge is low.

CAUTION **Sulfuric acid, the active ingredient in battery electrolyte, is very corrosive. It can destroy most things it touches. It will cause painful and serious burns if it gets on the skin. It can cause blindness if it gets into eyes. If you get battery acid (electrolyte) on your skin, flush it off at once with water. Continue to flush for at least 5 minutes. Put baking soda (if available) on your skin. This will neutralize the acid. If you get acid in your eyes, flush your eyes out with water over and over again (Fig. 1-4). Then get to a doctor at once!**

CAUTION **The gases that form in the tops of the battery cells during charging are very explosive. Never light a match or a cigarette near a recently charged battery. It**

could blow up. Never blow off a battery with an air hose. The compressed air could lift the cell cover and splash electrolyte on you.

18-13 VISUAL INSPECTION OF THE BATTERY

Look the battery over for signs of leakage, a cracked case or top, corrosion, missing fill plugs, and loose or missing hold-down straps. A leakage sign which could indicate a cracked battery case is white corrosion on the battery carrier or motorcycle frame. If the top of the battery is covered with corrosion and the battery needs water frequently, the battery probably is being overcharged. Check the charging system, as discussed in Chap. 20.

The most common cause of a cracked case is improper installation of the hold-down straps and rubber insulating strips around the battery. Also, if the motorcycle should fall over, doing little or no other visible damage, cracking of the battery case may occur.

Motorcycle batteries have a breather tube, as shown in Fig. 18-5. Whenever you check the battery, check this tube. If the tube becomes kinked or clogged, pressure can build up in the battery as a result of the gassing that accompanies battery charging. This pressure can become great enough to cause the battery to explode. Always check that the breather tube is clear so gases can exhaust from the battery.

18-14 CHECKING THE ELECTROLYTE LEVEL AND ADDING WATER

The electrolyte level in all battery cells should be checked periodically. A typical recommendation is to check the electrolyte level every 15 days to 1 month.

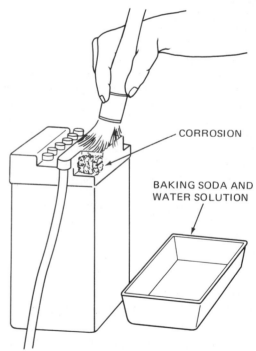

CORROSION

BAKING SODA AND WATER SOLUTION

Fig. 18-8 Cleaning corrosion off a battery with a solution of baking soda and water.

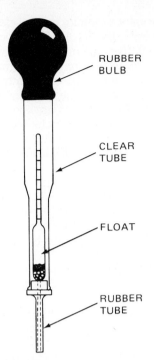

Fig. 18-9 A battery hydrometer.

If the battery has a transparent case, you can check the electrolyte level at a glance. On other batteries, you must remove the fill plugs to check the level. If the electrolyte level is low, add water to bring the electrolyte up to its proper level. Distilled water is recommended, but any water that is fit to drink can be used.

CAUTION **Don't add too much water! Too much water will cause the electrolyte to leak out. This will corrode, or eat away, any metal it touches and damage the paint.**

18-15
CLEANING CORROSION OFF THE
BATTERY   Battery terminals and cables on top of the battery may corrode. To get rid of the corrosion and to clean the battery top, mix some common baking soda in a can of water. Brush on the solution, wait until the foaming stops, and then flush off the battery top with water (Fig. 18-8).

If the buildup of corrosion around the terminals is heavy, detach the cables from the terminals. Then use a wire brush to clean the terminal posts and cables. Some technicians coat the terminals with grease or an anticorrosion compound to retard additional corrosion.

18-16
TESTING THE CONDITION OF THE
BATTERY   There are several ways to test battery condition. The most common way is with a battery hydrometer. Other methods use a testing meter such as a voltmeter.

As a battery discharges, acid disappears from the electrolyte in direct proportion to the amount of electricity taken from the battery. The hydrometer, which checks the specific gravity (the amount of acid in the electrolyte), shows the state of charge of the battery.

The hydrometer has a rubber bulb at the top, a clear tube, a float, and a rubber tube at the bottom, as shown in Fig. 18-9. You use it by squeezing the bulb, putting the end of the rubber tube into the battery cell, and then releasing the bulb. This will draw electrolyte up into the tube. The float, with its stem projecting, will float in this electrolyte. The battery's state of charge is indicated by the length of the stem that sticks out of the electrolyte as shown in Fig. 18-10. Take the reading at eye level.

CAUTION **Do not drip electrolyte from the hydrometer tube onto the motorcycle or on yourself! Electrolyte will burn you, eat holes in your clothes, and ruin the paint on the motorcycle.**

If some cells test much lower than others, it means there is something wrong with those cells. It could be that a cracked case has allowed electrolyte leakage, or perhaps there is internal damage to the plates or separators. If the variation is only a few specific-gravity points, then the battery probably can continue in service. But if a cell measures 50 points lower, then that cell is defective and the battery should be discarded.

The decimal point is not normally referred to in talking about gravity (specific gravity). For example, "twelve twenty-five" means 1.225, and "eleven fifty" means 1.150.

After you have checked the electrolyte in the battery cell, squeeze the bulb to return the electrolyte to the cell from which you drew it. If the battery is low, it should be recharged. If the battery is low and old, it may be worn out and a new battery may be needed.

Another type of hydrometer can be used. It is much smaller and simpler to use than the hydrometer discussed above. The small hydrometer has four or five small plastic balls in it instead of a float (Fig. 18-11). When electrolyte is drawn into the tube, the condition of the cell is told by the number of balls that float. If all

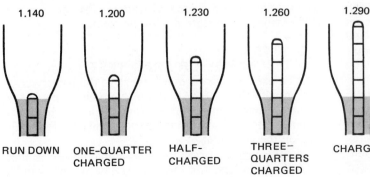

| 1.140 | 1.200 | 1.230 | 1.260 | 1.290 |

RUN DOWN   ONE–QUARTER CHARGED   HALF– CHARGED   THREE– QUARTERS CHARGED   CHARGED

Fig. 18-10 Various specific-gravity readings. *(Delco-Remy Division of General Motors Corporation)*

163

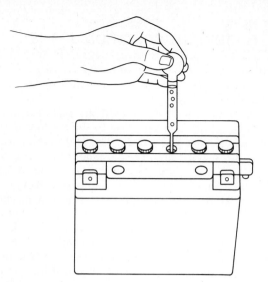

Fig. 18-11 A ball-type hydrometer for testing batteries. (*ATW*)

the balls float, the cell is fully charged. If no balls float, the cell is dead.

18-17 VARIATIONS OF SPECIFIC GRAVITY WITH TEMPERATURE

As the temperature of the electrolyte goes down, it gets thicker. This increases its specific gravity. Unless you take this into account, your reading of the gravity of a cold battery could fool you. You might think the battery is charged even though it is partly run down.

For example, suppose the battery temperature is 10°F [−12.2°C]. You read the gravity as 1.230, which looks to be the reading of a half-charged battery (Fig. 18-10). Actually, the electrolyte gained in gravity 0.028 points simply because it gets thicker when it gets cold.

NOTE For every 10°F [6.5°C] that the temperature of the electrolyte drops below 80°F [26.7°C], the electrolyte gains 0.004 points in gravity (gets that much thicker). Since the electrolyte temperature was 70°F below the 80°F standard (80 − 10), the gravity gained 0.028 points (7 × 4). The actual reading is only 1.202. The battery is only one-quarter charged.

Some hydrometers, such as the ball type shown in Fig. 18-11, are self-compensating for temperature. These are direct reading, and require no additional calculations to find the corrected specific gravity.

Usually you don't have to worry about temperature too much if the battery temperature is in the neighborhood of 60 to 90°F [15.6 to 32.2°C]. For every 10°F [6.5°C] below 80°F [26.7°C], subtract 0.004 points to get an accurate reading. For every 10°F above 80°F, add 0.004 points. The electrolyte loses gravity (becomes thinner) as its temperature goes up.

18-18 LOSS OF SPECIFIC GRAVITY

As the battery ages, the electrolyte gradually loses specific gravity. This is because active material is lost from the plates (as it sheds and drops into the bottom of the cells) and because gassing causes the loss of acid. Over a period of two years, for example, battery electrolyte may drop to a top specific gravity, when fully charged, of not more than 1.240, from the original top gravity of 1.280. Little can be done to restore specific gravity, since the loses are an indication of an aging battery.

There is always some chemical activity in a battery, even when the battery is not connected to a circuit and delivering current. Such chemical action, which does not produce current, is called *self-discharge*. When the battery is not in use, it discharges at the rate of about 0.5 to 1 percent per day.

Self-discharge varies with temperature and with the strength of the electrolyte. The higher the temperature, the faster the self-discharge, since the chemical actions are stimulated by the higher temperatures. A battery kept at 100°F [37.8°C] loses half its charge in 30 days. A battery kept at 0°F [−17.8°C] has almost no loss of charge during the same time. A strong electrolyte, with its higher percentage of sulfuric acid, also causes more rapid self-discharge.

One disadvantage to self-discharge is that the lead sulfate produced by self-discharge is harder to break down during recharging of the battery. If batteries are not recharged periodically to compensate for self-discharge, they may be severely damaged or even completely ruined. Older batteries and batteries that have impurities in them (often introduced in the water) tend to self-discharge more rapidly.

Batteries operating in hot climates are often readjusted so that their gravity is reduced. For example, instead of a 1.280 specific gravity, the electrolyte may be reduced to 1.240 for a fully charged battery. The reduction of specific gravity prolongs the life of the battery and reduces the amount of self-discharge. On discharge, the specific gravity may drop as low as 1.120 before the battery ceases to deliver current. When there is no danger of freezing, these lower gravities may be used with safety.

18-19 FREEZING POINT

The higher the specific gravity, the lower the temperature required to freeze the electrolyte. Freezing must be avoided, since it may crack the case and ruin the battery.

Figure 18-12 shows the freezing temperature of electrolytes of various specific gravities. A discharged battery must never be left out in the cold. In winter a person may try to start an engine and do nothing more than run the battery down. If the battery remains out in the cold, it may freeze. Then a new battery will have to be installed and the original trouble corrected before the engine can be started with the electric starter.

18-20 DISCHARGE OR DRAW TEST

A voltmeter can be used to make a quick check of the battery condition with the battery in the motorcycle. This test is made by turning on the ignition and the headlight. Then connect the voltmeter to the battery and note the reading on the voltmeter.

A fully charged 6-volt battery should have a reading of 5.6 volts or higher. If the reading is between 5.6 and 4 volts, the battery should be charged. If the reading is less than 4 volts, the battery may be defective.

A 12-volt battery should read 11.2 volts or higher during the draw test. Voltage readings between 11.2 and 10 volts indicate that the battery should be charged. Readings of less than 10 volts may indicate a defective battery.

18-21 BATTERY TROUBLE DIAGNOSIS
When battery trouble is found, the cause should be determined and eliminated. That way, the same problem will not occur again. Following are various battery troubles and their possible causes.

1. Overcharging. If the battery requires water frequently, the battery is probably being overcharged. This means that too much current is being forced through the battery. This is a damaging condition that overworks the active materials in the battery and shortens battery life. In addition, overcharging speeds up the loss of water from the battery electrolyte.

Unless this water is replaced frequently, the electrolyte level is likely to fall below the tops of the plates. This exposes the plates and separators to air and could ruin them. Also, battery overcharge will make battery plates buckle and crumble. Therefore, a battery that is severely overcharged will soon be ruined. Where overcharging is experienced or suspected, check the charging system. Adjust it if necessary to prevent overcharging. This procedure is explained in Chap. 20.

2. Undercharging. If the battery is discharged, recharge it as outlined later. In addition, try to find out why the battery is discharged. This condition can be caused by

  a. A charging-system malfunction
  b. Defective connections in the charging circuit between the alternator and the battery
  c. Excessive load demands on the battery
  d. A defective battery
  e. Permitting the battery to stand idle for long periods so that it self-discharges excessively
  f. Running the engine at too slow a speed while riding

In addition, an old battery may have a low specific-gravity reading because it is approaching failure.

3. Sulfation. The active materials in the plates are converted into lead sulfate during discharge. This lead sulfate is reconverted into active materials during recharge. However, if the battery stands for long periods in a discharged condition, the lead sulfate is converted into a hard, crystalline substance. This substance is difficult to reconvert into active materials by normal charging processes.

A sulfated battery should be charged at half the normal rate for 60 to 100 hours. Even though this long charging period may reconvert the sulfate to active materials, the battery may remain damaged. As the crystalline sulfate forms, it tends to break the plate grids.

4. Cracked Cases. Cracked cases may result from excessively loose hold-down straps, from the battery freezing, or from dropping the motorcycle.

Specific Gravity	Freezing temperature, degrees Fahrenheit [°C]
1.100	18 [−8]
1.160	1 [−17]
1.200	−17 [−27]
1.220	−31 [−35]
1.260	−75 [−59]
1.300	−95 [−71]

Fig. 18-12 Table showing freezing temperature of electrolytes of various specific gravities.

5. Bulged Cases. Bulged cases result from high temperatures or a plugged or kinked vent tube. Check that the vent tube is routed away from the exhaust system and clamped in place securely.

6. Corroded Terminals and Cable. Corrosion occurs naturally on batteries. Remove the excessive corrosion from terminals and cables periodically. Cables should be disconnected from the terminal and the terminal posts and cables cleaned, as explained in 18-15.

7. Corroded Battery Holder. As the battery is being charged, some of the electrolyte commonly sprays from it. This electrolyte should be carried away through the vent tube. However, some may get on the battery holder and cause it to become corroded. With the battery removed, the corrosion may be cleaned off with a wire brush and a baking-soda solution.

8. Dirty Battery Top. Dirt and corrosion may accumulate on the battery top. This should be cleaned off periodically, as explained previously.

If a motorcycle is operated only infrequently and only for a short time when it is used, the battery will tend to run down. For one thing, the operating time may not be long enough to allow the alternator to put back into the battery the current used up in starting. Second, a battery sitting idle, especially at higher temperatures, tends to self-discharge, as explained earlier. Batteries, during this kind of short-use, long-idle period, should be recharged periodically.

18-22 BATTERY CHARGING
Most localities have alternating current only. The job of the battery charger is to convert this alternating current to direct current and supply it to the battery.

Recharging the battery is necessary when it gets run down. This condition can be determined by a hydrometer or a voltmeter test. Dim lights and a weak horn indicate a low battery that should be recharged. A trickle charger must be used, perferably one that has an adjustable charging rate. Motorcycle batteries must be charged at a very low rate. The maximum charging rate should not exceed one-tenth of the ampere-hour capacity of the battery. A 10-ampere-hour battery, for example, should be charged at a rate of 1 ampere.

To charge the battery, connect the charger as shown in Fig. 18-7. Leave the battery on the charger until the battery starts gassing freely and the specific gravity of

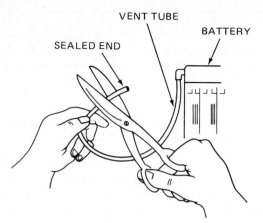

VENT TUBE
SEALED END
BATTERY

Fig. 18-13 Cut off the sealed end of the vent tube when activating a dry-charged motorcycle battery. (*Yuasa Battery Company, Ltd.*)

the electrolyte reaches 1.260, or its fully charged specification. This may take about 10 hours.

NOTE Never connect a motorcycle battery to an automotive-type quick charger. The minimum charging rate on most quick chargers is so high that it will destroy a motorcycle battery.

18-23
BATTERY ADDITIVES Sometimes electrolyte may be added to a battery if some acid has been lost through spraying or spilling. But other chemicals, or *dopes,* should never be added. Some of these chemicals may give a battery a temporary boost, but this condition will not last long. Shortly afterward, the battery will probably fail completely, having been ruined by the added chemicals. Furthermore, the use of such chemicals voids the battery manufacturer's warranty. All battery manufacturers condemn the use of additives in batteries.

18-24
ACTIVATING DRY-CHARGED BATTERIES Dry-charged batteries have no electrolyte in them and

are sealed. Therefore, they are chemically inert and can be stored for a long time without deterioration. However, since the plates may oxidize slowly if moisture is present, dry-charged batteries should be kept in a dry, clean place and protected from moisture. Never unscrew the fill plugs until you are ready to fill the battery and use it.

Dry-charged batteries are usually packed in shipping cartons. These cartons should be inspected whenever a battery shipment arrives. If the cartons are damaged or damp, they should be opened so that the batteries themselves can be inspected. The electrolyte for dry-charged batteries is shipped separately in large containers.

CAUTION Handle electrolyte containers with great care, since electrolyte is highly dangerous and corrosive. Handle electrolyte in an area where plenty of baking soda and water is available for flushing it away if it should come in contact with the skin or clothes. Wear goggles or eye shields.

To prepare a dry-charged battery for use, or to activate it, proceed as follows:

1. Remove the battery from the carton.
2. Remove the fill plugs. Cut off the sealed end of the vent tube, as shown in Fig. 18-13. On other batteries, remove the short sealed tube and attach the long vent tube that is packaged with the battery.
3. Fill each cell to the upper-level mark with electrolyte.
4. Wait 30 minutes to allow the plates and separators to absorb electrolyte. Then, if necessary, add more electrolyte to fill it to the upper-level mark again.
5. Although the battery can be put into immediate operation when first filled, a dry-charged battery is only at about 65 percent of full strength. Good battery operation can be ensured by charging the battery for 3 to 5 hours.
6. If the electrolyte level falls during charging, refill the battery with distilled water.

CHAPTER 18
REVIEW QUESTIONS

1. What is the purpose of the battery?
2. Where is the battery usually located on a motorcycle?
3. What does the size of a battery determine?
4. How can you tell a 6-volt battery from a 12-volt battery?
5. What could happen if a battery is installed backward?
6. Why do motorcycle batteries have a vent tube?
7. What is the voltage of a fully charged battery cell?
8. How is a battery recharged?
9. Name the factors that affect battery capacity.
10. What is the ampere-hour-capacity rating of a battery?
11. How do batteries wear out?
12. What affects battery life?
13. List the six steps in battery maintenance.
14. Can you repair a battery with a cracked case?
15. What type of water should be added to a battery?
16. How do you clean corrosion from the terminals of a battery?
17. How do you use a hydrometer to determine the state of charge of a cell?
18. What causes a battery to self-discharge?
19. What happens if a battery freezes?
20. Explain how to use a voltmeter to check a battery.
21. When a battery requires water frequently, what trouble should you suspect?
22. At what rate should a motorcycle battery be charged?

CHAPTER 19

STARTERS AND STARTER SERVICE

After studying this chapter,
you should be able to:

1. Explain how kick starters work and how they are serviced.

2. Discuss starting-motor construction and operation.

3. Describe starting-motor overrunning clutches and explain how they work.

4. Explain how the starter relay and the starter solenoid work.

5. Discuss starting-motor troubleshooting and possible causes of two starting-motor troubles.

6. Describe the various steps in starting-motor service, including starting-motor rebuilding and the repair of damaged parts.

19-1 KICK STARTERS

There are two general types of motorcycle starters, the mechanical kick-start type and the electric type. The kick starter was used almost exclusively for many years. But as motorcycle engines became bigger and more powerful, the electric starter became popular. It takes a strong kick to crank a high-compression multicylinder engine fast enough to start it. We will discuss kick starters first, and then electric starters.

The kick starter uses leg power for its operation and is a popular starter for motorcycles. All kick starters operate in a similar manner. Figure 19-1 shows the gear train for a typical kick starter. When the kick pedal is kicked down using leg power, the rotary motion is carried through the gear train to the engine crankshaft, causing it to spin. When the pedal is released, a heavy spring returns it to the former raised position. It may take several kicks to start a cold engine.

Note that the gear train in Fig. 19-1 has an increase in gear ratio from the kick-pedal gear to the gear on the crankshaft. This causes the crankshaft to spin rapidly when the kick-pedal gear rotates. Once the engine is running, the starter motion is achieved in different ways, depending on the design.

The kick starter shown in Fig. 19-2 illustrates how one-way starter motion is possible. The kick gear is free to rotate on the kick shaft. A ratchet wheel, or gear, can move back and forth on splines of the kick shaft. When the engine is running, the arm on the ratchet gear is resting behind the stopper guide. This holds the ratchet gear away from the kick gear. However, when the kick pedal is pushed down the kick shaft turns, forcing the ratchet gear to turn. The arm on the ratchet gear moves out from behind the stopper guide. The spring back of the ratchet gear now forces the ratchet forward so that its teeth engage the kick gear. Further movement of the

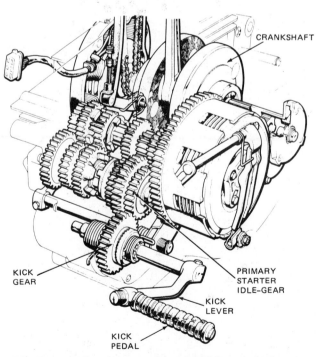

Fig. 19-1 Gear train for a kick starter and transmission gears for a one-cylinder engine. (*Honda Motor Company, Ltd.*)

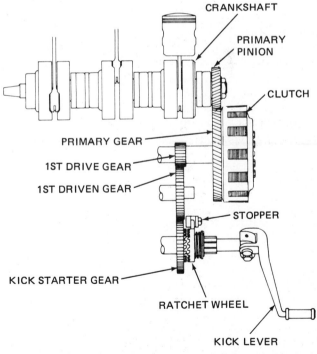

Fig. 19-2 Gear train from the kick lever to the crankshaft for a three-cylinder engine. (*Suzuki Motor Company, Ltd.*)

167

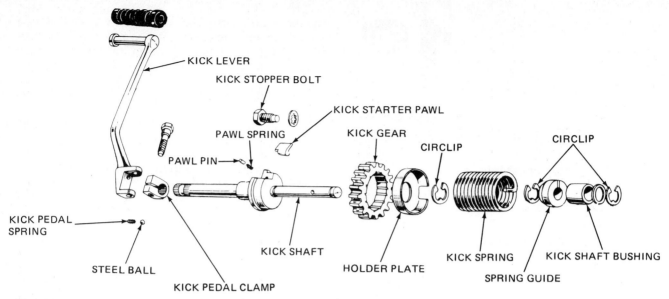

Fig. 19-3 Disassembled view of a kick-starter system using a kick pawl. (*Kawasaki Heavy Industries, Ltd.*)

kick pedal forces the kick gear to turn. This transmits motion through the gears, causing the crankshaft to spin.

As the engine starts, it drives the kick gear. The ratchet is a one-way device, so the kick gear runs without driving the ratchet gear. That is only a momentary condition, however. As soon as the kick pedal is released, the ratchet gear rotates with the kick-pedal shaft, and the ratchet-gear arm hits the stopper guide. As the arm slides on back of the curved stopper guide, the ratchet gear is pulled back away from the kick gear. The ratchet teeth are now disengaged.

A second clutch-declutch system for the kick starter is shown in disassembled view in Fig. 19-3. It uses a pawl that locks into a notch on the inner diameter of the kick gear. Here is the way it works. When the engine is running, the outer end of the kick pawl is held in against its spring tension by the kick stopper. This is a round section on the end of a bolt.

When the kick pedal is pushed down to start the engine, the kick shaft rotates, carrying around with it the cutaway collar assembled on the shaft. The kick pawl is located inside this collar. As the collar moves, the kick pawl passes out from under the kick stopper. This allows the kick-pawl spring to push the kick pawl out. The end of the pawl now catches in a notch in the inside of the kick gear. This forces the kick gear to rotate, and the gear train spins the engine crankshaft as shown in Fig. 19-4.

After the engine starts and the kick pedal is released, the kick shaft, with its collar, returns to its original position. As the kick pawl moves into this position, the kick stopper forces the end of the kick pawl in and away from the notches in the kick gear. Now, the kick gear can run freely with no connection with the kick pawl. The heavy spring to the right in Fig. 19-3 has the job of returning the kick pedal to its upper position when it is released.

Kick starters are light and reliable. However, it is difficult to kick-start a stalled engine without having the passenger dismount. To use a kick starter, the rider must set up the motorcycle properly for the kick. Otherwise the body motion after the kick may cause the rider to drop the motorcycle.

Because it takes time to kick-start a motorcycle, there may be danger. For example, the motorcycle may have stalled on a hill or in the path of oncoming traffic. An advantage of the electric starter is its ability to crank the engine quickly on demand and without having the passenger dismount.

19-2 ELECTRIC STARTING SYSTEMS The typical electric starting system on a motorcycle includes a

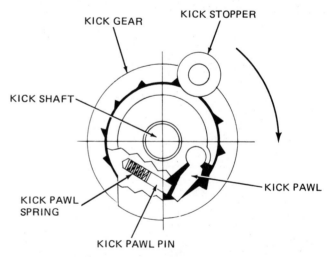

Fig. 19-4 The kick pawl is released when the kick shaft is rotated by the movement of the kick lever. This allows the pawl to lock in a notch in the kick gear, thereby spinning the gear. (*Kawasaki Heavy Industries, Ltd.*)

168

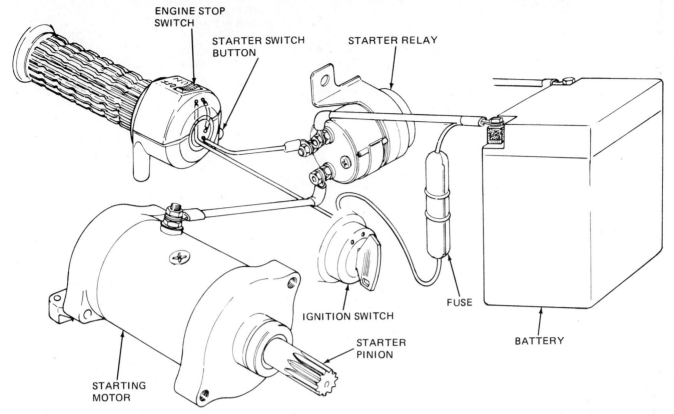

Fig. 19-5 Electric-starting system for a motorcycle. (*Suzuki Motor Company, Ltd.*)

6- or 12-volt battery, a starter relay, a starting motor, an ignition switch, and an engine stop switch (Fig. 19-5). The starting motor may be a separate unit attached to the engine, or it may be combined with the flywheel alternator to form a *starter-generator*. This type of starter is discussed further in Chap. 20, "Charging Systems."

To start the engine, both the ignition switch and the engine stop switch must be on. Then when the starter button on the right handlebar is pressed, current flows to the starter relay (Fig. 19-5). Contacts close inside the relay, allowing current to flow directly from the battery to the starting motor as long as the starter button is pressed.

To shut off the engine quickly, as in an emergency, the rider moves the engine stop switch to the OFF position. This kills the ignition.

Space and weight are at a premium on a motorcycle. Therefore, the electric starter, with its battery, must be as light and as compact as possible, consistent with good performance and durability. This means that the electric starting motor must work efficiently, and it must have a relatively long service life.

19-3 ELECTRIC STARTERS Starting motors—also called *cranking motors* and *starters*—are small but powerful electric motors that spin the crankshaft to get the engine started. Starting motors are not very complicated, and they seldom need service. Their job is to

convert electric energy from the battery into mechanical energy.

The starting motor is operated by electromagnetism. Electric current flowing through wires and through coils of wire, or windings, produces electromagnetism. The magnetized area around an electromagnet is called the *magnetic field*.

Two separate magnetic fields are produced in the starting motor, one by field windings and the other by the armature (Fig. 19-6). The field windings inside the field frame are stationary and produce a stationary field winding. The armature, which is supported on bearings, produces a rotating magnetic field. The rotating field opposes the stationary field, and this opposition forces the armature to rotate. The rotary motion is

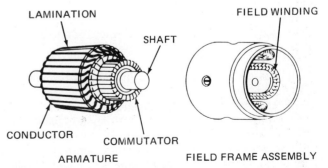

Fig. 19-6 The two major parts of a starting motor: the armature and the field-frame assembly.

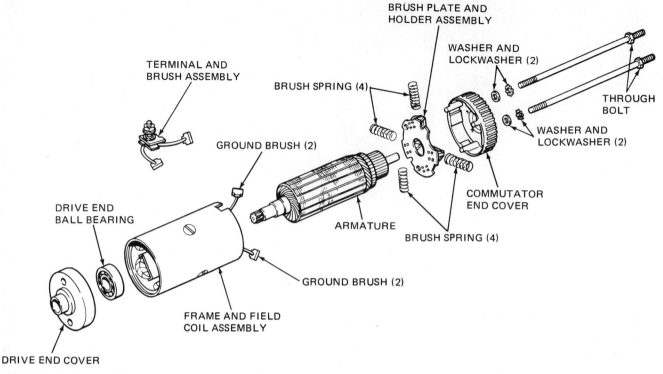

Fig. 19-7 A disassembled starting motor. *(Harley-Davidson Motor Company, Inc.)*

carried through gears to the engine crankshaft, making it rotate and starting the engine.

In addition to the field frame and the armature, the starting motor has other parts (Fig. 19-7). These include spring-loaded brushes which ride on the armature commutator. These brushes feed current into the armature windings. The same current flows through the field windings. This produces the two magnetic fields which cause the armature to spin.

19-4
STARTING-MOTOR DRIVES The gear ratio between the starting-motor armature and the crankshaft is 10:1 or higher. The armature turns 10 times or more to turn the crankshaft once. This enables the armature to turn fast—up to 3000 rpm—where it can develop high cranking power.

After starting, the engine may speed up to several thousand rpm. This would spin the armature at very high speed, and the armature would be ruined. The windings would be thrown from the armature by centrifugal force. To prevent this, starting-motor drives have a means of coupling for starting and of uncoupling from the crankshaft after the engine is started (Fig. 19-8).

The device that does the coupling and uncoupling is called a *one-way clutch,* or an *overrunning clutch.* Figure 19-9 shows one clutch arrangement. When the starting motor is operated to start the engine, the three rollers in the clutch are rolled into the smaller ends of the notches in the clutch. There, they jam to lock the gear to the crankshaft so the engine is cranked. Then, when the engine starts, the crankshaft tries to drive the starting motor through the rollers. However, this

causes the rollers to roll back into the other end of the notches, where they are free. The engine runs without driving the starting motor.

A similar starting-motor drive is shown in Fig. 19-10. Compare this figure with the kick-starter system for the same engine (Fig. 19-2). The clutch is located in the gear train at the transmission clutch (Fig. 19-10). The clutch works the same way as the one pictured in Fig. 19-9 and described above.

Figure 19-11 is a disassembled view of a starting motor which has a separate overrunning clutch. The overrunning clutch is shown two times in Fig. 19-11, once assembled (14) and once disassembled (18). This clutch works in the same way as others previously

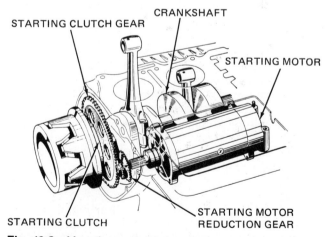

Fig. 19-8 Mounting and drive arrangement of an electric-starting motor for a four-cylinder engine. *(Honda Motor Company, Ltd.)*

170

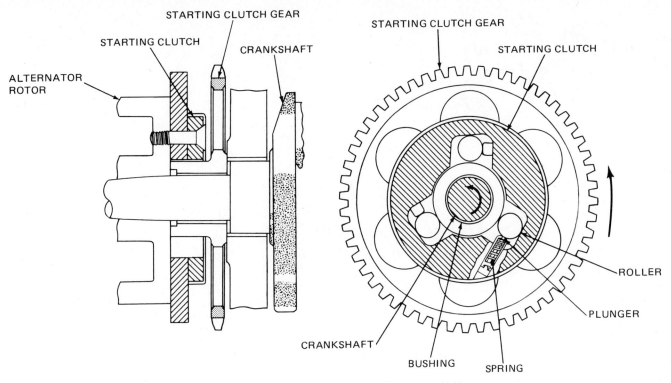

Fig. 19-9 Details of the one-way, or overrunning, clutch. (*Honda Motor Company, Ltd.*)

described. The basic difference is that the clutch is moved along a driveshaft to produce a meshing of the clutch drive pinion with the crankshaft gear. When the engine starts, the clutch drive pinion is pulled back from the crankshaft gear and out of mesh. The solenoid (� 19-5) moves the clutch back and forth.

19-5 STARTING-MOTOR CIRCUIT   The starting motor requires a large current. It is not practical to carry this heavy current up to the handlebar starter switch. A large cable would be required. Instead, the starter switch is wired to a starter relay (Fig. 19-12).

When the starter button is pushed, it connects the relay winding to the battery. Current flows through the winding. This produces a magnetic field which pulls a metal plunger down. This motion pulls down a contact plate which connects the battery directly to the starting motor. The engine is cranked. When the starter button is released, a spring in the starter relay lifts the contact plate so the circuit between the battery and starting motor is opened. The starting motor stops.

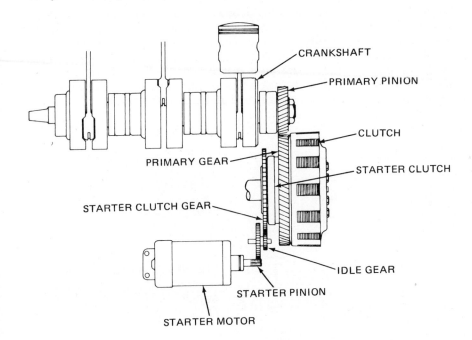

Fig. 19-10 Drive train between the starting motor and the engine crankshaft. (*Suzuki Motor Company, Ltd.*)

171

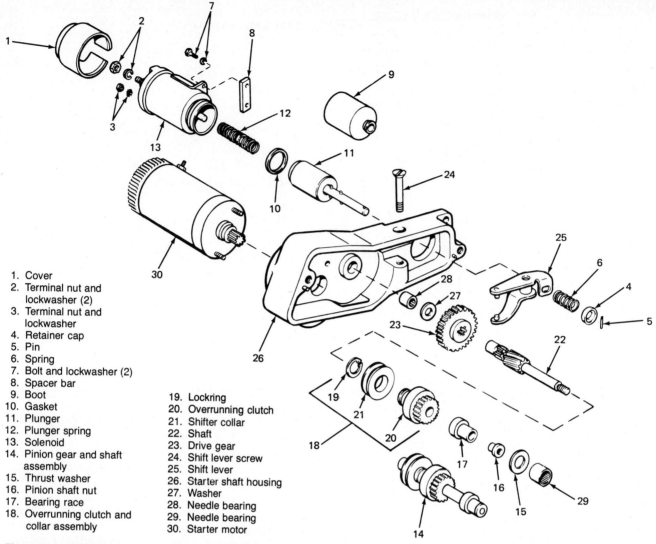

1. Cover
2. Terminal nut and lockwasher (2)
3. Terminal nut and lockwasher
4. Retainer cap
5. Pin
6. Spring
7. Bolt and lockwasher (2)
8. Spacer bar
9. Boot
10. Gasket
11. Plunger
12. Plunger spring
13. Solenoid
14. Pinion gear and shaft assembly
15. Thrust washer
16. Pinion shaft nut
17. Bearing race
18. Overrunning clutch and collar assembly
19. Lockring
20. Overrunning clutch
21. Shifter collar
22. Shaft
23. Drive gear
24. Shift lever screw
25. Shift lever
26. Starter shaft housing
27. Washer
28. Needle bearing
29. Needle bearing
30. Starter motor

Fig. 19-11 Disassembled view of a starting motor using an overrunning clutch. (*Harley-Davidson Motor Company, Inc.*)

In some starting motors, the starter relay is given an additional job to do. One arrangement is shown in Fig. 19-11. The relay (called a *solenoid* in Fig. 19-11) is mounted on the starting motor. In addition to moving the contact plate to connect the battery to the starting motor, it also moves the clutch (🖝 19-4). When the starter button is pressed, the solenoid is connected to

the battery. Its magnetic field pulls the plunger (11) in, and this operates the shift lever (25). The shift lever pushes the clutch along the shaft so the pinion meshes with the crankshaft gear. At the same time, the plunger movement pulls in the contact plate to complete the circuit between the battery and starting motor. The starting motor runs and cranks the engine.

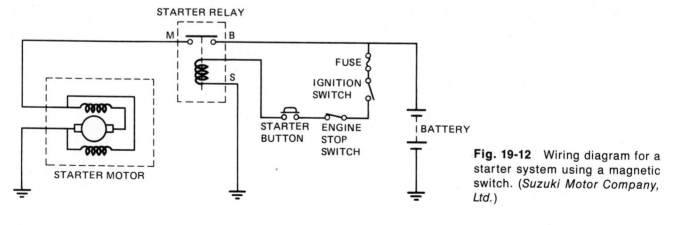

Fig. 19-12 Wiring diagram for a starter system using a magnetic switch. (*Suzuki Motor Company, Ltd.*)

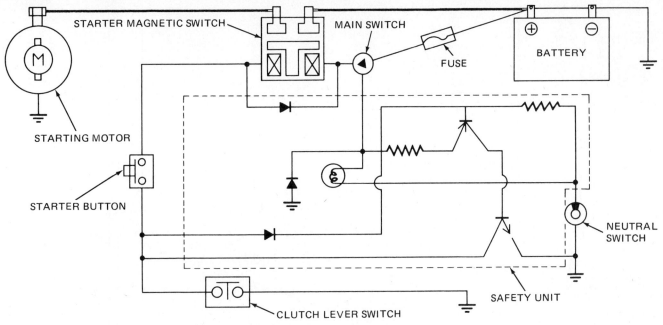

Fig. 19-13 Wiring diagram of a motorcycle starter safety-switch circuit. (*Honda Motor Company, Ltd.*)

As soon as the engine starts and the starter button is released, a spring pulls the clutch out of mesh. Also, the plunger moves back into the solenoid, and this moves the contact plate out to open the circuit to the battery. The armature stops rotating.

19-6
STARTER SAFETY SWITCH
Motorcycles with electric starters are equipped with a safety switch that prevents starting if the transmission is in gear and the clutch is applied. Figure 19-13 shows the wiring diagram of one such system. Starting is prevented if the neutral switch is in a transmission-in-gear position. However, when the clutch lever is squeezed to declutch, the clutch-lever switch will be closed, and starting can take place. The system protects the rider and motorcycle from a sudden and unexpected takeoff when starting the engine.

19-7
TROUBLESHOOTING ELECTRIC
STARTERS
Electric starters are highly reliable. Some manufacturers imply in their manuals that their starters require no routine servicing beyond an occasional inspection. Starters and wiring circuits do fail, however. The trouble symptoms can range from slow starting to complete failure to crank. When faced with these complaints, you will have to diagnose the trouble and make the necessary repairs.

Troubleshooting is a systematic, logical procedure of finding the causes of trouble symptoms. You begin your troubleshooting by noting the symptoms of trouble.

The basic problems with the starting motor are as follows:

1. The starting motor does not crank.

2. The starting motor cranks slowly, but the engine does not start.

3. The starting motor cranks the engine at normal speed, but the engine does not start.

Problem 3 cannot be blamed on the starting motor. If it spins the engine at normal cranking speed, the starting motor has done its job. Now let's look at the other two problems.

19-8
STARTING MOTOR DOES NOT CRANK
When you turn the ignition key to ON and press the start button, and nothing happens, the first thing you probably think about is a dead battery. You may be right. But before you check the battery, turn on the headlight and try cranking. Five things could happen when you do this:

1. No Cranking, No Lights. When you try to start, if the starting motor does not do anything and the light does not come on, either the battery is dead or a connection is bad. If you think there may be a bad connection, check the connections at the battery, at the starting-motor solenoid, and at the starter switch or relay.

2. No Cranking, Light Goes Out as You Press the Button. If the light goes out as you press the button, there may be a bad connection at the battery. The bad connection lets only a little current through—enough for the light to go on. But when you try to start, all the current goes to the starting motor because the starting motor has much less resistance than the light. Therefore the light goes out. Try wiggling the battery cables to see if this helps.

3. No Cranking, Light Dims Only Slightly When You Try to Start. The trouble probably is in the starting motor. Either the pinion is not engaging with the engine, or there is an open circuit inside the starting motor. If you

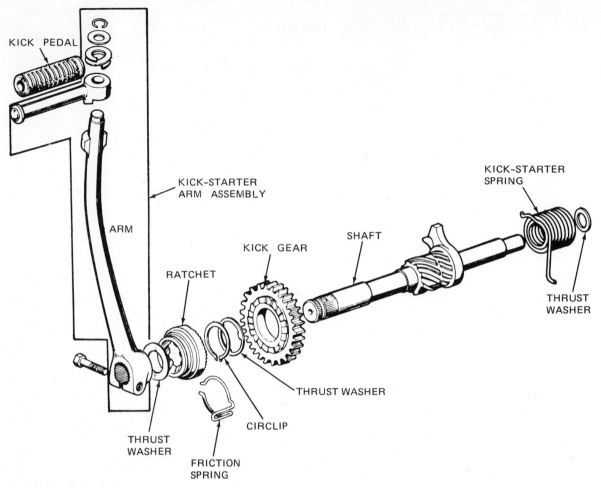

Fig. 19-14 Disassembled ratchet-type kick starter. (*Honda Motor Company, Ltd.*)

hear the starting-motor armature spin, then the overrunning clutch is slipping.

4. No Cranking, Light Dims Heavily When You Try to Start. This is most likely due to a run-down battery. The battery has enough charge to burn the light but not enough charge to deliver the current needed to the starting motor. Low temperatures make it tough on the battery. The starting motor needs more current to start a cold engine because the engine oil is much thicker. The battery should be in good condition and fully charged in the winter to ensure starting. There is one other thing to consider when you get no cranking and the light dims heavily. The starting motor or the engine may be seized or dragging.

5. No Cranking, Light Stays Bright When You Try to Start. The trouble probably is either in the starting motor or in the circuit between the starter button and the solenoid. You have to check to find the problem. If the trouble is not in the wiring, then it is in the starting motor.

⚙19-9
STARTING MOTOR CRANKS SLOWLY BUT THE ENGINE DOES NOT START This condition probably is due to a discharged battery. The battery doesn't have enough power to crank the engine fast enough for starting. Low temperature could be a factor here, as it was in item 4 of ⚙ 19-8, above.

Also, the rider may have run down the battery trying to start the engine. For example, there might be a problem in the engine, ignition, or fuel system that is preventing the engine from starting. The rider continued to crank until the battery ran down.

NOTE Never operate the starting motor for more than 30 seconds at a time. Pause for a few minutes to allow it to cool off. Then try again, if necessary. It takes a very high current to crank the engine. This can overheat the starting motor if it is used for too long a time. Overheating can ruin the starting motor.

The procedure here is to test the battery and replace it or recharge it, if it is low. Or connect a jumper battery and then to try to start. If you still can't get the engine started, the trouble is in the engine, not in the battery. As long as the starting motor cranks the engine normally, the starting motor is working properly.

⚙19-10
KICK-STARTER SERVICE The mechanical kick starter is usually easy to service. However, sometimes the compactness of its installation may require removal of several surrounding parts to get to it. The kick starter generally uses a ratchet or a pawl-engagement type of starter-drive mechanism.

Figure 19-1 shows a ratchet-type kick starter installed on an engine. Figure 19-14 shows the starter dis-

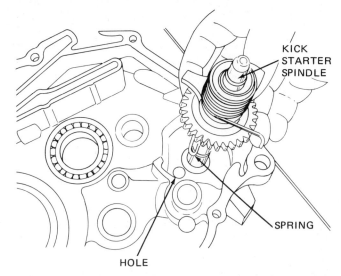

Fig. 19-15 Installing the kick starter. Note that the end of the spring fits into the hole in the case. (*Honda Motor Company, Ltd.*)

assembled. To reach the starter, you may have to remove the cylinder head, cylinder, right crankcase cover, oil filter, oil pump, and clutch. Then, the gearshaft itself and the alternator must be removed. Next, split the case and remove the kick starter. Inspect the starter ratchet for wear and for tooth damage. Check the shaft and bearing for wear. Figure 19-15 shows how the starter assembly is installed. Note that the hook on the end of the starter spring fits into the hole in the case.

Figure 19-3 shows a disassembled view of a pawl-type kick starter. The starter has a one-way clutch. When the kick pedal is in the up position, the pawl is held up out of the way by a stopper bolt, shown in Fig. 19-3. But when the kick pedal is pushed down, the pawl moves out from under the stopper bolt and locks into the gear to transmit cranking power.

After removal from the engine, this starter is taken apart by removing the Circlip and then the thrust washer, bushing, and spring guide. Then remove another Circlip, and the kick gear can be removed from the shaft. On this type of starter, inspect the inner teeth of the kick gear for broken and worn teeth. Also check that the pawl is not worn. When you reassemble the starter, make sure that the pawl is able to move freely and that it can lock into the kick gear. To properly install the stopper bolt in the crankcase, turn the kickshaft so the pawl is out of the way.

19-11
STARTING-MOTOR SERVICE Most starting motors require service only when the engine is overhauled. However, if a starting motor has very heavy use, it may require more frequent service. Also, if a starting motor is damaged or becomes defective, it requires service.

The major steps in rebuilding a starting motor are as follows:

Replace the bushing supporting the armature.
Test the armature and the field coils.

Turn the commutator, if required.
Undercut the mica between the commutator bars as recommended in the manufacturer's service manual.
Replace the field coils if they are damaged.
Check the solenoid.
Replace the brushes.

19-12
DAMAGED STARTING-MOTOR PARTS
Several kinds of defects may develop in a starting motor, as follows:

1. Thrown Armature Windings. This condition results from an excessive armature speed that has thrown the windings from the armature. Opening the throttle too wide after starting puts an excessive burden on the overrunning clutch. It overheats, seizes, and causes the armature to be spun at high speed. A defective overrunning clutch produces the same condition.

2. Burned Commutator Bars. Burned commutator bars usually indicate an open-circuited armature. The open circuit normally will be found at one or more commutator riser bars. It is most often caused by excessively long cranking periods. Such long cranking periods overheat the starting motor and melt the solder at the riser-bar connection. This throws solder on the cover band; it also causes the connection to loosen. Arcing then takes place each time the bar with the bad connection passes under the brushes. The bar soon burns. If the bars are not too badly burned, the armature can be repaired.

3. Dirty or Gummy Commutator. The commutator sometimes becomes covered with a film of dirt or gum. This can be cleaned off with a brush-seating stone or with No. 00 sandpaper held against the commutator while the starting motor is being operated (Fig. 19-16). However, it is usually best to correct this condition by turning the commutator on a lathe.

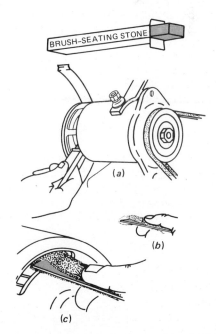

Fig. 19-16 Cleaning a commutator with a brush-seating stone (*a*) or sandpaper (*b* and *c*).

19-13

REBUILDING THE STARTING MOTOR To disassemble the starting motor, first remove the solenoid or switch, where present. Next, the cover band (where present) is removed, and the brush leads are disconnected. Where leads are soldered, the brushes are removed from the holders. Then, after the through bolts are taken out, the commutator end frame, field frame, and drive-end frame can be separated. Figure 19-7 shows a disassembled starting motor.

On many overruning-clutch starting motors, the overrunning clutch can be slid off. Figure 19-11 is a disassembled view of a starting motor using an overrunning clutch.

1. Cleaning Starting-Motor Parts. The armature and fields should never be cleaned in any solution that dissolves or damages the insulation. They should be wiped off with a clean cloth. Never clean the overrunning clutch in a solvent tank. The solvent will dissolve the clutch lubrication and ruin the clutch.

2. Field-Winding Service. Test for a grounded field with the test-light leads on the terminal stud and frame. If the lamp lights, the field is grounded. Test for opens with the test light at the two ends of the field circuit. The lamp should light. Replace the field windings, if necessary. Rapping the frame with a plastic hammer while the screws are being tightened helps align the shoes properly. When resoldering connections, use rosin-core solder.

3. Armature Service. The causes and correction of thrown armature windings and burned commutator bars have been discussed. Inspect the armature laminations for rub marks. These mean a worn bearing or a bent shaft has allowed the laminations to rub on the pole shoes. A check for a bent shaft can be made by putting the armature in V blocks. Rotate the armature while a dial indicator is in position to measure runout. The runout or out-of-roundness of the commutator can be checked at the same time.

The armature is tested for grounds by placing one test-light lead on the laminations and the other on the

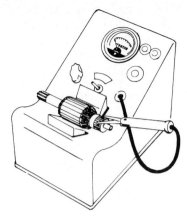

Fig. 19-18 Checking an armature for an open circuit. (*Suzuki Motor Company, Ltd.*)

commutator, as shown in Fig. 19-17. If the lamp lights, the armature is grounded. It is tested for short circuits on the growler. The armature is placed on the growler and slowly revolved while a hacksaw blade is held above the armature core. The hacksaw blade vibrates against the core when it is above a slot containing a shorted winding. A shorted or grounded armature should be discarded.

After checking for short circuits in the armature, remove the hacksaw blade. Then place each of the growler tester prods on each two segments or bars of the commutator (Fig. 19-18). Go completely around the commutator while watching the current flow indicated on the ammeter in the growler. All readings should be the same. A difference of several amperes in current flow with the prods connected to any two segments indicates an open circuit.

If the commutator is out of round or worn, or if it has high mica, it should be turned on a lathe. The cut should be as smooth and as light as possible. Then the mica between the commutator bars should be undercut.

4. Brush Service. Brushes that are worn to one-half their original length should be replaced. If a brush lead is soldered, unsolder it and unclinch the lead from the connector. Where the lead terminal clip is riveted to the frame, unsolder and unclamp the lead from the clip. Then the lead of a new brush can be clamped and soldered to the clip. With new brushes in place, put the armature into position so that the brushes rest on the commutator. If the brushes do not align with the commutator bars, the brush holders are bent. This requires replacement of the brush holders or the end frame.

The brush-spring tension should be checked with a spring scale. Note the pull required to raise the brushes, brush arms, or holders from the contact position. Replace the springs if the tension is not correct.

5. Testing the Overrunning Clutch. The overrunning-clutch pinion should turn freely and smoothly in the overrunning direction. It should not slip in the cranking position with normal cranking torque applied. If the pinion turns roughly in the overrunning direction, the rollers are chipped or worn, and the clutch should be replaced. If the pinion slips in the cranking direction, the clutch should be replaced.

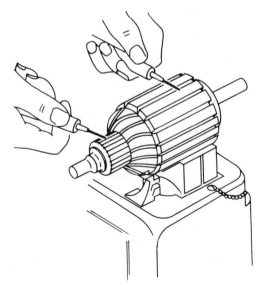

Fig. 19-17 Testing an armature for grounds.

6. Starting-Motor Lubrication. During reassembly of the starting motor, all bearings should be lubricated with a few drops of light engine oil. Many starting motors have oilless bearings that have no provision for oiling. However, they should be lubricated before reassembly with a few drops of SAE 20 oil.

7. Starting-Motor Assembly. The assembly procedure is the reverse of disassembly. Soldered connections should be made with rosin-core solder.

19-14
INSTALLING THE STARTING MOTOR

Before a starting motor is removed or installed, the battery ground cable should be disconnected from the battery terminal. This avoids shorting the battery by an accidental grounding of the insulated cable. When installing the starting motor, connect the cable from the battery after the motor is bolted into place on the engine. Finally, reconnect the battery ground cable.

CHAPTER 19
REVIEW QUESTIONS

1. What are the two types of starters used on motorcycles?
2. When the kick-starter pedal is released, what returns it to the proper position for cranking?
3. How is the kick starter disengaged from the engine after starting?
4. What are the advantages of a kick starter?
5. What are the advantages of an electric starter?
6. Name the components in an electric-starting system.
7. What operates a starting motor?
8. What are the two main parts of a starting motor?
9. Why is some type of starter drive required?
10. Explain why a starter relay is needed.
11. Describe the operation of the starter relay when the starter button is pressed.
12. How does an overrunning clutch drive operate?
13. What is the purpose of mounting a solenoid on the starting motor?
14. Why is a starter safety switch used on motorcycles equipped with electric starters?
15. List the three basic problems with starting motors.
16. What causes burned commutator bars on the starting-motor armature?
17. How can the commutator be cleaned without disassembling the starting motor?
18. Explain how to test the field coils for grounds, opens, and shorts.
19. Explain how to test the armature for grounds, opens, and shorts.
20. When should brushes be replaced?

CHAPTER **20**

CHARGING SYSTEMS

After studying this chapter, you should be able to:

1. Explain the difference between a dc generator and an alternator.
2. Describe the construction and operation of a typical alternator.
3. Discuss the operation of a rectifier.
4. Explain how alternator regulators work, and discuss the difference in operation between the mechanical and the electronic regulator.
5. Discuss charging-system trouble diagnosis, and list the possible causes of troubles.
6. List and explain the five charging-system service precautions.
7. Explain how to check the operation of the charging-system indicator light.
8. Discuss alternator service and why you should refer to the manufacturer's shop manual for specific instructions.

20-1 MOTORCYCLE CHARGING SYSTEMS

Today, many motorcycles have electric starters. To operate the starting motor, a battery is required. The purpose of the charging system is to keep the battery charged. However, many motorcycles without a battery or a starting motor have electric equipment such as lights and horn. On these bikes, the only job the alternator has is to supply current to operate this electric equipment.

Figure 17-1 shows the complete electric system of a motorcycle. Notice that this motorcycle uses an ac generator, or alternator. There are two basic types of generators. One type uses an armature with a commutator and brushes to provide direct current. This type of generator often is called a *dc generator* or, simply, a *generator*. It is seldom used today.

The second type of generator provides alternating current at its output terminal. This type of generator is called an *ac generator* or an *alternator*. However, most of the electric equipment on the motorcycle will not run on alternating current. Therefore the alternating current must be converted into direct current. The device that does this job is the rectifier (17-14). In addition, most generators and alternators require a regulator to prevent damaging high voltage.

When you take current out of the battery, you have to put it back in, or you will end up with a run-down battery. The alternator does this job by converting mechanical energy taken from the engine into electric energy.

At the start, the battery must supply current to crank the engine and to operate all electric devices that are turned on. When the engine is running fast enough, the alternator takes over the job as the source of electric

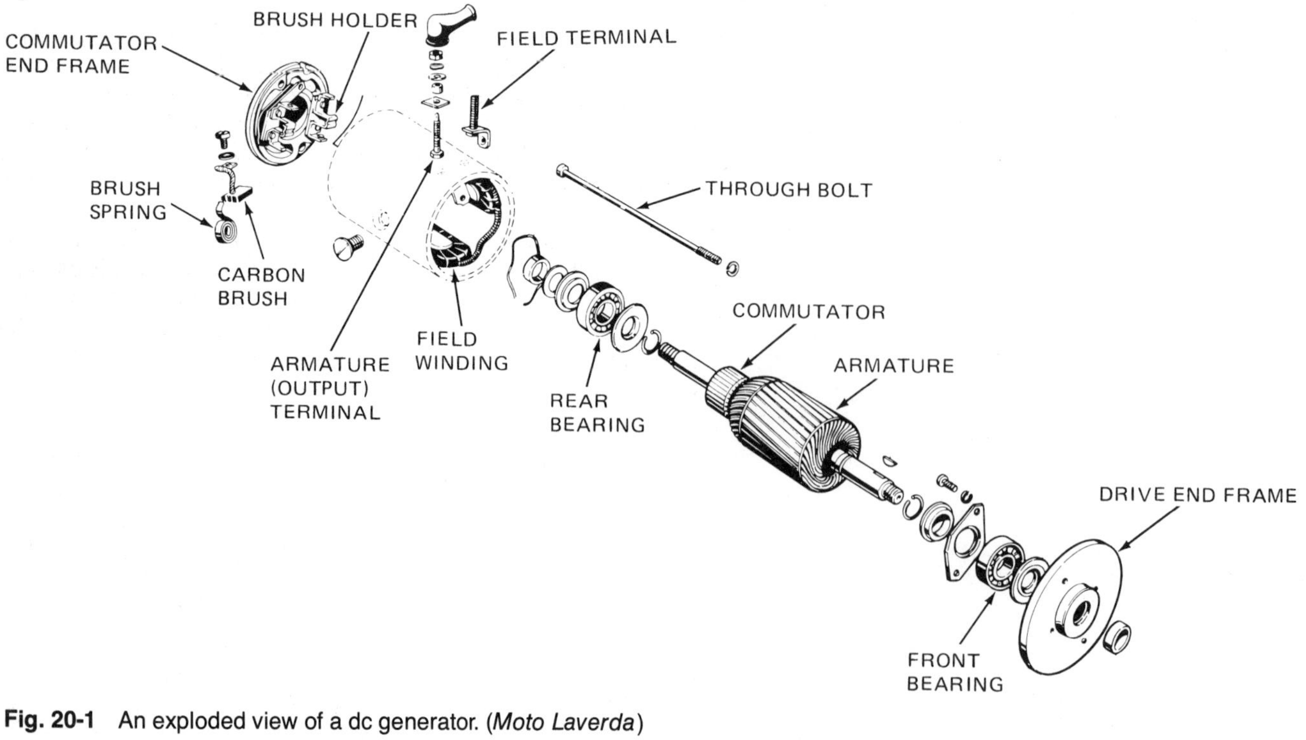

Fig. 20-1 An exploded view of a dc generator. (*Moto Laverda*)

current. At this time, the alternator begins to put back into the battery the current taken out for starting. (This is how the battery is kept charged.) The charging system consists of the alternator along with the rectifier, regulator, and wiring.

20-2 GENERATOR

For many years, motorcycles used dc (direct-current) generators. The action of the brushes and commutator on the armature provided direct current at the output terminal of the generator. You won't see this type of generator today except on older motorcycles and some small engines and farm tractors. Figure 20-1 shows an exploded view of a generator used on motorcycles. Generators are all very similar in construction and operation.

The generator produces electric current when the armature is rotated in a stationary magnetic field. This magnetic field is created by passing a small current through the field windings. The output current is generated in the armature. It passes through the armature commutator, brushes, and output terminal to the external circuit (Fig. 20-2). A regulator is required to control the output of the generator.

Figure 20-2 shows a wiring diagram for a charging system using a generator. In operation, the regulator controls how much current flows into the field windings through the F, or field, terminal of the generator. This determines how much current is generated in the windings of the armature.

20-3 STARTER-GENERATOR

Some motorcycles have a combination starter-generator. It cranks the engine for starting like the starting motors discussed in Chap. 19. After the engine is running, the armature is revolving in a magnetic field. Then the starter-generator acts like the dc generator discussed above.

20-4 ALTERNATOR

The alternator (Fig. 20-3) may be a separate unit or it may be built into the crankcase.

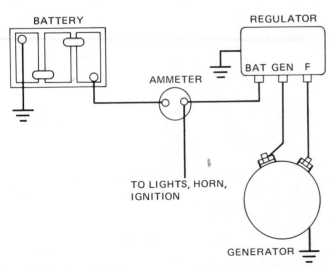

Fig. 20-2 Wiring diagram of a dc charging system.

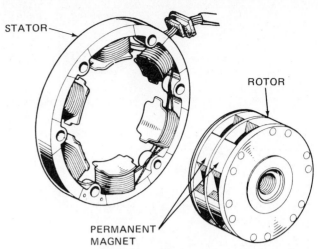

Fig. 20-3 Basic parts of an alternator. (*Honda Motor Company, Ltd.*)

Both operate in the same way. Today, almost all motorcycle alternators are on the side of the crankcase and are driven directly by the crankshaft. The alternator has replaced the generator on motorcycles for several reasons. It is lighter in weight and simpler in construction. It has fewer parts that wear. This gives it a long life, and makes it easy to service. The charging system using an alternator requires much less service than the generator and regulator used years ago.

The alternator produces current in stationary windings called *stator coils*. The current is produced by a rotating magnetic field produced by the rotor. Some rotors have permanent magnets (Fig. 20-3). When the rotor rotates, the magnetic fields of these magnets sweep through the stationary coils, or windings, of the stator. This movement produces an electric current in the coils.

Other rotors have field windings in them (Fig. 20-4). Current is fed to these windings through brushes and slip rings. When current flows through the field windings, they produce a magnetic field which rotates with the windings. The magnetic field sweeps through the stationary coils of the stator, and this produces current in the coils.

A simple type of alternator is shown in Fig. 20-5. It is called a *flywheel magneto and alternator* and is used on many mopeds, minibikes, and off-road motorcycles. One stator coil produces current to operate the ignition system. The second stator coil produces current to

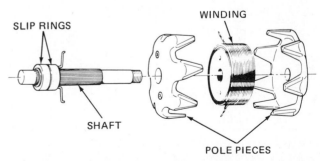

Fig. 20-4 The rotor of an alternator, partly disassembled.

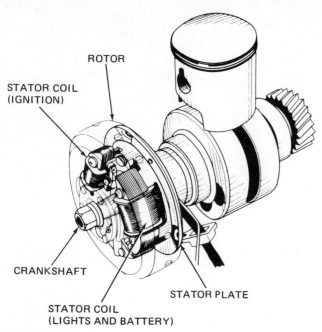

STATOR COIL
(IGNITION)

ROTOR

CRANKSHAFT

STATOR PLATE

STATOR COIL
(LIGHTS AND BATTERY)

Fig. 20-5 Phantom view of a flywheel magneto and alternator. (*Suzuki Motor Company, Ltd.*)

operate the lights and to charge the battery, if the motorcycle has one. Note that in Fig. 20-5 the rotor is outside the stator. Other alternators have the rotor inside the stator (Fig. 20-4).

A third type of alternator is shown in Fig. 20-6. In this alternator, both the stator and the field coil are stationary. A drum-shaped rotor is positioned between the stator and the field coil. The rotor has a series of permanent magnets. When it rotates, it carries the magnetic field around with it.

The field coil is connected through wires to the battery so it produces a magnetic field. When the rotor carries the magnetic field of the permanent magnets through this magnetic field, it causes the field-coil magnetic field to sway back and forth through the stator windings. This induces a current in the stator windings. Note that the alternator shown in Fig. 20-6 has no brushes. There is nothing to wear but the bearings that hold the rotor and allow it to rotate.

**20-5
RECTIFIER** The alternator produces alternating current in its stator. As the rotor rotates, its magnetic field cuts through the stator winding, first in

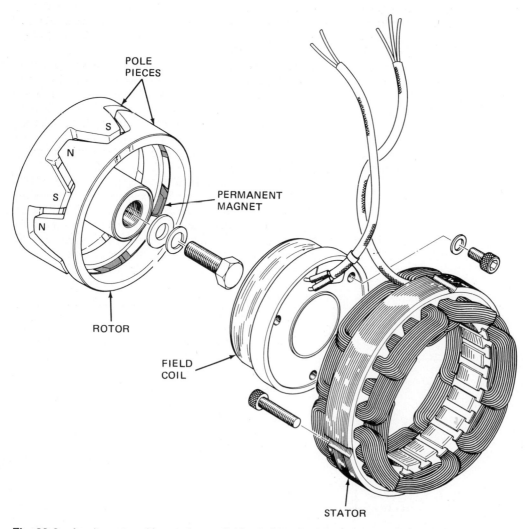

POLE
PIECES

PERMANENT
MAGNET

ROTOR

FIELD
COIL

STATOR

Fig. 20-6 An alternator with a stationary field coil. (*Yamaha Motor Company, Ltd.*)

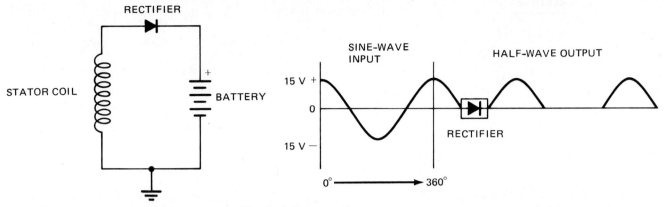

Fig. 20-7 A single-phase charging system with a half-wave rectifier.

one direction and then in the other. This means that the current induced flows first in one direction and then in the other. Alternating current cannot be used in the motorcycle system. The battery requires direct current to charge it. Other electric devices are also dc units.

Diodes are used to change the alternating current to direct current (rectify the direct current). The diode is discussed in ☑ 17-14. It is a one-way electric valve. Some diodes are also called *silicon rectifiers*. Some alternators use only one diode; others use four or six.

Rectifiers are classified as single-phase half-wave, single-phase full-wave, and three-phase full-wave. Figure 20-7 shows the wiring diagram for a charging system that includes a flywheel alternator like the one shown in Fig. 20-5. This type of charging system is found on motorcycles with very little electric equipment.

By using one diode as a rectifier, as shown in Fig. 20-7, half of the current generated by the alternator gets

through to charge the battery. The other half is cut off. For this reason, this type of rectifier is known as a *half-wave rectifier*. It also is a *single-phase rectifier* because there is only a single winding in the stator. Some other alternators have three electrically separate windings.

Figure 20-8 shows in phantom view the parts of a charging system, their locations on a motorcycle, and, at the upper right, the wiring circuit. The symbol indicates a diode. The direction of the arrow indicates the direction the current must take to flow through the diode. Note that there are four diodes in the rectifier, which produces single-phase full-wave output. For this reason, it is called a *full-wave rectifier*. Figure 20-9 shows another charging system using a four-diode rectifier to provide full-wave output.

Figure 20-10 shows how the diodes do this job. Notice that the four diodes are numbered 1, 2, 3, and 4. Now look at the top illustration in Fig. 20-10. Current is

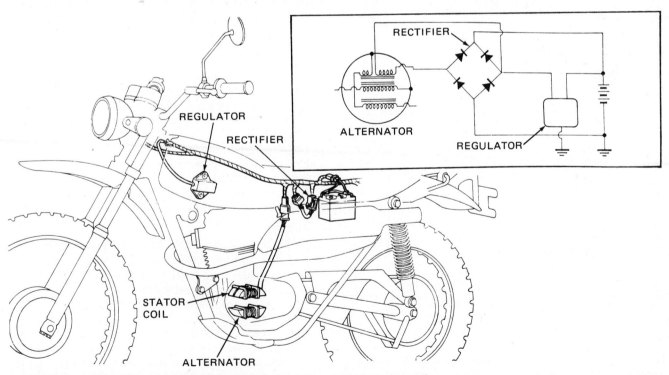

Fig. 20-8 Voltage regulator used with a flywheel magneto and alternator type of charging system. (*Honda Motor Company, Ltd.*)

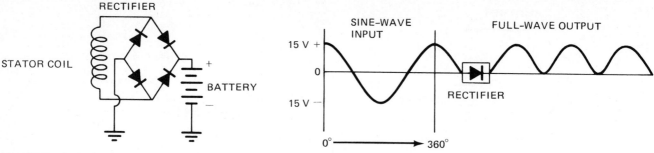

Fig. 20-9 A single-phase charging system with a full-wave rectifier.

flowing up through the right lead from the alternator, which is the stator-coil lead (Fig. 20-5). As the current reaches the rectifier, only diode 3 lets the current flow through. From there, the current flows up to the negative (−) terminal of the battery, through the battery, and back to the rectifier. As the current returns to the diodes, only diode 1 lets the current flow through.

A moment later, when the current alternates and starts flowing in the opposite direction, the situation is as shown at the bottom in Fig. 20-10. Now the current is flowing up the left lead from the alternator. The current cannot pass through diode 1, but it can move through diode 2 and from there to the battery. On its return from the battery, the current passes through diode 4 and then down to the alternator.

One way to quickly identify whether a rectifier is a full-wave or a half-wave rectifier is to count the number of wires attached to it. A half-wave rectifier usually has

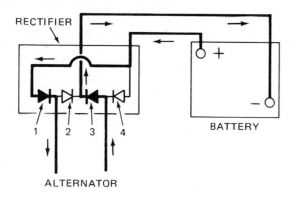

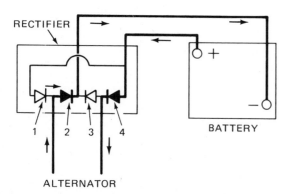

Fig. 20-10 A rectifier using four diodes connected to an alternator. The diodes rectify the alternating current and charge it to direct current for charging the battery.

two wires, as shown in Fig. 20-7. A full-wave rectifier has three or four wires, as shown in Figs. 20-9 and 20-10.

The charging system shown in Fig. 20-9 is single-phase because there is only a single ac source. This is the single stator coil. A single source results in a pulsating current that has a series of peaks and valleys even after it is rectified by a full-wave rectifier. This can be compared to a single-cylinder engine which does not provide a smooth flow of power. There are a series of peaks between which no power is delivered.

To provide a smooth flow of current, most large motorcycle and automobile alternators are three-phase (Fig. 20-11). They are built with three stator circuits which, in effect, give overlapping pulses of alternating current. When these overlapping pulses are rectified, a comparatively smooth flow of direct current is obtained.

20-6
ALTERNATOR REGULATORS The alternator could increase its output with speed until, at high speed, it would be producing too much output. This could overcharge the battery, burn out the headlight, and do other damage. To prevent this, a current limiter, or voltage regulator, is used. The voltage regulator regulates the amount of current being fed to the field windings.

When high alternator output is required, the regulator allows more current to flow. This produces a strong magnetic field which causes the alternator output to go up. But when low alternator output is required (because the battery is being charged and no electric load is turned on), the regulator cuts down the field current. The magnetic field is weak, and only a small amount of current is produced.

There are two types of alternator regulators. One is mechanical, and the other is electronic.

20-7
MECHANICAL VOLTAGE REGULATOR
Figure 20-12 is a wiring diagram of an alternator charging system with a mechanical regulator. The regulator has a coil which is connected between the alternator-rectifier output lead and ground. The alternator voltage is impressed on this coil. The armature is a flat metal plate with contact points. When the alternator is rotating slowly, it does not produce enough voltage to pull the armature down. This is because the voltage on the coil does not produce enough current flow in the coil. Its magnetism is weak.

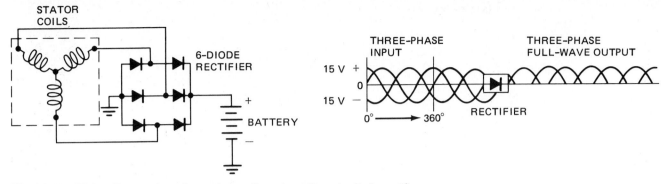

Fig. 20-11 Wiring diagram for a three-phase alternator with a six-diode rectifier.

However, as the alternator speed and voltage go up, the magnetism gets stronger. When the voltage reaches its safe upper limit, the magnetism in the coil is strong enough to pull the armature down. This separates the low-speed points, which puts a resistance into the field-coil circuit. This causes less field current to flow, and the magnetic field in the alternator is weaker.

With a weaker magnetic field, the alternator output and voltage fall. The magnetic field in the regulator coil weakens, and the armature is released. It moves up, and the low-speed points close. Now, with the resistance shorted out, the alternator output increases. The whole cycle is repeated many times a second as the points vibrate. This action puts just enough resistance into the field-coil circuit to regulate the voltage at the safe limit.

The alternator speed can increase further so that the voltage starts to climb even with the resistance in the field-coil circuit. When this happens, the higher voltage pulls the armature all the way down so the high-speed points close. This connects the insulated end of the field coil to ground.

With both ends of the field coil connected to ground, no current can flow, and the magnetism of the field coil drops off to practically zero. As a result, the alternator voltage drops as the points vibrate. However, the vibration is of the lower, or high-speed, points.

20-8 ELECTRONIC VOLTAGE REGULATOR

Figure 20-13 shows a charging system which includes an alternator, a rectifier, and an electronic voltage regulator. Figure 20-14 shows a schematic wiring diagram for this charging system. In the voltage regulator, notice the *Zener diode* and the *silicon-controlled rectifier* (SCR). The rotor contains permanent magnets, so no field coil is needed in the alternator.

A Zener diode is a type of diode that will conduct current in the normal direction. But when the voltage across the Zener diode reaches a certain predetermined value, it will begin to conduct in the reverse direction. The Zener diode will continue to conduct until the excess voltage is no longer applied. This characteristic allows the Zener diode to be used on a solid-state current limiter in some alternator charging systems.

The SCR is another special type of diode. It is also called a *thyristor*. Normally the SCR acts as an open circuit and does not conduct. No current can pass through in either direction. But when a voltage is applied to the gate of the SCR, it begins to conduct. As you can see in Fig. 20-14, regular diodes (in the rectifier) and Zener diodes (in the voltage regulator) have two leads each. The SCR has three leads.

In Fig. 20-14, the battery, voltage regulator, and the electric load form three branches of a parallel circuit. A

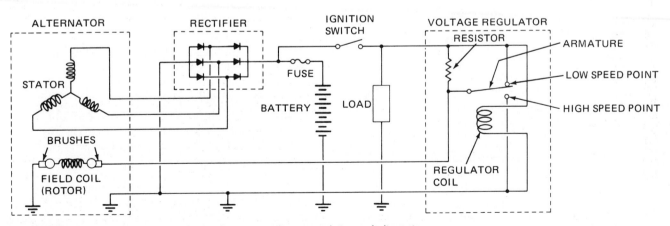

Fig. 20-12 Circuit of a mechanical, or point-type, voltage regulator and alternator. (*Suzuki Motor Company, Ltd.*)

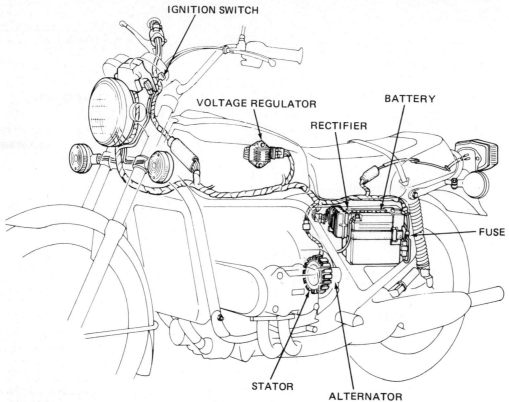

Fig. 20-13 A charging system on a motorcycle using a solid-state voltage regulator. (*Honda Motor Company, Ltd.*)

portion of the current from the rectifier flows through the battery to charge it. The rest of the current flows through the electric equipment which is turned on. In addition, a small current flows through the two resistors in the voltage regulator. This applies a small voltage to the Zener diode, but not enough to make it conduct.

As the battery becomes fully charged and engine speed increases, the voltage applied to the Zener diode also increases. At some predetermined voltage, called the *breakdown voltage,* the Zener diode suddenly allows a small current through it in the reverse direction.

This small current acts as a signal. When it is applied to the gate of the SCR, the SCR begins to conduct.

When the SCR is conducting, the output from the alternator is reduced by as much as one-third. The current from winding C in the stator (Fig. 20-14) now flows through the SCR to ground, instead of joining with the main current flow from the rectifier. This reduces the generated voltage. Therefore, the Zener diode stops conducting.

Because the Zener diode has stopped conducting, the signal voltage no longer is applied to the SCR, which

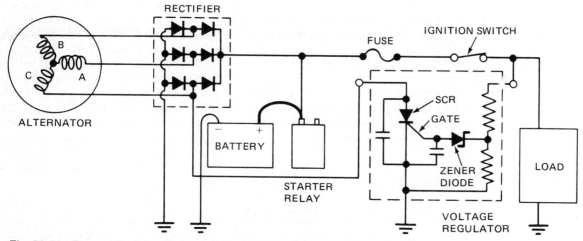

Fig. 20-14 Schematic wiring diagram of the charging system using the solid-state voltage regulator shown in Fig. 24-13. (*Honda Motor Company, Ltd.*)

also stops conducting. Now the alternator voltage again starts to rise. This cycle is repeated as necessary to limit the voltage to a safe maximum.

The advantage of the electronic regulator is that it has no moving parts. In the mechanical voltage regulator, a slight arcing of the points occurs each time they open. However, electronic devices such as Zener diodes and SCRs can operate at very high speed to electronically open and close circuits. Since no arc is created by their operation, *theoretically* an electronic voltage regulator will never wear out or need adjustment.

20-9 CHARGING-SYSTEM TROUBLE DIAGNOSIS

Two abnormal conditions that occur with the charging systems are

1. A charged battery and a high charging rate
2. A discharged battery and a low charging rate

There could be other problems, such as a noisy alternator or faulty operation of an ammeter or an indicator light. Noise is due to trouble inside the alternator. If the problem is inside the alternator, it must be inspected. Bad bearings and some types of diode failure make noise. Faulty indicator-light or ammeter action can be caused by a burned-out light bulb, by defective wiring, or by trouble in the regulator. If the problem is a bad regulator, usually a new regulator must be installed.

1. A Charged Battery and a High Charging Rate. If the alternator continues to push a high charging rate into a charged battery, something is wrong. If it is not corrected, there will be more trouble. The voltage will be high, the headlight will burn out, and other electric devices may be damaged. The battery will be overcharged and will have a very short life.

The most likely cause of a high charging rate with a charged battery is trouble in the regulator. A defective regulator can be checked and adjusted or replaced.

2. A Discharged Battery and a Low Charging Rate. With a low battery, the charging rate should be high. If the battery is run down and the alternator is producing little or no current, there is trouble. It could be caused by some defect in the alternator or the regulator.

Look at the wiring and the connections. A loose connection in the charging circuit can prevent current flow to the battery. Another possibility is trouble in the alternator or regulator. This requires checking and servicing of the alternator or regulator.

NOTE You need a voltmeter and an ammeter to check alternator output. The meters tell you the voltage and current output from the alternator. Many motorcycles have a charge-indicator light instead of an ammeter. On these, the only way to tell how much current the alternator is putting out is with an ammeter. Each motorcycle manufacturer recommends its own special charging-system testing procedure. Follow the procedure in the manufacturer's service manual to make the electrical check of the charging system you are testing.

20-10 CHARGING-SYSTEM SERVICE PRECAUTIONS

The following precautions must be observed when working on the charging system.

Failure to observe these precautions may result in serious damage to the electric equipment.

1. Do not polarize an alternator.
2. Do not short across or ground any of the terminals in the charging system except as specifically instructed in the manufacturer's testing procedure.
3. Never operate the alternator with the output terminal disconnected.
4. Make sure the alternator and the battery are of the same ground polarity.
5. When connecting a battery charger or a jumper battery to the motorcycle battery, observe the polarity of the battery. Be careful not to cause any sparks around the battery.

20-11 VISUAL CHARGING-SYSTEM CHECKS

Before making any electrical test, visually inspect all charging-system connections and slip-on connectors. Make sure all connections at the alternator, regulator, and engine are clean and tight.

Inspect all wiring for cracked, frayed, or broken insulation.

Check the fuse located between the battery and the alternator on some motorcycles. Replace the fuse if it is blown.

Check the battery and cable terminals for clean and tight connections. If they are corroded, remove the battery cables. Clean and install the cables securely.

Be sure that the alternator is properly grounded.

Check the state of charge of the battery with a hydrometer. The specific gravity must be at least 1.200 to perform electrical tests of the charging system.

Carefully note the customer's complaint about the charging system. This information will aid you in locating the part of the charging system causing the problem.

20-12 INDICATOR-LIGHT CHECK

Improper operation of the charging-system indicator light or ammeter indicates trouble in the charging system. For checking indicator-light operation, the normal conditions of the indicator light are shown in the chart below.

NORMAL INDICATOR-LIGHT OPERATION

Ignition switch	Light	Engine
Off	Off	Stopped
On	On	Stopped
On	Off	Running

If the indicator light operates normally and the battery is undercharged, check the battery with a battery tester. If the battery is okay, follow the charging-system testing procedure in the manufacturer's service manual. Be sure that an undercharged battery was not caused by the ignition or lights having been left on for long periods. Also, riding a motorcycle with the engine running too slowly will cause this condition.

If the indicator light is on when the ignition switch is

off, follow the charging-system testing procedure in the manufacturer's service manual.

If the indicator light is off with the engine stopped and the ignition switch on, an open circuit is indicated. Check for a blown fuse, a burned-out indicator-light bulb, a defective bulb socket, or an open circuit between the alternator or regulator and the ignition switch. If none of these conditions is found, follow the charging-system testing procedure in the manufacturer's service manual.

If the ignition switch is on with the engine running and the indicator light is on, follow the charging-system testing procedure in the manufacturer's service manual.

20-13 ALTERNATOR SERVICE Alternators are of very simple construction and should operate for long periods without trouble. The only wearing parts in the alternator are the bearings, the brushes, and the slip rings. Also, it is possible for a diode in the rectifier to become defective. The exact procedure to follow in servicing an alternator depends upon the type and model of alternator. Refer to the manufacturer's shop manual for specific instructions on how to check and service the alternator you are working on.

Diodes can be checked with an ohmmeter. Never try to test a diode with a 110-volt test light. You will ruin the diode.

20-14 VOLTAGE-REGULATOR SERVICE Some mechanical (contact-point) type of regulators can be adjusted. Refer to the manufacturer's shop manual for specific instructions. Electronic regulators require no service and usually have no provision for adjustment. If an electronic regulator is suspected of causing trouble, temporarily install a regulator known to be good. If this does not fix the trouble, look for the cause elsewhere.

CHAPTER 20
REVIEW QUESTIONS

1. What is a generator?
2. What is the difference between a generator and an alternator?
3. How does a dc generator provide direct current at the output terminals?
4. What is a starter-generator?
5. Why have alternators replaced generators on motorcycles?
6. In an alternator, what is the name of the part that rotates?
7. What is the name of the part that contains the stationary windings?
8. What is the simplest type of alternator?
9. Why are slip rings used in some alternators?
10. Describe how a brushless alternator generates electricity.
11. What is a rectifier?
12. What is a diode?
13. What is the difference between a mechanical regulator and an electronic regulator?
14. Describe the operation of the voltage regulator used with a flywheel magneto and alternator.
15. How do you service a defective electronic regulator?
16. What is a Zener diode?
17. Explain the operation of a silicon-controlled rectifier (SCR).
18. List and explain the possible causes of two abnormal conditions that can occur in the charging system.
19. Explain how to use the indicator light on the motorcycle to determine if the charging system is operating properly.

CHAPTER **21**

IGNITION SYSTEMS

After studying this chapter,
you should be able to:

1. Explain the purpose of the ignition system.

2. Describe the three basic types of motorcycle-engine ignition systems.

3. Discuss the differences between ignition systems for two-cycle and four-cycle engines.

4. Explain how the three basic types of motorcycle-engine ignition systems work.

5. Discuss advance mechanisms and explain how the centrifugal and vacuum-advance mechanisms work.

6. Explain how to check the spark and what could cause no spark.

7. Describe contact-point service.

8. Discuss ignition timing and explain how it is done.

9. Discuss spark-plug service.

21-1 INTRODUCTION TO THE IGNITION SYSTEM

A variety of ignition systems have been used with internal combustion engines. Ignition systems can be divided into two general categories—magneto ignition and battery ignition. Most small engines, such as those used in lawnmowers, trimmers, chain saws, and blowers, use magneto ignition. Most motorcycle engines had magneto ignition until a few years ago, when four-cycle engines for motorcycles began to use battery ignition. Battery ignition is used in all automobiles, trucks, and buses (except when the vehicle has a diesel engine, which requires no separate electric ignition system).

Figure 21-1 shows the components of a typical ignition system on a one-cylinder motorcycle. The ignition system produces the sparks that ignite the compressed air-fuel mixture in the engine cylinders. The sparks have to be hot enough to ignite the mixture. Also, they have to arrive at the engine cylinders at exactly the right time. This means that the ideal ignition system must do the following things:

1. Produce sparks at the spark plug or plugs to ignite the compressed air-fuel mixture in the cylinder.
2. Advance the timing of the sparks (that is, move them ahead) as engine speed increases, so the mixture is ignited earlier and is given enough time to burn and deliver its power to the downward-moving piston.
3. Advance the timing at part-throttle because less mixture gets to the cylinder and the mixture burns slower.

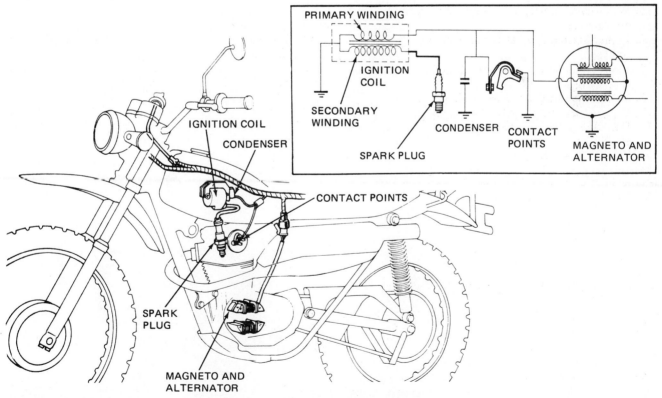

Fig. 21-1 Magneto ignition system on a motorcycle. The drawing to the upper right shows the wiring diagram of the system. (*Honda Motor Company, Ltd.*)

187

Many motorcycle engines do not provide for item 3. In general, only the larger motorcycle engines have part-throttle advance control. In later sections of this chapter, we discuss how the ignition timing is advanced.

21-2 MOTORCYCLE-ENGINE IGNITION SYSTEMS

Motorcycle engines have one of three types of ignition systems. The first is the magneto ignition system (Fig. 21-1). It is similar to the flywheel magneto charging system, covered in Chap. 20. The second is the battery ignition system, which is similar to the ignition system used in automobiles. The third is the capacitor-discharge ignition (CDI) system.

In the magneto ignition system, the magneto generates the primary current. No battery is required. To stop the engine, you move the engine stop switch to the OFF position. This grounds the ignition system by grounding the magneto primary winding.

With the battery ignition system, a battery furnishes the primary current. A CDI system uses either a battery or a magneto to furnish the primary current. However, the difference in the CDI system is in how the high-voltage spark is created.

Some electronic ignition systems are used in which the contact points are replaced by a small rotor and a field, or pickup, coil. The operation of this system is discussed in the section on CDI systems (21-7).

21-3 MAGNETO IGNITION SYSTEM FOR A FOUR-CYCLE ENGINE

The magneto ignition system used in motorcycle engines is often called a *flywheel-magneto system* because the system is incorporated in the flywheel. Figure 21-1 shows a magneto ignition system on a motorcycle with a single-cylinder four-cycle engine. The schematic wiring diagram to the upper right shows how the various components are connected. The magneto-alternator assembly has three windings. We are concerned with only the center wind-

ing at this time. The contact points are opened and closed by a breaker cam that is driven off the camshaft.

As the breaker cam rotates, its lobe (or high point) opens and closes the contact points. When the points are closed, both ends of the center winding, or *source coil,* in the magneto-alternator assembly are grounded. The magnets that are rotating past the winding produce a voltage in the winding, but this voltage goes nowhere. It just alternates in the winding.

However, when the points separate, the alternating voltage in the magneto is suddenly released. It surges into the primary winding (Fig. 21-1) of the ignition coil. This voltage produces a very strong magnetic field in the ignition coil. A *condenser,* or *capacitor,* is connected between the movable point and ground. The purpose of the condenser is to prevent excessive arcing of the points as they separate and to aid in the collapse of the magnetic field.

The buildup of the magnetic field sends magnetic lines of force cutting across the many turns of wire in the secondary winding of the ignition coil (Fig. 21-1). The action induces a high voltage in the secondary winding. The voltage goes high enough to send a high-voltage surge to the spark plug. This causes a spark at the spark-plug gap so that the compressed air-fuel mixture in the engine cylinder is ignited.

The opening and closing of the contact points is controlled by a breaker cam which is driven by the engine. The ignition system shown in Fig. 21-1 includes a mechanical spark advance which works on engine speed. As engine speed increases, the spark advances. Therefore, the spark appears earlier so that the compressed air-fuel mixture has enough time to burn.

Figure 21-2 shows the advance mechanism. It includes two advance weights, springs, and advance levers. Only one of these is shown in the small box to the left in the illustration. As engine speed increases, the advance weights are thrown outward by centrifugal force, against the tension of the springs. This outward motion causes the advance levers to pivot, pushing the

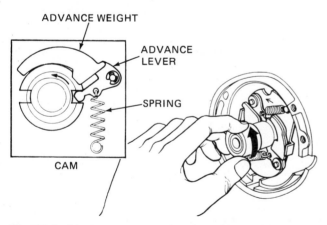

Fig. 21-2 Mechanical advance mechanism. To the right, the operation of the mechanism is being checked. As it is turned, the weights are pushed out against the spring tension. To the left, one of the two advance weights and springs is shown. (*Honda Motor Company, Ltd.*)

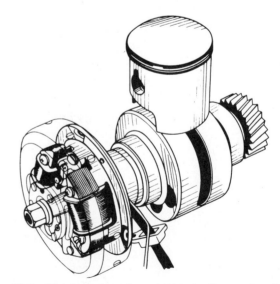

Fig. 21-3 Phantom view of a magneto ignition system for a one-cylinder two-cycle engine. (*Suzuki Motor Company, Ltd.*)

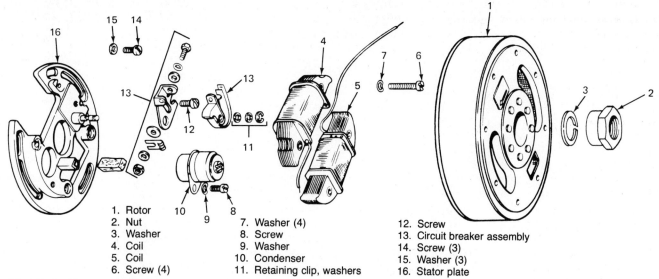

1. Rotor	7. Washer (4)	12. Screw
2. Nut	8. Screw	13. Circuit breaker assembly
3. Washer	9. Washer	14. Screw (3)
4. Coil	10. Condenser	15. Washer (3)
5. Coil	11. Retaining clip, washers	16. Stator plate
6. Screw (4)		

Fig. 21-4 Disassembled view of a magneto ignition system. This system also includes a generator. (*Harley-Davidson Motor Company, Inc.*)

cam ahead. The greater the engine speed, the more the advance weights move out and the farther the cam is moved ahead. This advances the spark in accordance with engine speed. Centrifugal, or mechanical, advance is discussed in detail in ⚙ 21-9.

⚙ 21-4 MAGNETO IGNITION SYSTEM FOR A TWO-CYCLE ENGINE

Figure 21-3 shows in phantom view a magneto ignition system for a two-cycle engine. Figure 21-4 shows the system in disassembled view. The breaker cam which opens and closes the breaker points is mounted on the end of the crankshaft and turns at crankshaft speed. This is different from the system described previously and shown in Figs. 21-1 and 21-2. In that ignition system, the breaker cam was driven by the camshaft at half crankshaft speed. In a four-cycle engine, the spark plug fires once every *two* crankshaft revolutions. That is the reason why the breaker cam is driven off the camshaft (which turns at half crankshaft speed).

Here is why there is a difference in the speed with which the breaker cam rotates. The ignition system shown in Figs. 21-3 and 21-4 is used on a two-cycle engine. In this engine, a power stroke takes place with every revolution of the crankshaft. Therefore, the breaker points must open every revolution of the crankshaft.

Not all magnetos are built into the engine flywheel. Some motorcycles have used a separately mounted external magneto. Basically, its operation is the same as described above.

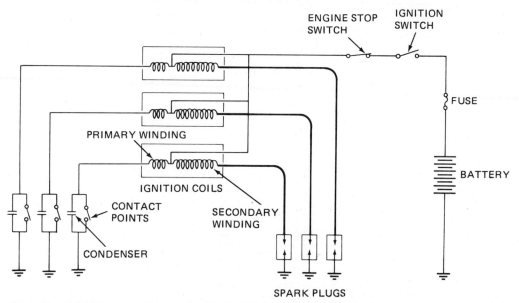

Fig. 21-5 Battery ignition system for a three-cylinder two-cycle motorcycle engine. Note that this is, in effect, three separate ignition systems, one for each cylinder. (*Suzuki Motor Company, Ltd.*)

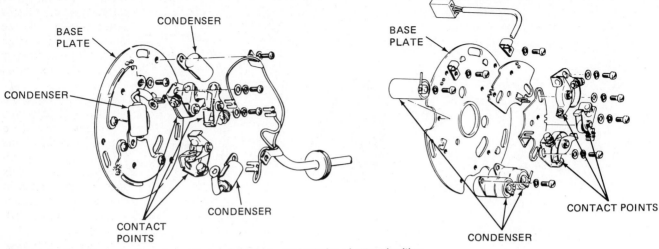

Fig. 21-6 Two designs of breaker plates and contact-point sets for a battery ignition system used in a three-cylinder motorcycle engine. (*Suzuki Motor Company, Ltd.*)

21-5
BATTERY IGNITION SYSTEM FOR TWO-CYCLE ENGINES

Figure 21-5 shows a wiring diagram for a battery ignition system used on a three-cylinder two-cycle motorcycle engine. The system has three ignition coils and three sets of contact points. Figure 21-6 shows the way the three sets of contact points and the three condensers are mounted on a base plate. Two designs of base plate are shown. The system is, in effect, three separate ignition systems, one for each cylinder, operating off a single battery and being actuated by a single breaker cam.

The cam mounts on the end of the crankshaft in the same manner as in the engine shown in Fig. 21-3. The cam turns at the same speed as the crankshaft. With every crankshaft revolution, the cam opens and closes the three sets of contact points. They open and close 120° of crankshaft rotation apart. Every time a set of points opens, a spark is delivered to one of the spark plugs. Let's follow the complete sequence of events in this type of ignition system.

As the cam lobe moves out from under a contact arm, that set of contact points closes. Now, current from the battery can flow through the primary winding of the ignition coil connected to the set of contact points. A magnetic field builds up in that ignition coil. As the cam continues to rotate, the cam lobe comes around under the contact arm, forcing the contact arm away so the contact points separate.

Now, the current stops flowing in the ignition coil primary winding. The magnetic field collapses, and a high-voltage surge is induced in the secondary winding of the ignition coil. This secondary winding high-voltage surge is delivered to the spark plug connected to the

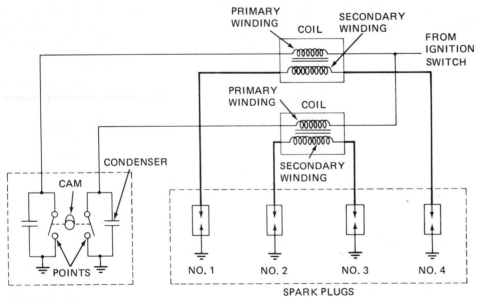

Fig. 21-7 Wiring diagram of a battery ignition system for a four-cylinder four-cycle motorcycle engine. Note that there are, in effect, two independent ignition systems, each firing two plugs. (*Suzuki Motor Company, Ltd.*)

190

Fig. 21-8 Breaker plate with two sets of contact points and two condensers for a battery ignition system used in a four-cylinder four-cycle motorcycle engine. (*Honda Motor Company, Ltd.*)

winding. The plug fires, and a power stroke starts in the cylinder.

A condenser is connected across each set of contact points, as shown in Fig. 21-5. The purpose of the condenser is to prevent excessive arcing across the contact points as they separate. This helps bring the current flow in the battery winding of the ignition coil to a quick stop. This quick stopping of the current flow produces a very rapid collapse of the magnetic field. The faster the magnetic field collapses, the higher the voltage goes in the secondary winding. Therefore, the condenser, in speeding up the collapse of the magnetic field, helps the secondary winding produce the high voltage needed to fire the plug.

The same action described above for one set of contact points, one ignition coil, and one spark plug, takes place with the other contact points, coil, and plug. However, the actions are spaced 120° of cam rotation apart because the three cylinders in the engine fire 120° apart.

The arrangement described above for a three-cylinder two-cycle engine can also be used for a two-cylinder two-cycle engine. A breaker plate with two sets of contact points and two condensers is used with a two-cylinder two-cycle engine. This system produces, in effect, two separate ignition systems, each with its own set of contact points and its own condenser, ignition coil, and spark plug.

21-6
BATTERY IGNITION SYSTEM FOR FOUR-CYCLE ENGINES The battery ignition system is widely used on street-legal motorcycles with four-cycle engines. Many different variations have been used, some with an automotive-type distributor and others with as many sets of points and coils as the engine has cylinders. One important variation fires two spark plugs at the same time. This type of battery ignition system is shown in Fig. 21-7 and discussed below.

In Fig. 21-7, notice that this ignition system has two ignition coils and two sets of contact points. The two ends of the secondary windings in each ignition coil are connected in series to two spark plugs. Because of this connection, both spark plugs fire simultaneously, although one of the plugs fires with reverse polarity. This type of ignition system can be used to fire spark plugs in any two cylinders whose firing orders are 360° of crankshaft rotation apart. You will find this system on 360° twins and on four- and six-cylinder engines.

When the points open, one of the spark plugs fires to ignite the compressed air-fuel mixture. At the same time, the other plug also fires. However, it fires in the other cylinder toward the end of the exhaust stroke. This has no effect, since the burned exhaust gases cannot be reignited. Here is how the system works.

The breaker cam is mounted on the end of the crankshaft and turns at the same speed as the crankshaft. The cam has a single lobe. As the cam rotates, the single lobe opens the two sets of contact points, one after the other. They open 180° of cam rotation apart. Figure 21-8 shows the two sets of contact points mounted on the base plate.

We first look at the actions at one set of contact points and one spark plug. A contact-point set closes, connecting the ignition-coil primary winding to the battery. Current flows through the primary winding, producing a magnetic field in the ignition coil. Then the lobe on the breaker cam comes around and pushes the contact arm away from the stationary point. The points are separated. Now the current stops flowing in the ignition-coil primary winding, and the magnetic field collapses. This produces a high voltage in the secondary winding. As a result, the secondary winding sends out a high-voltage surge that produces a spark at the two spark plugs, as noted above.

To see how this works in the complete engine, first look at the firing order in the engine. The firing order is the sequence in which the engine delivers power strokes. The firing order in the system shown in Fig. 21-7 is 1, 2, 4, 3. The number 1 cylinder spark plug fires first, followed by the number 2 cylinder spark plug, then number 4, and then number 3. The cylinders are num-

Spark-plug firing order at end of compression stroke	Spark-plug firing order at end of exhaust stroke
1	4
2	3
4	1
3	2

Fig. 21-9 The firing order of the spark plugs in the ignition system shown in Fig. 21-7.

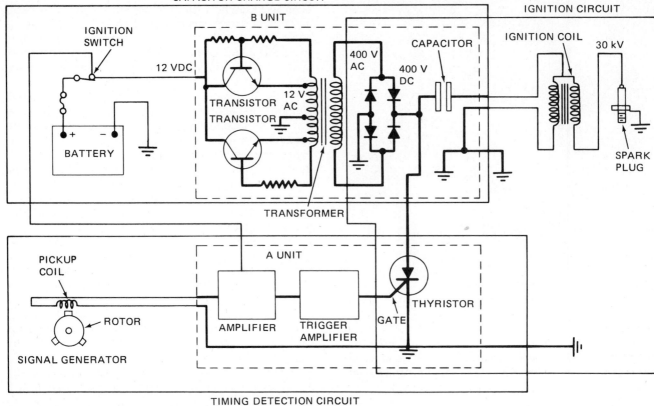

Fig. 21-10 Wiring diagram of a capacitor-discharge ignition (CDI) system. (*Kawasaki Heavy Industries, Ltd.*)

bered from left to right, as viewed by the rider sitting on the seat of the motorcycle.

The spark plugs for cylinders 1 and 4 are both connected to the secondary winding of one of the ignition coils (Fig. 21-7). This means that these two plugs fire at the same time. Likewise, the plugs in cylinders 2 and 3 also fire together.

Figure 21-9 relates the compression and exhaust strokes and the spark plugs that fire together. When cylinder 1 spark plug fires at the end of the compression stroke, cylinder 4 spark plug is firing at the end of the exhaust stroke. When plug 2 fires at the end of the compression stroke, plug 3 fires at the end of the exhaust stroke. And so on. A spark plug firing at the end of the exhaust stroke has no effect. The piston is just finishing the exhaust stroke, and no fresh charge of air-fuel mixture has entered the cylinder.

21-7 CAPACITOR-DISCHARGE IGNITION SYSTEM

The capacitor (or condenser) discharge ignition (CDI) system usually does not have contact points. But the CDI system does the same job as the ignition systems described previously. It fires the spark plugs at the right time to ignite the compressed air-fuel mixture in the engine cylinders. The system uses several electronic devices, including a large capacitor, diodes, and transistors similar to those used in modern automotive electronic ignition systems. In addition, the

CDI system uses an SCR (silicon-controlled rectifier). Let's review these electronic devices.

1. Diode. The diode is a one-way valve for electric current. It is discussed in ✍ 17-14.

2. Transistor. The transistor acts as an electronic switch or as an amplifying device in which a small current flowing in will cause a large current to flow through. It also is discussed in ✍ 17-14.

3. SCR. This is a variation of the diode. It also is called a *thyristor.* It is shown in wiring diagrams as in Fig. 21-10 (lower right). The SCR operates as described in ✍ 20-8 and is shown in a voltage regulator in Fig. 20-14.

Figure 21-10 is a schematic wiring diagram of a complete CDI system. The action starts in the *signal generator,* in the lower left corner of Fig. 21-10. The signal generator takes the place of the breaker cam and contact points. It includes a rotor and a pickup coil in place of the breaker cam and points. Sometimes the rotor is called a *reluctor.*

The rotor has the same number of tips on it as there are cylinders in the engine. In Fig. 21-10, the rotor has three tips because the engine has three cylinders. The rotor is mounted on the end of the crankshaft and rotates with it.

The tips of the rotor shown in Fig. 21-10 are small magnets. As the rotor revolves, the magnetic fields surrounding the magnets sweep through the pickup coil and generate voltage in it.

When a voltage pulse arrives at the amplifier, the pulse is amplified and sent to the trigger amplifier. The pulse is greatly strengthened and sharpened by the trigger amplifier and then sent on to the SCR. The amplifier and trigger amplifier use transistors to increase and shape the pulse.

When the pulse from the amplifier arrives at the SCR, it enters the gate. Before we explain what happens then, we must take a look at the upper part of Fig. 21-10. Starting at the left, the battery is connected to the B unit of the system. The 12-volt direct current from the battery is converted into 12-volt alternating current by the two transistors. This 12-volt alternating current is imposed on the primary winding of the transformer. The transformer steps up this low voltage to 400-volt alternating current. Then the set of four diodes changes the alternating current to direct current. Now 400 dc volts are applied to one plate of the capacitor, which charge it.

Now we can go back to the SCR and Fig. 21-10. When the pulse from the trigger amplifier hits the SCR gate, the SCR becomes conductive. It acts as a short circuit across the capacitor. As a result, the capacitor discharges very suddenly through the primary winding of the ignition coil. The fast buildup of the magnetic field produces a high voltage in the ignition coil secondary winding. The voltage may go as high as 30,000 volts (30 kV). As the voltage builds up, a spark occurs at the spark plug.

The capacitor and primary winding of the ignition coil form a closed loop. When the capacitor discharges through the primary winding, it sets up a flow of current. Now, even after the secondary voltage has gone up to 30 kV and a high-voltage pulse goes to the spark plug, current flows in the primary winding. It continues to flow until it has built up a voltage of 400 volts or more on the condenser in the opposite direction. This opposite voltage, as it reaches the SCR, causes the SCR to turn off. The SCR stops conducting so that the next charging cycle can begin. Then, when the next tip of the rotor passes the pickup coil, the whole cycle is repeated.

The signal generator in this system is located on the left side of the engine, under the left cover. One other item to discuss is the distributor.

21-8 IGNITION DISTRIBUTOR

When only one ignition coil is used in the ignition system for a multicylinder engine, an ignition distributor is required. Under the right cover of the engine discussed above, there is a plastic distributor cap to which four high-voltage cables are connected. Three of the cables are connected to the spark plugs at one end and to metal terminals inside the cap at the other end (Fig. 21-11). These metal terminals are evenly spaced around the cap, 120° apart.

A rotor is centered under the cap. It is mounted on a shaft that is driven at crankshaft speed. The rotor has a metal blade from its center to its tip (Fig. 21-11). The fourth cable coming in to the distributor cap is connected to the center of the metal blade on the rotor.

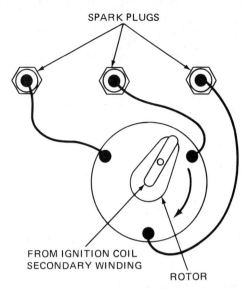

Fig. 21-11 In a distributor, the rotor, as it turns, connects the coil secondary winding to the spark plugs in the firing order.

The ignition distributor is a distributing system for the ignition sparks. As the rotor rotates, its metal blade completes the circuit to each of the three outer terminals in turn. Then, when a high-voltage pulse from the ignition-coil secondary winding arrives through the center cable, the pulse goes through the rotor blade to one of the outside terminals. Everything is timed so that the outside terminal which receives the high-voltage pulse is connected by the ignition cable to the spark plug in the cylinder that is ready to fire. As the engine runs, the ignition system continues to produce high-voltage pulses and the distributor delivers the pulses to the right spark plug.

21-9 CENTRIFUGAL ADVANCE

When the engine is idling, the spark is timed to occur just before the piston reaches TDC (top dead center) on the compression stroke. At higher speeds, it is necessary to deliver the spark to the combustion chamber earlier. This gives the mixture time to burn and deliver its power to the piston.

To provide this advance, a centrifugal-advance mechanism is used (Fig. 21-12). It consists of two weights that are thrown out against spring tension as engine speed increases. This movement is transmitted through a toggle arrangement to the breaker cam (or to the pickup coil or the rotor of an electronic ignition system). This causes the cam (or pickup coil or rotor) to advance, or move ahead, with respect to the shaft on which the cam is mounted.

On the contact-point distributor, this advance causes the cam to open the contact points earlier in the compression stroke at high speeds. On the electronic distributor, the rotor is advanced so that the pickup coil advances the timing of its signals to the electronic control unit. By using a centrifugal-advance mechanism, the timing of the spark to the cylinder varies from no advance at low speed to full advance at high speed

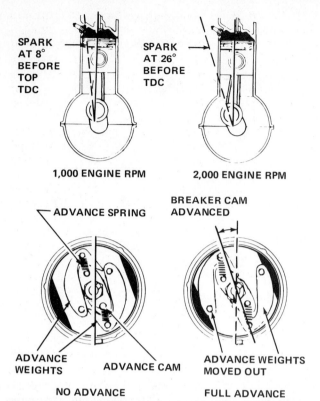

SPARK AT 8° BEFORE TOP TDC

SPARK AT 26° BEFORE TDC

1,000 ENGINE RPM   2,000 ENGINE RPM

ADVANCE SPRING

BREAKER CAM ADVANCED

ADVANCE WEIGHTS   ADVANCE CAM   ADVANCE WEIGHTS MOVED OUT

NO ADVANCE   FULL ADVANCE

Fig. 21-12 Centrifugal advance mechanism in no-advance and full-advance positions. Typically, as in the example shown, the ignition is timed at 8° BTDC (before top dead center) on idle. There is no centrifugal advance at 1000 engine rpm. There is 26° total advance (18° centrifugal plus 8° due to the original timing) at 2000 engine rpm. (*Delco-Remy Division of General Motors Corporation*)

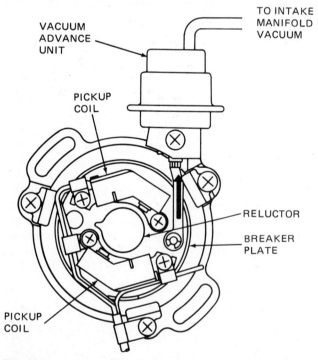

VACUUM ADVANCE UNIT

TO INTAKE MANIFOLD VACUUM

PICKUP COIL

RELUCTOR

BREAKER PLATE

PICKUP COIL

Fig. 21-13 An electronic distributor with two pickup coils and a vacuum advance unit attached. (*Yamaha International Corporation*)

194

(when the weights have reached the outer limits of their travel).

Maximum advance may be as much as 45° of crankshaft rotation before the piston reaches TDC. The amount of the advances varies with different makes and models of engines. The weights and springs are designed to provide the correct advance for the desired engine performance.

21-10 VACUUM ADVANCE

Under part throttle, a partial vacuum develops in the intake manifold. This means that less air and fuel will be admitted to the cylinder. There is less fuel to burn, and the mixture will burn more slowly when ignited. In order to realize full power from it, the spark should be advanced. To obtain this spark advance, a vacuum-advance mechanism is used in many ignition systems.

Figure 21-13 shows a vacuum-advance unit used on an electronic distributor. The vacuum-advance unit contains a spring-loaded, airtight diaphragm. The diaphragm is connected by a linkage, or lever, to the breaker plate. The breaker plate is supported on a bearing so it can turn inside the distributor housing. Actually, the plate turns only a few degrees. The linkage to the spring-loaded diaphragm prevents any greater rotation than this.

The spring-loaded side of the diaphragm is connected through a vacuum line to an opening in the carburetor. This opening is on the atmospheric side of the throttle valve when the engine is idling. There is no vacuum advance in this position.

As soon as the throttle is opened, however, it moves past the opening of the vacuum passage. The intake-manifold vacuum can then draw air from the vacuum line and the airtight chamber in the vacuum-advance mechanism. This causes the diaphragm to move against the spring. The linkage to the breaker plate then rotates the breaker plate. This movement carries the pickup coils around. Therefore, the rotor, as it rotates, starts and stops current flow to the coil earlier in the cycle. The spark then appears at the spark-plug gap earlier in the compression stroke.

As the throttle is opened wider, there is less vacuum in the intake manifold and less vacuum advance. At wide-open throttle, there is no vacuum advance at all. The spark advance under this condition is provided entirely by the centrifugal-advance mechanism.

Ignition systems with breaker points also operate as described above.

21-11 COMBINATION OF CENTRIFUGAL AND VACUUM ADVANCES

At any particular engine speed, there will be some centrifugal advance due to engine speed. There may be an additional spark advance due to the operation of the vacuum-advance mechanism. Figure 21-14 illustrates this.

In this example, at 40 mph [64 km/h], the centrifugal-advance mechanism provides 15° of spark advance. The vacuum mechanism will supply up to 15° of additional advance under part-throttle conditions. However, if the engine is operated at wide-open throttle, there will be no vacuum advance.

Total spark advance usually varies between the straight line (centrifugal advance) and the curved line (centrifugal advance plus total possible vacuum advance) as the throttle is closed and opened.

21-12 INTRODUCTION TO IGNITION-SYSTEM SERVICE

So far, we have described the different kinds of ignition systems used on motorcycles. The engine may have a magneto ignition system, and the magneto may be either built into the engine flywheel or mounted separately. Or a battery ignition system or a CDI system may be used. And the system may have contact points and condenser, or it may be an electronic or solid-state ignition system without them.

Each type of ignition system has some special parts and certain test procedures that apply only to it. However, there are three widely performed services on the ignition system that you should know how to do:

1. Service points and condenser
2. Check and adjust ignition timing
3. Service spark plugs

Now, we will discuss how to perform each of the ignition-system services listed above. For information on other ignition-system services, refer to the shop manual for the motorcycle you are servicing.

21-13 CHECKING THE SPARK

One of the checks to be made on any ignition system is the spark test. To make it, disconnect the high-voltage lead from the spark plug. Put a bolt into the spark-plug boot to get a metal contact. Hold the bolt about 3/16 inch [5 mm] from the cylinder head and crank the engine. If strong sparks jump to the cylinder head, the ignition system is probably working properly. If no spark occurs, then the ignition system is probably at fault and it should be checked. Some possible causes of trouble are dirty or worn contact points, points out of adjustment, a defective capacitor (condenser), a defective high-voltage lead that lets voltage leak off to ground, a defective ignition switch, and a defective magneto coil.

If a spark does jump from the bolt to the cylinder head, examine the spark plug to see if it can deliver the spark to the engine. Remove the plug and reattach the high-voltage lead to it. Lay or hold the plug against the cylinder head and crank the engine. Watch for a spark at the plug gap. If no spark jumps, the spark plug is probably at fault. Examine it for wetness from gasoline or oil and for cracks, black sooty deposits on the porcelain or electrodes, burned electrodes, or a wide gap (Fig. 21-15). Any of these could prevent a good spark. Spark-plug service is covered in detail in 🔲 21-16.

If you do not get a spark on the spark test, then check for the following:

1. Bad insulation or poor connections in the wiring
2. A grounded ignition switch which prevents the opening of the primary circuit so that primary current is not interrupted when the contact points open
3. A shorted condenser, which would have the same effect as a grounded ignition switch
4. A magneto coil that is shorted, open, or grounded so it cannot produce high voltage
5. A loss of magnetism in permanent magnets on the flywheel or in the external magneto rotor
6. Contact points that are dirty, worn, or out of adjustment
7. An engine kill switch that is not in the RUN position

If the engine backfires or kicks back when starting, the timing may be too advanced, or the breaker-point gap may be too wide, causing ignition to occur too early in the compression stroke. When this happens, the resulting increase in pressure forces the piston back down before it can reach TDC. An early spark will also cause detonation when the engine is running. The remedy is to reset the timing or points. On some magnetos, the only adjustment is to change the breaker-point opening. On others, you can also move the breaker plate to change the timing.

21-14 BREAKER-POINT SERVICE

The breaker points have a stationary point and a movable point on a contact arm. The design and arrangement of the points vary with different engines. On some engines, the stationary point is on the end of the condenser. On others, it is mounted on a bracket. The breaker arm, on which the movable point is mounted, is pivoted so that it can move the point up against or away from the stationary point. There are various arrangements for moving the contact arm. Regardless of the method, when the high

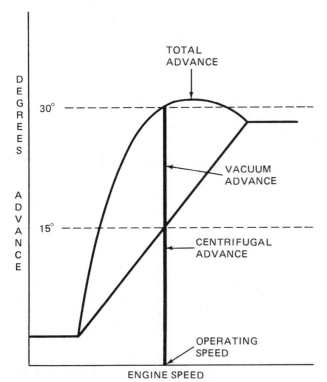

Fig. 21-14 Centrifugal and vacuum advance curves for one particular engine.

NORMAL

Brown to grayish tan color and slight electrode wear. Correct heat range for engine and operating conditions.

RECOMMENDATION: Properly service and reinstall.

SPLASHED DEPOSITS

Spotted deposits. Occurs shortly after long-delayed tune-up. After a long period of misfiring, deposits may be loosened when normal combustion temperatures are restored by tune-up. During a high-speed run, these materials shed off the piston and head and are thrown against the hot insulator.

RECOMMENDATION: Clean and service the plugs properly and reinstall.

CARBON DEPOSITS

Dry soot.

RECOMMENDATION: Dry deposits indicate rich mixture or weak ignition. Check for clogged air cleaner, high float level, sticky choke, or worn breaker contacts. Hotter plugs will temporarily provide additional fouling protection.

HIGH-SPEED GLAZING

Insulator has yellowish, varnish-like color. Indicates combustion chamber temperatures have risen suddenly during hard, fast acceleration. Normal deposits do not get a chance to blow off, instead they melt to form a conductive coating.

RECOMMENDATION: If condition recurs, use plug type one step colder.

OIL DEPOSITS

Oily coating.

RECOMMENDATION: Caused by poor oil control. Oil is leaking past worn valve guides or piston rings into the combustion chamber. Hotter spark plug may temporarily relieve problem, but positive cure is to correct the condition with necessary repairs.

MODIFIER DEPOSITS

Powdery white or yellow deposits that build up on shell, insulator, and electrodes. This is a normal appearance with certain branded fuels. These materials are used to modify the chemical nature of the deposits to lessen misfire tendencies.

RECOMMENDATION: Plugs can be cleaned or, if replaced, use same heat range.

TOO HOT

Blistered, white insulator, eroded electrodes and absence of deposits.

RECOMMENDATION: Check for correct plug heat range, overadvanced ignition timing, cooling system level and/or stoppages, lean air-fuel mixtures, leaking intake manifold, sticking valves, and if car is driven at high speeds most of the time.

PREIGNITION

Melted electrodes. Center electrode generally melts first and ground electrode follows. Normally, insulators are white, but may be dirty due to misfiring or flying debris in combustion chamber

RECOMMENDATION: Check for correct plug heat range, overadvanced ignition timing, lean fuel mixtures, clogged cooling system, leaking intake manifold, and lack of lubrication.

Fig. 21-15 Appearance of spark plugs as it relates to the causes of spark-plug problems. (*Champion Spark Plug Company*)

point or lobe of the cam comes around under the rubbing block, the contact arm is moved and the points separate. The breaker cam is on the crankshaft on two-cycle engines. On four-cycle engines, the breaker cam may be on the camshaft or on the crankshaft.

Cleaning Points Once the contact points are exposed, examine them for oxidation or pits. If they are only slightly burned or pitted, they can be cleaned with

an ignition file, as shown in Fig. 21-16. It is not necessary to file the points until they are smooth. Just remove the worst of the high spots. Blow out all dust after cleaning the contacts. Pull a strip of clean bond paper between the points (with points closed) to remove the last traces of filings.

Never use emery cloth or sandpaper to clean the points. Particles of emery or sand will embed in the points and cause erratic operation and possible point burning.

Installing New Points If the points are badly burned, worn, or pitted, they should be replaced. Severe burning of the points could be due to a defective condenser, improper adjustment, or oil on the contact surfaces. Check for these conditions before replacing the points. Various methods of attaching the stationary point and breaker arm are used.

On one type of distributor, the point assembly is removed by removing the condenser wire from the breaker-point clip and then loosening the screw holding the post in position. The stationary contact is on the condenser and is removed along with the condenser by loosening the condenser-clamp screw.

On the type of breaker arm that uses a rubbing block, as shown in Fig. 21-16, check for rubbing-block wear. As the rubbing block wears, it changes the breaker-point opening, which in turn changes the timing.

Examine the breaker cam for wear. On some engines, the cam is a separate collar locked to the crankshaft by a key. On these, the cam can be replaced if it is worn.

Check for a leaky crankshaft seal. A leaky seal will allow oil to get on the breaker points, which will then burn rapidly. The seal should be replaced.

After removing the old points, install the new points. Check for even contact of the point faces, and adjust if necessary. Then check the point opening and adjust it as necessary. Finally, check the ignition timing. These steps are discussed below.

Adjusting Points To adjust the breaker points, first make sure that they are properly aligned. Usually, the points are properly aligned and no adjustment is required. However, if new points are misaligned, adjust them by slightly bending the bracket supporting the stationary point.

The point opening is a critical adjustment. If it is excessive, ignition timing can be too advanced. This can cause engine backfiring on starting, and detonation when the engine is running. A typical point gap is 0.012 to 0.016 inch [0.3 to 0.4 mm].

To adjust the point opening, turn the crankshaft in the direction of normal rotation until the cam opens the points to the widest position. Then use a feeler gauge of the proper thickness to measure the gap between the points (Fig. 21-17). Make sure the feeler gauge is clean

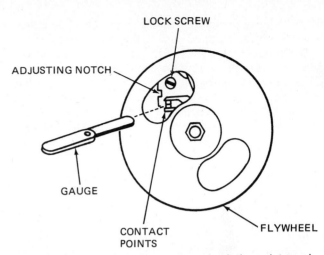

Fig. 21-17 Using a feeler gauge to check the point gap by inserting the gauge through the slot in the flywheel. (*Honda Motor Company, Ltd.*)

so you do not get oil or dirt on the points. The thickness of the feeler gauge selected to make the measurement varies with different engines. Always check the specifications for the engine being checked.

The point gap can also be checked on some motorcycles with a *dwell meter*. This test instrument is widely used in automotive service. It measures the length of time that the points are closed during one revolution of the contact-point cam. This measurement is given either in terms of degrees of cam rotation or as a percent. Some manufacturers provide dwell specifications for various models of motorcycles.

Changing the point gap changes dwell, and vice versa. For example, increasing the point gap decreases dwell. Decreasing the point gap increases dwell.

Adjustments are made in different ways according to the method of point attachment. On some magnetos, the adjustment is made as shown in Fig. 21-17. The lock screw holding the bracket on which the stationary point is mounted is loosened slightly. Then a screwdriver is inserted into the slot and twisted to move the stationary point the correct amount to get the proper point opening. Then the lock screw is tightened.

21-15
TIMING THE IGNITION To time the ignition means to make an adjustment that will cause the spark to occur at exactly the right time before the piston reaches TDC on compression. This starts the ignition process at the correct moment so that maximum power will be realized on the power stroke. If the timing is early, the engine will backfire on starting and detonate when running. If the timing is late, the power stroke will be weak, because ignition will not start until after the piston has begun to move down on the power stroke.

Various devices can be used to time the ignition. These include the *stroboscopic light*, or *timing light*, which is used on a running engine. For timing engines that are stopped (*static timing*), a continuity light, a self-powered test light, a buzzer, an ohmmeter, or any of several types of special timing tools can be used. On

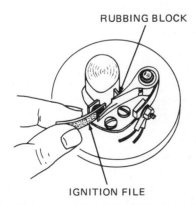

Fig. 21-16 The breaker points can be cleaned with an ignition file.

many engines, the ignition timing can be checked either with the engine stopped or with the engine running.

The sequence shown in Fig. 21-18 shows the static ignition-timing procedure for many small two-cycle engines. After installing the points (1), align them using the special tool shown to bend the stationary point support (2). Then measure the point opening and adjust it as required (3). Next, clean the points with lint-free paper (4), and use a timing tool or rule to locate the TDC position of the piston (5, 6). Back off the piston by turning the crankshaft backwards (7).

Find the timing dimensions in the manufacturer's specifications, and adjust the tool to that dimension. Then tighten the thumb screw to lock the dimension (8, 9). Next, slowly rotate the crankshaft in the normal running direction until the piston touches the bottom of the tool (10). Then install a test light, connected across the contact points (11).

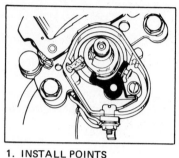

1. INSTALL POINTS

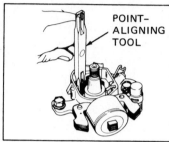

2. ALIGN POINTS

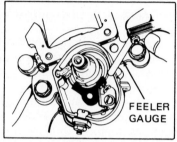

3. POINT OPENING ADJUSTMENT

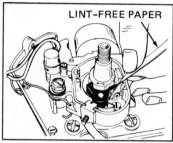

4. CLEAN POINTS

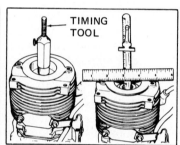

5. INSTALL TIMING TOOL OR RULE

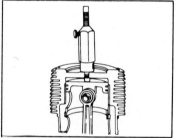

6. FIND TDC (TOP DEAD CENTER)

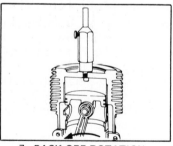

7. BACK OFF ROTATION (OPPOSITE NORMAL RUNNING ROTATION)

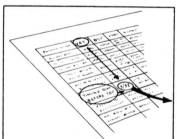

8. FIND BTDC (TIMING DIMENSION SPECIFICATIONS)

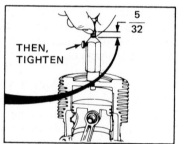

9. APPLY DIMENSION TO TOOL

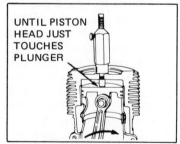

10. BRING UP ON STROKE (NORMAL RUNNING ROTATION)

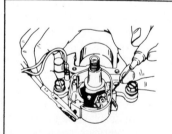

11. INSTALL TIMING LIGHT (OR USE CELLOPHANE)

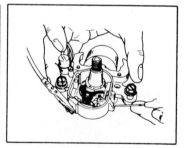

12. ROTATE STATOR UNTIL POINTS JUST OPEN

Fig. 21-18 The complete sequence of actions in timing one type of single-cylinder two-cycle engine. (*Tecumseh Products Company*)

With the stator hold-down screws loosened slightly, shift the stator (12) until the points just open. When this occurs, the light goes out. Tighten the hold-down screws. As an alternative, you can use a strip of thin cellophane between the points. It will fall out as the points separate. After completing the timing, install the flywheel and cover.

NOTE Most engines with a flywheel ignition system require that the flywheel be installed when the timing is set. This is because the timing marks are on the flywheel, and also because the breaker cam may be attached to it.

Figure 21-19 shows how to time a running engine by using a timing light. This is the most accurate method because the timing is checked and adjusted with the engine running. It is the only way that advance and retard can be checked on an engine with mechanical or vacuum advance of the ignition timing.

To use the timing light, connect it to the spark-plug cable for the number 1 cylinder. Each time the plug fires, a momentary flash of light is produced by the timing light. During the timing operation, the light is directed to the flywheel. The flywheel has a timing mark on it that should align with a mark on the case when the timing is correct.

If the marks do not align, adjustment is made by loosening the point-opening adjusting screw. Then shift the breaker plate with a screwdriver. When the marks align, tighten the breaker-plate screw. Ignition timing is checked and set with the engine running at a specified speed. Before timing an engine, get the specification from the service manual.

21-16 SPARK-PLUG SERVICE

Spark plugs may fail for a variety of reasons. They are subjected to high temperatures, high pressures, and high voltages. Spark plugs must withstand these conditions and operate at the proper temperature. If a plug becomes too hot, it will wear rapidly and may burn. If it does not become hot enough, it may foul, since oil and fuel soot, or carbon, may deposit on it and not burn away. If enough material is deposited, the high-voltage current will leak to ground through the deposit instead of jumping the spark gap. Then the plug will not fire and the engine will miss.

The temperature the plug reaches is governed by the heat range of the plug. Heat range depends on the shape of the plug and the distance heat must travel from the center electrode of the plug to reach the cylinder head (Fig. 21-20). If the path that the heat must travel through the insulator is long, then the plug will run hot. If it is short, the plug will run cool.

Plugs in motorcycle engines should be checked and serviced or replaced periodically to maintain top engine performance. There are spark-plug cleaners which will clean the plug with a blast of abrasive sand against the electrodes and porcelain interior. You can also clean deposits out of the plug with a sharp stick or a small-bladed knife.

Because spark plugs are relatively cheap and labor costs are high, many mechanics find it less expensive to install new plugs rather than service the old.

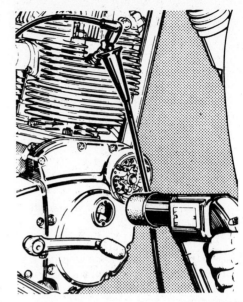

Fig. 21-19 Using a timing light to set the ignition timing on a running engine. (*Castrol, Limited*)

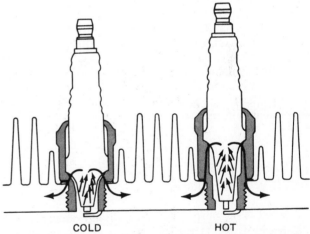

COLD   HOT

Fig. 21-20 The heat range of spark plugs. The longer the heat path (indicated by the arrows), the hotter the plug runs. (*Champion Spark Plug Company*)

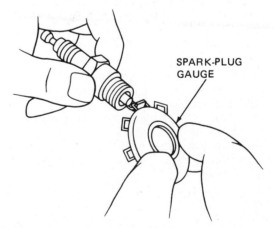

SPARK-PLUG GAUGE

Fig. 21-21 Using a spark-plug gauge to check the gap between the electrodes.

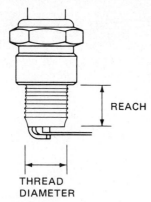

Fig. 21-22 Thread diameter and thread length, or reach. (*Kawasaki Heavy Industries, Ltd.*)

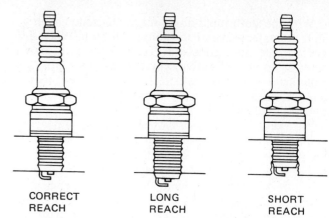

| CORRECT REACH | LONG REACH | SHORT REACH |

Fig. 21-23 Correct and improper spark-plug reach.

You can tell from its appearance whether a plug is of the correct heat range for the application. Figure 21-15 illustrates several spark-plug conditions and explains their causes.

After cleaning the plug, regap it. Measure the gap between the electrodes. Do not use a flat gauge, because this would result in too great a gap. Figure 21-21 shows how to check the spark-plug gap.

Some riders now install CB radios on their motorcycles. If there is excessive ignition static in the radio during reception or transmission, a different set of spark plugs may be required. Resistor spark plugs have a device inside them to suppress ignition static in the radio. This will improve the operation of the CB radio and will not affect engine performance. Resistor spark plugs are available in normal heat ranges for each engine.

Always be sure to install the correct spark plug for the engine. Spark plugs are made in standard sizes that are determined by *thread diameter* and *thread reach* (Fig. 21-22). Thread diameter is the diameter across the threads, measured in millimeters. Various sizes of motorcycle spark plugs have a thread diameter of 10, 12, 14, or 18 mm.

A spark plug with the wrong thread diameter cannot be properly installed in an engine. However, a plug may have an improper reach which will not interfere with its installation. But when the engine is cranked, damage to the engine or misfiring may result. The correct spark-plug reach is shown in Fig. 21-23, along with examples of improper reach. The typical thread length, or reach, of a motorcycle spark plug is 1/2 inch [12.7 mm] or 3/4 inch [19 mm].

CHAPTER 21
REVIEW QUESTIONS

1. What is the purpose of the ignition system?
2. Name three types of ignition systems used on motorcycle engines.
3. Why can a magneto ignition system be used without a battery?
4. In a magneto ignition system, does the spark occur when the points close or when they open?
5. In a two-cycle engine, why is the breaker cam mounted to the crankshaft?
6. What is the difference between a magneto ignition system and a battery ignition system?
7. What is the purpose of the condenser in the battery ignition system?
8. How many sets of points are used in an ignition system that has three ignition coils?
9. What happens in an engine when the system is designed to fire two spark plugs simultaneously?
10. Define *firing order*.
11. How do you locate the number 1 cylinder in a multicylinder engine?
12. What is the difference between a battery ignition system and a CDI system?
13. What is an SCR?
14. In an electronic ignition system, what parts replace the points and condenser?
15. In a CDI system, does the spark at the plug occur as the magnetic field builds up or as the magnetic field collapses?
16. What is an ignition distributor?
17. In a distributor, how does the rotor transfer the high-voltage surge from the coil wire to the spark-plug wire?
18. What is the purpose of centrifugal advance?
19. What is the purpose of vacuum advance?
20. Which advance mechanism is working at full throttle?
21. How do you make a spark test?
22. Explain how to clean breaker points.
23. Describe the conditions to look for when checking a breaker cam.
24. Explain how to time the ignition when the engine is not running.
25. Explain how to time the ignition using a timing light.

CHAPTER 22

ELECTRIC INSTRUMENTS AND WIRING

After studying this chapter,
you should be able to:

1. List and describe the electric instruments on the motorcycle.

2. Explain the purpose of wiring harnesses and how they are made.

3. Discuss headlights and their adjustment.

4. Describe the operation of stoplights and how to service them.

5. Explain the purpose and operation of a flasher.

6. Discuss the key ignition switch and how it works.

22-1 MOTORCYCLE ELECTRIC EQUIPMENT

A completely equipped motorcycle will have the following, in addition to a battery, a starter, a charging system, and an ignition system:

Headlights
Taillight
Stoplight
Turn signals
Horn
Oil-pressure switch
Neutral switch

A motorcycle will have other switches, also, such as the ignition switch, light switch, horn button, and stop switch. All of the electric devices on the motorcycle are connected by wires, with the frame of the motorcycle serving as the return circuit.

Not all motorcycles will have all the equipment we cover in this chapter. In fact, some motorcycles, such as motocrossers, have almost none of the equipment. A manufacturer's instructions covering the conversion of one model for motocross competition describe removal of the headlight, battery, taillight, main switch, and regulator. These are not needed in competition.

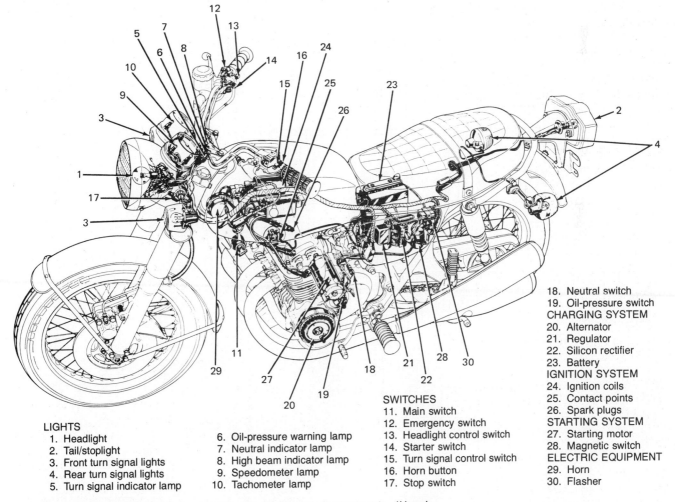

LIGHTS
1. Headlight
2. Tail/stoplight
3. Front turn signal lights
4. Rear turn signal lights
5. Turn signal indicator lamp
6. Oil-pressure warning lamp
7. Neutral indicator lamp
8. High beam indicator lamp
9. Speedometer lamp
10. Tachometer lamp

SWITCHES
11. Main switch
12. Emergency switch
13. Headlight control switch
14. Starter switch
15. Turn signal control switch
16. Horn button
17. Stop switch
18. Neutral switch
19. Oil-pressure switch

CHARGING SYSTEM
20. Alternator
21. Regulator
22. Silicon rectifier
23. Battery

IGNITION SYSTEM
24. Ignition coils
25. Contact points
26. Spark plugs

STARTING SYSTEM
27. Starting motor
28. Magnetic switch

ELECTRIC EQUIPMENT
29. Horn
30. Flasher

Fig. 22-1 Motorcycle completely equipped with electric components. (*Honda Motor Company, Ltd.*)

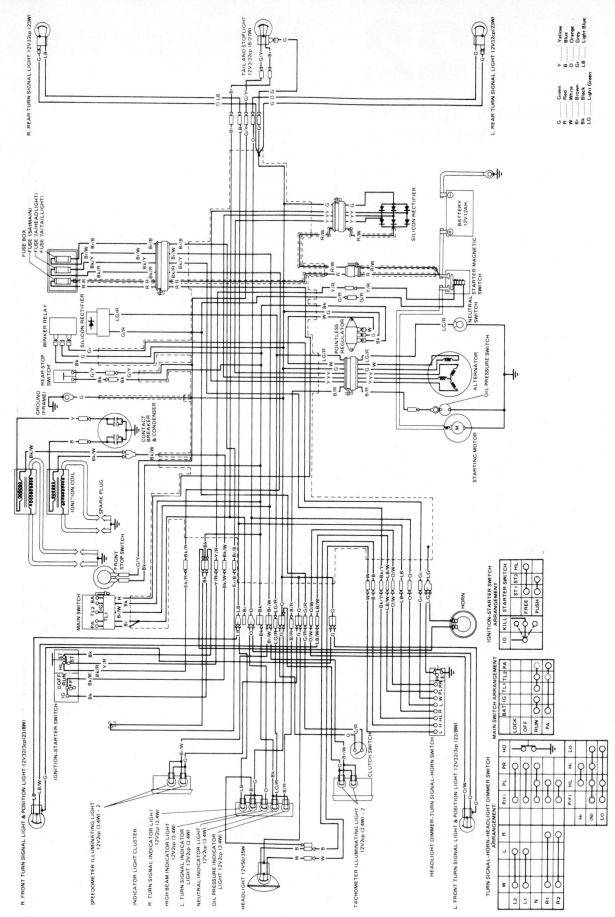

Fig. 22-2 Complete wiring diagram for a four-cylinder street motorcycle. (*Honda Motor Company, Ltd.*)

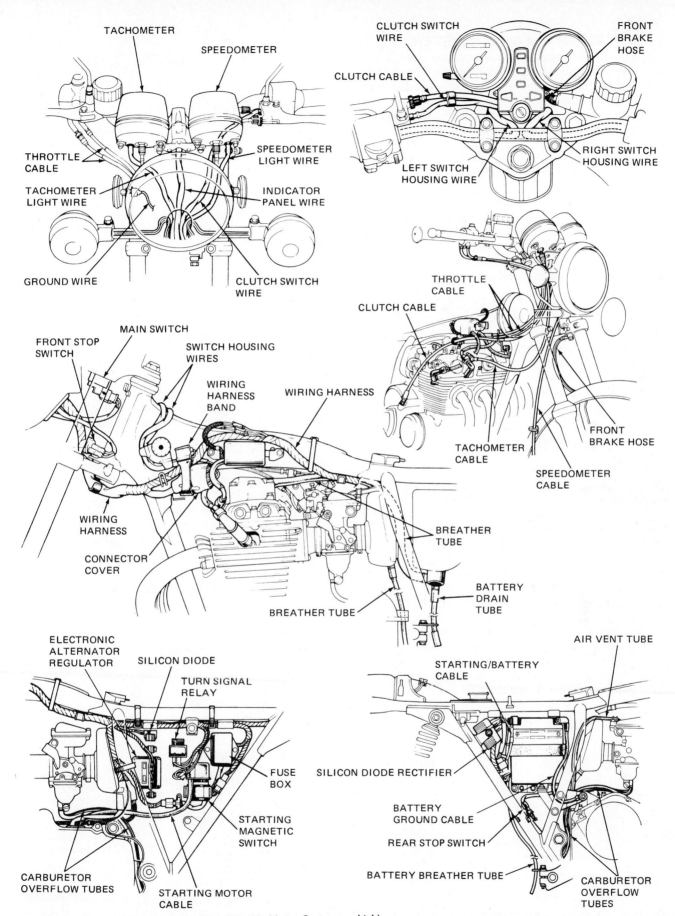

Fig. 22-3 Routing of wires and cables. (*Honda Motor Company, Ltd.*)

TACHOMETER

SPEEDOMETER

THROTTLE CABLE

TACHOMETER LIGHT WIRE

GROUND WIRE

SPEEDOMETER LIGHT WIRE

INDICATOR PANEL WIRE

CLUTCH SWITCH WIRE

CLUTCH SWITCH WIRE

CLUTCH CABLE

FRONT BRAKE HOSE

LEFT SWITCH HOUSING WIRE

RIGHT SWITCH HOUSING WIRE

THROTTLE CABLE

CLUTCH CABLE

TACHOMETER CABLE

SPEEDOMETER CABLE

FRONT BRAKE HOSE

FRONT STOP SWITCH

MAIN SWITCH

SWITCH HOUSING WIRES

WIRING HARNESS BAND

WIRING HARNESS

WIRING HARNESS

CONNECTOR COVER

BREATHER TUBE

BREATHER TUBE

BATTERY DRAIN TUBE

ELECTRONIC ALTERNATOR REGULATOR

SILICON DIODE

TURN SIGNAL RELAY

FUSE BOX

STARTING MAGNETIC SWITCH

CARBURETOR OVERFLOW TUBES

STARTING MOTOR CABLE

AIR VENT TUBE

STARTING/BATTERY CABLE

SILICON DIODE RECTIFIER

BATTERY GROUND CABLE

REAR STOP SWITCH

BATTERY BREATHER TUBE

CARBURETOR OVERFLOW TUBES

22-2 COMPLETE ELECTRIC SYSTEM

Figure 22-1 shows a motorcycle with a complete electric system. The motorcycle is a street bike with a four-cylinder OHC (overhead-camshaft) engine. Note the locations of the lights, switches, alternator, regulator, rectifier, and battery in the charging system. Also, locate the ignition coils, contact points, spark plugs, starting motor, and magnetic switch in the starting system.

Figure 22-2 is the complete wiring diagram of the system. Figure 22-3 shows the routing of all wires in the motorcycle. Study each part of the illustration to become familiar with where each electric component is located and how the wires to the components are routed. Notice that some wires go through the inside of the handlebars. Figure 22-3 also shows the locations of various cables, such as the clutch and front-brake cables and the speedometer and tachometer cables.

NOTE Distinguish between the electric wiring, which is sometimes called *cable,* and the mechanical cables that connect the

1. Clutch lever with the clutch
2. Brake lever with the front brake
3. Tachometer to the engine
4. Speedometer to the front wheel

If a switch has to be removed from the handlebars or if the handlebars have to be replaced, the switch wires must be routed through the handlebars. The procedure is as follows.

With the handlebars detached, attach a stiff wire to the ends of the switch and push the wire through the handlebar from the end hole to the center hole. Then pull this wire on through to bring the switch wires into place, as shown in Fig. 22-4. If you must remove a switch from a handlebar, attach a stiff wire to the end of the switch wires, as shown in Fig. 22-5, before pulling the switch. Then, when you pull the switch, detach the stiff wire, leaving it inside the handlebar. It will be there when you reinstall the switch and this will make it easier to pull the switch wires back into place.

The wires are gathered together into a harness wherever possible. You can see wiring harnesses to the middle left in Fig. 22-3. Using wiring harnesses in this manner makes the installation much neater. It also protects the wires by enclosing them in an additional protective cover.

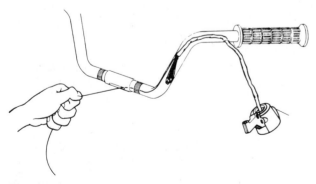

Fig. 22-4 Using a wire to pull the switch wires through the handlebars. (*Honda Motor Company, Ltd.*)

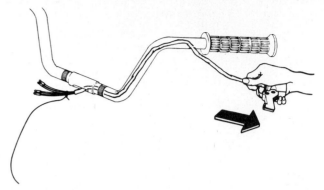

Fig. 22-5 Before pulling the switch wires through the handlebars, attach a wire. Then leave the wire in place when you remove the switch and wires. The wire will then be ready to pull the switch wires back into place in the handlebar. (*Honda Motor Company, Ltd.*)

22-3 HEADLIGHT

The motorcycle headlight is either a halogen type with a replaceable bulb, or the sealed-beam type (Fig. 22-6). Either type is adjustable in both the vertical and horizontal directions. To remove the sealed-beam lamp, loosen the three headlight mounting screws and take the headlamp from the case. Disconnect the leads from the terminals on the back of the lamp. Then unscrew the two adjusting screws and remove the lamp.

If a filament is broken or the unit is cracked, discard it. Make sure the wiring is in good condition and that the headlight socket makes good contact with the terminals on the lamp when it is installed.

Check and adjust headlight aiming as follows:

1. The vertical adjustment is made by loosening the bolts which mount the headlight assembly. The headlight is adjusted in the vertical direction so that the center of the beam hits the ground at a point 164 feet [50 m] in front of the motorcycle with the motorcycle in the riding attitude.

1. Beam adjusting screw
2. Beam adjusting spring
3. Unit holder screw
4. Headlight rim
5. Cotter pin
6. Unit holder nut
7. Cross screw
8. Retaining ring
9. Sealed-beam unit
10. Mounting ring
11. Headlight cord socket
12. Beam adjusting nut
13. Cross screw
14. Spring washer
15. Headlight setting collar
16. Headlight case collar
17. Headlight case

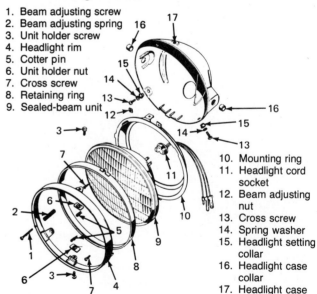

Fig. 22-6 Disassembled headlight assembly. (*Honda Motor Company, Ltd.*)

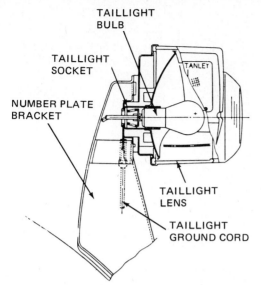

Fig. 22-7 Sectional view of tail/stoplight bulb case. (*Honda Motor Company, Ltd.*)

2. The horizontal beam adjustment is made with the adjusting screw located on the left side of the headlight when facing the motorcycle. Turning the screw in will move the beam toward the left side of the rider and turning the screw out will move the beam toward the right side. Adjust the beam to coincide with the center line of the motorcycle.

22-4
TAIL/STOPLIGHT
The tail/stoplight contains two filaments, one for the taillight and the other for signaling when the brake is applied. Figure 22-7 shows how the bulb is mounted. To replace the bulb, remove the lens. The bulb is removed by pressing down on it and turning it counterclockwise a few degrees.

Check the operation of the stoplight switch on the front-brake master cylinder and at the rear-brake pedal separately. The switch on the front brake is not adjust-

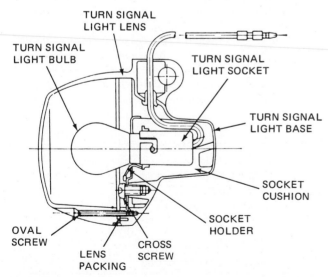

Fig. 22-8 Sectional view of a turn-signal light case. (*Honda Motor Company, Ltd.*)

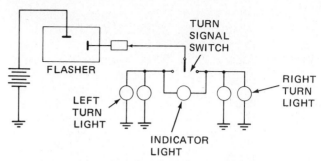

Fig. 22-9 Wiring diagram of a turn-signal system. (*Honda Motor Company, Ltd.*)

able, and the one on the rear brake is adjustable. Therefore, a malfunctioning front-brake switch has to be replaced.

Adjust the rear-brake stoplight switch so that the stoplight will come on when the brake pedal is depressed to the point where the brake just starts to take hold. If the stoplight switch is late in switching on the stoplight, screw in the switch locknut. If the stoplight comes on too early, screw out the switch locknut.

22-5
TURN-SIGNAL LIGHT AND FLASHER
Figure 22-8 is a sectional view of the turn-signal case. The bulb is replaced in the same way the tail/stoplight bulb is replaced. Remove the lens, press down on the bulb, and turn it a few degrees counterclockwise.

The turn-signal lights are connected to a flasher through a turn-signal switch, as shown in Fig. 22-9. When the turn switch is operated to signal a right or left turn, the turn-signal light on the right or left is connected to the battery through the flasher. The flasher repeatedly opens and closes its points to disconnect and then connect the light to the battery. The light therefore flashes.

A flashing light is much more noticeable than a steady light. At the same time that the light flashes, the indicator light by the turn-signal switch also flashes, telling the rider that the turn-signal light is working.

If the lights do not flash properly, do not come on, or come on without flashing, the flasher may be at fault. To remove the flasher, first determine its location. In the motorcycle we are discussing, the flasher is close to the battery, and the battery cover must be removed to get at it. Disconnect the leads to remove the flasher. The flasher can be checked by connecting it to a battery in series with the proper bulb. A 12-volt 25-watt bulb is specified for the motorcycle we are discussing. The flasher should flash the light 65 to 90 cycles per minute.

NOTE If the flasher is not properly grounded on the motorcycle, the lights may come on and stay on and the flasher will buzz.

22-6
KEYED IGNITION SWITCH
The motorcycle has two ignition switches, one on the handlebar, which is simply an off-on flip switch, and the main switch, which is operated by a key (Fig. 22-10). This switch has three positions—OFF, RUN, and PARK (Fig. 22-11). The

PARK

RUN

OFF

Fig. 22-10   Keyed ignition switch. (*ATW*)

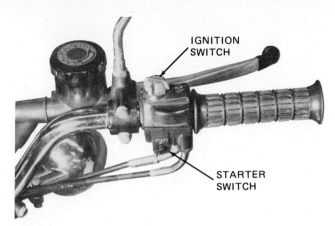

IGNITION
SWITCH

STARTER
SWITCH

Fig. 22-12   Location of the starter switch and the ignition switch on the right handlebar. (*ATW*)

switch controls the entire electrical circuit. When the switch is turned to OFF, everything is disconnected. When the switch is turned to RUN, everything can be operated. This requires the use of the key, and in the RUN position the key cannot be removed. However, in the PARK position, only the taillight is on, and the key can be removed.

To remove the keyed ignition switch, remove the fuel tank and then unscrew the switch locknut. Disconnect the switch connector and remove the switch. To check the switch and leads, use a 12-volt battery and a 12-volt test light connected in series. Replace the leads or the switch if defects are found.

22-7
STARTER AND IGNITION SWITCHES
These switches are located on the right handlebar, as shown in Fig. 22-12. They are combined into a unit which is removed as follows. Loosen the switch mounting screws. Move the switch out of the way and disconnect the throttle-cable connector from the lower side of the switch. Disconnect the wiring and remove the switch.

When reinstalling the switch, make sure the locating pin is inserted into the hole in the handlebar. Refer to Figs. 22-4 and 22-5 for the method of pulling the switch wires through the handlebar. After reconnecting the switches, check each system for proper operation.

22-8
TURN-SIGNAL SWITCH, HORN BUTTON, AND DIMMER SWITCH
These are located on the left handlebar, as shown in Fig. 22-13. Turn-signal system operation was discussed in ⧉ 22-5. Pressing on the horn button connects the horn to the battery. This

causes a diaphragm in the horn to vibrate. It is this vibration that produces the horn sound.

To remove the turn-signal switch, dimmer switch, and horn button assembly, first remove the headlight unit and disconnect the wiring inside the headlight case. Then unscrew the two switch mounting screws and separate the two halves of the switch. Figures 22-4 and 22-5 show how to pull the switch wire through the handlebar. When reattaching the switch, be sure to locate the switch properly on the handlebar.

The horn can be adjusted, but adjustment is not advised if it is operating properly. To adjust it, remove the horn cover and turn the adjusting screw. Turning the screw in increases the loudness.

22-9
OIL-PRESSURE SWITCH
On four-cycle engines, an oil-pressure switch is used to give the rider an indication of oil pressure in the engine. Figure 22-14 shows the location of the oil-pressure switch on one engine. The oil-pressure switch is connected to an indicator light. When the ignition switch is first turned on, the light should come on to show no oil pressure. But as soon as the engine is started and oil pressure builds up, the oil-pressure switch opens its contacts and the light goes off.

If the light fails to go off, the oil pressure is probably low, and the engine should be stopped so the cause of the low oil pressure can be determined. However, the oil-pressure switch could be defective and not open its contacts when the oil pressure builds up.

Switch position	BAT lead	IG lead	Lead 3	Lead 2	Function	Key
OFF					Electric equipment is inoperative and the engine cannot be started.	Removed
RUN	O-----O		O-----O		Electric equipment is operative, the engine will start.	In switch
PARK	O----------------------O				Parking light is operative, engine cannot be started.	Can be removed

Fig. 22-11   The three positions of the keyed ignition switch. (*Honda Motor Company, Ltd.*)

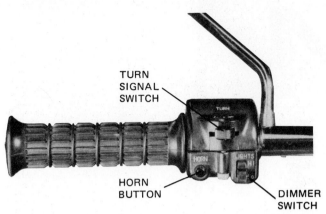

Fig. 22-13 Location of the turn-signal switch, headlight dimmer switch, and horn button. (*ATW*)

If the oil-pressure switch requires replacement, disconnect the lead and unscrew the switch from the crankcase.

22-10
NEUTRAL SWITCH
The neutral switch operates to turn on the neutral indicator lamp on the tachometer or instrument cluster when the transmission is in neutral. When the lamp is on, the transmission is in neutral and the key ignition switch is turned on.

This is a safety signal designed to keep the rider from trying to start when the transmission is in any gear. It is

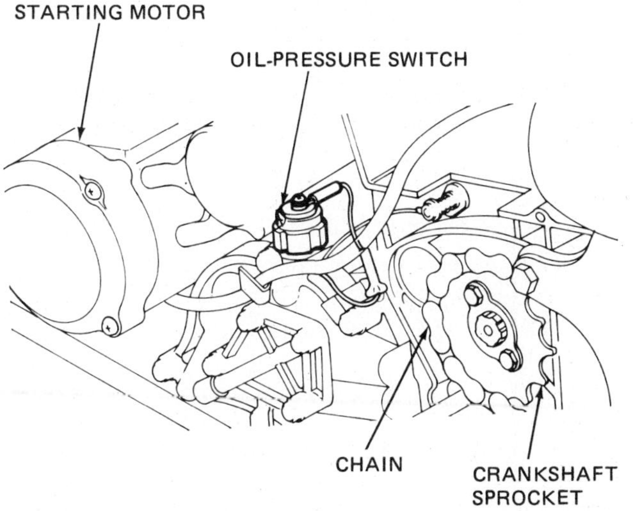

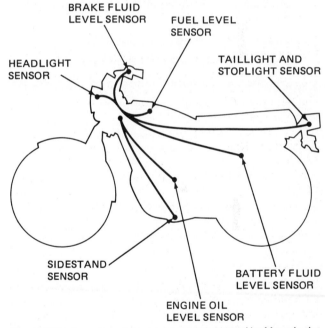

Fig. 22-14 Location of the oil-pressure switch. (*Honda Motor Company, Ltd.*)

usually installed under the lower crankcase. To remove the switch, disconnect the lead, unscrew the mounting bolt, and take off the switch.

22-11
SELF-DIAGNOSTIC SYSTEMS
For many years, motorcycle engineers and riders both have wanted a motorcycle with self-diagnostic capabilities. With this system, sensors placed in certain parts and in the fluids can provide notice to the rider that immediate attention is needed.

Figure 22-15 shows the location of the sensors on one model of Yamaha motorcycle. There are seven sensors, plus a small computer and a liquid-crystal diode (LCD) display panel. As long as the ignition key is turned on, the sensors monitor seven conditions. These are the position of the sidestand, brake-fluid level, engine-oil level, battery-fluid level, headlight, taillight and stoplight, and fuel level.

When something is wrong, the main warning light on the display panel will begin flashing. At the same time, the LCD for the area requiring attention will be displayed. When nothing is wrong, only the fuel gauge LCDs will be on. As long as the key is turned on, they show the level of the fuel in the tank.

Fig. 22-15 Location of the seven sensors used by Yamaha in the Computerized Monitor System. (*Yamaha Motor Corporation*)

CHAPTER 22
REVIEW QUESTIONS

1. List the electric devices on the motorcycle and explain how each works.
2. What is the purpose of a wiring harness and how is it made?
3. How do you remove and install wiring in a handlebar?

4. How do you adjust the headlight?
5. How does the flasher work?
6. What is the purpose of the keyed ignition switch and how does it work?
7. How does the oil-pressure switch work?
8. What is the purpose of the neutral switch?

PART **4**

MOTORCYCLE ENGINE SERVICE

Part 4 covers the maintenance and servicing of motorcycles and motorcycle engines. The first chapter in Part 4 discusses maintenance, trouble diagnosis, and tune-up. It includes maintenance schedules that cover all motorcycle components, and it includes preride and after-race checkups. The following chapters describe the servicing of two-cycle and four-cycle engine components.

There are four chapters in Part 4. They are:

MOTORCYCLE MAINTENANCE, TROUBLE DIAGNOSIS, AND TUNE-UP

After studying this chapter,
you should be able to:

1. Discuss preride inspection and list and explain the 10 items that should be checked.

2. Explain the need for maintenance schedules for two-cycle and four-cycle engines.

3. With the proper tools and instruction, perform complete maintenance on motorcycles with two-cycle and four-cycle engines.

4. Explain how to use the trouble diagnosis charts.

5. Diagnose engine troubles on various motorcycles.

23-1 PRERIDE INSPECTION

Motorcycle manufacturers urge riders to always inspect a motorcycle before riding it. This applies to anyone who wants to drive down the highway or follow a trail into the woods or across the desert. It is essential for the competition rider who is about to race the motorcycle. If the bike is in good condition, then the rider has fewer worries about trouble during the ride.

These are the items that should be checked and the actions that should be taken:

1. Check the gasoline level in the fuel tank. Add fuel as necessary to fill the tank.

2. Check the level of the oil in the oil tank or crankcase. Add oil if necessary.

3. Check the operation of the front and rear brakes. Adjust the cable and the linkage on drum brakes, as necessary, to get the proper free play and braking action. If the brake linings are worn excessively, install new shoes. On disk brakes, if the brake-lever action feels soft or spongy, there is a problem in the hydraulic system. Brake service is covered in Chap. 31. Do not ride a motorcycle with defective, improperly adjusted, or worn brakes.

4. Check the condition of the tires and the tire pressure. If the pressure is low, add air to get the tires up to the proper pressure. If the tires are worn excessively, install new tires. Do not ride a motorcycle with damaged or worn-out tires. Wheel and tire service is covered in Chap. 32.

5. Check the condition of the chain. Measure the chain slack. Adjust the chain if the slack is excessive.

Lubricate the chain if it is dry, and replace it if it is damaged or badly worn. Check the condition of the chain oiler (where present) to see if it is working. Note the condition of the sprocket teeth. If they are worn, install new sprockets. The service of motorcycle final drives is covered in Chap. 29.

6. Check the throttle operation as you swing the front wheel from side to side. The throttle should operate freely as the handlebars are turned to any steering position. Check the free play. Make any adjustments required on the throttle cable. Sometimes it is necessary to reroute the cable or to restore it to its original routing to get free operation in all steering positions.

7. Check the operation of the clutch to make sure it works freely. Adjust the clutch linkage, as necessary, to get full disengagement of the clutch when the clutch lever is squeezed and full engagement of the clutch when the lever is released.

8. Check the steering by turning the front wheel from side to side. It should turn freely with no binding spots. On motorcycles having adjustable steering, tighten or loosen the adjustable steering damper to select the type of ride for the conditions you anticipate. Steering noise is covered in Chap. 30.

9. Give the motorcycle a careful "once-over" to check for loose bolts, leaking fork tubes, loose wheel axles, and so on. You can check for a loose rear axle by holding the frame and seeing how much wobble, if any, the rear wheel has when you push the frame from one side to the other. The front wheel axle can be checked in a similar manner. Make any necessary adjustments.

10. Check all the lights and the horn. This includes checking the stoplight operation as each brake is applied. Set the turn-signal switch in the left-turn position. Check for proper flashing of the left-front and the left-rear turn-indicator lights. Repeat the procedure with the switch in the right-turn position. Check for proper operation of the headlight high beam and low beam. Check the rearview mirror brackets for looseness, and tighten if necessary. Then, sit on the motorcycle in your normal riding position and adjust the rearview mirrors.

Note that the preride inspection includes other items to be checked in addition to those that apply to the engine itself. The steps listed above make up a complete inspection of the safety items that should be checked before each motorcycle ride.

23-2 PERIODIC MAINTENANCE SCHEDULE

All motorcycle manufacturers publish maintenance schedules which list the necessary maintenance operations and the intervals at which these operations should be performed. The maintenance intervals are based on average operating conditions. When the motorcycle is given severe usage or is ridden in unusually rough or dusty conditions, it should have more frequent maintenance.

Item	Initial 750 miles [1000 km]	Every 2000 miles [3000 km]	Every 4000 miles [6000 km]	Every 8000 miles [12,000 km]
1. Air-cleaner element		Wash		Replace
2. Carburetor	Adjust with throttle valve stop screw and pilot air screw	Adjust with throttle valve stop screw and pilot air screw		Overhaul and clean
3. Clutch	Adjust	Adjust		
4. Contact breaker points	Check contact point gap and ignition timing	Check contact point gap and ignition timing		Replace contact points
5. Cylinder head and cylinder	Retighten cylinder head nuts	Retighten cylinder head nuts	Remove carbon	
6. Drive chain	Adjust	Adjust	Wash	
7. Exhaust pipe and muffler	Retighten exhaust pipe fitting nuts	Retighten exhaust pipe fitting nuts	Remove carbon	
8. Oil pump	Check operation and adjust control lever aligning marks	Check operation and adjust control lever aligning marks		
9. Spark plug	Clean	Clean and adjust gap	Replace	
10. Transmission oil	Change	Change		
11. Battery	Check and service	Check and service		
12. Bolts, nuts, and spokes	Retighten		Retighten	
13. Front brake	Check fluid level, leakage, and pad	Check fluid level, leakage, and pad		
14. Fuel cock	Clean fuel strainer		Clean fuel strainer	
15. Rear brake	Adjust play	Adjust play		
16. Throttle grip	Adjust play	Adjust play		
17. Tire		Check tire tread condition		

Fig. 23-1   Maintenance schedule for a three-cylinder two-cycle motorcycle engine.

Most manufacturers indicate the maintenance-operation intervals in both miles and kilometers. At one time, it was common practice to indicate service intervals in months. However, this was not always satisfactory, because of the great variation in distances motorcycles might travel in a month. One month a bike might sit with no usage. Another month it might be in use every day and cover great distances. Now, service intervals are usually given in miles or kilometers of travel.

Figures 23-1 and 23-2 are the maintenance and lubrication schedules for a motorcycle with a three-cylinder two-cycle engine. Figure 23-3 is the maintenance schedule for a motorcycle with a four-cylinder four-cycle engine.

Item	Initial 750 miles [1000 km]	Every 2000 miles [3000 km]	Every 4000 miles [6000 km]
1. Transmission	Check oil	Check oil	
2. Brake camshaft		Grease	
3. Brake cable		Oil	
4. Clutch cable		Oil	
5. Drive chain		Chain lube	
6. Oil-pump cable		Oil	
7. Throttle cable		Oil	
8. Contact breaker cam oil felt			Grease
9. Swinging arm pivot shaft			Grease
10. Throttle grip			Grease

Fig. 23-2   Lubrication schedule for a three-cylinder two-cycle motorcycle engine.

	Initial service period, 500 miles [800 km]	REGULAR SERVICE PERIOD—Perform at every indicated month or mileage interval, whichever occurs first.			
		1 month, 500 miles [800 km]	3 months, 1500 miles [2400 km]	6 months, 3000 miles [4800 km]	12 months, 6000 miles [8600 km]
ENGINE OIL—Change	●		○		
OIL-FILTER ELEMENT—Replace	●			○	
OIL-FILTER SCREEN—Clean					○
CHECK ENGINE OIL PRESSURE			○		
SPARK PLUGS—Clean and adjust gap or replace if necessary				○	
CONTACT POINTS AND IGNITION TIMING*—Clean, check, and adjust or replace if necessary	●			○	
VALVE TAPPET CLEARANCE*—Check, and adjust if necessary	●			○	
CAM CHAIN TENSION*—Adjust	●			○	
AIR-FILTER ELEMENT—Clean				○ (service more frequently if operated in dusty areas)	
AIR-FILTER ELEMENT—Replace					○
CARBURETORS*—Check and adjust if necessary	●			○	
THROTTLE OPERATION—Inspect cables. Check and adjust free play	●			○	
FUEL FILTER SCREEN—Clean				○	
FUEL LINES—Check					○
MAKE COMPRESSION TEST OF ENGINE	Any time the engine is tuned				
CLUTCH*—Check operation and adjust if necessary	●			○	
DRIVE CHAIN—Check, lubricate, and adjust if necessary	● (initial service period 200 miles)	○			
BRAKE-FLUID LEVEL—Check, and add fluid if necessary	●			○	
FRONT BRAKE PADS*—Inspect, and replace if worn				○	
REAR BRAKE SHOES*—Check wear indicator				○	
BRAKE CONTROL LINKAGE—Check linkage, and adjust free play if necessary	●			○	
WHEEL RIMS AND SPOKES*—Check. Tighten spokes and true wheels, if necessary	●			○	
TIRES—Inspect and check air pressure	●	○			
FRONT FORK OIL—Drain and refill	● (initial service period 1500 miles)				○
FRONT AND REAR SUSPENSION—Check operation	●			○	
REAR FORK BUSHING—Grease, check for excessive looseness				○	
STEERING HEAD BEARINGS*—Adjust					○

*Items marked with an asterisk should be serviced by a competent mechanic who has the proper tools and is mechanically proficient. Other maintenance items are simple to perform and may be serviced by the owner.

(Continued)

Fig. 23-3 Maintenance schedule for a four-cylinder four-cycle overhead-camshaft motorcycle engine.

Fig. 23-3 (Continued)

	Initial service period, 500 miles [800 km]	REGULAR SERVICE PERIOD—Perform at every indicated month or mileage interval, whichever occurs first.			
		1 month, 500 miles [800 km]	3 months, 1500 miles [2400 km]	6 months, 3000 miles [4800 km]	12 months, 6000 miles [8600 km]
BATTERY—Check electrolyte level, and add water if necessary	●	○			
LIGHTING EQUIPMENT—Check and adjust if necessary	●	○			
ALL NUTS, BOLTS, AND OTHER FASTENERS—Check security and tighten if necessary					
ROAD TEST	After any service work				

NOTE The inspection procedures and corrections or adjustments are *in addition* to the preride inspection that should be made *every time* a motorcycle is ridden.

Note that the first column in Figs. 23-1, 23-2, and 23-3 refers to the initial check after the motorcycle has been operated only a few hundred miles. This checkup is very important because during initial running, or *break-in,* many parts "wear in." Checks and adjustments are often required.

Motorcycle manufacturers caution against racing or overspeeding a new engine during the first few hundred miles of operation. Look at Fig. 23-4. For the first 100 miles [160 km], keep engine speed below 3500 rpm. Up to 500 miles [800 km] keep engine speed below 4000 rpm. Up to 1000 miles [1600 km] keep engine speed below 5000 rpm.

The maintenance procedures listed in Figs. 23-1, 23-2, and 23-3 are discussed elsewhere in the book, in the chapters on fuel, ignition, cooling, charging, and starting systems. Checking, maintenance, and servicing procedures on clutches, transmissions, final drives, frames, suspension, brakes, wheels, and tires are covered in later chapters.

23-3 ENGINE TUNE-UP Following the recommended maintenance procedure will keep the engine and other motorcycle components in their best operat-

ing condition. However, when a bike is brought in for service, the technician may do a tune-up job on it, regardless of the maintenance it has had.

The technician uses the proper tools and test instruments to check every operating component on the bike. Then any part needing attention is adjusted, serviced, or replaced. Other chapters in this book cover all of these services, adjustments, and repairs.

23-4 ENGINE TROUBLE DIAGNOSIS Trouble diagnosis, or *troubleshooting,* requires a careful analysis of the trouble and careful consideration of possible causes. A specific trouble usually is caused by certain specific conditions. For example, failure to start could be due to no fuel, an improper air-fuel ratio, ignition-system trouble, a loss of compression, or a defective valve (in four-cycle engines). The charts that follow (Figs. 23-5 and 23-6) show the relationships among the various troubles in two-cycle and four-cycle engines. Figure 23-7 lists the possible causes for each trouble. To use the charts, follow the example given below.

EXAMPLE
A. Your problem engine is two-cycle.
B. The problem is that the engine idles poorly. On the two-cycle chart (Fig. 23-5), locate "Idles Poorly" on the vertical symptom column.

FIRST 100 MILES [160 km]   UP TO 500 MILES [800 km]   UP TO 1000 MILES [1600 km]

Fig. 23-4 Do not overspeed or race the engine during the break-in period. The tachometer readings shown should not be exceeded in the distances shown. (*Suzuki Motor Company, Ltd.*)

SYMPTOMS \ POSSIBLE CAUSE	1. No fuel	2. Improper fuel	3. Improper air-fuel ratio	3A. Improper oil or fuel/oil ratio	4. No spark	5. Ignition system	6. Battery condition	7. Improper cooling	8. Improper lubrication	9. Low compression	10. Carbon buildup	11. Faulty governor	12. Engine overloaded	13. Exhaust restriction
Will not start	●		●		●	●	●			●				
Hard starting	●		●	●		●	●			●				●
Stops suddenly	●			●	●	●		●	●	●				
Lacks power			●	●		●		●	●	●			●	●
Operates erratically			●			●						●		
Knocks or pings		●	●	●		●		●	●		●		●	
Misfires or "skips"		●	●	●		●	●							●
Backfires			●			●								
Overheats		●	●	●		●		●	●		●	●	●	
Idles poorly			●			●				●				●

Fig. 23-5 Trouble diagnosis chart for two-cycle motorcycle engines. (*Champion Spark Plug Company*)

SYMPTOMS \ POSSIBLE CAUSE	1. No fuel	2. Improper fuel	3. Improper air-fuel ratio	4. No spark	5. Ignition system	6. Battery condition	7. Improper cooling	8. Improper lubrication	9. Low compression	10. Carbon buildup	11. Faulty governor	12. Engine overloaded	13. Exhaust restriction	14. Stuck, burnt, or damaged valve
Will not start	●		●	●	●	●			●					●
Hard starting	●		●		●	●			●				●	●
Stops suddenly	●			●	●		●	●	●					●
Lacks power			●		●		●		●			●	●	●
Operates erratically			●		●						●			
Knocks or pings		●	●		●					●		●		
Misfires or "skips"		●	●		●	●							●	
Backfires			●		●									●
Overheats		●	●		●		●	●		●		●		●
Idles poorly			●		●				●				●	●

Fig. 23-6 Trouble diagnosis chart for four-cycle motorcycle engines. (*Champion Spark Plug Company*)

C. At each dot across consider the "Possible cause" given.

D. "Idles Poorly" lists four possible causes:
  3. Improper air-fuel ratio
  5. Ignition system
  9. Low compression
  13. Exhaust restriction

E. Locate each "Possible Cause" in Fig. 23-7. Then consider and check each item.

Complaint	Possible cause
1. No fuel	**a.** Tank empty
	b. Fuel shutoff valve OFF
	c. Filler cap vent plugged
	d. Filter or delivery lines clogged
	e. Fuel pump faulty
	f. Carburetor needle and seat inoperative
2. Improper fuel	**a.** Stale fuel
	b. Water in fuel tank
	c. Octane rating too low
	d. Two-cycle oil not to engine manufacturers' specs
3. Improper air-fuel ratios	**a.** Improper choke operation
	b. Improper carburetion settings and adjustments
	c. Restricted air intake
	d. Dirty carburetor, restricted internally
	e. Air leak in intake system
	f. Damaged head gasket or cracked head or cylinder
	g. Leaking crankcase seals (two-cycle)
3A. Improper fuel/oil ratios	**a.** Improper mix
	b. Fuel/oil separation
	c. Main bearing seal leaking (two-cycle) (if main bearing is pressure fed)
4. No spark	**a.** Ignition switch OFF
	b. Wiring in primary or secondary circuit disconnected, broken, or corroded
	c. Contact breakers stuck or oxidized
	d. Coil and condenser faulty
	e. Battery condition
5. Ignition system	**a.** Faulty ignition switch
	b. Broken, damaged, or corroded wire (abnormally high resistance)
6. Battery condition	**a.** Low voltage—inadequate charge
	b. Internal short circuit
	c. Corrosion
	d. Poor or loose connections
7. Improper cooling	**a.** Restriction in cooling system or fins
	b. Lack of coolant
	c. Cooling fin damage
8. Improper lubrication	**a.** Out of oil
	b. Improper oil
	c. Improper fuel/oil ratio (two-cycle)
9. Low compression or loss of compression	**a.** Cracked or broken piston rings
	b. Blown head gasket or cracked cylinder or head
	c. Valve sticking or broken push rod
	d. Preignition damage
	e. Detonation damage
10. Carbon buildup	**a.** Normal accumulation
	b. Excessive rich mixtures
	c. Excessive fuel/oil ratios
	d. Incorrect oil type
11. Faulty governor	Governor malfunctioning

(Continued)

Fig. 23-7 Possible causes for each condition given in the charts in **Figs. 23-5** and **23-6**. (*Champion Spark Plug Company*)

Fig 23-7 (Continued)

Complaint	Possible cause
12. Engine overload	Engine operated in conditions above those for which designed
13. Exhaust restriction	**a.** Damaged exhaust system
	b. Clogged or restricted baffles
	c. Clogged or restricted exhaust port
14. Valve problems	**a.** Improper valve clearance
	b. Improper seating due to burned, bent, or stuck valve

CHAPTER 23
REVIEW QUESTIONS

1. What are the preride inspection checks and how are they performed?
2. What are the basic steps in the maintenance schedule for a three-cylinder two-cycle motorcycle engine?
3. What are the basic steps in the lubrication schedule for a three-cylinder two-cycle motorcycle engine?

4. What are the basic steps in the maintenance schedule for a four-cylinder four-cycle overhead-camshaft motorcycle engine?

CHAPTER 24

TWO-CYCLE-ENGINE TOP-END SERVICE

After studying this chapter,
you should be able to:

1. Explain why cleanliness is important in engine-service work.

2. Describe the typical methods of cleaning engines.

3. Explain in detail how to do a top-end overhaul job on a two-cycle engine.

24-1
TOP-END OVERHAUL   Top-end overhaul consists of disassembling the upper end of the engine and servicing the parts in the upper end. In the two-cycle engine, this includes the cylinder head, cylinder, and piston assembly. In the four-cycle engine, it would also include the valves, as explained in Chap. 25.

24-2
CLEANLINESS   The major enemy of good engine-service work is dirt. A trace of dirt or abrasive in a bearing, on the cylinder wall, or on other working parts can ruin an otherwise good service job. Before disassembling any engine, clean its outside thoroughly. Depending on how dirty the engine is, use a scraper, an old broom, or a stiff bristle brush to knock off the larger chunks of dirt. Then brush the remaining dirt, oil, and caked grease with a chemical cleaner, or a strong mixture of detergent and water.

Rinse off the dirt with a hose, and allow the engine to dry. Some shops steam-clean engines before working on them. Do not get water into the air cleaner, carburetor, muffler, or ignition.

While servicing an engine, be careful to keep all parts clean. When reassembling an engine or installing engine parts, dirty parts are likely to cause trouble in the engine. Parts should be cleaned as explained in the chapters dealing with servicing the different engine components. Several cleaning methods and cleaners are in use. Some methods use hot water mixed with solvent in which the parts are soaked. Other methods include steam jets and vapor degreasers.

As soon as a metal part is cleaned and dried, a light coating of oil should be applied to brightly finished surfaces so that rust will not form. Be sure that parts are thoroughly clean and thoroughly dry.

CAUTION **If you use an air hose to dry parts, always wear safety goggles. The compressed-air stream drives dirt particles at high velocity, and these particles could injure your eyes. Be careful where you point the air hose. Never point it at others in the shop. Always wear safety goggles when using the air hose.**

24-3
DISASSEMBLY   Depending on the model of engine and motorcycle, you may have to remove shrouding or other parts that block access to the engine. On some motorcycles you will have to remove the engine from the bike. On other engines, you can do a top-overhaul job on the engine without removing it from the motorcycle. The bike shown in Fig. 24-1 has enough room above the engine to permit you to work within the frame and lift out the parts as you remove

Fig. 24-1   Top-end overhaul in this motorcycle does not require removal of the engine from the frame. (*Harley-Davidson Motor Company, Inc.*)

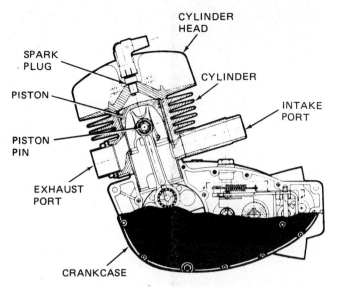

Fig. 24-2 Sectional view of a single-cylinder two-cycle engine. (*Husqvarna*)

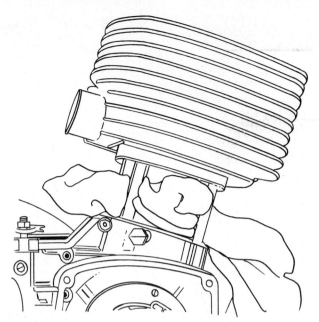

Fig. 24-4 Put a clean cloth around the connecting rod and in the crankcase opening to prevent dirt from falling into the crankcase.

them. If you don't have to remove the engine, don't do it.

Figure 24-2 is a sectional view of a single-cylinder two-cycle engine, showing the parts in the upper end that are to be removed for a top-end overhaul.

NOTE Always have the shop manual for the engine you are servicing. The procedure that follows is general. But many engines require servicing procedures that may differ in some details from the general procedure outlined below.

Disconnect the fuel line from the fuel tank. Remove the choke and throttle linkage, if necessary. Remove the spark plug, exhaust pipe, and carburetor air cleaner. Then remove the carburetor.

Remove any screws or nuts holding the cylinder head and cylinder to the crankcase (Fig. 24-3). Take off the cylinder head. Pull the cylinder up about 2 inches [50 mm]. Stuff a clean cloth or shop towel around the connecting rod and in the crankcase opening, as shown in Fig. 24-4. This will help prevent dirt from falling into the crankcase as you remove the cylinder. Now lift the cylinder off the crankcase.

1. Nut
2. Lockwasher
3. Washer
4. Bolt
5. Lockwasher
6. Plug
7. Gasket
8. Cylinder head
9. Gasket
10. Cylinder
11. Gasket
12. Stud
13. Bolt
14. Gasket
15. Exhaust adaptor
16. Lockwasher
17. Spring
18. Spark plug
19. Carburetor adaptor
20. Lockwasher
21. Nut
22. Insulator
23. Gasket
24. Clamp
25. Screw

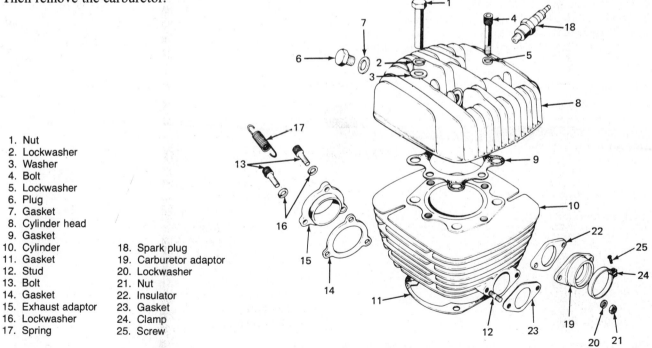

Fig. 24-3 Cylinder head and cylinder of a two-cycle one-cylinder engine, with related parts. (*Kawasaki Heavy Industries, Ltd.*)

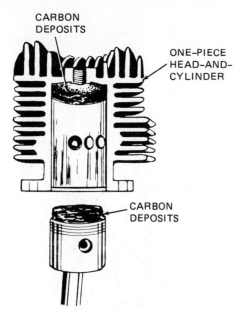

Fig. 24-5 A one-piece head-and-cylinder assembly removed from the crankcase. Notice the scored cylinder walls caused by lack of lubrication, clogged exhaust ports, and carbon deposits on the head of the piston and in the combustion chamber.

Store the cylinder, with the cylinder head-end down, on a piece of heavy cardboard. This will prevent any damage to the crankcase sleeve or to threads on the exhaust port. With the cylinder removed, the piston-and-connecting-rod assembly protrudes through the cylinder opening in the crankcase.

On some two-cycle engines, the head and cylinder are one piece. They are made in a combined head-and-cylinder assembly, as shown in Fig. 24-5. To remove this type of cylinder assembly, unbolt it from the crankcase. Then pull the cylinder from the crankcase and off of the piston. Remember to pause when the cylinder is

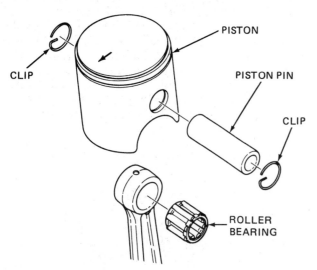

Fig. 24-6 Exploded view of the piston-and-connecting-rod assembly for a two-cycle engine. (*Yamaha Motor Company, Ltd.*)

lifted about 2 inches [51 mm] from the crankcase. Then, place a clean cloth around the connecting rod and in the crankcase opening to prevent dirt from entering the crankcase.

The next part of the top-end service job is to remove the piston from the connecting rod. In most engines, the piston pin is held in place by Circlips, snap rings, or lock rings, as shown in Fig. 24-6. To remove the lock ring from the piston, grasp the ring with needlenose pliers and remove the ring from the piston. Then turn the piston around and remove the lock ring from the other side of the pin.

Wrap the fingers of your hand around the piston to support it. Use a small wooden dowel in your other hand to push the piston pin out of the piston. Sometimes the pin will move partway out, then become hard to move. If this should happen, grasp the pin with needle-nose pliers, and work it out of the piston. However, pliers might mar the pin so that you would not want to use it again. If this happens, a new pin must be installed during reassembly of the engine.

NOTE Never drive the pin out of the piston using a hammer and a punch. This may remove the pin, but the force of the hammer blows will bend the connecting rod.

Some manufacturers make available a special piston-pin puller which can be used on most hollow pins. Another method of removing the pin is to insert a long bolt through the pin. Screw a nut on the bolt, being sure that the nut is small enough to pass freely through the pin hole in the piston. Then pull on the head of the bolt to remove the pin.

24-4
CLEANING ENGINE PARTS With the top-end of the engine disassembled, the next step is to clean the parts. This is necessary so that they can be checked, inspected, and measured. The job of cleaning top-end parts often is called *decarboning* the engine. Here is why it is sometimes necessary to decarbon a two-cycle engine. The two-cycle engine requires a mixture of oil and gasoline. Part of the oil burns away during the combustion process, but some of it becomes a hard

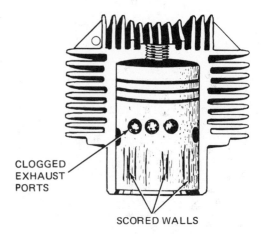

Fig. 24-7 Cutaway view of a cylinder and head showing scored walls caused by carbon deposits in the exhaust ports.

carbon deposit. This deposit forms in the transfer port, in the exhaust ports and exhaust passages, on the top of the piston, and on combustion-chamber surfaces.

The exhaust ports in the cylinder can become so clogged that the engine will barely run (Fig. 24-7). To remove the carbon, use a screwdriver or a hardwood scraper to scrape away the accumulations, as shown in Fig. 24-8. Very fine sandpaper can be used to finish removing any remaining carbon from the parts.

This job often can be done on an engine without disassembling it. To remove the deposits on an assembled engine, take off the exhaust muffler. Then turn the crankshaft so that the piston covers the exhaust ports. Use the screwdriver or scraper to remove the carbon, as described above. The piston will keep carbon particles from falling into the crankcase where they could cause trouble. Be very careful to avoid scratching the piston. Blow out all loose particles from the ports.

Remove the old gasket from the cylinder head, if the head is detachable, and from the cylinder-to-crankcase surface. Clean any sticking gasket material from the metal surfaces. Wash all parts in clean solvent. Dry the parts with air, or by wiping with a clean cloth. Take a look at the spark-plug threads. If you can see carbon deposits in the threads, clean them by running a tap of the correct size through the spark-plug hole (14 mm is correct for most engines).

24-5 SERVICING THE PISTON AND RINGS

Remove the piston rings from the piston. Inspect the piston for scuffing and scoring, cracks in the head or skirt, and damaged or broken ring lands. If the piston skirt is rough or scored or if it shows signs of seizure, it must be smoothed. Reinstalling a piston with a rough skirt will damage the cylinder. Polish the piston by rubbing it with a soap-filled steel wood pad. Then, rinse the piston clean by holding it under running water. Dry the piston, and apply a light coat of oil. Another way to smooth a rough piston skirt is to use an oilstone. Hold the piston in your hand and work the oilstone over the scuffed area, following the pattern shown in Fig. 24-9. A piston with damage that does not clean up must be discarded.

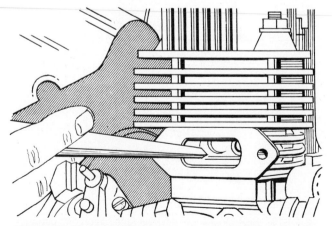

Fig. 24-8 Use a hardwood scraper or screwdriver to remove carbon from the exhaust ports.

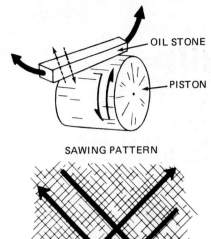

Fig. 24-9 Using an oilstone to clean up a scuffed piston. (Yamaha Motor Company, Ltd.)

Clean the carbon from the ring grooves in the piston. This step is necessary because carbon on the sides of the ring groove may cause a new ring to stick. Carbon in the bottom or back side of a ring groove, behind a new ring, may cause the ring to stick out too far. This makes installation in the cylinder difficult and may cause scoring and seizure when the engine starts.

To clean the carbon out of the ring groove, make a tool by breaking in two the ring taken from the groove. Use the sharp edge to clean the groove. Another way to clean the groove is by using a piston-ring-groove cleaner such as shown in Fig. 24-10. The important point to remember about cleaning ring grooves is to remove carbon—not metal—from the grooves. The removal of metal from the ring groove can weaken the piston and rapidly increase ring-groove wear and blowby.

After you have scraped as much carbon from the grooves as possible, soak the piston in a liquid chemical cleaner. Many shops use old carburetor cleaner for this purpose. Whatever chemical cleaner you use, be sure the label states that it is safe to use on aluminum. After the carbon has been softened by the cleaner, very carefully scrape out any carbon remaining in the grooves.

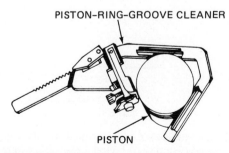

Fig. 24-10 Piston-ring-groove cleaner.

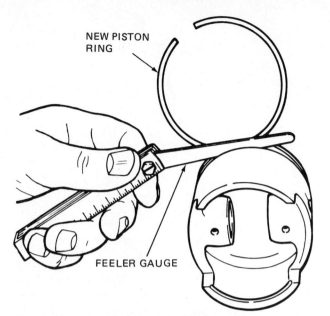

NEW PISTON RING

FEELER GAUGE

Fig. 24-11 Checking the side clearance of the piston ring in the ring groove. (*Kohler Company*)

NOTE Never use a wire brush of any type on a piston. The steel-wire bristles of the wire brush will scratch the soft aluminum piston and will round off severely the outside edges of the piston lands. This reduces support for the piston ring and may increase wear and blowby.

After cleaning and inspecting the piston, check the ring grooves for wear. In normal operation the top ring groove wears the most because it is closest to the hot combustion temperatures. Also, any dirt that enters the combustion chamber (through a defective air cleaner, for example) may lodge in the top ring groove. New rings will not seal in worn grooves and will soon break.

Piston-ring side clearance between the side of the piston ring and the ring groove may be checked with a feeler gauge, as shown in Fig. 24-11. Install a new piston ring in the groove to be checked. Then try to slip a 0.004-inch [0.10-mm] feeler gauge between the top of the ring and the land.

NOTE When checking for ring-groove wear, check at several points around the piston. Many manufacturer's specifications call for piston-ring side clearance of less than 0.004 inch [0.10 mm]. Follow the manufacturer's specifications for the engine you are servicing if you have them available.

If the feeler gauge slides in 1/16 inch [1.59 mm] or more from the edge of the land, the groove is worn excessively. Discard the piston and install a new one.

Some two-cycle engines use a keystone-shaped piston ring instead of a plain square-cut piston ring. Figure 24-12 shows the difference between the two types. Notice that the top of the keystone piston ring and groove is tapered, or slanted. This allows the side clearance to change as the piston goes up and down in the cylinder. Figure 24-13 shows this action. The result of the changing side clearance is that the scrubbing action of the sides of the ring in the groove reduces the formation of deposits. This prevents the ring from sticking and provides longer engine life.

Be careful not to try installing a plain piston ring in a keystone piston ring groove. The rings are not interchangeable. Clean the keystone groove very carefully. Do not gouge or cut into the sides of the groove when cleaning it. All other service procedures for a piston with a keystone ring are the same as for a conventional piston and ring.

A piston that has been in a running engine for some time will wear. This means that the ring grooves will wear, as we discussed. It also means that the piston skirt will wear and create excessive clearance between it and the cylinder wall. Sometimes this is called piston collapse, especially if excessive clearance between the piston skirt and the cylinder wall suddenly develops. This could be the case, for example, should an engine

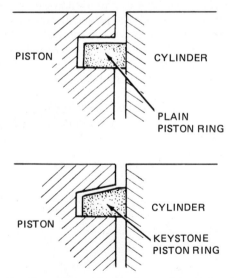

Fig. 24-12 Comparison of a regular, or plain, piston ring (top) with a keystone piston ring (bottom). (*Yamaha Motor Company, Ltd.*)

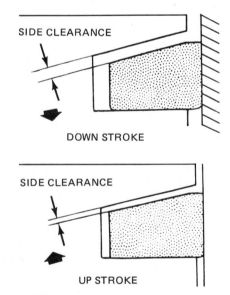

Fig. 24-13 Side clearance of a keystone piston ring changes as the piston moves up and down in the cylinder. (*Yamaha Motor Company, Ltd.*)

overheat severely. Figure 24-14 (left) shows the fit of a piston in the cylinder of a cold engine. Notice that the piston tapers toward the top. This type of piston design is used in some two-cycle engines. Other pistons for two-cycle engines are straight. Figure 24-14 (right) shows the proper fit of a piston in a cylinder after the engine reaches normal temperature. Note how the shape of the piston changes.

Here's what happens when the piston overheats. For example, suppose someone buys a new two-cycle engine and fails to read the owner's manual about allowing the engine to run slowly at light load to break in properly. The engine is operated immediately at full throttle, with a heavy load, and for a long time. Excessive friction from this type of operation causes the piston to overheat. The overheating causes the piston, as shown in Fig. 24-14 (right), to expand some more. As it expands, the piston and rings break through the oil film providing lubrication with the cylinder wall. When the piston begins to drag, or rub against the cylinder wall, the engine *seizes* and the engine stops.

Sometimes the rings get so hot they momentarily weld to the cylinder wall. This could happen when the piston is at TDC when the rings are momentarily at rest. However, when the piston starts down again, the welds break loose from the cylinder wall. The welded spots now scratch the cylinder wall. With severe cylinder-wall scores, the engine will soon be inoperative because of excessive blowby. Damage to the piston and cylinder also will occur.

In addition, the excessive expansion of the piston due to the excessive heat causes another trouble. The engine develops a new noise. It will range from a heavy whispering or scratching sound to a ringing knock. This noise is due to piston-skirt collapse. It is characteristic of an engine that has excessive piston-to-cylinder clearance.

The cause of piston collapse is as follows. Once the piston overheats, it tries to continue expanding from the heat. However, the piston cannot expand any further than the cylinder wall. But the piston keeps trying to, because the heat is causing the metal in all parts of the piston to expand. As a result, the forced expansion from the heat permanently damages the internal structure of the piston. This damage, called *piston collapse,*

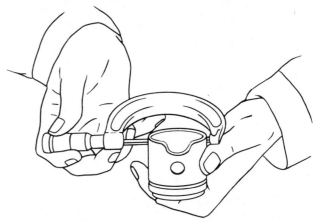

Fig. 24-15 Measuring the skirt diameter of the piston with an outside micrometer.

occurs to some extent every time a piston overheats and seizes. Because of the internal damage to the pistons, when the engine cools the piston returns to a smaller diameter than it had originally.

Here are a couple of general definitions to keep in mind. Piston wear is the reduction in piston-skirt diameter as a result of normal operation of the engine for long periods of service. Piston collapse is the rapid change in skirt diameter as a result of severely overheating the engine for a short period of time. When checking piston-skirt diameter, wear is what we normally look for and expect to find, although checking for a collapsed skirt is done the same way.

Earlier in this chapter we explained how to clean a piston, make a visual inspection, and repair minor skirt damage with an oilstone. In addition, piston skirt diameter should be checked with a micrometer, as shown in Fig. 24-15. Then compare the measurement to the manufacturer's specifications.

Some manufacturers recommend that the fit of the piston to the cylinder bore be checked by inserting the piston into the bore with a feeler gauge along its side as shown in Fig. 24-16. The thickest feeler gauge that can move alongside the piston is the piston clearance. When clearance is excessive, hone or rebore the cylinder and install a new oversize piston. This procedure is discussed in detail later.

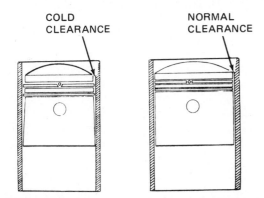

Fig. 24-14 When cold, the piston is tapered (left). With the engine running at normal temperature, the piston expands to a round shape (right). (*Yamaha Motor Company, Ltd.*)

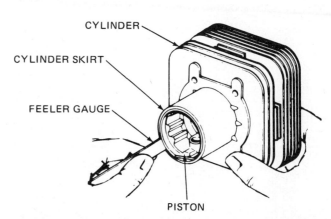

Fig. 24-16 Measuring piston clearance with a feeler gauge. (*Outboard Marine Corporation*)

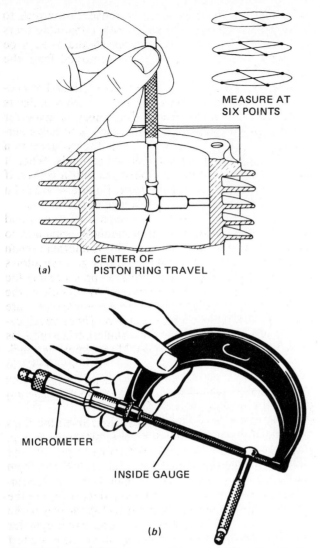

MEASURE AT SIX POINTS

CENTER OF PISTON RING TRAVEL

(a)

MICROMETER

INSIDE GAUGE

(b)

Fig. 24-17 Taking bore measurements with a telescoping gauge and an outside micrometer. First you set the gauge to the bore diameter (a), and then you determine the diameter by using the micrometer as shown at (b).

24-6 CYLINDER SERVICE

Examine the cylinder for cracks, stripped threads in the bolt holes, broken fins, or scores or other damage in the cylinder bore.

Any of these types of damage must be repaired, or the cylinder must be discarded. If the cylinder appears to be in good condition, use an inside micrometer or a telescoping gauge to check the cylinder bore for wear, as shown in Fig. 24-17. In a two-cycle engine the fit between the piston and the cylinder wall is very important. Make several measurements of the cylinder bore, both above and below the ports. Yamaha, for example, suggests that eight different cylinder-bore measurements be made, as shown in Fig. 24-18. The cylinder should be checked for wear, taper, and out-of-round. Excessive cylinder-bore wear means that the cylinder must be honed or bored oversize and that an oversize piston must be installed. This procedure is covered later.

Here is another important check to make on the cylinder. Many small engines have cylinders made of aluminum instead of cast iron. An aluminum cylinder is lighter and provides better cooling than a cast-iron cylinder. However, the piston and rings cannot operate directly against the aluminum. Therefore, an aluminum cylinder has a cast-iron liner, or sleeve, inside it. A cylinder of this type is shown in Fig. 24-19. The liner serves as the cylinder bore.

Under certain conditions, the cast-iron liner can work loose in the aluminum cylinder. If this happens, the excess heat from combustion is prevented from reaching the cooling fins. The piston and cylinder overheat, and the cylinder discolors. Usually, overheating causes the cylinder to turn blue in spots from the excessively high temperatures. On aluminum cylinders, always make a quick check to see that the cast-iron liner remains tight in the cylinder. If you find the liner loose or find blue areas on the cylinder walls, replace the cylinder with a new one. Other types of aluminum cylinders are coated with a thin layer of hard chrome to serve as the surface for the piston and rings to run against.

Shiny and glazed cylinder walls should be lightly honed to remove the glaze, as shown in Fig. 24-20. This is necessary on many engines to ensure that new piston rings will seat after they are installed. After the cylinder walls are honed, wash them. Use clean cloths with plenty of strong soap and water to wash out the cylinder bore. Dry the cylinder bore with a clean, dry cloth. Coat the walls with a thin film of oil to prevent rusting.

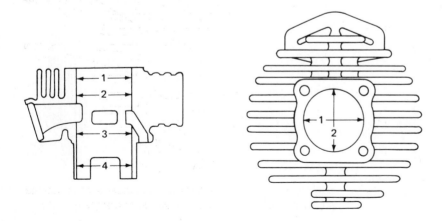

Fig. 24-18 Cylinder measuring points for a two-cycle-engine cylinder. (*Yamaha Motor Company, Ltd.*)

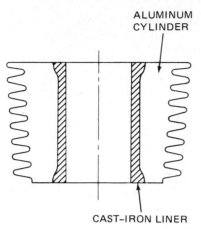

Fig. 24-19 Aluminum cylinder with a cast-iron liner. (*Yamaha Motor Company, Ltd.*)

Honing and boring the cylinder larger so that an oversize piston can be installed is covered later.

NOTE Some cylinder bores are chrome plated. This is done to improve the wear characteristics of the cylinder. You can identify a chromed cylinder by noting that the entire cylinder bore has a very shiny surface of hard chrome. It looks and feels similar to the surface on the chrome bumper of a car. Chrome-plated cylinders cannot be refinished in any way. If the cylinder shows signs of wear or damage, you must replace it.

24-7 PISTON-RING SERVICE

Rings that show any type of damage must be replaced. This is also true of piston rings that are removed from an engine that has been in service a long time. When the rings are removed from an engine that has operated only a short time, you may be able to reuse the rings. Wipe them clean with a cloth, and carefully examine the face of each ring. If the rough marks, machine marks, or coating has not worn

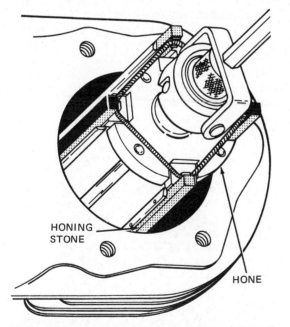

Fig. 24-20 Honing the cylinder of a two-cycle engine. (*Onan Corporation*)

off the face of the ring, it can be reused, according to some manufacturers. However, other manufacturers recommend that new piston rings should always be installed whenever the piston is removed from the cylinder.

With the cylinder cleaned and reconditioned as necessary, check the end-gap clearance of each ring that is to be installed on the piston. This check is made for several reasons. One important reason is to make certain the rings are the correct size for the cylinder. In a running engine, the ring gets hot and expands. When it does so, the ends of the ring must not butt together. If they do touch, the ring may break. Engine seizure can then occur and cause severe damage to the engine.

All piston rings must have at least a minimum end gap. While the end gap is not particularly critical as to its size, it must not be too large. This is another reason for checking piston-ring end gap. Too large a gap allows excessive blowby of the compression pressure and the combustion gases into the crankcase. Always check the manufacturer's specifications for the engine you are servicing to find the correct ring gap. These specifications may also be printed on the installation instructions that come with new piston rings. Many times the specifications are given as a range, for example, 0.008 to 0.014 inch [0.20 to 0.36 mm]. This means that the ring gap should measure not less than 0.008 inch [0.20 mm] nor more than 0.014 inch [0.36 mm].

To check the end gap of a piston ring, insert the rings one at a time into the cylinder bore, as shown in Fig. 24-21. Some manufacturers recommend placing the piston ring squarely in the bore, 1 inch [25.4 mm] from the top of the cylinder. Other manufacturers recommend checking the ring in the lower, unworn part of the cylinder. The piston rings do not travel all the way to the bottom of the cylinder. When you look into a cylinder bore, you can see this. Piston-ring wear stops a short distance from the bottom end of the bore.

Square the ring in the cylinder using the piston to push the ring into the cylinder, as shown in Fig. 24-22. When you don't have a piston, move the ring so that it is 1 inch [25.4 mm] from the end of the cylinder on all sides. Check the ring gap with a feeler gauge, as shown in Fig. 24-23.

Compare the measurement with the manufacturer's

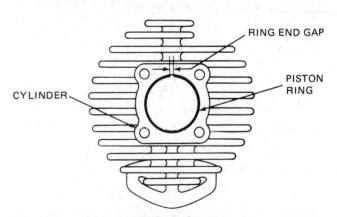

Fig. 24-21 Piston ring installed in a cylinder bore so that the ring gap can be checked. (*Yamaha Motor Company, Ltd.*)

specifications. If you are checking a used ring from the engine, and the ring gap is too large, the ring is worn excessively. This means that a new ring set must be installed on the piston. When one ring on a piston is replaced, all rings on that piston must always be replaced at the same time.

If you are checking a new piston ring, and the ring gap is excessive, you may have the wrong size ring set for the engine. Double check on the ring cylinder sizes. For example, the number 10 stamped on the top of a piston or on the extended skirt of a cylinder indicates that the piston and cylinder are 0.010 inch [0.25 mm] oversize. Also, the possibility exists that the wrong size rings have been placed in the package of new rings.

Another check for piston-ring wear can be made with the piston ring properly fitted in the cylinder. Place a sheet of white paper under the cylinder. Then carefully look for any gap between the piston ring and the cylinder wall. With the white paper acting as a reflector, a thin strip of white will be seen wherever the ring is not in contact with the cylinder wall. There is a good seal between the piston ring and the cylinder wall when no strip of white is visible.

Check each piston ring in its ring groove for tightness and binding. Place the ring in the groove as shown in Fig. 24-24. Roll the ring completely around the groove in the piston. The ring should roll freely. Any metal burr or remaining carbon deposits will cause the ring to stick or fail to roll freely. The groove must be cleaned before the rings are installed on the piston and the engine assembled. A ring that sticks may protrude from the groove too far to permit installation of the piston in the cylinder. A sticking ring will not work free in a running engine. Ring breakage, scoring of the cylinder walls, excess blowby, and other serious engine damage can result when a piston is installed with a stuck ring.

24-8 PISTON-PIN SERVICE
Before installing the rings on the piston, check the fit of the pin in the piston. You can measure the pin with an outside micrometer and the pin hole with a telescoping gauge. Compare the measurements with the manufacturer's specifications.

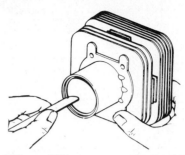
Fig. 24-23 Using a thickness gauge to check the ring end-gap measurement, with the piston ring inserted in the cylinder bore. (*Outboard Marine Corporation*)

If they are not within the specifications in the manufacturer's service manual, correction must be made. Some manufacturers supply oversize piston pins. If these are available for the engine you are servicing, you can bore the piston or bushings (if used) and install the oversize pin. This means boring the connecting-rod bushing also. Other manufacturers supply new bushings which can be installed so that a standard-size pin can be used. All this takes special equipment and is not recommended for a shop that does not have the proper tools.

Some piston pins are a *hand-press fit* or a *palm-push fit* into the piston, according to the service manual. This means that when coated with a thin film of oil the pin should slide into the piston as you push on the pin with the palm of your hand. What you are checking is that the piston and pin are not worn so much that the pin will push through the piston too easily or fall through of its own weight. If it does, there is excess clearance caused by wear on the pin, in the bushings or pin bores, or both.

Figure 24-6 shows a piston, pin, and roller bearing assembly in disassembled view. The roller bearing fits inside the connecting-rod small end and is used instead of a bushing. Other engines use smaller needle bearings in the small end of the connecting rod. In most engines, roller and needle bearings wear so little that their wear is difficult to check. Always make a thorough visual inspection of the needles, rollers, and bearing cage for abrasions, rough spots, flat spots, any blue color from overheating, and any other damage. If you find any damage, or suspect that some part of the needle or roller bearing is damaged, install a new bearing.

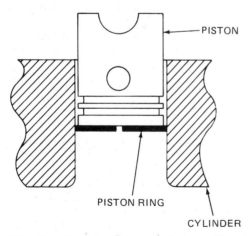
Fig. 24-22 Squaring a ring in the cylinder bore with a piston in preparation for measuring ring end gap.

Fig. 24-24 Checking the piston ring for tightness, or binding, by rolling it around the groove. (*Outboard Marine Corporation*)

24-9
CONNECTING-ROD BIG-END BEARING

Any time you perform a top-end overhaul, check the connecting-rod bearing on the crankshaft. Figure 24-25 shows how to check for wear in the big-end bearing and crankpin. Move the rod to one side to eliminate the rod side clearance. Then move the piston end of the connecting rod as far as it will move in both directions. The distance that the small end moves is the axial looseness. It can tell you a lot about the big-end bearing conditions. Yamaha specifies that when the small end moves 2 mm [0.080 inch] or less, the crankpin and big-end bearing are all right. When the axial play exceeds 2 mm [0.080 inch], the crankcase must be split and the crankshaft disassembled to replace the worn parts.

Not all manufacturers give a specification for axial looseness. However, get in the habit of checking every engine as outlined above. After you have checked several engines, you will begin to develop a "mechanic's feel" for spotting defective big-end bearings.

24-10
REASSEMBLING A TWO-CYCLE ENGINE
TOP-END A sheet of installation instructions may be packaged with new piston rings. Sometimes, this information is printed on the wrapper. Before installing rings on the piston, always read the instruction sheet completely. Although you may have installed piston rings before, the instructions may contain time-saving tips, new information, and the proper procedure for installing the rings on the engine you are servicing.

NOTE Some two-cycle engines use rings of special design, such as keystone rings or Dykes rings. Always follow the installation instructions carefully to insure proper operation after the engine is assembled.

To install rings on the piston, use your thumbs or a ring expander as shown in Fig. 24-26. Start with the bottom ring. Depending on the engine, there may be four, three, or two piston rings. Some engines use only a single piston ring. Place the ring to be installed on the

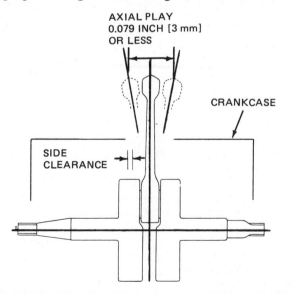

Fig. 24-25 Checking for crankpin and big-end wear. (*Yamaha Motor Company, Ltd.*)

AXIAL PLAY
0.079 INCH [3 mm]
OR LESS

CRANKCASE

SIDE
CLEARANCE

PISTON RING

RING EXPANDER

Fig. 24-26 One type of piston-ring expander for removing or installing rings on a piston.

ring expander. Check the instruction sheet to be sure that you are not installing the piston ring upside down. Rings are usually installed with the marked side facing up. Be very careful not to overexpand the ring and break it. Most rings are very brittle. Spread the ring just enough to slip over the piston head, and place the ring in its groove. Check that the ring is free in the groove after installation.

Two-cycle engines have lockpins in the piston-ring groove. A typical piston-ring lockpin is shown in Fig. 24-27. The purpose of the lockpin is to hold the ring in one position. This prevents the ring from rotating in its groove. In these engines, there is a danger that should the ring turn in its groove, the edge of the ring at the gap will catch on the ports in the cylinder. This causes the ring to break and may result in major damage to the engine. As you can see in Fig. 24-27, the lockpin is toward the top of the groove. This allows the piston ring to fit in only one way, preventing the ring from being installed upside down.

24-11
INSTALLING THE PISTON PIN After the
piston rings are installed, the next step is to install the piston pin. There are several different methods of fastening the piston to the connecting rod, as we have discussed before. In general, the pin usually is installed by reversing the procedure you followed to remove it.

Here are a couple of important tips about installing the piston and pin on two-cycle engines. The head, or top, of a piston may be flat, domed, or irregular in shape. Some pistons used in two-cycle engines have a

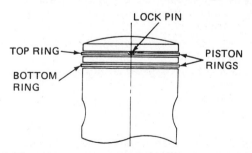

Fig. 24-27 Lockpin used to hold the piston ring in position on a two-cycle engine. (*Yamaha Motor Company, Ltd.*)

LOCK PIN

TOP RING

BOTTOM
RING

PISTON
RINGS

dome-type deflector on the piston head. One side of the dome has a very steep, almost vertical, face, or *baffle,* as shown in Fig. 24-28. The purpose of the baffle is to prevent the incoming air-fuel charge from passing directly across the top of the piston and out the exhaust ports. As the air-fuel charge strikes the baffle, the baffle deflects the air-fuel charge up the cylinder into the combustion chamber. Escape of the incoming air-fuel charge is reduced. The point to remember is that a piston of the type shown in Fig. 24-28 is installed with the baffle facing the transfer ports in the cylinder.

Some piston pins used in two-cycle engines are closed on one end and open on the other. This type of pin is installed with the closed end toward the exhaust ports.

Coat the pin, bushings, and bearings with oil. On many engines, the pin is installed by starting it about ⅛ inch [3 mm] into the pin bore in the piston. Then lower the piston over the connecting rod until the pin and the hole in the rod align. Push the pin through the rod until

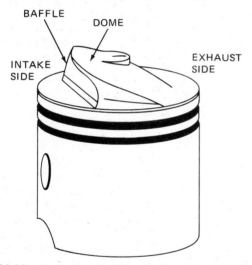

Fig. 24-28 A domed piston having a baffle deflector is installed with the deflector facing the incoming air-fuel charge.

the pin is centered between the grooves for the piston-pin locks. Use needlenose or snap-ring pliers and install new spring clips or locks in the pin lock grooves.

Check that the rings are properly positioned against each ring lockpin. On two-ring pistons, the ring end gaps will be about 180° apart.

24-12
INSTALLING THE CYLINDER
Coat the cylinder wall with oil. Remove the cloth that you placed around the connecting rod to prevent dirt from entering the crankcase. Install a new cylinder base gasket on the through bolts, and slide the gasket into place on the crankcase. Place the cylinder over the through bolts. Slide the skirt of the cylinder over the head of the piston. Use your fingers or a hinged ring compressor to compress each ring into the cylinder. When all rings are in the cylinder, slide the cylinder into place in the crankcase.

If a separate cylinder head is used, place a new head gasket on the cylinder. Then properly position the head and set it in place. Reinstall the washers and nuts on the through-bolt threads. Turn the nuts until they are finger-tight. Then use a torque wrench to torque the nuts to the manufacturer's specifications. Be sure to follow the torquing sequence recommended by the manufacturer.

Install the carburetor, being careful not to over-tighten the nuts that hold it in place. Overtightening may cause the base of the carburetor to break off. Reinstall the shrouding and all other parts removed when you began the top-end overhaul.

Check that the engine has a supply of oil and gasoline mixed to the proper ratio in the fuel tank or that the oil-injection reservoir is full. This assures ample lubrication during start-up. Then start the engine.

Some manufacturers indicate that no special break-in procedure is needed. However, operate the engine for the first few times at light load to give the piston rings and other parts a chance to seat. After 10 hours of operation, no further break-in precautions are required.

CHAPTER 24
REVIEW QUESTIONS

1. What is a top-end overhaul?
2. When is it necessary to remove the engine from the motorcycle to do a top-end overhaul?
3. While the cylinder is off of the crankcase, why should the crankcase opening be covered with a shop towel?
4. List the different ways that the piston can be removed from the connecting rod.
5. What causes the exhaust ports to clog in a two-cycle engine?
6. What three conditions of a cylinder can be checked with an inside micrometer?
7. How can you tell if a cylinder has a cast-iron liner?
8. What is the difference between a chrome-plated cylinder bore and a cast-iron liner?
9. Explain how to hone a cylinder.
10. After honing, how is the cylinder cleaned?
11. What do you do about a piston that has a broken ring land?
12. Explain how to check piston clearance.
13. Why should a wire brush never be used to clean a piston?
14. How do you check for ring-groove wear?
15. When can piston rings be reused?
16. List the types of piston rings used in two-cycle engines.
17. Describe how to check the piston-pin bearing.
18. How do you check for connecting-rod bearing wear without disassembling the engine?
19. What usually causes piston collapse?
20. Which way does the baffle on the top of the piston face during reassembly?

FOUR-CYCLE-ENGINE VALVE SERVICE

After studying this chapter,
you should be able to:

1. List six valve troubles and explain the causes of each.

2. Describe the procedure for removing the cylinder head.

3. With the proper tools and instructions, remove cylinder heads from four-cycle engines.

4. Explain how to remove, inspect, and service valves.

5. With the proper tools and instructions, service valves.

6. Service and adjust valves on various engines.

7. Service valve guides and valve seats.

8. Reassemble a four-cycle engine.

25-1 SERVICING VALVES IN FOUR-CYCLE ENGINES

In addition to the cylinder, piston, and piston-ring services discussed in Chap. 24, the four-cycle engine also may require valve-train service. This includes removing the cylinder head, removing and servicing the valves, checking and servicing valve guides as necessary, checking and servicing the camshaft and bearings, and checking and servicing the camshaft drive chain or belt. All of these services are covered in following sections.

Cleanliness in engine work is very important. A particle of dirt can cause serious trouble in the motorcycle engine. Reread 24-2 on the need for cleanliness in engine-service work.

25-2 VALVE TROUBLE DIAGNOSIS CHART

The chart that follows on p. 228 (Fig. 25-1) lists possible valve troubles, possible causes, and checks or corrections to be made.

25-3 VALVE STICKING

Valves will stick from gum or carbon deposits on the valve stem. Worn valve guides, which pass excessive amounts of oil, speed up the formation of deposits since the oil carbonizes on the hot valve stem. If the valve stem warps, it will stick in the valve guide. Warpage could result from overheating, an eccentric seat which throws pressure on one side of the valve face, or a cocked spring or retainer which puts bending pressure on the stem. Insufficient oil will also cause valve sticking. Sometimes valves will stick when the engine is cold, but work themselves free and function normally as the engine warms up.

When valves and piston rings have become so clogged with deposits that they no longer operate properly, it is usually necessary to overhaul the engine. However, some mechanics suggest the use of special compounds in the oil and fuel which help in freeing valves and rings. One of these compounds comes in a pressurized can and is sprayed into the running engine through the carburetor with the air cleaner off. When parts are not too badly worn and the major trouble seems to be from deposits, use of these compounds may postpone engine overhaul.

25-4 VALVE OVERHEATING AND BURNING

Valve overheating and burning is usually an exhaust-valve problem. Any condition that causes the valve to stick so that it does not close tightly will cause valve burning. Not only does the poor seat prevent normal valve cooling through the valve seat, but it also allows hot gases to blow by, further heating the valve. The valve is cooled through both the valve seat and the valve guide.

Poor seating or a worn guide can cause overheating and burning. Also, in a liquid-cooled engine, if the water jackets or distributing tubes in the cooling system are clogged, local hot spots may develop around valve seats. These hot spots may cause seat distortion, which then prevents normal seating and permits blowby and valve burning. Valve-seat distortion can also result from improper tightening of the cylinder-head bolts. Other conditions that prevent normal seating include a weak or cocked valve spring and insufficient valve-tappet clearance. If the tappet clearance is too closely adjusted, the valve may be held open.

On engines equipped with valve rotators, check the valve-stem tip of valves that have burned to see whether or not the rotators are working. If the tip shows no rotation or a partial rotation pattern, the rotator should be replaced.

A lean air-fuel mixture may cause exhaust-valve burning since some combustion may still be going on (the lean mixture burns slowly) when the valve opens. If a lean air-fuel mixture is the cause, the fuel system should be serviced.

Preignition and detonation, both of which produce excessively high combustion pressures and temperatures, have an adverse effect on valves and on other engine parts. They can be eliminated by cleaning out carbon, retiming the ignition, or using a higher-octane fuel.

In some persistent cases of valve-seat leakage, especially where deposits on the valve seat and face prevent adequate sealing, the use of an interference angle has proved helpful. The valve is faced at an angle 0.5° to 2° flatter than the valve-seat angle, as shown at the top of Fig. 25-2. This gives greater pressure at the lower edge of the valve seat, which tends to cut through any

Complaint	Possible cause	Check or correction
1. Valve sticking	a. Deposits on valve stem	See item 6
	b. Worn valve guide	Replace guide
	c. Warped valve stem	Replace valve
	d. Insufficient oil	Service lubricating system; add oil
	e. Cold-engine operation	Valves free up as engine warms up
	f. Overheating valves	See item 2
2. Valve burning	a. Valve sticking	See item 1
	b. Distorted valve seat	Check cooling system; tighten cylinder-head bolts
	c. Valve-tappet clearance too small	Readjust
	d. Valve spring cocked or worn	Replace
	e. Overheated engine	Check cooling system
	f. Lean air-fuel mixture	Service fuel system
	g. Preignition	Clean carbon from engine; use cooler plugs
	h. Detonation	Adjust ignition timing; use higher-octane fuel
	i. Valve-seat leakage	Use an interference angle
	j. Overloaded engine	Reduce load or try heavy-duty valves
	k. Valve-stem stretching from strong spring or overheated engine	Use weaker spring; eliminate overheating
3. Valve breakage	a. Valve overheating	See item 2
	b. Detonation	Adjust ignition timing; use higher-octane fuel; clean carbon from engine
	c. Excessive tappet clearance	Readjust
	d. Seat eccentric to stem	Service
	e. Cocked spring or retainer	Service
	f. Scratches on stem from improper cleaning	Avoid scratching stem when cleaning valves
4. Valve-face wear	a. Excessive tappet clearance	Readjust
	b. Dirt on valve face	Check air cleaner
	c. See also causes listed under item 2	
5. Valve-seat recession	a. Valve face cuts valve seat away	Use coated valves and valve-seat inserts
6. Valve deposits	a. Gum in fuel (intake valve)	Use proper fuel
	b. Carbon from rich mixture (intake valve)	Service fuel system
	c. Worn valve guides	Replace
	d. Carbon from poor combustion (exhaust valve)	Service fuel, ignition system, or engine as necessary
	e. Dirty or wrong oil	Service lubricating system; replace oil

Fig. 25-1 Valve trouble diagnosis chart for four-cycle engines.

deposits that have formed and thereby establishes a good seal.

Figure 25-2 illustrates one manufacturer's recommendation for the valve and seat angles to get interference. Note that this manufacturer does not recommend an interference angle on stellite-faced exhaust valves and induction-hardened exhaust-valve seats. These surfaces are so hard that no appreciable improvement in seating would be obtained by use of an interference angle.

Any condition that causes the engine to labor hard or overheat will also overheat the valves. If the engine must be operated under heavy load and this causes valve trouble, heavy-duty valves should be installed.

In some engines, valve stems have been found to stretch because of a combination of heavy springs and overheating. Lighter springs should be used and the overheating eliminated.

25-5
VALVE BREAKAGE Any condition that causes the valve to overheat or to be subjected to heavy pounding, as from excessive detonation or tappet clearance, may cause valves to break. Excessive tappet

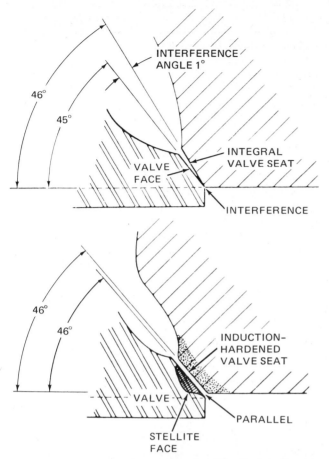

Fig. 25-2 Valve and valve-seat angles. Top, the interference angle recommended for many intake and exhaust valves and seat. Bottom, the parallel faces recommended for some stellite-faced exhaust valves and induction-hardened exhaust-valve seats.

clearance permits heavy impact seating. If the seat is eccentric to the stem or if the valve spring or retainer is cocked, then the valve will be subjected to side movement or pressure every time it seats. This may cause the valve to fatigue and break. If the stem has been scratched during cleaning, the scratch may serve as a starting point for a crack and a break in the stem.

25-6
VALVE-FACE WEAR   In addition to the conditions discussed earlier, excessive tappet clearance or dirt on the valve face or seat can cause valve-face wear. Excessive tappet clearance causes heavy impact seating that is wearing on the valve and may cause valve breakage. Dirt may cause valve-face wear if the engine operates in dusty conditions or if the carburetor air cleaner is not functioning properly. The dirt enters the engine with the air-fuel mixture, and some dirt deposits on the valve seat. The dirt will also cause bearing, cylinder-wall, piston, and ring wear.

25-7
VALVE-SEAT RECESSION   Valve-seat recession is caused by the wearing away of the valve seat. This is produced by the action of the valve face which,

under certain conditions, can cut the seating surface of the valve seat. Valve-seat recession has become more of a problem in recent years because lead has been removed from gasoline. Lead additives in the gasoline form a lubricant between the valve face and the valve seat. This lubricant prevents iron particles that flake off the valve seat from sticking on the valve face. Without the lead coating, the particles build up into tiny bumps or warts, which gradually cut away the valve seat, as shown in Fig. 25-3. The resulting valve-seat recession causes lash loss, or a decrease in valve-tappet clearance. As the valve gradually cuts into the valve seat, clearance in the valve train is reduced. In an engine using mechanical valve lifters, the result can be a complete loss of clearance so that the valve can no longer close completely. The result will be valve and valve-seat burning.

To prevent valve-seat recession in engines run on lead-free gasoline, the valves are given a very thin coating of aluminum or other metal. This coating, less than 0.002 inch [0.051 mm] in thickness, prevents the iron particles from adhering to the valve face and prevents valve-seat recession. The coating gives the valve face a dull, almost rough, appearance. The natural tendency for the mechanic would be to reface the valve. However, this must not be done. Coated valves should not be refaced or lapped. Doing so would remove the coating and deny the valve seat the protection produced by the coating. The result could be very short valve and valve-seat life.

25-8
VALVE DEPOSITS   If the fuel has excessive amounts of gum in it, some of this gum may deposit on the intake valve as the air-fuel mixture passes the valve on the way to the engine cylinder. Carbon deposits may form either from an excessively rich mixture or from oil passing a worn intake valve guide. Improper combustion due to a rich mixture, a defective ignition system, loss of compression in the engine, a cold engine, and so on will result in carbon deposits on the exhaust valves. Dirty or improper oil will cause deposits to form on the valves.

25-9
STAINLESS-STEEL VALVES   For extra-heavy-duty performance, some motorcycle technicians recommend stainless-steel valves. These valves are

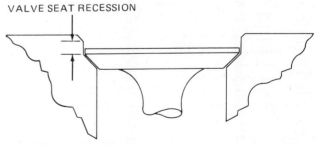

Fig. 25-3 Valve-seat recession can occur in some engines operating on lead-free fuel.

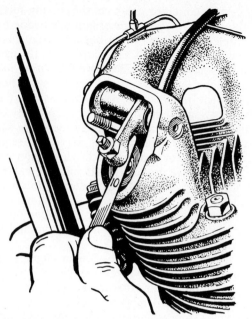

Fig. 25-4 Adjusting valve-tappet clearance on an overhead-valve engine. (*Norton Triumph Corporation*)

lighter and stronger than standard valves. Also, the valve stems are chrome plated for improved wear resistance under extreme operating conditions.

25-10
VALVE SERVICE In servicing valves, several components must be checked. These include valves, valve seats and guides, valve springs and retainers,

rocker-arm mechanisms (in overhead-valve engines), valve tappets, camshaft, camshaft drive, and bearings.

The service jobs on valves include adjusting valve-tappet clearances (also called *adjusting valve lash*), grinding valves and valve seats, installing new seat inserts (on engines so equipped), cleaning or replacing valve guides, removing and checking the camshaft, servicing camshaft bearings, and timing the valves.

25-11
ADJUSTING VALVE-LIFTER CLEARANCE
The procedure for checking and adjusting valve-tappet, or valve-lifter, clearance (or adjusting valve lash) varies with the type and model of the engine. Some engines with hydraulic valve lifters normally require no clearance adjustment. Others require checking and adjustment whenever valve-service work is performed. The following procedures are typical.

25-12
OVERHEAD-VALVE ENGINES WITH ROCKER ARMS Most specifications call for making the check with the engine cold and not running. First, remove the valve cover. Measure the clearance between the valve stem and the rocker arm, as shown in Fig. 25-4. The clearance is measured with the valve lifter, or rocker arm, on the base circle of the cam. Turn the crankshaft until the base circle of the cam is under the valve lifter.

There are two kinds of rocker arms. One is shaft-mounted and the other is mounted on a ball stud. The shaft-mounted type usually has an adjustment screw. This screw is normally self-locking and does not require

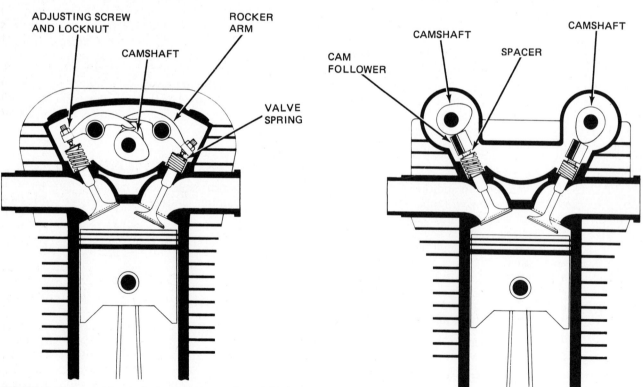

Fig. 25-5 Valve-and-camshaft arrangement for a SOHC engine and for a DOHC engine. (*Honda Motor Company, Ltd.*)

a locking nut. Use a box wrench to turn the adjustment screw and adjust the clearance to specifications. Do not use an open-end wrench. This could damage the screw head.

On ball-stud-mounted rocker arms, turn the self-locking rocker-arm stud nut to make the adjustment. Turning the nut down reduces clearance.

25-13 OVERHEAD-CAMSHAFT ENGINES

OHC (overhead camshaft) engines have several arrangements for carrying the cam action to the valve stems. In some engines, cam action is carried directly to the valve stem through a cap, called the *valve tappet*. This cap fits over the valve stem and spring. In other engines, the cam action is carried through a rocker arm. Checks and adjustments are made with the engine cold. This means that the engine has cooled overnight or has not been operated for at least 4 hours.

Figure 25-5 shows two arrangements that are used to actuate the valves by means of an overhead camshaft. In some engines the cam operates the valve directly. Other engines use rocker arms to transfer cam motion to the valve. When only one camshaft is used, as shown in the left illustration of Fig. 25-5, the engine is identified as having a single overhead camshaft. This is often abbreviated SOHC. When an engine has two camshafts, one camshaft to operate the intake valves and a second camshaft to operate the exhaust valves, the engine is known as a DOHC (double overhead-camshaft) engine.

A valve-clearance adjustment on an overhead-camshaft engine using rocker arms is made in the same manner as for the overhead-valve engine shown in Fig. 25-4. The adjustment is made with the piston at TDC on the compression stroke, when both valves are closed.

Most engines have timing marks indicating this position. However, in a four-cycle engine, when the timing marks line up, the engine could be at TDC ending the compression stroke or at TDC ending the exhaust stroke. A quick way to tell if the valves are in position to adjust or if the engine should be cranked one complete revolution, is to wiggle the rocker arms up and down. Both should have a slight amount of free movement up and down. If either rocker arm is tight, then turn the engine one full revolution.

On multicylinder engines, crank the engine until the piston in each cylinder is in the proper position for valve adjustment.

Insert a feeler gauge of the specified thickness in the space between the rocker arm and the valve stem, as shown in Fig. 25-6. If the gauge goes in with a slight drag, the valve has the proper clearance. However, if the gauge won't go in, the valve does not have enough clearance. When the gauge slips through the space freely with no resistance, the clearance is excessive and must be reduced.

The adjuster and locknut on many rocker arms can be set using a wrench and a screwdriver. This is the method shown in Fig. 25-4. Some engines require a special adjusting wrench, as shown in Fig. 25-6, to fit the rocker-arm adjuster. To set the clearance, first use a

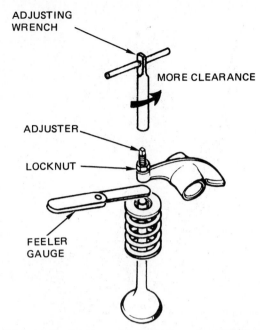

Fig. 25-6 Adjusting the valve clearance on an OHC engine that has rocker arms. (*Honda Motor Company, Ltd.*)

wrench to loosen the locknut. Then, use the adjusting wrench to make the clearance adjustment. Basically, the adjuster is a machine screw. Turning it clockwise lengthens the distance the screw sticks out below the rocker arm. This reduces the clearance. Turning the adjuster counterclockwise increases the clearance between the end of the screw and the valve stem.

When you feel a slight drag on the feeler gauge while turning the adjuster, the clearance is correct. Remove the feeler gauge, and tighten the locknut. Then, recheck the clearance again. Sometimes tightening the locknut changes the clearance slightly.

On some engines, the cam works directly on a valve tappet that fits over the end of the valve stem, as shown to the right in Fig. 25-5 and in Figs. 25-7 and 25-8. On this type, the adjustment is made by changing the tappet shim (9 in Fig. 25-8).

25-14 REMOVING THE CYLINDER HEAD

Removing the cylinder head of a four-cycle engine is a little more complicated than removing the head from a two-cycle engine. The typical motorcycle four-cycle engine has the valves and camshaft in the head. As a first step, remove all parts and disconnect all wires that would interfere with head removal. Release the camshaft chain or belt tensioner so the chain or belt can be taken off the camshaft sprocket or pulley. Then slightly loosen all cylinder-head bolts to ease the tension on the head.

Remove the bolts and take off the head. If the head sticks, work it loose by tapping it with a soft hammer. Do not pry it off if you can help it. If you do have to use a pry bar, use it carefully to avoid scratching or denting the mating surfaces. Lift off the head and put it on a clean piece of wood or cardboard.

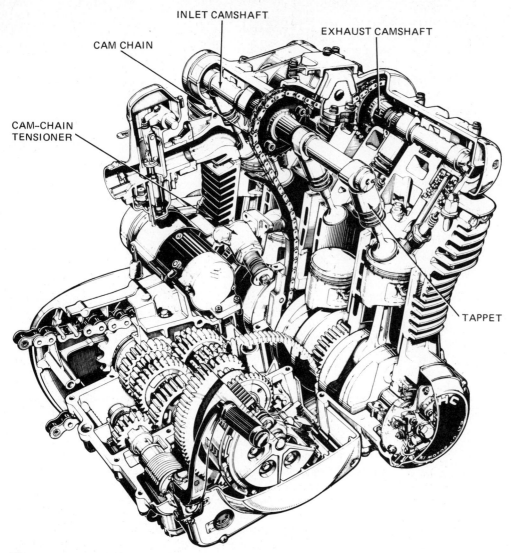

INLET CAMSHAFT

EXHAUST CAMSHAFT

CAM CHAIN

CAM-CHAIN
TENSIONER

TAPPET

Fig. 25-7 Cutaway view of a four-cylinder four-cycle engine with double-overhead camshafts, showing how the tappets are in direct contact with the cams. (*Suzuki Motor Company, Ltd.*)

NOTE Never remove a cylinder head from a hot engine. Wait until the engine cools. If the head is removed hot, it might warp so it cannot be used again.

25-15
REMOVING THE VALVES   First, take off the rocker arms and camshaft or camshafts. Also remove the valve tappets if present (Fig. 25-8). Next, use a valve-spring compressor as shown in Fig. 25-9 to compress the valve springs. With a spring compressed, you can remove the valve locks, valve-spring retainer, spring or springs, valve oil seal, and valve guide ring (Figs. 25-9 and 25-10).

Do not interchange parts between valves or cylinders. Use a rack like the one shown in Fig. 25-11 to keep valves and other parts in proper order.

25-16
SERVICING VALVES   Valves should be inspected for wear, burned spots, pits, cracks, and other

damage. If the valve face appears to be in good condition but worn, it can be refaced on the valve-refacing machine. Figure 25-12 shows the valve parts to be checked. If a valve appears to be in good condition except for needing refacing, put it back into the valve rack.

NOTE   Not all valves can be refaced. Some valve faces are made of stellite or coated with some other material that must not be removed. Do not attempt to grind or reface these valves. Refer to the manufacturer's service manual for valve-refacing instructions and specifications.

After all valves are inspected, service one valve at a time. First, clean the carbon off the valve with a wire wheel.

CAUTION   Wear goggles when using the wire wheel. Particles of metal can fly off the wheel. You must protect your eyes from these particles.

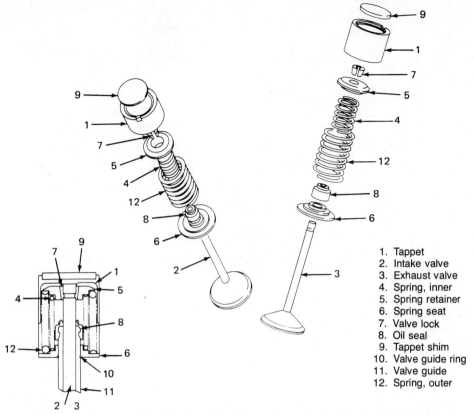

1. Tappet
2. Intake valve
3. Exhaust valve
4. Spring, inner
5. Spring retainer
6. Spring seat
7. Valve lock
8. Oil seal
9. Tappet shim
10. Valve guide ring
11. Valve guide
12. Spring, outer

Fig. 25-8 Exploded view of the valve train of an engine with direct-acting tappets. (*Suzuki Motor Company, Ltd.*)

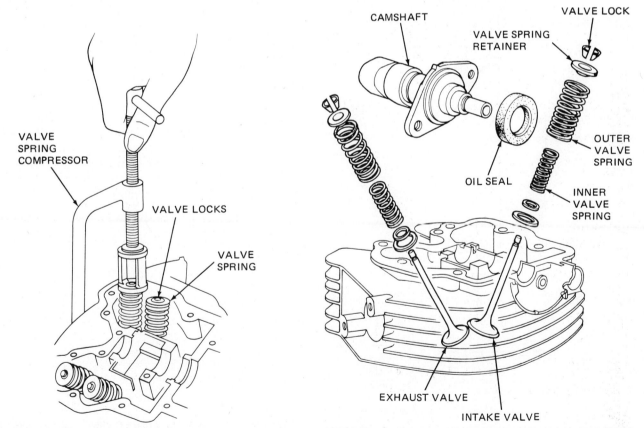

Fig. 25-9 Using a valve-spring compressor. (*Honda Motor Company, Ltd.*)

Fig. 25-10 Valve retainer, spring, and other parts assembled on the valve stem.

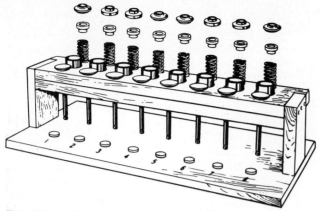

Fig. 25-11 Valve rack for holding valves and valve-train parts.

Next, if the valve appears to be in good condition, reface the valve in the valve machine (Fig. 25-13). Follow the instructions supplied by the machine manufacturer. The chuck should be set to grind the valve face at the angle specified by the engine manufacturer. The first cut should be a light one. If this cut removes metal from

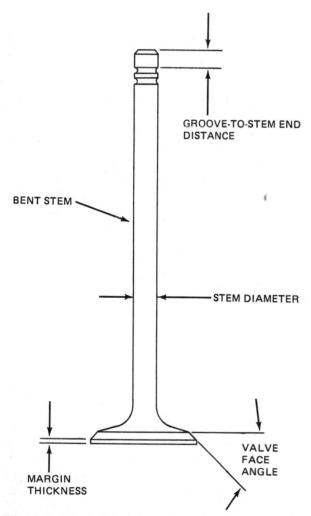

Fig. 25-12 Parts of the valve to be checked. For the dimensions, refer to the manufacturer's specifications.

GROOVE-TO-STEM END DISTANCE

BENT STEM

STEM DIAMETER

MARGIN THICKNESS

VALVE FACE ANGLE

CHUCK FOR VALVE

GRINDING WHEEL

Fig. 25-13 Valve-refacing machine, also called a *valve grinder* or a *valve refacer*. (*Black and Decker Manufacturing Company*)

only half or a third of the valve face, the valve may not be centered in the chuck. Or the valve stem may be bent, in which case the valve must be discarded.

Cuts, after the first one, should remove only enough metal to true up the surface and remove pits. Do not take heavy cuts. If so much metal must be removed that the margin is lost (Fig. 25-14), discard the valve. Loss of the margin will cause the valve to run hot, and it will soon fail.

NOTE If new valves are required, they will not need to be refaced. Seating should be checked, however. Never reface or lap coated valves.

If the tip end of a valve is rough or worn unevenly, it can be polished in the valve-refacing machine (Fig. 25-15). The attachment allows you to swing the valve end across the side of the grinding wheel while slowly rotating the valve. This produces a slight crown, or rounded end. One recommendation is to grind off the

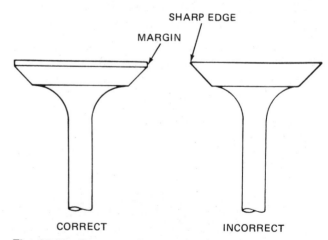

SHARP EDGE

MARGIN

CORRECT

INCORRECT

Fig. 25-14 Correct and incorrect valve-face grinding. The valve to the right has no margin and would soon fail. (*TRW, Inc.*)

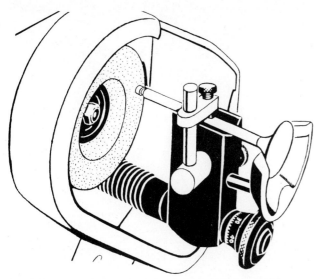

Fig. 25-15 Grinding the tip-end of a valve stem. (*Snap-on Tools Corporation*)

same amount from the stem that you ground off the valve face. That way, you make up for the amount the valve sinks into the valve seat as a result of face grinding.

25-17
CHECKING THE VALVE SPRINGS AND TAPPETS Valve springs should be tested for proper tension and for squareness. A valve-spring tester, shown in Fig. 25-16, is required to check spring tension. The pressure required to compress the spring to the proper length should be measured. Then, the spring should be checked for squareness, as shown in Fig. 25-17. Stand the spring on a surface plate and hold a steel square next to it. Rotate the spring slowly against the square and see whether the top coil moves away from the square. If the spring is excessively out of square or lacks sufficient tension, discard it.

Check the valve-tappet faces which ride on the cams for roughness or wear. The tappet must not be worn concave, or dished in. Check the adjusting-screw head which is in contact with the valve stem, or the stem end of the tappet on tappets which do not have adjusting screws, for wear. If you find wear or roughness, install new tappets.

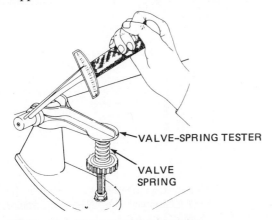

Fig. 25-16 Checking valve-spring tension.

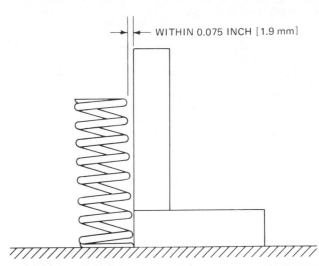

WITHIN 0.075 INCH [1.9 mm]

Fig. 25-17 Checking valve-spring squareness. (*Kawasaki Heavy Industries, Ltd.*)

25-18
SERVICING VALVE GUIDES The valve guide must be clean and in good condition for normal valve seating. It must be serviced before the valve seats are ground if grinding is required. As a first step, the valve guide should be cleaned with a wire brush or adjustable-blade cleaner. Then the valve guide should be checked for wear. If it is worn, it requires service. The type of service depends on whether the guide is replaceable or integral. If it is replaceable, the old guide should be pressed out. Then a new guide should be installed and reamed to size.

When installing a new guide, some mechanics recommend heating the head so it will expand. This makes guide installation easier. If the guide is integral, it can be serviced by reaming it to a larger size and installing a valve with an oversize stem.

The valve guide may wear bellmouthed or oval-shaped because the valve tends to wobble as it opens and closes. The bellmouth wear shown in Fig. 25-18, is exaggerated. A small-hole gauge will detect oval or bellmouth wear. The split ball is adjusted until it is a light drag fit at the point being checked. Then, the split ball is measured with a micrometer. By checking the guide at various points, any eccentricity will be detected.

25-19
GRINDING VALVE SEATS Valve seats are of two types. The integral type is actually the cylinder head. The insert type is a ring of special metal set into the head. Grinding valve seats is described below.

If the valve seat is worn, burned, pitted, or otherwise damaged, it should be trued with a valve-seat grinder or a valve-seat cutter (Fig. 25-19). If the seat is so badly worn or burned that it will not clean up, it is possible to counterbore the seat and install a seat insert.

As a first step in grinding a valve seat, make sure that the valve guide is in good condition. The reason for this is that the seat grinding stone is centered in the valve guide. We explained how to check and service valve guides in the previous section.

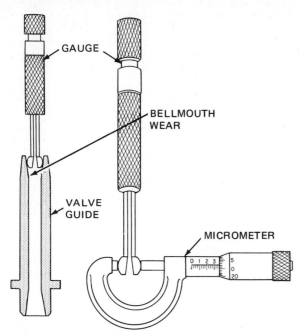

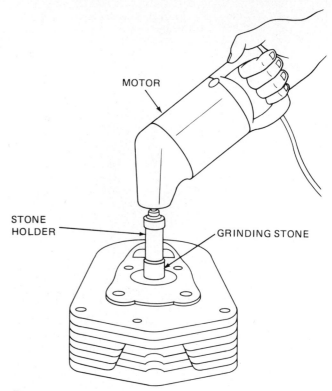

Fig. 25-18 A small-hole gauge is the most accurate device for measuring valve-guide wear. The gauge is adjusted so that the split ball is a drag fit in the guide (left). Then the split ball can be measured with the micrometer (right).

Fig. 25-20 Grinding a valve seat. (*ATW*)

The valve-seat grinder rotates a grinding stone of the proper shape on the valve seat, as shown in Fig. 25-20. The stone is kept concentric with the valve seat by a pilot installed in the valve guide, as shown in Fig. 25-21. This means that the valve guide must be cleaned and serviced before the valve seat is ground. In operation, an electric or air-powered motor rotates the grinding stone at high speed to smooth the seat. The angle of the

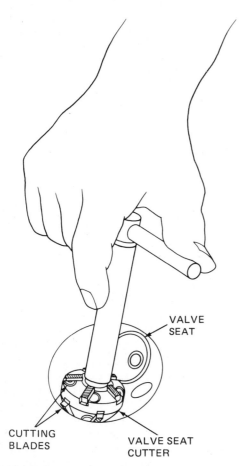

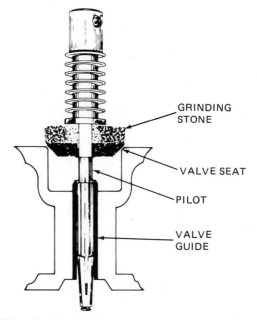

Fig. 25-19 Using a valve-seat cutter with carbide blades to recondition a valve seat. (*Neway Manufacturing, Inc.*)

Fig. 25-21 Pilot on which the grinding stone rotates. The pilot keeps the stone concentric with the valve seat. (*Black and Decker Manufacturing Company*)

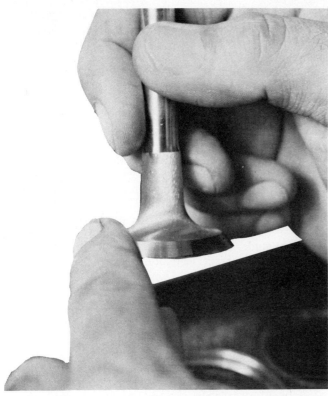

Fig. 25-22 Applying lapping compound to the valve face. (*TRW, Inc.*)

stone determines the angle to which the seat will be ground. This angle matches the angle to which the valve face is ground in the valve-refacing machine.

NOTE Follow the operating instructions furnished by the valve-seat-grinder manufacturer. The grinding stone must be dressed frequently with the diamond-tipped dressing tool.

After the valve seat is ground, it may be too wide. It must be narrowed with upper and lower grinding stones to grind away the upper and lower edges of the seat. A steel scale can be used to measure the valve-seat width.

Fig. 25-23 Using a valve-lapping tool to check and improve the fit of the valve face to the valve seat. (*ATW*)

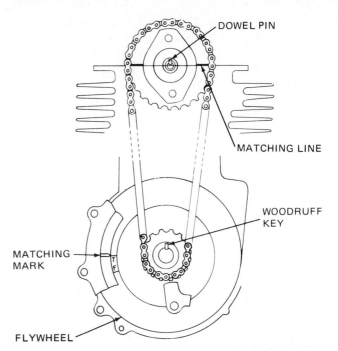

Fig. 25-24 One method of timing valves. (*Honda Motor Company, Ltd.*)

Some engine manufacturers recommend that after the valve and valve seat are ground, the two should be lapped together to check and perfect the fit. Lapping compound is an abrasive paste that comes in a tube or a small can. To use it place a small amount on your finger.

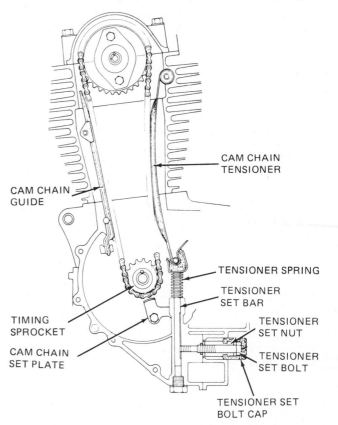

Fig. 25-25 Adjusting the cam-chain tensioner. (*Honda Motor Company, Ltd.*)

237

Then apply the lapping compound to the valve face as shown in Fig. 25-22. When there is a light coat of lapping compound around the entire valve face, place the valve in its proper guide.

To lap the valve, a lapping tool is used. It is a turning device or stick with a small rubber suction cup on one end which holds to the valve head. The stick-type lapping tool is rotated back and forth between your hands several times while lightly bouncing the valve up and down. This operation is shown in Fig. 25-23. Remove the valve from the guide and wipe the valve face clean with a cloth. After the lapping operation is completed, the valve seat and valve must be thoroughly cleaned to remove all traces of the lapping compound.

25-20 REASSEMBLING THE ENGINE

When reinstalling the cylinder head, tighten the cylinder-head bolts in the proper sequence, as shown by the diagram in the manufacturer's shop manual. Run through the tightening sequence several times. Each time bring the bolts down tighter until they are tightened to the proper torque.

When reinstalling the chain or belt, make sure you locate the sprockets properly so that the valves are timed correctly. Figure 25-24 shows one method of timing the valves. The T mark on the flywheel is aligned with the matching mark on the left-hand crankcase cover. Then the matching line on the cam sprocket is aligned with the upper-end face of the cylinder head, with the camshaft dowel pin facing upward.

The cam-chain tensioner is then adjusted, after it is installed (Fig. 25-25), as follows. The piston must be at TDC on the compression stroke. Slightly rotate the timing sprocket counterclockwise to apply tension to the chain guide. Loosen the tensioner set bolt. Chain tension is then correct. Retighten the tensioner set bolt and nut.

CHAPTER 25
REVIEW QUESTIONS

1. What is the biggest difference between servicing a two-cycle engine and servicing a four-cycle engine?
2. Describe the procedure for adjusting the valves on an OHC engine that has the cam lobes operating directly on the valves.
3. How do you remove the mushroomed end of a valve stem so the valve can be removed?
4. Why should the cylinder head never be removed until after the engine has cooled?
5. What tool is used to compress valve springs so that the locks and retainers can be removed?
6. What is the margin of a valve?
7. During the use of the valve-refacing machine, what tool must be used periodically to ensure that the face of the grinding wheel is clean, straight, and smooth?
8. Explain how to service the tip end of the valve stem.
9. How are valve guides checked?
10. Why are valve guides serviced before the valve seats are refinished?
11. What are the two general types of valve guides?
12. What is the interference angle?
13. How do you lap a valve?
14. Why must the timing marks on the camshaft and crankshaft be aligned during installation of the camshaft?
15. Can a valve tappet be reused if it is dished in on the face that rides against the cam lobe?
16. Where do you find the bolt-tightening sequence to use when installing the bolts in a cylinder head?
17. Should new valves be refaced on the valve-refacing machine before installation?
18. What causes a valve to stick?
19. What causes a valve to burn?
20. What causes a valve to break?

CHAPTER **26**

ENGINE CYLINDER AND CRANKSHAFT SERVICE

After studying this chapter,
you should be able to:

1. Inspect and refinish the cylinder.

2. Remove and install the engine in a motorcycle.

3. Disassemble and assemble the crankcase.

4. Replace the connecting rod and bearing.

5. Inspect and replace the crankshaft bearings.

6. Replace crankcase oil seals.

7. Inspect and replace the reed valve.

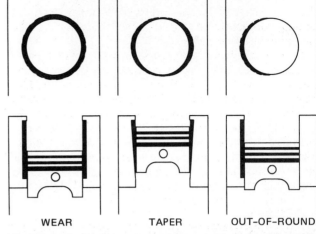

WEAR   TAPER   OUT-OF-ROUND

Fig. 26-2 Cylinder wear, taper, and out-of-roundness. (*ATW*)

26-1 INSPECTING THE CYLINDER

As a first step in servicing the cylinder, clean and inspect it as explained in ☑ 24-6. Then do whatever refinishing is required.

Examine the cylinder for cracks, stripped threads in the bolt holes, broken fins, and scores or other damage in the cylinder bore. Any of these require replacement of the cylinder. Sometimes stripped threads can be repaired by installing a thread insert, as shown in Fig. 26-1. The repair is made by drilling out the damaged threads. Then the hole is tapped with a special tap that comes with the repair kit. Finally, a threaded insert is screwed into the hole to bring it back to its original thread size.

If the cylinder appears to be in good condition, use an inside micrometer or a cylinder-bore gauge to check the cylinder bore for wear, taper, and out-of-round (Fig. 26-2). A telescoping gauge and an outside micrometer can also be used to check the cylinder bore (Fig. 24-17). Take the measurements at several places, as shown in Fig. 24-18.

Some engines have cylinders of aluminum with cast-iron liners (Fig. 24-19). The cast-iron liner serves as the bore and the wearing surface. Cast iron wears very little

compared with aluminum. When you find a cylinder of this type, check to see if the cast-iron liner has worked loose. A loose liner causes piston and cylinder over-heating. The heat cannot escape easily if the liner is loose. If there are blue spots on the bore (from the cast iron overheating) or if the liner is loose, discard the cylinder.

Other engines have chrome-plated cylinder bores. Chrome is harder and wears less than cast iron. You can identify chrome-plated cylinders by their shiny appearance. These cylinders cannot be refinished. If they show signs of wear or scoring, replace the cylinder.

26-2 REFINISHING THE CYLINDER

If the cylinder is scored, worn, tapered, or out-of-round, it must be bored or honed to a larger size so that a larger piston and rings can be installed. Pistons are supplied in standard oversizes, such as 0.010, 0.020, 0.030, and 0.040 inch [0.25, 0.50, 0.75, and 1.00 mm]. The cylinder, unless it is a chrome-plated cylinder, must be refinished to take one of these *standard oversize pistons*. Chrome-plated cylinders cannot be refinished.

Figure 24-20 shows the honing procedure for a cylinder of a one-cylinder two-cycle engine with a detach-able cylinder head. The honing should be done from the crankcase end of the cylinder. Honing also is done in a drill press and in special shop hones that have fixtures for holding the cylinder. Follow the instructions supplied by the hone manufacturer for installation of the hone in the cylinder, operating speed, and lubrication. Remove the hone and measure the cylinder periodically so you do not remove too much metal.

When the cylinder is within approximately 0.002 inch [0.05 mm] of the desired size, change to fine stones to finish the honing operation. Usually, rough honing is done with 60-grit stones. Finish honing is done with 220-grit stones. When the honing job is finished, the cylinder wall should have a *crosshatch pattern*, as shown in Fig. 26-3. This finish requires that the hone be moved up and down at the proper rate while it is rotating at the specified speed.

A one-piece cylinder-block-and-head assembly should be machine-bored and not honed when cylinder-

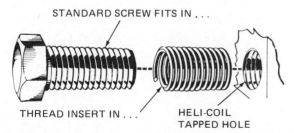

STANDARD SCREW FITS IN . . .

THREAD INSERT IN . . .   HELI-COIL TAPPED HOLE

Fig. 26-1 Installing a threaded insert to replace damaged threads. (*Heli-Coil Products Division of Mitre Corporation*)

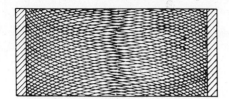

Fig. 26-3 Crosshatch appearance of a properly honed cylinder bore.

bore oversizing is necessary. However, when cylinder oversizing is not necessary, use the hone to break the glaze on the cylinder wall. Roughen the cylinder wall slightly by running the hone through the cylinder several times. This will help new piston rings seat faster in a rebuilt engine.

NOTE The cylinder wall must be cleaned very carefully after honing. This is to remove all particles of grit and metal that may have become embedded in the cylinder wall. The best way to clean the cylinder wall is to use soap and water with clean rags. Wash the cylinder wall thoroughly or until you can rub a clean cloth on it without getting the cloth dirty. Then dry the cylinder wall and coat it with engine oil. Do not use kerosene or gasoline to clean the cylinder wall. They will not remove all the grit.

If the cylinder wall is damaged or if the wear is too great to be cleaned up by honing, the cylinder must be bored. This requires the use of a fixture to hold the

cylinder and a boring machine, or *boring bar* (Fig. 26-4). The size to which the cylinder is rebored depends on the amount of metal that must be removed from the cylinder wall. It also depends on the sizes of oversize pistons available.

26-3
REMOVING AND INSTALLING THE ENGINE
Many service jobs can be performed on the engine with it in the motorcycle. Other jobs, such as work on the crankshaft bearings, require removal of the engine from the frame. Specific removal procedures vary. Always check the manufacturer's service manual for the motorcycle you are servicing before starting the job. There is a great deal of difference between trying to remove a small single-cylinder engine and trying to remove a large multicylinder engine. The steps that follow are a typical procedure. However, each step does not apply to all motorcycles.

1. Remove all dirt, mud, dust, and grease from the frame of the motorcycle and from the outside of the engine. This will make removal easier and prevent any dirt from entering the engine.
2. Place the motorcycle on its center stand, or place a stand under it.
3. Drain the cooling system, including the cylinder block (on liquid-cooled engines).
4. Disconnect the battery and remove it, if necessary.
5. Drain the crankcase oil, and remove the oil filter, if necessary (on four-cycle engines).
6. Check that the fuel valve is turned to OFF. Then remove the fuel line to the carburetor.
7. Remove the fuel tank and seat, if necessary.
8. Disconnect the exhaust pipe.
9. Remove the foot rests, if necessary.
10. Remove the shift lever and left crankcase cover, if necessary.

BORING BAR

CYLINDER-HOLDING FIXTURE

CYLINDER BLOCK

Fig. 26-4 Using a boring bar to bore a cylinder held in a holding fixture. (*Kwik-Way Manufacturing Company*)

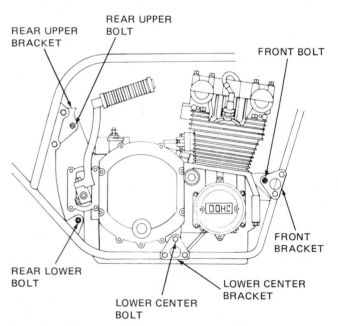

REAR UPPER BRACKET

REAR UPPER BOLT

FRONT BOLT

FRONT BRACKET

REAR LOWER BOLT

LOWER CENTER BOLT

LOWER CENTER BRACKET

Fig. 26-5 Brackets and bolts that attach the engine to the frame of the motorcycle. (*Kawasaki Heavy Industries, Ltd.*)

11. Remove the master link from the drive chain, and remove the chain from its sprocket on the engine.
12. Disconnect the compression-release cable (on some two-cycle engines), starter cable, ignition wiring, and all other wires to the engine.
13. Disconnect the throttle cable from the linkage at the carburetor. Drain the oil tank and disconnect the oil line and cable from the oil pump (on two-cycle engines). If necessary, remove the oil pump.
14. Remove the spark-plug caps from the spark plugs, and disconnect the tachometer cable and clutch cable.
15. Remove the carburetor and air cleaner.
16. Remove the mount bolts and remove the engine from the frame. Typical mounting brackets and bolts are shown in Fig. 26-5. If you are removing a large multicylinder engine, taking off the cylinder head and cylinders first will make the engine lighter and easier to handle. Head and cylinder removal is covered in Chap. 24.

Engine installation is essentially the reverse of the removal procedure.

26-4 SERVICING THE ENGINE-CASE ASSEMBLY

In most motorcycle engines, the engine-case assembly includes the crankcase, crankshaft, transmission, kick starter, magneto cover, and shifter.

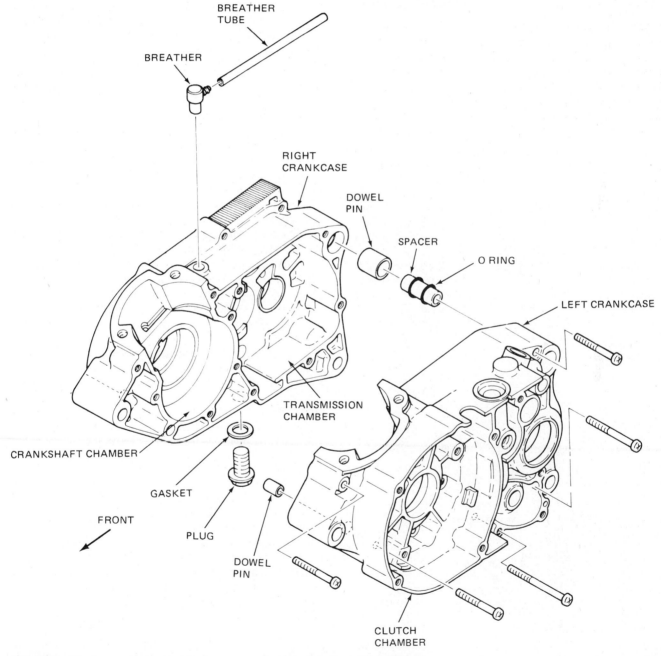

Fig. 26-6 The two crankcase halves for a one-cylinder two-cycle engine. (*Yamaha Motor Corporation*)

If a complete engine overhaul is required, then the top-end work described in Chaps. 24 and 25 must also be performed. Following sections in this chapter discuss the jobs that are performed after the engine is out of the frame. These include disassembling and assembling the crankcase and servicing connecting-rod bearings, crankshaft main bearings, crankcase reed valves, and oil seals and gaskets.

26-5 DISASSEMBLING THE CRANKCASE

To perform almost any service on the crankshaft and bearings, the crankcase of the motorcycle engine must be split apart. The crankcase is made in two pieces and then, after the crankshaft, transmission, and other parts are installed, the crankcase halves are bolted together.

The crankcase on most single-cylinder engines splits along the vertical center line into a right and left half (Fig. 26-6). For many multicylinder motorcycle engines, the crankcase splits horizontally into a top and bottom section (Fig. 26-7). The cylinders are bolted to the top section.

Before attempting to disassemble the crankcase, refer to the manufacturer's service manual for the motorcycle you are servicing. There is some variation in the steps required on different engines. Special pullers or case separators may be needed to prevent damage to the cases.

The motorcycle-engine crankcase is made of aluminum alloy, which must be handled carefully. You cannot pound on the cases with a hammer. Crankcase halves are put together with liquid sealer, positioned by dowel pins, and tightened with screws.

In the two-cycle engine, the crankcase consists of the crankshaft chamber and the transmission chamber (Fig. 26-6). The transmission chamber connects with the clutch chamber, which is on the outside of the left crankcase (Fig. 26-6). Both chambers contain a spec-

ified amount of oil to provide lubrication and cooling for the transmission and clutch.

The top of the transmission chamber has a breather hole. Its purpose is to release any pressure that could build up inside when the temperature rises. When the crankcase is assembled, it must be accurately positioned to hold the crankshaft, transmission output shaft, and other parts in proper alignment. The details of removing the parts necessary to split the crankcase are given in Chap. 28. On many engines, the crankcase separating tool is used to remove the crankshaft from the case.

26-6 CONNECTING-ROD SERVICE

The rod big-end bearing can be checked for looseness while it is still attached to the crankshaft, as explained in 24-9. The rod small end may have a needle bearing or a bushing (Fig. 2-12). If the bushing or sleeve bearing is worn, it can be replaced in many rods. In other rods, the bushing can be reamed to a larger size and an oversize pin fitted. In some engines, the bushing is not serviceable and, if worn, the rod is replaced.

In many motorcycle engines, a built-up crankshaft is used (Fig. 2-12b). In these, the crankshaft, connecting rod, and rod big-end bearing may be replaced as an assembly. The big-end bearing usually is the needle type. Other engines have needle bearings in the rod big end which can be replaced.

26-7 CLEANING AND INSPECTING CASE COMPONENTS

After disassembling the crankcase, as shown in Fig. 26-8, wash each part (except the seals) in solvent. Then dry the parts with air or a clean cloth. Be sure to clean the crankshaft-bearing oil passage in the case and the transmission breather. Remove all traces of gasket sealer from the mating faces of the case halves.

Inspect the ball bearings for wear by placing each bearing face down on a clean bench. Then hold both the inner and outer races with your fingers and try to push the bearing retainer and balls around with a wood stick. If the retainer and balls can be slipped between the races, replace the bearing.

Check the bearings for galled or pitted conditions by rotating the bearing with your fingers. If the bearing action is rough or catchy, replace the bearing.

Inspect the crankcases for cracks. Replace the case if any cracks are found around the bearing bores. Then check that the crankcase mating surfaces are clean and free of any damage such as gouges or dents that would prevent an oil-tight case-to-case seal on reassembly. Replace the case if any such condition is found. Try to slip each bearing into its proper bore in the case. If the bearing is loose and the outer bearing can spin in the case, replace the crankcases.

NOTE Because of the alignment required between the two cases after reassembly, crankcases usually are supplied only in pairs.

Examine the transmission parts for wear and

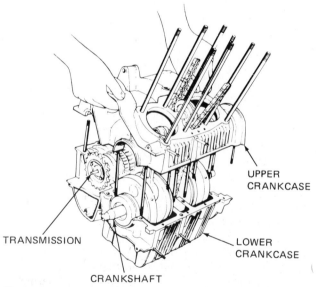

TRANSMISSION

UPPER CRANKCASE

LOWER CRANKCASE

CRANKSHAFT

Fig. 26-7 The crankcase of a multicylinder motorcycle engine which splits into an upper half and a lower half. (*Moto Laverda*)

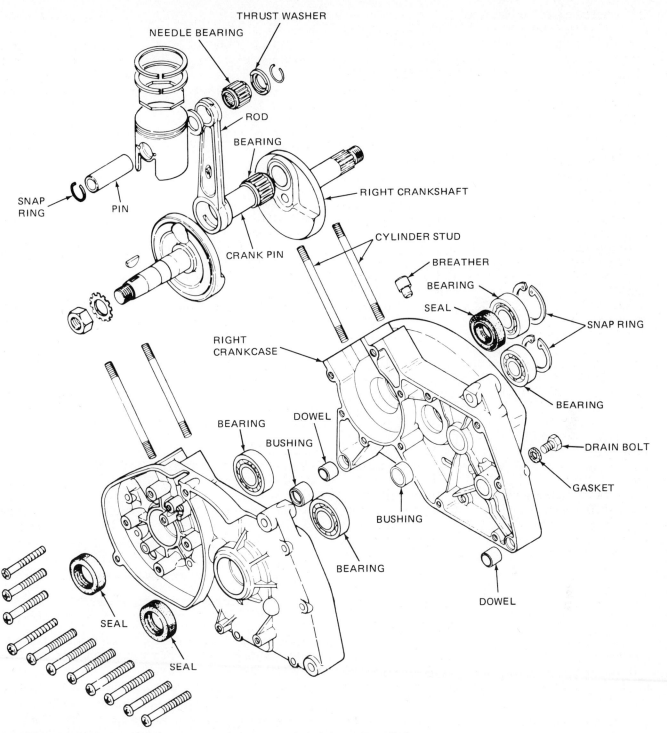

Fig. 26-8 Disassembled view of the crankcase and crankshaft for a one-cylinder two-cycle engine. (*Pacific Basin Trading Company*)

damage, as outlined in Chap. 28. Then check the kick starter, as covered in Chap. 19.

26-8
CHECKING THE CRANKSHAFT ASSEMBLY Examine the crankshaft assembly for the following conditions:

1. Galled bearing-mounting surfaces
2. A chipped keyway
3. Worn spots on the taper
4. Worn or broken clutch-hub splines
5. Damaged threads at shaft ends
6. A discolored connecting-rod big end
7. Chewed or damaged thrust washers
8. Rough and catchy action of a rod needle bearing
9. An excessive radial movement in the rod big end

Any of these conditions requires that the crankshaft

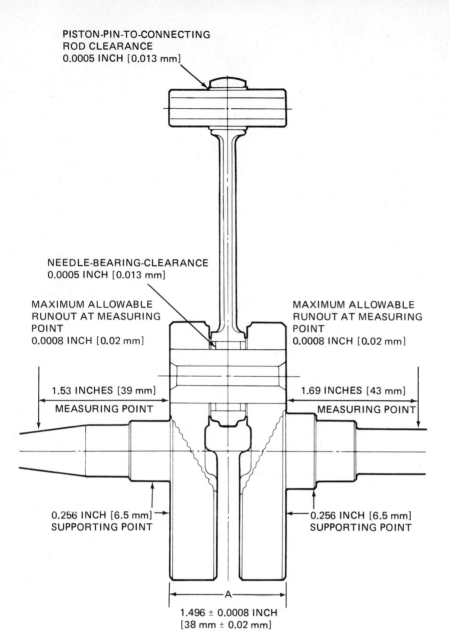

PISTON-PIN-TO-CONNECTING
ROD CLEARANCE
0.0005 INCH [0.013 mm]

NEEDLE-BEARING-CLEARANCE
0.0005 INCH [0.013 mm]

MAXIMUM ALLOWABLE
RUNOUT AT MEASURING
POINT
0.0008 INCH [0.02 mm]

MAXIMUM ALLOWABLE
RUNOUT AT MEASURING
POINT
0.0008 INCH [0.02 mm]

1.53 INCHES [39 mm]
MEASURING POINT

1.69 INCHES [43 mm]
MEASURING POINT

0.256 INCH [6.5 mm]
SUPPORTING POINT

0.256 INCH [6.5 mm]
SUPPORTING POINT

A

1.496 ± 0.0008 INCH
[38 mm ± 0.02 mm]

Fig. 26-9 Measurements that should be made before disassembling the crankshaft assembly. Specifications are for one model of single-cylinder two-cycle engine. (*Pacific Basin Trading Company*)

assembly be disassembled and the defective parts replaced.

If the crankshaft assembly passes the above visual inspection, then make the following measurements (Fig. 26-9):

1. Measure the clearance between the piston pin and the connecting-rod bearing. (This measurement is with the piston pin installed in the needle bearing.) If the clearance is in excess of the amount specified, replace the connecting rod.
2. Measure the crankshaft bearing-surface runout. Measure the runout in an alignment jig or in a device capable of measuring both right and left bearing surfaces at the same time. Crankshaft runout, or *drift*, may be corrected by using a brass hammer and a wood wedge, as shown in Fig. 26-10. Then recheck the alignment in the alignment jig.

If the crankshaft assembly requires disassembly, as shown in Fig. 26-8, heat the area around the crankpin with a butane torch. Then use a puller to pull the flywheel from the crankpin.

NOTE Never press the crankpin needle-bearing surface through the mounting bores in the flywheels to disassemble the crankshaft. This will ruin the crankpin mounting bores.

Repeat the heating process on the opposite flywheel, and use the puller to push the crankpin out of the flywheel mounting bore. If the connecting rod or needle bearing requires replacement, many manufacturers recommend replacing the crankpin, connecting rod, and bearing as an assembly.

**26-9
CONNECTING-ROD SLEEVE-BEARING SERVICE** The sleeve-type bearing (Fig. 26-11) is used with a split-rod big end. The rod has a bearing cap so the two halves of the sleeve bearing can be installed

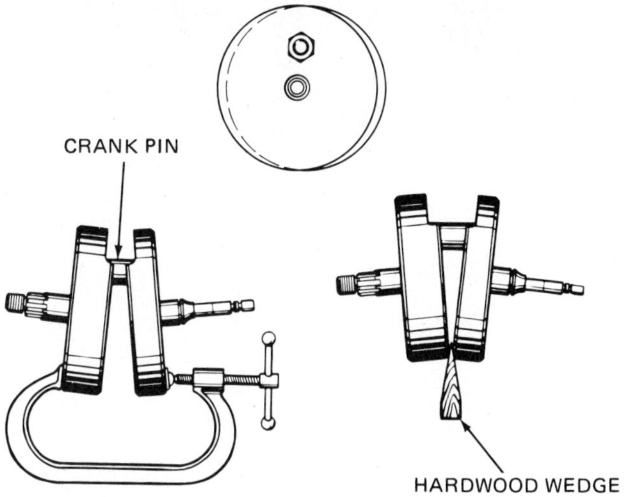

Fig. 26-10 Correcting flywheel alignment. (*Harley-Davidson Motor Company, Inc.*)

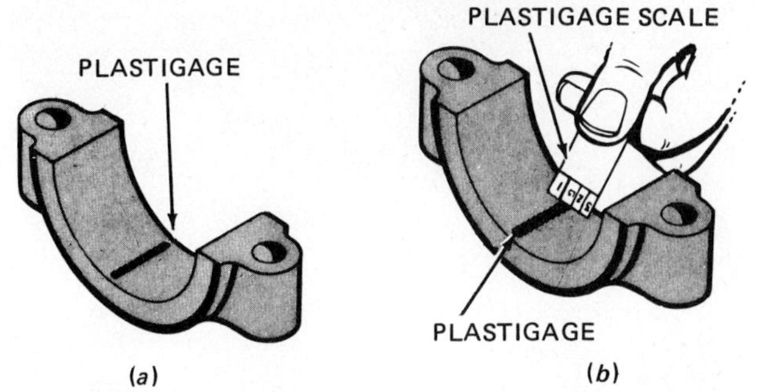

Fig. 26-12 Using Plastigage to check bearing clearance. (*a*) Lay a strip of Plastigage on the bearing in the rod cap. (*b*) After installing the cap and then removing it, measure the amount that the Plastigage has flattened to determine the bearing clearance.

(Fig. 2-12*a*). The clearance between the sleeve bearings and the crankshaft should be checked with Plastigage.

Before you check the bearing clearance, inspect the crankpin for wear and roughness. If the crankpin is worn, it will require service or the crankshaft will require replacement (see 26-8).

Plastigage is a plastic wire that comes in strips. It flattens when pressure is applied to it. To use Plastigage, first make sure the bearing and crankpin are wiped clean of dirt and oil. Lay a strip of the Plastigage on the bearing in the rod cap, as shown in Fig. 26-12*a*. Then install the cap and rod on the crankpin, and tighten the nuts to the specified torque. Do not move the crankshaft while the Plastigage is in place.

Remove the cap and measure the amount that the Plastigage has flattened, as shown in Fig. 26-12*b*, using the scale that is printed on the Plastigage package. If the clearance is small, the Plastigage will have flattened considerably. If the clearance is relatively large, the Plastigage will not have flattened as much.

26-10 INSTALLING NEW SLEEVE BEARINGS

New connecting-rod bearings are required if the old bearings are defective or have worn so much that the clearances are excessive. They also are required if the crankpins have become out-of-round or tapered. In such engines, a new or reground crankshaft with new bearings must be installed.

Always check the crankpin as explained in 26-8 to make sure it is not out-of-round or tapered. With either of these conditions, new bearings would soon fail.

When installing new bearings, make sure your hands, the workbench, your tools, and all engine parts are clean. Keep the new bearings wrapped until you are ready to install them. Handle them carefully. Wipe each bearing with a clean cloth just before installing it. Be sure that the bore in the cap and rod are clean and not out-of-round. Some manufacturers recommend a check of bore roundness with the bearing halves removed. The cap is attached and the nuts drawn up to specifications. Then a telescoping gauge and micrometer are used to check the bore. If it is excessively out-of-round, a new rod should be installed. If the bore is satisfactory, install the bearing (Fig. 26-13). If the bearing halves have locking tangs, be sure they enter the notches provided in the rod and cap.

Bearing Spread Bearing halves, or shells, are usually manufactured with *spread*. The shell diameter is slightly greater than the diameter of the rod cap and rod bore into which the shell will fit. This is shown in Fig. 26-11. When the shell is installed in the cap or rod, it snaps into place and holds its seat during later assembly operations.

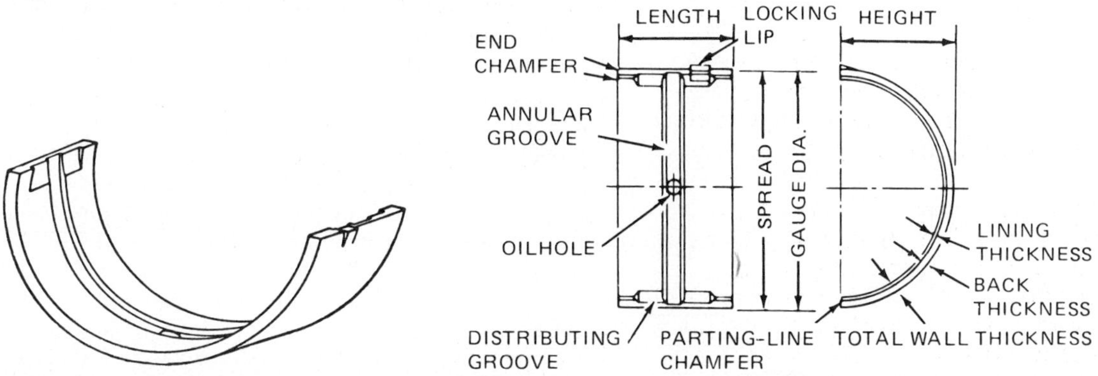

Fig. 26-11 (Left) A typical sleeve-type bearing half. (Right) A sleeve-type bearing half with the parts named. (*Federal Mogul Corporation*)

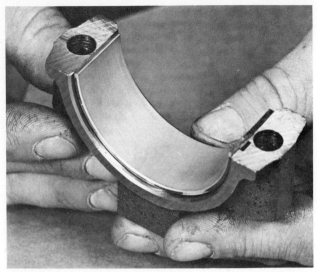

Fig. 26-13 Inserting a new bearing in the connecting-rod cap.

Bearing Crush To make sure that the bearing shell will "snug down" into its bore in the rod cap or rod when the cap is installed, the bearings have *crush*. This is shown in Fig. 26-14. They are manufactured to have a slight additional height over a full half. This additional height must be crushed down when the cap is installed. Crushing down the additional height forces the shells into the bores in the cap and rod. It ensures firm seating and snug contact with the bores.

Never file off the edges of the bearing shells in an attempt to remove crush. When you select the bearings recommended by the engine manufacturer for an engine, they will have the correct crush. Precision-insert bearings must not be shimmed or filed to make them "fit better." This usually leads only to early bearing failure.

26-11
CRANKSHAFT-BEARING SERVICE
The crankshaft of a single-cylinder engine is held at its ends by bearings. Crankshafts in multicylinder engines may have additional crankshaft bearings, or *main bearings*, located between the crankpins. A variety of bearing types are used: needle, ball, tapered roller, and sleeve. Sleeve bearings usually are of the split type, which are

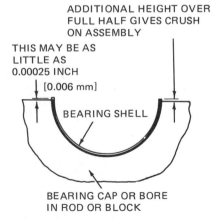

Fig. 26-14 Bearing crush.

246

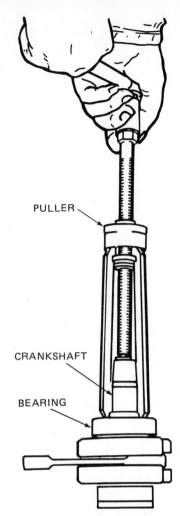

Fig. 26-15 Removing a bearing from a crankshaft with a puller.

checked and serviced the same as connecting-rod bearings. Refer to 26-7 and 26-8 for the procedure.

To gain access to the main bearings, the crankshaft usually must be removed. This requires splitting of the crankcase (26-5).

26-12
CRANKSHAFT NEEDLE-, ROLLER-, AND BALL-BEARING SERVICE
To service ball, needle, or tapered roller bearings, first determine if the bearings are damaged or worn. After the crankshaft is removed from the engine, wash the bearing and then dry it. Do not spin-dry the bearing with compressed air. Depending on the engine, the bearing will remain in the crankcase or on the crankshaft. Do not remove the bearing until you have decided that it must be replaced. After the bearing is clean and dry, make a thorough visual inspection of it for pits and discoloration. If the bearing appears to be in good condition, coat it with oil. Then rotate the inner race of the bearing so you can determine by feel whether the bearing is tight or has rough spots.

If the bearings are worn or damaged, they must be replaced. If the bearings are on the crankshaft, they should be pulled with a puller (Fig. 26-15) or pressed off with a press. Then a new bearing can be pressed on.

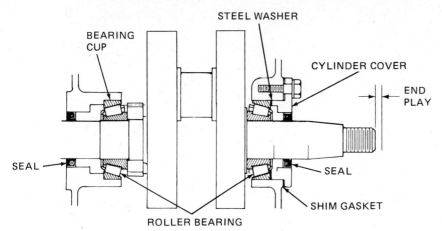

Fig. 26-16 Crankshaft mounted on tapered roller bearings.

When the crankshaft is mounted on roller bearings, as shown in Fig. 26-16, you can replace the outer race in the housing by pulling the race. Another way is to heat the housing with a butane torch until the race drops out. Then install a new race. The inner race on the crankshaft must be pulled out with a puller and a new race pressed on.

Crankshaft needle bearings should be cleaned, dried, and coated with oil. Then check the needle bearings and their cage for wear. Replace the needle bearing when the needles are very loose or fall out of their cage. To install a new needle bearing, always drive the bearing on the end with the identification marks.

NOTE If the new needle bearing assembly is damaged during installation, it will quickly damage the crankshaft.

**26-13
OIL SEALS** On a two-cycle engine, the crankcase must be sealed. Although no oil is carried in the crankcase, air leaks must be prevented. Otherwise, the air-fuel ratio will be changed and the engine may not run right. Oil seals on each end of the crankshaft prevent these leaks.

Oil seals should be discarded and new seals installed every time the engine is given a complete overhaul. Usually, oil seals are damaged during removal. One oil-seal arrangement is shown in Fig. 26-17. On some engines the seal is held in place by a retainer and snap ring. To remove the snap ring and seal, use a pointed tool to pry the snap ring out of the spiral groove. This permits

removal of the spring, retainer, and seal. Figure 26-17 shows how a seal remover is used to remove the seal.

When installing new seals, many technicians coat the outside of the seal case with Permatex No. 3 or other liquid gasket sealer. Then, while the seal is being driven into place, the liquid sealer will fill in any slight out-of-round of the seal or the seal bore. Some seals are made with a neoprene (plastic) coating for the same purpose. These can be installed without the use of liquid gasket sealer.

If you use a liquid sealer, be sure that it is applied to the seal and not to the bore in the block. Do not coat the bore in the block and then drive the seal in. Doing so allows the gasket sealer to get into the lip and may cause it to leak. Also, the sealer could possibly cause a leak by running into and blocking off the oil drain hole. Drive the seal into its bore until the seal is flush with the case. The seal must not be cocked or driven in too far (Fig. 26-18).

**26-14
GASKETS** Always use new gaskets on engine reassembly. Old gaskets are probably hard and will not provide a good seal. In addition, they may have been damaged or destroyed during engine disassembly. Make sure that the sealing surfaces on the engine are clean, but do not scrape them. Instead, use lacquer thinner on a clean cloth to wipe traces of sealer or gasket material from the surfaces.

The two halves of the crankcase are sealed by a bead of liquid gasket sealer. Apply the sealer to the contact face of one of the halves, and then assemble the crank-

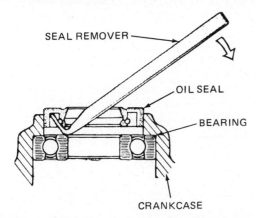

Fig. 26-17 Removing a crankcase oil seal from a two-cycle-engine case. (*Suzuki Motor Company, Ltd.*)

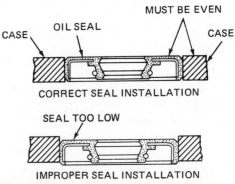

Fig. 26-18 Crankshaft oil-seal installation. (*Suzuki Motor Company, Ltd.*)

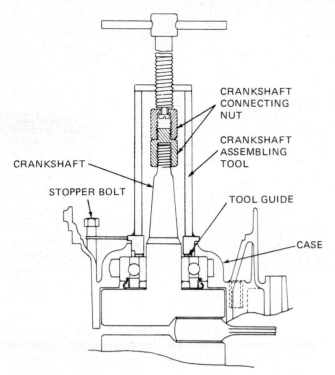

Fig. 26-19 Using a crankcase assembling tool to reassemble the crankcase halves. (*Suzuki Motor Company, Ltd.*)

case. To properly assemble the cases of an engine with a vertically split crankcase, a crankcase assembling tool may be needed, as shown in Fig. 26-19.

The gaskets in a two-cycle-engine crankcase must not leak. Depending on which gasket leaked, this could cause a lean air-fuel mixture or transmission-oil consumption and exhaust smoke. Various pressure testers are available for checking for crankcase leaks. After plugging the intake and exhaust ports, a small pump is operated to slightly pressurize the air in the crankcase. If the pressure drops too quickly, then the defective gaskets must be located and replaced.

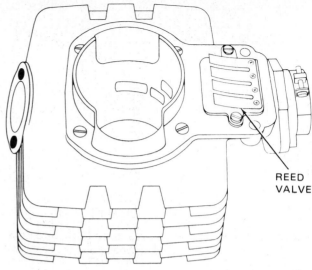

Fig. 26-20 Reed valves on two-cycle engines must be checked during engine overhaul.

26-15
REED VALVES

Some two-cycle engines use reed valves. Those that do will not run right with a defective reed valve. When overhauling an engine, always clean all dirt and oil from the reeds and the adapter, also called the *base plate* or *reed-valve plate* (Fig. 26-20). Do this carefully to avoid damaging reeds. If reeds are bent, damaged, or broken, replace the reed-valve assembly. On engines using a reed-valve stop, make sure the stop is not bent or broken. Use a feeler gauge to check how much the reeds bend away from the plate. One manufacturer specifies a maximum of 0.010 inch [0.25 mm]. If the reeds bend more than this or are otherwise damaged, replace them.

Some manufacturers recommend that you do not attempt to check reed-valve action with compressed air. This can damage the reeds. In these engines, reed valves are checked by visual inspection only.

CHAPTER 26
REVIEW QUESTIONS

1. List the conditions to check for when inspecting the cylinder.
2. How can stripped threads in aluminum cases be repaired?
3. Explain how to refinish a cylinder that does not need boring.
4. Why must a new piston and rings be installed after a cylinder is bored?
5. What steps are required to remove an engine from the frame?
6. What type of engine usually has a crankcase that splits apart along its vertical centerline?
7. What must be done with a connecting rod that has turned blue in the big-end bore?
8. How is the condition of a ball bearing checked?
9. List eight checks to make on the crankshaft assembly.
10. How is excessive crankshaft runout corrected?
11. Why is it sometimes necessary to heat the cases with a torch before the bearings can be removed?
12. Explain how to use Plastigage to check bearing clearance in a sleeve-type bearing.
13. What are *bearing spread* and *bearing crush*?
14. What types of bearings may be found supporting the crankshaft in motorcycle engines?
15. How are needle bearings cleaned?
16. What happens when an oil seal allows air to leak into the crankcase of a two-cycle engine?
17. When can old gaskets be used to reassemble an engine?
18. How are reed valves checked?

PART **5**

MOTORCYCLE
POWER TRAINS

Part 5 covers the maintenance and servicing of motorcycle power trains. This includes motorcycle clutches, motorcycle transmissions, and motorcycle final drives. The chapter on final drives covers chain-and-sprocket drives and shaft-and-gear drives.

There are three chapters in Part 5. They are:

Chapter 27   Motorcycle Clutches and Clutch Service

**Chapter 28   Motorcycle Transmissions and
Transmission Service**

Chapter 29   Motorcycle Final Drives

CHAPTER 27

27-1 MOTORCYCLE POWER TRAIN The power developed by the engine in a motorcycle is transmitted to the rear wheel by a power train which consists of a primary drive, clutch, transmission, and final drive (Fig. 27-1). The primary drive, which transfers power from the crankshaft to the clutch, may be gears, or sprockets and chain or belt. The drive gear or sprocket is mounted on the engine crankshaft. As the crankshaft rotates, power is transferred through the primary drive to the clutch.

With the clutch engaged, power is transmitted through the clutch to the transmission and final drive. The final drive may be either a chain drive (using a chain and sprockets) or a shaft drive (using gears and shafts).

It connects the final-drive sprocket (Fig. 27-1) or gear to the rear wheel.

Torque multiplication with speed reduction between the engine and the rear wheel results from the larger sprocket or gear that is used as the driven member of the primary drive and of the final drive. A torque increase and speed reduction occurs between the primary drive on the engine and the clutch. A further torque increase and speed reduction occurs between the final drive and the rear wheel. In addition, the various transmission-gear ratios provide torque multiplication.

27-2 PRIMARY DRIVES In recent years, most motorcycles have been built with the engine and the transmission combined into a single unit. This has the advantage of allowing gears to be used to transfer power from the engine crankshaft to the clutch. However, some motorcycles, especially older models, have a separate *primary drive* (Fig. 27-2). Its purpose is to transfer the power from the engine crankshaft to the clutch and transmission.

Typically, the primary-drive sprocket on the crankshaft is about half the diameter of the clutch sprocket. This provides a speed reduction through the primary drive of about 2:1. On some motorcycles, the primary-drive ratio can be varied by changing the sizes of the sprockets. This cannot be done when gears are used in the primary drive.

Most primary drives run in oil. These are called *wet-type primary drives*. Many are lubricated by the transmission oil. Others have their own oil supply. However, the oil must be changed frequently. The oil can be contaminated by particles thrown off the clutch, chain, or gears.

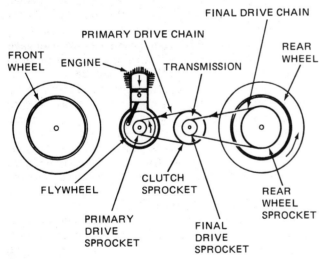

Fig. 27-1 A typical motorcycle power train, which consists of a primary drive, clutch, transmission, and final drive.

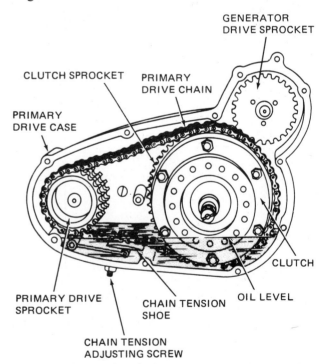

Fig. 27-2 A wet-type primary drive, which uses a primary chain running in oil.

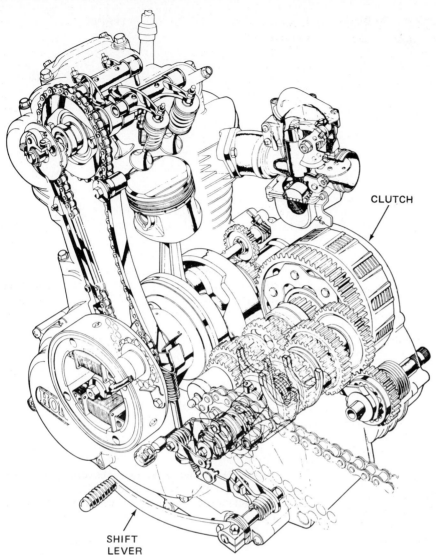

CLUTCH

SHIFT
LEVER

Fig. 27-3 Cutaway view of a one-cylinder four-cycle engine, showing the transmission and the clutch. The clutch is to the lower right. It is driven from the crankshaft by a pair of gears. (*Honda Motor Company, Ltd.*)

When a chain is used in the primary drive, the chain is often called the *primary chain*. Like most other chains, it will stretch in use. To remove the excess slack from some primary chains, a slack adjuster is used. The chain can be adjusted by changing the tension on the chain-tension shoe, which presses against the chain to maintain tension. On some motorcycles, primary chain tension is adjusted by moving either the transmission and clutch or the engine. Other motorcycles have non-adjustable primary chains.

27-3 INTRODUCTION TO MOTORCYCLE CLUTCHES

The clutch is located between the engine and the transmission. Figure 27-3 is a cutaway view of a one-cylinder engine which shows the transmission and the clutch. The clutch is the round drum to the middle right with the large gear. This large gear is meshed with a gear on the engine crankshaft so the clutch drum turns when the engine is running.

The purpose of the clutch is to couple the engine to the transmission or to uncouple it during gearshifting. When the clutch is engaged, which is the normal run-

ning position, the power flows from the engine through the clutch to the transmission and then to the motorcycle rear wheel. The clutch is operated by a hand lever on the left handlebar (Fig. 4-14). When the lever is pulled toward the handlebar, a cable from the lever to the clutch causes the clutch to disengage. It is necessary to interrupt the power flow from the engine—to disengage the clutch—when the gears are shifted. Transmissions and gearshifting are described in Chap. 28.

The transmission is needed to provide different *gear ratios* between the engine and the wheel. The gear ratio is the difference between the speeds at which the engine crankshaft and the motorcycle's rear wheel are turning. When first starting out, the engine crankshaft must be turning fast for the engine to produce enough torque and power to get the motorcycle moving and accelerate it. This requires a high gear ratio—the engine turns fast while the wheel turns slowly.

Then, while the motorcycle is moving at a low speed, the gear ratio is changed to allow the wheels to turn faster without higher engine speeds. This gear changing is repeated as the transmission is shifted up through intermediate to high speed. And each time the gears are

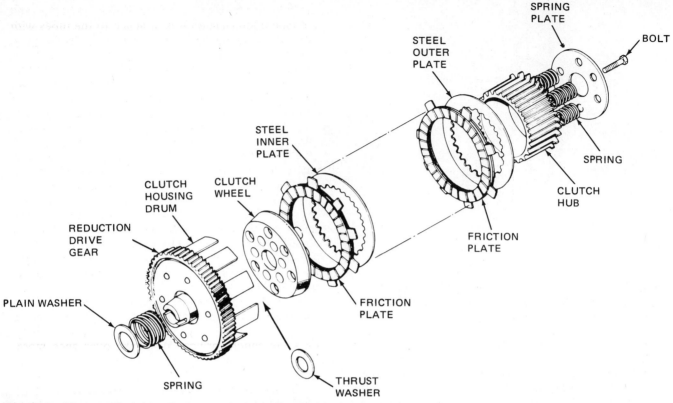

Fig. 27-4 Disassembled view of a motorcycle clutch. Not all of the friction disks are shown. (*Kawasaki Heavy Industries, Ltd.*)

shifted, the power from the engine must be interrupted. It is difficult to shift gears while power is flowing through them. Also, meshing and demeshing gears that are transmitting power may damage the transmission. The job of the clutch is to interrupt the power flow so that shifts can be made without transmission damage.

27-4
CONSTRUCTION AND OPERATION OF MOTORCYCLE CLUTCHES
The typical motorcycle clutch has two sets of round disks. One set is keyed to the clutch housing, or *outer drum*. The second set is keyed to the clutch hub, or *clutch center* (Fig. 27-4). When the two sets of disks are pressed together by the clutch springs, the clutch is engaged. Power can flow through the clutch. But when the spring force is relieved, the two sets of disks can revolve independently. The clutch is disengaged, and no power can flow through it.

Figure 27-5 shows the effect when the force between the disks is relieved. There is space between the disks so that the clutch housing disks can revolve independently of the hub disks. Figure 27-6 shows what happens when the spring force is applied. The disks are forced together, and the friction between the disks forces the hub disks to turn along with the drum disks.

Figure 27-7 is a sectional view of a motorcycle clutch. Notice how the clutch disks are alternately connected by tangs to the clutch hub and the clutch housing. Figure 27-8 shows a similar clutch, viewed from an angle different from the angle shown in Fig. 27-6. The tangs on the outer diameter of one set of disks fit into the slots in the clutch housing (the drum). The tangs on the inner diameter of the other set of disks fit into the slots cut in the surface of the clutch hub.

Figure 27-9 shows how the clutch assembly fits into the engine and transmission. While this is a common arrangement, it is not the only way the clutch is in-

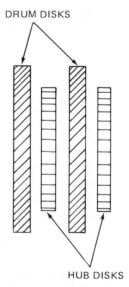

Fig. 27-5 When the clutch is released, there is space between the drum disks and the hub disks. The two sets of disks can revolve independently of each other.

252

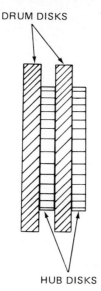

Fig. 27-6 When the clutch is engaged, the two sets of disks are clamped together. Now, friction between the disks causes the two sets to rotate together.

stalled. However, all clutches are of the same general design.

When the clutch is engaged, the four springs (item 5 in Fig. 27-9), apply force to the clutch hub (6). Note that the pressure plate has four long tubes that stick out toward the hub. These four tubes go through holes in the hub. The springs are placed around the tubes, and the clutch lifter plate (3) is attached to the tubes with bolts. This compresses the springs and pulls the pressure plate toward the hub. Therefore, spring force is applied to the disks, holding them together. Friction between the disk faces forces the disks to rotate together. Now the clutch is engaged.

To declutch, or disengage the clutch, the rider operates the clutch lever on the left handlebar. A cable from this lever to the clutch lever at the clutch (12 in Fig. 27-9) causes the shaft of the clutch-operating lever to rotate. Rotation of this shaft causes the clutch-operating lever (15) to pivot. The lower end of this lever pushes against the ball bearing (2) which is assembled inside the lifter plate (3). This pushes the lifter plate and the pressure plate (9), which is attached to the lifter plate (to the right), thereby compressing the springs. This relieves the spring force on the disks so that the two sets of disks (hub and housing) can rotate independently.

When the rider releases the lever on the handlebar, spring action allows the clutch-operating lever to move back, releasing the force on the ball bearing. This allows the clutch springs (5) to take over once more, forcing the disks together so the clutch is again engaged.

Most motorcycle clutches are designed to run in oil. This type of clutch is called a *wet clutch*. Other clutches are *dry clutches*, such as the ones used in automobiles.

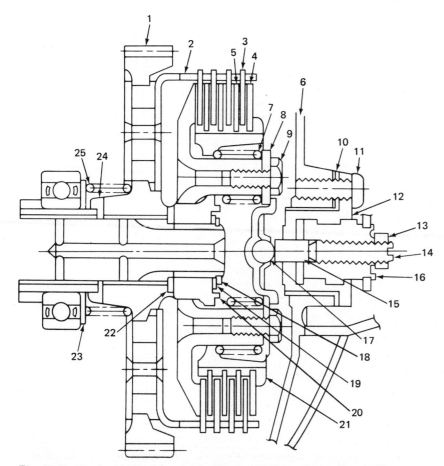

1. Housing gear
2. Clutch housing (drum)
3. Friction plate
4. Steel outer plate
5. Steel inner plate
6. Right engine cover
7. Spring
8. Spring plate
9. Bolt
10. Gasket
11. Screw
12. Outer clutch release worm gear
13. Nut
14. Adjusting screw
15. Pin
16. Inner clutch release worm gear
17. Spring plate
18. Circlip
19. Thrust washer
20. Clutch wheel
21. Clutch hub
22. Thrust washer
23. Thrust washer
24. Idle gear
25. Spring

Fig. 27-7 Sectional view of a clutch. (*Kawasaki Heavy Industries, Ltd.*)

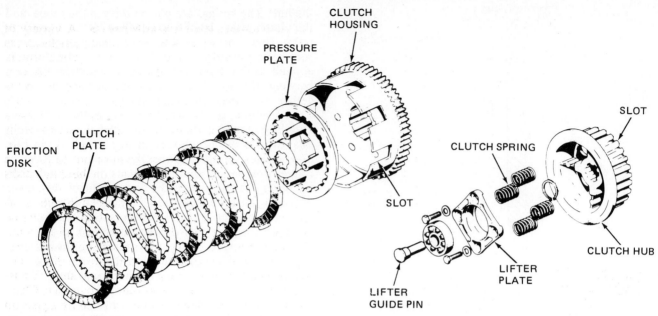

Fig. 27-8 Disassembled view of a motorcycle clutch. (*Honda Motor Company, Ltd.*)

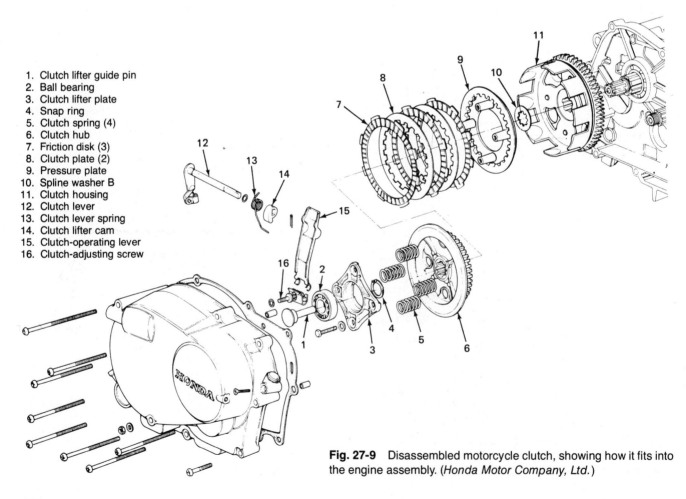

1. Clutch lifter guide pin
2. Ball bearing
3. Clutch lifter plate
4. Snap ring
5. Clutch spring (4)
6. Clutch hub
7. Friction disk (3)
8. Clutch plate (2)
9. Pressure plate
10. Spline washer B
11. Clutch housing
12. Clutch lever
13. Clutch lever spring
14. Clutch lifter cam
15. Clutch-operating lever
16. Clutch-adjusting screw

Fig. 27-9 Disassembled motorcycle clutch, showing how it fits into the engine assembly. (*Honda Motor Company, Ltd.*)

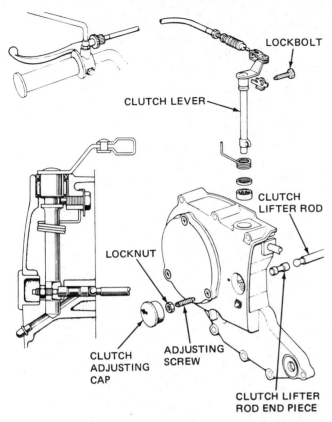

Fig. 27-10 Linkage arrangement between the lever at the handlebar and the clutch. (*Honda Motor Company, Ltd.*)

LINKAGE ARRANGEMENTS

A variety of linkage arrangements has been used between the clutch lever on the handlebar and the lever at the clutch. Figure 27-10 shows a typical arrangement. This illustration shows the linkage from the handlebar lever to the clutch lever. How this linkage fits into the clutch itself is shown in Fig. 27-11. The lifter rod (in Fig. 27-10) is shown in Fig. 27.11. When the handlebar clutch lever is operated, the clutch lever (in Fig. 27-10) is rotated, and this forces the lifter rod to push out toward the clutch. This action releases the force on the clutch disks and disengages the clutch.

Figure 27-11 also shows how the clutch hub is attached to the transmission. The main shaft has external splines which match the internal splines in the hub. When the clutch is engaged, the clutch housing is turning and driving the clutch hub through the disks. The hub is then driving the transmission main shaft. Transmission construction and operation is covered in Chap. 28. The clutch housing or drum is driven by a gear on the crankshaft, as shown in Fig. 27-3, or through sprockets and a chain, as shown in Fig. 27-12.

A second clutch-operating arrangement is shown in Fig. 27-13. Moving the clutch lever at the handlebar pulls on the cable, causing the inner release gear to rotate. The release gear is shown in Fig. 27-14. Note that it is a sort of worm gear with teeth that spiral from one end to the other. These spiral teeth match internal teeth in the outer release gear.

In these, the friction disk must be kept oil-free for proper operation.

Although the clutch must be located in the power train between the engine crankshaft and the transmission, not all motorcycle clutches are actually attached to the main shaft. Some motorcycles have the clutch mounted directly on the end of the crankshaft.

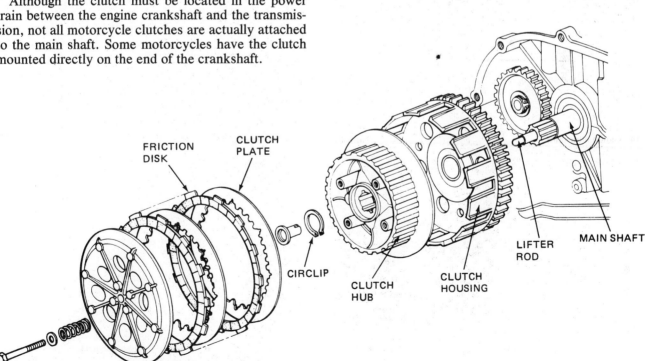

Fig. 27-11 Disassembled view of a motorcycle clutch. (*Honda Motor Company, Ltd.*)

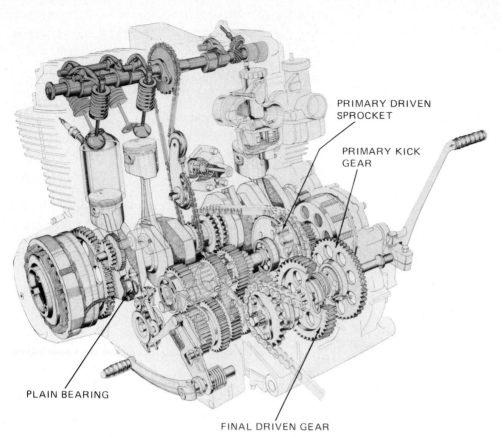

PRIMARY DRIVEN
SPROCKET

PRIMARY KICK
GEAR

PLAIN BEARING

FINAL DRIVEN GEAR

Fig. 27-12 Partial cutaway view of a four-cylinder four-cycle motorcycle engine, showing the transmission and clutch. The clutch is to the lower right. A chain and a sprocket carry engine power from the crankshaft to the clutch and the transmission. (*Honda Motor Company, Ltd.*)

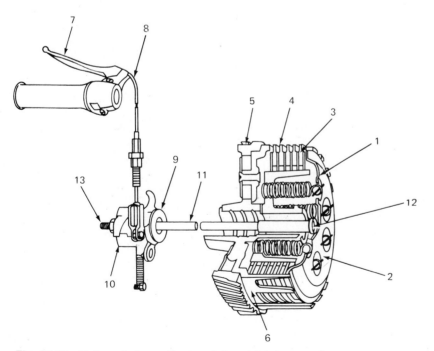

1. Clutch spring
2. Pressure plate
3. Cork plate
4. Steel plate
5. Primary gear
6. Clutch housing
7. Clutch lever
8. Clutch cable
9. Release screw
10. Release screw guide
11. Push rod
12. Release rod
13. Adjusting screw

Fig. 27-13 Linkage between the handlebar clutch lever and the clutch. (*Suzuki Motor Company, Ltd.*)

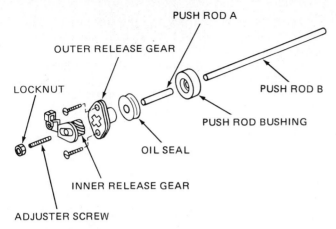

Fig. 27-14 Details of release gears for the clutch-operating mechanism. Note the spiral splines or spiral gear teeth on the inner release gear and inside the outer release gear. (*Kawasaki Heavy Industries, Ltd.*)

When the inner release gear rotates, the spiral teeth push the outer release gear away. This movement pushes against the two push rods—push rod A and push rod B in Fig. 27-14. The push rods are centered in the countershaft. Push rod B bears against the release rod. As the push rods are pushed inward, the release rod is moved, and this pushes the pressure plate out, relieving the pressure on the clutch disks. Figure 27-15 is another view of the clutch and release mechanism.

The clutch can be adjusted to compensate for internal wear of the disks. For example, in Fig. 27-10 the adjusting screw can be turned in to push the lifter-rod end piece and lifter rod in, thereby taking up any excessive clearance caused by wear. To make the adjustment, the adjusting cap has to be removed and the locknut loosened. Then the adjusting screw is turned to make the adjustment. This adjustment is covered in a later section of this chapter. The adjusting screw is numbered 14 in Fig. 27-7. It is numbered 17 in Fig. 27-15.

Adjustment is also made at the handlebar, but this is to establish the correct free play of the lever. Free play is the distance the lever moves before the clutch begins to release. Figure 27-16 shows one adjusting method. With the adjuster locknut loose, adjust the cable adjuster so that there is 0.200 to 0.240 inch [5 to 6 mm] of free play at the clutch lever. Then tighten the locknut.

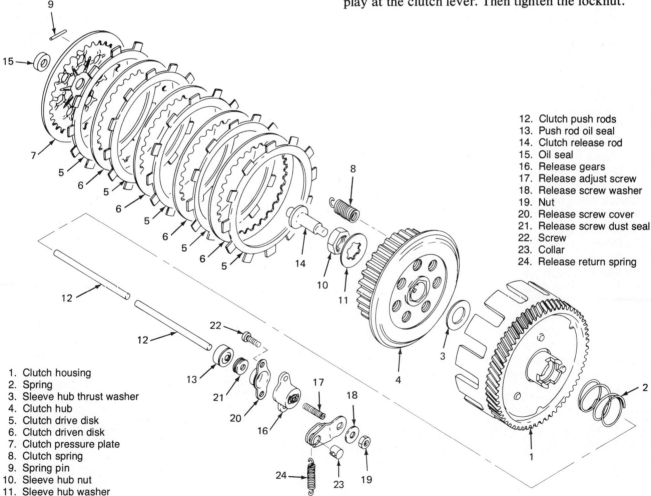

12. Clutch push rods
13. Push rod oil seal
14. Clutch release rod
15. Oil seal
16. Release gears
17. Release adjust screw
18. Release screw washer
19. Nut
20. Release screw cover
21. Release screw dust seal
22. Screw
23. Collar
24. Release return spring

1. Clutch housing
2. Spring
3. Sleeve hub thrust washer
4. Clutch hub
5. Clutch drive disk
6. Clutch driven disk
7. Clutch pressure plate
8. Clutch spring
9. Spring pin
10. Sleeve hub nut
11. Sleeve hub washer

Fig. 27-15 Disassembled view of a motorcycle clutch using release gears, as shown in the previous illustration. (*Kawasaki Heavy Industries, Ltd.*)

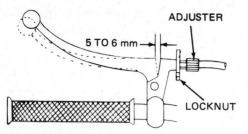

Fig. 27-16 Adjusting the clutch linkage at the handlebar lever. (*Kawasaki Heavy Industries, Ltd.*)

27-6 CLUTCH TROUBLES

The three basic clutch troubles are:

1. Clutch disengaging incorrectly
2. Clutch slipping
3. Clutch noise

Now, let's discuss the possible causes of each trouble.

1. The clutch not disengaging properly can be caused by
   a. Excessive clutch-lever play
   b. Warped or rough clutch disks
   c. Uneven clutch-spring tension
   d. Old transmissin oil
   e. Heavy transmission oil
   f. Clutch housing hanging up on transmission shaft
   g. Defective clutch-release mechanism
   h. Unevenly worn clutch hub or housing
   i. Missing or broken parts
2. A slipping clutch can be caused by:
   a. No clutch-lever free play
   b. Worn clutch disks
   c. Weak clutch springs
   d. Clutch cable hanging up
   e. Defective clutch-release mechanism
   f. Unevenly worn clutch hub or housing
3. Clutch noise may be caused by:
   a. Too much backlash between the primary gear and the clutch gear
   b. Damaged gear teeth
   c. Too much clearance between the clutch disk tangs and the clutch housing
   d. Deteriorated damper rubber
   e. Weak or damaged shock-absorber spring
   f. Metal chips in the clutch-housing gear teeth

The remedy in each case is to make the required repair. This may be an adjustment, replacing oil, or a complete overhaul and replacement of defective parts. The following section describes typical clutch servicing procedures.

27-7 SERVICING A CLUTCH FOR A TWO-CYLINDER FOUR-CYCLE ENGINE

Figure 27-17 is a disassembled view of the clutch covered in this section. The servicing procedure follows:

1. Disassembly. Drain the engine oil. Remove the right exhaust muffler (on models where it is in the way).

Remove the right foot peg and the starter kick pedal. Place an oil pan in position to catch oil, and remove the right crankcase cover.

Remove bolts and the clutch springs and clutch pressure plate. Then the clutch friction disks and plates can be removed (Fig. 27-17). Remove the clutch release rod, the external snap ring, and the clutch hub. Then remove the oil-filter rotor, as follows.

To remove the oil-filter rotor, remove the oil-pump idle gear by pulling on the idle shaft. Then remove the oil-filter screen by taking out the bolts. Next, remove the oil pump. The oil-filter cap can then be removed by removing the internal snap ring, screwing in a 6-mm bolt, and pulling. Finally, the locking lugs of the lock washer can be straightened so the special lock-washer removing tool can be used to remove the lock washer. The oil-filter rotor can now be removed.

With the oil-filter rotor off, the clutch housing can be removed. Remove the stop ring and the clutch plate from the hub.

2. Inspection. Check the friction disks and plates for wear, roughness, and thickness. Measure thickness with a micrometer or a vernier caliper. Lay the disks and plates separately on a flat surface and check them for warpage with a feeler gauge. Discard any disks or plates that show any defects or are excessively worn. Check the springs for length and discard all for new springs if any spring is short or shows signs of having been heated (blued, burned).

Measure the clearance between the tangs on the friction disks and the slots in the clutch housing. If this clearance is excessive, the clutch will be noisy. Replace the disks if the tangs have worn excessively. If the housing slots have worn excessively, replace the housing.

3. Reassembly. To reassemble the clutch, follow the disassembly procedure in reverse. Here are some special steps to follow.

When installing the clutch plate be sure to have the chamferred side of the clutch plate facing out. Secure the plate with the stop ring.

Install the clutch hub on the clutch housing, and install the eight friction disks and seven plates alternately. Attach the clutch assembly to the main shaft, and secure it with the external snap ring.

Install the clutch release rod (10 in Fig. 27-17), and then install the clutch pressure plate and the clutch springs. Secure them with attaching bolts.

Reinstall the oil-filter rotor, oil-filter cap, oil pump, oil-filter screen, and oil-pump idle gear. Then adjust the clutch.

4. Clutch Adjustment. The normal free play of this clutch is 0.400 to 0.800 inch [10 to 20 mm] at the lever tip. To adjust, loosen the locknut and turn the clutch-cable upper adjuster all the way into the clutch-lever bracket. Turn the clutch-cable lower adjuster to loosen the clutch cable.

Then loosen the clutch-adjuster locknut and turn the clutch-adjuster screw until a slight resistance is felt. From this position, turn the adjuster in one-quarter turn. Tighten the locknut.

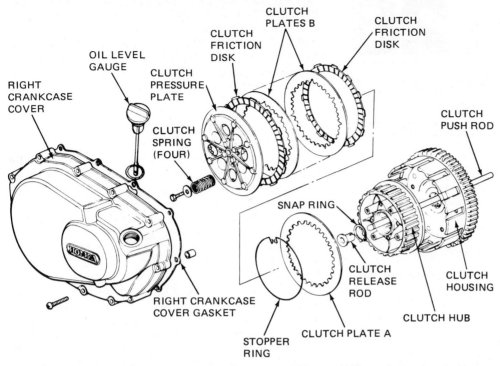

Fig. 27-17 Disassembled view of a motorcycle clutch. (*Kawasaki Heavy Industries, Ltd.*)

Turn the clutch-cable lower adjuster so that there is 0.400 to 0.800 inch [10 to 20 mm] of free travel at the clutch lever. Then tighten the locknut. Make any further adjustments at the upper cable adjuster.

Test the clutch to make sure it is not slipping and that the clutch engages properly. Start the engine, declutch by pulling in on the lever, and shift into gear. The engine should not stall, and the motorcycle should not start to creep. Gradually release the clutch lever and open the throttle. Clutch engagement should be smooth but firm, and the motorcycle should start smoothly and accelerate gradually.

CHAPTER 27
REVIEW QUESTIONS

1. In the motorcycle power train, where is the clutch located?
2. What is the purpose of the clutch?
3. Why does a motorcycle require a transmission with various gear ratios?
4. Describe the construction of a typical motorcycle clutch.
5. How is the clutch operated?
6. What provides the force that causes the clutch to lock up?
7. How can the clutch work when it is running in oil?
8. What action in the clutch causes it to release?
9. What are the three basic clutch troubles?
10. When a clutch jerks on engagement, what can be the causes?
11. What are the causes of clutch slippage?
12. List five possible causes of clutch noise.
13. Explain how to overhaul a clutch.
14. During an overhaul, why must the thickness of the clutch disks and plates be measured?
15. How is the clutch free play adjusted?

CHAPTER 28

MOTORCYCLE TRANSMISSIONS AND TRANSMISSION SERVICE

After studying this chapter,
you should be able to:

1. Discuss the purpose and describe the operation of transmissions.

2. Describe what happens when shifts occur and describe how to shift transmission gears.

3. Discuss gears and dogs and explain how they produce the various gear ratios in the transmission.

4. Explain what the drum is in a transmission and how it works.

5. Discuss transmission troubles and their possible causes.

6. Describe how to disassemble, inspect the parts, and reassemble a transmission.

7. Overhaul a motorcycle transmission.

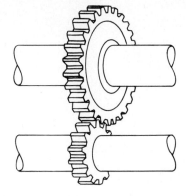

GEARS MESHED

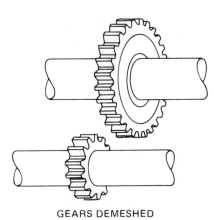

GEARS DEMESHED

Fig. 28-1 When two gears are meshed (top), the gears and their shafts must turn together. However, when one of the gears is moved along its shaft (bottom), it moves out of mesh so the two gears no longer rotate together.

28-1
INTRODUCTION TO MOTORCYCLE TRANSMISSIONS
A transmission is necessary because an engine will not produce much power or torque at low engine speed. And it takes high torque and considerable power to move a motorcycle away from the curb and bring it up to speed. Therefore, a series of gears is necessary between the engine and the wheel.

When first starting out, the gears in the transmission are moved to produce a high gear ratio. This means that the engine turns fast to turn the wheels slowly. That way, the engine can produce enough torque and power to get the motorcycle moving. Then, when the bike is on the way at slow speed, the gear ratio in the transmission

is again changed to allow the wheel to turn faster without higher engine speeds. This gear changing is repeated until the motorcycle is cruising in top gear.

28-2
GEARS AND GEAR RATIOS
The gears in motorcycle transmissions are spur gears. Spur gears are shown in Fig. 28-1. A spur gear is a metal wheel with a series of teeth on its outer edge. A pair of spur gears is shown meshed in Fig. 28-1 (left). When one gear ro-

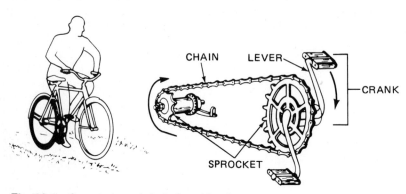

Fig. 28-2 Sprockets and chain for a bicycle.

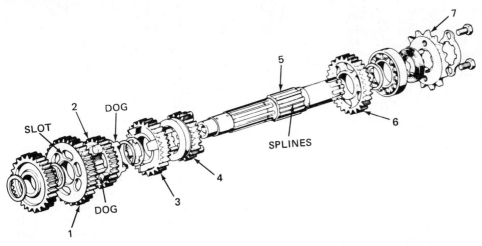

Fig. 28-3 Disassembled view of gears on one transmission shaft. (1) Gear with slots. (2) Gear with dogs splined to the shaft. (3) Gear with dogs. (4) Gear with dogs splined to the shaft. (5) Shaft. (6) Gear with slots. (7) Sprocket. (*Honda Motor Company, Ltd.*)

tates, the other gear must also rotate because the teeth are interlocked, or meshed. The teeth of the driving gear push against the teeth of the driven gear, making the driven gear turn. The gears are mounted on shafts so that motion can be carried from one shaft to another.

The sizes of the two gears determine the relative speed with which the two gears turn. A big driven gear turns slower than a small driving gear. But the small gear has a greater turning force. This turning force is called *torque*. Suppose, for example, that when a motorcycle transmission is in low gear, the engine crankshaft turns 10 times to make the wheel turn once. Speed is lost, but torque is gained. The engine turns at relatively high speed to turn the wheel slowly. The increased torque causes the motorcycle to accelerate rapidly.

When the speed is reduced through a pair of gears, the torque goes up. If the two gears were the same size and if both had the same number of teeth, they would turn at the same speed.

28-3
SPROCKETS AND CHAIN The sprockets and chain form another combination to transmit torque and power. Figure 28-2 shows a chain drive for a bicycle. It has two sprockets and a chain. Many motorcycles use a chain drive from the transmission to the rear wheel. Most four-cycle engines use a chain and sprockets to drive the camshaft (Fig. 2-1*d, e,* and *f*). Figure 27-12 shows the chains and sprockets in a four-cylinder OHC engine. The chain at the upper center connects the camshaft sprocket at the top with a crankshaft sprocket at the bottom. The multiple-link chain at the center connects the crankshaft sprocket with the clutch sprocket. The large chain to the lower center connects the transmission sprocket to the rear-wheel sprocket (not shown).

Figure 27-3 shows another engine partly cut away. It uses gears to carry the engine power and torque to the clutch. The clutch is the large drum to the right. You can see the chain and sprockets that drive the overhead camshaft and the sprocket and part of the chain that carries the power and torque from the transmission to the rear wheel. The pedal to the lower left is the gear-change, or shift, lever, which is described in following sections.

28-4
GEARS AND DOGS IN MOTORCYCLE TRANSMISSIONS Gears on separate shafts can be meshed and demeshed by sliding one of the gears on its shaft (Fig. 28-1). To the left in Fig. 28-1 the two gears are meshed, and power is passing through the gears. To the right, the lower gear has been moved along its shaft so it is demeshed from the upper gear. Now, no power can pass through the gears. Early transmissions used this type of gear shifting. It is no longer used because it is difficult to achieve shifts. The gear teeth have to be moving at exactly the same speed to avoid gear clash. Gear clash can break teeth.

Motorcycle transmissions use gears that are constantly in mesh. Some of the gears are fixed on shafts; others can slide back and forth on their shafts. The gear teeth are always in mesh, but *dogs* on the sides of the gears can lock to make two gears turn together. Dogs are described later. Figure 28-3 shows the gears on one shaft in a transmission. These gears are connected with other gears to build up the complete transmission.

Look at gears 1 and 2 in Fig. 28-3. Notice that gear 1 has a number of curved slots in its side. Now look at gear 2. Notice that it has a series of dogs sticking out from its side. Gear 1 is free to turn on the shaft (5) as long as gear 2 stays away from it. Gear 2 has internal splines that match external splines on the shaft. Splines are square teeth cut in the inner diameter of the gear and on the surface of the shaft. They match so that the gear can slide along on the splines. But the gear and shaft must turn together. Therefore, gear 1 can turn freely on the shaft, but gear 2 must turn with the shaft.

As long as gear 2 stays away from gear 1, gear 1 is free

Fig. 28-4 Cutaway view of a four-cylinder four-cycle OHC engine, showing the transmission and the clutch. (*Suzuki Motor Company, Ltd.*)

to turn on the shaft. But it cannot move along the shaft as gear 2 can. When a shift is made, gear 2 moves along the shaft, and the dogs on its side enter the curve slots in the side of gear 1. This locks the two gears together. Now, the two gears must turn together. The combination of dogs and slots form what is called a *dog clutch*. Several such clutches are used in motorcycle transmissions.

Look at gears 4 and 6 in Fig. 28-3. Here, the position of the gears is reversed so you can see what the other side of such gears looks like. Gear 4 has internal splines that match the shaft splines so it can slide along on the shaft, turning with the shaft at all times. Gear 6 is free to turn on the shaft as long as gear 4 stays away from it. Gear 6 has a bearing that permits it to rotate on the shaft, but it cannot move along the shaft as gear 4 can. Snap rings hold it in its place on the shaft. Now you can see what happens when gear 4 moves up to gear 6 so the dogs on gear 4 enter the slots in gear 6. Both must turn together.

In the actual transmission, the shaft (5) is the *output shaft* (also called the *countershaft*), and it carries on its end the sprocket (7) that is connected to the rear wheel by a chain. Gears 1 and 6 are in constant mesh with gears on another shaft. This other shaft is the main shaft, which is driven by the engine. Therefore, when the engine is running, gears 1 and 6 are rotating. If gear 2 is then moved so its dogs enter the slots in gear 1, the output shaft will be driven. The speeds of the main shaft and the output shaft are determined by the gear ratio between gears 1 and 2.

TRANSMISSION GEARS The gears in transmissions vary with different models of motorcycles. Some transmissions have four or six speeds and neutral. Most have five speeds and neutral. Some have a drive sprocket that is connected by a chain to the rear-wheel sprocket directly on the output shaft, as shown in Fig. 28-4. Others have an additional shaft to carry the output sprocket, as shown in Fig. 27-12. This additional shaft is driven by an extra gear (the *final driven gear*) from the output shaft of the transmission.

There are several gear arrangements, set up in different ways. We will look at a typical five-speed transmission and see how the five speeds are attained.

Figure 28-5 shows the gears and shafts in a five-speed transmission in disassembled view. The input shaft, driven by the engine, has five gears. These are, from left to right in Fig. 28-5, the second drive gear (1), the fifth drive gear (3), the third drive gear (6), the fourth drive gear (7), and the first drive gear (8).

The *output shaft* is driven though the gears from the input shaft. It also has five gears. These are, from left to right in Fig. 28-5, the second drive gear (11), the fifth driven gear (12), the third driven gear (13), the fourth driven gear (14), and the first driven gear (17).

Take a close look at Fig. 28-5 and notice the differences in the sizes of these gears.

Now let's put all the gears together (Fig. 28-6). Note that the gears and shafts are numbered in the same way in Figs. 28-5 and 28-6. This will enable you to compare Fig. 28-5 to Fig. 28-6, so you can identify each gear.

Some of the gears can be shifted along their supporting shafts. Others cannot. Let us examine Fig. 28-6 in detail. To the upper left, there is no power flow through the transmission. The transmission is in neutral. Now look to the upper right. Here the transmission is in low, or first speed. To achieve this, gear 14, which is the fourth driven gear, is shifted to the right so its dogs engage the slots in gear 17, the first driven gear. Gear 17 is free to turn on the output shaft (10) so long as gear 14 stays away from it. It is in mesh with the first drive gear (8) on the input shaft (9). Therefore, it is turning at all times.

This has no effect in the transmission until gear 14 moves over to gear 17, as shown to the upper right in Fig. 28-6. Gear 14 is splined to the output shaft (10). When the gear 14 dogs enter the slots in gear 17, gear 14 is forced to turn. This turns the output shaft (10) so that the drive chain sprocket (18) is driven. Note that a small gear (8) is driving a big gear (17). So there is considerable gear reduction through the transmission.

Now let us see what happens when a shift is made to second speed. This is shown in the middle left of Fig. 28-6. When the shift is made to second, gear 14 (the fourth driven gear), is shifted away from gear 17 (the first driven gear). This shifts the transmission out of first gear.

At the same time, gear 12 (the fifth driven gear) is shifted to the left. The dogs on gear 12 enter the slots in gear 11 (the second driven gear). Gear 11 is free to turn on the output shaft (10) as long as gear 12 stays away from it. Gear 11 is driven by gear 1 (the second drive

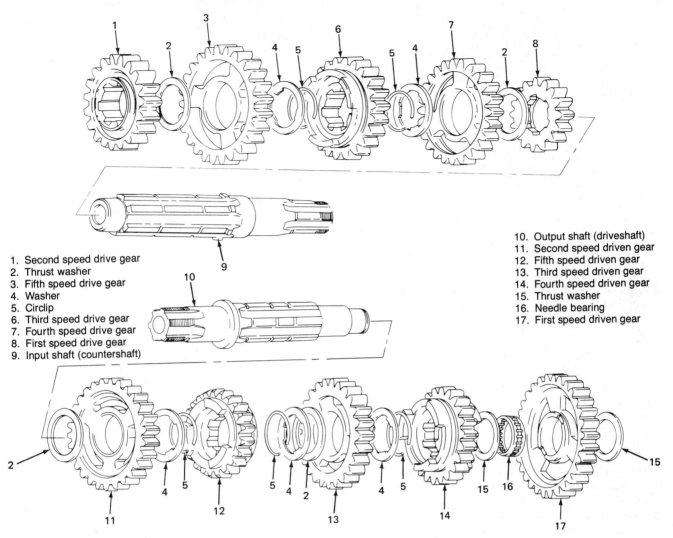

1. Second speed drive gear
2. Thrust washer
3. Fifth speed drive gear
4. Washer
5. Circlip
6. Third speed drive gear
7. Fourth speed drive gear
8. First speed drive gear
9. Input shaft (countershaft)

10. Output shaft (driveshaft)
11. Second speed driven gear
12. Fifth speed driven gear
13. Third speed driven gear
14. Fourth speed driven gear
15. Thrust washer
16. Needle bearing
17. First speed driven gear

Fig. 28-5 Disassembled view of the gears and shafts in a five-speed motorcycle transmission. (*Suzuki Motor Company, Ltd.*)

gear). But when gear 12 locks into gear 11, gear 12 is forced to rotate with gear 11. Since gear 12 is splined to the output shaft (10), the output shaft is forced to turn with gear 12. Note that the two gears are more nearly alike in size than the first-speed gears are. This means that the gear ratio through the transmission has been reduced.

Now look at what happens when a shift is made to third speed (middle right in Fig. 28-6). As this happens, gear 12 is moved away from gear 11 so that the shift is made out of second speed. At the same time, gear 14 is moved to the left so the dogs on its left side can enter the slots in gear 13 (the third driven gear). Now the transmission is shifted into third. The power flows through, as shown by the arrows, from the input shaft, through the third drive gear (6), and to the third driven gear, the fourth driven gear (14), the gear 14 splines, and the output shaft (10).

When a shift is made to fourth speed (lower left in Fig. 28-6), gear 14 (the fourth driven gear) is moved away from gear 13. This demeshes third gear. At the same time, gear 6 (the third drive gear) on the input

shaft, is moved to the right, as shown, so its dogs enter the slots in gear 7 (the fourth drive gear). Now the power flow is as shown to the lower left in Fig. 28-6. Compare the sizes of the drive and driven gears (7 and 14). A further gear reduction through the transmission has been made.

When the shift is made to high, or fifth speed, the conditions are as shown to the lower right in Fig. 28-6. Note that the third drive gear (6) has been moved to the left so its dogs enter the slots in the fifth drive gear (3). Now the power flow is as shown by the arrows in Fig. 28-6 (lower right).

28-6
SHIFTING THE GEARS We have seen how shifting gears 6, 12, and 14 in Figs. 28-5 and 28-6 produces the different gear ratios through the transmission. Now let us see how the gears are moved back and forth on their shafts.

Figure 28-7 shows a typical gearshift mechanism. Figure 28-8 shows a transmission using the type of gearshifting mechanism shown in Fig. 28-7. Figure 28-9

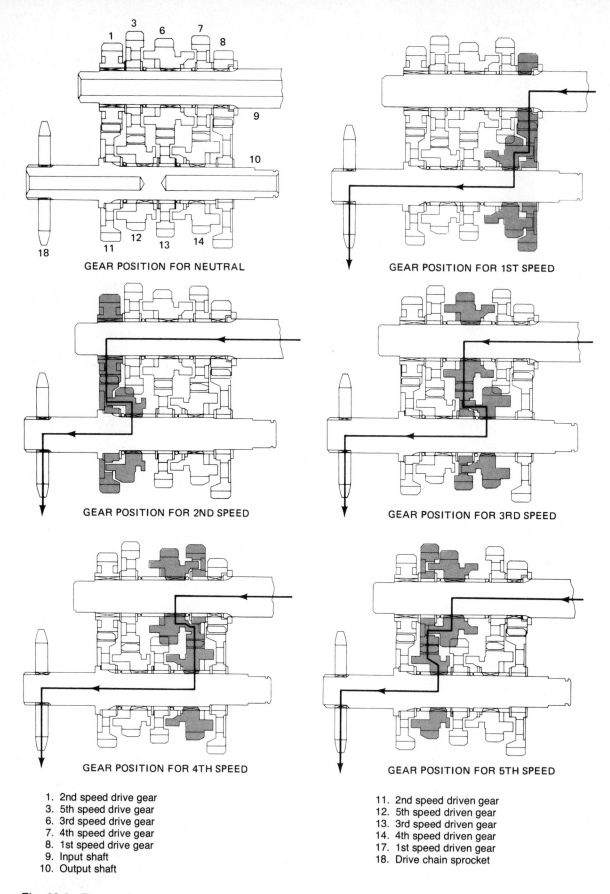

GEAR POSITION FOR NEUTRAL

GEAR POSITION FOR 1ST SPEED

GEAR POSITION FOR 2ND SPEED

GEAR POSITION FOR 3RD SPEED

GEAR POSITION FOR 4TH SPEED

GEAR POSITION FOR 5TH SPEED

1. 2nd speed drive gear
3. 5th speed drive gear
6. 3rd speed drive gear
7. 4th speed drive gear
8. 1st speed drive gear
9. Input shaft
10. Output shaft

11. 2nd speed driven gear
12. 5th speed driven gear
13. 3rd speed driven gear
14. 4th speed driven gear
17. 1st speed driven gear
18. Drive chain sprocket

Fig. 28-6 The positions of the gears and the power flow (shown by arrows) in neutral and at the various speeds—first to fifth. (*Suzuki Motor Company, Ltd.*)

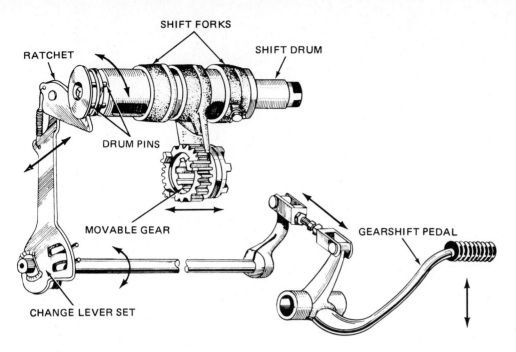

SHIFT FORKS

RATCHET

SHIFT DRUM

DRUM PINS

MOVABLE GEAR

GEARSHIFT PEDAL

CHANGE LEVER SET

Fig. 28-7 Gearshift mechanism for one transmission design. (*Kawasaki Heavy Industries, Ltd.*)

shows the way various gears are meshed and related. Even though the gear arrangement is different from that shown in Figs. 28-5 and 28-6, the end effect is the same.

When the gearshift pedal is moved up or down, the linkage between the pedal lever and the change (shift) drum causes the shift drum to rotate. There is a ratchet on the upper end of the linkage which works against the pins in the end of the drum. As the pedal moves, the ratchet catches against one of the pins and causes the drum to rotate. The drum has a series of slots cut in its surface, as shown in Fig. 28-10. It is these slots that force the movable gears to move.

The gears have shift forks (6, 7, and 31 in Fig. 28-10)

which straddle collars on the gears. When the shift forks are moved back and forth, the gears also move back and forth. Note that the shift forks are mounted on shift rods (8 and 32 in Fig. 28-8). The shift forks are free to move on these rods. The upper ends of the rods have pins which enter the slots in the shift drum (21) when the transmission is assembled.

When the drum rotates, the pins must follow the slots in the drum. This forces the pins to move back and forth as the drum turns. When the pins move, the forks and gears move with them. This action produces the shift patterns shown in Fig. 28-6.

Figure 28-11 shows the linkage of Fig. 28-7 com-

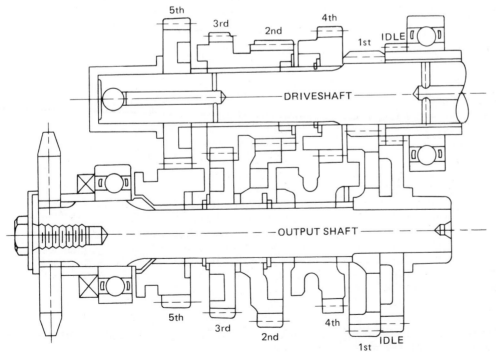

5th 3rd 2nd 4th 1st IDLE

DRIVESHAFT

OUTPUT SHAFT

5th 3rd 2nd 4th 1st IDLE

Fig. 28-8 Gears, shafts, and related parts of a transmission using the type of gearshift mechanism shown in Fig. 28-7. (*Kawasaki Heavy Industries, Ltd.*)

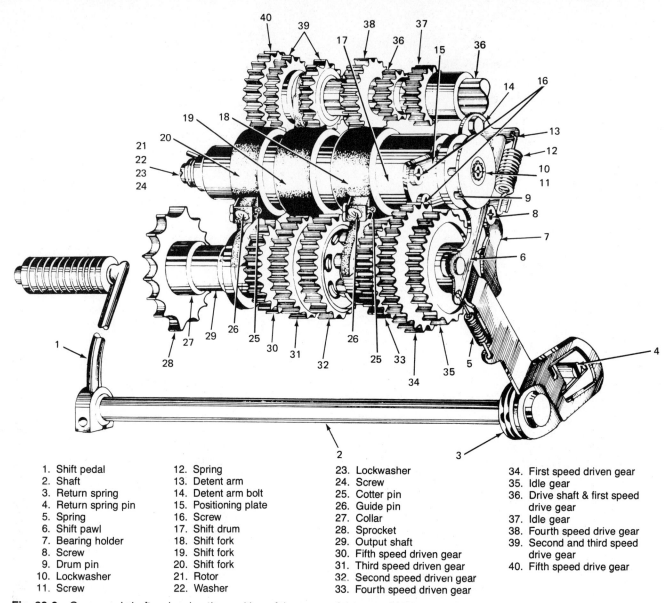

Fig. 28-9 Gears and shafts, showing the position of the gears of the transmission shown in Fig. 28-8. (*Kawasaki Heavy Industries, Ltd.*)

1. Shift pedal
2. Shaft
3. Return spring
4. Return spring pin
5. Spring
6. Shift pawl
7. Bearing holder
8. Screw
9. Drum pin
10. Lockwasher
11. Screw
12. Spring
13. Detent arm
14. Detent arm bolt
15. Positioning plate
16. Screw
17. Shift drum
18. Shift fork
19. Shift fork
20. Shift fork
21. Rotor
22. Washer
23. Lockwasher
24. Screw
25. Cotter pin
26. Guide pin
27. Collar
28. Sprocket
29. Output shaft
30. Fifth speed driven gear
31. Third speed driven gear
32. Second speed driven gear
33. Fourth speed driven gear
34. First speed driven gear
35. Idle gear
36. Drive shaft & first speed drive gear
37. Idle gear
38. Fourth speed drive gear
39. Second and third speed drive gear
40. Fifth speed drive gear

pletely disassembled. The gearshift pedal is located, in most motorcycles, on the left. Figure 28-12 shows the gearshift procedure. Neutral is located between first and second gear. First gear is engaged by fully depressing the pedal from the neutral position. Shifting into successively higher gears is produced by pulling up on the shift lever once for each gear. When shifting from first to second gear, neutral is automatically missed. When shifting to neutral, depress or raise the lever half a stroke between first and second.

There are several drum-and-fork arrangements in different transmission models. Figure 28-13 shows a design which has two of the shift forks installed directly on the shift drum, with the third fork (3) installed on a separate shift rod. The system works in exactly the same way as the arrangement previously discussed. Figure 28-14 is a closeup of one of the forks installed on the drum. This illustration shows the right and wrong

way to install the cotter pin holding the shift-fork pin in place.

Figure 28-15 shows the gearshift mechanism for a four-speed transmission in which both shift forks are mounted on the drum. This illustration shows another feature of the drum type of gearshift mechanisms. This is the drum-stopper mechanism, shown to the right. In this transmission, the drum-stopper mechanism includes a stopper lever with a roller on its end. This roller rides in a cam on a stopper plate (13). As the drum turns, the roller moves up and down in the cam. A spring keeps the roller in contact with the cam.

As the roller drops into each of the valleys in the cam, its spring tends to hold the cam and, therefore, the drum. In effect, this locks the drum in a specific gear position. A push from the gearshift pedal is needed to turn the drum against the tension of the stopper-lever spring.

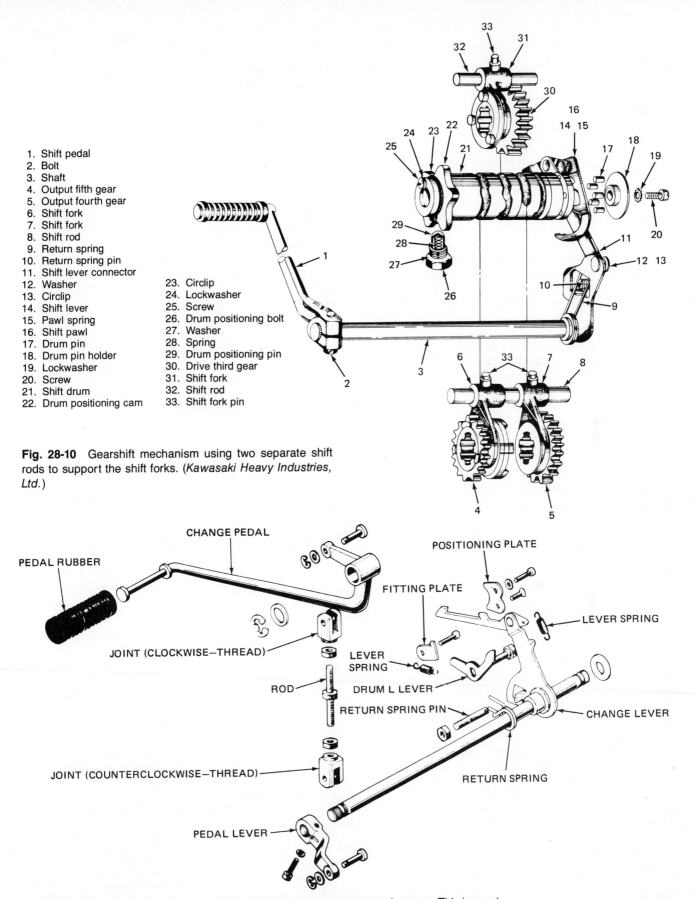

1. Shift pedal
2. Bolt
3. Shaft
4. Output fifth gear
5. Output fourth gear
6. Shift fork
7. Shift fork
8. Shift rod
9. Return spring
10. Return spring pin
11. Shift lever connector
12. Washer
13. Circlip
14. Shift lever
15. Pawl spring
16. Shift pawl
17. Drum pin
18. Drum pin holder
19. Lockwasher
20. Screw
21. Shift drum
22. Drum positioning cam

23. Circlip
24. Lockwasher
25. Screw
26. Drum positioning bolt
27. Washer
28. Spring
29. Drum positioning pin
30. Drive third gear
31. Shift fork
32. Shift rod
33. Shift fork pin

Fig. 28-10 Gearshift mechanism using two separate shift rods to support the shift forks. (*Kawasaki Heavy Industries, Ltd.*)

Fig. 28-11 Gearshift mechanism, disassembled so separate parts can be seen. This is used with the shift mechanism shown in Fig. 28-7. (*Kawasaki Heavy Industries, Ltd.*)

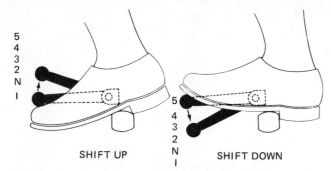

Fig. 28-12 Gearshift procedure. Moving the shift lever up or down, as shown, produces the various gear positions in the transmission.

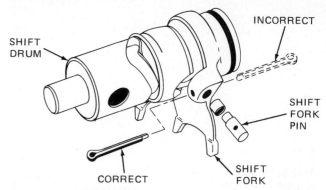

Fig. 28-14 Shift drum, showing the right and wrong way to fit the cotter pin that holds the shift-fork pin in the fork. (*Suzuki Motor Company, Ltd.*)

28-7 OTHER GEARSHIFT ARRANGEMENTS

Instead of a round drum being used to shift the gears, some transmissions use a flat plate with slots cut in it. Figure 28-18 shows this flat plate, called the *gearshifter cam,* installed in the assembly. The gearshifter cam is shown separately as number 5 in Fig. 28-19. The transmission has four speeds and uses two shifter forks (10 in Fig. 28-19). The basic operation is the same as in the transmissions previously discussed.

As the gearshifter cam is turned, the pins, or finger rollers, on the shift forks (11) follow the slots cut in the gearshifter cam (5). This moves the shift forks, and therefore the gears, to achieve the four gear ratios through the transmission.

The purpose of the stopper is to prevent the drum from drifting out of a gear position. The stopper holds the drum in the gear position that has been selected until a gearshift is made by movement of the gearshift pedal.

Other types of stoppers, or drum-positioning arrangements, are used. For example, in Fig. 28-10, the stopper plate is called the *drum-positioning cam* (22). A spring-loaded positioning pin rides on this cam. As the drum is turned, the pin first retracts and then is pushed out by its spring. When the drum is turned to a specific gear position, the pin, because it is spring-loaded in a valley between two cam lobes, keeps the drum from turning away from this position.

Figure 28-16 is a disassembled view of a five-speed transmission in which all three forks are assembled on the same shift rod. Figure 28-17 shows the complete assembly on an engine. Notice that the two illustrations also include the kick starter. The kick starter is covered in Chap. 19.

1. Gearshift fork
2. Gearshift fork
3. Gearshift fork
4. Shifting fork pin
5. Shifting fork roller
6. Cotter pin
7. Shift drum
8. Shifting cam drive pin
9. Shifting cam stopper pin
10. Drive pin retainer
11. Screw
12. Gearshift cam plug
13. Cam guide
14. Screw
15. Cam stopper pawl
16. E ring
17. Gearshift cam stopper
18. Stopper spring
19. Stopper washer
20. Stopper bolt
21. Shifting cam stopper
22. Stopper spring
23. Stopper housing gasket
24. Stopper housing
25. Shift rod
26. Gearshift shaft comp.
27. Pawl return spring
28. Shaft return spring
29. Shifting shaft oil seal
30. Shifting arm stopper
31. Lockwasher
32. Gearshifting switch
33. Switch gasket

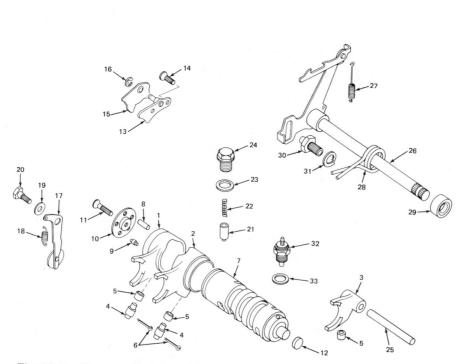

Fig. 28-13 Disassembled view of the gearshift mechanism for a five-speed transmission. (*Suzuki Motor Company, Ltd.*)

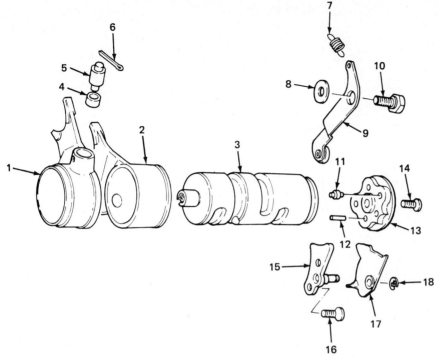

1. High speed gearshift fork
2. Low speed gearshift fork
3. Gearshift drum
4. Gearshift fork pin roller
5. Gearshift fork pin
6. Cotter pin
7. Gearshift drum stopper spring
8. Gearshift drum stopper washer
9. Gearshift drum stopper lever
10. Gearshift drum stopper bolt
11. Gearshift drum stopper pin (short)
12. Gearshift drum pin
13. Gearshift drum stopper plate
14. Screw
15. Gearshift drum guide
16. Screw
17. Gearshift drum stopper pawl

Fig. 28-15 Gearshift mechanism for a four-speed transmission. Note the drum-stopper mechanism in the gear into which it has been shifted. (*Suzuki Motor Company, Ltd.*)

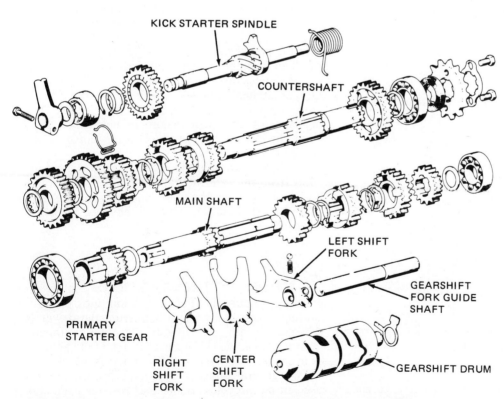

Fig. 28-16 Complete gears and shafts for a five-speed transmission. (*Honda Motor Company, Ltd.*)

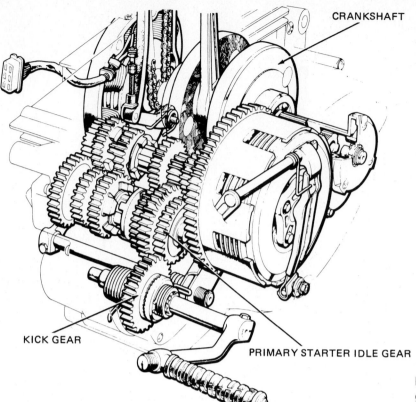

CRANKSHAFT

KICK GEAR

PRIMARY STARTER IDLE GEAR

Fig. 28-17 Kick starter and the transmission gears for a one-cylinder engine. (*Honda Motor Company, Ltd.*)

28-8 DUAL-RANGE TRANSMISSIONS
A few motorcycles have an auxiliary transmission attached to one side of the main transmission (Fig. 28-20). By changing the final-drive gear ratio from the transmis-

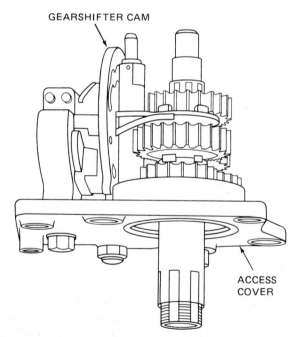

GEARSHIFTER CAM

ACCESS COVER

Fig. 28-18 Transmission access cover with gears, forks, and flat gearshifter cam for a four-speed transmission. (*Harley-Davidson Motor Company, Inc.*)

sion, a high and low, or *dual-range*, transmission is provided. This doubles the number of speed ratios available from the transmission. Using a five-speed transmission and a two-speed intermediate gearbox, the motorcycle shown in Fig. 28-20 has 10 forward speeds.

In the power train shown in Fig. 28-20, power flows by chain from the engine crankshaft through the clutch and transmission to the final drive gear. However, the ratio of the final drive gear is selected by the rider. For more rapid acceleration, the low range is used. When high-speed touring with maximum fuel economy is desired, the intermediate gearbox (or *subtransmission*) is shifted to high.

To absorb shock in the power train, the final drive shaft from the intermediate gearbox incorporates a heavy spring shock absorber. Note also that this motorcycle has shaft drive, which is covered in detail in Chap. 29.

28-9 AUTOMATIC TRANSMISSIONS
In the automobile, the automatic transmission does the job of shifting gears without any help from the driver. Although there are some motorcycles with "automatic" transmissions, the shifting action is not fully automatic as in the automotive automatic transmission.

Two general types of automatic transmissions are used in motorcycles. Some trail bikes and minibikes have been equipped with a centrifugal clutch, or a V-belt torque converter (Fig. 28-21). This type of auto-

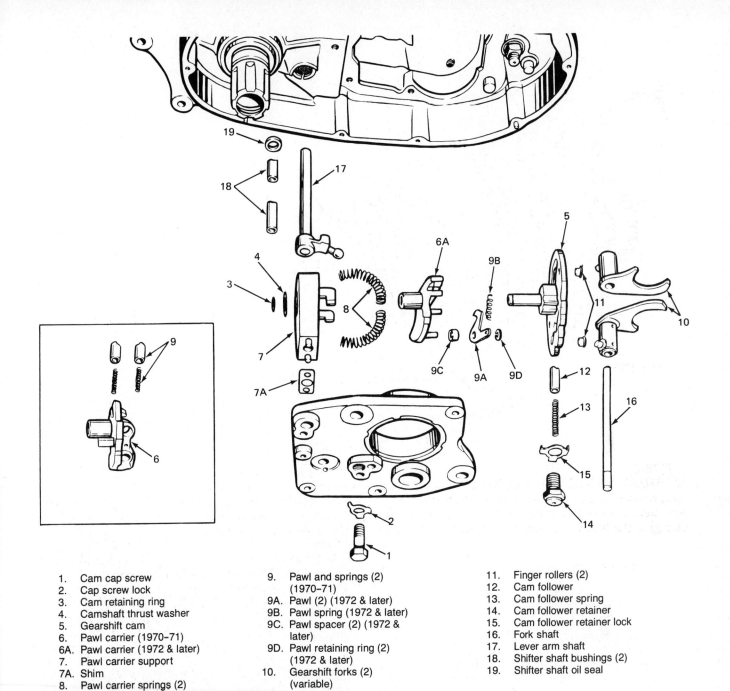

Fig. 28-19 Gearshift mechanism for a transmission using a flat gearshifter cam (5). *(Harley-Davidson Motor Company, Inc.)*

1. Cam cap screw
2. Cap screw lock
3. Cam retaining ring
4. Camshaft thrust washer
5. Gearshift cam
6. Pawl carrier (1970–71)
6A. Pawl carrier (1972 & later)
7. Pawl carrier support
7A. Shim
8. Pawl carrier springs (2)

9. Pawl and springs (2) (1970–71)
9A. Pawl (2) (1972 & later)
9B. Pawl spring (1972 & later)
9C. Pawl spacer (2) (1972 & later)
9D. Pawl retaining ring (2) (1972 & later)
10. Gearshift forks (2) (variable)

11. Finger rollers (2)
12. Cam follower
13. Cam follower spring
14. Cam follower retainer
15. Cam follower retainer lock
16. Fork shaft
17. Lever arm shaft
18. Shifter shaft bushings (2)
19. Shifter shaft oil seal

matic transmission may be used alone or with a gearbox that has two or three forward speeds.

The centrifugal clutch is basically two variable-width pulleys connected by a V-type drive belt. One pulley, the drive pulley, is attached to the engine crankshaft. The other pulley, the driven pulley, is connected to the rear wheel. At idle speed, a spring holds the sides of the drive pulley so far apart that they do not grip the belt. Therefore the belt does not turn. This is shown in Fig. 28-21a.

As engine speed increases, the centrifugal force overcomes the spring and pushes the sides of the drive pulley closer together until they grip the belt. Now the belt begins to turn the driven pulley (Fig. 28-21b). This condition provides maximum torque to the driven pulley.

With further increases in engine speed, the increased centrifugal force causes the sides of the drive pulley to move even closer together. At the same time the sides of the driven pulley are moving apart an equal distance. This changes the gear ratio through the centrifugal clutch, as shown in Fig. 28-21c. Now the gear ratio through the pulleys decreases the torque and increases the speed of the driven pulley.

The second type of automatic transmission is found on some mid-size and larger street and touring motorcy-

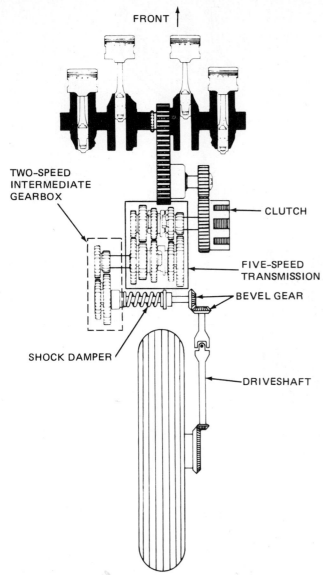

Fig. 28-20 Motorcycle with a two-speed, or dual-range, auxiliary gearbox which provides 10 forward speeds. (*Honda Motor Company, Ltd.*)

cles. This automatic transmission has a two-speed gearbox coupled with a fluid-coupling type of torque converter (upper left in Fig. 28-22). The transmission does not shift automatically. The rider must shift it from low to high, although there is no clutch to operate. An almost 2:1 torque increase is available through the torque converter. When multiplied by the gear ratio through the transmission, this provides the acceleration needed for most riding in the high range. However, maximum low-speed acceleration is made available to the rider by shifting the transmission to the low range.

28-10
TRANSMISSIONS FOR SHAFT DRIVE

Most motorcycles have a chain that transmits power from the transmission to the rear wheel. However, some mid-size and larger street and touring bikes have a shaft type of final drive. Final drives are discussed in detail in Chap. 29.

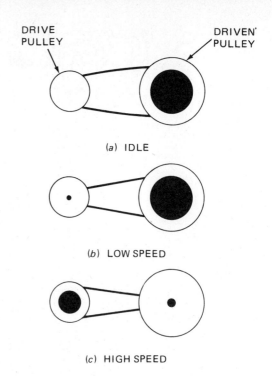

(a) IDLE

(b) LOW SPEED

(c) HIGH SPEED

Fig. 28-21 Operation of a centrifugal clutch. (*ATW*)

Most motorcycles with shaft drive have a longitudinal crankshaft. This means that the crankshaft is in a straight line with the drive shaft to the rear wheel. However, some shaft-drive motorcycles have a transverse engine (Figs. 28-20 and 28-23). As you can see by studying these illustrations, to get power from the crankshaft to the rear wheel, another shaft and a pair of bevel gears must be added to the transmission.

28-11
INTRODUCTION TO MOTORCYCLE TRANSMISSION SERVICE
On previous pages, we described the construction and operation of various transmissions used in motorcycles. We saw that the transmissions are constant-mesh units with various gears always in mesh. Shifting is done by moving cer-

Fig. 28-22 An automatic transmission used by Honda. It combines a two-speed gearbox, which is shifted by the rider, with a fluid-coupling type of torque converter. (*Honda Motor Company, Ltd.*)

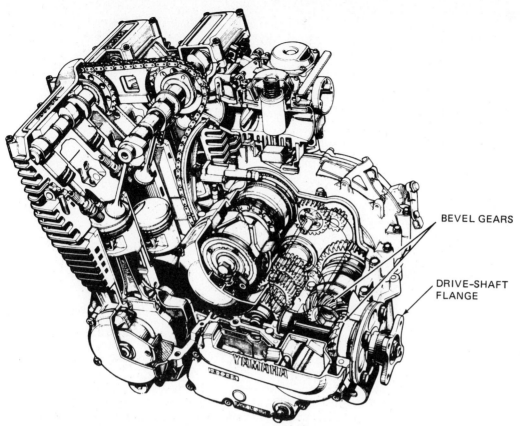

BEVEL GEARS

DRIVE-SHAFT
FLANGE

Fig. 28-23 Cutaway view of an engine and transmission, showing the use of bevel gears to deliver power from the transmission to the drive-shaft flange. (*Yamaha Motor Corporation*)

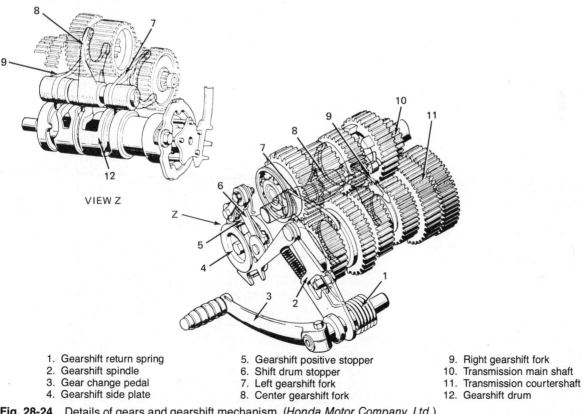

VIEW Z

1. Gearshift return spring
2. Gearshift spindle
3. Gear change pedal
4. Gearshift side plate
5. Gearshift positive stopper
6. Shift drum stopper
7. Left gearshift fork
8. Center gearshift fork
9. Right gearshift fork
10. Transmission main shaft
11. Transmission courtershaft
12. Gearshift drum

Fig. 28-24 Details of gears and gearshift mechanism. (*Honda Motor Company, Ltd.*)

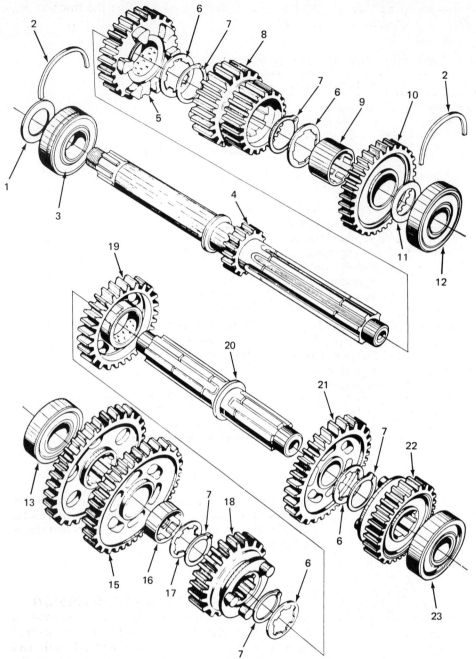

Fig. 28-25 Exploded view of the gears and shafts in a transmission. (*Honda Motor Company, Ltd.*)

1. Thrust washer
2. Ball bearing set ring A
3. Special ball bearing
4. Transmission main shaft
5. Main shaft fourth gear (37T)
6. Thrust washer
7. Circlip
8. Main shaft second & third gear (24T & 27T)
9. Bushing
10. Main shaft top gear (33T)
11. Thrust washer
12. Radial ball bearing
13. Radial ball bearing
14. Final drive gear
15. Countershaft low gear (47T)
16. Bushing
17. Thrust washer
18. Countershaft fourth gear (34T)
19. Countershaft third gear (36T)
20. Transmission countershaft
21. Countershaft second gear (41T)
22. Countershaft top gear (31T)
23. Ball bearing

tain gears from one side to the other, thereby engaging the dogs in the sides of those gears in the slots in the sides of other gears. This locks the two gears together so that both rotate as a unit.

Now we discuss transmission troubleshooting, adjustments, disassembly, inspection, and reassembly. When you are working on a specific transmission, you should have the shop manual that applies in front of you. Disassembly and reassembly procedures and adjustment specifications are different for different models of transmissions.

28-12
TROUBLESHOOTING THE
TRANSMISSION   Motorcycle transmissions seldom cause trouble. However, if trouble does occur, you will want to know what can cause transmission troubles and how to fix them. Transmission troubles can be divided into three categories:

1. Difficult gearshifting
2. Excessive gear noise
3. Gears that slip out of mesh

The chart that follows lists these troubles, along with probable causes and corrections. Then, after the chart, the repair procedures required to fix the troubles are covered.

TRANSMISSION TROUBLE DIAGNOSIS CHART

Trouble	Probable Cause	Correction
1. Difficult gearshifting	a. Improper clutch disengagement	Adjust clutch
	b. Damaged gear	Replace
	c. Foreign object in transmission	Remove and repair unit
	d. Gearshift fork damaged	Repair
	e. Improper operation of drum stopper and shift-pedal linkage	Repair or replace
	f. Main shaft and countershaft out of alignment	Align and repair
	g. High-viscosity oil	Replace with more suitable oil
2. Excessive gear noise	a. Excessive gear backlash	Repair and replace defective parts
	b. Worn bearings	Replace
3. Gears slip out of mesh	a. Worn fingers (pins) on gearshift forks	Replace
	b. Worn dog holes in gears	Replace worn gears
	c. Worn splines	Replace shaft and gears

⚙ 28-13
DISASSEMBLING A FIVE-SPEED
TRANSMISSION As an example of a complete overhaul procedure, we cover the transmission of the four-cylinder engine shown in Fig. 27-12. This is a four-cycle OHC engine.

To get at the transmission, you must first remove the cylinder head, cylinder, and cam chain tensioner. Next, the oil must be drained and the crankcase must be

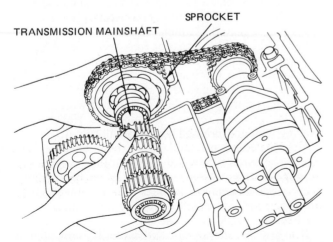

Fig. 28-26 Removing the transmission main shaft and sprocket. (*Honda Motor Company, Ltd.*)

disassembled. This exposes the transmission, as shown in Fig. 28-24, so you can remove the transmission parts. Figure 28-25 is an exploded view of the gears and shafts used in the transmission.

⚙ 28-14
DISASSEMBLING THE TRANSMISSION
Figure 28-26 shows the removal of the transmission mainshaft from the crankcase. After the main-shaft assembly is out, remove the final-shaft oil guide and assembly from the upper crankcase. Next, pull out the gearshift-fork shaft. Take out the gearshift forks. Unscrew the neutral stopper bolt and remove the stopper. Take out the gearshift from the crankcase.

Remove the countershaft top gear (Fig. 28-27). Now you can remove the countershaft gear assembly (Fig. 28-27) from the lower crankcase. Pull the countershaft bearing from the crankcase with the bearing puller. After checking gear backlash, as explained in the following section, the gears can be removed from the shafts.

Be very careful to identify each gear as it is removed, so you can put it back onto the shaft in its original position. Place the gears and other parts on a clean workbench in the exact order in which you remove them. This will make it easier to put everything back together again in the original order.

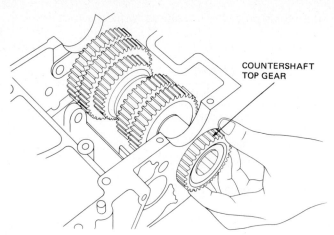

Fig. 28-27 Removing the countershaft top gear. (*Honda Motor Company, Ltd.*)

28-15
INSPECTING TRANSMISSION PARTS

After the transmission is disassembled, but before the main shaft and the countershaft are removed from the crankcase, the gear backlash should be checked, as shown in Fig. 28-28. Attach a dial indicator with the finger against a tooth. Hold the meshing gear on the countershaft and turn the meshing gear on the main shaft to see how much backlash there is between the gears. Check each set of matching gears in this manner.

The backlash, when the transmission is new, is 0.0018 to 0.0055 inch [0.046 to 0.140 mm]. If the backlash, because of wear, has increased to 0.008 inch [0.20 mm] or more, the pair of meshing gears should be replaced. On the first-gear set, the specifications are 0.0017 to .0052 inch [0.044 to 0.140 mm] when new, but the service limits are the same.

Check the dogs on the gears and replace the gears if the dogs are worn. Make sure the gears slide smoothly on their shafts. Some of the gears have bushings which enable them to turn on their shafts, and the fit of these gears should be checked. This check is made by mea-

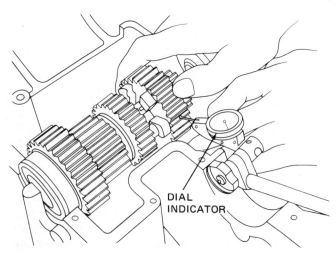

Fig. 28-28 Using a dial indicator to check gear backlash. (*Honda Motor Company, Ltd.*)

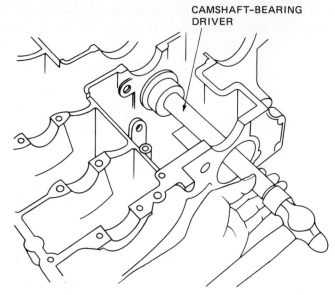

Fig. 28-29 Installing a countershaft bearing with a bearing driver. (*Honda Motor Company, Ltd.*)

suring the bore of the gear with an inside micrometer or a small-hole gauge and then checking the shaft with a micrometer. The clearance when the transmission is new is 0.0016 to 0.0032 inch [0.04 to 0.082 mm]. Gears should be replaced if the clearance is over 0.0072 inch [0.182 mm].

Check the gear teeth for wear, chips, or cracks. Replace any gear with defective teeth. When replacing a gear, also replace the gear with which it meshes.

Check the gearshift forks as follows. Measure the fingers on the gearshift fork with a micrometer. Discard the gearshift fork if fingers are worn to less than 0.240 inch [6.1 mm], or if the fork dog (the pin that rides in the gearshift drum groove) is worn to less than 0.260 inch [6.6 mm]. Check the inside diameter of the fork bushing. Discard the fork if it has worn to more than 0.513 inch [13 mm]. Check the fork shaft with a micrometer and replace it if it has worn to less than 0.508 inch [13 mm].

Check the gearshift drum outside diameter with a micrometer. Replace it if the large diameter has worn to less than 1.414 inch [36 mm] or if the small diameter has worn to less than 0.515 inch [12 mm].

Check the ball bearings for free operation. A sealed bearing should never be cleaned in solvent because this will remove the lubricant and ruin the bearing. The open type of bearing (ball or roller) should be cleaned by slowly rotating it while it is covered with solvent. After it is cleaned, remove and air-dry it. Never spin a bearing with compressed air! This will ruin it.

Hold the center race and slowly rotate the outer race to see if it turns freely and without noise, a feeling of roughness, or excessive sloppiness. If the bearing feels gritty, clean it again and recheck it. If it still feels gritty, the bearing races or balls probably are damaged, and the bearing should be discarded.

If a bearing checks out satisfactorily, immediately lubricate it, wrap it in clean, lint-free cloth, and put it aside until you are ready to reinstall it.

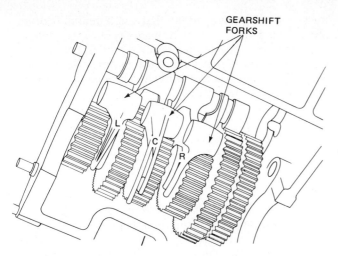

Fig. 28-30 Locations of the gearshift forks. (*Honda Motor Company, Ltd.*)

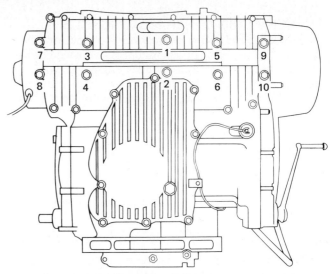

Fig. 28-31 Tightening sequence for the lower crankcase attaching bolts. (*Honda Motor Company, Ltd.*)

Check the crankcase for damage, such as cracks or nicks in the mating surfaces. Nicks should be filed off with a fine-cut file. Wash away all filings with solvent and then air-dry the crankcase parts. Stripped threads in tapped holes can be repaired with a threaded insert (Fig. 26-1). First, drill out the worn threads. Then tap the hole with the special tap that comes with the threaded-insert installation set. Then screw the threaded insert into the new threads, bringing the hole back to its original thread size. The original bolt can then be used in the hole.

Damaged studs may be repaired with a thread chaser. This is a sort of die that is run down over the damaged threads and straightens them back to their original condition, provided the damage is not too severe.

28-16 REASSEMBLING A FIVE-SPEED TRANSMISSION

After all parts have been inspected and either discarded or replaced with new parts, you are ready to reassemble the transmission. Essentially, reassembly is just the reverse of disassembly. Proceed as follows.

Mount the primary chain tensioner on the lower crankcase. Reinstall all gears on their shafts. Use new Circlips and make sure they are properly seated in the shaft grooves. Drive the countershaft bearing into the lower crankcase with a bearing driver, as shown in Fig. 28-29. With the countershaft fifth gear off the countershaft, install the countershaft in the crankcase. The countershaft fifth gear is installed later from the outside of the case (Fig. 28-27).

Mount the gearshift drum, and install the neutral stopper with a bolt. The neutral position on the drum is at the depression on the drum.

Install the gearshift forks. Refer to Fig. 28-30 for their proper locations. The forks are stamped with the letters R, C, and L. The L and R forks are used with the countershaft, and the fingers of these forks therefore fit into the collars of countershaft fourth and fifth gears.

The C fork is used with main-shaft second-and-third gear. The dogs, or pins, on the backs of the forks fit into the grooves in the gearshift drum, as shown in Fig. 28-30.

Install the final shaft in the upper crankcase. Install the final-shaft oil guide. Mount the primary sprocket on the transmission main-shaft assembly, and install the complete unit into the upper crankcase.

Install the two dowel pins, oil collar, and "D" ring in the upper crankcase. Apply liquid gasket on the mounting flange, and assemble the lower crankcase. Make sure all the gears are in neutral and that the center gearshift fork is inserted into the main-shaft second-and-third gear collar.

Next, assemble the camshaft chain and primary chain on the crankshaft, and install it in the upper crankcase. Assemble the primary chain on the primary sprocket, and install the sprocket on the main shaft. Set the lower crankcase on top. Install the mounting bolts and tighten them in the pattern shown in Fig. 28-31 to the torque specified in the shop manual.

Turn the crankcase assembly so you can torque down the upper crankcase. Install the countershaft bearing, and assemble the gear-change positive stopper, drum stopper, and gearshift arm.

Install the clutch for proper location of parts. Then install the spark-advance mechanism with the pin on the back side of the advancer fitting into the crankshaft pin. Install the contact-breaker assembly and washer. Install the starting-motor reduction gear and clutch gear. Install the alternator with the mounting bolts, torquing the bolts to specifications.

Next, install the cylinder and cylinder head, following the proper tightening sequence. Add the proper grade and amount of oil to the engine.

NOTE The procedure of installing the cylinder and head includes timing the valves, adjusting the spark advance, and adjusting the valve-tappet clearance. These procedures are covered in other chapters.

SERVICING OTHER MOTORCYCLE TRANSMISSIONS

In the previous sections, we covered the servicing of one model of five-speed transmission used with a four-cylinder engine. If you can understand the service procedures on that transmission, you should have little problem with other transmissions. All transmissions that use a gearshift drum are serviced in a very similar manner. However, whenever you are working on a specific model, try to have the shop manual that covers the motorcycle you are servicing. Then you can follow the procedures and the specifications that apply.

CHAPTER 28
REVIEW QUESTIONS

1. Why is a transmission necessary in a motorcycle?
2. Define *gear ratio*.
3. What is the relationship between torque and the speed of gears?
4. Explain the difference between a sliding-gear transmission and a constant-mesh transmission.
5. How are shifts made using dogs?
6. What causes the shift drum to rotate?
7. Explain why a motorcycle transmission cannot be shifted directly from third to fifth.
8. What is the purpose of the drum-stopper mechanism in the transmission?
9. Describe how a slotted flat plate is used in some transmissions to shift gears.
10. What is a dual-range transmission?
11. Name two types of automatic transmissions used in motorcycles.
12. Describe the operation of a centrifugal clutch.
13. In an automatic transmission that has a torque converter and a two-speed gearbox, how is the transmission shifted from low to high range?
14. Discuss why some transmissions used with shaft drive must have a set of bevel gears that other transmissions do not require.
15. List the three categories of transmission trouble.
16. What steps must be performed before a transmission can be worked on?
17. Explain how to clean and inspect the parts of a transmission after it is disassembled.
18. What must be done when an inspection reveals a gear with a cracked tooth?
19. How are transmission bearings cleaned?
20. What type of oil is used in most motorcycle transmissions?

CHAPTER **29**

MOTORCYCLE FINAL DRIVES

After studying this chapter,
you should be able to:

1. Describe the final-drive chain and explain how to maintain and service it.

2. Describe a shaft drive and explain why a universal joint and a slip joint are needed.

3. Replace the sprockets and drive chain.

4. Replace the universal joint and slip joint.

5. Overhaul a shaft-type final drive.

29-1 INTRODUCTION TO MOTORCYCLE FINAL DRIVES

In this chapter, we will cover the parts of the motorcycle that carry power from the engine and transmission to the rear wheel and the parts that support the motorcycle. This engine power rotates the rear wheel, which in turn propels the motorcycle.

Most motorcycles use a chain and sprockets to carry the power to the rear wheel. There are some motorcycles, however, that use a shaft and gears instead of a chain. Both systems, called *final drives,* are covered in detail in this chapter.

29-2 FUNDAMENTALS OF CHAIN DRIVE

There are from one to four chains on a motorcycle. The chain that is visible is the one that carries power from the drive sprocket on the transmission output shaft to the driven sprocket on the rear wheel. This is called the *final-drive chain.* You can see this chain in many of the pictures of motorcycles in the book. The other chain or chains are inside the engine-transmission assembly.

The chain consists of a series of rollers, with bushings, mounted on pins which are connected by small metal plates. Figure 29-1 shows top and side views of a short length of chain. The rollers of the chain fit into the valleys between the teeth of the sprocket.

Let us look at the chain a little more closely. It is made up of two types of links: inside links and outside links. Figure 29-2 shows the construction of both types. To the left, we see the parts of the inside link. It includes two plates, two bushings, and two rollers. At the bottom of the drawing, you see an inside link assembled. To the right, from the top, you see the parts of an outside link. It consists of two plates and two pins.

At the bottom right of the drawing you see how an inside link and an outside link are connected. The two pins are secured to, or *staked* into, one plate of the outside link. The two pins are then inserted through the plates, bushings, and rollers of two inside links. Then the second plate of the outside link is installed and the pins are secured to the second plate. The rollers can turn on the bushings, and the bushings can turn on the pins for low friction at the joints.

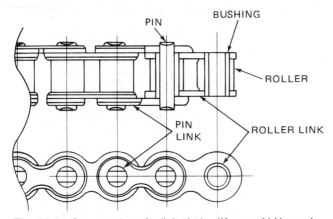

Fig. 29-1 Construction of a link chain. (*Kawasaki Heavy Industries, Ltd.*)

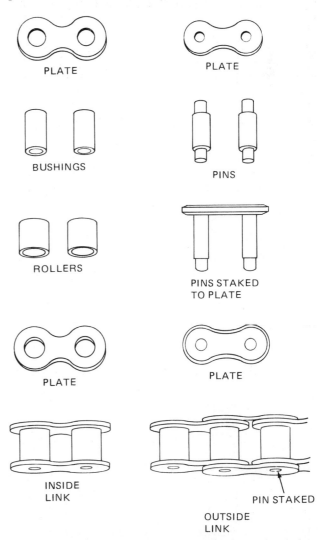

Fig. 29-2 Details of the inside and outside links of a chain.

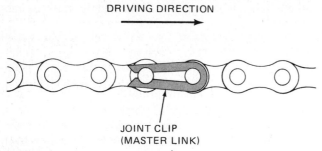

DRIVING DIRECTION

JOINT CLIP
(MASTER LINK)

Fig. 29-3 Joint clip on a drive chain.

In some roller chains, the pins are not staked, but are locked into position by a joint clip, as shown in Fig. 29-3.

29-3 CHAIN LUBRICATION AND LUBRICATORS

A chain should be kept lubricated to minimize wear. Lubrication reduces friction between the joints of the chain and between the chain and the sprocket. It also helps keep out dirt that could cause accelerated wear. The dirtier the environment in which a chain is used, the faster the chain will wear. Therefore, it is important that the chain be lubricated periodically.

If the chain does not have an automatic oiler or lubricator, you should lubricate the chain at frequent intervals. Under normal conditions, you should lubricate the chain every 500 miles [800 km] with SAE 90 gear lube. If the chain is very dirty, wash it first with solvent.

CAUTION Use the solvent *outside* or in a safe place where there is no flame or sparks that could set off an explosion of the solvent fumes!

Use a bristle brush to brush on the solvent. Wipe it off with a clean shop cloth. Rotate the rear wheel so you get the entire chain clean.

Then lubricate each pin and roller in each link. Do not simply pour the oil on, but apply it carefully. Excess amounts of oil will collect dirt or be thrown off as the sprockets turn.

If the chain is very dirty or appears worn, you should remove it from the motorcycle so that you can clean it and check it for length and wear. We will describe these services later.

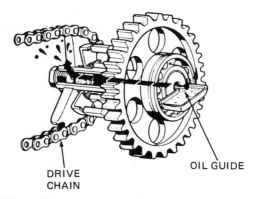

DRIVE CHAIN

OIL GUIDE

Fig. 29-4 Drive-chain oiler, located at the drive sprocket. (*Honda Motor Company, Ltd.*)

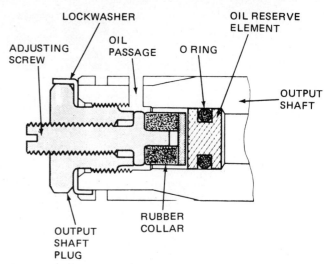

LOCKWASHER

ADJUSTING SCREW

OIL PASSAGE

O RING

OIL RESERVE ELEMENT

OUTPUT SHAFT

OUTPUT SHAFT PLUG

RUBBER COLLAR

Fig. 29-5 Sectional view of the chain-oiler adjustment arrangement. (*Honda Motor Company, Ltd.*)

Some motorcycles have a chain *lubricator* that feeds oil to the chain as the motorcycle operates. Figure 29-4 illustrates one type. The oil feeds through the hollow output shaft to the outer surface of the drive sprocket. From there, it flows outward to the chain, as shown in Fig. 29-4.

Figure 29-5 shows the details of the adjustment which changes the amount of oil being fed to the chain. Oil feeds through the hollow shaft to the oil-reserve element. This is a porous ceramic plug that allows oil to seep through. The oil then must pass the hole through the center of the rubber collar (Fig. 29-5). If the adjusting screw is turned in, the rubber collar is squeezed so that it expands in diameter. This reduces the oil passage and cuts down on the amount of oil that can get through. If the adjusting screw is backed off, the rubber collar can shrink in diameter and allow more oil to flow through.

Before a motorcycle leaves the factory, the adjusting screw is adjusted to maximum flow to assure adequate chain lubrication during the initial running period. If there is excessive oil on the wheel rim, spokes, and fender, the adjusting screw should be turned in a clockwise direction about 1/4 turn. Figure 29-6 shows the

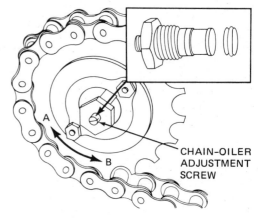

A

B

CHAIN-OILER ADJUSTMENT SCREW

Fig. 29-6 Location of the chain-oiler adjustment screw (*Honda Motor Company, Ltd.*)

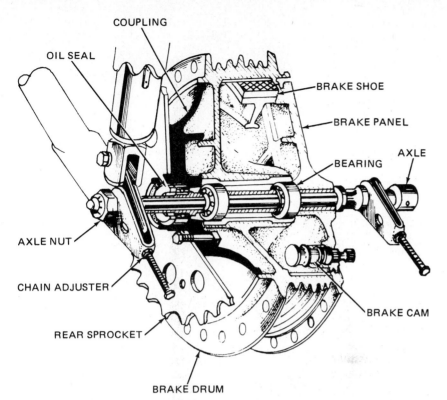

COUPLING

OIL SEAL

BRAKE SHOE

BRAKE PANEL

BEARING

AXLE

AXLE NUT

CHAIN ADJUSTER

REAR SPROCKET

BRAKE CAM

BRAKE DRUM

Fig. 29-7 Rear axle and support, showing how the chain adjusters are assembled. When the locknuts are loosened and the screws are turned in, the axle is moved toward the rear of the motorcycle. This takes up chain slack. (*Kawasaki Heavy Industries, Ltd.*)

location of the chain-oiler adjustment screw. Remove the rear crankcase cover to get to the screw. Then turn the screw in direction A to reduce the amount of oil going to the chain.

After making the adjustment, wipe all oil off the chain with a clean shop cloth. Install the rear crankcase cover. Then ride the motorcycle briefly at about 50 mph [80 kph]. Examine the chain for oil. The adjustment is correct if the chain links and rollers are wet with oil and other areas are free of oil. Continue to readjust the screw as necessary to obtain this condition.

To assure proper lubrication of the chain, some motorcycles have an enclosed chain drive. The engine drive sprocket is surrounded by an aluminum case. Another aluminum case surrounds the rear sprocket. A pair of rubber tubes connects the two cases. About one liter of lithium grease is enclosed in the system with the chain and sprockets. As the chain runs through the grease, it heats up and melts. Then the liquid grease provides proper lubrication of the chain.

29-4 REMOVING AND INSTALLING DRIVE CHAINS
Occasionally, it is necessary to remove a drive chain to repair it or to install a new chain. Removing a chain is a two-step process. You first slacken the chain and slide it off the sprockets. Then you break the chain or disconnect one link so that you can remove the chain completely.

Back off the adjusting screws at the rear wheel to slacken the chain. The adjusting screws on a typical rear-wheel assembly are shown in Fig. 29-7. Turn the screws in the direction that allows the rear wheel to move forward. (On some motorcycles, you have to loosen the axle to move the wheel.) When

there is enough slack in the chain, lift the chain off the sprockets.

If the chain has a joint clip, as shown in Fig. 29-3, the clip can be pulled off with pliers so the chain can be broken and taken off. After the clip is removed, one plate is taken off. The other plate, with pins staked to it, can be pulled from the other side of the chain. Figure 29-8 shows the two plates and pins removed. This breaks the chain.

On the type of chain with a joint clip, when you reinstall the clip, be sure the closed end is facing in the direction the chain moves, as shown in Fig. 29-3.

Some chains do not have a joint clip. On these, if the chain has to be broken for any reason, a special tool must be used to press the pins out of one plate of an outside link. A chain might be broken to add or remove links, for example, if the sizes of the sprockets are changed. Sprocket sizes might be changed to change the drive ratio between the drive sprocket and the driven sprocket.

Figure 29-9 shows the complete procedure for break-

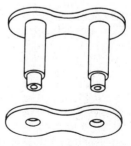

Fig. 29-8 One link of a chain, with one plate removed. This is an outside link. (*Suzuki Motor Company, Ltd.*)

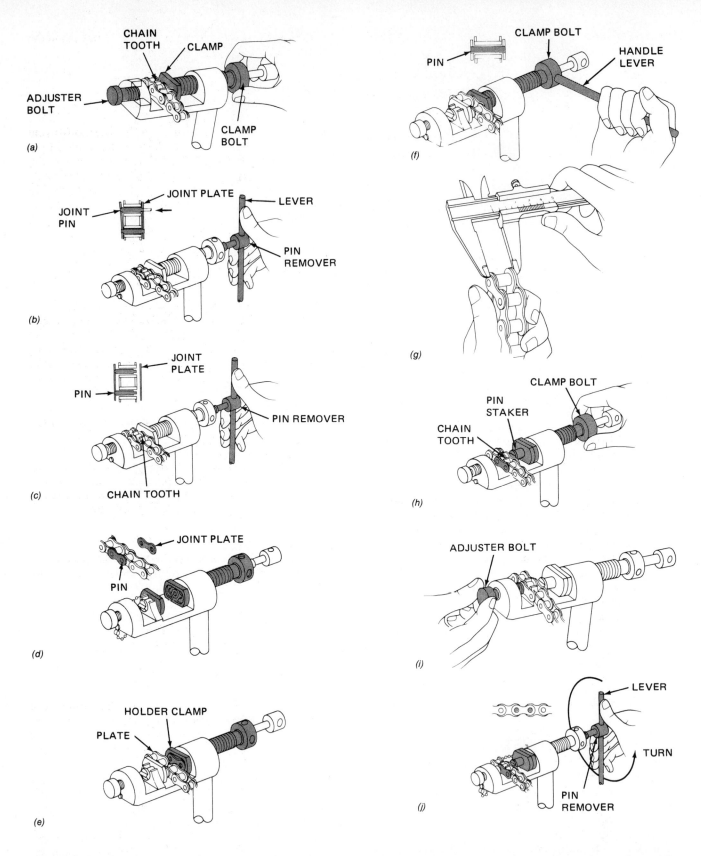

Fig. 29-9 (*a*) Turning the clamp bolt to clamp the chain in the chain holder. (*b*) Turning the pin remover to press pin out of one plate. (*c*) Turning the pin remover to press the second pin out of the plate. (*d*) The plate removed from the link. (*e*) Preparing to reinstall the plate. (*f*) Tightening the clamp bolt to press the plate onto the pins. (*g*) Measuring the distance between the two plates on an outside link. (*h*) Preparing to stake the pins. (*i*) Turning the adjuster screw in against the pin to be staked. (*j*) Making the first stake. (*Honda Motor Company, Ltd.*)

ing and reconnecting a chain that does not have a joint clip.

1. Select the outside link that is to be removed to break the chain. Position it in the chain holder, as shown in Fig. 29-9a. The chain holder has teeth that fit between the chain rollers. Back off the adjuster bolt so it does not interfere with pin removal. Screw in the clamp bolt so the clamp holds the chain firmly.
2. Use the lever in the pin remover (shown in Fig. 29-9b) to apply pressure to the pin of the link you are cutting. Turn the pin remover in just enough to push the pin out of the plate, as shown in the insert to the upper left in Fig. 29-9b.
3. Unclamp the chain by backing off the clamp bolt. Move the chain in the chain holder so the next pin of the outside link is in position to be pressed out (Fig. 29-9c). Reclamp the chain by turning the clamp bolt in. Turn the pin remover (Fig. 29-9c) in with the lever to press the pin out. Now, both pins of the link are pressed out of the plate, as shown to the upper left in Fig. 29-9c. Unclamp the chain. Remove the chain from the chain holder. The link with the two pins still attached to it can now be pulled away from the chain, so the chain is broken. The chain should be cleaned and inspected, as explained later.
4. To reconnect the chain, install the link with pins into the two end rollers and plates of two inside links. Insert the pins into the end rollers, as shown in Fig. 29-9d, thereby joining the two ends of the chain.
5. Apply a thin coat of grease to the recess of the clamp. Set the plate into the recess of the clamp, as shown in Fig. 29-9e. The chamfered side, which has the chain code stamped on it, should face inward. The grease will hold the plate in place.
6. Position the chain on the chain holder, as shown in Fig. 29-9e, in readiness to press the plate onto the pins. Make sure the plate is lined up with the pins. Turn the clamp bolt in to press the plate onto the ends of the pins, as shown in Fig. 29-9f. Turn until the link moves up against the steps on the pins.
7. To make sure that the link has been pressed on far enough, measure the distance between the two links, as shown in Fig. 29-9g. Refer to the manufacturer's shop manual for the correct measurement. If the measurement exceeds the maximum allowable, put the chain back into the chain holder and press the plate tighter onto the pins.
8. Stake the pins as follows. Put the pin staker into the chain holder, as shown in Fig. 29-9h. The wedge end of the staker should be in line with the center of the pin to be staked. Tighten the clamp bolt finger tight. Then turn in the adjuster bolt until it is tight against the end of the pin to be staked (Fig. 29-9i). Tighten the adjuster bolt finger tight.
9. Use the lever to turn the pin remover three-fourths of one turn, as shown in Fig. 29-9j. This stakes the pin in one direction.
10. Back off the pin remover about two turns. Rotate the wedge end of the staker 90°. Repeat Step 8. This stakes the pin in two directions 90° apart.

11. Repeat the staking operation for the other pin in the outside link.

29-5 ADJUSTING DRIVE CHAINS

A chain with too much slack will sag, and it may snap or jump off the sprockets. To adjust the drive chain, put the motorcycle on the stand with the rear wheel off the floor. Move the chain up and down at a midpoint between the two sprockets. Carefully measure the total movement. The actual dimension specified by motorcycle manufacturers varies. A typical specification is that the total movement should be between 0.5 and 1.0 inch [12 to 25 mm].

NOTE Chain slack should be checked with the rider sitting on the motorcycle. This compensates for normal compression of the suspension due to the rider's weight.

If adjustment is required, first examine the adjustment arrangement at the rear axle. The usual arrangement is shown in Fig. 29-7. Raise the rear wheel off the ground and loosen the locknuts on the axle. Then turn the adjustment screws inward to move the axle back. Be sure to turn both screws the exact same amount. This will keep the rear wheel in alignment. Most motorcycles have adjusting marks on the swing arm and on the adjusters. These marks should be referred to when making adjustments.

After the adjustment is complete, tighten the locknuts. Now, rotate the rear wheel and note its relationship to the frame. It should be exactly in line with the frame. If it is not, readjust the screw that will move the axle as necessary to bring the wheel into line.

29-6 INSPECTING AND CLEANING CHAINS AND SPROCKETS

Check the drive chain for the following:

Damaged rollers
Loose pins
Dry or rusted plates
Kinked or bent plates
Excessive wear
Acid spots (from battery overflow)

To check for excessive wear, lay the chain out on the bench and measure between a specified number of pins. For example, Suzuki specifies measuring a span of 20 pins, with the chain stretched to its maximum. In this specific instance, the new length of the chain should be 11⅞ inch [301.6 mm]. If the distance is greater than 12⅛ inch [308.0 mm], the chain is too worn to be used any more. It should be discarded and a new chain installed.

Clean the chain thoroughly in a suitable solvent. Use a bristle brush (not a wire brush) to make sure you get all the caked dirt and grease off. It is during this cleaning that you can inspect the chain, as noted in the previous section. Rinse the chain in clean solvent and allow it to dry. Then put the chain in a pan containing a mixture of 10 parts of SAE 10W-40 engine oil and 1 part of petroleum jelly. This is 1 pint of oil to 5 ounces of pe-

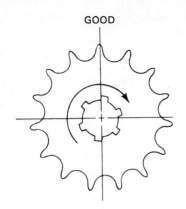

GOOD

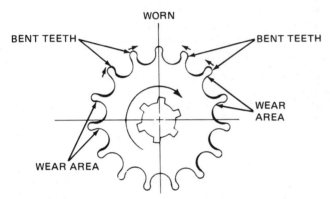

WORN

BENT TEETH → ← BENT TEETH

WEAR AREA

WEAR AREA

Fig. 29-10 (Top) A good sprocket. (Bottom) Various types of sprocket wear and damage. (*Yamaha Motor Company, Ltd.*)

troleum jelly. Heat the pan to 150° to 250°F [66° to 100°C] for about 10 minutes.

Remove the pan from the heat and carefully agitate the chain with a screwdriver. This gets the lubricant into all the bushings. When the lubricant and chain have cooled off, remove the chain. Allow it to hang over the pan and drain off the lubricant. Then use a clean cloth to wipe off the excess lubricant. The chain is now ready for installation.

Check the sprockets for worn or damaged teeth. Figure 29-10 shows how the teeth on a sprocket wear. Worn teeth make the chain noisy and wear the chain rapidly. Figure 29-10 also shows where to measure the

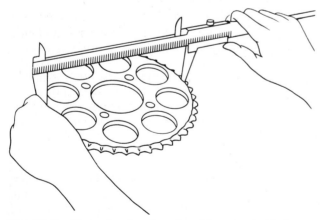

Fig. 29-11 Measuring the diameter of the sprocket between the base of the teeth. (*Kawasaki Heavy Industries, Ltd.*)

diameter of the sprocket at the base of the teeth. Figure 29-11 shows the measurement being made with a vernier caliper. If the wear is excessive, the sprocket should be discarded.

29-7 SHAFT DRIVES
In most motorcycles, a chain and sprocket are used as the final drive to transmit engine power from the transmission to the rear wheel. However, some motorcycles use shaft drive instead. Figure 29-12 shows a motorcycle with shaft drive.

The *drive shaft*, also called the *propeller shaft*, transmits power from the transmission output shaft to the final-drive gearcase at the rear wheel. The final-drive gearcase contains the ring gear and the pinion gear. With shaft drive, the rotary motion of the transmission output shaft is carried through the drive shaft to the pinion gear. The pinion gear is mounted on the end of the drive shaft, as shown in Fig. 29-13. The pinion gear meshes with the ring gear, which is attached to the final-driven flange in the rear-wheel hub. As the drive shaft turns, the pinion gear turns the ring gear, causing the rear wheel to rotate.

Shaft drive eliminates many of the problems associated with chain drive. Gone are the noise, the thrown oil, and the need for frequent lubrication and frequent slack adjustments of the chain. The only regular maintenance required is to check the oil level in the final-drive gearcase.

29-8 DRIVE SHAFT COUPLINGS
The engine-transmission assembly in a motorcycle is mounted rigidly in the frame. Because of the swing arm and rear springs, the rear wheel moves up and down in a slight arc. This means two things:

1. The drive shaft must change in length slightly as the rear wheel moves up and down, because the distance between the transmission and the rear wheel changes.
2. The angle of drive must change as the rear wheel moves up and down, because the transmission output shaft is stationary while the wheel hub is moving up and down.

To allow for the two variations, two different kinds of joints, or couplings, may be necessary on the drive shaft. *A universal joint takes care of the changes in drive angle. A slip joint takes care of the changes in shaft length.* When a chain and sprockets are used, the chain automatically takes care of the changes in drive angle. At the same time, the drive chain does undergo some change in length as the rear wheel moves up and down. This contributes to the wear of the chain and sprockets.

To transmit power between two shafts that are at an angle to each other, a *universal joint* is used. Figure 29-14 shows a simple universal joint. It is a double-hinge joint consisting of two Y-shaped yokes and a cross-shaped member called a *spider*. One of the yokes is on the driving shaft, and the other is on the driven shaft. The four arms of the spider, called the *trunnions*, are as-

Fig. 29-12 A motorcycle that has shaft drive. Notice the use of a drive shaft, instead of a chain, to the rear wheel. (*Yamaha Motor Company, Ltd.*)

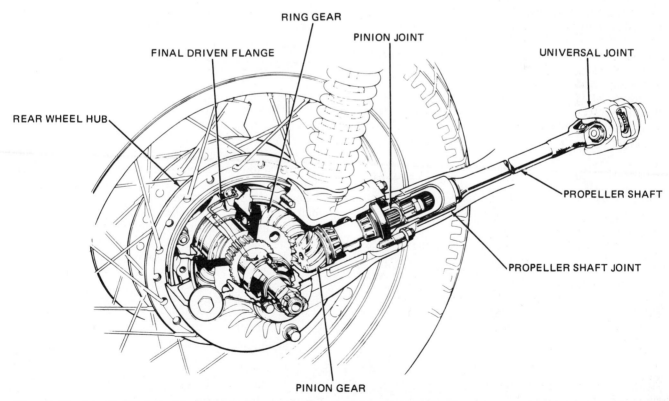

RING GEAR

FINAL DRIVEN FLANGE

PINION JOINT

UNIVERSAL JOINT

REAR WHEEL HUB

PROPELLER SHAFT

PROPELLER SHAFT JOINT

PINION GEAR

Fig. 29-13 A sectional view of the drive shaft and hub. (*Honda Motor Company, Ltd.*)

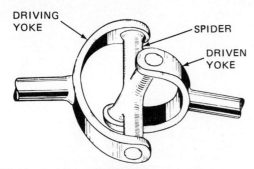

Fig. 29-14 A simple universal joint.

sembled into bearings in the ends of the two shaft yokes. The driving shaft and yoke cause the spider to rotate, and the other two trunnions on the spider cause the driven shaft to rotate. When the two shafts are at an angle to each other, the bearings in the yokes permit the yokes to swing around on the trunnions with each revolution. A variety of universal joints has been used, but the ones in common use now are the spider-and-two-yoke type and the constant-velocity type.

Figure 29-15 is a disassembled view of a practical spider-and-two-yoke type of universal joint. Note the similarity between it and the simple universal joint shown in Fig. 29-14. As you can see, the practical joint has needle bearings on each trunnion of the spider. The bearings are held in place by snap rings that drop into undercuts in the yoke-bearing holes. This type of universal joint is sometimes called a *Cardan* universal joint.

The Cardan universal joint has one important drawback. When the driving shaft and the driven shaft are at an angle to each other, the driven shaft will rotate in jerks or spurts, even though the driving shaft is rotating smoothly. This problem is overcome by using the *constant-velocity,* or *double-Cardan,* universal joint. When a constant-velocity universal joint is used, the driving shaft and the driven shaft always have the same speed.

The constant-velocity universal joint includes two separate universal joints, as shown in Fig. 29-16. They are linked by a ball and seat which split the angle of the

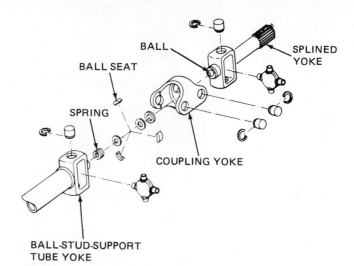

Fig. 29-16 Disassembled view of a constant-velocity universal joint.

two shafts between the two universal joints. Because the two joints operate at the same angle (half the total angle), the variations in driven shaft speed that could result from a single joint are canceled out.

Figure 29-17 shows a *slip joint.* In the power train, a slip joint is a variable-length connection that permits the drive shaft to change its effective length. It has outside splines on one shaft and matching internal splines on a mating hollow shaft. The splines cause the two shafts to rotate together but permit the two to move endwise in relation to each other. This allows changes in the length of the drive shaft as the rear wheel moves toward or away from the transmission. To minimize wear and maximize spline life, the splines should be lubricated with a high-temperature, high-pressure grease.

29-9
FINAL-DRIVE GEARCASE The rotation of the drive shaft transmits torque through the ring gear to the rear wheel. The wheel rotates and moves the motorcycle forward, as the rear axle pushes against the rear fork. The torque not only attempts to rotate the wheel in one direction, but also attempts to rotate the final-drive gearcase in the opposite direction. To understand this, let's review the construction of the final drive.

The pinion gear is mounted on the end of the drive shaft. You can see this in Fig. 29-13. Teeth on the pinion gear mesh with teeth on the ring gear. The ring gear is

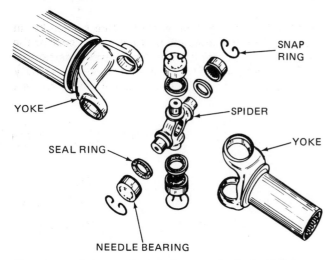

Fig. 29-15 Spider-and-two-yoke type of universal joint.

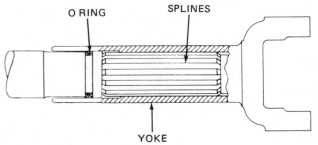

Fig. 29-17 Cutaway view of a slip joint.

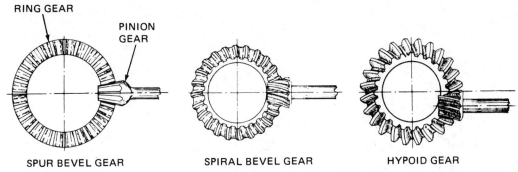

RING GEAR

PINION GEAR

SPUR BEVEL GEAR   SPIRAL BEVEL GEAR   HYPOID GEAR

Fig. 29-18 Spur bevel, spiral bevel, and hypoid pinion gears and ring gears.

bolted to the final-driven flange, which is bolted to the rear-wheel hub. So, indirectly, the ring gear is connected to the rear-wheel hub.

The torque applied through the pinion gear forces the ring gear and rear wheel to rotate. It is the side thrust of the pinion-gear teeth against the ring-gear teeth that makes the ring gear rotate. This side thrust also causes the pinion-gear shaft to push against the pinion-shaft bearings. The thrust against the shaft bearings is in a direction opposite to the thrust of the pinion-gear teeth against the ring-gear teeth. Since the pinion-shaft bearings are held in the gearcase, it tries to rotate in a direction opposite to the ring-gear and rear-wheel rotation. This action is called *rear-wheel torque*. One of the jobs performed by the rear fork and rear springs is to prevent excessive gearcase movement from this torque.

On acceleration, for example, the rear end of some shaft-drive motorcycles will lower slightly.

Since the ring gear has many more teeth than the pinion gear, a gear-ratio reduction occurs in the gearcase. Gear ratios in the final drive vary. The Honda GL1000 has 7 teeth on the pinion gear and 33 teeth on the ring gear. This means that the ring gear has 4.714 times as many teeth as the pinion gear. Therefore, the pinion gear has to rotate 4.714 times to rotate the ring gear one complete revolution.

The gear ratio in the gearcase may be referred to as the *axle ratio*, the *secondary-drive ratio*, or the *final-drive ratio*. However, this is not necessarily the same as the overall gear ratio, which is the ratio of engine revolutions to wheel revolutions.

If you want to calculate the axle ratio and you have the ring gear and the pinion gear, do this. Count the number of teeth on each. Divide the number of teeth on the ring gear by the number of teeth on the pinion gear. The answer is the axle ratio.

Figure 29-18 shows different types of final-drive gears. At one time, straight bevel gears were used for the pinion gear and the ring gear. Then spiral bevel gears, which are quieter, were used. Hypoid gears are also used. These are similar to spiral bevel gears. The difference is that the tooth formation permits the pinion gear to be placed below the center line of the ring gear, as you can see in Fig. 29-18. Also, there is a wiping action between the teeth as they mesh and unmesh. This wiping action is always found in hypoid gears.

Because of the wiping action, a special hypoid-gear lubricant must be used.

Figure 29-19 illustrates gear-tooth nomenclature. The mating teeth to the left show clearance and backlash. The tooth to the right has its various parts named. *Clearance* is the distance between the tip of the tooth of one gear and the valley between adjacent teeth of the mating gear. *Backlash* is the distance between adjacent meshing teeth in the driving and driven gears. It is the distance one gear can rotate backward, or backlash, before it will cause the other gear to move. The *toe* is the smaller section of the gear tooth, and the *heel* is the larger section.

29-10 DIAGNOSING SHAFT-DRIVE TROUBLES

Usually, the first sign of trouble within the final-drive gearcase is noise. The kind of noise you hear can help you determine what is causing the trouble. Be sure that the noise is actually coming from inside the gearcase before you take it apart. Sometimes you can be fooled by universal-joint, wheel-bearing, or tire noise. Note whether the noise is a hum, growl, or knock and whether the noise is produced when the motorcycle is operating on a smooth road or on rough pavement where the rear wheel is moving up and down. Note whether the noise is more evident when the engine is driving the motorcycle or when the motorcycle is coasting.

Humming A humming noise is often caused by an incorrect internal adjustment of the pinion gear or the ring gear. An incorrect adjustment prevents normal tooth contact and can cause rapid tooth wear and early failure of the gear set. The humming noise will take on a

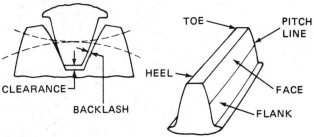

TOE   PITCH LINE

HEEL   FACE

CLEARANCE   FLANK

BACKLASH

Fig. 29-19 Gear-tooth nomenclature.

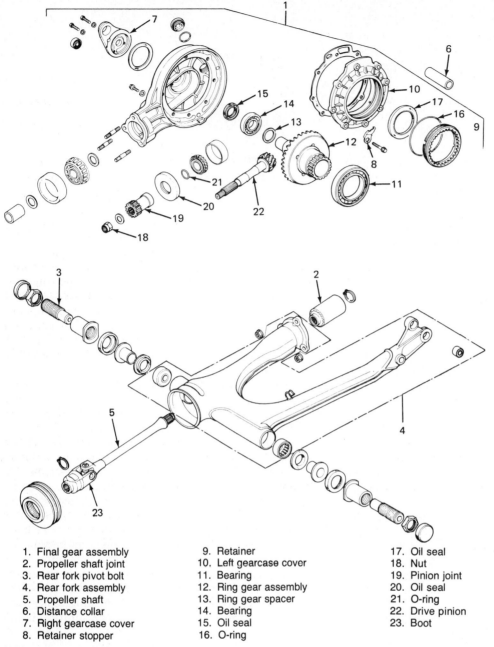

1. Final gear assembly
2. Propeller shaft joint
3. Rear fork pivot bolt
4. Rear fork assembly
5. Propeller shaft
6. Distance collar
7. Right gearcase cover
8. Retainer stopper
9. Retainer
10. Left gearcase cover
11. Bearing
12. Ring gear assembly
13. Ring gear spacer
14. Bearing
15. Oil seal
16. O-ring
17. Oil seal
18. Nut
19. Pinion joint
20. Oil seal
21. O-ring
22. Drive pinion
23. Boot

Fig. 29-20 Disassembled view of the drive shaft and the gearcase assembly. (*Honda Motor Company, Ltd.*)

growling sound as the wear progresses. Check the shop manual for the motorcycle you are servicing when you are adjusting the ring gear or the pinion gear.

Noise on Acceleration Noise that is more evident when the motorcycle is accelerating probably means there is heavy contact on the heel ends of the gear teeth. Noise that is more evident when the motorcycle is coasting probably means there is heavy toe contact. Both these conditions must be corrected. Refer to the manufacturer's shop manual for the procedures.

Other noises may be caused by damaged ring-gear bearings or pinion-gear bearings. Any bearing damage

in the final-drive gearcase may prevent the rear wheel from rotating freely.

Damaged splines on the ends of the propeller shaft may make noise. Also, noise will be heard from within the gearcase when the lubricant level is low. Oil leaks from the gearcase can be caused by a high oil level, damaged seals, or a clogged hub breather pipe.

The breather pipe allows any pressure buildup within the gearcase to escape. One end of the breather pipe is close to the center of the gearcase, which has little splashing oil. The other end is open to a vent hole in the left gearcase cover. Any oil that is forced up the pipe by escaping pressure is trapped in two small storage chambers in the gearcase cover, called the *primary chamber*

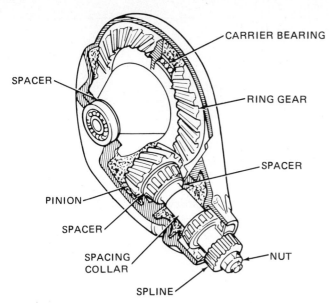

Fig. 29-21 A motorcycle ring-and-pinion-gear assembly. (*Honda Motor Company, Ltd.*)

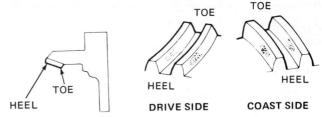

Fig. 29-22 Ring-gear-to-pinion-gear tooth-contact pattern. (*Honda Motor Company, Ltd.*)

and the *secondary chamber*. When the pressure drops inside the gearcase, the trapped oil from the chambers returns to the gearcase. The oil should be SAE 80 in winter and SAE 90 in summer.

29-11
SERVICING SHAFT DRIVES Repair and overhaul procedures on shaft-type final drives vary among motorcycle models. Try to have the manufacturer's shop manual that covers the model you are working on when you begin to repair or adjust a final drive. Many shaft-drive motorcycles have nonrepairable universal joints. When defective, the complete universal-joint assembly is replaced as a unit.

Shaft drive does not require any external adjustments to compensate for wear. Ring-gear-to-pinion-gear backlash is adjustable. The depth of the gear-tooth engagement, or the clearance, also is adjustable. To make either of these adjustments, you must disassemble the drive hub.

Figure 29-20 shows the complete shaft drive and gearcase for the Honda GL1000 in disassembled view. Note that the drive shaft is covered and protected by the rear fork assembly. The driveshaft passes through the right arm of the rear fork. A rubber boot covers the universal joint and its connection to the end of the transmission output shaft.

To remove the drive hub, place the motorcycle on its center stand. Then drain the oil. A drain plug is located at the bottom of the hub. Remove the shock absorbers and the brake-caliper bolt from the rear fork. Place a block under the rear tire, and remove the cotter pin, nut, and rear axle. Be sure the caliper is out of the way, and then disengage the rear wheel from the hub drive spline. Remove the wheel.

Reinstall the left shock absorber. This will support the rear fork. Then remove the three attaching nuts and slide the hub free.

Figure 29-21 shows the ring-and-pinion-gear assembly. To disassemble it, two special tools are required: a four-pin spanner wrench and a spline wrench. To remove the ring gear from the housing, start by taking off the ring-gear-seal lock. After removing this lock, the ring-gear seal can be removed with the spanner wrench by turning counterclockwise. Remove the ring of 8-mm screws. Apply force on opposite sides of the ring-gear bearing support until the ring gear disengages from the housing. On the small end of the ring gear, which engages the bearing on the right side of the housing, you will find a spacer. This spacer controls the depth of engagement of the ring gear in the pinion and is the only ring-gear adjustment.

To remove the pinion shaft, use the spline spanner wrench to hold the spline, and then remove the castle nut. The spline can then be removed, revealing a large seal. Use a seal puller to remove the seal. Next, remove the tapered roller bearing on the forward side of the pinion shaft by pulling it out of the front of the housing. The pinion shaft and rear tapered roller bearing are removed through the center of the housing.

To inspect the tooth-contact pattern, assemble the pinion gear, ring gear, left gearcase cover, and retainer to the final-drive gearcase. It is not necessary to have the seals installed when checking this adjustment. Install the seals on final assembly.

Paint several of the teeth on the ring gear with a light coating of Prussian blue, white lead, or red lead. These are various types of marking pastes. Turn the pinion gear by hand in its normal direction of rotation until the painted sections make contact with the pinion gear. Compare the pattern with the drive-side pattern shown in Fig. 29-22. If the tooth-contact pattern is distributed over the center part of each pinion-gear tooth toward the heel, the adjustment is correct.

Next, turn the pinion gear by hand in the opposite direction. Check the pattern for the coast side, as shown in Fig. 29-22. If either pattern is abnormal, you must adjust the ring gear and the pinion gear.

Notice the two spacers located on either side of the pinion-gear bearing in Fig. 29-21. These two spacers control the position of the pinion gear in relation to the ring gear.

After the tooth-contact pattern is properly adjusted, reassemble the final drive and reinstall it on the motorcycle. Then fill the hub with the proper type and amount of hypoid gear lubricant. The hub is filled to the proper level when the lubricant reaches the lower threads of the oil fill-plug hole.

1. In how many places can chains be used in the power train of a motorcycle?
2. Describe the construction of a chain.
3. What steps are performed to properly clean, inspect, and lubricate a chain?
4. How does a chain lubricator work?
5. Explain how to remove a chain that does not have a master link or joint clip.
6. How do you remove a chain that has a master link?
7. Describe how to adjust the chain.
8. Explain how to clean and inspect a sprocket.
9. What is shaft drive?
10. What are the advantages of shaft drive?
11. What is a universal joint?
12. Explain why a slip joint is used with shaft drive.
13. Describe how to service the ring-gear-and-pinion of a shaft-drive motorcycle.
14. How do you find the gear-reduction through the gearcase of a shaft-drive motorcycle?
15. Define *clearance* and *backlash*.
16. What can cause a humming from the gearcase of a shaft-drive motorcycle?
17. List the possible causes of noise on acceleration that may come from the gearcase of a shaft-drive motorcycle.
18. Describe how to service the final drive of a shaft-drive motorcycle.
19. Explain how to adjust the ring-gear-and-pinion to obtain the proper tooth-contact pattern.
20. What type of lubricant is used in the gearcase of a final-drive gearcase?

MOTORCYCLE CHASSIS

Part 6 covers the maintenance and servicing of motorcycle frames, suspension, steering, brakes, wheels, and tires.

There are three chapters in Part 6. They are:

CHAPTER 30

MOTORCYCLE FRAMES, SUSPENSION, AND STEERING

After studying this chapter,
you should be able to:

1. Describe various types of motorcycle frames.

2. Discuss the modern rear-suspension systems used on motorcycles and explain how the swinging fork works.

3. Discuss the springing and damping arrangements for rear wheels.

4. Describe shock absorbers and explain how they work and how they are adjusted.

5. Service rear-suspension systems.

6. Discuss front-suspension and steering systems and explain how they work.

7. Adjust the steering damper, front springs, steering stability, and the steering stem.

8. Service the front suspension.

30-1 FUNDAMENTALS OF MOTORCYCLE FRAMES, SUSPENSION, AND STEERING

In Chap. 4, you were introduced to motorcycle frames, suspension, and steering. Now, in this chapter, we discuss the details of these motorcycle components. The purpose of the frame is to support the engine, the transmission assembly, and the rider. The frame provides attachments for the wheels so that the frame is supported by the wheels. The front wheel is mounted so that it can be pivoted from side to side, which permits the motorcycle to be steered. The frame must be strong yet light, rigid under stress, and formed so that the wheels, engine, seat, and rider can be easily placed on the frame.

Figures 4-2 to 4-6 show some frame types, rear and front suspension, and steering. Many frames are made

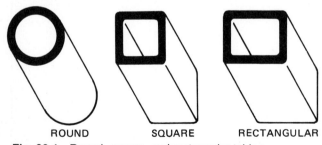

Fig. 30-1 Round, square, and rectangular tubing.

of round tubing. Other motorcycles have frames made of rectangular or square tubing (Fig. 30-1).

The advantage of using a square or rectangular tube is that it has a flat surface to which lugs can more easily be brazed or welded. In addition, it is easier to attach accessories to flat surfaces, with screws or bolts, than to round surfaces. A possible disadvantage is that a square or rectangular frame is somewhat less strong on a comparative weight basis.

Another type of frame construction is called a *spine frame*. This name comes from the use of a single strong large-diameter tube, or box-section. It serves as the sole means for tying together the front and rear wheels and for tying the engine to the transmission. The spine frame, shown in Fig. 4-2c, is made of pressed heavy-gauge steel plate which has been welded together. The front end contains a support for the front-wheel steering head. The rear end, in the construction shown in Fig. 4-2c, includes the rear fender and attachments for the pivoted fork that supports the rear wheel. There will be more on suspension later.

On some models, the spine doubles as an oil tank. It is hollow and large enough to hold several ounces. Some spines use the engine and transmission assembly as an integral part of the frame itself.

The *reverse spine frame,* or *open frame,* shown in Fig. 4-2d is used on motor scooters and lightweight bikes. The advantage of this design to the rider is that the rider sits "in" the bike, rather than straddling a frame member.

30-2 REAR SUSPENSION

Early motorcycles had what was called a *rigid frame*. The rear-wheel axle was fastened to a rigid rear section of the frame, as on most bicycles today. This was called a *hardtail* and is shown in Fig. 30-2. However, a rear-suspension system was desired that would allow the rear wheel to move up and down for better control and riding comfort.

One problem with rear suspension is that the distance between the drive sprocket on the transmission and the driven sprocket on the wheel changes as the wheel moves up and down. On early rear-suspension systems, the rear-wheel axle was supported by two tubes. The axle moved up and down in a straight line to absorb road shocks. This design was much like the modern front-suspension system which we will cover later. The tubes

Fig. 30-2 An early motorcycle with a rigid frame to which the rear-wheel axle is fastened. (*Smithsonian Institution*)

292

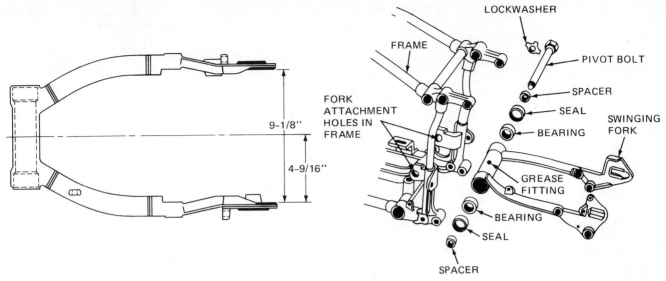

Fig. 30-3 Details of a rear fork and attaching parts. The drawing to the left shows the correct dimensions of the fork. (*Harley-Davidson Motor Company, Inc.*)

contained springs and dampers. The rear-wheel axle was attached to the lower end of the tubes. The upper ends of the tubes were attached to the frame.

With this design, movement of the rear wheel up and down caused the distance between the sprockets to change. The drive chain was first pulled tight and then slackened excessively. This was unsatisfactory because it put great stress on the chain and resulted in a short chain life.

Later, the swinging-fork design was adopted for practically every type of motorcycle. The principle of the swinging fork is shown in Fig. 30-3. The fork consists of a one-piece assembly, as shown in Fig. 30-3. The inner

end is attached, through bearings, to the frame. This attachment point is close to the drive sprocket on the side of the transmission. The ends of the two legs of the fork are attached to the rear-wheel axle. As the wheel moves up and down, the fork swings up and down. The wheel axle and the outer ends of the fork move in an arc, as shown in Fig. 30-4. As a result, the distance between the two sprockets changes very little. Chains are not stressed as severely and last longer.

Figure 30-3 shows one swinging-fork design. Figure 30-5 shows a swinging fork for a lightweight motorcycle. Note its simpler construction. It uses a pair of bushings on which the arm pivots. The design shown in Fig. 30-6 is similar. It also uses a pair of bushings which support the front end of the fork and allow the fork to pivot. Note that this design includes a pair of footrest bars. The design also includes two chain adjusters (10 in Fig. 30-6). When the nuts are turned on these adjusters, they move the wheel axle to change the distance between the chain sprockets. Other models use screws which are turned to make the adjustment.

A variety of springing and damping arrangements has

Fig. 30-4 As the fork swings up and down, the axle moves in an arc. Therefore the distance between the sprockets changes very little.

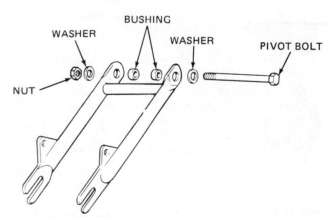

Fig. 30-5 Rear fork for a lightweight motorcycle. (*Harley-Davidson Motor Company, Inc.*)

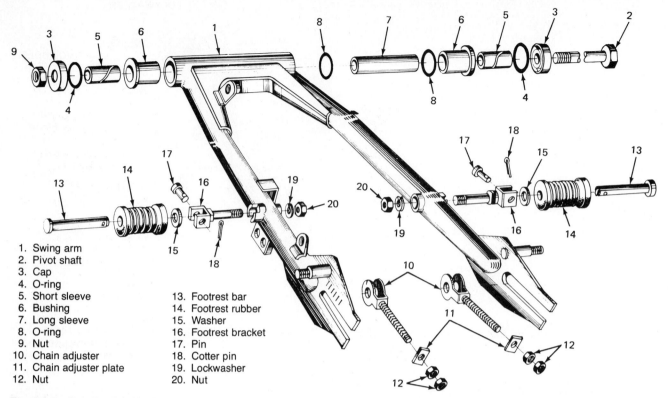

1. Swing arm
2. Pivot shaft
3. Cap
4. O-ring
5. Short sleeve
6. Bushing
7. Long sleeve
8. O-ring
9. Nut
10. Chain adjuster
11. Chain adjuster plate
12. Nut

13. Footrest bar
14. Footrest rubber
15. Washer
16. Footrest bracket
17. Pin
18. Cotter pin
19. Lockwasher
20. Nut

Fig. 30-6 Details of a rear fork, or swing arm. (*Kawasaki Heavy Industries, Ltd.*)

been used. The most common includes a pair of spring-damper assemblies, one on each side of the rear wheel. The upper ends are attached to the frame on swinging pivots. The lower ends are attached to the two legs of the swinging fork, just at or near the rear-wheel axle. Figure 30-7 shows this arrangement. As the fork swings up and down, the spring and damper assemblies shorten (telescope) and extend.

Figure 30-8 shows a disassembled view of a rear suspension system. Included in the illustration is the

FRAME
ATTACHING
BOLT

SPRING-
DAMPER

FORK
ATTACHING
BOLT

FRONT-WHEEL
AXLE

Fig. 30-7 A damper-and-spring assembly is attached on each side of the rear wheel between the motorcycle frame and the swinging fork. (*Honda Motor Company, Ltd.*)

drive-chain case (1). Note how the springs (8) are assembled around the outside of the dampers (12). Two types of springs are used on motorcycles—straight wound and progressive springs. The springs shown in Fig. 30-8 are straight wound. As the load increases, the springs will compress evenly. However, a progressive spring gets progressively stronger, as it is compressed.

30-3
SHOCK ABSORBERS The damper, or shock absorber, is usually mounted inside the spring, as shown in Figs. 30-7 to 30-9. Note the two adjusting cams (Fig. 30-9). These adjust the ride from soft, to medium, or hard, as explained later. The purpose of the shock absorber is to prevent excessive wheel movements and to damp out secondary movements of the wheel after a road irregularity has passed.

A spring alone will not give a good ride. You can demonstrate for yourself why a spring alone will not be satisfactory for a motorcycle suspension. Hang a weight on a spring. Then lift the weight and let it drop. It will expand the spring as the weight drops. The spring takes over and pulls the weight back up. This is called *rebound*. After the weight has been pulled up, it starts down again, expanding the spring once more. The spring will therefore keep the weight moving up and down, or oscillating. These oscillations will gradually die out.

On the motorcycle, a very similar action would take place with a spring alone. The spring is under an initial compression, due to the load imposed on it. As the wheel passes over a bump, the spring is further compressed. After the bump is passed, the spring attempts

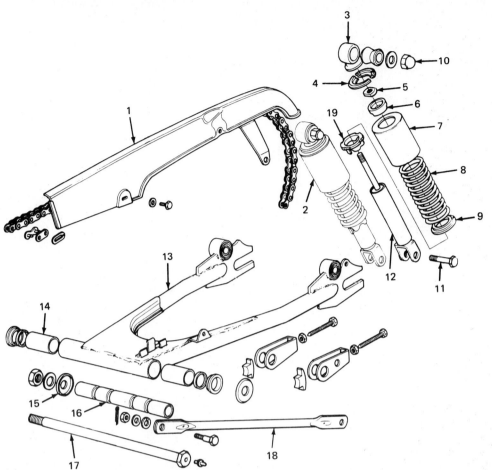

1. Drive-chain case (2)
2. Rear suspension (2)
3. Upper joint (2)
4. Spring seat stopper (4)
5. 9-mm locknut (2)
6. Rear cushion stopper rubber (2)
7. Rear cushion upper case (2)
8. Rear cushion spring (2)
9. Spring under seat (2)
10. Rear cushion upper nut (2)
11. Hex bolt 10 x 32 (2)
12. Rear damper (2)
13. Rear fork
14. Rear fork pivot bush (2)
15. Rear fork dust-seal cap (2)
16. Rear fork center collar
17. Rear fork pivot bolt
18. Rear brake stopper arm
19. Adjusting cam

Fig. 30-8 Disassembled view of a rear suspension. Note that Honda calls the damper-and-spring assembly a *cushion*. (*Honda Motor Company, Ltd.*)

to return to its original position. But it overrides this position and expands too much. This causes the motorcycle frame to be thrown upward. Now, having overexpanded, the spring compresses. Again it overrides and compresses too much. As this happens, the wheel may be raised clear of the road and the frame may drop. Now the spring expands again and the oscillations continue, gradually dying out. But every time the wheel meets a bump or hole in the road, the same series of oscillations would take place if a spring alone were used.

Such spring actions on a motorcycle would give a very rough and unsatisfactory ride. On a bumpy road or on curves, it might become impossible to control the motorcycle. The wheel would not be in contact with the road enough of the time for control. This is the reason that shock absorbers must be used to quickly dampen out the spring oscillations after a bump or hole has been passed.

The shock absorber uses the principles of hydraulics. It contains a quantity of oil which must pass from one space into another whenever the shock absorber is expanded or shortened. Restricting valves and holes, or orifices, prevent the oil from flowing freely. It takes time for oil to flow through these small openings. This restricts the spring and wheel movement.

Shock absorbers are double acting. They work when the wheel is moving up after meeting a bump in the road. They also work when the wheel moves down after meeting a hole in the road.

Figure 30-10 is a partial sectional view of a rear shock absorber and spring assembly. Note that this is somewhat different in construction from the one shown in Fig. 30-9. The shock absorber in Fig. 30-9 has an adjustment arrangement that includes two adjusting cams and an adjusting cup. The design in Fig. 30-8 has a single adjusting cam (19). We will describe these adjustments later.

The shock absorber shown in Fig. 30-10 is very similar in construction and action to the shock absorbers used on automobiles. Figure 30-11 shows the actions in the shock absorber during compression (wheel moving up) and extension (wheel moving down). When the wheel meets a bump it is pushed upward. The spring outside of the shock absorber is compressed.

At the same time, the cylinder of the shock absorber moves up into the outer shell. This puts pressure on the oil under the piston. The oil is forced through the piston orifice, and it pushes the nonreturn valve up, as shown in Fig. 30-11a. The oil can then flow through the valve and enter the space above the piston. A small part of the oil also flows through the opening of base valve A. It pushes down base valve B and enters the oil chamber between the cylinder and the outer shell. The resistance to the oil flow, plus spring tension, dampens the wheel movement. If the wheel moves up the maximum distance, the cylinder will strike the rubber stopper at the top of the shock absorber (Fig. 30-10).

When the wheel meets a hole, the wheel moves down

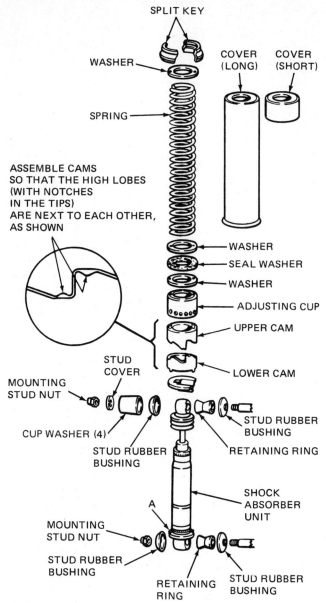

SPLIT KEY

WASHER

SPRING

COVER (LONG)

COVER (SHORT)

ASSEMBLE CAMS
SO THAT THE HIGH LOBES
(WITH NOTCHES
IN THE TIPS)
ARE NEXT TO EACH OTHER,
AS SHOWN

WASHER

SEAL WASHER

WASHER

ADJUSTING CUP

UPPER CAM

LOWER CAM

STUD COVER

MOUNTING STUD NUT

CUP WASHER (4)

STUD RUBBER BUSHING

STUD RUBBER BUSHING

RETAINING RING

SHOCK ABSORBER UNIT

A

MOUNTING STUD NUT

STUD RUBBER BUSHING

RETAINING RING

STUD RUBBER BUSHING

Fig. 30-9 Disassembled view of a rear-spring-and-shock-absorber assembly. The spring tension is adjusted by turning the adjusting cup which turns the upper cam. (*Harley-Davidson Motor Company, Inc.*)

and the shock absorber extends. It grows longer as shown in Fig. 30-11*b*. The oil in the space above the piston goes through the piston orifice. It pushes the piston valve down and goes through the valve into the space under the piston. At the same time, the oil in the space between the cylinder and the outer shell pushes valve A open and returns to the space under the piston.

Note the arrows in Fig. 30-11*b*. The resistance to the oil as it flows through the valves and orifices checks the tendency of the spring to extend to its full length. If the shock absorber does extend to its maximum length, the inner spring hits the stopper at the top of the cylinder. This absorbs the force of the blow.

In addition to the shock absorber described above,

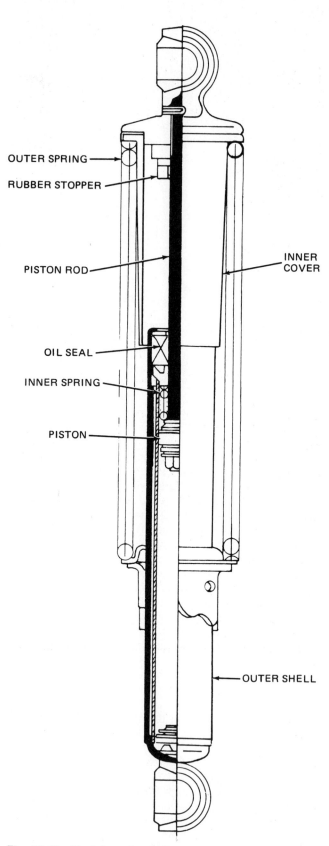

OUTER SPRING

RUBBER STOPPER

PISTON ROD

INNER COVER

OIL SEAL

INNER SPRING

PISTON

OUTER SHELL

Fig. 30-10 Partial sectional view of a rear shock absorber (*Kawasaki Heavy Industries, Ltd.*)

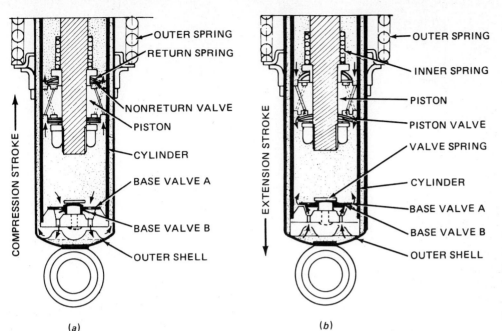

Fig. 30-11 (a) Action in the shock absorber during compression. Arrows show the flow of oil. (b) The action in the shock absorber during extension. Arrows show the flow of oil.

air-filled and gas-filled types also are used on motorcycles. Other types of rear suspension, such as the monoshock swing arm and the progressive-linkage swing arm, have a single shock absorber and spring for the rear wheel.

30-4 ADJUSTING THE RIDE

The ride can be varied to suit the road conditions and the load being carried. Figure 30-12 shows one adjustment method. The cam at the lower end of the spring can be turned with a cam adjuster. The adjustment moves the cam up or down. If the cam is moved up, the spring end is pushed up, compressing the spring an added amount. This compensates for any increased load at the rear wheel.

One widely used type of spring-and-shock-absorber assembly has five adjustments on the adjusting cam, as shown in Fig. 30-13. Note that the graph to the left in Fig. 30-13 shows the spring loads on the spring for the various adjustments, and the increase in spring loading as the spring is compressed.

The cams on the two sides of the motorcycle must be

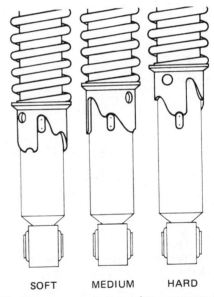

Fig. 30-12 The cam can be turned to compress the spring varying amounts, thus varying the ride from soft, to medium, to hard. (Castrol, Limited)

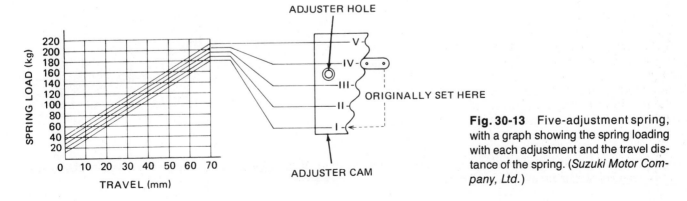

Fig. 30-13 Five-adjustment spring, with a graph showing the spring loading with each adjustment and the travel distance of the spring. (Suzuki Motor Company, Ltd.)

297

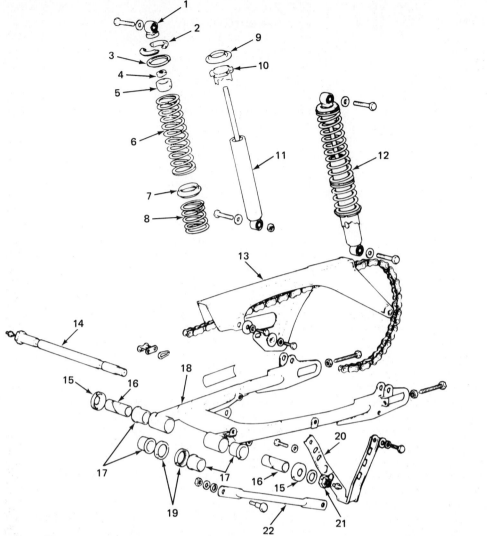

1. Upper joint
2. Spring seat stopper
3. Rear cushion spring seat
4. Locknut
5. Stopper rubber
6. Rear cushion spring B
7. Rear cushion spring joint
8. Rear cushion spring A
9. Under spring seat
10. Spring adjuster
11. Rear damper
12. Rear cushion assembly
13. Drive-chain case
14. Rear fork pivot bolt
15. Dust-seal rubber
16. Rear fork center collar
17. Fork pivot bush
18. Rear fork
19. Dust-seal cap
20. Chain guide
21. Self-locknut
22. Rear brake stopper arm

Fig. 30-14 Disassembled view of a rear-suspension system. (*Honda Motor Company, Ltd.*)

adjusted the same. If one is set differently from the other, a severe side strain will be put on the suspension system, and the ride could be unstable.

30-5 SEAT POSTS
In some motorcycles, the seats are sprung. They are supported by a spring or springs to improve riding comfort. The springs soften the ride by absorbing most of the up-and-down motion of the motorcycle frame.

30-6 REAR-SUSPENSION SERVICE
Rear-suspension systems for most motorcycles are very similar in general construction. They include a pair of spring-and-shock-absorber assemblies—one on each side of the rear wheel—and a swinging rear fork.

As an example of a disassembly procedure, we will take apart the rear-suspension system. It is shown disassembled in Fig. 30-14. As a first step, remove the spring-and-shock-absorber assemblies by removing the attaching bolts. Then use the spring compressing tool,

as shown in Fig. 30-15, to compress the spring so the spring stopper (2 in Fig. 30-14) can be removed. This permits you to separate the assembly into the parts shown in Fig. 30-16.

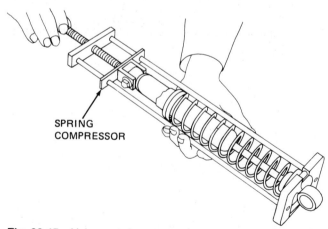

SPRING
COMPRESSOR

Fig. 30-15 Using a spring compressor on a rear-spring-and-shock-absorber assembly. (*Honda Motor Company, Ltd.*)

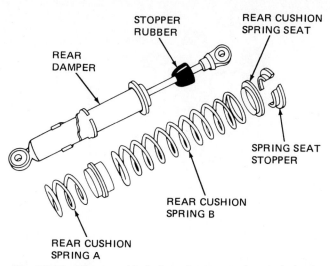

Fig. 30-16 Disassembled view of a rear-spring-and-shock-absorber assembly. (*Honda Motor Company, Ltd.*)

Check the free length of the springs, and discard them if they are shortened. Shortened springs have lost tension and will not provide a normal ride.

Detach the fork from the frame by removing the pivot shaft. Check the bushings inside the rear fork for wear. Replace them if they are worn. Figure 30-17 shows one construction. Bushings can be removed with a long drift punch and a hammer. New bushings can then be pressed into place. On some motorcycles, the bushings will then require reaming to size to take the pivot shaft. Some manufacturers recommend checking the pivot shaft for distortion in vee blocks with a dial indicator.

On reassembly, apply a coating of grease to the shaft and bushings on models not equipped with grease fittings. On models with grease fittings, apply the grease gun to inject the proper amount of grease. The pivot shaft and bushings are protected by dust-seal caps at both ends. These are fitted over the ends of the fork

collar, as shown in Fig. 30-17. Caps made of flexible material can be put into place by folding the edge back. Then, when the fork is in place and attached with the pivot shaft, the caps may be folded down over the ends of the fork collar.

Some models have two positions for attaching the upper end of the spring-and-shock-absorber assembly. Since the upper position shortens the spring, the ride is somewhat stiffer.

30-7
STEERING HEAD AND SUSPENSION
SYSTEM Up front, all frames have a means of supporting the front wheel and permitting the wheel to pivot from side to side. Figure 4-2 shows the steering collar, which is welded onto the front of the frame. The steering collar supports the steering-shaft-and-bracket assembly. This assembly, with bearings, is called the *steering head*. One version is shown in disassembled view in Fig. 30-18. There are two sets of balls, one above the frame support (the collar) and the other below the support. The balls, with their upper and lower cups, form a rolling support for the stem and brackets. The brackets, with the two parallel tube members, or fork legs, form the front fork, as shown in Fig. 30-19. The front-wheel axle is attached to the lower ends of the two fork legs, as shown in Fig. 30-7. The tubes are combination springs and shock absorbers. The ball bearings allow the brackets and fork, with the wheel, to pivot easily from side to side.

Figure 30-20 shows the steering stem and other parts installed on a motorcycle. The collar is cut away to show the details of the bearings and other parts. Figure 30-21 shows details of one of the tubes of the front fork and steering system. Each leg contains a long spiral spring that compresses and expands as the wheel meets bumps and holes in the road. The leg also contains a damper, similar to the shock absorber used at the rear wheels. The damper restricts wheel movement and

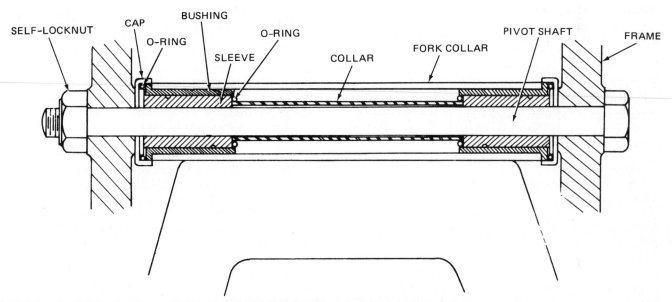

Fig. 30-17 Sectional view through the collar of a rear fork, showing how the rear fork is attached to the frame by the pivot shaft. (*Kawasaki Heavy Industries, Ltd.*)

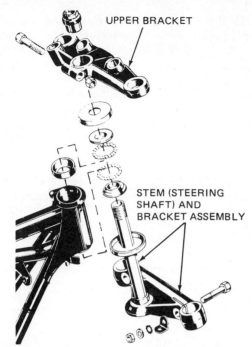

Fig. 30-18 Cup-and-ball steering-head assembly, disassembled. Note that this arrangement uses loose encaged balls, rather than assembled ball bearings. (*Castrol, Limited*)

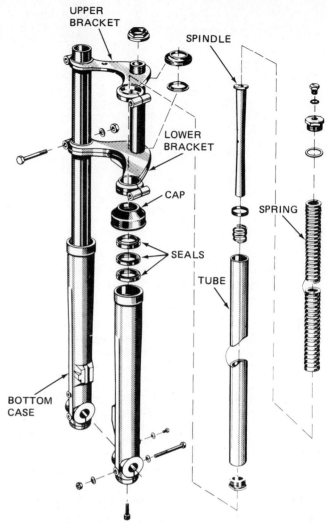

Fig. 30-19 Disassembled view of one front-fork leg. (*Husqvarna*)

dampens secondary spring movements after a bump or hole has been passed.

In addition to the spring, each leg has a bottom case in which a piston moves up and down as the wheel meets bumps and holes in the road. The assembly is filled with oil. When the piston moves up and down in the bottom case, oil must flow through a valve. This restricts the flow of oil. The assembly acts in the same manner as the shock absorbers used at the rear wheel, already described.

Some motorcycles have an *antidive* front suspension. This design connects the hydraulic system of the front brake with the passages for the fork oil to help reduce front-fork dive during braking. The system works automatically. A valve is located near the bottom of each fork leg. As the fork is compressed, the fork oil flows through the valves. When the front brake is applied, the brake-fluid pressure closes the valve.

With the valves closed, the flow of oil is greatly restricted. This causes the fork to resist compression during braking. However, if the front wheel strikes a bump, the pressure of the front-fork oil increases. This opens the valves automatically, allowing the fork to absorb the shock.

Instead of a valve, some models use the arrangement shown in Fig. 30-19. This design uses a spindle of varying outside diameters. The main tube is filled with oil. As the front wheel moves up and down, the springs expand and shorten to absorb the shock of meeting bumps and holes. This movement forces the oil to flow past the spindle. This somewhat restricts the spring movement. Because of the shape of the spindle, the oil has an easier time moving in a central position. But as the wheel approaches the upper or lower limits of its

travel, the oil must pass the larger diameter of the spindle. This furnishes greater resistance, restricting additional wheel movement.

There are other front-fork designs that are very similar, but all work on the same general principle. They allow the front wheel to move up and down, but provide some restraint to keep the wheel from excessive movement. Also, they prevent second and third rebounds of the wheel after a hole or bump has been passed. Without some restraint, as previously explained, the springs would tend to keep on expanding and shortening after the road irregularity had passed. The tubes telescope (or shorten) and expand (or lengthen). This is the reason for the name usually applied to the front suspension—*telescope suspension*.

Figure 30-22 shows another design of front steering and suspension which is similar to the others previously described. This design also uses a separate shock-absorber assembly (11 in Fig. 30-22) instead of a tapered spindle. Springs in the front fork may be straight wound or of the progressive type, as in the rear-suspension system.

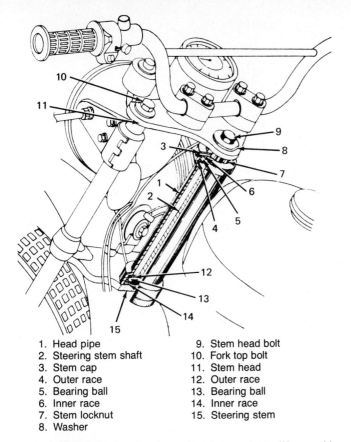

1. Head pipe
2. Steering stem shaft
3. Stem cap
4. Outer race
5. Bearing ball
6. Inner race
7. Stem locknut
8. Washer
9. Stem head bolt
10. Fork top bolt
11. Stem head
12. Outer race
13. Bearing ball
14. Inner race
15. Steering stem

Fig. 30-20 Details of a front steering system. (*Kawasaki Heavy Industries, Ltd.*)

NOTE Specifications for motorcycles call for changing the oil in the two fork tubes periodically. Late-model Harley-Davidsons require changing the oil every 5000 miles [8047 km]. If leakage occurs, the cause of the leak must be corrected. Then, the oil should be changed. Several ounces of oil are required to refill each fork tube. For hard riding over rough surfaces, a heat-resistant oil of a heavier grade must be used.

For winter, a heat-resistant oil of a lighter grade should be used. The grade of oil is a measure of its viscosity, or its ability to flow. The easier the oil flows, the lower the grade. An SAE 10 oil flows more easily than an SAE 30 oil. The oil used should be of the proper grade to produce the best damping. Most imported motorcycle manufacturers recommend the use of automotive automatic-transmission fluid (ATF) for front-fork oil. Fork oil also is available from dealers in various weights, such as 10, 20, 30, and 40. The higher the number, the thicker the oil and the greater damping action it provides.

One of the problems with the telescope suspension is that dirt has a tendency to work into the upper end of the main tube. This can be overcome by a cap, as shown separately in Fig. 30-19. The cap is secured to the bottom case and allows the tube to slide up and down through the cap hole. Seals under the cap prevent the entrance of dirt and water.

A second method of protecting the internal mechanism from dirt and water is to seal the joint with an expandable rubber boot, as shown in Fig. 30-21. The

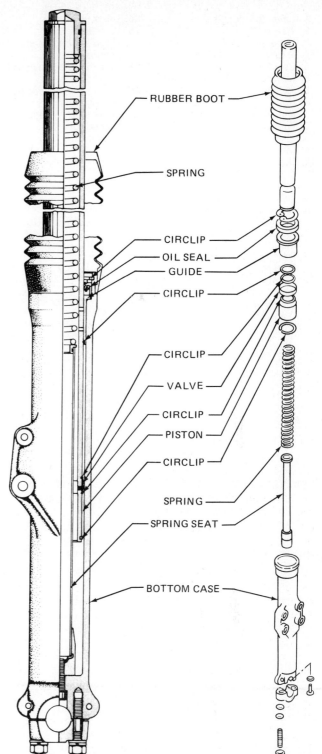

Fig. 30-21 Cutaway and disassembled views of one leg of a front fork. (*Suzuki Motor Company, Ltd.*)

rubber boot is secured at the bottom to the bottom case. It is secured at the top to the upper, or main, tube. As the tube moves up and down in the bottom case, the boot expands or shortens. It maintains at all times a complete seal of the joint between the bottom case and the tube.

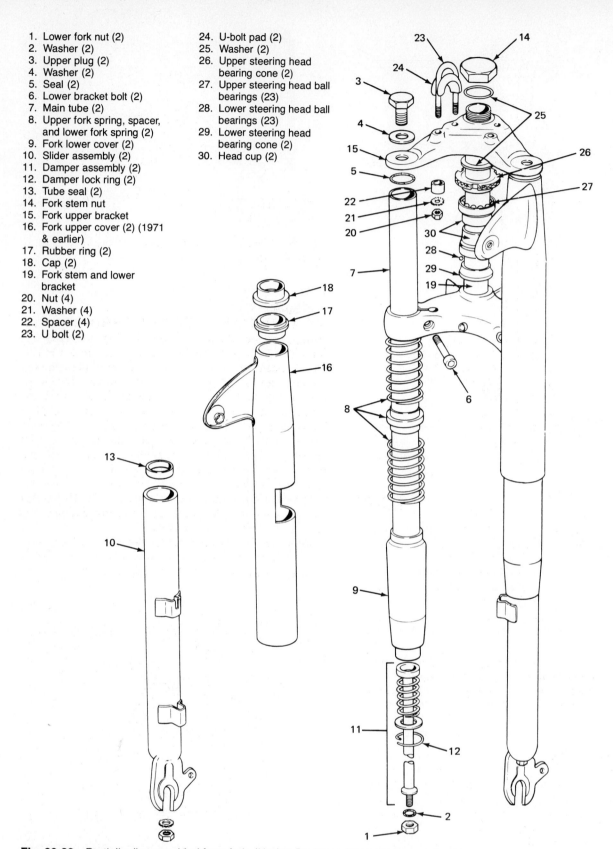

1. Lower fork nut (2)
2. Washer (2)
3. Upper plug (2)
4. Washer (2)
5. Seal (2)
6. Lower bracket bolt (2)
7. Main tube (2)
8. Upper fork spring, spacer, and lower fork spring (2)
9. Fork lower cover (2)
10. Slider assembly (2)
11. Damper assembly (2)
12. Damper lock ring (2)
13. Tube seal (2)
14. Fork stem nut
15. Fork upper bracket
16. Fork upper cover (2) (1971 & earlier)
17. Rubber ring (2)
18. Cap (2)
19. Fork stem and lower bracket
20. Nut (4)
21. Washer (4)
22. Spacer (4)
23. U bolt (2)

24. U-bolt pad (2)
25. Washer (2)
26. Upper steering head bearing cone (2)
27. Upper steering head ball bearings (23)
28. Lower steering head ball bearings (23)
29. Lower steering head bearing cone (2)
30. Head cup (2)

Fig. 30-22 Partially disassembled front fork. (*Harley-Davidson Motor Company, Inc.*)

30-8
ADJUSTABLE STEERING DAMPER

Some steering arrangements include an adjustment to change the stiffness of the steering. This changes the ease with which the handlebars and front wheel can be turned for steering. Figure 30-23 shows one design. If the knob is turned clockwise, the tanged spring at the bottom is pulled up, thereby forcing the friction plates more

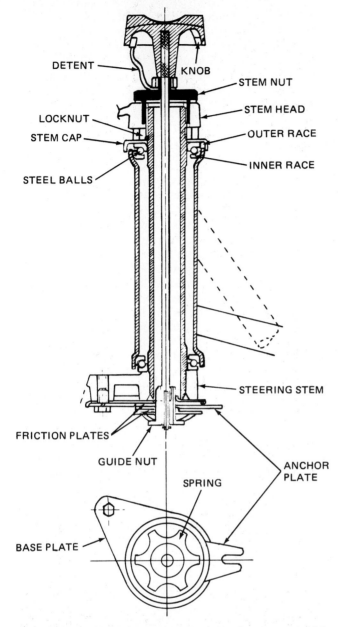

DETENT
KNOB
STEM NUT
STEM HEAD
LOCKNUT
STEM CAP
OUTER RACE
INNER RACE
STEEL BALLS

STEERING STEM

FRICTION PLATES
GUIDE NUT
SPRING
ANCHOR PLATE
BASE PLATE

Fig. 30-23 Sectional view of a front steering system which includes a means of adjusting the steering stiffness. The knob at the top can be turned to change the stiffness. (*Kawasaki Heavy Industries, Ltd.*)

tightly together. This makes it harder to turn the handlebar and wheel. If the knob is backed off, the pressure between the friction plates is lessened so that the handlebar is easier to turn. This permits the rider to change the steering stiffness to meet different road, track, or field conditions. Steering should be free for smooth road surfaces and tight for rough roads or trails.

Instead of a knob that can be adjusted while the motorcycle is actually in operation, some designs use an adjusting bolt or screw. One manufacturer uses a small damper unit attached to the frame and to the steering stem. In operation, the unit acts like a hydraulic shock absorber.

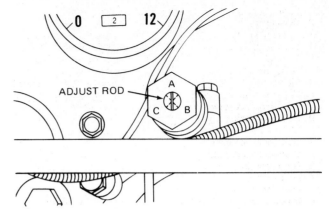

ADJUST ROD

0   2   12

A
C   B

Fig. 30-24 Front-fork spring adjustment. (*Kawasaki Heavy Industries, Ltd.*)

**30-9
ADJUSTABLE FRONT SPRINGS** Rear springs can be adjusted to give varying riding characteristics from soft to medium to hard, as shown in Fig. 30-12. Some front-suspension systems also have a means of adjusting the spring tension to vary the spring action. Figure 30-24 is a top view of the adjusting rod that is located on top of the fork leg on one model of motorcycle. The three adjusting positions are shown. The normal (A) position is for average, relatively low-speed highway riding. To stiffen the springs, the protective rubber cap is removed and the rod is turned clockwise to position B. Maximum stiffness is attained by turning the rod clockwise to position C. The stiffer springing action is desirable for cornering at high speed and for driving off the highway.

Many large touring motorcycles have an air-assist type of front suspension which can be pumped up or deflated to change the front-spring action.

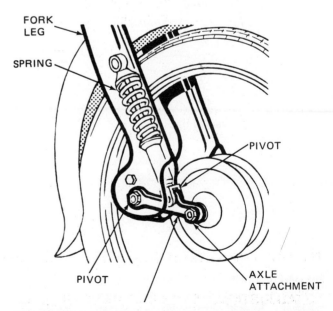

FORK LEG
SPRING
PIVOT
PIVOT
AXLE ATTACHMENT

Fig. 30-25 Leading-link front-suspension system. (*Castrol, Limited*)

Fig. 30-26 One leg of a front-suspension system in which the trail can be adjusted. Note the two holes at the lower end of the leg. The forward, or off-center, hole is empty in the picture. The axle is shown installed on the hole that is in line with the leg centerline. (*Kawasaki Heavy Industries, Ltd.*)

30-10
TRAILING AND LEADING LINKS

Some front-suspension systems use a bottom link, as shown in Figs. 30-25 and 30-26. The bottom link is pivoted at one end and attached at the other end to the bottom of the fork leg. At an intermediate point, the link is pivoted to the lower end of the spring assembly. As the wheel

moves up and down, the link pivots and causes the spring to expand or contract. The bottom-link suspension, shown in Fig. 30-25, is called a *leading-link system.* The link is positioned so that the wheel axle is ahead of the spring. In the *trailing-link system,* shown in Fig. 30-26, the wheel axle is trailing, or behind, the spring.

30-11
ADJUSTING STEERING STABILITY

The position of the wheel axle and wheel with respect to the centerline of the steering head has a considerable effect on the stability of the motorcycle. Stability, in this case, means the tendency of the motorcycle to self-steer in a straight line while moving forward. Some motorcycles have a means of changing the amount that the wheel trails the steering stem, and this changes the stability. Figure 30-27 shows one arrangement. The lower ends of the legs have two axle holes, as shown in Fig. 30-27. One is on the centerline of the leg. The other hole is offset. This permits three axle positions in relation to the legs. One position is shown in Fig. 30-27 (left). Another position would be to move the axle forward to the front holes on the legs (Fig. 30-27) (center). The third position would be to rotate the legs 180° and again install the axle in the offset holes (Fig. 30-27, right).

Let's see how this all works. In Fig. 30-27a we show the offset hole in the leg to the rear and the wheel axle installed in this hole. This gives the maximum trail between the line through the steering axis of the steering head and the point of contact of the tire with the

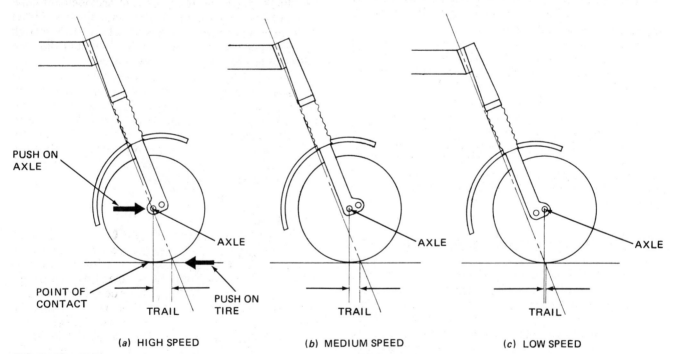

Fig. 30-27 The three positions of the leg and axle. (*a*) The off-center hole is to the rear, and the axle is installed in it. (*b*) The leg has been rotated so the off-center hole is forward. The axle is installed in the hole that is on the leg centerline. (*c*) The axle is installed in the hole that is forward of the leg centerline. The "trails" are exaggerated so you can clearly see the effect of changing the axle position.

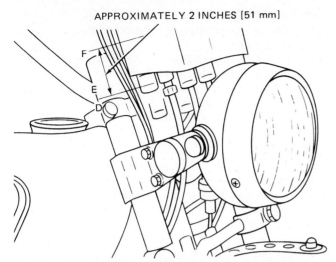

APPROXIMATELY 2 INCHES [51 mm]

Fig. 30-28 Steering-stem adjustment. (*Kawasaki Heavy Industries, Ltd.*)

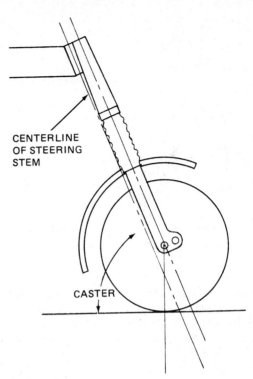

CENTERLINE OF STEERING STEM

CASTER

Fig. 30-29 Caster angle is the angle between the centerline of the steering stem and the horizontal.

ground. This provides stability, or a tendency for the motorcycle to self-steer straight ahead.

Here's the reason. The forward push on the wheel is through the axle, as shown by the heavy arrow in Fig. 30-27*a*. The backward push of the road on the tire is at the point of contact, as shown by the other heavy arrow. Since the trail, or distance between the two pushes, is considerable, the wheel has a strong tendency to self-steer straight ahead. As a result, it takes more force to make a turn.

For a lighter steering effort, the axle can be moved to the position shown in Fig. 30-27*b*. Now the trail has been reduced and less effort is required to turn the motorcycle. However, some steering stability has been lost with the axle in this position.

For the lightest steering effort, the legs can be turned 180°, as shown in Fig. 30-27*c*, and the axle mounted forward in the offset holes. This produces the smallest trail and the easiest steering control.

The reason for changing the axle position is to set up the motorcycle for various operating conditions. For example, for high-speed operation, the maximum trail and steering stability are desired. However, for quick maneuvering and off-road conditions, the minimum trail and steering stability are desirable. This makes it easier to flip the wheel toward one side or the other, as required for quick turns.

30-12
HYDRAULIC STEERING DAMPER Some motorcycles have a steering damper, which is a form of shock absorber, connected between the steering stem and the frame. It has a piston inside an oil-filled cylinder. As the handlebars are turned from side to side for steering, the piston moves back and forth inside the cylinder. This forces oil to flow through a small opening in the piston. As a result, the steering damper offers resistance to any sudden movement of the handlebars and steering stem. The purpose of the steering damper is to minimize handlebar vibration at high speeds. Some late-model steering dampers have a thumbscrew adjustment which permits adjustment of the damping effect.

30-13
ADJUSTING THE STEERING STEM Some motorcycles also have a means of raising or lowering the steering stem in relation to the frame, as shown in Fig. 30-28. The purpose of this is to provide additional trail for high-speed riding. To make the adjustment from the standard position, which is D in Fig. 30-28, loosen the four clamp bolts on the steering stem and slide the right and left fork legs up to position E or F.

Both adjusting the steering stability by changing the trail and adjusting the steering stem, as shown in Fig. 30-28, change the caster. Figure 30-29 illustrates caster. It is the angle between the steering stem and the horizontal. Changing this angle also changes steering stability. For example, when raising the fork legs up to positions E or F, you lower the front end of the frame. This decreases the caster angle.

30-14
STEERING-STEM SERVICE Figure 30-30 shows the steering stem we will discuss in this section. Proceed as follows to disassemble, inspect, and reassemble it. Note that the motorcycle using this design has a hydraulic disk brake. Similar designs are used on motorcycles with drum brakes. The procedure that follows will apply, in general, to all motorcycles having a design like the one shown in Figs. 30-28 and 30-30.

Disassembly Disassemble the steering stem as follows:

1. Remove the front wheel and caliper assembly.
2. Remove the handlebar.

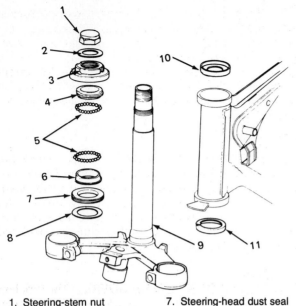

1. Steering-stem nut
2. Steering-stem nut washer
3. Steering top nut
4. Steering top cone race
5. Steel balls (37)
6. Steering bottom cone race
7. Steering-head dust seal
8. Dust-seal washer
9. Steering stem
10. Steering top ball race
11. Steering bottom ball race

Fig. 30-30 Disassembled view of a steering stem. (*Honda Motor Company, Ltd.*)

3. Remove the headlight unit from its case, and disconnect the wiring at the harness in the case. Then remove the case from the steering stem.
4. Disconnect the brake hose at the steering stem.
5. Remove the speedometer and the tachometer. Disconnect the meter cables at the engine and the fork legs.
6. Loosen the front-fork bolt at the bottom bridge of the steering stem, and loosen the bolts securing the forks at the fork top bridge. Then pull out the front-fork assembly.
7. Loosen the steering-stem nut on top of the stem, and remove the fork top bridge.
8. Remove the steering-head top nut (3 in Fig. 30-30) to remove the steering stem. Be careful not to lose any of the 37 balls (19 upper and 18 lower).

Inspection Inspect the parts as follows:

1. Check the steering stem for damage, such as nicks, a bent condition, rust, and so on.
2. Clean the steering top and bottom cone races and balls in solvent, and check them for wear or other damage. Make sure the balls are in good condition.
3. Make sure the dust seal is in good condition.

Reassembly Reassemble the steering stem as follows:

1. Install the balls—19 in the upper race and 18 in the lower race—securing them in place with grease. Put the stem in place.
2. Carefully tighten the steering top nut to take up all the play in the balls. Do not overtighten or you will

damage the balls and races. Then, back off the nut just enough to permit free rotation without rattles or excessive play.
3. Complete the assembly by reinstalling the fork and other parts removed during disassembly. On the hydraulic disk brake system, the hydraulic system should be serviced if it has been opened. Add brake fluid and bleed the system. This procedure is explained in Chap. 31.

NOTE While the procedure outlined above applies generally to all steering stems, there are some variations in construction that require some changes in the procedure. Always refer to the manufacturer's shop manual that covers the motorcycle you are working on.

30-15
FRONT-SUSPENSION SERVICE The oil in the front-fork legs should be changed periodically. The length of time or distance driven before an oil change is recommended varies with the type of operation. If the

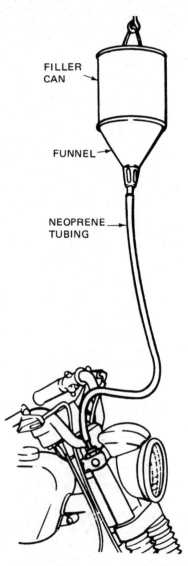

FILLER CAN

FUNNEL

NEOPRENE TUBING

Fig. 30-31 Adding oil to one leg of the front fork. (*Harley-Davidson Motor Company, Inc.*)

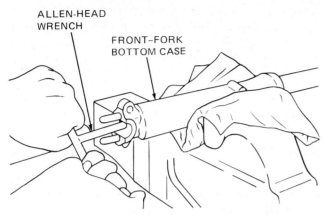

Fig. 30-32 Clamping the bottom case in a vise and using a special wrench to loosen the bottom bolt. (*Honda Motor Company, Ltd.*)

motorcycle is operated in very dusty or damp conditions or is run over very rough trails that stress the suspension to the limit, then the oil should be changed more often. A typical recommendation is to change the oil every year or 5000 miles [8047 km]. Riders who participate in high-performance competition may change the oil much more frequently.

On some motorcycle models, the manufacturer supplies a method of checking the level of the oil in the front-fork legs. You raise the rear end of the motorcycle so the fork is vertical. Then you remove the top bolt from the inner tube and insert a rod down into the tube to measure the height of the oil. If it is low, you add oil.

A device like the one shown in Fig. 30-31 makes it easier to add new oil. Note that it is made with a can of the proper size and a funnel. Holes are punched in the bottom of the can, and the funnel is soldered to the bottom of the can. Do not use a rubber hose. The oil will attack rubber, and this will contaminate the oil. Instead, use neoprene tubing. Figure 30-31 shows the filler can in use.

Before adding oil, the old oil must be drained out. This is done by removing the drain plug located at the bottom of the fork leg. Allow the oil to drain. Operate the suspension by flexing the fork to speed the draining process. After all of the oil is drained, reinstall the plug. Then, measure out the exact amount of the recommended grade and kind of fork oil. (Some manufacturers recommend automatic-transmission fluid.) Pour it into the filler can. The oil will flow in faster if the fork is worked up and down. When the oil has all run into the fork leg, install the upper bracket bolts.

30-16
INSPECTING THE FRONT FORK The front fork should be inspected frequently for leaks or damage. If the leak is around the joint between the bottom case and the tube that slides up and down in the case, the oil seal is bad and must be replaced. If the oil is leaking from the vent hole at the top of the fork leg, there probably is too much oil in the leg.

You can check the fork action by locking the front brake. Then pump the fork up and down vigorously. Check for stiffness or excessively soft action.

If the fork action is stiff or soft and spongy, either there is not enough oil in the fork legs or the valves are defective. If draining the old oil and adding the correct amount of fresh oil does not correct the condition, the fork should be removed so it can be disassembled for valve replacement.

30-17
SERVICING THE FRONT FORK There are several front-fork designs, differing in some details. For this reason, always have the manufacturer's shop manual in front of you when you are servicing a motorcycle. We cover one model of front fork here. Others are very similar, so the procedure we outline can be considered to be typical. Disassemble as follows.

30-18
FRONT-FORK LEG REMOVAL The fork legs are attached at three places: the wheel axles, the steering stem, and the steering-stem head. The fork leg must be detached from these three points before it can be removed. Remove the wheel first. Then loosen the attaching bolts on the two steering-stem bridges, or *brackets*. Now the fork leg can be pulled down and out.

30-19
FRONT-FORK LEG SERVICE Drain the oil from the leg. Then clamp the bottom case in a vise, as shown in Fig. 30-32. Note that the case is protected by a heavy padding of shop cloth. An old inner tube can also be used—anything to protect the case from damage. Do not clamp the case too tightly or you will distort and ruin it.

Use the proper wrench to unscrew the bolt at the bottom of the bottom case. With this bolt out, the assembly can be taken apart, as follows.

First remove the front-fork inner tube with the damper unit as an assembly. Then remove the front-fork bolt on top of the fork inner tube to take apart the assembly.

To remove the oil seal, remove the Circlip. A new seal can then be installed with the special seal driver, as shown in Fig. 30-33. Coat the seal and the inside of the case with automatic-transmission oil or the oil recommended for use in the fork. Secure the seal with a Circlip.

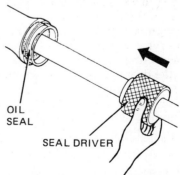

Fig. 30-33 Installing an oil seal in a bottom case. (*Honda Motor Company, Ltd.*)

30-20
INSPECTION OF PARTS
Measure the free length of the spring, and discard it if it is short. A short spring has low tension and gives a relatively poor ride.

Check the tube for any damage or distortion. A slight misalignment can be corrected by applying pressure in the proper place. But this must be done very carefully to avoid making the condition worse. Do not attempt to straighten a tube that has been bent enough to wrinkle it. The metal has been stretched and you cannot restore alignment. You can check alignment with vee blocks and a dial indicator. As you rotate the tube in the vee blocks, any misalignment will show up on the dial indicator.

Figure 30-34 shows how to use special straightening blocks which have the same inner curvature as the tube. Careful application of pressure to the high point can often bring it back into alignment. However, realigning tubes requires a great deal of skill.

30-21
FRONT-FORK REASSEMBLY AND INSTALLATION
Put the damper and inner-tube parts together.

A new seal must be installed every time the fork is disassembled. Installing a new seal has already been covered. Lubricate the tube with the recommended oil and insert it into the bottom case. Secure it with the bolt. First, apply locking sealant to the bolt. Install the fork legs by sliding them up into the steering-stem brackets and tightening the attaching bolts. Then, install the wheel and axle.

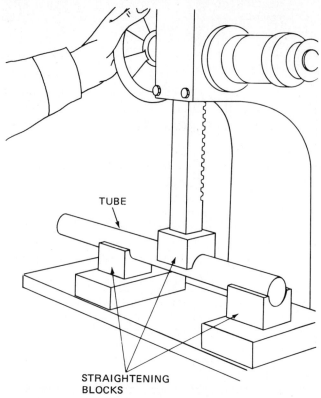

TUBE

STRAIGHTENING BLOCKS

Fig. 30-34 Applying force with an arbor press to straighten a tube. (*Harley-Davidson Motor Company, Inc.*)

CHAPTER 30
REVIEW QUESTIONS

1. What is the purpose of the frame?
2. Describe three types of motorcycle frames.
3. What is a *rigid frame?*
4. Why does a motorcycle need a rear-suspension system?
5. Explain the operation of the swinging fork for the rear wheel.
6. What is a spring-damper assembly?
7. How does a spring-damper assembly operate?
8. Explain how to adjust a spring-damper assembly to get a harder ride.
9. What services can be performed on the rear suspension?
10. What is a steering head?
11. Describe the operation of the front fork.
12. How do you select the proper oil for use in the front forks?
13. In the front-fork assembly, what protects the internal parts from dirt and water?
14. Explain the use of the adjustable steering damper.
15. Describe how to adjust the front springs on some motorcycles.
16. Define *trailing link* and *leading link.*
17. Why is steering stability important on a motorcycle?
18. What is a hydraulic steering damper?
19. Explain how to adjust the steering stem.
20. Describe how to service the steering stem.
21. Name the services that can be performed on the front suspension.
22. What do you look for when inspecting the front fork?
23. Describe how to remove and service a front-fork leg.
24. Explain how to change oil in the front forks.
25. Describe how to straighten a bent front fork.

CHAPTER 31

MOTORCYCLE BRAKES

After studying this chapter,
you should be able to:

1. Explain how friction in the brakes slows or stops the motorcycle.

2. Describe drum brakes and explain how they work.

3. Describe disk brakes and explain how they work.

4. Discuss hydraulic pressure and explain how it works to apply the brakes in a disk-brake system.

5. Explain why brakes require periodic adjustment.

6. Adjust front and rear brakes.

7. Replace drum-brake shoes and drums.

8. Service master cylinders and calipers.

9. Bleed the hydraulic system.

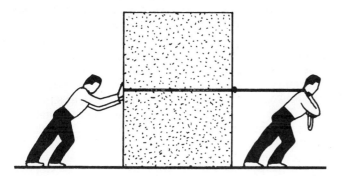

FRICTION OF REST

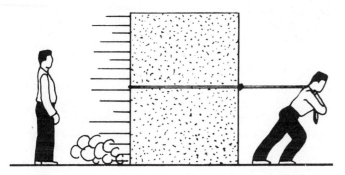

FRICTION OF MOTION

Fig. 31-1 Friction of rest is greater than friction of motion. In the example shown, it takes two men to overcome the friction of rest. But one man can keep the object moving by overcoming the friction of motion.

31-1 INTRODUCTION TO MOTORCYCLE BRAKES
There are two basic types of motorcycle brakes—drum and disk. Drum brakes are operated by means of a mechanical linkage from the rider's right hand and right foot to the front and rear brakes. The front brake is operated by a hand lever on the right handlebar. The rear brake is operated by a foot pedal on the right side of the motorcycle. Disk brakes are operated by a hydraulic system, which we cover later in the chapter.

31-2 FRICTION OF REST AND MOTION
It requires more force to put an object into motion than it does to keep it in motion, as shown in Fig. 31-1. In the example shown, it takes two people to get the object started. Once it is started, one person can keep it moving. Therefore, the friction of an object at rest is greater than the friction of an object in motion.

Engineers refer to these two kinds of friction as *static friction* and *kinetic friction*. Static friction is friction of rest, and kinetic friction is friction of motion.

31-3 FRICTION IN MOTORCYCLE BRAKES
Friction is used in motorcycle brake systems. The friction between the brake drums or disk and brake shoes slows or stops the rotation of the wheels. Then, friction between the tires and the road slows the motion of the motorcycle. However, if the brakes are applied so hard that the wheels lock, the friction between the tires and road is kinetic friction (caused by the motion of tires skidding on the road).

When the brakes are applied a little less hard, the wheels are permitted to continue rotating. Then it is static friction that works between the tires and the road. The tire surface is not skidding on the road, but is instead rolling on it. Since this produces static friction between the road and the tires, there is greater braking effect. The motorcycle stops more quickly if the brakes are applied just hard enough to get maximum static friction between the tires and road. If the brakes are applied harder than this, then the wheels will lock, the tires will skid or slide, and a lesser kinetic friction will result.

One example that illustrates the static-kinetic friction idea is the rider who takes a turn too fast. As long as the tires are not skidding, the bike will stay on course. But the instant the tires break loose (lose friction) the bike is uncontrollable. Skidding tires will not hold on the road, for they have little friction. An expert rider knows just how much lean is needed and how much speed to have when negotiating a turn.

Motorcycles use two kinds of brakes, drum and disk. Drum brakes were used universally on motorcycles until recently. Then, manufacturers began fitting disk brakes to front wheels and later to rear wheels. While the disk brake is more complicated because it requires a hydraulic system, it provides stronger and smoother braking with less force applied to the controls. Both drum and disk brakes are covered in following sections.

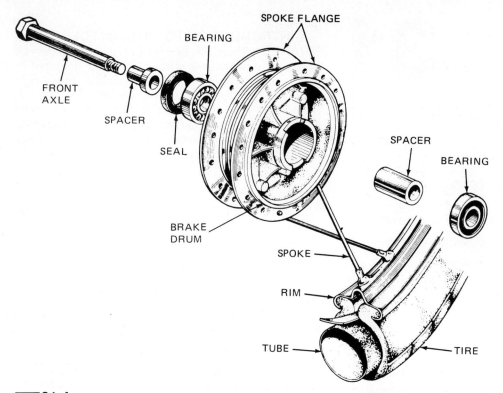

Fig. 31-2 Drum with spokes and wheel attached. The axle and the bearings support the wheel. (*Honda Motor Company, Ltd.*)

31-4
DRUM BRAKES The drum in drum brakes is a round metal rotor shaped as shown in Fig. 31-2. The drum, which has an inside diameter of about 5 to 7 inches [127 to 178 mm], forms the supporting part of the wheel. A flange on its outer diameter has holes in it for fastening the spokes that support the wheel rim. The inside of the drum is round and smooth. When the brake is assembled, two brake shoes fit inside the drum. Brake drums, which include the wheel hubs, are made of aluminum with an iron or steel band cast in. This design reduces the unsprung weight of the wheel assembly while allowing heat to be dissipated quickly.

Figure 31-3 shows a brake shoe. It is made of aluminum or steel and has a facing, or lining, of tough asbestos or other material that can stand the heat and the dragging effect resulting from brake application. The lining is curved to fit against the inside diameter of the drum. There are two shoes for each brake. When the brake is applied, the shoes are forced outward and into hard contact with the rotating drum. The frictional drag of the stationary shoes on the rotating drum slows or stops the drum and wheel.

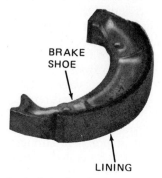

Fig. 31-3 A motorcycle brake shoe.

31-5
FRONT DRUM BRAKES Figure 31-4 shows a disassembled view of a front brake assembly. When the parts are assembled, the two brake shoes fit inside the drum and are supported by the brake panel or backing plate. In some brakes, a pair of cams fits between the two ends of the shoes. Other brakes use a single cam at one end of the shoes and a pivot at the other end. When the brake is not applied, the cam is vertical, as shown in Fig. 31-5a. But when the brake is applied, the linkage between the handlebar lever and the cam causes the cam to turn, as shown in Fig. 31-5b. This pushes the brake shoes out. They are forced tightly against the brake drum. The friction between the shoes and the drum slows or stops the drum and wheel so the bike is stopped.

When a drum brake is applied, as shown in Fig. 31-5b, the cam pushes the brake shoes out toward the rotating drum. The leading shoe, or primary shoe, is the shoe which comes into contact with the drum first. The friction between the primary shoe and the drum forces the brake assembly to shift in the direction of drum rotation. It can shift only a little because the pivot, or anchor pin, at the bottom permits only a very limited movement. However, the movement forces the primary shoe more tightly against the revolving drum, greatly increasing the braking action. This self-energizing action of the leading shoe in the drum brake causes strong braking when only a light force is applied.

In Fig. 31-5b, the secondary shoe, or trailing shoe, is forced away from the rotating drum instead of into it. For this reason, some drum brakes have a separate anchor pin, or pivot point, for each shoe. Other brakes have a separate cam and anchor for each shoe. This makes both shoes self-energizing leading shoes and greatly increases braking. A brake of this type is sometimes referred to as a *two-leading-shoe* design.

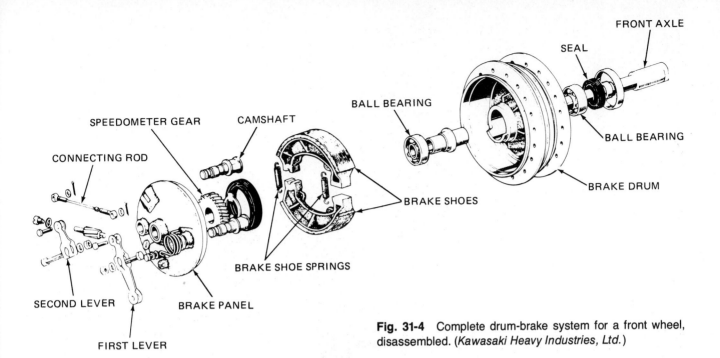

SPEEDOMETER GEAR
CAMSHAFT
CONNECTING ROD
BALL BEARING
SEAL
FRONT AXLE
BALL BEARING
BRAKE SHOES
BRAKE DRUM
SECOND LEVER
BRAKE PANEL
FIRST LEVER
BRAKE SHOE SPRINGS

Fig. 31-4 Complete drum-brake system for a front wheel, disassembled. (*Kawasaki Heavy Industries, Ltd.*)

Figure 31-6 shows the brake system for a motorcycle. The front-brake lever is on the right handlebar, as shown in Fig. 31-7. When the front brake lever is pulled, the cable pulls on a lever at the brake, which rotates the brake cam to the position shown in Fig. 31-5b. This applies the brakes by forcing the shoes against the drum.

Some brakes have two cams. Both brake cams are turned when the brakes are applied. This means there must be a linkage between the two cams. You can see this linkage disassembled in Fig. 31-4. When the brake

cable is pulled by the operation of the brake lever, the two levers pivot, thereby rotating the cams between the ends of the brake shoes.

Figure 31-8 shows the front hub and brake assembled and partially cut away. The axle is supported on its two ends by the two ends of the front fork, as explained in Chap. 30. The speedometer gear is connected by a cable to the speedometer mounted on the handlebars. This is shown in Fig. 31-7. The axle has two ball bearings which support the drum-and-hub assembly. Some front brakes, such as those shown in Fig. 31-9, have only one

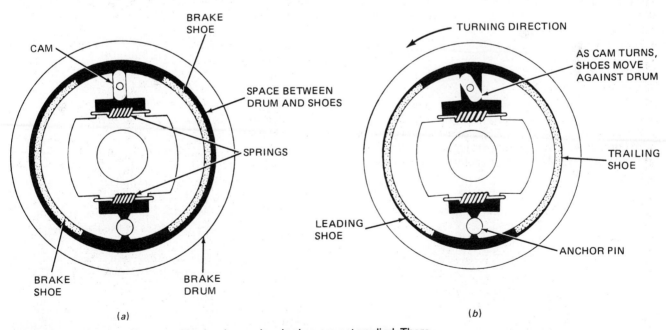

BRAKE SHOE
CAM
SPACE BETWEEN DRUM AND SHOES
SPRINGS
BRAKE SHOE
BRAKE DRUM

TURNING DIRECTION
AS CAM TURNS, SHOES MOVE AGAINST DRUM
TRAILING SHOE
LEADING SHOE
ANCHOR PIN

(a)   (b)

Fig. 31-5 (a) Position of cam and brake shoes when brakes are not applied. There is clearance between the brake shoes and drum. (b) Position of cam and brake shoes when brakes are applied. The shoes are being pressed against the brake drum.

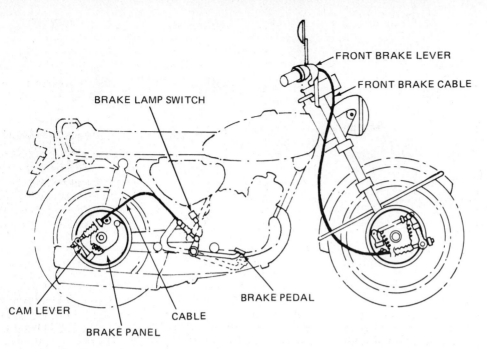

Fig. 31-6 Brake system for a motorcycle using drum brakes front and rear. (*Kawasaki Heavy Industries, Ltd.*)

brake cam. Therefore, no second lever or connecting rod is needed.

Some front brakes for larger and heavier motorcycles have two sets of brake shoes and two drum surfaces, as shown in Fig. 31-10. Each set of brake shoes has its own two cams. Linkages between the two sets of shoes cause them to apply at the same time.

The reason for the second set of brake shoes and drum is that when the front brakes are applied, most of

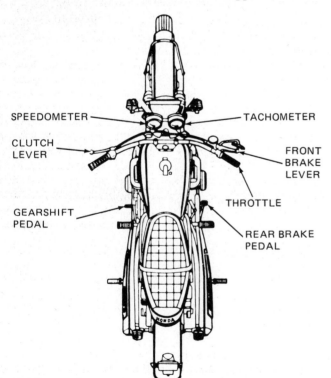

Fig. 31-7 Motorcycle controls. This arrangement is used on most late-model bikes. However, there is some variation, especially on older motorcycles. (*Honda Motor Company, Ltd.*)

the weight of the motorcycle and rider tends to shift forward onto the front wheel. This action puts extra stopping requirements on the front brake. In larger motorcycles, a single set of shoes is not always sufficient to do the job properly.

Because of the stricter front-braking requirements for heavier motorcycles, many manufacturers now use disk brakes. We cover disk brakes later, after we have described the construction and operation of rear brakes.

For better cooling of the front brakes, air ventilation is sometimes provided. Keeping the brakes cool improves their efficiency. Hot brakes lose braking ability. Very hot brakes can lead to burned linings which would require new shoes. Figure 31-11 shows one brake-cooling arrangement.

The covers and caps can be removed if air cooling is required. For most operating conditions, however, the covers and caps are kept in place to protect the drum and shoes from dust which could damage them.

31-6
REAR DRUM BRAKES
Rear drum brakes are very similar in construction and action to front drum brakes. Figure 31-12 shows disassembled view of a rear brake and hub assembly. Notice the rubber damper and coupling. The rubber damper fits between the drive sprocket and the wheel and helps to damp out changes in driving torque from the engine. Note also the two chain adjusters at the two ends of the axle. These may be turned to tighten the chain as it wears.

Figure 31-13 shows another rear brake, hub, and wheel assembly in disassembled view. The rear-wheel damper shown here is in four pieces. You can see how the chain fits around the sprocket in this illustration.

Regardless of the arrangement of the parts, all rear-brake systems work the same way. Figure 31-6 shows how the rear brake is connected through linkage to the foot pedal. When the foot pedal is pushed down by the

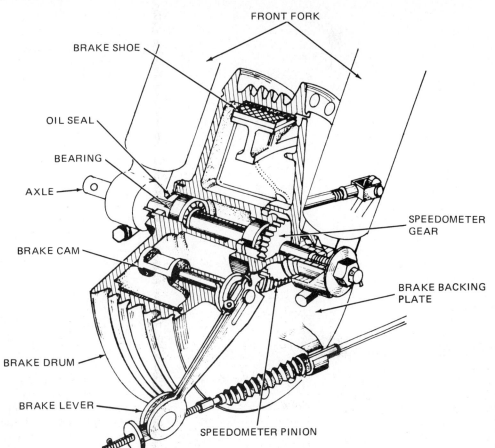

FRONT FORK

BRAKE SHOE

OIL SEAL

BEARING

AXLE

BRAKE CAM

BRAKE DRUM

BRAKE LEVER

SPEEDOMETER PINION

SPEEDOMETER GEAR

BRAKE BACKING PLATE

Fig. 31-8 The front axle is supported by the front fork. (*Kawasaki Heavy Industries, Ltd.*)

rider, the rear brake is applied. The brake cable pulls on the lever, and the lever rotates the brake cam or cams. This forces the brake shoes out and into contact with the brake drum.

**31-7
DISK BRAKES** Disk brakes for the front wheels of motorcycles have been installed in recent years, particularly on the larger and heavier bikes. Now, the rear wheels on some motorcycles are equipped with disk brakes. They provide stronger braking and require less hand or foot effort. Disk brakes use a hydraulic system. We will now cover the hydraulic system and then look at the disk brake itself.

**31-8
HYDRAULICS** Hydraulics is the study of liquids or fluids, such as oil and water, under different physical conditions. Our special interest, so far as motorcycle disk brakes are concerned, is the effect of pressure on liquids. This is called *hydraulic pressure*. Hydraulic pressure is used in the brake system, in shock absorbers, and in engine-lubricating systems. Hydraulic pressure also is used in liquid-cooled engines to produce circulation of the coolant through the engine water jackets.

When pressure is put on a liquid in one cylinder, the liquid can flow through a tube to another cylinder. When this happens, the movement of an applying piston in one cylinder can make an output piston move

in another cylinder (Fig. 31-14). This effect is used in disk brakes. Figure 31-15 shows how it works. When the hand brake lever is moved by the rider, it pushes a piston into the master cylinder. This pushes liquid out of the master cylinder, through the brake line, and into the wheel caliper. As the liquid flows into the wheel caliper, it causes the brake to apply.

Figure 31-16 shows a disassembled hydraulic disk-brake system for the front wheel of a motorcycle. The master cylinder is shown disassembled and in sectional view in Fig. 31-17. Movement of the piston (7 in Fig. 31-17) forces liquid out of the master cylinder, as already noted.

This liquid flows through the brake line and into the caliper. There, it pushes against a pair of pistons. These pistons are then forced inward against the rotating disk (Fig. 31-18). The disk is pinched between the two pads on the inner ends of the pistons. This applies friction to the disk so that it slows or stops. This is the braking action that slows or stops the motorcycle.

The brake pads are always in light contact with the disk. This is not actual heavy braking contact, but a light sliding contact that keeps the disk wiped clean of mud and other foreign matter. Because of this "zero" clearance, relatively little brake-lever movement is required to produce braking action.

Disk brakes are self-adjusting. This effect is produced by the piston seal. When the piston moves to apply the brakes, the piston seal is distorted, as shown to the left in Fig. 31-19. Then, when the brake is re-

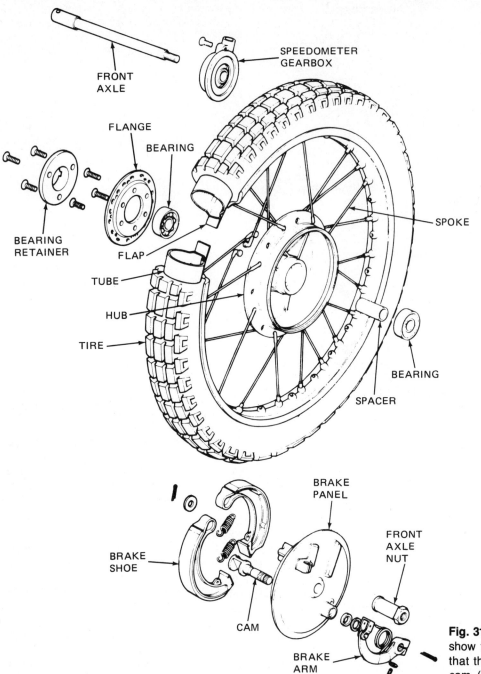

FRONT AXLE

SPEEDOMETER GEARBOX

FLANGE

BEARING

BEARING RETAINER

FLAP

TUBE

HUB

TIRE

SPOKE

BEARING

SPACER

BRAKE PANEL

FRONT AXLE NUT

BRAKE SHOE

CAM

BRAKE ARM

Fig. 31-9 Front end, disassembled, to show the brake and other parts. Note that this system uses only one brake cam. (*Honda Motor Company, Ltd.*)

leased, relaxation of the seal draws the piston slightly away from the disk. As the brake lining on the pads wears, piston travel tends to exceed the limit of deflection that the seal is capable of. This allows the piston to slide outward slightly through the seal to compensate for lining wear. Because of this action, disk brakes are self-adjusting.

**31-9
TYPES OF DISK BRAKES** Two methods of mounting the caliper are used. These are called the *fixed caliper* and the *floating caliper*. Figure 31-18 shows a simplied fixed caliper. It has two pistons and two pads,

one on each side of the disk. The floating caliper has two pads but only one piston, as shown in Fig. 31-16. When the brake fluid enters the caliper, the fluid pushes the piston against its pad and into the disk to provide braking action. But at the same time, the fluid pushes the caliper in the opposite direction with the same force.

As a result, the caliper "floats" or slides slightly on its special mounting bolts. This pulls the other leg of the caliper, which has a brake pad fastened to it, toward the disk. Now both pads are acting against the disk with the same force.

Some motorcycles equipped with disk brakes at the front and rear wheels have a *unified brake system*. This system can be used on a motorcycle that has triple disk

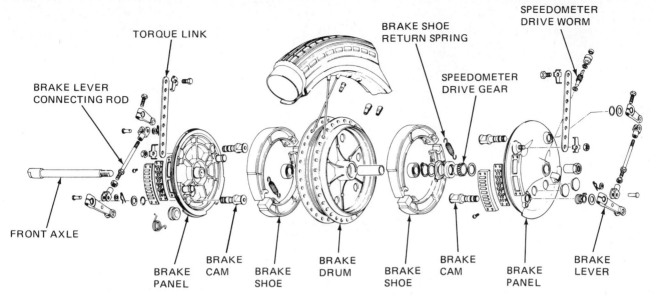

Fig. 31-10 Brake system using two sets of brake shoes and a double drum. (*Suzuki Motor Company, Ltd.*)

brakes—two on the front wheel and one on the rear. When the front-brake lever on the right handlebar is operated, the right front caliper operates. However, when the brake pedal is pressed, both the left front caliper and the rear caliper work at the same time.

The brake-pedal master cylinder is connected to both the left front caliper and the rear caliper. Because of the weight transfer to the front wheel that occurs during braking, a proportioning valve is located in the hydraulic system. If the brake pedal is pushed lightly, both front and rear calipers receive the same pressure. But when the pressure increases, the proportioning valve limits the pressure to the rear brake caliper. This helps prevent rear-wheel lockup and skidding. Full pressure continues to be applied to the left front caliper. When additional braking is needed, the rider can use the brake lever to apply the right front caliper.

31-10 BRAKE FLUID

BRAKE FLUID   Brake fluid is *not oil!* Variations in temperature have little effect on this special fluid. In addition, brake fluid does not damage the metal and rubber parts in the braking system, whereas ordinary

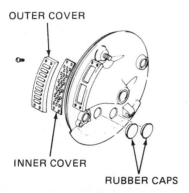

Fig. 31-11 Details of a ventilation system for a front brake. (*Suzuki Motor Company, Ltd.*)

mineral oil will damage these parts. For this reason, only the brake fluid recommended by the manufacturer should be put into the brake system. Most manufacturers recommend the use of extra-heavy-duty brake fluid that has the marking D.O.T. 3 on the container.

NOTE   Never put ordinary oil in a brake system. Engine oil, transmission fluid, or anything other than brake fluid will cause rubber parts in the system, such as the piston cups, to swell or dissolve. This could cause complete brake failure and lead to an accident. Never use anything but the brake fluid recommended by the motorcycle manufacturer.

31-11 MOTORCYCLE BRAKE SERVICE

MOTORCYCLE BRAKE SERVICE   Service includes adjustment and replacement of worn parts. Disk brakes also require checking the hydraulic system, including the master cylinder, caliper, and brake-fluid level. On drum brakes, the adjustments are made for two reasons. One reason is to compensate for brake-lining wear. The other is to correct the brake adjustment if the chain tensioner on the rear wheel has been adjusted. Disk-brake service is a little more complicated because it requires checking of the hydraulic system, and the caliper and brake pads. We will discuss all of these services.

31-12 DRUM-BRAKE ADJUSTMENTS

DRUM-BRAKE ADJUSTMENTS   Brake adjustment should be checked periodically—at least every 5000 miles [8064 km]. As wear takes place, the hand lever and foot pedal must be moved farther from the rest position before braking takes effect. The purpose of the adjustment is to reduce this free play to the specified value. For example, a typical recommendation is that if the front-wheel brake is properly adjusted, the hand lever will move about one quarter of its full movement before the brakes start to take effect. If adjusted tighter, the brakes may drag, causing rapid

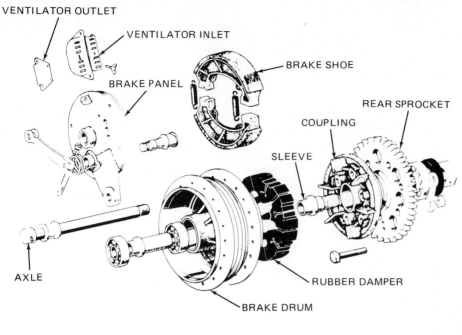

VENTILATOR OUTLET

VENTILATOR INLET

BRAKE PANEL

BRAKE SHOE

COUPLING

REAR SPROCKET

SLEEVE

AXLE

RUBBER DAMPER

BRAKE DRUM

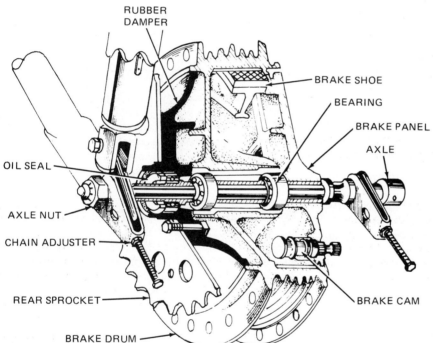

RUBBER DAMPER

OIL SEAL

AXLE NUT

CHAIN ADJUSTER

REAR SPROCKET

BRAKE DRUM

BRAKE SHOE

BEARING

BRAKE PANEL

AXLE

BRAKE CAM

Fig. 31-12 (*Top*) Disassembled view of rear-brake system. (*Bottom*) Cutaway view of assembled brake system for a rear wheel.

lining and drum wear. A typical motorcycle brake system is shown in Fig. 31-6.

31-13
ADJUSTING FRONT BRAKES
Several linkage arrangements have been used to connect the brake hand lever with the brake levers and to connect the two brake levers together. One arrangement is shown in cutaway view in Fig. 31-8 and disassembled in Fig. 31-4.

Only one brake lever and brake cam are used in some models, as shown in Fig. 31-9. Figures 31-20, and 31-23 show other arrangements of front brakes, using two levers and brake cams. The brake shown in Figs. 31-10 and 31-20 has two pairs of brake shoes.

When the hand lever is operated, the brake cable pulls on the brake levers at the wheel. This motion rotates the brake cam or cams, causing the brake shoes to move out and into contact with the brake drum. As the brake shoes wear, the hand lever must be moved farther so the brake cam or cams turn enough to push the brake shoes into contact with the brake drum. To compensate for this wear, the brake cable must be shortened.

The system shown in Fig. 31-21 has an adjustment in the cable. To make the adjustment on this bike, loosen the locknut on the adjusting sleeve. Turn the sleeve nut in toward the cable-support tube to decrease the free movement of the hand lever. Turn it away from the

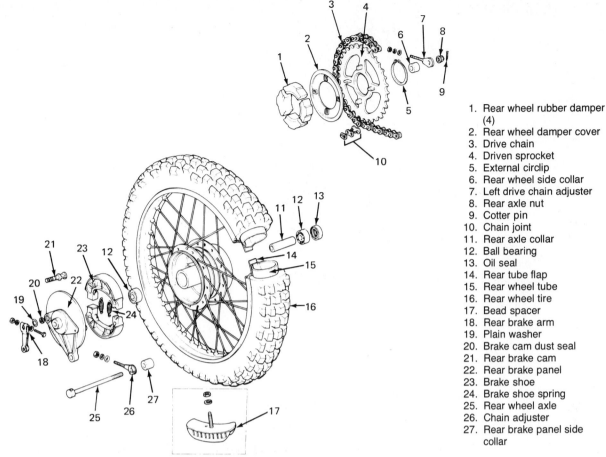

1. Rear wheel rubber damper (4)
2. Rear wheel damper cover
3. Drive chain
4. Driven sprocket
5. External circlip
6. Rear wheel side collar
7. Left drive chain adjuster
8. Rear axle nut
9. Cotter pin
10. Chain joint
11. Rear axle collar
12. Ball bearing
13. Oil seal
14. Rear tube flap
15. Rear wheel tube
16. Rear wheel tire
17. Bead spacer
18. Rear brake arm
19. Plain washer
20. Brake cam dust seal
21. Rear brake cam
22. Rear brake panel
23. Brake shoe
24. Brake shoe spring
25. Rear wheel axle
26. Chain adjuster
27. Rear brake panel side collar

Fig. 31-13 Disassembled rear wheel and brake showing the rear-wheel damper and the drive chain and driven sprocket. (*Honda Motor Company, Ltd.*)

support tube to increase the free movement. When the free movement is correct, tighten the locknut. Rotate the wheel to make sure it turns freely and is not dragging on the brake shoes. If the brake drags with the proper hand-lever free movement, loosen the front brake-shoe pivot stud (4 in Fig. 31-21) and axle nut (5 in Fig. 31-21). Spin the front wheel. While the wheel is turning, apply

APPLYING PISTON   OUTPUT PISTON

CYLINDER A   CYLINDER B

Fig. 31-14 Motion can be transmitted through a tube from one cylinder to another by liquid, or hydraulic, pressure.

the brake and then tighten the pivot stud and axle nut. Recheck the brake for correct adjustment, as previously outlined.

On some brakes there is a takeup adjustment at the handlebar. If this adjustment is inadequate because the cable has stretched, an additional adjustment can be made by loosening the locknut and turning the adjusting nut. Tighten the locknut after the adjustment is completed.

Some models require a different adjusting procedure. For example, in the system shown in Fig. 31-22*a* and *b,* the recommended procedure is to make the adjustment at the wheel. If this is insufficient, then make additional adjustments of the brake lever, as shown. In this same model, checks should be made before adjusting the brake to see if internal brake parts, such as the brake cam, have worn excessively. This check is done by applying the brake lightly. Then check the angle between the brake lever and the brake cable, or rod, as shown in Fig. 31-22*c.* If the angle is much greater than 90°, braking effectiveness will be reduced. This can be corrected by removing the brake lever and remounting it in a new position on the brake cam. The position is correct if the angle is between 80° and 90°, as shown in Fig. 31-22*c.*

The front-brake system shown in Fig. 31-10 and 31-20

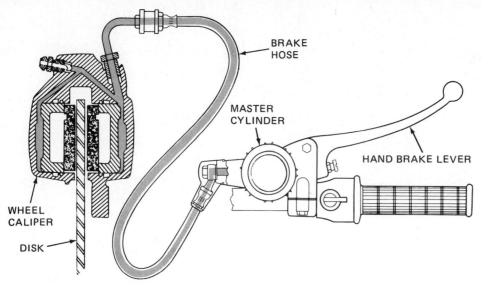

Fig. 31-15 Schematic diagram of a disk-brake system for the front wheel of a motorcycle. (*Castrol, Limited*)

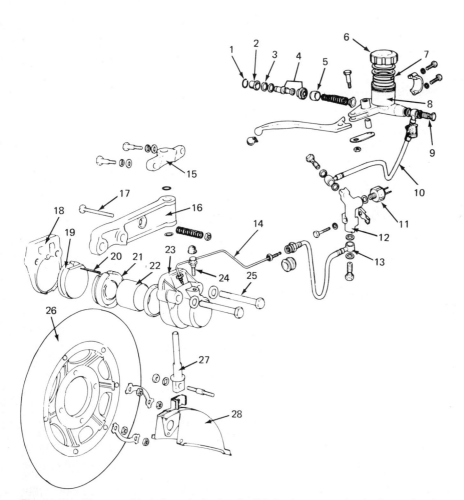

1. Boots stopper
2. Boots
3. Internal circlip
4. Piston
5. Primary cup
6. Oil cup cap
7. Diaphragm
8. Master cylinder
9. Brake-fluid bolt
10. Front brake hose B
11. Stop switch
12. Three-way joint
13. Front brake hose A
14. Front brake pipe
15. Caliper holder joint
16. Caliper holder
17. Caliper adjusting bolt
18. Caliper B
19. Pad B
20. Cotter pin
21. Pad A
22. Piston
23. Caliper A
24. Bleeder valve
25. Caliper attaching bolts (2)
26. Front brake disk
27. Caliper holder
28. Disk cover

Fig. 31-16 Disassembled view of a hydraulic disk-brake system for the front wheel of a motorcycle. (*Honda Motor Company, Ltd.*)

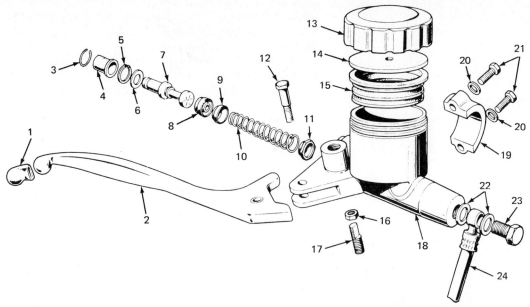

1. BRAKE LEVER CAP	9. PRIMARY CUP	17. LEVER ADJUSTING BOLT
2. BRAKE LEVER	10. RETURN SPRING	18. MASTER CYLINDER BODY
3. LOCK RING	11. CHECK VALVE	19. MASTER CYLINDER HOLDER
4. BOOT	12. HANDLE LEVER PIVOT BOLT	20. LOCKWASHER
5. SNAP RING	13. BRAKE-FLUID CAP	21. HEX BOLT
6. WASHER	14. MASTER CYLINDER PLATE	22. BRAKE-FLUID BOLT WASHER
7. PISTON	15. DIAPHRAGM	23. BRAKE-FLUID BOLT
8. SECONDARY CUP	16. LOCKNUT	24. FRONT-BRAKE HOSE

(a)

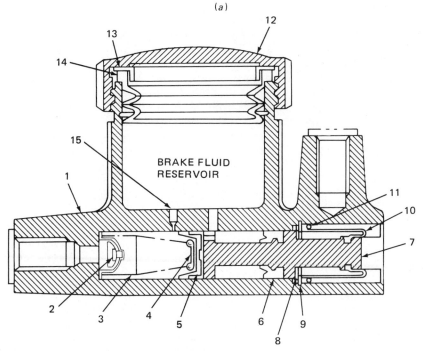

1. MASTER CYLINDER BODY	6. SECONDARY CUP	11. STOPPER, DUST SEAL
2. CHECK VALVE	7. PISTON	12. CAP
3. SPRING	8. STOPPER, PISTON	13. PLATE
4. SPRING SEAT	9. CIRCLIP	14. CAP SEAL (DIAPHRAGM)
5. PRIMARY CUP	10. DUST SEAL	15. RELIEF PORT

(b)

Fig. 31-17 (a) Disassembled view of the master cylinder for a hydraulic disk-brake system for the front wheel of a motorcycle. (b) Sectional view of a master cylinder for the hydraulic system of a disk-brake system. (*Honda Motor Company, Ltd.; Kawasaki Heavy Industries, Ltd.*)

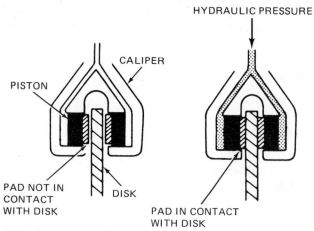

HYDRAULIC PRESSURE

CALIPER

PISTON

PAD NOT IN CONTACT WITH DISK   DISK

PAD IN CONTACT WITH DISK

Fig. 31-18 (*Left*) When the brakes are not applied, the brake pads are not in contact with the disk. (*Right*) When the brakes are applied, hydraulic pressure forces the brake pads against the rotating disk. The friction between the pads and the disk slows or stops the rotation of the wheel. (*Yamaha International Corporation*)

requires an additional adjustment because it has two pairs of brake shoes. The recommended procedure is as follows.

First adjust the connecting rod. Loosen the locknut. Shorten the distance between the two levers (A and B) so that the brake shoe operated by lever A touches the drum before the brake shoe operated by lever B touches the drum as the brake is applied. Then extend the connecting rod, while holding lever A so its brake shoe is applied, until lever B stops moving. This means that the brake shoe operated by lever B is also up tight against the brake drum. Tighten the locknut. Then make the adjustment to the adjuster, as shown in Fig. 31-22*b*, to get the correct free movement of the brake lever. If the adjustment here is not sufficient, make an additional adjustment at the upper end of the brake cable at the brake hand lever.

NOTE The change in the angle between the cam lever and the connecting rod, or cable, shown in Fig. 31-22*c,* is caused by wear of internal parts. If the angle is over 90°, check the internal parts for wear.

31-14
ADJUSTING REAR BRAKES
The rear brake is adjusted in about the same way as the front brake. The brake's cable length is adjusted so that the brake pedal has the correct free movement before the brake is

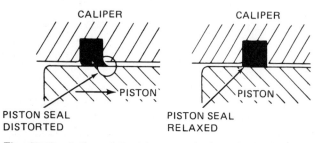

CALIPER   CALIPER

PISTON   PISTON

PISTON SEAL DISTORTED   PISTON SEAL RELAXED

Fig. 31-19 Action of the piston seal when the brakes are applied and released. (*Yamaha International Corporation*)

applied. Figure 31-12 is a cutaway and assembled view of a similar brake. Figure 31-22*d* shows the adjustment on one model of motorcycle.

There are two reasons that the rear brake may require adjustment. One is wear of the brake shoes. The other is a problem caused by a chain adjustment. When the chain is adjusted to take up the slack caused by wear, the wheel is moved back. This reduces free travel of the brake pedal and could cause the brake to drag if the proper adjustment is not made. Figure 31-12 shows the chain adjuster on one model of motorcycle.

31-15
DRUM-BRAKE SERVICE
Brake shoes and drums should be checked periodically, and replaced if excessively worn. Brake drums on most motorcycles are not serviceable by turning or grinding the inner diameter. Most manufacturers state that if the drum is worn or grooved, it must be discarded and a new drum must be installed. However, some motorcycle manufacturers state that the drum can be turned. They supply the maximum diameter to which the drum can be safely enlarged.

Motorcycle brake shoes have their linings bonded to the shoes. If the lining is worn, the shoe must be replaced. Never replace only one shoe at a wheel. Shoes must be replaced as pairs. A worn shoe working with a new shoe will not brake effectively.

31-16
REPLACING BRAKE SHOES
Figure 31-23 is a disassembled view of a front-brake system. To replace the brake shoes, the brake pedal must be removed from the wheel. The shoes are attached to the brake panel. To remove the panel, first remove the front wheel from the motorcycle. Support the frame so that the wheel is raised from the floor. Then disconnect the speedometer and brake cables and remove the wheel axle. This frees the wheel, which can now be laid on its side so the brake panel can be removed. Remove the brake cam lever or levers. The shoes with springs can then be lifted off the brake panel.

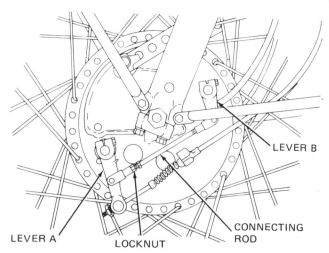

LEVER B

LEVER A   LOCKNUT   CONNECTING ROD

Fig. 31-20 Front brake using two brake cams. Note the connecting rod between the two levers (A and B). (*Suzuki Motor Company, Ltd.*)

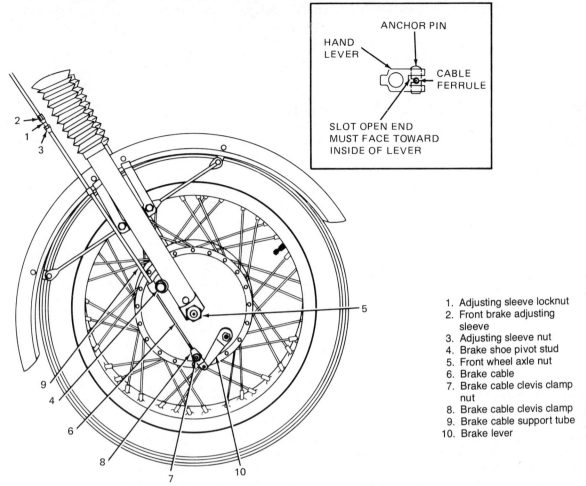

Fig. 31-21 Front brake using two brake cams with the brake cable connected directly to the shafts of the cams. *(Harley-Davidson Motor Company, Inc.)*

1. Adjusting sleeve locknut
2. Front brake adjusting sleeve
3. Adjusting sleeve nut
4. Brake shoe pivot stud
5. Front wheel axle nut
6. Brake cable
7. Brake cable clevis clamp nut
8. Brake cable clevis clamp
9. Brake cable support tube
10. Brake lever

Check the linings for wear, grease, or oil. If a lining is oil soaked, it will not give good braking. The shoe should be discarded and a new pair of shoes installed. Measure the thickness of the lining. If it is worn excessively, new shoes will be required. The typical thickness for front and rear brake linings is 0.200 inch [5 mm] when new. If linings are worn down to 0.120 inch [3 mm], the shoes should be replaced.

NOTE When handling new brake shoes, or shoes that you intend to reuse, do not get any grease or oil on them. Grease from your hands can be enough to seriously reduce the braking effectiveness of the shoes.

31-17
BRAKE-SHOE SPRINGS Examine the springs for damage and check their free length. If a spring has stretched beyond its service limit, replace the pair of springs. A typical specification is that a new spring will be 2.620 inches [66.5 mm] in length and should be discarded if it has stretched to a free length of 2.740 inches [69.5 mm].

31-18
BRAKE DRUMS Many manufacturers recommend that a new drum be installed if the old drum is excessively bell-mouthed, worn, or grooved. Other manufacturers supply specifications beyond which a drum should not be turned. For example, a new front drum on one model has an inside diameter of 7.874 inches [200 mm]. It is permissible to refinish this drum up to an inside diameter of 7.904 inches [200.75 mm]. But if more material than this is removed, the drum's safety limit will be exceeded, and the drum should be discarded. Use calipers or an inside micrometer to check the inside diameter of a drum.

Cast-iron drums can be either turned or ground. Steel drums, however, because of their hardness, usually require grinding. Follow the instructions from the manufacturer of the bike or the servicing equipment.

31-19
DISK-BRAKE SERVICE A disk brake requires servicing of the hydraulic system, the master cylinder, the caliper, and the disk. Figure 31-16 shows a disassembled view of a disk-brake system. We will start with the master cylinder and work our way down to the disk, describing the servicing of each element of the system. The procedure that follows applies to one specific motorcycle model, but it covers generally the procedures for all motorcycle disk-brake systems. Before you start to service a disk-brake system, check the service manual covering the motorcycle you are working on.

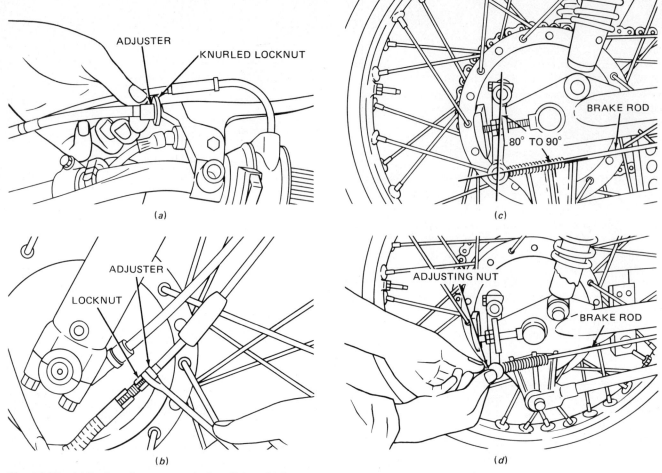

Fig. 31-22 (*a*) Brake adjustment at the handlebar. (*b*) Brake adjustment at the front wheel. (*c*) Correct position of the brake rod, or cable, and the brake lever. (*d*) Adjusting the rear brake at the wheel. (*Kawasaki Heavy Industries, Ltd.*)

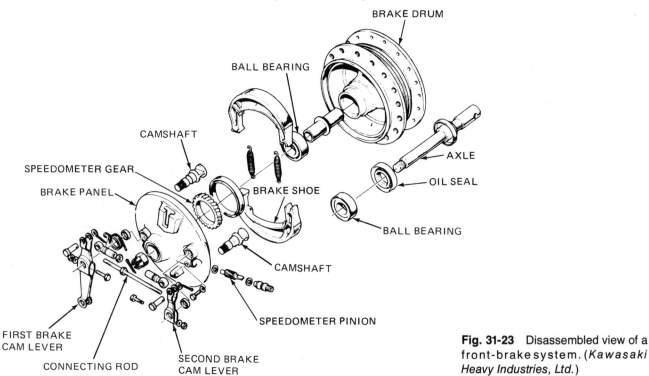

Fig. 31-23 Disassembled view of a front-brake system. (*Kawasaki Heavy Industries, Ltd.*)

31-20
MASTER-CYLINDER SERVICE Figure 31-17a is a disassembled view of a master cylinder. To remove the master cylinder from the handlebars, disconnect the brake line by removing the brake-fluid bolt. Tape the end of the line shut, so that no dirt gets into the line. Unscrew the two bolts which hold the master cylinder to the handlebar, and remove the master cylinder.

To disassemble the master cylinder, refer to Fig. 31-17a. Remove the brake-lever adjusting bolt and locknut (17 and 16), and remove the brake lever (2). Take off the lock ring (3) and boot (4). Use snap-ring pliers to remove the snap ring (5). Now the internal parts can be removed. These include the washer, piston, secondary cup, primary cup, return spring, and check valve (6 to 11). You may need to apply light air pressure through the brake-hose connector to force out the primary cup, as shown in Fig. 31-24. Be careful to avoid damaging parts or injuring yourself. Before you apply air pressure, point the piston end of the master cylinder down into a soft cloth on the workbench.

Inspect the piston, the cylinder, the primary and secondary cups, and the check valve for damage, and replace any damaged parts. Measure the inside diameter of the cylinder with an inside dial gauge and the outside diameter of the piston with a micrometer. Compare the measurements. If the clearance is greater than 0.0045 inch [0.115 mm], replace the parts. Use a new primary cup on reassembly.

To reassemble the master cylinder, make sure all parts are clean. Do not clean the parts with gasoline as this will ruin the cups and other rubber parts. Instead, use brake fluid. Then, apply a thin coat of brake fluid to the inside of the cylinder. Install the check valve and spring. Make sure the check valve is installed facing in the correct direction (Fig. 31-17a).

Now apply a thin coat of brake fluid on the new primary cup, and push it into the cylinder, as shown in Fig. 31-25. Make sure the cup is facing the correct direction. Then install the other parts in proper order, as shown in Fig. 31-17a. Secure with the snap ring (5), and install the boot and lock ring. Install the assembly on the handlebars, and reattach the brake hose. Fill the

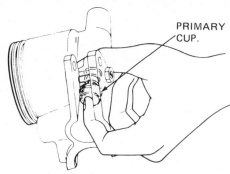

Fig. 31-25 Installing a primary cup. (*Honda Motor Company, Ltd.*)

master cylinder and bleed the system, as explained later.

31-21
CALIPER SERVICE Refer to Fig. 31-16. The front wheel must first be removed. Raise the front wheel off the floor by putting a support under the engine. Disconnect the speedometer cable from the front-wheel hub assembly. Remove the axle-holder attaching nuts and remove the wheel.

Disconnect the front-brake pipe from the caliper, and allow the fluid to drain out. Remove the front fender if it is in the way. Examine the caliper and the caliper holder (16 in Fig. 31-16) to determine how many attaching bolts are used. Remove the disk cover, if present. Then take out the caliper attaching bolts to separate the two caliper parts (18 and 23). Remove the brake pads from the caliper. The pad on one side is held in place by a cotter pin (19 and 20). The pad on the other side comes out when the piston is removed.

Check the pads for excessive wear. On some models, there is a red-line groove. Replace the pads if the lining is worn down to this limit groove. Measure the inside diameter of the caliper cylinder and the caliper piston. If the clearance is excessive, replace both. Note also if there are scratches on the cylinder or piston surfaces. Replace the cylinder or piston if the scratches are noticeable. They could cause poor braking. They will also damage the piston seal and cause brake-fluid leakage.

Check the condition of the seal on the piston. Replace

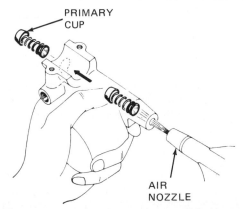

Fig. 31-24 Using compressed air to remove the primary cup. Be careful to avoid injury. (*Honda Motor Company, Ltd.*)

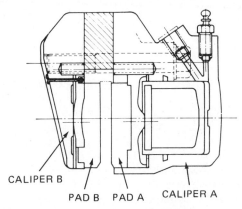

Fig. 31-26 Sectional view of an assembled caliper. (*Honda Motor Company, Ltd.*)

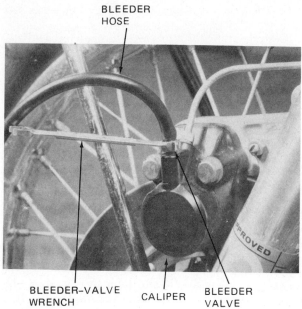

BLEEDER
HOSE

BLEEDER–VALVE WRENCH   CALIPER   BLEEDER VALVE

Fig. 31-27 Attaching a bleeder hose to the caliper to bleed the hydraulic system. (*ATW*)

the seal if it is damaged in any way. When installing a new seal, be sure to put it on in the same position as the original. Handle the seal with care to avoid damaging it.

On reassembly, apply a light coat of silicone sealing grease to the sliding surfaces of the caliper, as shown in Fig. 31-26. Do not get any grease on the pad surfaces. Be very careful not to get any dirt in the caliper during assembly. Even a trace of dirt can produce wear and poor braking action.

After the caliper is assembled, install it on the motorcycle. Reinstall all other parts that were removed, such as the disk cover and wheel. The hydraulic system must then be filled with brake fluid and bled.

**31-22
FILLING AND BLEEDING THE HYDRAULIC SYSTEM**   Whenever the hydraulic system has been opened, air probably has gotten in. This can also happen if brake fluid has leaked out, resulting in a low brake-fluid level in the master cylinder. Air in the system will reduce or prevent braking. The brake lever will

feel soft and spongy. Excessive lever travel may be required to produce braking. The correction is to fill and bleed the hydraulic system. As a first step, remove the reservoir cap and fill the reservoir with the specified brake fluid.

NOTE   The proper grade of brake fluid must be used. To use a brake fluid that fails to meet or exceed the manufacturer's specifications is to risk damage to the hydraulic system. Engine oil, gasoline, or kerosene will ruin the rubber parts in the system and thereby prevent braking action.

Remove the dust cap from the bleeder valve, and attach a bleeder hose, as shown in Fig. 31-27. Put the other end of the hose into a clean container of clean brake fluid. The end of the hose should be in the brake fluid. Rapidly pump the brake lever until pressure can be felt. Then, holding the brake lever to maintain pressure, open the bleeder valve about half a turn and squeeze the brake lever all the way down. Do not release the lever until you close the bleeder valve. Release the lever and repeat the operation—open the valve, squeeze the lever, close the valve. Repeat this until the fluid runs out of the bleeder hose without any air bubbles. This means that the air has been eliminated from the system.

NOTE   Keep filling the reservoir in the master cylinder during the procedure so it does not become empty.

When the fluid runs out of the hose without bubbles, close the bleeder valve and install the cap. Refill the reservoir to the proper level. Install the reservoir diaphragm and cap.

NOTE   Never reuse brake fluid that has been pumped out of the system. Brake fluid can damage a paint finish, so avoid getting it on any motorcycle parts. Also, avoid leaving the reservoir cap off for any length of time, because the brake fluid can absorb moisture from the air, which can cause rusting and rubber deterioration.

**31-23
ADJUSTING THE BRAKE LEVER**   If excessive brake-lever movement is required for braking, and the hydraulic system is okay, readjust the lever free travel (Fig. 31-17a). Loosen the locknut (16) and turn the adjusting bolt (17) to change the lever travel as necessary to obtain the proper free travel.

CHAPTER 31
REVIEW QUESTIONS

1. What are the two types of brakes used on motorcycles?
2. What are the two types of friction?
3. How is friction used to provide braking action?
4. Describe the construction of a drum brake.
5. How does a drum brake operate?
6. Why do some brakes have two sets of shoes?
7. How is the front brake operated?
8. What operates the rear brake?
9. Define *hydraulic pressure*.
10. How does hydraulic pressure operate the disk brake?

11. On the disk brake, where are the pads located?
12. Why are disk brakes self-adjusting?
13. Discuss why nothing except brake fluid should ever be put into the master cylinder.
14. Why is it necessary to adjust drum brakes?
15. Explain how to adjust drum brakes.
16. How do you adjust the brake cable for the front wheel?
17. What steps are required to replace brake shoes?
18. What can be done with a badly scored brake drum?
19. How is the master cylinder overhauled?
20. Explain how to fill and bleed the hydraulic system.

CHAPTER 32

MOTORCYCLE WHEELS AND TIRES

After studying this chapter,
you should be able to:

1. Explain how to remove and replace front wheels.

2. Describe how to remove and install a rear wheel.

3. Discuss inspection of wheel axles and bearings.

4. Describe wheel balancing and perform this service.

5. Explain how to align wheels.

6. Discuss wheel spoking.

7. Describe the purpose and construction of tires.

8. Explain how to inspect, remove, service, and install a tire and tube.

32-1 MOTORCYCLE WHEELS AND AXLES

Wheels and axles are very important parts of a motorcycle. The wheels must be strong, yet light. They carry the driving, braking, and steering forces, and they support the weight of the motorcycle rider and passenger. At the same time, they should not adversely affect the handling or the riding comfort of the machine. The axles must allow the wheels to rotate freely while keeping them in proper alignment. In this chapter we cover the servicing of wheels, including alignment and spoking. We also cover tires and tire servicing.

Most motorcycle wheels are of the spoke type. Some motorcycles are equipped with aluminum or magnesium wheels. This type of wheel is often called a *mag wheel*. Other motorcycles are equipped with a split-rim type of wheel, as shown in Fig. 32-1. This type of wheel can be separated into two parts to mount or demount the tire.

Figure 32-2 shows a disassembled view of a front wheel. The hub contains the front brake and the speedometer drive gearcase. This motorcycle uses a mechanically operated drum type of front-wheel brake. The brake drum is formed into the wheel hub. Other motorcycles, equipped with disk brakes, have the disk assembly mounted to one side of the wheel.

The speedometer gearcase operates the speedometer mounted to the handlebars through a drive cable. The lower end of the cable plugs into the speedometer gearcase in the wheel assembly.

The wheel is secured to the motorcycle by means of the axle. The wheel rotates on wheel bearings, shown in Fig. 32-2. The bearings fit into recesses in the wheel

hub. The axle is mounted to the lower end of the front fork.

The rear wheel has the final drive attached to it. On most motorcycles, this is a sprocket driven by a chain from the transmission. Figure 32-3 is a disassembled view of a rear wheel and related parts.

32-2 REMOVING A FRONT WHEEL
The procedure for removing and installing front wheels with drum brakes differs from that for front wheels with disk brakes. Both procedures are covered in this chapter. Brakes and brake service are covered in Chap. 31.

Front Wheel with Drum Brake   To remove a front wheel that has a drum brake, raise the front end of the motorcycle so the wheel is off the ground. Disconnect the front-brake cable. Remove the axle nut (13 in Fig. 32-2) or axle-holder nuts (whichever are used). The wheel can then be removed. On most motorcycles, the brake panel and brake shoes come off with the wheel. On other models, the brake panel and drum are left on the motorcycle, as shown in Fig. 32-4. This requires removal of the wheel-mounting screws.

Front Wheel with Disk Brake   To remove a front wheel that has a disk brake, raise the front wheel and detach the speedometer cable from the front hub assembly. Remove the axle-holder mounting bolts or nuts. The wheel can now be removed.

NOTE   Do not depress the brake lever when the wheel is off the motorcycle. This can force the caliper piston out of the caliper and cause a loss of brake fluid. If this does happen, then you will have to service the brake hydraulic system, as explained in Chap. 31.

32-3 INSTALLING A FRONT WHEEL
After inspecting the bearings, axle, and other parts, as explained later, proceed as follows. On the motorcycle shown in Fig. 32-4, the brake drum and shoes are left on

Fig. 32-1   Motorcycle with split-rim wheels. (*Honda Motor Company, Ltd.*)

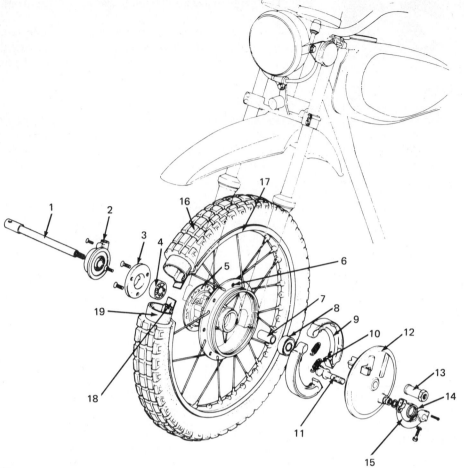

1. Front-wheel axle
2. Speedometer gear box
3. Bearing retainer
4. Ball bearing
5. Front spoke flange
6. Front-wheel hub
7. Front axle distance collar
8. Ball bearing
9. Brake shoe
10. Brake-shoe spring
11. Brake cam
12. Brake panel
13. Wheel axle nut
14. Brake arm return spring
15. Brake arm
16. Tire
17. Wheel rim
18. Dust seal
19. Tube

Fig. 32-2 Disassembled view of a front wheel and related parts. (*Honda Motor Company, Ltd.*)

the motorcycle. Therefore the wheel hub must be reattached to the drum with the wheel mounting screws. On motorcycles using an axle holder, install the axle holder and secure it with nuts or bolts.

If the axle is of the type with a nut, put the wheel in place, install the axle, and secure it with the nut. Some axle nuts are secured with a cotter pin (Fig. 32-4). On this type, install the cotter pin after tightening the nut. Now, reattach the speedometer cable and brake cable, and adjust the brake cable.

On a disk-brake front wheel, make sure that the brake works by trying it after the wheel is installed.

NOTE Balance the wheel, either before or after it is installed, as explained later. More accurate balancing can be done with the wheel off the motorcycle.

32-4
REMOVING AND INSTALLING A REAR
WHEEL   On some motorcycles, the recommendation is to disconnect the chain link so the chain can be parted and removed from the rear-wheel sprocket. On other models, the chain adjusters can be loosened enough so the wheel can be moved forward to allow the chain to be lifted off the sprocket. The muffler must be removed on

some models before the wheel comes off. A typical removal and installation procedure for a rear wheel with chain drive follows.

32-5
REMOVING A REAR WHEEL   The rear wheel
we are going to use as an example is shown in Fig. 32-5. To begin, put the motorcycle up on a stand so the rear wheel is off the ground. Remove the brake adjusting nut. Then separate the brake rod from the brake arm. Next, remove the brake stopper arm by removing the cotter pin, nut, spring washer, flat washer, and stopper bolt.

Remove the cotter pin from the right side of the rear axle and loosen the axle nut (Fig. 32-5). Loosen the drive-chain adjusting-bolt locknuts, and back out the adjusting bolts. Turn the chain adjusters down. Remove the rear-fork cap attaching bolts and caps. Push the wheel forward, lift the chain off the sprocket, and then pull the wheel to the rear and away from the rear fork.

To remove the rear sprocket, refer to Fig. 32-3. Unlock the washers (20) by bending down the tongues. Remove the nuts so the sprocket (18) can be taken off.

Next, remove the ball bearing. Remove the bearing retainer (13 in Fig. 32-3), and the bearing (11) will then come out.

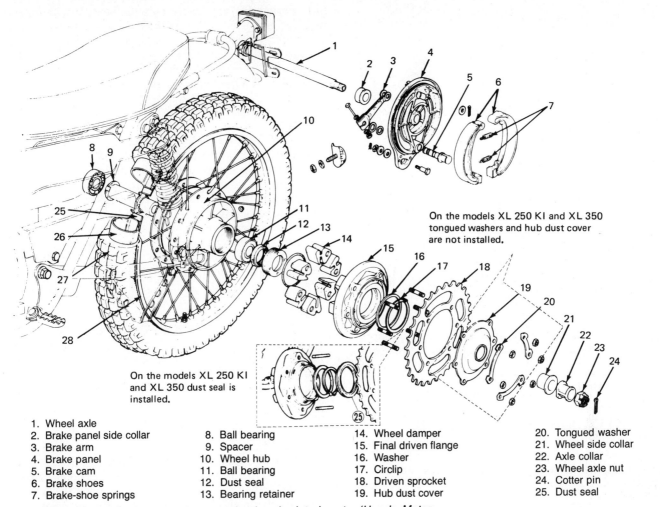

Fig. 32-3 Disassembled view of a rear wheel and related parts. (*Honda Motor Company, Ltd.*)

On the models XL 250 KI and XL 350 tongued washers and hub dust cover are not installed.

On the models XL 250 KI and XL 350 dust seal is installed.

1. Wheel axle
2. Brake panel side collar
3. Brake arm
4. Brake panel
5. Brake cam
6. Brake shoes
7. Brake-shoe springs

8. Ball bearing
9. Spacer
10. Wheel hub
11. Ball bearing
12. Dust seal
13. Bearing retainer

14. Wheel damper
15. Final driven flange
16. Washer
17. Circlip
18. Driven sprocket
19. Hub dust cover

20. Tongued washer
21. Wheel side collar
22. Axle collar
23. Wheel axle nut
24. Cotter pin
25. Dust seal

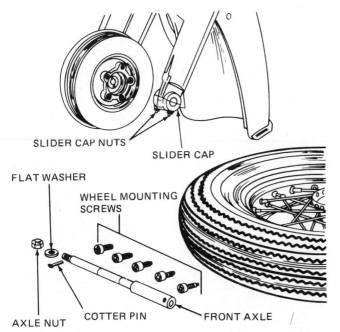

SLIDER CAP NUTS

SLIDER CAP

FLAT WASHER

WHEEL MOUNTING SCREWS

AXLE NUT   COTTER PIN   FRONT AXLE

Fig. 32-4 On some motorcycles, when the front wheel is removed, the brake drum remains attached to one fork leg. (*Harley-Davidson Motor Company, Inc.*)

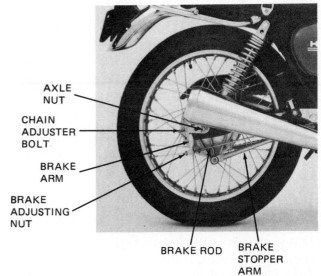

AXLE NUT

CHAIN ADJUSTER BOLT

BRAKE ARM

BRAKE ADJUSTING NUT

BRAKE ROD   BRAKE STOPPER ARM

Fig. 32-5 Locations of the parts to be removed to take off the rear wheel. (*Honda Motor Company, Ltd.*)

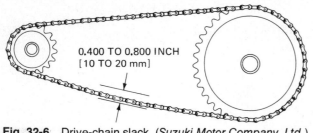

Fig. 32-6 Drive-chain slack. (*Suzuki Motor Company, Ltd.*)

32-6 INSTALLING A REAR WHEEL
To install a rear wheel, proceed as follows. Install the bearing and secure it with the bearing retainer (Fig. 32-3). Install the rear-wheel sprocket and secure it with the tongued lockwashers and attaching nuts. Bend the tongues up on flats of nuts to keep them from loosening.

Install the wheel on the frame. Put the chain on the sprocket. Assemble the chain adjuster, fork cap, and attaching bolt, as shown in Fig. 32-5. Tighten the adjusting bolts until there is a slack of 0.400 to 0.800 inch [10 to 20 mm], as shown in Fig. 32-6. Some manufacturers give closer tolerance specifications—for example, 0.600 to 0.800 inch [15 to 20 mm]. Adjust the brake.

NOTE The wheel should be balanced, as explained later, before it is installed.

32-7 INSPECTING WHEEL AXLES AND BEARINGS
The checking and servicing of brakes is covered in Chap. 31. The checking of bearings, wheel axles, and tires is covered in the following sections.

32-8 CHECKING THE BEARINGS
Do not wash sealed bearings in solvent. This will remove the lubricant and ruin the bearing. Sealed bearings should be checked to see if they are worn or damaged in any way. Hold the center race between the fingers and thumb of one hand, and slowly turn the outer race with the other hand. Check for grit, roughness, and looseness. Examine the races for any damage. Replace any bearing that is defective or damaged.

Other ball bearings should be washed in solvent to remove all old lubricant. Use compressed air to blow the bearing dry, but do not spin the bearing with compressed air. This will ruin it! Check the bearing, as explained above. If it passes inspection, immediately lubricate it and wrap it in a clean, lint-free shop cloth or paper. Put it in a safe place until you are ready to reinstall it. If a bearing is not oiled at once, it may begin to rust.

32-9 CHECKING THE WHEEL AXLES
A bent axle can cause wheel vibration and unstable handling. You can check an axle with V blocks. The axle is put on two V blocks, and the dial indicator gauge is positioned so the gauge finger touches the center of the axle. As the axle is revolved in the V blocks, a bent condition will show up as a movement of the gauge needle. One manufacturer specifies that the axle should be discarded if the runout, or out-of-line condition, is more than 0.028 inch [0.7 mm]. The runout on a new axle should not exceed 0.008 inch [0.2 mm].

32-10 CHECKING BEARING ON THE AXLE
Honda recommends checking the bearing installed on the axle for axial and radial runout, using V blocks and a dial indicator, as shown in Fig. 32-7. This check is made after the axle has been found to be okay. Excessive looseness or runout of the bearing means that the bearing is worn and should be discarded.

32-11 WHEEL BALANCING
Wheel balance can be checked *statically* or *dynamically*. Static balance can be checked either on the motorcycle or with the wheel removed from the motorcycle. A fairly accurate balance check can be achieved as follows.

32-12 STATIC BALANCE CHECK ON THE MOTORCYCLE
With the motorcycle on a stand so the wheel is off the ground, spin the wheel several times and see if it comes to rest with the same spot at the bottom each time. (The chain must be off the sprocket to perform this test on the rear wheel.) If the same spot

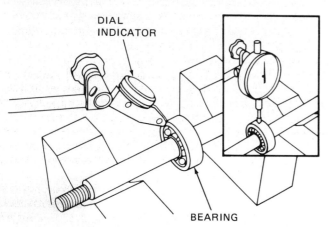

Fig. 32-7 Checking bearing on axle for axial and radial runout. (*Honda Motor Company, Ltd.*)

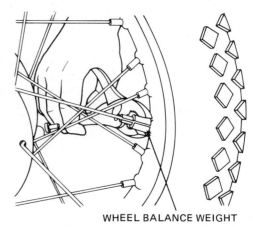

Fig. 32-8 Pinching a balance weight tight on wheel spoke with pliers. (*ATW*)

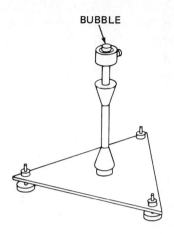

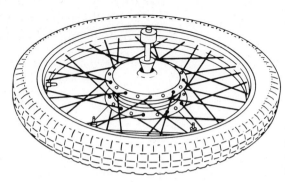

Fig. 32-9 (Left) Bubble type of static wheel balancer. (Right) Tire and wheel on balancer in readiness for balance check. (*ATW*)

comes to rest at the bottom each time, that spot is heavy. This shows that the wheel is unbalanced.

Small weights can be placed on the spokes that are opposite the heavy spot to balance the wheel. The weights are put on the spokes and pinched tight, as shown in Fig. 32-8. Start with a light weight and repeat the test, adding weights as necessary to achieve balance. The wheel is in balance when it does not come to rest in the same spot each time it is spun. Be sure the weights are pinched tight on the spokes.

32-13 STATIC BALANCE CHECK WITH THE WHEEL OFF THE MOTORCYCLE

In a static balance test of a detached wheel, the wheel and tire assembly are placed on a balancer, as shown in Fig. 32-9 (right). A bubble in the center of the balancer head centers under the cross in the head if the wheel is in balance. If the wheel is not in balance, spoke weights should be installed, as explained above, to achieve balance.

32-14 DYNAMIC BALANCE CHECK

For the most accurate balancing, a dynamic balancer should be used (Fig. 32-10). The dynamic balancer spins the wheel and can more exactly detect any imbalance. Spoke weights are used to achieve balance, as explained above. Dynamic balancing is especially recommended for the high-performance rider and is preferred by most speed racers and by most riders of touring bikes.

32-15 WHEEL ALIGNMENT

The wheel alignment can be checked with the wheel on the motorcycle. But a more accurate check can be made with the wheel off and placed in a wheel trueing stand, as shown in Fig. 32-11. Install the trueing arbor, which is part of the stand, in the wheel hub so the wheel will turn on its bearings.

Lateral Runout Rotate the wheel, as shown in Fig. 32-11, with the pointer positioned so the lateral runout (also called *side runout, sideways runout,* or *axial runout*) can be checked. If the runout is excessive (if the side clearance between the pointer and the rim varies too much), correction must be made. This is done by

loosening the spoke nipples at the point of minimum runout and tightening the spoke nipples on the opposite side. This will pull the rim into lateral alignment with the hub.

Radial Runout After the rim runs true laterally, adjust the pointer as shown in Fig. 32-12 to check the radial runout. If the rim runs eccentrically (has too much radial runout), loosen the spoke nipples at the points of maximum runout. Then tighten the spoke nipples at the point of minimum runout. This shifts the rim enough to eliminate the radial runout.

Fig. 32-10 Balancing a motorcycle wheel-and-tire assembly on a dynamic, or spin-type, wheel balancer. (*Phoenix International*)

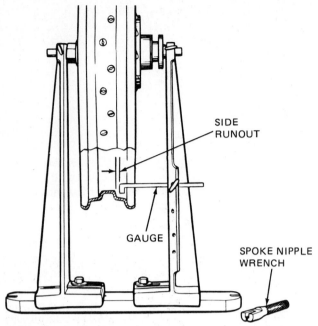

Fig. 32-11 Wheel installed on trueing stand with gauge (pointer) positioned to check side runout. (*Harley-Davidson Motor Company, Inc.*)

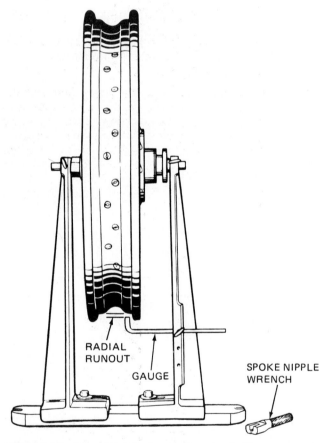

Fig. 32-12 Wheel installed on trueing stand with gauge positioned to check radial runout. (*Harley-Davidson Motor Company, Inc.*)

NOTE If the rim is bent (Fig. 32-13), replace it. You cannot align a wheel that has a bent rim.

After the wheel has been trued both laterally and radially, start at the tire valve and tighten the spoke nipples, one at a time, one complete turn. Work your way completely around the wheel. Repeatedly recheck the wheel for lateral and radial runout.

Do not overtighten the spokes. Overtightening may draw the nipples through the rim or cause the hub flanges to become distorted.

NOTE If the tire is off the rim, the spokes can be checked to make sure they are not sticking too far through the rim. This would allow the long spokes to puncture the tube. File or grind off the ends of any spoke that is too long.

32-16
SPOKING WHEELS The spokes are installed at different angles with the rim and hub, as shown in Fig. 32-14. The purpose of this is to support the load and provide reactions to acceleration and braking. For example, the spokes shown in Fig. 32-14*a* support the direct load—the weight of the vehicle and rider. The spokes in Fig. 32-14*b* provide support for acceleration. During acceleration, the hub is trying to turn faster than the rim and tire, so these spokes are pulling on the rim, trying to get it to move faster. The spokes in Fig. 32-14*c* provide support during braking. In this case, the tire and rim are trying to slow down and pull on the hub through the spokes. Notice that in all three patterns, the spokes are under tension. The load is pulling on the spokes.

A variety of spoke arrangments is used. The arrangement varies according to the width of the hub and rim. Here are some typical spoking instructions.

32-17
SPOKING THE HARLEY-DAVIDSON ELECTRA GLIDE This hub has two rows of spoke holes on each side, with 10 inner-row holes and 10 outer-row holes in each flange (Fig. 32-15*a*). A typical spoke is

Fig. 32-13 A bent rim must be replaced. (*ATW*)

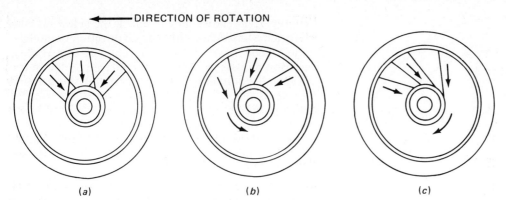

DIRECTION OF ROTATION

(a)   (b)   (c)

Fig. 32-14 Three directions spokes are installed in some models. (a) The spokes that support direct load. (b) The spokes that handle acceleration load. (c) The spokes that handle braking load. (*Kawasaki Heavy Industries, Ltd.*)

shown in Fig. 32-15b. All spokes must be inserted from the inside of the flanges on the hub. Proceed as follows.

Put the hub on the bench with the brake-drum end of the hub up. Insert spokes in the 10 inner spoke holes of the brake side flange. Swing the loose ends of the spokes counterclockwise as far as the hub will allow without turning the hub. This is the position of the spoke shown to the right in Fig. 32-15a.

Put the rim over the hub with the tire-valve hole 90° to 180° from the hub grease fitting. Insert the spokes in the upper row of holes that angle in the same direction as the spokes.

NOTE Some wheels have 16-inch rims; others have 18-inch rims. The 18-inch rim is placed over the hub with either side down. The 16-inch rim is placed over the hub with the tire-valve hole down, with the opposite side of the brake drum on the hub.

As you insert each spoke in the hub and rim, start the nipple onto the spokes but do not tighten it.

After you have installed all the spokes in the inner hub holes, start to install the spokes in the outer holes on the rim, swinging them clockwise, as shown in Fig. 32-15a. Cross the first outer spoke over four inner spokes (A, B, C, and D in Fig. 32-16), and insert the outer end of the spoke into the nearest upper-rim hole.

Start a nipple on the spoke. Follow this procedure with the remainder of the spokes for the outer row of holes in the brake-drum end of the hub.

Then turn the rim and hub over. Repeat the operations. Start with the inner row of holes in the hub flange, inserting a spoke at a time through the hub hole and the corresponding rim hole. However, when doing this, you swing the spokes going through the inner holes clockwise. Also, when inserting the spokes through the outer holes in the hub, you swing the spokes counterclockwise.

NOTE The outer spokes on both sides point in the same direction.

Not all wheels are spoked in the same way. Before you attempt to spoke a wheel, refer to the shop manual covering the motorcycle you are working on.

After installing all spokes and securing them with the nipples loosely turned down, install a trueing arbor in the wheel hub. Put the assembly on a wheel trueing stand. Tighten the arbor nuts so the hub will turn on its bearings. Figure 32-12 shows a wheel installed in the trueing stand. Tighten each nipple just enough to cover the spoke threads.

Then start at the valve hole and tighten all nipples

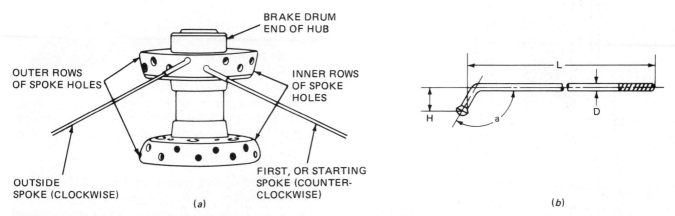

BRAKE DRUM
END OF HUB

OUTER ROWS
OF SPOKE HOLES

INNER ROWS
OF SPOKE
HOLES

OUTSIDE
SPOKE (CLOCKWISE)

FIRST, OR STARTING
SPOKE (COUNTER-
CLOCKWISE)

(a)

(b)

Fig. 32-15 (a) Starting the spokes in a wheel hub. (b) A typical wheel spoke. There are many different models, varying in length, diameter (D), angle at the head, or hub, end, and rise of the hub end (H). (*Harley-Davidson Motor Company, Inc.; Suzuki Motor Company, Ltd.*)

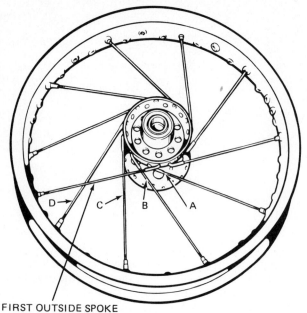

FIRST OUTSIDE SPOKE
(CROSS FOUR INSIDE SPOKES)

Fig. 32-16 Spoking a wheel, showing how the outside spokes cross over four inside spokes. Not all wheels are spoked in the same way. (*Harley-Davidson Motor Company, Inc.*)

three full turns each, using the nipple tightener shown in Fig. 32-12. If further tightening is needed, tighten all nipples one full turn at a time until the spokes are snug.

Check the rim for centering sideways on the hub, for running sideways, and for radial runout (concentricity). Centering the rim sideways with the hub and trueing the rim sideways must be done as one operation.

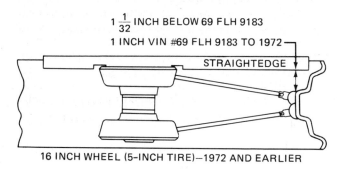

$1\frac{1}{32}$ INCH BELOW 69 FLH 9183
1 INCH VIN #69 FLH 9183 TO 1972
STRAIGHTEDGE

16 INCH WHEEL (5-INCH TIRE)—1972 AND EARLIER

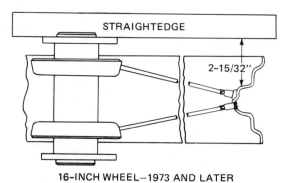

STRAIGHTEDGE

2-15/32″

16-INCH WHEEL—1973 AND LATER

Fig. 32-17 Centering a 16-inch [404.6-mm] wheel rim. (*Harley-Davidson Motor Company, Inc.*)

Figure 32-17 shows how to check the sideways centering of the wheel rim with the hub on different models. Some wheels have the rim off center. Later Harley-Davidson models have the rims centered on the hub.

Adjust the pointer (gauge) in the trueing stand until it is close to the side of the drop center of the rim, as shown in Fig. 32-11. Slowly rotate the wheel and note the lateral runout (eccentricity). Loosen the nipples at the point on the rim which comes closest to the gauge. Tighten the nipples at the point on the rim which passes farthest from the gauge. This will bring the rim into sideways alignment. At the same time you are doing this, loosen and tighten the nipples to shift the hub as necessary to center it in the rim, as shown in Fig. 32-17. Note that some rims are slightly offset, as shown in Fig. 32-17.

After the rim has been centered sideways with the wheel hub and after the rim runs true sideways, check it for radial runout. Adjust the gauge to the rim tire head, as shown in Fig. 32-12. Slowly rotate the wheel and note how much off center the rim is. If it runs off center (radial runout), loosen the nipples in the area of maximum runout and tighten the nipples in the area where the rim touches the gauge. This shifts the rim to make it concentric. While you are doing this, repeatedly recheck the rim, as shown in Fig. 32-11, for lateral runout, to make sure you do not throw the rim off sideways.

The rim should be trued to within 0.020 inch [0.5 mm] both axially and radially.

After the above operations have been completed, start at the valve stem hole and tighten all nipples one turn at a time all the way around the rim until the spokes are tight. Repeatedly check for lateral runout, as shown in Fig. 32-11.

As a final step, after the spokes have been pulled up to normal tightness, seat each spoke head and nipple into the rim and hub flange with a sharp blow, using a flat-nose punch and hammer. Then retighten all the nipples and finish trueing the wheel. This procedure seats the spoke heads in the flange so the spokes will not loosen soon after the wheel goes into service. Without this final step, the spoke heads will seat in the hub-flange holes soon after the wheel is installed and the motorcycle is ridden. The spokes will then become loose after a comparatively short time.

NOTE Do not tighten the spokes too much. The nipples may be drawn through the rim, or the hub flanges may become distorted. However, if the spokes are left loose, they will loosen further after the wheel is put into service.

Check the inside of the rim to see if any of the spokes are sticking through the nipples. If they are, file or grind them off. Otherwise, they could puncture the inner tube.

32-18
SPOKING THE HARLEY-DAVIDSON SUPER GLIDE Spoking of this model is shown in Fig. 32-18. There are 20 spoke holes equally spaced around each side flange of the hub, and 20 spoke holes are arranged in pairs on each side of the rim drop center. Spacing of the holes is the same on each side of the rim and hub.

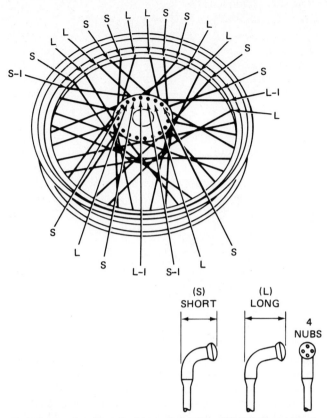

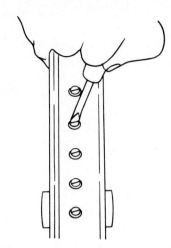

(S) SHORT (L) LONG 4 NUBS

Fig. 32-18 Spoking the front wheel of an FX (1973 and later). (*Harley-Davidson Motor Company, Inc.*)

There are two types of spokes, long and short at the bend or hub end, as shown in Fig. 32-18. One long spoke and one short spoke are used in each pair of spokes. The long spoke of each pair crosses over to the opposite side of the hub, while the short spoke connects to the same side of the hub. The procedure is the same as previously described.

Fig. 32-19 Motorcycle with a wheel hub having two flanges and mounting 18 spokes in each flange. (*Kawasaki Heavy Industries, Ltd.*)

32-19
SPOKING AN ENDURO WHEEL   Figure 32-19 shows the type of motorcycle and wheel discussed here. On this wheel, the hub has two flanges, and there are 18 spoke holes in each flange. The inner spokes are inserted into the flanges from the outside of the drum, and the outer spokes are inserted from the inside of the flange. Insert the inner and outer spokes alternately.

The wheel rim has 36 holes, but their angles are not the same. The inner and outer spokes are inserted into the hub flanges alternately, but they are fitted into every fourth hole in the rim. The order of insertion would be the inner spoke from one flange, outer spoke from the other flange, outer spoke from the first flange, and inner spoke from the other flange.

After the spokes are installed properly, screw on the spoke nipples from the inside of the rim by hand. Then use a screwdriver to tighten them, as shown in Fig. 32-20. Next, put the wheel on a trueing stand, as shown in Fig. 32-11. Check and correct the lateral and the radial runout by adjusting the nipples. The procedure has been outlined previously. Suzuki recommends the use of a dial indicator, as shown in Fig. 32-21, to check

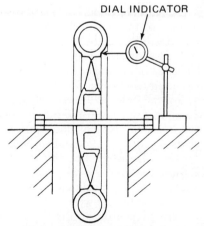

Fig. 32-21 Checking lateral runout with a dial indicator. (*Suzuki Motor Company, Ltd.*)

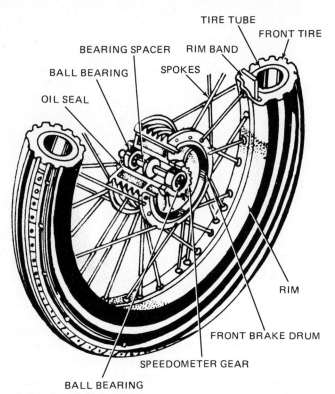

Fig. 32-22 Cutaway view of a tire, tube, and wheel. (*Kawasaki Heavy Industries, Ltd.*)

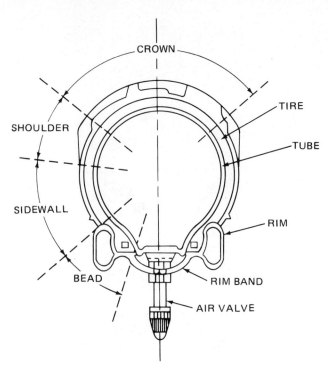

Fig. 32-23 Sectional view of a tire and tube, showing the construction. (*Kawasaki Heavy Industries, Ltd.*)

lateral runout. With this method, the actual amount of runout can be measured accurately. Suzuki recommends keeping the runout below 0.120 inch [3 mm].

**32-20
SERVICING SPOKES** If spokes become loose during the operation of the motorcycle, the wheel rim may become deformed and the spokes may be damaged. The tightness of the spokes can be checked by tapping them with a wrench or a similar tool. A tight spoke will give off a definite pinging sound. Suzuki recommends retightening the spokes every 1900 miles [3000 km]. Other manufacturers also recommend checking and tightening the spokes periodically.

**32-21
TIRE CONSTRUCTION** The tires used on motorcycles are of the inner-tube type. A doughnut-shaped inner tube is placed between the wheel rim and the tire itself, as shown in Figs. 32-22 and 32-23. The inner tube is made of natural or synthetic rubber. It has an air valve, as shown in Fig. 32-23.

When the tire and tube have been installed on the rim, compressed air is forced into the tube through the air valve so that the tube becomes filled with compressed air. This gives the tire its shock-absorbing capability. The compressed air also gives the tire the rigidity needed for good traction with the road.

A typical tire is shown in cutaway view in Fig. 32-24. The tire is made by starting with layers of cord, called *plies*, which are shaped on a form. The form has the shape of the inner surface of the tire that is being made. The number of plies placed on the form varies with

different tires. A two-ply tire would have two layers of plies, a four-ply tire would have four layers. The plies are then covered with rubber, which will form the tread and sidewalls of the tire. This assembly is then put into a mold and heated under pressure. This cures the rubber so that when the mold is opened, the tire in its final form can be removed.

Tires are made in a variety of sizes and treads, as shown in Fig. 4-9. Aside from the universal tread (Fig. 4-9, left), the other treads are special-purpose designs. Knobby tread gives the tire positive bite on soft dirt or rocky hills. Motocross tread is for dirt, track, hill climb-

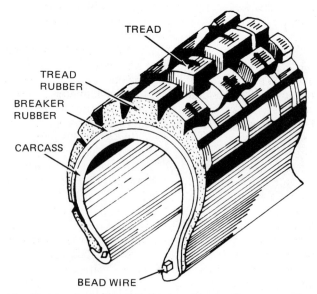

Fig. 32-24 Cutaway view of a tire, showing the construction. (*Kawasaki Heavy Industries, Ltd.*)

Fig. 32-25 Comparison of the amount of tread a racing tire and a standard tire put on the road. (*Castrol, Limited*)

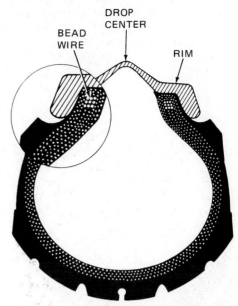

Fig. 32-26 The bead wire prevents the bead from expanding, holding the tire in place on the ledges of the rim. (*The Goodyear Tire & Rubber Company*)

ing, and cross-country riding. Street tread is for street and highway travel. Rib tread is especially designed for taking corners fast, and it has good road-holding ability. Studded tread is for scrambles, hill climbing, and heavy off-road use.

Sometimes different types of treads are installed on the front wheel to improve steering. A block-type tread might be installed on the rear wheel to ensure good traction for the driving wheel.

The tire size is given by one of the numbers molded on the tire sidewall. A typical size would be 3.50H-18. The first part of the number is the cross-sectional width of the tire. The last number is the rim diameter. A letter such as S, H, or V, appearing between the two parts of the tire size, indicates the speed rating for the tire. For example, a tire that is size 3.50H-18 is 3.5 inches in cross-sectional width, can be used on motorcycles capable of a maximum speed of 130 mph, and must be mounted on a rim of the proper width and having an 18-inch diameter.

Racing tires tend to have a profile like the one shown at the top in Fig. 32-25. The advantage of this tire is that a relatively large amount of tread is put on the road with the motorcycle leaning at a 45° angle when rounding a curve. Compare this with the amount of tread the standard tire puts on the road when the motorcycle is leaning at 45° rounding a curve (Fig. 32-25, lower). The racing tire, with its somewhat pointed profile, places about twice as much tread on the road when rounding a curve. This gives the tire much better holding ability.

The tire bead has a bead wire in it. This wire prevents the bead from expanding. The bead must fit firmly and snugly on the ledges on the two sides of the rim, as shown in Fig. 32-26. Notice that the center of the rim is recessed. It is of a smaller diameter. The name for this construction is *drop center*. The purpose of the drop center is to permit the tire to be removed from the rim. The first step is to let the air out of the tire. Then the tire bead can be pushed off the ledge into the drop center. Now the tire bead can be pushed off center so that it can be worked over the rim.

32-22
TIRE-BEAD CLAMP Tires are subjected to severe forces when the motorcycle is accelerated or braked. When the motorcycle is accelerated, the rim tends to slip ahead of the tire. In a similar way, when the motorcycle is braked, the tire tends to slip ahead of the rim. During severe operating conditions, an unprotected tire can actually slip on the rim. This could take the tube around with it, pulling the tube valve hard enough to rip the tube and ruin the tube and tire.

To prevent this from happening, special tire security locks, or tire-bead clamps, are used. Figure 32-27 shows how a bead clamp is installed. It is positioned so that it clamps the tire bead to the rim as the attaching nut is tightened. This holds the tire bead firmly to the rim so the tire cannot slip.

32-23
TUBELESS TIRES Up to a point, motorcycle tires are similar in construction to automobile tires. However, automobile tires are considerably larger and heavier. Automobile tires do not use inner tubes, but heavy-duty tires for trucks and other such equipment

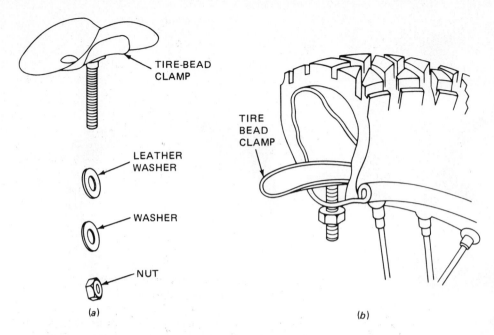

TIRE-BEAD CLAMP

LEATHER WASHER

WASHER

NUT

(a)

TIRE BEAD CLAMP

(b)

Fig. 32-27 (a) Tire-bead clamp. (b) Tire-bead clamp installed. (*Harley-Davidson Motor Company, Inc.; Kawasaki Heavy Industries, Ltd.*)

do use inner tubes. Automotive tubeless tires have three basic designs, as shown in Fig. 32-28. These are bias ply, belted-bias, and belted-radial. The belted-radial tire has become popular for cars and trucks in recent years. However, it is not recommended for use on motorcycles.

Tubeless tires are beginning to be made for motorcycles. Until cast wheels became available, all motorcycle tires had to use inner tubes. This is because air leaks out of the wheels between the spoke nipples and their holes in the rim when an inner tube is not used on a spoked rim. However, the rim of a cast wheel has only one hole in it, which is for the valve stem. Figure 32-29 shows the difference in construction between the spoked-wheel rim and a cast wheel. You can see how tubeless tires can be used with wheels similar in construction to the cast wheel. However, tubeless tires cannot be used on all cast wheels.

32-24
TIRE INSPECTION AND INFLATION Tires should be checked frequently with an accurate tire gauge. Keep the tires inflated to the specified pressure. A tire that is run under-inflated will be damaged. The sidewalls will flex excessively, causing the cords to break so that the tire loses strength. Loss of strength can lead to a blowout. Also, excessive pressure can damage a tire. Excessive pressure results in a rough ride, poor traction with the road, and possibly ruptured cords. With excessive tire pressure, the cords cannot give normally when the tire meets bumps. As a result, the cords can be broken. This may also lead to a blowout.

Examine the tires for cracks, cuts, splits, tread chunking out, and other damage that could lead to tire failure. *Chunking out* means that pieces of the tread have been broken or torn out, usually resulting from

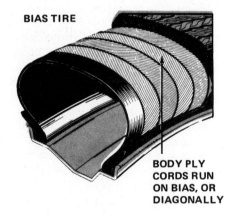

BIAS TIRE

BODY PLY CORDS RUN ON BIAS, OR DIAGONALLY

BODY PLY CORDS RUN ON BIAS FROM BEAD TO BEAD. BUILT WITH 2 TO 4 PLIES. CORD ANGLE REVERSED ON EACH PLY. TREAD IS BONDED DIRECTLY TO TOP PLY.

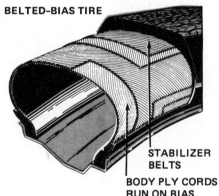

BELTED–BIAS TIRE

STABILIZER BELTS

BODY PLY CORDS RUN ON BIAS

STABILIZER BELTS ARE APPLIED DIRECTLY BENEATH THE TREAD. BODY PLY CORDS RUN ON BIAS, SIMILAR TO BIAS TIRE CONSTRUCTION.

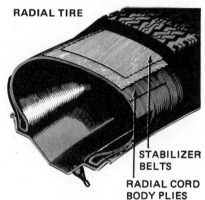

RADIAL TIRE

STABILIZER BELTS

RADIAL CORD BODY PLIES

RADIAL PLY CORDS RUN STRAIGHT FROM BEAD TO BEAD WITH STABILIZER BELTS APPLIED DIRECTLY BENEATH THE TREAD.

Fig. 32-28 Cutaway views of tubeless tires, showing the construction. (*Firestone Rubber Company*)

Fig. 32-29 Comparison of a spoked-wheel rim and a cast wheel. (*ATW*)

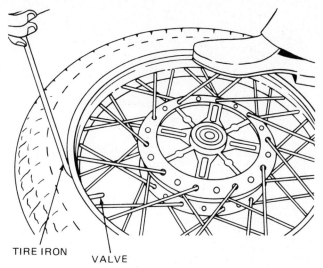

Fig. 32-30 Using tire iron to push tire bead off the rim ledge. (*Kawasaki Heavy Industries, Ltd.*)

running over very rough surfaces. If you plan a high-performance run, the tires must be in top condition. Worn treads or other damage will lower performance and can be dangerous. Remove stones from the treads of tires used at high speeds. Stones can work themselves deeper into the treads and damage the tire.

If a tire shows some evidence of damage on the outside, it should be removed from the wheel and examined from the inside. Look for separated plies, cracks in the casing, or internal roughness that might not show on the outside. Separated plies or cracks in the casing can lead to a blowout. Internal roughness can wear the tube to the point where it will lose air so the tire goes flat. Do not try to repair a tire with cracked casing or separated plies. Such a tire is dangerous and should be discarded.

32-25
TIRE REMOVAL AND INSTALLATION In this section, we describe the procedure for removing a tire from a one-piece rim, as in Fig. 32-30.

To begin with, the wheel with its tire should be removed from the motorcycle. You usually cannot remove a tire from a wheel on the motorcycle. Remove the valve cap and valve core to release all the air from the tube. Put a chalk mark on the tire next to the valve so you can put the tire back on in the same position. This helps to maintain wheel-and-tire balance.

Next, remove the valve-stem nut. If the tire uses a bead clamp, loosen the clamp nut. Then push both beads off the rim ledges and into the drop center of the rim. You can do this by hitting the side of the tire with a rubber mallet, by stepping on the side of the tire, or by using a tire iron, as shown in Fig. 32-30. Do not use sharp instruments. Make sure the tire iron does not have any sharp edges that could damage the tire or tube.

After both tire beads have been pushed into the drop center, use two tire irons, as shown in Fig. 32-31, to lift the bead up over the wheel rim. Start at the valve stem. Work carefully to avoid damaging the tire bead. If you damage the tire bead, the tire may be ruined and will

have to be discarded. Do not use force because this could stretch or break the bead wires and ruin the tire.

Before you work on the other bead, remove the tube. Then start raising the other bead up over the rim. Once you have the second bead partly off, discard the tire tools and complete the tire removal by hand.

Before you install a tire or tube, make sure it is in good condition. Remove all dirt or dust from the inside of the tire. Wipe the tube and the inside of the tire with a clean, dry cloth. Inspect the wheel rim. If it is dirty, clean it with a wire brush. If the rim flange is dented or bent and cannot be straightened, the rim should be discarded.

Make sure the rim does not have any rough spots which could cause the tube to wear. Smooth out rough spots with steel wool or emery cloth, and be sure to clean any filings off the rim. Roughness, unevenness, and dirt can chafe the tube and cause early tube and tire failure. If the wheel has a rubber rim strip, make sure it is in place and that the rim-strip valve hole registers with the valve hole in the rim.

Be sure to use the correct tube for the tire if you must use a new tube. A tube of the wrong size will probably have a very short life.

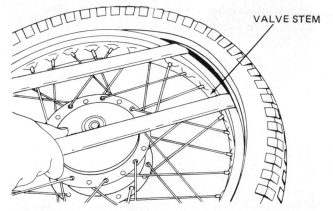

Fig. 32-31 Using two tire irons to lift the tire bead up over rim. (*Kawasaki Heavy Industries, Ltd.*)

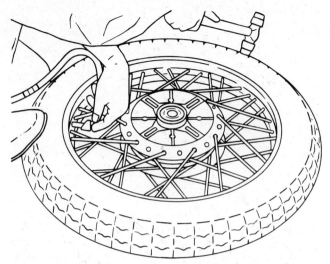

Fig. 32-32 Tapping a tire with a mallet during inflation to assure good alignment of the tube in the tire. (*Kawasaki Heavy Industires, Ltd.*)

32-26
REPAIRING TIRES AND TUBES If a tire tube has been punctured but is otherwise in good condition, it can be repaired with a patch. First, you have to find the hole. Inflate the tube after it is out of the tire and submerge the tube in water. Bubbles will appear where the leak is. Mark the spot with anything that will make a light scratch on the rubber. Deflate the tube and dry it.

There are two ways to patch a tube leak, the cold-patch and the hot-patch methods. With the cold-patch method, first make sure the rubber is clean, dry, and free of grease or oil. Then roughen the area around the hole and cover the area with rubber cement. Let the cement dry until it is tacky, then peel off the back of a patch and apply the patch firmly. Recheck the tube for leaks by reinflating it and submerging it in water.

With the hot-patch method, prepare the tube in the same way as for the cold-patch method. Put the hot patch into place and clamp it. Then, with a match, light the fuel on the back of the patch. The heat ensures a good bond. After the patch has cooled, recheck for leaks by submerging the inflated tube in water.

Another kind of hot patch uses an electric vulcanizing hot plate which supplies the heat required to bond the patch to the tube.

NOTE The hot-patch method usually is considered better than the cold-patch method.

If a tire has chunked out or has damaged cords or large punctures, it is beyond repair. Discard it. Small punctures can be repaired with a rubber plug or by applying a patch inside the tire. If a rubber plug is used, the puncture area inside the tire is buffed with a wire brush to roughen it. Then the plug, puncture hole, and buffed area are coated with cement. After the cement is tacky, the plug is inserted to seal the puncture. The purpose of repairing a puncture in this manner is not to seal off any air leak—the tube does that. Rather, it is to prevent the entrance of dirt through the hole which could chafe the tube and shorten its life.

Either a cold patch or a hot patch can be applied to the puncture from inside the tire. The same methods as for repairing tube punctures are used.

32-27
INSTALLING TIRE ON RIM First, insert the tube in the tire, placing the air valve at the chalk mark you made before removing the tire. Swab the entire tube and the inside of the tire with a heavy suds solution of tire mounting compound and water. Do not get any compound on the bead seat of the tire. Inflate the tube just enough to round it out. With the wheel lying flat, place the tire on the rim and align the valve with the hole in the rim.

Start the bottom bead into the drop center of the rim near the valve, and hold it while pushing the remainder of the bottom bead into the drop center. You may need tire tools to complete this. Spread the tire and insert the tube valve stem through the hole in the rim. Make sure the valve stem enters the hole without straining in one direction or the other. If you have to pull it along to get the stem to enter the hole, it means that the tube is not properly positioned.

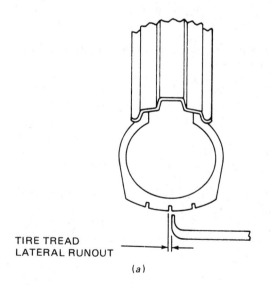

TIRE TREAD
LATERAL RUNOUT

(a)

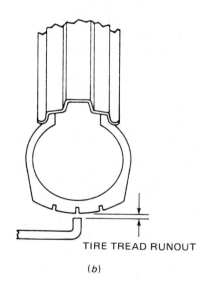

TIRE TREAD RUNOUT

(b)

Fig. 32-33 (a) Checking tire lateral runout. (b) Checking tire radial runout. (*Harley-Davidson Motor Company, Inc.*)

338

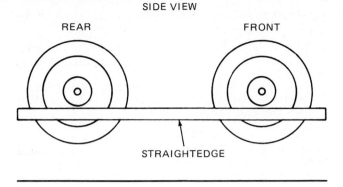

SIDE VIEW

REAR   FRONT

STRAIGHTEDGE

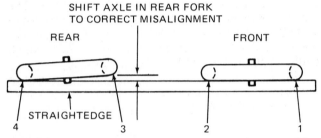

TOP VIEW

SHIFT AXLE IN REAR FORK
TO CORRECT MISALIGNMENT

REAR   FRONT

STRAIGHTEDGE

4   3   2   1

Fig. 32-34 Using a straightedge to check the alignment of the front and rear wheels of a motorcycle.

Now work on the upper bead, forcing it over the rim flange and into the drop center. Stand or kneel on the side of the tire to hold it while working the bead over the rim. Be careful not to damage the bead or pinch the tube. Then inflate the tire, little by little, stopping several times to hit the tire with a soft mallet to make sure the tube is not getting caught between the tire and the rim (Fig. 32-32). After the tube has the recommended pressure in it, check the valve for leaks. Deflate the tube and then reinflate it to the proper pressure. This allows the tube to settle into place.

Tighten the nuts on the tube stem and the bead clamp. Then check the tire for trueness, as described in the following section.

32-28
CHECKING TIRE TRUENESS
A tire should run true. If it does not, the motorcycle will have a tendency to wobble and will have poor riding characteristics. Two factors determine tire trueness: the alignment of the rim and the alignment of the tire itself. Checking rim and wheel alignment was covered earlier in this chapter. Here is how the tire itself should be checked for trueness. We are assuming that the wheel itself runs true.

With the tire-and-wheel assembly on its axle, position a pointer, as shown in Fig. 32-33a. Locate the tip of the pointer near the centerline of the tire, or at one side of the tire. Rotate the tire and note the amount of lateral runout. If it is excessive ($^3/_{64}$ inch [1.191 mm] is the maximum allowable according to one manufacturer), the tire or wheel is at fault. If you have already checked the wheel, then the tire itself is at fault and should be discarded.

Next, check the radial runout by positioning the pointer as shown in Fig. 32-33b. Note how the clearance between the tire and the pointer varies as the wheel is revolved. If the runout exceeds the specifications (one manufacturer specifies a limit of $^3/_{32}$ inch [2.381 mm]) and the wheel is not at fault, the tire is defective and should be replaced.

Check the alignment of the front and rear wheels. Put a straight wood board or string against the tire sidewalls as high up as possible, as shown in Fig. 32-34. The straightedge should be parallel to the tires as shown. If the rear wheel is misaligned, it can be aligned by shifting the rear axle in the rear fork. As a final step, check the balance of the wheel.

NOTE On motorcycles using different size tires front and rear, the smaller tire will be offset from the straightedge.

CHAPTER 32
REVIEW QUESTIONS

1. What two types of wheels are used on motorcycles?
2. Explain how to remove a front wheel with a drum brake.
3. Explain how to remove a front wheel with a disk brake.
4. Describe how to remove the rear wheel from a motorcycle with chain drive.
5. Explain how to clean and check the front-wheel bearings.
6. What are the two ways that wheels can be balanced?
7. How can you make a quick static-balance check of a wheel on the motorcycle?
8. What is lateral runout?
9. What is radial runout?
10. Can a bent rim be straightened or repaired?
11. Define *spoking wheels.*
12. Why are there different arrangements used for spoking patterns?
13. Explain how to spoke a wheel.
14. What can be done with a wheel that has a few broken spokes but no other rim or hub damage?
15. How are spokes adjusted?
16. What prevents tubeless tires from being used on most spoked rims?
17. What is the purpose of knobs on some motorcycle tires?
18. Explain how a tire-bead clamp prevents tire slippage.
19. Describe how to inspect a tire for damage.
20. How can an inner tube be patched?

GLOSSARY

AC (or ac)   Abbreviation for *alternating current*.

Accelerator pump   In the carburetor, a pump which is linked to the throttle and which momentarily enriches the air-fuel mixture when the throttle is opened at low speed.

Additive   A substance added to gasoline or oil to improve some property of the gasoline or oil.

Adjust   To bring the parts of a component or system to a specified relationship, dimension, or pressure.

Adjustments   Necessary or desired changes in clearances, fit, or settings.

Advance   The moving ahead of the timing of the ignition spark in relation to piston position; produced either electronically or by centrifugal or vacuum devices in accordance with engine speed and the intake-manifold vacuum.

Air bleed   An opening into a fuel passage through which air can pass, or bleed, into the fuel as it moves through the passage.

Air cleaner   A device, mounted on or connected to the carburetor, for filtering dirt and dust out of the air being drawn into the engine.

Air-cooled engine   An engine that is cooled by the passage of air around the cylinders, not by the passage of a liquid through water jackets.

Air filter   A filter that removes dirt and dust particles from air passing through it.

Air-fuel mixture   The air and fuel traveling to the combustion chamber after being mixed by the carburetor.

Air-fuel ratio   The proportion of air to fuel (by weight) in the mixture supplied for combustion.

Air gap   A small space between parts that are related magnetically, as in an alternator, or electrically, as the electrodes of a spark plug.

Air pollution   Contamination of the air by natural or manufactured pollutants.

Air pressure   Atmospheric pressure; also, the pressure produced by an air pump or by the compression of air in a cylinder.

Alignment   The act of lining up, or the state of being in a true line.

Alternating current   Electric current that first flows in one direction and then alternates and flows in the opposite direction.

Alternator   The device in the motorcycle electric system that converts mechanical energy into electric energy for charging the battery and operating electric accessories. Also known as an *ac generator*.

Aluminum cylinder block   An engine cylinder block cast from aluminum alloy and usually provided with cast-iron sleeves for use as cylinder bores.

Ammeter   A meter for measuring the amount of current (in amperes) flowing through an electric circuit.

Amperage   The amount of current, in amperes.

Ampere   A unit of measure for current. One ampere equals a flow of 6.28×10^{18} electrons per second.

Antifreeze   A chemical, usually ethylene glycol, that is added to the engine coolant to raise its boiling temperature and lower its freezing temperature.

Antifriction bearing   A name given to almost any type of ball, roller, or tapered roller bearing.

Antiknock compound   An additive put into gasoline to suppress spark knock, or detonation.

Antilock system   A system installed with the brakes to prevent wheel lockup during braking.

Arcing   The spark that jumps an air gap between two electric conductors; for example, the arcing of the ignition breaker points.

Armature   A part moved by magnetism, or a part moved through a magnetic field to produce current.

ATDC   Abbreviation for *after top dead center*; any position of the piston between TDC and BDC on the downward stroke.

Atmospheric pressure   The weight of the atmosphere per unit area. Atmospheric pressure at sea level is 14.7 psi absolute [101.35 kPa]; it decreases as altitude increases.

Automatic choke   A device that positions the choke valve automatically in accordance with engine temperature or time.

Automatic transmission   A transmission in which gear ratios are changed automatically, eliminating the necessity of shifting gears by hand or foot.

Axle   A crossbar supporting the front or rear wheel of a motorcycle.

Axle ratio   The ratio between the rotational speed (rpm) of the drive shaft and that of the driven wheel; gear reduction in the final drive, determined by dividing the number of teeth on the ring gear by the number of teeth on the pinion gear.

Backfiring   Preexplosion of the air-fuel mixture so that the flame passes back around the opened intake valve and through the intake manifold and carburetor; also, the loud explosion of overly rich exhaust gas in the exhaust system.

Backlash   In gearing, the clearance between the meshing teeth of two gears.

Back pressure   Pressure in the exhaust system. The higher the back pressure, the lower the volumetric efficiency.

Ball bearing   An antifriction bearing with an inner race and an outer race, and one or more rows of balls between them.

Ball joint   A flexible joint consisting of a ball within a socket, used in valve-train rocker arms.

Band   In an automatic transmission, a hydraulically controlled brake band installed around a metal clutch drum; used to stop or permit drum rotation.

Barrel   A term sometimes applied to the cylinder of an engine.

Battery   An electrochemical device for storing energy in chemical form so that it can be released as electricity; a group of electric cells connected together.

Battery acid   The electrolyte used in a battery; a mixture of sulfuric acid and water.

BDC   Abbreviation for *bottom dead center*.

Bead   That part of the tire which is shaped to fit the rim; the bead is made of steel wires, wrapped and reinforced by the plies of the tire.

Bearing   The part which transmits the load to the support and, in so doing, takes the friction caused by moving parts in contact.

Bearing caps   In the engine, caps held in place by bolts or nuts which, in turn, hold bearing halves in place.

Bearing crush   The additional height over a full half which is purposely manufactured into each bearing half. This ensures complete contact of the bearing back with the housing bore when the engine is assembled.

Bearing spin A type of bearing failure in which a lack of lubrication causes the bearing to overheat until it seizes on the shaft, shearing the locking lip and causing the bearing to rotate in the housing or block.

Bearing spread A purposely manufactured small extra distance across the parting faces of the bearing half, in excess of the actual diameter of the housing bore.

Bell-shaped wear Deterioration of an opening (such as a valve guide or brake drum) in which one end is worn most, causing the opening to flare out like a bell.

Belt In a tire, a flat strip of material, such as fiberglass, rayon, or woven steel, which underlies the tread around the circumference of the tire.

Bevel gear A gear shaped like the lower part of a cone; used to transmit motion through an angle.

bhp See *Brake horsepower*.

Bias-ply tire A tire in which the plies are laid diagonally, crisscrossing one another at an angle of about 30 to 40°.

Big end The crankpin end of the connecting rod.

Bleeding A process by which air is removed from a brake hydraulic system by draining part of the fluid or operating the system to work out the air.

Block See *Cylinder block*.

Blowby Leakage of compressed air-fuel mixture and some burned gases past the piston rings into the crankcase during the compression and combustion strokes.

Bore The diameter of an engine cylinder; the diameter of any hole. Also used to describe the process of enlarging or accurately refinishing a hole, as "to bore an engine cylinder."

Boring bar An electric-motor-powered cutting tool used to machine, or bore, an engine cylinder, thereby removing metal and enlarging the cylinder bore, or diameter.

Bottom dead center (BDC) The piston position when the piston has moved to the bottom of the cylinder and the cylinder volume is at its maximum.

Brake An energy-conversion device used to slow, stop, or hold a vehicle or mechanism; a device which changes the kinetic energy of motion into useless and wasted heat energy.

Brake drum A metal drum mounted on a motorcycle wheel to form the outer shell of the brake; the brake shoes press against the drum to slow or stop drum-and-wheel rotation for braking.

Brake fluid A special oil used in the hydraulic braking system to transmit pressure through a closed system of tubing known as the brake lines.

Brake horsepower (bhp) The power delivered by the engine available for doing work; bhp = torque × rpm/5252.

Brake lining A high-friction material, often a type of asbestos, attached to the brake shoe by rivets or a bonding process. The lining takes the wear when the shoe is pressed against the brake drum or rotor.

Brake shoe In drum brakes, arc-shaped metal pieces lined with a high-friction material (the brake lining) which are forced against the revolving drums to produce braking action. In disk brakes, flat metal pieces lined with brake lining which are forced against the rotor face.

Brake system A combination of one or more brakes and their operating and control mechanisms.

Breather The opening used on engines without emission-control devices that allows air to circulate through the crankcase to provide ventilation.

Brush A block of conducting substance such as carbon which rests against a rotating ring or commutator to form a continuous electric circuit.

BTDC Abbreviation for *before top dead center*; any position of the piston between BDC and TDC on the upward stroke.

Bushing A one-piece sleeve placed in a bore to serve as a bearing surface.

Cables Stranded conductors, usually covered with insulating material, used for connections between electric devices.

Calibrate To check or correct the initial setting of a test instrument.

Caliper A tool that can be set to measure the thickness of a block, the diameter of a shaft, or the bore of a hole (inside caliper). In a disk brake, a housing for pistons and brake shoes, connected to the hydraulic system; holds the brake shoes so that they straddle the disk.

Cam A rotating lobe, or eccentric, which can be used with a cam follower to change rotary motion to reciprocating motion.

Cam follower See *Valve lifter*.

Camshaft The shaft in the engine which has a series of cams for operating the valve mechanisms. It is driven from the crankshaft by gears, by sprockets and a chain, or by sprockets and a toothed belt.

Canister In an evaporative control system, a special container that contains charcoal to trap vapors from the fuel system.

Capacitor See *Condenser*.

Capacitor-discharge ignition An ignition system in which the primary energy is stored in a large capacitor that discharges as the points close or as a transistor operates to complete the primary circuit.

Capacity The ability to perform or to hold.

Carbon A black deposit left on engine parts by the combustion of fuel. Carbon forms in ports and on pistons, rings, valves, and other parts, inhibiting their action.

Carbon dioxide (CO_2) A colorless, odorless gas which is formed when gasoline is burned completely.

Carbon monoxide (CO) A colorless, odorless, tasteless, poisonous gas which is formed when gasoline is burned incompletely.

Carburetor The mixing device in the fuel system which meters gasoline into the air stream (vaporizing the gasoline as it does so) in varying proportions to suit the engine operating conditions.

Casing The outer part of the tire assembly, made of fabric or cord to which rubber is vulcanized.

Caster Tilting of the steering axis forward or backward to provide directional steering stability.

Catalyst A substance that can speed or slow a chemical reaction between substances, without itself being consumed by the reaction. In the catalytic converter, platinum and palladium usually are the active catalysts.

Catalytic converter A mufflerlike device for use in an exhaust system. It converts harmful exhaust gases into harmless gases by promoting a chemical reaction between a catalyst and the pollutants.

CDI See *Capacitor-discharge ignition*.

Celsius In the metric system, a temperature scale on which water boils at 100° and freezes at 0°; a reading on the Celsius scale is equal to a reading on a Fahrenheit thermometer of $5/9$ (°F − 32). Also called *centigrade*.

Centigrade See *Celsius*.

Centimeter (cm) A unit of linear measure in the metric system equal to approximately 0.390 inch.

Centrifugal advance A rotating-weight mechanism that advances and retards ignition timing through the centrifugal force resulting from changes in the rotational speed of a shaft.

Charcoal canister A container filled with activated charcoal; used to trap gasoline vapor from the fuel tank and carburetor while the engine is off.

Charging rate The amperage flowing from the alternator into the battery.

Chassis The assembly of mechanisms that make up the major operating part of the motorcycle; assumed to include everything except the engine and the electric system.

Check To verify that a component, system, or measurement complies with specifications.

Check valve A valve that opens to permit the passage of air or fluid in one direction only; also, a valve that operates to prevent (check) some undesirable action.

Chemical reaction The formation of one or more new substances when two or more substances are brought together.

Choke In the carburetor, a device used when starting a cold engine that chokes off the air flow for greater fuel delivery and a richer mixture.

Chopper A customized motorcycle in which the front wheel has been "chopped" off and reattached extended forward.

Chrome-plated ring A piston ring that has its cylinder-wall face lightly plated with hard chrome.

CID Abbreviation for *cubic inch displacement*.

Circuit The complete path of an electric current, including the current source. When the path is continuous, the circuit is closed and current flows. When the path is broken, the circuit is open and no current flows. Also used to refer to fluid paths, as in hydraulic systems.

Circuit breaker A protective device that opens an electric circuit to prevent damage when the circuit is overheated by excess current flow. One type contains a thermostatic blade that warps to open the circuit when the maximum safe current is exceeded.

Clearance The space between two moving parts or between a moving and a stationary part, such as a journal and a bearing. Bearing clearance is considered to be filled with lubricating oil when the mechanism is running.

Closed-crankcase ventilation system A system in which the crankcase vapors (blowby gases) are discharged into the engine intake system and pass through to the engine cylinders instead of being discharged into the air.

Clutch In the motorcycle, the mechanism in the power train that connects the engine crankshaft to, or disconnects it from, the transmission.

Clutch disk See *Friction disk*.

Clutch lever A lever, usually on the left handlebar, that operates the clutch.

CO The chemical formula for carbon monoxide.

CO₂ The chemical formula for carbon dioxide.

Coated ring A piston ring having its cylinder-wall face coated with ferrous oxide, soft phosphate, or tin. This thin coating helps new rings seat by retaining oil and reducing scuffing during break-in.

Coil In the ignition system, a transformer used to step up the primary voltage (by induction) to the high voltage required to fire the spark plugs.

Coil spring A spring made of an elastic metal such as steel, formed into a wire and wound into a coil.

Cold patching A method of repairing a punctured tire or tube by glueing a thin rubber patch over the hole.

Combustion (burning) In the engine, the rapid burning of the air-fuel mixture in the cylinder.

Combustion chamber The space at the top of the cylinder and in the cylinder head in which combustion of the air-fuel mixture takes place.

Commutator A series of copper bars at one end of a generator or starting-motor armature, electrically insulated from the armature shaft and insulated from one another by mica. The brushes rub against the bars of the commutator, which form a rotating connector between the armature windings and the brushes.

Compression Reduction in the volume of a gas by squeezing it into a smaller space. Increasing the pressure reduces the volume and increases the density and temperature of the gas.

Compression ignition The ignition of fuel solely by the heat generated when air is compressed in the cylinder; the method of ignition in a diesel engine.

Compression pressure The pressure in the combustion chamber at the end of the compression stroke.

Compression ratio The volume of the cylinder and combustion chamber when the piston is at BDC divided by the volume when the piston is at TDC.

Compression ring The upper ring or rings on a piston, designed to hold the compression pressure in the combustion chamber and prevent blowby.

Compression stroke The piston stroke from BDC to TDC during which both valves are closed and the air-fuel mixture is compressed.

Compression tester A gauge for measuring the pressure, or compression, developed in an engine cylinder during cranking.

Condensation A change of state during which a gas turns to liquid, usually because of temperature or pressure changes. Also, moisture from the air deposited on a cool surface.

Condenser Also called a *capacitor*. In the breaker-point ignition system, it is connected across the points to reduce arcing by providing a storage place for electricity (electrons) as the points open.

Conductor Any material or substance that allows current or heat to flow easily.

Connecting rod In the engine, the rod that connects the crank on the crankshaft with the piston.

Connecting-rod bearing See *Rod bearing*.

Connecting-rod cap The part of the connecting-rod assembly that attaches the rod to the crankpin.

Constant-velocity joint Two closely coupled universal joints arranged in such a way that their acceleration-deceleration effects cancel out. This results in an output-shaft speed that is identical with the input-shaft speed, regardless of the angle of drive.

Contact points In the breaker-point ignition system, the stationary and the movable points which open and close the ignition primary circuit.

Coolant The liquid mixture of antifreeze and water used in the liquid-cooling system.

Cooling system In the engine, the system that removes heat by the circulation of liquid coolant or of air to prevent engine overheating.

Corrosion A chemical action, usually by an acid, that eats away, or decomposes, a metal.

Countershaft The shaft in the transmission which is driven by the clutch; gears on the countershaft drive gears on the main shaft when the latter are shifted into gear.

Crank An offset section of a rotating shaft used with a connecting rod to convert reciprocating motion of the piston into rotary motion of the crankshaft.

Crankshaft The lower part of the engine in which the crankshaft rotates; it splits in half to allow removal of the crankshaft.

Crankcase dilution Dilution of the lubricating oil in a four-cycle engine by liquid fuel seeping down the cylinder walls.

Crankcase emissions Pollutants emitted into the atmosphere from the engine crankcase.

Crankcase ventilating system The system that permits air to flow through the engine crankcase when the engine is running to carry out the blowby gases and relieve any pressure buildup.

Cranking motor See *Starting motor*.

Crankpin That part of the crankshaft to which the connecting rod is attached.

Crankpin ridging A type of crankpin failure typified by deep ridges worn into the crankpin bearing surfaces.

Crankshaft The main rotating member, or shaft, of the engine with cranks to which the connecting rods are attached; may be a one-piece or a built-up type.

Crankshaft gear A gear or sprocket mounted on the crankshaft to drive the camshaft through a gear, chain, or toothed belt.

Crank throw One crankpin with its two webs.

Cross-firing In a multicylinder engine, the jumping of a high-voltage surge in the ignition secondary circuit to the wrong high-voltage lead so that the wrong spark plug fires. Usually caused by improper routing of the spark-plug wires, by faulty insulation, or by a defective distributor cap or rotor.

Cubic centimeter (cc) A unit in the metric system used to measure volume; equal to approximately 0.061 cubic inch.

Cubic inch displacement The cylinder volume swept out by the piston of an engine as it moves from BDC to TDC, measured in cubic inches.

Current A flow of electrons, measured in amperes.

Cycle Any series of events which continuously repeats. In the engine, the two or four piston strokes that complete the working process and produce power.

Cylinder A circular, tubelike opening in an engine cylinder casting in which a piston moves up and down.

Cylinder block The basic framework of the multicylinder engine, in and on which the other engine parts are attached. It includes the engine cylinders and the upper part of the crankcase.

Cylinder-compression tester See *Compression tester*.

Cylinder head The part that encloses the cylinder bores. It contains the valves on overhead-valve engines.

Cylinder hone An expandable rotating tool with abrasive stones turned by a small motor, used to clean and smooth the inside surface of a cylinder.

Cylinder liner See *Cylinder sleeve*.

Cylinder sleeve A replaceable cast-iron sleeve, or liner, inset into the aluminum cylinder casting to form the cylinder bore.

DC (or dc) Abbreviation for *direct current*.

Decleration A decrease in velocity or speed; also, allowing the motorcycle or engine to coast to idle speed from a higher speed with the throttle at or near the idle position.

Degree Part of a circle. One degree is $1/360$ of a complete circle.

Detent A small depression in shaft, rail, or rod into which a pawl or ball drops when the shaft, rail, or rod is moved; this provides a locking effect.

Detergent A chemical added to engine oil that helps keep internal parts of the engine clean by preventing the accumulation of deposits.

Detonation In the engine, an uncontrolled second explosion after the spark occurs, with excessively rapid burning of the compressed air-fuel mixture, resulting in spark knock or a pinging noise.

Device A mechanism, tool, or other piece of equipment designed to serve a special purpose or perform a special function.

Diagnosis A procedure followed in locating the cause of a malfunction; the procedure answers the question "What is wrong?"

Diaphragm A thin dividing sheet or partition which separates an area into compartments; used in fuel pumps, modulator valves, vacuum-advance units, and other control devices.

Dial indicator A gauge that has a dial face and a needle to register movement; used to measure variations in size, movements too little to be measured conveniently by other means, and so on.

Dieseling A condition in which an engine continues to run after the ignition is shut off.

Dimmer switch A two-position switch usually located on the left handlebar, operated by the rider to select the high or low headlight beam.

Diode A solid-state electronic device which allows the passage of an electric current in one direction only. Used in the alternator to convert alternating current to direct current for charging the battery.

Dipstick The oil-level indicator stick in the engine or transmission.

Direct current Electric current that flows in one direction only.

Directional signal A device on the motorcycle that flashes lights to indicate the direction in which the rider intends to turn.

Dirt bike A motorcycle designed for a particular type of off-road use.

Disassemble To take apart.

Disk In a disk brake, the rotor, or revolving piece of metal, against which shoes are pressed to provide braking action.

Disk brake A brake in which brake shoes on a viselike caliper grip a revolving disk to stop it.

Dispersant A chemical added to oil to prevent dirt and impurities from clinging together in lumps that could clog the engine lubricating system.

Displacement In an engine, the total volume of the air-fuel mixture an engine is theoretically capable of drawing into all cylinders during one operating cycle. The space swept through by the piston in moving from one end of a stroke to the other.

Distributor Any device that distributes. In the ignition system, the rotary switch that directs high-voltage surges to the engine cylinders in the proper sequence. See *Ignition distributor*.

Distributor advance See *Centrifugal advance; Ignition advance; Vacuum advance*.

Distributor cam The cam on the top end of a shaft which rotates to open and close the contact points.

Distributor timing See *Ignition timing*.

DOHC See *Double-overhead-camshaft engine*.

Double-overhead-camshaft engine An engine with double, or two, camshafts over each cylinder.

Driven disk A friction disk in a clutch.

Drive pinion A small gear on a rotating shaft that transmits torque to a larger gear.

Drive shaft An assembly of one or two universal joints and slip joints connected to a metal shaft; used to transmit power from the transmission to the final drive in a motorcycle with shaft drive. Also called the *propeller shaft*.

Drop-center wheel A wheel which has a well, or drop, in the center for one tire bead to fit into while the other bead is being lifted over the rim flange.

Drum brake A brake in which curved brake shoes press

against the inner circumference of a metal drum to produce braking action.

Dry friction The friction between two dry solids.

Dwell The number of degrees the ignition cam rotates while the breaker points are closed.

Dwell meter A precision electric instrument used to measure the cam angle, or dwell, or number of degrees the breaker points are closed while the engine is running.

Dynamic balance The balance of an object when it is in motion (for example, the dynamic balance of a rotating wheel).

Dynamometer A device for measuring the power output, or brake horsepower, of an engine; may be an engine dynamometer, which measures power output at the flywheel, or a chassis dynamometer, which measures the power output at the rear wheel or final drive.

Eccentric A disk or offset section (of a shaft, for example) used to convert rotary to reciprocating motion. Sometimes called a *cam*.

ECU See *Electronic control unit*.

Efficiency The ratio between the effect produced and the power expended to produce the effect; the ratio between the actual and the theoretical.

Electric current A movement of electrons through a conductor such as a copper wire; measured in amperes.

Electric system The system that electrically cranks the engine for starting, furnishes high-voltage sparks to the engine cylinders to fire the compressed air-fuel charges, lights the lights, and operates the other electric equipment. It consists, in part, of the starting motor, wiring, battery, alternator, regulator, and ignition system.

Electrode In a spark plug, the spark jumps between two electrodes. The wire passing through the insulator is the center electrode. The small piece of metal welded to the spark-plug shell (and to which the spark jumps) is the side, or ground, electrode.

Electrolyte A mixture of sulfuric acid and water used in lead-acid storage batteries. The acid enters into chemical reaction with active material in the plates to produce voltage and current.

Electromagnetic induction The characteristic of a magnetic field that causes an electric current to be created in a conductor if it passes through the field or if the field builds and collapses around the conductor.

Electron A negatively charged particle that circles the nucleus of an atom. The movement of electrons is an electric current.

Electronic control unit A solid-state device that receives information from sensors and is programmed to operate various circuits and systems based on that information.

Electronic fuel-injection system A system that injects gasoline into a spark-ignition engine and includes an electronic control unit to time and meter the fuel flow.

Electronic ignition system An ignition system using transistors which does not have mechanical contact points. Also called *solid-state ignition*.

Electronics Electric assemblies, circuits, and systems that use electron devices such as transistors and diodes.

Element A substance that cannot be further divided into simpler substances. In a battery, the group of unlike positive and negative plates, separated by insulators that make up each cell.

Emission control Any device or modification added onto or designed into a motor vehicle for the purpose of reducing air-polluting emissions.

Emission standards Allowable emission levels, set by local, state, and federal legislation.

End play The distance that a shaft can be moved forward and back.

Enduro A type of motorcycle that has the required equipment for street riding and adequate suspension and tires for off-road use.

Energy The capacity or ability to do work. Usually measured in work units of pound-feet (kilogram-meters) but also expressed in heat-energy units such as Btu (joules).

Engine A machine that converts heat energy into mechanical energy. The assembly that burns fuel to produce mechanical power; sometimes referred to as a *power plant*.

Engine tune-up The procedure of checking and adjusting various engine components so that the engine is restored to top operating condition.

Ethyl See *Tetraethyl lead*.

Ethylene glycol Chemical name of a widely used type of antifreeze for liquid-cooling systems.

Evaporation The transformation of a liquid to the gaseous state.

Evaporative emission-control system A system which prevents the escape of fuel vapors from the fuel tank or carburetor to the atmosphere while the engine is off. The vapors are stored in a canister or in the crankcase until the engine is started.

Exhaust emissions Pollutants emitted into the atmosphere through any opening downstream of the exhaust port of an engine.

Exhaust gas The burned and unburned gases that remain (from the air-fuel mixture) after combustion.

Exhaust-gas analyzer A device for sampling the exhaust gas from an engine to determine the amounts of pollutants in the exhaust gas. Most analyzers used in the shop check HC and CO, while analyzers used in testing laboratories can also check NO_x.

Exhaust pipe The pipe connecting the exhaust port with the muffler.

Exhaust stroke The piston stroke from BDC to TDC during which the exhaust valve is open so that the burned gases are forced from the cylinder.

Exhaust system The system through which exhaust gases leave the engine. Consists of the exhaust port, exhaust pipe, muffler, and tail pipe.

Exhaust valve The valve which opens to allow the burned gases to exhaust from the engine cylinder during the exhaust stroke.

Expansion plug A plug that is slightly dished out and used to seal core passages in the cylinder block and cylinder head of a liquid-cooled engine. The plug flattens and expands when driven into place to fit tightly.

Expansion tank A tank at the top of an engine radiator which provides room for heated coolant to expand and give off any air that may be trapped in the coolant. Also used in some fuel tanks to prevent fuel from spilling from the tank because of expansion.

Fan The bladed device on the front of the engine that rotates to draw cooling air through the radiator or around the engine cylinders.

Fatigue failure A type of metal failure resulting from repeated stress which finally alters the character of the metal so that it cracks. In engine bearings, frequently caused by excessive idling or slow engine idle speed.

Field coil A coil, or winding, in a generator or starting motor which produces a magnetic field as current passes through it.

Field relay A relay that is part of some alternator charging systems; connects the alternator field to the battery when the engine runs and disconnects it when the engine stops.

Filter That part in the lubricating or fuel system through which fuel, air, or oil must pass so that dust, dirt, and other contaminants are removed.

Fins Thin metal projections on an air-cooled engine cylinder and head which greatly enlarge the total heat-transferring surface and help provide cooling of the engine cylinder. In a radiator, the thin metal projections over which cooling air flows to carry heat away from the hot coolant tubes.

Firing order The order in which the engine cylinders fire or deliver their power strokes, beginning with the number 1 cylinder.

Flasher An automatic-reset circuit breaker used in the directional-signal circuit.

Flat rate Method of paying mechanics and technicians by use of a manual which indicates the time normally required to do each service job.

Float bowl In some carburetors, the reservoir from which fuel feeds into the passing air.

Float level The float position at which the needle valve closes the fuel inlet to the carburetor, to prevent further delivery of fuel.

Float system In the carburetor, the system that controls the entry of fuel and the fuel level in the float bowl.

Flooded Term used to indicate that the engine cylinders received "raw," or liquid, gasoline or an air-fuel mixture too rich to burn.

Fluid Any liquid or gas.

Fluid coupling A device in the power train consisting of two rotating members; transmits power from the engine, through a fluid, to the transmission gears.

Flywheels Rotating metal wheels attached to the crankpin which help even out the power surges from the power strokes and engine cranking system.

Force Any push or pull exerted on an object.

Four-cycle See *Four-stroke cycle*.

Four-speed A manual transmission having four forward gears.

Four-stroke cycle The four piston strokes of intake, compression, power, and exhaust which make up the complete cycle of events in the four-stroke-cycle engine. Also called *four-cycle* and *four-stroke*.

Frame The assembly of metal structural tubes that supports the engine and rider and provides attachment points for the rear wheel and steering.

Friction The resistance to motion between two bodies in contact with each other.

Friction bearing Bearing in which there is sliding contact between the moving surfaces. Sleeve bearings, such as those used in some connecting rods, are friction bearings.

Friction disk In the clutch, a flat disk faced on both sides with friction material and splined to the clutch shaft. It is positioned between the clutch pressure plate and the engine crankshaft. Also called the *clutch disk* or *driven disk*.

Friction horsepower (fhp) The power used up by an engine in overcoming its own internal friction; usually it increases as engine speed increases.

Front fork Attached to the steering head of the frame, the front fork connects the frame with the front wheel, which is steered by turning the handlebars. The front fork may be rigid or telescopic, with spring movement and damping action built into each tube.

Fuel The substance that is burned to produce heat and create motion in an engine.

Fuel filter A device located in the fuel line ahead of the carburetor; removes dirt and other contaminants from fuel passing through.

Fuel gauge A gauge that indicates the amount of fuel in the fuel tank.

Fuel injection A fuel-delivery system replacing the carburetor, which sprays fuel under pressure into the intake air before it enters the cylinder.

Fuel line The pipe or tube through which fuel flows from the fuel tank to the carburetor.

Fuel nozzle The tube in the carburetor through which fuel feeds into the passing air. In a fuel-injection system, the tube that delivers the fuel into the air.

Fuel pump A device in the fuel system which forces fuel from the fuel tank to the carburetor.

Fuel system In the engine, the system that delivers to the engine cylinders the combustible mixture of vaporized fuel and air. It consists of fuel tank, lines, gauge, carburetor, fuel pump, and intake ports or manifold.

Fuel tank The storage tank for fuel on the motorcycle.

Fuel-vapor recovery system See *Vapor-recovery system*.

Full throttle Wide-open throttle position, with the throttle grip turned all the way open.

Fuse A device designed to open an electric circuit when the current is excessive to protect equipment in the circuit. An open, or "blown," fuse must be replaced after the circuit problem is corrected.

Fuse block A boxlike unit that holds the fuses for the various electric circuits in the motorcycle.

Fusible link A type of fuse in which a special wire melts to open the circuit when the current is excessive. An open, or "blown," fusible link must be replaced after the circuit problem is corrected.

Gap The air space between two electrodes, as the spark-plug gap or the contact-point gap.

Gas A state of matter, neither solid nor liquid, which has neither definite shape nor definite volume. Air is a mixture of several gases. In the engine, the discharge from the muffler is called the *exhaust gas*. Also, *gas* is a slang term used to refer to the liquid fuel gasoline.

Gasket A flat strip, usually of cork or metal or both, placed between two machined surfaces to provide a tight seal between them.

Gasket cement A liquid adhesive material, or sealer, used to install gaskets; in some applications, a bead of sealer is used as the gasket.

Gasoline A liquid blend of hydrocarbons, obtained from crude oil; used as the fuel in most automotive engines.

Gassing Hydrogen gas escaping from a battery; the gas is formed during battery charging.

Gear lubricant A type of grease or oil designed especially to lubricate gears.

Gear ratio The number of revolutions of a driving gear required to turn a driven gear through one complete revolution. For a pair of gears, the ratio is found by dividing the number of teeth on the driven gear by the number of teeth on the driving gear.

Gears Mechanical devices that transmit power or turning effort from one shaft to another; gears contain teeth that interlace, or mesh, as the gears turn.

Gearshift The mechanism by which the gears in the transmission are engaged.

Gear-type pump A pump using a pair of matching gears that rotate; meshing of the gears forces oil (or other liquid) between the teeth and through the pump outlet.

Generator A device that converts mechanical energy into electric energy; it can produce either alternating current or direct current. In general usage, the term applies to a dc generator.

Glaze A very smooth, mirrorlike finish that develops on engine-cylinder walls.

Glaze breaker An abrasive tool rotated by a motor, used to remove the glaze from engine-cylinder walls.

Grease Lubricating oil to which thickening agents have been added.

Grommet A device, usually made of hard rubber or a similar material, used to encircle or support a component.

Ground Connection of an electric unit to the engine or frame to return the current to its source.

Ground-return system Common system of electric wiring in which the chassis and frame are used as part of the electric return circuit to the battery or alternator; also known as the *single-wire system*.

HC Abbreviation for *hydrocarbon*.

Head See *Cylinder head*.

Headlight The light at the front of a motorcycle designed to illuminate the road ahead.

Heat A form of energy released by the burning of fuel.

Heat of compression An increase in temperature brought about by the compression of air or an air-fuel mixture.

Helical gear A gear in which the teeth are cut at an angle to the center line of the gear.

Heli-coil A thread insert used to repair worn or damaged threads. It is installed in a retapped hole to bring the screw thread back to original size.

Hemispheric combustion chamber A combustion chamber resembling a hemisphere, or a round ball cut in half.

High-speed system In the carburetor, the system that supplies fuel to the engine at speeds above about 25 mph [40 km/h]. Also called the *main-metering system*.

High-voltage cables The secondary (or spark-plug) cables, or wires, that carry high voltage from the ignition coil to the spark plugs.

Hone A tool with abrasive stones that is rotated in a bore or bushing to remove metal.

Horn An electric noise-making device on a vehicle, used for signaling.

Horn relay A relay connected between the battery and the horn. When the horn button is pressed, the relay is energized and connects the horn to the battery.

Horsepower A measure of mechanical power, or the rate at which work is done. One horsepower equals 33,000 ft-lb (foot-pounds) of work per minute; it is the power necessary to raise 33,000 pounds a distance of 1 foot in 1 minute.

Hot patching A method of repairing a tire or tube by using heat to vulcanize a patch onto the damaged surface.

Hub The center part of a wheel.

Hydraulic brakes A braking system that uses hydraulic pressure to force the brake shoes against the brake drums, or rotors, as the brake pedal is depressed.

Hydraulic pressure Pressure exerted through the medium of a liquid.

Hydraulics The use of a liquid under pressure to transfer force or motion or to increase an applied force.

Hydraulic valve lifter A valve lifter that by means of oil pressure maintains zero valve clearance so that valve noise is reduced.

Hydrocarbon (HC) A compound made of the elements hydrogen and carbon. Gasoline is a blend of hydrocarbons refined from crude oil.

Hydrometer A test instrument used to measure the specific gravity of a liquid. Consists of a float inside a tube, used to measure the specific gravity of battery electrolyte and the freeze protection of the coolant in the liquid-cooling system.

IC See *Internal combustion engine*.

Idle Engine speed when the throttle grip is fully released and there is no load on the engine.

Idle mixture The air-fuel mixture supplied to the engine during idling.

Idle-mixture screw The adjustment screw (on some carburetors) that can be turned in or out to lean out or enrich the idle mixture.

Idle speed The speed (in rpm) at which the engine runs without load when the throttle is closed.

Idle system In the carburetor, the passages through which fuel is fed when the engine is idling.

Ignition In an engine, the act of the spark in starting the combustion process in the engine cylinder.

Ignition advance The moving forward, in time, of the ignition spark relative to the piston position. TDC or 1° ATDC is considered advanced as compared with 2° ATDC.

Ignition coil That part of the ignition system which acts as a transformer to step up the battery voltage to several thousand volts; the high-voltage surge then produces a spark across the spark-plug gap.

Ignition distributor That part of the ignition system which closes and opens the circuit to the ignition coil with correct timing and distributes to the proper spark plugs the resulting high-voltage surges from the ignition coil.

Ignition resistor A resistance connected into the ignition primary circuit to reduce the battery voltage to the coil during engine operation.

Ignition retard The moving back in time of the ignition spark relative to the piston position. TDC or 1° BTDC is considered retarded as compared with 2° BTDC.

Ignition switch The switch in the ignition system which is operated with a key to open and close the ignition primary circuit.

Ignition system The electric system that furnishes high-voltage sparks to the engine cylinders to fire the compressed air-fuel mixture.

Ignition timing The delivery of the spark from the coil to the spark plug at the proper time for the power stroke, relative to the piston position.

ihp See *Indicated horsepower*.

Impeller A rotating finned disk; used in centrifugal pumps, such as water pumps, and in torque converters.

Indicated horsepower (ihp) The power produced within the engine cylinders before deducting any frictional loss.

Indicator A device using a light or a dial and pointer to make some condition known; for example, the temperature indicator or the oil-pressure indicator.

Induction The action of producing a voltage in a conductor or coil by moving the conductor or coil through a magnetic field or by moving the field past the conductor or coil.

Inertia The property of an object that causes it to resist any change in its speed or in the direction of its travel.

Infrared analyzer A test instrument used to measure very small quantities of pollutants in exhaust gas. See *Exhaust-gas analyzer*.

In-line engine An engine in which all the cylinders are located in a single row, or line.

Inspect To examine a component or system for surface condition or function.

Install To set up for use on a motorcycle any part, accessory, option, or kit.

Insulation Material that stops the travel of electricity (electric insulation) or heat (heat insulation).

Insulator A poor conductor of electricity or heat.

Intake manifold A series of passages from the carburetor to the engine cylinders through which the air-fuel mixture can flow.

Intake stroke The piston stroke from TDC to BDC during which the intake valve is open and the cylinder receives a charge of air-fuel mixture.

Intake valve   The valve that opens to permit the air-fuel mixture to enter the cylinder on the intake stroke.

Integral   Built into as part of the whole.

Internal combustion (IC) engine   An engine in which the fuel is burned inside the engine itself, rather than in a separate device (as in a steam engine).

Internal gear   A gear with teeth pointing inward, toward the hollow center of the gear.

Jet   A calibrated passage in the carburetor through which fuel flows.

Journal   The part of a rotating shaft which turns in a bearing.

Key   A wedgelike metal piece, usually rectangular or semicircular, inserted in grooves to transmit torque while holding two parts in relative position; the small strip of metal with coded peaks and grooves used to operate a lock, as in an ignition.

Kilogram (kg)   In the metric system, a unit of weight and mass; approximately equal to 2.2 pounds.

Kilometer (km)   In the metric system, a unit of linear measure equal to 0.621 mile.

Kilowatt (kW)   A unit of power, equal to about 1.34 hp.

Kinetic energy   The energy of motion; the energy stored in a moving body through its momentum; for example, the kinetic energy stored in a rotating flywheel.

Knock   The heavy metallic sound created in an engine, varying with engine speed and usually caused by a loose or worn bearing.

kW   See *Kilowatt*.

Laminated   Made up of several thin sheets or layers.

Lapping   A method of seating engine valves by which the valve is turned back and forth on the seat.

Lash   The amount of free motion in a gear train, between gears, or in a mechanical assembly, such as the lash in a valve train.

Lead   A cable or conductor that carries electric current (pronounced "leed"). A heavy metal; used in lead-acid storage batteries (pronounced "led").

Leaded gasoline   Gasoline to which small amounts of tetraethyl lead are added to improve engine performance and to reduce detonation.

Lean mixture   An air-fuel mixture that has a relatively high proportion of air and a relatively low proportion of fuel. An air-fuel ratio of 16:1 is a lean mixture, compared with an air-fuel ratio of 13:1.

Lifter   See *Valve lifter*.

Light   A gas-filled bulb enclosing a wire that glows brightly when an electric current passes through it; a lamp. Also, any visible radiant energy.

Linear measurement   A measurement taken in a straight line; for example, the measurement of crankshaft end play.

Line boring   Using a special boring machine, centered on the original center of the cylinder-block main-bearing bores, to rebore the crankcase into alignment.

Lines of force   See *Magnetic lines of force*.

Lining   See *Brake lining*.

Linkage   An assembly of rods, or links, used to transmit motion.

Liquid-cooled engine   An engine that is cooled by the circulation of liquid coolant around the cylinders.

Liter (L)   In the metric system, a measure of volume; approximately equal to 0.26 gallon (U.S.), or about 61 cubic inches. Used as a metric measure of engine-cylinder displacement.

Lobe   A projecting part, such as a rotor lobe or a cam lobe.

Locknut   A second nut turned down on a holding nut to prevent loosening.

Low beam   A headlight beam used to illuminate the road ahead when the motorcycle is meeting or following another vehicle.

Low-speed system   The system in the carburetor that supplies fuel to the air passing through during low-speed, part-throttle operation.

Lubricating system   The system in the engine that supplies moving engine parts with lubricating oil to prevent contact between the metal surfaces.

Lugging   Low-speed, full-throttle engine operation in which the engine is heavily loaded and overworked.

Machining   The process of using a machine tool to remove metal from a metal part.

Magnetic   Having the ability to attract iron. This ability may be permanent, or it may depend on a current flow, as in an electromagnet.

Magnetic field   The area or field of influence of a magnet, within which it will exhibit magnetic properties; extends from the north pole of the magnet to its south pole. The strength of the field of an electromagnet increases with the number of turns of wire around the iron core and the current flow through the wire.

Magnetic lines of force   Imaginary lines by which a magnetic field may be visualized.

Magnetic switch   A switch with a winding (a coil of wire); when the winding is energized, the switch is moved to open or close a circuit.

Magnetism   The ability, either natural or produced by a flow of electric current, to attract iron.

Magneto   An engine-driven device that generates its own primary current, transforms that current into high-voltage surges, and delivers the surges to the proper spark plugs.

Mag wheel   A magnesium wheel assembly; also frequently used to refer to any chromed, aluminum, or magnesium wheel of spoke design.

Main bearings   In the engine, the bearings that support the crankshaft.

Main jet   The fuel nozzle, or jet, in the carburetor that supplies fuel when the throttle is partially to fully open.

Malfunction   Improper or incorrect operation.

Manifold   A device with several inlet or outlet passageways through which a gas or liquid is gathered or distributed.

Manifold vacuum   The vacuum in the intake ports or manifold that develops as a result of the pistons moving down the cylinders.

Master cylinder   The liquid-filled cylinder in the hydraulic braking system where hydraulic pressure is developed when the rider operates a brake lever or brake pedal.

Matter   Anything that has weight and occupies space.

Measuring   The act of determining the size, capacity, or quantity of an object.

Mechanical efficiency   In an engine, the ratio between bhp and ihp.

Mechanism   A system of interrelated parts that make up a working assembly.

Meshing   The mating or engaging of the teeth of two gears.

Meter (m)   A unit of linear measure in the metric system, equal to 39.37 inches. Also, the name given to any test instrument that measures a property of a substance passing through it, as an ammeter measures electric current. Also, any device that measures and controls the flow of a substance passing through it, as a carburetor jet meters fuel flow.

Metering rod and jet   A device consisting of a small movable rod which has a varied diameter and a jet that increases or decreases fuel flow according to engine throttle opening, engine load, or a combination of both.

Millimeter (mm)   In the metric system, a unit of linear measure approximately equal to 0.039 inch.

Minibike   A small motorcycle, usually for off-road use by children.

Missing   In the engine, the failure of the air-fuel mixture in a cylinder to ignite when it should.

Modification   An alteration; a change from the original.

Modulator   A pressure-regulated governing device; used, for example, in automatic transmissions.

Moisture   Humidity, dampness, wetness, or very small drops of water.

Molecule   The smallest particle into which a substance can be divided and still retain the properties of that substance.

Moped   A motorized bicycle.

Motor   A device for converting electric energy into mechanical energy—for example, the starting motor.

Motor vehicle   A vehicle propelled by a means other than muscle power; usually mounted on rubber tires, it does not run on rails or tracks.

mph   Abbreviation for *miles per hour*; a measure of speed.

Muffler   In the engine-exhaust system, a device through which the exhaust gases must pass to deaden or muffle their sound.

Multiple-viscosity oil   An engine oil which has a low viscosity when cold for easier cranking and a higher viscosity when hot to provide adequate engine lubrication.

Mutual induction   A condition in which a voltage is induced in one coil by a changing magnetic field caused by a changing current in another coil. The magnitude of the induced voltage depends on the number of turns in the two coils.

Needle bearing   A roller-type antifriction bearing, in which the rollers are very small in diameter (needle-size).

Needle valve   A small, tapered, needle-pointed valve which can move into or out of a valve seat to close or open the passage through the seat. Used to control the carburetor float-bowl fuel level.

Negative   One of the two poles of a magnet, or one of the two terminals of an electric device.

Negative terminal   The terminal from which electrons flow in a complete electric circuit. On a battery, the negative terminal can be identified as the battery post with the smaller diameter; a minus sign (−) is often used to identify the negative terminal.

Neutral   In a transmission, the setting in which all gears are disengaged and the engine is disconnected from the transmission output shaft.

Neutral-start switch   A switch wired into the ignition switch to prevent engine cranking unless the transmission is in NEUTRAL.

Nitrogen (N)   A colorless, tasteless, odorless gas that constitutes 78 percent of the atmosphere by volume and is a part of all living tissues.

Nitrogen oxides (NO_x)   Any chemical compound of nitrogen and oxygen. Nitrogen oxides result from high temperature and pressure in the combustion chambers during the combustion process. When combined with hydrocarbons in the presence of sunlight, nitrogen oxides form smog.

Nonconductor   See *Insulator*.

North pole   The pole from which the lines of force leave a magnet.

NO_x   Abbreviation for nitrogen oxides.

Nozzle   The opening, or jet, through which fuel passes when it is discharged into the carburetor venturi.

Octane rating   A measure of the antiknock properties of a gasoline. The higher the octane rating, the more resistant the gasoline is to spark knock, or detonation.

Odometer   The meter that indicates the total distance a vehicle has traveled, in miles or kilometers; usually located in the speedometer.

OHC engine   See *Overhead-camshaft engine*.

Ohm   A unit of electric resistance.

Ohmmeter   An instrument used to measure electric resistance.

OHV engine   See *Overhead-valve engine*.

Oil   A liquid lubricant usually made from crude oil and used to provide lubrication between moving parts.

Oil-control ring   The lower ring or rings on a piston in a four-cycle engine, designed to prevent excess oil from getting past the rings and into the combustion chamber.

Oil cooler   A small radiator through which the lubricating oil flows to lower its temperature.

Oil dilution   The dilution of oil in the crankcase of a four-cycle engine, caused by the leakage of liquid fuel from the combustion chamber past the piston rings.

Oil filter   The filter through which oil passes to remove any impurities.

Oil-level indicator   The indicator, usually called the *dipstick*, that is removed to check the level of oil in the crankcase or transmission case.

Oil-pressure indicator   A gauge that indicates to the rider the oil pressure in the engine lubricating system.

Oil pump   In the lubricating system, the device that forces oil from the reservoir to the moving engine parts.

Oil pumping   Leakage of oil past the piston rings and into the combustion chamber, usually as a result of defective rings or worn cylinder walls.

Oil ring   See *Oil-control ring*.

Oil seal   A seal placed around a rotating shaft or another moving part to prevent the leakage of oil.

Oil strainer   A wire-mesh screen placed at the inlet end of the oil-pump pickup tube to prevent dirt, sludge, and other large particles from entering the oil pump.

One-wire system   On motorcycles, the use of the engine and frame as a path for the grounded side of the electric circuits; eliminates the need for a second wire as a return path to the battery or alternator.

Open circuit   In an electric circuit, a break, or opening, which prevents the passage of current.

Orifice   A small opening or hole into a cavity.

O-ring   A type of sealing ring made of a special rubberlike material; in use, the O-ring is compressed into a groove to provide the sealing action.

Oscilloscope   A high-speed voltmeter which visually displays voltage variations on a television-like picture tube. Used to check engine ignition systems, charging systems, and electronic fuel-injection systems.

Output shaft   The shaft that delivers torque from the transmission to the final drive.

Overcharging   The continued charging of a battery after it has reached the charged condition. This action damages the battery and shortens its life.

Overdrive   Transmission gearing that causes the output shaft to overdrive, or turn faster than the engine crankshaft.

Overflow   Spilling of the excess of a substance; also, to run or spill over the sides of a container, usually because of overfilling.

Overflow tank   See *Expansion tank*.

Overhaul To completely disassemble a unit, clean and inspect all parts, reassemble it with the original or new parts, and make all adjustments necessary for proper operation.

Overhead-camshaft (OHC) engine An engine in which the camshaft is located in the cylinder head instead of in the cylinder block.

Overhead valve (OHV) engine An engine in which the valves are mounted in the cylinder head above the combustion chamber; the camshaft is usually mounted in the cylinder block or crankcase, and the valves are actuated by push rods.

Overheat To heat excessively; also, to become excessively hot.

Overrunning clutch drive A type of clutch drive which transmits rotary motion in one direction only. When rotary motion attempts to pass through in the other direction, the then driving member overruns and does not pass the motion to the other member. Widely used as the drive mechanism for starting motors.

Oversquare A term applied to engines which have a bore larger than the length of the stroke.

Oxides of nitrogen See *Nitrogen oxides*.

Oxygen (O) A colorless, tasteless, odorless, gaseous element which makes up about 21 percent of air. Capable of combining rapidly with all elements except the inert gases in the oxidation process called *burning*. Combines very slowly with many metals in the oxidation process called *rusting*.

Pancake engine An engine with two rows of cylinders which are opposed and on the same plane, usually set horizontally.

Parallel The quality of being the same distance from each other at all points; usually applied to lines and to machined surfaces.

Parallel circuit The electric circuit formed when two or more electric devices have their terminals connected positive to positive and negative to negative, so that each may operate independently of the others from the same power source.

Particle A very small piece of metal, dirt, or other impurity which may be contained in the air, fuel, or lubricating oil used in an engine.

Passage A small hole or gallery in an assembly or casting, through which air, coolant, fuel, or oil flows.

Pawl An arm pivoted so that its free end can fit into a detent, slot, or groove at certain times to hold a part stationary.

PCV Abbreviation for *positive crankcase ventilation*.

PCV valve The valve that controls the flow of crankcase vapors in accordance with ventilation requirements for different engine speeds and loads.

Petroleum The crude oil from which gasoline, lubricating oil, and other such products are refined.

Photochemical smog Smog caused by hydrocarbons and nitrogen oxides reacting photochemically in the atmosphere. The reactions take place under low wind velocity, bright sunlight, and an inversion layer in which an air mass is trapped (as between the ocean and mountains in Los Angeles). Can cause eye and lung irritation.

Pickup coil In an electronic ignition system, the coil in which voltage is induced by the reluctor.

Pilot shaft A shaft that is used to align parts and which is removed before the final installation of the parts; a dummy shaft.

Ping The sound resulting from the sudden ignition of the air-fuel charge in the engine combustion chamber; the characteristic sound of detonation.

Pinion gear The smaller of two meshing gears.

Piston A movable part fitted into a cylinder which can receive or transmit motion as a result of pressure changes in the cylinder. In the engine, the cylindrical part that moves up and down within a cylinder as the crankshaft rotates.

Piston displacement The cylinder volume displaced by the piston as it moves from the bottom to the top of the cylinder during one complete stroke.

Piston pin The cylindrical or tubular metal piece that attaches the piston to the connecting rod. Also called the *wrist pin*.

Piston rings Rings fitted into grooves in the piston. There are two types: compression rings for sealing the compression and combustion pressure (that is, pressure in the combustion chamber) and oil-control rings to scrape excessive oil off the cylinder wall of a four-cycle engine. See *Compression ring; Oil-control ring*.

Piston skirt The lower part of a piston, below the piston-pin hole.

Piston slap A hollow, muffled, bell-like sound made by an excessively loose piston slapping the cylinder wall.

Pivot A pin or shaft upon which another part rests or turns.

Planetary-gear system A gear set consisting of a central sun gear surrounded by two or more planet pinions which are, in turn, meshed with a ring (or internal) gear; used in overdrives and automatic transmissions.

Planet carrier In a planetary-gear system, the carrier or bracket that contains the shaft upon which the planet pinion turns.

Planet pinions In the planetary-gear system, the gears that mesh with, and revolve about, the sun gear; they also mesh with the ring (or internal) gear.

Plastic gasket compound A plastic paste in a tube which can be laid in any shape to make a gasket.

Plastigage A plastic material available in strips of various diameter; used to measure clearances in sleeve-type bearings.

Plate In a battery, a rectangular sheet of spongy lead. Sulfuric acid in the electrolyte chemically reacts with the lead to produce an electric current.

Plies The layers of cord in a tire casing; each of these layers is a ply.

Polarity The quality of an electric component or circuit that determines the direction of current flow.

Pollutant Any gas or substance in the exhaust gas from the engine or evaporating from the fuel tank or carburetor that adds to the pollution of the atmosphere.

Pollution Gases or other substances in the air which make the air less fit to breathe. *Noise pollution* is the name applied to excessive noise from machinery or vehicles.

Poppett valve A mushroom-shaped valve used in four-cycle engines.

Port In an engine, the opening through which the air-fuel mixture or burned gases pass.

Positive crankcase ventilating (PCV) system A crankcase ventilating system in which the blowby gas in the crankcase is returned to the intake system of the engine to be burned. This prevents blowby gas from escaping into and polluting the atmosphere.

Positive terminal The terminal to which electrons flow in a complete electric circuit. On a battery, the positive terminal can be identified as the battery post with the larger diameter; the plus sign (+) is used to identify the positive terminal.

Post A point at which a cable is connected to a battery.

Potential energy Energy stored in a body because of its position. A weight raised to a height has potential energy because it can do work coming down. Likewise, a tensed or compressed spring contains potential energy.

Power The rate at which work is done. A common power-measuring unit is the horsepower, which is equal to 33,000 foot-pounds per minute.

Power piston In some carburetors, a vacuum-operated piston that allows additional fuel to flow at wide-open throttle; permits delivery of a richer air-fuel mixture to the engine.

Power plant The engine, or power source, of a motorcycle.

Power stroke The piston stroke during which the air-fuel mixture burns and forces the piston down so that the engine produces power.

Power train The group of mechanisms that carry the rotary motion developed in the engine to the rear wheel.

ppm Abbreviation for *parts per million*; the unit used in measuring the level of hydrocarbons in exhaust gas with an exhaust-gas analyzer.

PR Abbreviation for *ply rating*; a measure of the strength of a tire, based on the strength of a single ply of designated construction.

Precision-insert bearings A type of bearing that can be installed in an engine without reaming, honing, or grinding.

Preignition Ignition of the air-fuel mixture in the engine cylinder by any means before the ignition spark occurs at the spark plug.

Preload In roller bearings, the amount of load placed on a bearing before actual operating loads are added.

Press fit A fit so tight that the pin has to be pressed into place, usually with an arbor or a hydraulic press.

Pressure Force per unit area, or force divided by area. Usually measured in pounds per square inch (psi) and kilopascals (kPa).

Pressure cap A radiator cap with valves which causes the cooling system to operate under pressure at a higher and more efficient temperature.

Pressure plate That part of the clutch which exerts pressure against the friction disks.

Pressure-relief valve A valve in the oil line that opens to relieve excessive pressure.

Pressure tester An instrument that clamps in the radiator filler neck; used to pressure-test the cooling system for leaks.

Pressurize To apply more than atmospheric pressure to a gas or liquid.

Primary circuit The low-voltage circuit of the ignition system.

Primary winding The outer winding of relatively heavy wire in an ignition coil.

Printed circuit An electric circuit made by applying a conductive material to an insulating board in a pattern that provides current paths between components mounted on or connected to the board.

Propeller shaft See *Drive shaft*.

psi Abbreviation for *pounds per square inch*; often used to indicate the pressure of a liquid or gas.

Pump A device that transfers gas or liquid from one place to another.

Push rod In an OHV engine, the rod between the valve lifter and the rocker arm.

Quench The space in some combustion chambers which absorbs enough heat to quench, or extinguish, the combustion flame front as it approaches a relatively cold cylinder wall. This prevents the detonation of the end gas but results in hydrocarbon emissions.

Quick charger A battery charger that produces a high charging current which charges, or boosts, a battery in a short time.

Races The metal rings on which ball or roller bearings rotate.

Radiator In the cooling system, the device that removes heat from liquid passing through it; takes hot coolant from the engine and returns the coolant to the engine at a lower temperature.

Radiator pressure cap See *Pressure cap*.

Ratio Proportion; the relative amounts of two or more substances in a mixture. Usually expressed as a numerical relationship, as in 2:1.

Reassembly The putting back together of the parts of a device.

Rebore To increase the diameter of a cylinder.

Recharging The action of forcing electric current into a battery in the direction opposite to that in which current normally flows during use. Reverses the chemical reaction between the plates and the electrolyte.

Reciprocating motion Motion of an object between two limiting positions; motion in a straight line, back and forth or up and down.

Rectifier A device which changes alternating current to direct current; in the alternator, a diode.

Reed valve A type of valve used in the crankcase of some two-cycle engines. the air-fuel mixture enters the crankcase through the reed valve, which then closes as pressure builds up in the crankcase.

Regulator In the charging system, a device that controls alternator output to prevent excessive voltage.

Relay An electric device that opens or closes a circuit in response to a voltage signal.

Relief valve A valve that opens when a preset pressure is reached. This relieves or prevents excessive pressure.

Reluctor In an electronic ignition system, the metal rotor (with a series of tips) which replaces the conventional ignition cam.

Remove and reinstall (R & R) To perform a series of servicing procedures on an original part or assembly; includes removal, inspection, lubrication, all necessary adjustments, and reinstallation.

Replace To remove a used part or assembly and install a new part or assembly in its place; includes cleaning, lubricating, and adjusting as required.

Reserve capacity A battery rating; the number of minutes a battery can deliver a 25-ampere current before the cell voltages drop to 1.75 volts per cell.

Resistance The opposition to a flow of current through a circuit or electric device; measured in ohms. A voltage of 1 volt will cause 1 ampere to flow through a resistance of 1 ohm. This is known as Ohm's law, which can be written in three ways: ampers = volts/ohms; ohms = volts/amperes; and volts = amperes × ohms.

Retard Usually associated with the spark-timing mechanisms of the engine; the opposite of spark advance. Also, to delay the introduction of the spark into the combustion chamber.

Return spring A pull-back spring, often used in drum-brake systems.

Rich mixture An air-fuel mixture that has a relatively high proportion of fuel and a relatively low proportion of air. An air-fuel ratio of 13:1 indicates a rich mixture, compared with an air-fuel ratio of 16:1.

Ring See *Compression ring*; *Oil-control ring*.

Ring gap The gap between the ends of the piston ring when the ring is in place in the cylinder.

Ring gear   The large gear driven by the pinion in the final drive of a motorcycle with shaft drive.

Ring ridge   The ridge formed at the top of a cylinder as the cylinder wall below is worn away by piston-ring movement.

Rocker arm   In an OHV engine, a device that rocks on a shaft or pivots on a stud as the cam moves the push rod, causing the valve to open.

Rod bearing   In an engine, the bearing in the connecting rod in which a crankpin of the crankshaft rotates. Also called a *connecting-rod bearing*.

Rod big end   The end of the connecting rod that attaches around the crankpin.

Rod bolts   Special bolts used on the connecting rod to attach the cap.

Rod small end   The end of the connecting rod through which a piston pin passes to connect the piston to the connecting rod.

Room temperature   68 to 72°F [20 to 22°C].

Rotary   Term describing the motion of a part that continually rotates or revolves.

Rotor   A revolving part of a machine, such as an alternator rotor, disk-brake rotor, distributor rotor, or Wankel-engine rotor.

Rotor oil pump   A type of oil pump using a pair of rotors, one inside the other, to produce the oil pressure required to circulate oil to engine parts.

rpm   Abbreviation for *revolutions per minute*; a measure of rotational speed.

Run-on   See *Dieseling*.

Runout   Wobble.

SAE   Abbreviation for *Society of Automotive Engineers*. Used to indicate a grade or weight of oil measured according to SAE standards.

Schematic   A pictorial representation, most often in the form of a line drawing. A systematic positioning of components and their relationship to one another or to the overall function.

Schrader valve   A spring-loaded valve through which a connection can be made to the air chamber in a tire or tube.

Scope   See *Oscilloscope*.

Scored   Scratched or grooved, as a cylinder wall may be scored by abrasive particles moved up and down by the piston rings.

Scraper ring   On a piston, an oil-control ring designed to scrape excess oil back down the cylinder into the crankcase.

Screen   A fine-mesh screen in the fuel and lubricating system that prevents large particles from entering the system.

Scuffing   A type of wear of moving parts characterized by the transfer of metal from one to the other part and by pits or grooves in the mating surfaces.

Seal   A material shaped around a shaft, used to close off the operating compartment of the shaft which prevents oil leakage.

Sealed-beam headlight   A headlight that contains the filament, reflector, and lens in a single sealed unit.

Sealer   A thick, tacky compound, usually spread with a brush which may be used as a gasket or sealant to seal small openings or surface irregularities.

Seat   The surface upon which another part rests, as a valve seat. Also, to wear into a good fit; for example, new piston rings seat after a few miles of riding.

Secondary circuit   The high-voltage circuit of the ignition system.

Segments   The copper bars of a commutator.

Self-discharge   Chemical activity in a battery which causes the battery to discharge even though it is furnishing no current to the external circuit.

Self-induction   The inducing of a voltage in a current-carrying coil of wire because the current in that wire is changing.

Semiconductor   A material that acts as an insulator under some conditions and as a conductor under other conditions.

Sensor   Any device that receives and reacts to a signal, such as a change in voltage, temperature, or pressure.

Series circuit   An electric circuit in which the devices are connected end to end, positive terminal to negative terminal. The same current flows through all the devices in the circuit.

Service manual   A book published by each motorcycle manufacturer, listing the specifications and service procedures for each model of motorcycle. Also called a *shop manual*.

Service rating   A designation that indicates the type of service for which an engine lubricating oil is best suited.

Servo   A device in a hydraulic system that converts hydraulic pressure to mechanical movement. Consists of a piston which moves in a cylinder as hydraulic pressure acts on it.

Shift pedal   The foot pedal used to change gears in a transmission.

Shift valve   In an automatic transmission, a valve that moves to produce the shift from one gear ratio to another.

Shim   A slotted strip of metal used as a spacer.

Shimmy   Rapid oscillation. In wheel shimmy, for example, the front wheel turns in and out alternately and rapidly; this causes the front end of the motorcycle to oscillate, or shimmy.

Shock absorber   A hydraulic device which prevents excessive wheel movements.

Shoe   In the brake system, a metal plate that supports the brake lining and absorbs and transmits braking forces.

Short circuit   A defect in an electric circuit which permits current to take a short path, or circuit, instead of following the desired path.

Shrink fit   A tight fit of one part in another achieved by heating or cooling one part and then assembling it with the other part. If heated, the part then shrinks on cooling to provide a shrink fit. If cooled, the part expands on warming to provide the fit.

Side clearance   The clearance between the sides of moving parts when the sides do not serve as load-carrying surfaces.

Single-overhead-camshaft (SOHC) engine   An engine in which a single camshaft is mounted over the cylinder head to operate the valves.

Slip joint   In the power train, a variable-length connection that permits the drive shaft to change its effective length.

Slip rings   In an alternator, the rings that form a rotating connection between the armature windings and the brushes.

Sludge   An accumulation of water, dirt, and oil in the engine; sludge is very viscous and tends to reduce lubrication.

Smog   A term coined from *smoke* and *fog* which is applied to the foglike layer that hangs over many areas under certain atmospheric conditions. Smog is compounded from smoke, moisture, and numerous chemicals which are produced by combustion (from power plants, automotive engines, incinerators, etc.) and from numerous natural and industrial processes. The term is used generally to describe any condition of dirty air and/or fumes or smoke.

Smoke   Small gas-borne or air-borne particles, exclusive of water vapor, that result from combustion; such particles emitted by an engine into the atmosphere in sufficient quantity to be observable.

Smoke in exhaust A visible blue or black substance often present in the engine exhaust. A blue color indicates excessive oil in the combustion chamber; black indicates excessive fuel in the air-fuel mixture.

Snap ring A metal fastener, available in two types; the external snap ring fits into a groove in a shaft; the internal snap ring fits into a groove in a housing. Snap rings must be installed and removed with snap-ring pliers.

SOHC engine See *Single-overhead-camshaft engine*.

Solenoid An electromechanical device which, when connected to an electric source such as a battery, produces a mechanical movement. This movement can be used to control a valve or to produce other movements.

Solenoid relay A relay that connects a solenoid to a current source when its contacts close; specifically, the starting-motor solenoid relay.

Solenoid switch A switch that is opened and closed electromagnetically, by the movement of a solenoid core. Usually, the core also causes a mechanical action, such as the movement of a drive pinion into mesh with gear teeth for cranking.

Solid-state regulator An alternator regulator encapsulated in a plastic material and mounted in the alternator.

South pole The pole at which magnetic lines of force enter a magnet.

Spark advance See *Advance*.

Spark duration The length of time a spark is established across a spark gap, or the length of time current flows in a spark gap.

Spark knock See *Detonation*.

Spark plug The assembly, which includes a pair of electrodes and an insulator, that has the purpose of providing a spark gap in the engine cylinder.

Spark-plug heat range The distance heat must travel from the center electrode to reach the outer shell of the plug and enter the cylinder head.

Spark test A quick check of the ignition system; made by holding the metal spark-plug end of a spark-plug cable about 1/4 inch [6 mm] from the cylinder head, cranking the engine, and checking for a spark.

Specifications Information provided by the manufacturer that describes each motorcycle system and its components, operation, and clearances. Also, the service procedures that must be followed for a system to operate properly.

Specific gravity A measure of the weight per unit volume of a liquid as compared with the weight of an equal volume of water.

Specs See *Specifications*.

Speedometer An instrument that indicates road speed; usually driven from the front wheel.

Spline A slot or groove cut in a shaft or bore; a splined shaft onto which a hub, wheel, gear, or other such part with matching splines in its bore is assembled so that the two must turn together.

Spool valve A rod with indented sections, used to control oil flow in automatic transmissions.

Spring A device that changes shape under stress or pressure, but returns to its original shape when the stress or pressure is removed; the component of the wheel suspension system that absorbs road shocks by flexing and twisting.

Spring retainer In the valve train, the piece of metal that holds the spring in place and is itself locked in place by the valve-spring-retainer locks.

Sprung weight That part of the motorcycle which is supported on springs (includes the engine, frame, and body).

Spur gear A gear in which the teeth are parallel to the center line of the gear.

Square engine An engine having a bore and stroke of equal measurements.

Squish The action in some combustion chambers in which the last part of the compressed mixture is pushed, or squirted, out of a decreasing space between the piston and the cylinder head.

Starter See *Starting motor*.

Starting motor The electric motor that cranks the engine by turning the crankshaft for starting.

Starting-motor drive The drive mechanism and gear on the end of the starting-motor armature shaft; used to couple the starting motor to, and disengage it from, the driven gear teeth.

Static balance The balance of an object while it is not moving.

Stator In the torque converter, a third member (in addition to the turbine and pump) which changes the direction of fluid flow under certain operating conditions (when the stator is stationary). In an alternator, the assembly that includes the stationary conductors.

Steering and ignition lock A device that locks the ignition switch in the OFF position and locks the handlebars so they cannot be turned.

Step-through frame A type of frame construction used on girls' bicycles, motor scooters, and some light motorcycles.

Stoplight The light at the rear of a motorcycle which indicates that the rider is applying a brake.

Stoplight switch The switch that turns the stoplight on and off as a brake is applied and released.

Storage battery A lead-acid electrochemical device that changes chemical energy into electric energy; that part of the electric system which acts as a reservoir for electric energy, storing it in chemical form.

Street bike A motorcycle with all equipment required for legal riding on the street.

Stroke In an engine cylinder, the distance that the piston moves in traveling from BDC to TDC or from TDC to BDC.

Sulfation The lead sulfate that forms on battery plates as a result of the battery action that produces electric current.

Sulfuric acid See *Electrolyte*.

Sun gear In a planetary-gear system, the center gear that meshes with the planet pinions.

Supercharger In the intake system of the engine, a pump that pressurizes the ingoing air-fuel mixture. This increases the amount of mixture delivered to the cylinders, which increases the engine output. If the supercharger is driven by the engine exhaust gas, it is called a *turbocharger*.

Suspension The system of springs and other parts which supports the motorcycle on its axles and wheels.

Swing arm A rear fork with a rear wheel attached, which pivots on the frame and whose travel is controlled by one or two springs and shock absorbers.

Switch A device that opens and closes an electric circuit.

Synchronize To make two or more events or operations occur at the same time or at the same speed.

Synthetic oil An artificial oil that is manufactured; not a natural mineral oil made from petroleum.

Tachometer A device for measuring engine speed, or rpm.

Taillight The steady-burning low-intensity light used on the rear of a motorcycle.

Tank unit The part of the fuel-indicting system that is mounted in the fuel tank.

Taper A shaft or hole that gets gradually smaller toward one end. In an engine cylinder, the uneven wear which is more at the top than at the bottom.

Tappet See *Valve lifter*.

TDC Abbreviation for *top dead center*.

Temperature A measure of heat intensity, in degrees. Temperature is not a measure of heat quantity.

Temperature gauge A gauge that indicates to a rider the temperature of the coolant in the engine cooling system.

Temperature indicator See *Temperature gauge*.

Temperature-sending unit A device in contact with the engine coolant whose electric resistance changes as the coolant temperature increases or decreases; these changes control the movement of the indicator needle in the temperature gauge.

Tetraethyl lead A chemical mixed into engine fuel which increases octane rating, or reduces spark-knock tendency. Also called *ethyl* and *TEL*.

Thermal Of or pertaining to heat.

Thermal efficiency The relationship between the power output and the energy in the fuel burned to produce the power.

Thermistor A heat-sensing device with a negative temperature coefficient of resistance; as its temperature increases, its electric resistance decreases. Used as the sensing device in engine-temperature indicators.

Thermometer An instrument which measures heat intensity (temperature) by the thermal expansion of a liquid.

Thermostat A device for the automatic regulation of temperature; usually contains a temperature-sensitive element that expands or contracts to open or close off the flow of air, a gas, or a liquid.

Thermostatic gauge An indicating device (for fuel quantity, oil pressure, engine temperature) that contains a thermostatic blade or blades.

Threaded insert A threaded coil that is used to restore the original thread size to a hole with damaged threads; the hole is drilled oversize and tapped, and the insert is threaded into the tapped hole.

Throttle A disk valve in a fixed-venturi carburetor that pivots in response to throttle-grip position; allows the rider to regulate the volume of the air-fuel mixture entering the engine, thereby controlling the engine speed. Also called the *throttle plate* or *throttle valve*.

Thrust bearing In the engine, the main bearing that has thrust faces to prevent excessive end play, or forward and backward movement of the crankshaft.

Thyristor A type of semiconductor device that acts as a switch. It turns on when a certain voltage is applied to the gate, and it turns off when the current flowing between the other two terminals stops or reverses.

Timing In the engine, refers to timing of valves, timing of ignition, and their relation to the piston position in the cylinder.

Timing chain A chain that is driven by a sprocket on the crankshaft and that drives the sprocket on the camshaft.

Timing gear A gear on the crankshaft that drives the camshaft by meshing with a gear on it.

Timing light A light that can be connected to the ignition system to flash each time the number 1 spark plug fires; used for adjusting the timing of the ignition spark.

Tire The casing-and-tread assembly (with or without a tube) that is mounted on a wheel to provide pneumatically cushioned contact and traction with the road.

Tire tread See *Tread*.

Top dead center (TDC) The piston position when the piston has reached the upper limit of its travel in the cylinder and the center line of the connecting rod is parallel to the cylinder walls.

Torque Turning or twisting effort; usually measured in pound-feet or kilogram-meters. Also, a turning force such as that required to tighten a connection.

Torque converter In an automatic transmission, a fluid coupling which incorporates a stator to permit a torque increase.

Torsional vibration Rotary vibration that causes a twist-untwist action on a rotating shaft, so that a part of the shaft repeatedly moves ahead of, or lags behind, the remainder of the shaft; for example, the action of a crankshaft responding to the cylinder firing impulses.

Trail bike A motorcycle made strictly for riding on trails and not equipped with required equipment for riding on the street.

Transistor An electronic device that can be used as an electric switch; used to replace the breaker points in electronic ignition systems.

Transmission An assembly of gears that provides the different gear ratios, as well as neutral, through which engine power is transmitted to the final drive to rotate the rear wheel.

Tread A part of a tire that contacts the road. It is the thickest part of the tire and is cut with grooves to provide traction for riding and stopping.

Trike A three-wheel motorcycle. Some models with large tires are known as *all-terrain vehicles*.

Trouble diagnosis The detective work necessary to find the cause of a trouble.

Tubeless tire A tire that holds air without the use of a tube.

Tuneup A procedure for inspecting, testing, and adjusting an engine and for replacing any worn parts, to restore engine performance.

Turbocharger A supercharger driven by the engine-exhaust gas.

Turn signal See *Directional signal*.

Twin A motorcycle engine with two cylinders in line.

Two-cycle See *Two-stroke cycle*.

Two-stroke cycle A series of events taking place in a two-stroke-cycle engine, which are intake, compression, power, and exhaust, all of which take place in two piston strokes. A two-stroke-cycle engine is also called a *two-cycle engine* or a *two-stroker*.

Unit An assembly or device that can perform its function only if it is not further divided into its components.

Universal joint In the power train, a jointed connection in the drive shaft that permits the driving angle to change.

Unleaded gasoline Gasoline to which no lead compounds have been intentionally added.

Upper beam A headlight beam intended primarily for distant illumination, not for use when other vehicles are being met or followed.

Upshift To shift a transmission into a higher gear.

Unsprung weight The weight of that part of the motorcycle which is not supported on springs; for example, the wheels and tires.

Vacuum An absence of air or other substance.

Vacuum advance Ignition-spark advance resulting from partial vacuum in the intake port or manifold.

Vacuum gauge In engine service, a device that measures vacuum in the intake port or manifold and thereby indicates the actions of engine components.

Vacuum-gauge set One or more vacuum gauges attached to a manifold (a pipe fitted with several outlets for connecting pipes) and used for measuring the vacuum in each intake port of a multicylinder engine.

Valve A device that can be opened or closed to allow or stop the flow of a liquid, gas, or vapor from one place to another.

Valve clearance The clearance in the valve train when the valve is closed.

Valve float A condition in which the engine valves do not close completely or fail to close at the proper time.

Valve grinding Refacing a valve in a valve-refacing machine.

Valve guide A cylindrical part in the cylinder head in which a valve is assembled and in which it moves up and down.

Valve lash See *Valve clearance*.

Valve lifter Also called *lifter, tappet, valve tappet,* and *cam follower*. A cylindrical part of the engine which rests on a cam of the camshaft and is lifted by cam action so that the valve is opened.

Valve overlap The number of degrees of crankshaft rotation during which the intake and exhaust valves are open together.

Valve refacer A machine for removing material from the seating face of a valve to true up the face.

Valve rotator A device used in place of the valve-spring retainer; it has a built-in mechanism to rotate the valve slightly each time it opens.

Valve seat The surface against which a valve comes to rest to provide a seal against leaking.

Valve-seat inserts Metal rings inserted in cylinder heads to act as valve seats. They are made of special metals able to withstand very high temperatures.

Valve-spring retainer The device on the valve stem that holds the spring in place.

Valve-spring retainer lock The locking device on the valve stem that locks the spring retainer in place.

Valve stem The long, thin section of the valve that fits into the valve guide.

Valve-stem seal A device placed on or around the valve stem to reduce the amount of oil that can get on the stem and then work its way down into the combustion chamber.

Valve tappet See *Valve lifter*.

Valve timing The timing of the opening and closing of the valves in relation to the piston position.

Valve train The valve-operating mechanism of an engine; includes all components from the camshaft to the valve.

Vane A flat, extended surface that is moved around an axis by or in a fluid. Part of the internal revolving portion of an air-supply pump.

Vapor A gas; any substance in the gaseous state, as distinguished from the liquid and solid states.

Vaporization A change of state from liquid to vapor, or gas, by evaporation or boiling; a general term including both evaporation and boiling.

Vapor lock A condition in the fuel system in which gasoline vaporizes in the fuel line or fuel pump; bubbles of gasoline vapor restrict or prevent fuel delivery to the carburetor.

Vapor-recovery system An evaporative emission-control system that recovers gasoline vapor escaping from the fuel tank and carburetor. See *Evaporative emission-control system*.

Variable-venturi carburetor A carburetor in which the size of the venturi changes according to engine speed and load.

Vent An opening through which air can leave an enclosed chamber.

Venturi In the carburetor, a narrowed passageway or restriction which increases the velocity of air moving through it; produces the vacuum responsible for the discharge of gasoline from the fuel nozzle.

Vertical twin A two-cylinder engine with the cylinders arranged in line.

Vibration A rapid back-and-forth motion; an oscillation.

Viscosity The resistance to flow exhibited by a liquid. A thick oil has greater viscosity than a thin oil.

Viscosity rating An indicator of the viscosity of engine oil. There are separate ratings for winter riding and for summer riding. The winter grades are SAE 5W, SAE 10W, and SAE 20W. The summer grades are SAE 20, SAE 30, SAE 40, and SAE 50. Many oils have multiple viscosity ratings, as, for example, SAE 10W-50.

Viscous Thick, tending to resist flowing.

Viscous friction Friction between layers of a liquid.

Volatility A measurement of the ease with which a liquid vaporizes.

Volumetric efficiency Ratio between the amount of air-fuel mixture that actually enters an engine cylinder and the theoretical amount that could enter under ideal conditions.

Voltage The force which causes electrons to flow in a conductor. The difference in electric pressure (or potential) between two points in a circuit.

Voltage regulator A device that prevents excessive alternator or generator voltage by alternately inserting and removing a resistance in the field circuit.

Voltmeter A device for measuring the potential difference (voltage) between two points, such as the terminals of a battery or alternator or two points in an electric circuit.

V-type engine An engine with two banks or rows of cylinders set at an angle to each other to form a V.

VV carburetor See *Variable-venturi carburetor*.

Wankel engine A rotary engine in which a three-lobe rotor turns eccentrically in an oval chamber to produce power.

Water jackets The space between the inner and outer shells of the cylinder and head, through which coolant circulates.

Water pump In the liquid-cooling system, the device that circulates coolant between the engine water jackets and the radiator.

Wedge combustion chamber A combustion chamber resembling a wedge in shape.

Wheel A disk or series of spokes with a hub at the center which revolves around an axle and which has a rim around the outside for mounting the tire.

Wheel alignment A series of tests and adjustments to ensure that wheels and tires are properly positioned on the motorcycle and run true.

Wheel balancer A device that checks a wheel-and-tire assembly statically and/or dynamically for balance.

Wheelbase The distance between the center lines of the front and rear wheel axles.

Wheel cylinder In a hydraulic braking system, a hydraulic cylinder located in the brake mechanism at the wheel. Hydraulic pressure from the master cylinder causes the wheel cylinder to move the brake shoes into contact with the brake drum for braking.

Wheel tramp Tendency of a wheel to move up and down so it repeatedly bears down hard, or "tramps," on the road. Sometimes called *highspeed shimmy*.

Wiring harness A group of individually insulated wires wrapped together to form a neat, easily installed bundle.

Work The changing of the position of an object against an opposing force; measured in foot-pounds or meter-kilograms. The product of a force and the distance through which it acts.

Wrist pin See *Piston pin*.

WOT Abbreviation for *wide-open throttle*.

Zener diode A special type of diode that will conduct current in its normally blocked or reverse direction under certain conditions.

Two-cycle engines (*Cont.*):
   lubricating systems for, 121–127, 137–138
   oil pump for, 125–127
   operating characteristics of, 42–43
   port timing for, 40–41
   reed valve in, 38–40, 248
   rotary valve in, 40–41
   top-end overhaul, 216–226

U
Universal joint, 284–286
Upshift, transmission, 33

V
Vacuum, 6
Vacuum advance, 194–195
Valves, 47–53, 227–238
   adjusting clearance of, 230–231
   coated, 229
   deposits on, 229
   floating of, 51
   guides for, 235–236
   lapping of, 237–238
   location of, 51
   operating of, 47–53
   refacing of, 232–233
   rocker arms for, 49–51
   rotary, 40–41
   servicing of, 227–238
   servicing seats for, 229, 235–238

Valves (*Cont.*):
   spring retainer for, 47–49
   stainless-steel, 229–230
   timing of, 53, 237–238
   trouble diagnosis of, 227–228
   valve guides, 235–236
Valve lifters, 230–231, 235
Valve seats, 229, 235–238
   recession of, 229
   servicing of, 235–238
Valve springs, 47–49, 235
Valve tappets, 230–231, 235
Valve train, 46–52
Valve stem, tire, 337
Vaporization, 84
Variable-venturi carburetor, 85–94
   constant-vacuum type of, 87, 93–94
   idle port in, 90–91
   piston in, 85–86
   slide valve in, 85–86
   slide-valve types of, 87–93
V-belt torque converter, 270–272
Vegetable oil, 118, 122
Venturi, 83–96
   effect, 84–85
   fixed and variable, 85–86
   varying of, 87–94
Viscosity, oil, 118–119
Volatility, 66
Voltage, 153
Voltage, battery, 161
Voltage regulator, 182–184, 186
   electronic, 183–184

Voltage regulator (*Cont.*):
   mechanical, 182–183
   servicing of, 186
Voltmeter, 151
Volumetric efficiency, 61–63

W
Water pump, 140–141, 147, 148
   servicing of, 148
   testing, 147
Wet sump lubricating system, 128–130
Wheel alignment, 329–330
Wheel balancing, 328–329
Wheelbase, 17
Wheel bearings, 328
Wheels, 28, 325–335
   axial runout of, 329
   cast types of, 28
   drop center rim for, 335
   front, 325–326
   lateral runout of, 329
   mag, 28
   rear, 326–328
   spoke type of, 28
   spoking, 330–334
Wiring circuits, 154
Wiring harness, 154
Work, 58

Z
Zener diode, 183–185
   breakdown voltage of, 184–185